Lecture Notes in Computer Science 8434

Commenced Publication in 1973
Founding and Former Series Editors:
Gerhard Goos, Juris Hartmanis, and Jan van Leeuwen

T0213733

Xinyi Huang   Jianying Zhou (Eds.)

Information Security Practice and Experience

10th International Conference, ISPEC 2014
Fuzhou, China, May 5-8, 2014
Proceedings

 Springer

Volume Editors

Xinyi Huang
Fujian Normal University
Fuzhou, China
E-mail: xyhuang81@gmail.com

Jianying Zhou
Institute for Infocomm Research
Singapore
E-mail: jyzhou@i2r.a-star.edu.sg

ISSN 0302-9743   e-ISSN 1611-3349
ISBN 978-3-319-06319-5   e-ISBN 978-3-319-06320-1
DOI 10.1007/978-3-319-06320-1
Springer Cham Heidelberg New York Dordrecht London

Library of Congress Control Number: 2014936019

LNCS Sublibrary: SL 4 – Security and Cryptology

Typesetting: Camera-ready by author, data conversion by Scientific Publishing Services, Chennai, India

Printed on acid-free paper

Springer is part of Springer Science+Business Media (www.springer.com)

Preface

The 10th International Conference on Information Security Practice and Experience (ISPEC 2014) was held in Fuzhou, China, during May 5-8, 2014. The conference was hosted by Fujian Provincial Key Laboratory of Network Security and Cryptology, Fujian Normal University.

This year the conference received 158 submissions. They were evaluated on the basis of their significance, novelty, technical quality, and practical impact. Each paper was reviewed by three Program Committee members and the reviewing process was double-blind. After careful reviews and intensive discussions, 36 papers were selected for presentation at the conference and inclusion in this Springer volume (LNCS 8434), with an acceptance rate of 23%.

In conjunction with ISPEC 2014, there was a "Huawei Information Security Practice and Experience Forum" sponsored by Huawei. The forum consisted of seven keynote speeches being delivered to the ISPEC 2014 participants. The seven keynote speakers were Dieter Gollmann, Miroslaw Kutylowski, Javier Lopez, David Naccache, Mark Ryan, Pierangela Samarati, and Yang Xiang. The proceedings also contain the invited papers from the keynote speakers.

There is a long list of people who volunteered their time and energy to put together the conference and who deserve special thanks. Thanks to the Program Committee members and external reviewers for their hard work in evaluating the papers. We are also very grateful to all the people whose work ensured a smooth organization process: Honorary Chair Fegn Bao, General Chairs Robert Deng and Li Xu, Publication Chair Ying Qiu, Publicity Chairs Cheng-Kang Chu and Yu Wang, and Organizing Chair Wei Wu.

Last but certainly not least, our thanks go to all the authors who submitted papers and all the attendees.

May 2014   Xinyi Huang
                                                                        Jianying Zhou

ISPEC 2014

10th Information Security Practice and Experience Conference

Fuzhou, China
5-8 May 2014

Organized by Fujian Normal University, China

Sponsored by Huawei Technologies Co., Ltd.

Honorary Chair

Feng Bao   Huawei, Singapore

General Chairs

Robert Deng   Singapore Management University, Singapore
Li Xu   Fujian Normal University, China

Program Chairs

Xinyi Huang   Fujian Normal University, China
Jianying Zhou   Institute for Infocomm Research, Singapore

Publication Chair

Ying Qiu   Institute for Infocomm Research, Singapore

Publicity Chairs

Cheng-Kang Chu   Huawei, Singapore
Yu Wang   Deakin University, Australia

Organizing Chair

Wei Wu   Fujian Normal University, China

Program Committee

Cristina Alcaraz   University of Malaga, Spain
Basel Alomair   KACST, Saudi Arabia
Man Ho Au   University of Wollongong, Australia

Kühn, Ulrich
Lai, Russell W.F.
Lanotte, Ruggero
Li, Juanru
Li, Nan
Li, Shujun
Liang, Bei
Liang, Kaitai
Limniotis, Konstantinos
Lin, Suqing
Liu, Junrong
Liu, Liang
Liu, Weiran
Liu, Wen Ming
Liu, Ya
Liu, Zheli
Liu, Zhen
Lu, Jiqiang
Lu, Yang
Luo, Xizhao
Ming, Tang
Moyano, Francisco
Nieto, Ana
Nuñez, David
Parra-Arnau, Javier
Rebollo-Monedero, David
Rhouma, Rhouma
Rizomiliotis, Panagiotis
Sabeti, Vajiheh
Sajadieh, Seyed Mehdi
Sasaki, Yu

Schwabe, Peter
Shen, Yilin
Shparlinski, Igor
Soleimany, Hadi
Tang, Fei
Tesfay, Welderufael
Tian, Haibo
Trujillo, Rolando
Veseli, Fatbardh
Veshchikov, Nikita
Wang, Huaqun
Wang, Jianfeng
Wang, Qingju
Wang, Yujue
Watanabe, Dai
Wenger, Erich
Wu, Shuang
Xu, Jing
Yang, Shuzhe
Yap, Wun-She
Yesuf, Ahmed Seid
Zagorski, Filip
Zhang, Cong
Zhang, Huajun
Zhang, Jiang
Zhang, Tao
Zhang, Yinghui
Zhao, Yongjun
Zhao, Ziming
Zhenhua, Liu

Table of Contents

Security Practice

Security Protocols

Cloud Security

Digital Signatures

Encryption and Key Agreement

Theory

Access Control in and Around the Browser

Dieter Gollmann

Hamburg University of Technology
diego@tuhh.de

Abstract. We conduct an analysis of access control mechanisms in the browser and note that support for mashups and defences against cross-site scripting attacks are both moving from ad-hoc measures towards solutions where the browser enforces access control policies obtained from a host (CORS and CSP respectively). We also point out the degree of trust these solutions have to take for granted.

1 Introduction

Once Netscape 2.0 had furnished the browser with the means for processing executable elements in HTML pages, the browser had to implement a *reference monitor* regulating how code arriving in a page might use client side resources. Resources include objects managed by the browser, objects managed by the underlying operating system, and outgoing connections. Initially, executable elements in HTML pages were so-called applets written in Java. Today, JavaScript has become the favourite language for writing client-side scripts in web applications, with the Document Object Model (DOM) used for representing web pages in the browser and *XMLHttpRequest* used for exchanging data with a server.

Reference monitors enforce a security policy. The Same Origin Policy (SOP) had been introduced in Netscape 2.0 and was adopted as the de facto standard by browser developers. SOP in its various flavours remains highly influential today. This paper will trace how SOP became an impediment when the development of web applications progressed towards mashups, and how attackers found ways around this defence to execute unwanted code at the client. (To explain how to interpret "unwanted code", we still need to discuss who actually decides the policy enforced in the browser.) This paper will also analyze the approaches developed for dealing with these two issues. Our discussion will be conducted within the framework of access control. It will steer clear of most browser specific details, relevant as they are for practical deployment, but lay out a systematic way for analyzing access control in the web. It is not our goal to study the idiosyncrasies of different browsers and browser versions.

2 Access Control

The principles of access control can be expressed using the terms *principal*, *subject*, *object*, and *access operation* [4].

X. Huang and J. Zhou (Eds.): ISPEC 2014, LNCS 8434, pp. 1–7, 2014.

> A *principal* is an entity that can be granted access to objects or can make statements affecting access control decisions [3].

Principals are thus the entities security policies refer to. We use *authorization* to denote the act of granting an access right to a principal, i.e. of setting a policy[1]. A *subject* is an active entity within an IT system that *speaks for* a principal. Subjects are the entities sending access requests to (the implementation of) the reference monitor. An *object* is the passive entity an access request refers to. Objects can be accessed by various *access operations*. *Authentication* binds a subject to a principal. In the words of [6],

> if s is a statement *authentication* answers the question "Who said s?" with a principal. Thus principals make statements; this is what they are for.

This terminology has its origin in the area of operating systems. Principals were *user identities*, referring in the main to persons who had an account on a system. *Processes* were the subjects speaking for principals, take the real uid and effective uid of processes on a Linux system as examples. From the operating system perspective, authentication is the step whereby a new process bound to certain user identities is created. The objects were resources managed by the operating system. Typical access operations were *read*, *write*, and *execute*.

This kind of identity-based access control is still the familiar paradigm of access control, to the extent that it on occasion obscures the view on the general picture. It is not the type of access control applicable to web applications. Here, we need a decision criterion other than the user who had started a process for defining access control rules. Web pages are loaded from hosts; hosts can be addressed in the browser by entering *host names*. SOP follows this line of reasoning and uses host names as its principals. Informally, SOP rules state that a script may only connect back to the host it had been loaded from, and may only read and modify data loaded from that host. The rules typically also consider the scheme (protocol) and the port used for communicating with the server. The combination of scheme, host name, and port is known as *origin*. Note that policies on *reading* and *sending* data control data flow out of the client.

The term origin is intuitive but can be misleading. Formally, a reference monitor applies its rules to requests coming from subjects (considering, of course, the principals they speak for). In browsers, the *Document* objects in a *browsing context* play the rôle of subjects. By convention, the *document.domain* property in a *Document* denotes the principal it is speaking for. The terminology adopted suggests that code in a page was loaded from this origin. Section 4 will analyze to which extent this is true.

---

[1] In the research literature on access control, authorization also stands for evaluating whether a requestor has been granted the access rights required for a given request.

2.1 Cross-Windows Attacks

There exist exceptions to SOP. *Frame navigation*, i.e. modifying the *location* property of a frame, may be governed by different rules. Without restrictions on frame navigation, users can be deceived about the host that will receive data they are entering in a frame in a browser window [1]. Assume a user has opened two windows, one to the attacker's host and a second to some other host, in the following called the target. A script in the attacker's window *navigates* a frame in the target window to the attacker's host. Data the user enters in that frame, e.g. user name and password in a login frame, would now be passed to the attacker.

The *same window* policy (Mozilla, 2001) restricts frame navigation so that frames may only navigate frames within their own window. Cross-windows attacks will be blocked but the attack would still be possible if the attacker's web frame had been included in the target's window by design. The *descendant* policy adopted in HTML 5 restricts the permission to navigate frames even further. A frame can only navigate its own descendant frames.

Cross-windows attacks are termed *escalation (elevation) of privilege* attacks in [1]: a frame takes control of a region outside its bounding box. The object of access control is a region in the browser screen. By including a frame, the parent *delegates* the permission to use part of its region to the child frame. With the same window policy, it also delegates the permission to navigate within the entire window containing the parent frame. With the descendant policy, a frame cannot step up and across within – or out of – the logical structure of a window.

3 Mashups

Mashups are web applications where an *integrator* combines *gadgets* from multiple hosts. Integrator and gadgets may be intended to exchange data. Gadgets can be included in a way that treats them as separate subjects isolated by SOP. *Iframes* have been used for that purpose. Malicious gadgets could not attack the integrator but SOP would also get in the way of intended interactions between integrator and gadgets.

Gadgets can be included in a way that lets them speak for the integrator, e.g. by including *script tags* loaded from the gadget's site. When script tags are not subject to SOP, code in the gadgets would run with the permissions of the integrator. Interaction between integrator and gadgets is possible but the integrator has to trust the gadgets. Gadgets are trusted if they can hurt the integrator! This is the original meaning of *trust* in computer security.

Both approaches are unsatisfactory, albeit in different ways. We desire isolation of subjects (integrators, gadgets), but we also want selected communications channels. Mashup developers found that *fragment identifiers* could be used as a workaround for communication between frames. Return, for a moment, to a technical issue in access control. At which stage of an attempted frame navigation would SOP be evaluated? Assume, for the sake of the argument, that this happens after the *location* property has been changed and when the frame is

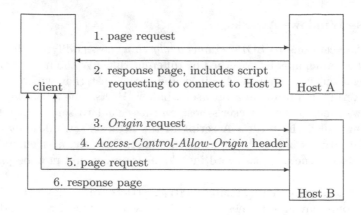

Fig. 1. Preflighted cross-origin resource sharing

reloaded from its new location. Frames are not reloaded when only the fragment identifier is changed, hence SOP will not be invoked, and frame identifiers become a message passing channel from the navigating frame to the frame navigated.

Later, the *postMessage* API was introduced, now part of HTML 5, as a dedicated message passing channel whereby a sending frame could post messages to a target origin[2] and a receiving frame could register events listening for messages from a specified sender. Advice on building secure communications channels on top of fragment identifiers and the *postMessage* API can be found in [1].

3.1 Cross-Origin Resource Sharing

With the *postMessage* API, the policy on who is authorised to send data to a frame is defined by the listening events in the frame itself, i.e. the policy is part of the code. From a design perspective it is desirable to separate policy and code. The W3C Recommendation on cross-origin resource sharing [8] provides this separation.

Figure 1 sketches the steps in a so-called preflight request. In steps 1 and 2 the client loads a page from *Host A* that contains a request for a resource on *Host B*. In step 3, the client asks *Host B* to authorize this request by sending an *Origin* request header indicating the origin of the request, *Host A* in our case. If the *Origin* header is missing or contains a value not in the access control list (list of origins) of *Host B*, the request cannot be authorized and the protocol run is terminated. If the request can be authorized, an *Access-Control-Allow-Origin* header and further headers specifying relevant policy rules are sent to the client (step 4). Steps 5 and 6 conclude the cross-origin request.

Employing the terminology of XACML [7], *Host B* serves as *Policy Information Point* in this example and initially also as *Policy Decision Point*. The client

---

[2] Here, the decision to refer to the triple (scheme, host, port) as origin leads to language that may appear counter-intuitive.

is the *Policy Enforcement Point*. The client furthermore caches the policies received from the server and may later act as a *Policy Decision Point* for requests that match a policy rule in its cache.

4 Cross-site Scripting

In a cross-site scripting (XSS) attack the client is deceived about the true source of a script and executes the script in a context it has not been authorized for. The effect is an *elevation of privilege attack* where the attacker's script gets executed with the permissions of a "trusted" server. Here, trust implies that the server is a principal that has permissions not granted to the attacker by the browser's security policy. In the context of SOP, it may just mean that server and attacker have different origins. Trust must no be mistaken as a statement about the server's trustworthiness.

To appreciate the possible attack patterns, consider the method the browser uses to authenticate subjects, i.e. for setting the value of *document.domain* in a *Document* in the browser context. When a page gets loaded, scheme, host, and port define the *origin* of that page. Any script in the DOM of that page gets the access rights of this origin. This authentication mechanism implicitly assumes that every script in the DOM of the page has been authorized by the host.

Access control can be broken by breaking this assumption. Dynamic web pages may be created by server-side scripts that include HTTP request parameters and data items from backend servers when constructing a response page. In *reflected XSS* the attacker's script is passed as an HTTP request parameter to the server (and the victim has to be tricked into sending the request so that the response is sent back to the victim). In *stored XSS*, the attacker's script is placed in a suitable data item held on a backend server. The client just has to load the vulnerable page to load the attacker's script.

DOM-based XSS exploits certain dynamic aspects of building the DOM in the browser. There exist document properties that do not correspond to the body of a web page but, e.g., to its location or URL. Frames in a web page may refer to such properties. Script elements injected in such a property would then be added to the DOM when the DOM is constructed and later be executed with the access rights of the web page.

4.1 Content Security Policy

Considering the mode of these attacks we observe that code gets injected and might defend against code injection attacks by applying filtering and blocking rules on the values that may serve as input to the construction of a web page. This can be tricky because it is up to the browser to interpret the data in the pages it receives. Server-side defences might not be aware of all client-side interpretations. Code-injection defences try to maintain the implicit assumption that all code in a page has been authorized to be there.

Content Security Policy (CSP) [2] makes authorization explicit and moves the removal of injected scripts to the browser. The server sends policy rules, so-called directives, in an HTTP header to the client. The client enforces the policy. For example, the **script-src** directive defines a white list of origins scripts are authorized to be loaded from. All *in-line* scripts are blocked. Only scripts loaded from the white listed origins will be included in the DOM and executed. Script tags or scripts sourced from the attacker's site can be injected at the server into a web page or into a URL passed to the browser but will not be included in the DOM and executed at the client.

The attacker could inject unintended scripts from white listed sources. This does not amount to an elevation of privilege attack, scripts will be using the rights they are authorized for, but the functionality of the web page would be altered. This can be viewed as a kind of confused deputy attack [5].

5   Conclusions

When the browser is asked to enforce origin-based policies on scripts, it has to be able to authenticate the origin of scripts. Authentication must be done in such a way that scripts authenticated as having a particular origin are indeed authorized to speak for that origin. The current authentication mechanism assumes that all scripts received in a page are authorized to speak for its origin. XSS attacks inject scripts either directly at the client into the DOM of a web page or at the server from where they are propagated into the DOM. CSP is a clean solution in terms of access control. The browser rejects all in-line scripts – their true source is uncertain – and loads scripts only from origins authorized by the host. The host is the Policy Information Point, the browser the Policy Enforcement Point.

When a browser enforces SOP, its security policy is too restrictive for mashups. The clean solution in terms of access control is to relax SOP and let the site targeted by a cross-origin request state its policy on sharing resources (CORS).

In both cases the browser enforces policies obtained from a server. From the user's angle, why should the server be trusted on policies? From the server's angle, why should the client be trusted on enforcement? CSP trusts the server to tell the truth and assumes that the white listed sources are not corrupted. Enforcement is in the user's interest as attacks may threaten the user's sensitive data such as cookies. CORS policies reflect the server's interest and the server trusts the client on enforcement.

This duality between CSP and CORS can be linked to different answers to the question "who owns the data in the browser". Data capturing the user's browsing history and access credentials belong to the user. Protecting these data is a privacy issue. Data loaded from a server may be the intellectual property of the hosting organization. Protecting these data is a matter of commercial confidentiality.

Next steps in the development of access control mechanisms for web applications could go in the direction of reducing trust in the other party and towards formal models of this access control system that has grown over the past twenty years.

Acknowledgements. This author gratefully acknowledges many fruitful discussions on the topic of this paper at the Dagstuhl Seminar 12401 "Web Application Security".

References

1. Barth, A., Jackson, C., Mitchell, J.C.: Securing frame communication in browsers. Communications of the ACM 52(6), 83–91 (2009)
2. Barth, A., Veditz, D., West, M.: Content security policy 1.1. W3C Working Draft (January 2014), http://www.w3.org/TR/CSP11/
3. Gasser, M., Goldstein, A., Kaufman, C., Lampson, B.: The Digital distributed system security architecture. In: Proceedings of the 1989 National Computer Security Conference (1989)
4. Gollmann, D.: Computer Security, 3rd edn. John Wiley & Sons, Chichester (2011)
5. Hardy, N.: The confused deputy. Operating Systems Reviews 22(4), 36–38 (1988)
6. Lampson, B., Abadi, M., Burrows, M., Wobber, E.: Authentication in distributed systems: Theory and practice. ACM Transactions on Computer Systems 10(4), 265–310 (1992)
7. OASIS. eXtensible Access Control Markup Language (XACML) Version V3.0. Technical report, OASIS Standard (January 2013)
8. van Kesteren, A.: Cross-origin resource sharing. W3C Recommendation (January 2014), http://www.w3.org/TR/cors/

Improving Thomlinson-Walker's Software Patching Scheme Using Standard Cryptographic and Statistical Tools

Michel Abdalla[1], Hervé Chabanne[2], Houda Ferradi[1,2],
Julien Jainski[3], and David Naccache[1]

[1] École normale supérieure
Équipe de cryptographie, 45 rue d'Ulm, F-75230 Paris CEDEX 05, France
given_name.name@ens.fr
[2] Morpho
11 boulevard Gallieni, F-92130 Issy-les-Moulineaux, France
given_name.name@morpho.com
[3] Diskrete Security LLC
1679 S. DuPont Highway, Suite 100, Dover, DE 19901. Kent County, USA
julienja@gmail.com

Abstract. This talk will illustrate how standard cryptographic techniques can be applied to real-life security products and services. This article presents in detail one of the examples given in the talk. It is intended to help the audience follow that part of our presentation. We chose as a characteristic example a little noticed yet ingenious Microsoft patent by Thomlinson and Walker. The Thomlinson-Walker system distributes encrypted patches to avoid reverse engineering by opponents (who would then be able to launch attacks on unpatched users). When the proportion of users who downloaded the encrypted patch becomes big enough, the decryption key is disclosed and all users install the patch.

1   Introduction

In a little noticed yet ingenious patent [11], Thomlinson and Walker describe a very original software patching system. Tomlinson and Walker describe their invention as follows:

"... *Computer programs are complex systems, and they typically have vulnerabilities that are not discovered until after the software is released. These vulnerabilities can be addressed after the initial software is released by distributing and installing an update to the software, which is designed to remedy, or protect against, the vulnerability. Typically, the vulnerability is discovered by the program's manufacturer, support entity, or partner before the vulnerability is generally known to the public.*

One problem with an update is that the update can normally be reverse engineered to reveal the existence of the vulnerability that the update is attempting to fix, which can be an invitation to attackers to try to exploit the vulnerability on machines without the fix applied. If updates could be delivered to every

X. Huang and J. Zhou (Eds.): ISPEC 2014, LNCS 8434, pp. 8–14, 2014.
© Springer International Publishing Switzerland 2014

machine at the same time, then the fact that the updates reveals the vulnerability would not be a significant problem, since all machines would be protected against the vulnerability at the same time that attackers learned of the vulnerability's existence. However, updates often take the form of large files, and there is not sufficient bandwidth, or other physical resources, to distribute the update to every machine at the same time. Thus, there is a window of time during which the update (and the vulnerability that it both fixes and reveals) is known to the public, but a significant number of machines are unprotected. It is desirable to update programs in such a manner that all, or a large number, of machines are protected very soon after the update is first made known to the public.

Updates can be provided in an encrypted form, such that being able to use the update (or to read it for reverse engineering purposes) requires a decryption key. The key can then be delivered after certain conditions have been met – e.g., only after the encrypted update has been delivered to a sufficient number of machines to ensure widespread protection, and/or after the update has undergone sufficient testing to ensure that it effectively remedies the vulnerability that it is designed to address. Since the key is small the key can be delivered to a large number of machines in a relatively short amount of time, as compared with how long it takes to distribute the update itself. Once the key is received by the machines on which the update is to be installed, the update, which has already been delivered in encrypted form, can be decrypted and installed. Since the update is encrypted, the update can be presumed not to be known to the world until the key is delivered. And, since the widespread distribution of the key takes a relatively short amount of time, the amount of time between when the update is first known, and the time at which a large number of machines are protected, is reduced, as compared with the time period that would exist if updates were distributed in unencrypted form ... "

While perfectly functional and useful, Tomlinson-Walker's original proposal suffers from two shortcomings:

Single Editor Support: Each software editor must manage his own keys. i.e. two editors cannot share keys without compromising the confidentiality of their respective patches.

Memory Increase: The list of published keys grows linearly with the number of updates. This is not a real-life problem because the number of software updates is usually small. However, it would be nice to come up with a system requiring only $O(1)$ or $O(\log^c n)$ memory for managing n updates[1].

The following sections will show how to improve Tomlinson-Walker's original proposal using standard cryptographic building-blocks such as one-way trapdoor functions, identity based encryption and tree-based hashing. The contribution of this invited talk is therefore the illustration of known techniques (e.g. [7,9])

---

[1] Note that throughout this paper complexities are expressed as a function of the number of updates and not as a function of the system's security parameter as is customary in cryptography. This is why, for instance, in Section 4, an IBE decryption operation is considered to require constant-time.

using a new problem rather than the design of new protocols. Throughout this paper τ denotes the moment at which the key is disclosed.

Related Work: The timed release of information is a widely researched area with an abundant bibliography. We do not overview these reference here but refer the reader to the excellent introduction found in [7].

2   Single Editor, Constant Memory, Linear Time

We first present a single-editor patch management method that requires constant storage from the editor but claims from the client $O(n)$ time.

Let N be an RSA modulus [8] generated by the editor. Let $3d = 1 \bmod \phi(N)$. The editor picks a random integer $r_0 \in \mathbb{Z}_N^*$. Everyday the editor computes $r_i = r_{i-1}^d \bmod N$ and updates the information on his website to (only) $\{N, r_i\}$. To retrieve the key of day $t < i$ the client (who knows the current date i) simply cubes r_i modulo N $i - t$ times to reach r_t. Note that exactly for the reasons described in [9], the client cannot speed-up computations and must spend $O(i-t)$ time to compute r_t from r_i.

This idea is also similar in concept to the reverse Canetti-Halevi-Katz [2] scheme suggested in section 5.4 of [1].

3   Single Editor, Polylogarithmic Memory, Polylogarithmic Time

We now use a hashing tree to achieve $O(\log^c n)$ time and storage. Instead of formally describing the algorithm, we illustrate the scheme's operation during 15 days. Pick a random r and derive a key tree by successive hashes as shown in Figure 1. The algorithm governing the management of this tree is straightforward.

4   Multiple Editors, Linear Memory, Constant Time

We will now extend Thomlinson-Walker's concept to multiple editors. As a typical example Microsoft, Google and Apple may want to use the same key distribution server for deploying patches for Windows, Chrome and iTunes without sharing any secret material. A technique for doing so was published by Mont *et alii* in [6]. [6] uses Identity Based Encryption (IBE). The concept of IBE was invented by Shamir in 1984 [10]. It allows a party to encrypt a message using the recipient's identity as a public key. The corresponding private-key is provided by a central authority. The advantage of IBE over conventional public-key encryption is that it avoids certificate management, which greatly simplifies the implementation of secure communications between users. With an IBE scheme, users can simply use their email addresses as their identities. Moreover, the recipient does not need to be online to present a public-key certificate before the sender encrypts a message, and the sender does not have to be online to check the validity of the certificate.

More formally, an IBE scheme consists of four algorithms :

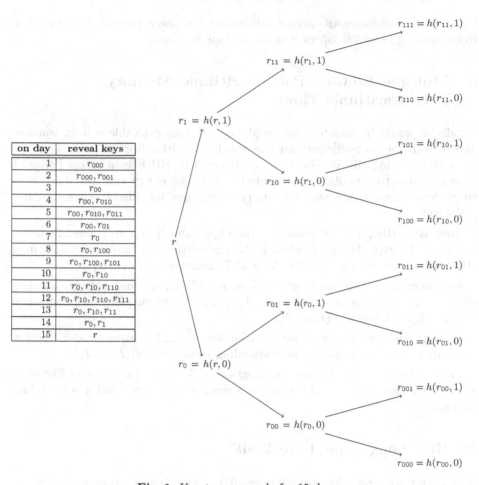

on day	reveal keys
1	r_{000}
2	r_{000}, r_{001}
3	r_{00}
4	r_{00}, r_{010}
5	r_{00}, r_{010}, r_{011}
6	r_{00}, r_{01}
7	r_0
8	r_0, r_{100}
9	r_0, r_{100}, r_{101}
10	r_0, r_{10}
11	r_0, r_{10}, r_{110}
12	$r_0, r_{10}, r_{110}, r_{111}$
13	r_0, r_{10}, r_{11}
14	r_0, r_1
15	r

Fig. 1. Key tree example for 15 days

Setup generates the system's public parameters π and a private master key μ.

KeyGeneration takes as input an identity v and computes v's private key d_v using μ.

Encrypt encrypts messages for an identity v using π.

Decrypt decrypts ciphertexts for identity v using π and the private-key d_v.

[6] considers time information as strings (*e.g.* [5]) and treats them as identities. A Trusted Third Party (TTP) generates π and maintains public list to which a new d_i is added every day. In other words, on day i the TTP reveals the keys $d_1, \ldots, d_i$. This allows different patch editors to encrypt patches into the future. The TTP also allows to preserve the editor's anonymity until τ. Indeed, an editor can post a patch on the TTP's website without indicating to which specific software the patch will be applied. This method forces all users to consult the

list at date τ but increases operational security because it prevents the opponent from knowing in which software he has to look for flaws.

5 Multiple Editors, Polylogarithmic Memory, Polylogarithmic Time

Finally, it would be nice to combine all the previous desirable system features and provide memory-efficient and time-efficient multi-editor support. This can be achieved using Hierarchical IBE (HIBE) [4,3,1]. HIBE generalizes IBE and allows to structure entities in a hierarchy. A level-i entity can distribute keys to its descendants but is unable to decrypt messages intended to ancestors and collaterals.

Just as an IBE, a HIBE comprises the algorithms Setup, KeyGeneration, Encrypt and Decrypt. However, while in IBE identities are binary strings, in a HIBE identities are ordered lists. As in IBE, Setup outputs $\{\pi, \mu\}$.

KeyGeneration takes as input an identity $(I_1, ..., I_k)$ and the private key $d[(I_1, ..., I_{k-1})]$ of the parent identity $(I_1, ..., I_{k-1})$ and outputs the private key $d[(I_1, ..., I_k)]$ for identity $(I_1, ..., I_k)$.

Encrypt encrypts messages for an identity $(I_1, ..., I_k)$ using π and Decrypt decrypts ciphertexts using the corresponding private key $d[(I_1, ..., I_k)]$.

We can hence adapt the tree construction of Section 3 as shown in Figure 2. We conveniently illustrate this idea for a week starting on Sunday and ending on Saturday.

6 How Long Should We Wait?

A last interesting question, totally unrelated to the above cryptographic discussion, is the determination of the optimal key release date τ. A plausible model can be the following: As an encrypted patch is announced, the opponent starts looking for the flaw. Let $\rho(t)$ be the probability that the vulnerability will be discovered by the opponent before t. Let $v(t)$ denote the proportion of users who downloaded the patch at time t. Here $\rho(0) = v(t) = 0$ and $\rho(\infty) = v(\infty) = 1$. It is easy to see that the optimal τ is the value that maximizes $(1 - \rho(t))v(t)$. It

Table 1. Optimal τ values solved for various p, q probabilities

Device connectivity	low exploit complexity $q = 0.1$	average exploit complexity $q = 0.01$	high exploit complexity $q = 0.001$
permanent $p = 0.8$	5	14	24
usual $p = 0.6$	3	8	12
intermittent $p = 0.2$	2	3	5

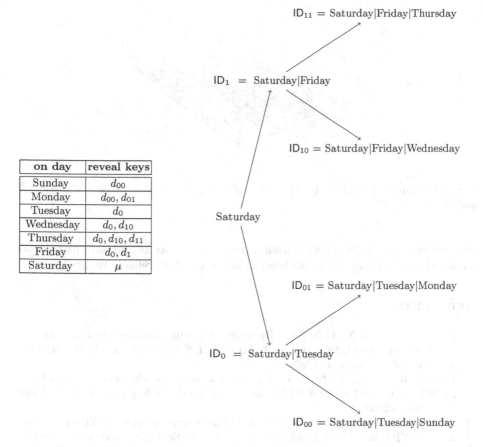

on day	reveal keys
Sunday	d_{00}
Monday	d_{00}, d_{01}
Tuesday	d_0
Wednesday	d_0, d_{10}
Thursday	d_0, d_{10}, d_{11}
Friday	d_0, d_1
Saturday	μ

Fig. 2. HIBE tree example for 7 days. d_X denotes the secret key of identity ID_X.

may be reasonable to assume that $v(t) \simeq 1 - p^t$ where p is the probability that a computer is not turned on by its owner during a day and $\rho(t) \simeq 1 - (1-q)^t$ where q is the probability to independently discover the flaw after a one day's work. Resolution for this simplified model reveals that for most "reasonable" values (e.g. $1/6 \leq p \leq 2/3$ and $10^{-4} \leq q \leq 0.1$) τ would typically range somewhere between 1 and 20 days (Figure 3).

To see what this model imply in practice, we consider three typical device categories: permanently connected devices (e.g. mobile telephones), usually connected devices (e.g. PCs, tablets) and intermittently connected devices (e.g. smart-cards). Exploits of different technical difficulties were assigned the q values given in Table 1.

Table 1 confirms the intuition that (for a fixed p) τ increases with the exploit's complexity, i.e. the model takes advantage of the exploit's non-obviousness to spread the patch to more devices. In addition, (for a fixed q) τ increases with the device's connectivity as it appears better to patch only some devices rather

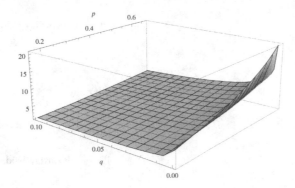

Fig. 3. Optimal τ for $\rho(t) = 1 - (1 - q)^t$ and $v(t) \simeq 1 - p^t$. Solved for $1/6 \leq p \leq 2/3$ and $10^{-4} \leq q \leq 0.1$

than let $v(t)$ slowly grow and maintain the entire device community at risk. We do not claim that this very simplified model accurately reflects reality.

References

1. Boneh, D., Boyen, X., Goh, E.-J.: Hierarchical identity based encryption with constant size ciphertext. In: Cramer, R. (ed.) EUROCRYPT 2005. LNCS, vol. 3494, pp. 440–456. Springer, Heidelberg (2005)
2. Canetti, R., Halevi, S., Katz, J.: A forward-secure public-key encryption scheme. In: Biham, E. (ed.) EUROCRYPT 2003. LNCS, vol. 2656, pp. 255–271. Springer, Heidelberg (2003)
3. Gentry, C., Silverberg, A.: Hierarchical ID-based cryptography. In: Zheng, Y. (ed.) ASIACRYPT 2002. LNCS, vol. 2501, pp. 548–566. Springer, Heidelberg (2002)
4. Horwitz, J., Lynn, B.: Towards hierarchical identity-based encryption. In: Knudsen, L.R. (ed.) EUROCRYPT 2002. LNCS, vol. 2332, pp. 466–481. Springer, Heidelberg (2002)
5. ISO 8601: 2004 Data elements and interchange formats Information interchange Representation of dates and times
6. Mont, M., Harrison, K., Lotspiech, J.: The HP ttime vault service: exploiting IBE for timed release of confidential information. In: Proceedings of the International World Wide Web Conference 2003, pp. 160–169. ACM (2003)
7. Paterson, K.G., Quaglia, E.A.: Time specific encryption. In: Garay, J.A., De Prisco, R. (eds.) SCN 2010. LNCS, vol. 6280, pp. 1–16. Springer, Heidelberg (2010)
8. Rivest, R., Shamir, A., Adleman, L.: A method for obtaining digital signatures and public-key cryptosystems. Communications of the ACM 21(2), 120–126 (1978)
9. Rivest, R., Shamir, A., Wagner, D.: Time-lock puzzles and timed-release crypto, Technical Report MIT/LCS/TR-684. MIT (February 1996)
10. Shamir, A.: Identity-based cryptosystems and signature schemes. In: Blakely, G.R., Chaum, D. (eds.) CRYPTO 1984. LNCS, vol. 196, pp. 47–53. Springer, Heidelberg (1985)
11. Thomlinson, M., Walker, C.: Distribution of encrypted software update to reduce attack winodow. United States Patent Application 2008/007327 (August 31, 2006)

Preserving Receiver-Location Privacy in Wireless Sensor Networks

Javier Lopez[1], Ruben Rios[1], and Jorge Cuellar[2]

[1] Network, Information and Computer Security (NICS) Lab,
Universidad of Málaga, Spain
[2] Siemens AG, Munich, Germany
{jlm,ruben}@lcc.uma.es,
jorge.cuellar@siemens.com

Abstract. Wireless sensor networks (WSNs) are exposed to many different types of attacks. Among these, the most devastating attack is to compromise or destroy the base station since all communications are addressed exclusively to it. Moreover, this feature can be exploited by a passive adversary to determine the location of this critical device. This receiver-location privacy problem can be reduced by hindering traffic analysis but the adversary may still obtain location information by capturing a subset of sensor nodes in the field. This paper addresses, for the first time, these two problems together in a single solution.

Keywords: Wireless sensor networks, location privacy, traffic analysis, node capture.

1 Introduction

Wireless sensor networks (WSNs) are highly distributed networks composed of two types of devices namely, the sensor nodes and the base station [1]. The sensor nodes are matchbox-sized computers which have the ability to monitor the physical phenomena occurring in their vicinity and to wirelessly communicate with devices nearby. To the contrary, the base station is a powerful device that collects all the information sensed by the sensor nodes and serves as an interface to the network. These networks are extremely versatile, making them suitable for countless application scenarios where sensor nodes are unobtrusively embedded into systems for monitoring, tracking and surveillance operations. Many of these applications are critical and thus security and privacy become essential properties.

Privacy problems in WSNs can been categorised as content-oriented or context-oriented [14]. Content-oriented privacy focuses on protecting the privacy of the packet contents. Therefore, the data to be protected may be the actual sensed data [21] or the queries issued to the network [8] by a user. Context-oriented privacy refers to the protection of the metadata associated with the measurement and transmission of data. These data include the time at which sensitive

X. Huang and J. Zhou (Eds.): ISPEC 2014, LNCS 8434, pp. 15–27, 2014.

information is collected (i.e., temporal privacy [13]) and the location of the nodes involved in the communication (i.e., location privacy [15]).

Similarly, there are two main types of location privacy problems affecting sensor networks: source- and receiver-location privacy. The former is concerned with hiding the area where a particular type of data messages are generated. This property is important in applications where these messages are related to the behaviour of individuals, business or valuable assets [12]. On the other side, receiver-location privacy solutions are focused on preventing an adversary from reaching the base station. This is essential for the survivability of the network since an adversary with physical access to this critical device may take control over the network or even render it useless by destroying it.

Preserving receiver-location privacy is especially challenging because all the traffic generated in the network is addressed to this single device using single-path multi-hop communications. This introduces obvious traffic patterns that an attacker can analyse to determine the location of the base station. Several traffic normalisation techniques [5,20,16] have been proposed to hinder traffic analysis but these solutions can only provide some means of protection when the attacker is passive. More sophisticated adversaries may also be able to capture a subset of sensor nodes, exploiting the fact that each node stores a routing table that contains information on the location or distance to the base station.

This paper presents a novel receiver-location privacy solution consisting of two complementary schemes that prevent the leakage of information about the location of base station in the presence of traffic analysis and node capture attacks. The first scheme uses a probabilistic approach to guide data packets to the base station and introduces controlled amounts of fake traffic to hide this flow of information. The second scheme consists of a tuneable routing table perturbation algorithm that reduces the negative effects of node capture attacks while ensuring the delivery of data to the base station. To the best of our knowledge there is no solution in the literature that considers both types of attacks to receiver-location privacy simultaneously.

The rest of this paper is organised as follows. Before describing our solution, some related works in the area are analysed in Section 2. Section 3 presents the network and attacker models together with the main assumptions adopted for the rest of this work. Section 4 first overviews the solution and then gives more details about the internals of each of the two schemes that comprise it. Next, Section 4 briefly discusses the benefits and downsides of the proposed solutions. Finally, some conclusions and future lines of research are sketched in Section 6.

2 Related Work

Receiver-location privacy solutions can be classified according to the capabilities of the adversary, which has traditionally been considered to be passive (with a local or global eavesdropping range). This classification can be further divided according to the main techniques used to counter these adversaries, as shown in Fig. 1. Since this work focuses on local adversaries, we only review these solutions

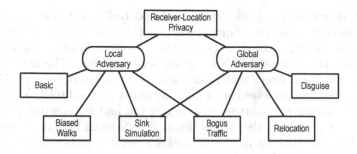

Fig. 1. Classification of Receiver-Location Privacy Solutions

but we refer the reader to [17] for a more exhaustive analysis of location privacy solutions in WSNs.

Deng et al. [6,5] were the first to propose a set of anti-traffic analysis techniques to protect the base station. They present a set of basic countermeasures consisting of applying hop-by-hop re-encryption, de-correlating packet sending times and establishing a uniform sending rate across the network. These solutions have some limitations and the authors try to alleviate them with the Multi-Parent Routing (MPR) scheme. The idea behind this scheme is balance the traffic load while reducing the distance to the base station at each hop. To that end, each node selects the next node uniformly at random from all its neighbours closer to the base station than itself. However, this countermeasure is insufficient to prevent parent-child correlation and the authors propose to make every node decide whether to send the packet to a random parent or to a random neighbour based on some probability.

A similar approach is proposed by Jian et al. [10,11]. They suggest to make each sensor node divide its neighbours into two groups: closer and further neighbours. Later, data packets are sent with higher probability to nodes belonging to the group of closer neighbours. This results in a traffic pattern biased towards the base station, which can be noticed by an attacker after a sufficient number of observations. This problem is reduced by injecting fake packets in the opposite direction with some probability. However, the attacker can still determine whether a packet is fake in some situations and therefore he is able to determine that the base station is on the other direction.

Some other approaches try to introduce more randomness in the communication pattern. Deng et al. [7,5] further improve MPR by generating fake paths of messages with some probability when a node observes the transmission of data packets in their vicinity. As a result, the random path grows fake branches. The main problem of this scheme is that nodes near the base station generate much more fake branches than remote nodes. To address this problem, the authors suggest that sensor nodes may adjust their probability of generating fake traffic based on the number of packet they forward.

Another scheme based on the injection of fake traffic is devised in [19]. Data messages are sent along the shortest path to the base station and when two of these paths converge at some point, the intersection node sends two fake packets to two fake data sinks after a given period of time. The idea is to have several points in the network that receive a similar number of packets. The main limitation is that the attacker gets a good intuition of the direction to the base station while tracing the shortest path before the first intersection point. This problem is also present in the Bidirectional Tree Scheme [3], which sends data messages along the shortest path and creates several branches of fake messages that flow into and out of the path.

Finally, sink simulation approaches try to emulate the presence of the base station at different locations. These techniques are also based on the generation of fake traffic but addressed to particular network areas. This results in areas with high volumes of traffic (i.e., hotspots) that are intended to draw the adversary away from the real base station. In [2], the base station selects the hotspots by sending some special messages to random locations which are at least h hops away from it. During data transmission, when a node receives a real packet it generates a fake message and forwards it to its closer maelstrom. Deng et al. [7,5] also devised a similar solution but hotspots are created in a decentralised way by keeping track of the number of fake packets forwarded to each neighbour. New fake traffic is more likely to be sent to neighbours who have previously received more fake traffic. The main drawback of hotspots is the high overhead needed to deceive local adversaries.

The solution presented in this paper is an evolution of our previous work [16], which can be classified as a biased random walk solution with fake packet injection. In the new version we introduce a new mechanism capable of increasing the safety time of the base station in the presence of node capture attacks. None of the solutions in the literature have considered this problem as a threat to receiver-location privacy.

3   Problem Description

This section presents the main assumptions as well as the network model and the capabilities of the attacker adopted for the rest of this paper.

3.1   Network Model

This work considers sensor networks deployed for monitoring purposes. These networks are usually deployed in vast areas and they are composed of a large number of sensor nodes and a single base station.

We assume that the connectivity of the network is relatively high and each node knows its neighbours based on some topology discovery protocol. This allows sensor nodes to build their routing tables in such a way that the node is aware of the distance of each of its neighbours to the base station. During data transmission the node may select the next communication hop from neighbours which are one hop closer, at the same distance than itself, or one hop further away from the base station. We denote these groups of nodes as L^C, $L^{\mathcal{E}}$ and $L^{\mathcal{F}}$, respectively.

Finally, we assume that every node shares pairwise cryptographic keys with each of its neighbours, which enables hop-by-hop re-encryption as well as the identification of fake messages.

3.2 Attacker Model

The adversary is considered to be mobile and capable of performing both traffic analysis and node capture attacks. Its hearing range is limited to a portion of the network, which we represent as $\mathcal{ADV}_n$ being n the number of hops controlled by the adversary. In the literature, the adversary is usually considered to have a monitoring range similar to an ordinary sensor node (i.e., $\mathcal{ADV}_1$).

A passive adversary decides its next move based on its observations. He may choose between a time-correlation or a rate-monitoring attack. In the former, the attacker observes the sending times of a nodes and its neighbours. Since a node forwards a packet immediately after it is received, the attacker may learn which neighbours are closer to the base station. The other attack is based on the assumption that nodes near the base station have a higher forwarding rate. Therefore, the attacker observes which node in its vicinity sends more packets and moves towards it.

An active adversary is interested in capturing nodes in order to retrieve their routing tables since these contain information on the distance to the base station. There are some works in the literature [4,18] devoted to the modelling and mitigation of node capture attacks but they are focused on the protection of the key distribution mechanisms. Some authors consider a random node capture strategy while others consider the capture of nodes in a particular area. In this work we consider that the attacker starts by capturing nodes at the edge of the network and moves according to the information he obtains. We also assume that the attacker cannot compromise all sensor nodes without being discovered. Only a fraction of the routing tables in the network can be captured.

4 Base Station Cloaking Scheme

This section presents our approach for protecting receiver-location privacy. We start by giving an overview of the two mechanisms comprising our solution and then we describe them in detail.

4.1 Overview

The devised solution consists of two complimentary schemes, a traffic normalisation scheme and a routing tables perturbation scheme. The former is intended to hinder traffic analysis attacks while the latter is used to diminish the threat of node capture attacks.

During data transmission, whenever a node has something to transmit, it sends two packets to different random nodes. One of the packets is more likely to be received by a node closer to the base station while the other packet is received by a neighbour at the same distance or further away with high probability. These probabilities are adjusted in such a way that every neighbouring node receives on average the same amount of traffic. Consequently, one of the packets can be used to carry real data and the other one as a mechanism to hide the data flow.

The second scheme complements the first one by introducing some perturbation to the routing tables. In this way, if an adversary is capable of capturing a node and retrieving its routing table he cannot be certain of which nodes in the table are closer to the base station. A parameter is introduced to control the degree of perturbation of the tables since modifying the routing tables affects the efficiency of the data transmission protocol.

4.2   Traffic Normalisation

The transmission protocol must satisfy a series of properties to ensure the security and usability of the system. First, it must guarantee the convergence of data packets to the base station. For this purpose, the expected value of the distance between the data sender and the base station must be larger than the expected value of the distance between the next node and the base station. This is a property for the usability of the system. Second, the protocol must ensure that the traffic generated by a node is evenly distributed among its neighbours. In other words, the average number of messages received by any pair of neighbours must be similar. This property is intended to locally normalise the traffic and thus make it difficult for the adversary to make a decision on its next move based on his observations. Finally, since the protocol sends pair of messages, we impose a third property to make sure that each of them is sent to a different node.

Sensor nodes always send two packets when they have something to transmit. Usually, real packets are sent out in conjunction with fake packets to hide the direction of the data flow because they are indistinguishable to an external observer. We devised a lightweight mechanism that ensures the three properties described above. This mechanism is based on the combinations without repetition of two elements from the routing table. If the routing table is sorted according to the distances of the neighbours to the base station (see Fig. 2a), we achieve that with high probability, any resulting combination has its first element from the list of closer nodes L^C. Consequently, if real packets are sent to the first element of the combination the convergence property is satisfied. Additionally, if combinations are picked uniformly at random, the node balances its transmission among all its neighbours since all the elements in the routing table appear in exactly $l - 1$ combinations, where l is the number of rows of the table. The combinations resulting from the routing table of node x are depicted in Fig. 2b, where we additionally count the number of combinations where the first and second element of the combination, n_1 and n_2 respectively, belong to each of the groups. From this figure it is easy to see that the probability of sending

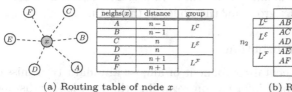

(a) Routing table of node x (b) Resulting combinations

Fig. 2. Neighbours Selection Process

Algorithm 1. Traffic normalisation

Input: $packet \leftarrow receive()$
Input: $combs \leftarrow combinations(sort(neighs), 2)$
Input: $FAKE\_TTL$
1. $\{n1, n2\} \leftarrow select\_random(combs)$
2. **if** $isreal(packet)$ **then**
3. $send\_random(n1, packet, n2, fake(FAKE\_TTL))$
4. **else**
5. $TTL \leftarrow get\_time\_to\_live(packet) - 1$
6.   **if** $TTL > 0$ **then**
7. $send\_random(n1, fake(TTL), n2, fake(TTL))$
8.   **end if**
9. **end if**

---

a data packet towards the base station, i.e., $\mathbb{P}(n_1 \in L^C) = 9/15$, is much higher than in order directions.

Since fake traffic is injected in the network, its propagation must be controlled in some way to minimise its impact on the lifetime of the network. In other words, fake traffic must be dropped at some point but this action must not give location information to the adversary. The whole process is represented in Algorithm 1. Upon the reception of a packet, the node first checks whether the packet contains actual data. In case the packet is real, the node selects two neighbours using the above mentioned mechanism and generates a new fake packet that contains a time-to-live value. The data packet is sent to node n_1 and the fake packet to node n_2. If the packet received is fake, the node must behave in the same way, that is, the node sends two packets. However, now both packets are fake. The time-to-live value is decremented at each hop and if the value reaches 0 no packets are forwarded. The initial value of this parameter is globally defined by the network administrator based on the eavesdropping power of the adversary. The goal is to allow fake traffic to propagate beyond the reach of the adversary.

This protocol works correctly under the assumption of highly connected networks where the number of further neighbours do not outnumber the number of closer neighbours. In [16] we showed this conditions are met even for randomly deployed sensor networks since the number of neighbours closer to the base station is roughly the same to the number of nodes further away. Still, the speed of convergence of data packets is affected by these values. The speed increases as the number of elements in $L^{\mathcal{C}}$ grows for the nodes in the path.

4.3   Routing Tables Perturbation

Routing tables are a fundamental component of almost any data transmission protocol. They contain relevant information regarding the location or distance to the data sink. Our traffic normalisation protocol relies on the table order[1] to determine suitable combinations of neighbours that satisfy the usability and privacy of the system. However, if an adversary gains access to the routing tables he is able to determine which nodes are closer to the base station regardless of the use of traffic analysis techniques.

We propose a routing table perturbation scheme that rearranges the elements of the table to generate some uncertainty on the adversary instead of giving him direct access to this privacy-relevant information. Since the perturbation affects the resulting combinations, it must be carefully tuned in such a way that the convergence property holds. Formally, we must ensure that $\mathbb{P}(n_1 \in L^{\mathcal{C}}) > \mathbb{P}(n_1 \in L^{\mathcal{F}})$. In other words, the routing table must continue to be biased towards the base station after the rearrangement of its elements.

The perturbation degree or bias is an important variable in this scheme because it determines both the speed of convergence of data packets to the base station and the uncertainty level of the attacker. We define the bias of a routing table r, $bias(r) \in [-1, 1]$, as the probability of sending data packets in the direction of or in the opposite direction to the base station. The closer the bias is to 1 the greater it is the probability that data packets are sent to nodes in $L^{\mathcal{C}}$. Likewise, a bias value close to -1 implies that it is highly likely that the resulting combinations have their first elements from $L^{\mathcal{F}}$. Consequently, the bias can be defined as the difference between the probability of sending the data packet to a node in $L^{\mathcal{C}}$ and the probability of sending it to $L^{\mathcal{F}}$.

$$bias(r) = \mathbb{P}(n_1 \in L^{\mathcal{C}}) - \mathbb{P}(n_1 \in L^{\mathcal{F}}) \tag{1}$$

Note that these probabilities depend on the positions of each of the elements in $L^{\mathcal{C}}$ and $L^{\mathcal{F}}$ in the routing table because the position determines the number of combinations that have a particular neighbour as the first element. For example, if we number the rows of the routing table in Fig. 2a from bottom to top, starting from 0, we can see in Fig. 2b that there are no combinations where the first element is F while A is the first element of 5 combinations. Therefore, we can generalise the probabilities in Equation 1 for any subset of elements in the table L as:

$$\mathbb{P}(n_1 \in L) = \frac{1}{C} \sum_{n \in L} pos(n) \tag{2}$$

where C is the total number of combinations resulting from the table. These equations allows us to check that $bias(r) = -1$ when the table is comprised

---

[1] Knowing the actual distance, as shown in Fig. 2b, is not necessary.

Algorithm 2. Perturbation Algorithm

Input: $br \leftarrow \{L^{\mathcal{C}}, L^{\mathcal{E}}, L^{\mathcal{F}}\}$
Input: $bias, MAX\_ITER$
1. $E \leftarrow energy(bias, br)$
2. $i \leftarrow 0$
3. **while** $(i < MAX\_ITER) \wedge (E \neq 0)$ **do**
4. $br' \leftarrow swap(br)$
5. $E' \leftarrow energy(bias, br')$
6.   **if** $(E' < E)$ **then**
7. $br \leftarrow br'$
8. $E \leftarrow E'$
9.   **end if**
10. $i \leftarrow i + 1$
11. **end while**
12. **return** br

---

solely of elements in $L^{\mathcal{F}}$ since $C = \sum_{n \in L^{\mathcal{F}}} pos(n)$. Likewise, if all the elements in the table are closer to the base station, then $bias(r) = 1$. In general, the bias must be greater than 0 in order to enable the eventual delivery of messages to the base station.

Finding a particular arrangement of the table that satisfies a particular bias value may be time consuming and may not always be feasible. This problem is conditioned by the number of elements of each group in the original table. Therefore, our perturbation scheme (see Algorithm 2) is modelled as an optimisation algorithm that receives as input a desired bias and the routing table, and returns the closest match. Our algorithm is inspired on evolutionary strategies [9] where simple mutations are applied to the routing table in order to minimise the distance to the desired bias. More precisely, we swap two elements from the routing tables and check whether this reduces the energy (i.e., the distance to the desired solution). In case the new state of the table reduces the energy we keep this arrangement. The process is repeated for a maximum number of iterations or until the energy is zero, which means that the optimal solution is found.

The main advantage of these solutions compared to deterministic algorithms is that the time to find a (pseudo-) optimal solution to the problem is reduced. The search space may be large for very dense network configurations where the routing tables contain a large number of nodes. In these cases, the computation time may be reduced several orders of magnitude. The main downside is that the desired solution is not always found although it converges to it.

The non-deterministic nature of the algorithm provides an additional means of protection to reversing attacks. Since the algorithm does not always reach the same solution, the attacker may not be able to undo the perturbation even if he learns the bias used by the algorithm. Nonetheless, it is more secure to completely remove this value from the node after use since it is no longer necessary for the operation of the data transmission protocol.

5   Discussion

A local eavesdropper eventually finds a data source and starts analysing the traffic it generates. If the attacker chooses to perform a time-correlation attack he moves to the neighbour who forwards the first packet, which may be real or fake. If the packet is real, the attacker is highly likely to reduce its distance to the base station but the probability of following a real packet is lower than the probability of following a fake packet. The reason is that the ratio of fake to real packets is greater or equal to 1 for typical attackers. Also, note that the adversary can only be sure that he followed a fake packet when it is no longer propagated but since they flow in any direction, this provides the attacker[2] with no relevant information. If the strategy is to perform rate monitoring, the attacker moves to the neighbour receiving the larger number of packets but our transmission protocol evenly distributes the traffic, which hinders this attack.

Dealing with an attacker capable of capturing sensor nodes and retrieving its routing table is an ambitious task. First, note that making the nodes store fake routing tables provides no protection to the real table. The reason is that the node must keep a pointer to the real table and the adversary may also have access to it. Even if this information is obfuscated in some way, the adversary can identify which table is in use in various ways. For example, if the node is transmitting packets, the adversary can observe which pairs of neighbours are actually receiving messages. Also, since the routing tables are updated after each topology discovery phase the fake routing tables should take into account topology changes to prevent the attacker from easily distinguishing the real table. The fact that routing tables are periodically updated, also implies that the perturbation must be performed by all nodes. If the decision is determined probabilistically, the adversary could compromise a set of nodes and wait until the next discovery phase to check whether the routing tables changed. In view of this, the attacker could identify which tables are real. In general, keeping the real tables in its original form within the nodes is unsafe.

The main drawback of our perturbation algorithm is that it negatively impacts the performance of the network by slowing the speed of convergence of data packets. However, it is the price to pay for protecting the location of the most important device of the network. Still, the attacker has an advantage that depends on the degree of perturbation introduced to the routing table. Since the resulting table must be slightly biased towards the base station in order to allow data packets to be delivered, the adversary can reproduce the behaviour of the node and generate pairs of messages whose first element is closer to the base station with higher probability. But this is true for any system where the attacker has access to all the secrets. Nevertheless, introducing the perturbation algorithm is much better than not modifying the routing tables. In the latter case, the adversary simply needs to move always to the first neighbour in the

---

[2] We are assuming that the network is configured correctly and thereby the adversary does not control the whole path of fake messages.

routing table and will reach the base station within the minimum number of captures.

6 Conclusions

This work presents a novel receiver-location privacy solution that reduces the chances of an attacker reaching the base station. The devised solution consists of two complementary schemes that hinder both traffic analysis and node capture attacks. The first scheme is a traffic normalisation protocol that injects controlled amounts of fake traffic to hide the flow of real data packets. This protocol satisfies several usability and security properties that ensure the eventual delivery of data packets to the base station while it is protected from being traced. The second scheme is an evolutionary algorithm that perturbs the routing tables of the nodes to interfere with adversaries capable of gaining location information about the base station after capturing a node. The algorithm is guided by a bias value, which determines the perturbation degree of the tables. This value introduces a tradeoff between the protection against these attacks and the mean delivery time of data packets.

As future work we aim to investigate new mechanisms to reduce the overhead introduced by the traffic normalisation scheme especially when the hearing range of the adversary is large. We also want to explore and develop more sophisticated attacker models and check the robustness of our solution against them. Additionally, we are working on the design of a privacy-friendly topology discovery protocol since traditional solutions reveal the location of the base station. Our final goal is to develop an integral solution capable of protecting both from attackers interested in finding the base station and data sources.

Acknowledgements. This work has been partially funded by the European Commission through the FP7 project NESSoS (FP7 256890), the Spanish Ministry of Science and Innovation through the ARES project (CSD2007-00004) and the Andalusian Government PISCIS project (P10-TIC-06334). The first author is supported by the Spanish Ministry of Education through the F.P.U. Program. Also, special thanks to Martín Ochoa for his valuable comments in preliminary versions of this work.

References

1. Akyildiz, I., Su, W., Sankarasubramaniam, Y., Cayirci, E.: A survey on sensor networks. IEEE Communications Magazine 40(8), 102–114 (2002)
2. Chang, S., Qi, Y., Zhu, H., Dong, M., Ota, K.: Maelstrom: Receiver-Location Preserving in Wireless Sensor Networks. In: Cheng, Y., Eun, D.Y., Qin, Z., Song, M., Xing, K. (eds.) WASA 2011. LNCS, vol. 6843, pp. 190–201. Springer, Heidelberg (2011)
3. Chen, H., Lou, W.: From Nowhere to Somewhere: Protecting End-to-End Location Privacy in Wireless Sensor Networks. In: 29th International Performance Computing and Communications Conference, IPCCC 2010, pp. 1–8. IEEE (2010)

4. Chen, X., Makki, K., Yen, K., Pissinou, N.: Node Compromise Modeling and its Applications in Sensor Networks. In: 12th IEEE Symposium on Computers and Communications (ISCC 2007), pp. 575–582 (July 2007)

5. Deng, J., Han, R., Mishra, S.: Decorrelating wireless sensor network traffic to inhibit traffic analysis attacks. Pervasive and Mobile Computing 2(2), 159–186 (2006)

6. Deng, J., Han, R., Mishra, S.: Intrusion tolerance and anti-traffic analysis strategies for wireless sensor networks. In: International Conference on Dependable Systems and Networks, DSN 2004, pp. 637–646. IEEE Computer Society, Los Alamitos (2004)

7. Deng, J., Han, R., Mishra, S.: Countermeasures Against Traffic Analysis Attacks in Wireless Sensor Networks. In: 1st International Conference on Security and Privacy for Emerging Areas in Communications Networks (SECURECOMM 2005), pp. 113–126 (2005)

8. Di Pietro, R., Viejo, A.: Location privacy and resilience in wireless sensor networks querying. Comput. Commun. 34(3), 515–523 (2011)

9. Eiben, A., Smith, J.: Introduction to Evolutionary Computing. Natural Computing, 2nd edn. Springer (2007)

10. Jian, Y., Chen, S., Zhang, Z., Zhang, L.: Protecting receiver-location privacy in wireless sensor networks. In: 26th IEEE International Conference on Computer Communications (INFOCOM 2007), pp. 1955–1963 (2007)

11. Jian, Y., Chen, S., Zhang, Z., Zhang, L.: A novel scheme for protecting receiver's location privacy in wireless sensor networks. IEEE Transactions on Wireless Communications 7(10), 3769–3779 (2008)

12. Kamat, P., Zhang, Y., Trappe, W., Ozturk, C.: Enhancing Source-Location Privacy in Sensor Network Routing. In: 25th IEEE International Conference on Distributed Computing Systems (ICDCS 2005), pp. 599–608 (2005)

13. Kamat, P., Xu, W., Trappe, W., Zhang, Y.: Temporal Privacy in Wireless Sensor Networks. In: 27th International Conference on Distributed Computing Systems, ICDCS 2007, p. 23. IEEE Computer Society, Washington, DC (2007)

14. Ozturk, C., Zhang, Y., Trappe, W.: Source-Location Privacy in Energy-Constrained Sensor Network Routing. In: 2nd ACM Workshop on Security of Ad Hoc and Sensor Networks (SASN 2004), pp. 88–93 (2004)

15. Proano, A., Lazos, L.: Perfect Contextual Information Privacy in WSNs under Colluding Eavesdroppers. In: 6th ACM Conference on Security and Privacy in Wireless and Mobile Networks, WiSec, April 17-19. ACM, Budapest (2013)

16. Rios, R., Cuellar, J., Lopez, J.: Robust Probabilistic Fake Packet Injection for Receiver-Location Privacy in WSN. In: Foresti, S., Yung, M., Martinelli, F. (eds.) ESORICS 2012. LNCS, vol. 7459, pp. 163–180. Springer, Heidelberg (2012)

17. Rios, R., Lopez, J.: Analysis of Location Privacy Solutions in Wireless Sensor Networks. IET Communications 5, 2518–2532 (2011)

18. Vu, T.M., Safavi-Naini, R., Williamson, C.: Securing wireless sensor networks against large-scale node capture attacks. In: Proceedings of the 5th ACM Symposium on Information, Computer and Communications Security, ASIACCS 2010, pp. 112–123. ACM, New York (2010)

19. Yao, L., Kang, L., Shang, P., Wu, G.: Protecting the sink location privacy in wireless sensor networks. Personal and Ubiquitous Computing, 1–11 (2012), doi:10.1007/s00779-012-0539-9

20. Ying, B., Gallardo, J.R., Makrakis, D., Mouftah, H.T.: Concealing of the Sink Location in WSNs by Artificially Homogenizing Traffic Intensity. In: 1st International Workshop on Security in Computers, Networking and Communications, pp. 1005–1010 (2011)
21. Zhang, L., Zhang, H., Conti, M., Di Pietro, R., Jajodia, S., Mancini, L.: Preserving privacy against external and internal threats in WSN data aggregation. Telecommunication Systems 52(4), 2163–2176 (2013)

Data Security and Privacy in the Cloud

Pierangela Samarati

Università degli Studi di Milano
Dipartimento di Informatica
Via Bramante 65 – 26013 Crema – Italy
pierangela.samarati@unimi.it

Abstract. Achieving data security and privacy in the cloud means ensuring confidentiality and integrity of data and computations, and protection from non authorized accesses. Satisfaction of such requirements entails non trivial challenges, as relying on external servers, owners lose control on their data. In this paper, we discuss the problems of guaranteeing proper data security and privacy in the cloud, and illustrate possible solutions for them.

Keywords: Cloud computing, confidentiality, integrity, honest-but-curious servers, data fragmentation, inferences, private access, shuffle index, query integrity.

1 Introduction

Cloud computing has emerged as a successful paradigm increasingly appealing to individuals and companies for storing, accessing, processing, and sharing information. The cloud provides, in fact, significant benefits of scalability and elasticity, allowing its users to conveniently offer and enjoy services at reduced costs thanks to the economy of scale that providers can exploit. Relying on the cloud for storing and managing data brings, together with all the benefits and convenience, also new security and privacy risks (e.g., [20,25,27,34]). In this paper, we address in particular the problems related to the protection of data and of computations on them. On one hand, cloud providers can be assumed to employ basic security mechanisms for protecting data outsourced to them, maybe even employing controls that would not be affordable by most individuals or small companies. On the other hand, however, relying on external parties for storing or processing data, users lose control on such data hence leaving them potentially exposed to security and privacy risks. Data could be sensitive and should be maintained confidential even with respect to the cloud provider itself that, while trustworthy for providing services, should not be allowed to know the actual data content (*honest-but-curious* servers). Even the integrity of data – or of computations on them – can be at risk as providers might behave not correctly (*lazy* or *malicious* servers).

X. Huang and J. Zhou (Eds.): ISPEC 2014, LNCS 8434, pp. 28–41, 2014.

Protecting data and computations entail then ensuring both confidentiality and integrity. Confidentiality issues arise since data externally stored or managed can contain sensitive information, or information that the owner wishes to maintain confidential. Confidentiality should be guaranteed also with respect to the server storing or processing data, hence introducing complications in query execution and in the enforcement of possible access restrictions. In addition to the stored data, even users' accesses on them may need to be maintained confidential. Integrity issues arise since external servers storing or processing data could misbehave. Guaranteeing integrity requires providing users with the ability of assessing that data are stored correctly, computations are performed correctly, and returned results are correct.

This paper is organized in two main sections. Section 2 illustrates confidentiality issues, presenting solutions for guaranteeing confidentiality of data in storage, enforcing access restrictions, and guaranteeing confidentiality of accesses over data. Section 3 illustrates integrity issues, presenting solutions for guaranteeing integrity of data as well as of computations on them.

2 Confidentiality of Data and Access Control

Guaranteeing confidentiality in the cloud entails ensuring confidentiality to the stored data (Section 2.1), enforcing of access restrictions on the data (Section 2.2), and maintaining confidentiality of the accesses performed on the data (Section 2.3).

2.1 Encryption and Fragmentation

A natural solution for protecting data confidentiality consists in *encrypting* data before releasing them to the external server for storage. Encryption can be applied at different granularity levels. In particular, when data are organized in relational tables, encryption can be applied at the level of *table*, *attribute*, *tuple*, and *cell* [7,22]. Encryption at the level of tuple appears to be preferred as it provides some support for fine-grained access while not requiring too many encryption/decryption operations. Also, for performance reasons, symmetric encryption is usually adopted.

A complication in dealing with encrypted data is that, since the server storing the data should not know the actual data content, data cannot be decrypted for query execution. A possible solution to this obstacle consists in evaluating queries on the encrypted values themselves. For instance, homomorphic encryption solutions provide such a capability but support limited kinds of queries and suffer from high performance overhead. An alternative solution consists in associating with the encrypted tuples some metadata, called *indexes*, which can be used for query execution (e.g., [7,22]). Intuitively an index column can be specified for every attribute on which conditions need to be evaluated. Conditions on plaintext values, known at the trusted client side, are then translated

PATIENT

SSN	Name	YoB	Job	Disease	Treatment
123-45-6789	A. Allen	1971	hairdressing	eczema	ointments
635-98-3692	B. Brown	1954	painter	asthma	bronchodilator
820-73-0735	C. Clark	1985	plastic worker	dermatite	corticosteroids
838-91-9634	D. Davis	1962	miners	silicosis	oxygen
168-87-4067	E. Evans	1977	lab techn	hepatitis	antiviral drug
912-83-7265	F. Fisher	1960	nurse	tuberculosis	antibiotics

(a)

PATIENT^e

tid	enc	I_n	I_y	I_j	I_d
1	τ	n_1	y_1	j_1	d_1
2	σ	n_2	y_1	j_2	d_2
3	λ	n_3	y_1	j_2	d_1
4	ρ	n_4	y_2	j_3	d_2
5	α	n_5	y_3	j_1	d_2
6	δ	n_6	y_3	j_3	d_2

(b)

Fig. 1. An example of plaintext relation (a) and of corresponding encrypted and indexed relation (b)

into conditions on index values to be evaluated at the server side. Figure 1 illustrates an example of relation and its corresponding encrypted and indexed version, where indexes have been defined over attributes Name, YoB, Job, and Disease of the plaintext relation. Query execution is enforced by: a query to be executed by the server over the index values and a further query to be executed by the client on the server's result once decrypted, to evaluate further conditions and producing the actual result. Index values should be well related to the plaintext values to provide effective in query execution, while at the same time not leak information on the plaintext values behind them. Different indexing functions have been proposed that differ in how plaintext values are mapped onto index values, such as [15]: *direct* indexing, providing a one-to-one mapping between plaintext values and index values; *hash and bucket-based* indexing, providing a many-to-one mapping between plaintext values and index values (thus generating collisions); and *flattened* indexing, providing a one-to-many mapping between plaintext values and index values (to not expose the indexing function to frequency-based inferences). All these types of indexing functions differ in the offered protection guarantees, the kinds of queries supported, and the performance overhead suffered. For instance, direct indexing allows precise evaluation of equality conditions, and even of range conditions if indexes are ordered but is also the one most exposed to inference attacks compromising the confidentiality of the indexing function.

As encryption makes query evaluation more complex or not always possible, alternative solutions have been devised trying to limit encryption, or depart from it. In particular, when what is sensitive are not the data values themselves but their association, confidentiality can be guaranteed breaking the association (i.e., its visibility) by storing the involved attributes in separate *data fragments*. The association is then protected by restricting visibility of the fragments or ensuring their un-linkability. A sensitive association can be represented as a set of attributes whose joint visibility (i.e., whose association) is sensitive. Attributes whose values are sensitive are also captured in such representation as they correspond to singleton sets. Figure 2(a) illustrates an example of relation and confidentiality constraints over it. Different fragmentation paradigms have been proposed differing in the use of encryption and in the assumptions required to ensure protection of the sensitive associations.

PATIENT

SSN	Name	YoB	Job	Disease	Treatment
123-45-6789	A. Allen	1971	hairdressing	eczema	ointments
635-98-3692	B. Brown	1954	painter	asthma	bronchodilator
820-73-0735	C. Clark	1985	plastic worker	dermatite	corticosteroids
838-91-9634	D. Davis	1962	miners	silicosis	oxygen
168-87-4067	E. Evans	1977	lab techn	hepatitis	antiviral drug
912-83-7265	F. Fisher	1960	nurse	tuberculosis	antibiotics

$c_1 = \{\text{SSN}\}$
$c_2 = \{\text{Name,Disease}\}$
$c_3 = \{\text{Name,Job}\}$
$c_4 = \{\text{Job,Disease}\}$

(a) Original relation and confidentiality constraints

F_1

tid	Name	YoB	Treatment	SSN^{1e}	Disease^{1e}
1	A. Allen	1971	ointments	α	η
2	B. Brown	1954	bronchodilator	β	ρ
3	C. Clark	1985	corticosteroids	γ	σ
4	D. Davis	1962	oxygen	δ	π
5	E. Evans	1977	antiviral drugs	ϵ	ϕ
6	F. Fisher	1960	antibiotics	θ	ε

F_2

tid	Job	SSN^{2e}	Disease^{2e}
1	hairdressing	χ	ξ
2	painter	τ	η
3	plastic worker	η	ζ
4	miners	ν	λ
5	lab techn	μ	ϱ
6	nurse	ω	ι

(b) Two can keep a secret

F_1

salt	enc	Name	YoB
s_{11}	Δ	A. Allen	1971
s_{12}	ν	B. Brown	1954
s_{13}	ρ	C. Clark	1985
s_{14}	σ	D. Davis	1962
s_{15}	ϵ	E. Evans	1977
s_{16}	π	F. Fisher	1960

F_2

sal	enc	Disease	Treatment
s_{21}	β	eczema	ointments
s_{22}	γ	asthma	bronchodilator
s_{23}	δ	dermatite	corticosteroids
s_{24}	μ	silicosis	oxygen
s_{25}	ϵ	hepatitis	antiviral drug
s_{26}	χ	tuberculosis	antibiotics

F_3

sal	enc	Job
s_{31}	ψ	hairdressing
s_{32}	ω	painter
s_{33}	Σ	plastic worker
s_{34}	Π	miners
s_{35}	λ	lab techn
s_{36}	ι	nurse

(c) Multiple fragments

F_o

tid	SSN	Name	Job
1	123-45-6789	A. Allen	hairdressing
2	635-98-3692	B. Brown	painter
3	820-73-0735	C. Clark	plastic worker
4	838-91-9634	D. Davis	miners
5	168-87-4067	E. Evans	lab techn
6	912-83-7265	F. Fisher	nurse

F_s

tid	YoB	Disease	Treatment
1	1971	eczema	ointments
2	1954	asthma	bronchodilator
3	1985	dermatite	corticosteroids
4	1962	silicosis	oxygen
5	1977	hepatitis	antiviral drug
6	1960	tuberculosis	antibiotics

(d) Keep a few

Fig. 2. A sample relation with confidentiality constraints and its fragmentation with different paradigms

— *Two can keep a secret* [1]. Data are split in two fragments stored at two independent external servers which are assumed to not communicate and not know each other. Sensitive attributes are obfuscated (e.g., encrypted). Sensitive associations are protected by splitting the attributes among the two servers. In addition to sensitive attributes, other attributes may be obfuscated if their plaintext storage at any of the two servers would expose some sensitive associations. The two fragments have a tuple identifier in common, allowing the data owner to correctly reconstruct the original relation. Figure 2(b) illustrates a sample fragmentation in two fragments for relation PATIENT of Figure 2(a), subject to the reported confidentiality constraints. Note that, while not sensitive by itself, attribute Disease is obfuscated since its plaintext storage in any of the two fragments would violate some constraint (c_2 for fragment F_1 and c_4 for fragment F_2).

– *Multiple fragments* [4,6,10,13]. It does not impose any assumption on the external servers or on the number of fragments. Sensitive attributes are stored in encrypted form. Sensitive associations are protected by splitting the involved attributes among different fragments. Fragments are assumed to be complete (every attribute is represented either in plaintext or in the encrypted chunk) and to not have attributes in common (to ensure their unlinkability). The encrypted chunk is produced with salts to avoid exposure of values with multiple occurrences. Figure 2(c) illustrates a sample fragmentation with multiple fragments for relation PATIENT; the use of three fragments permits to represent in plaintext form all attributes that are not sensitive by themselves.

– *Keep a few* [5]. It assumes the data owner (or a trusted party) to store a limited portion of the data and completely departs from encryption (i.e., all attributes are stored in plaintext form). Sensitive attributes are stored at the owner side. Sensitive associations are protected by ensuring that, for each constraint, at least one of the attributes in it is stored at the owner side. A tuple identifier is maintained in both fragments to allow the owner to correctly reconstruct the original relation. Figure 2(d) illustrates a sample fragmentation for relation PATIENT with this approach, where F_o is the fragment stored at the owner side.

The advantage of fragmentation over encryption is the availability of data in the clear and therefore the ability of the server to evaluate any condition on them; by contrast encrypted data or indexes provide limited support for evaluating conditions. In any of the strategies above, fragmentation should be enforced trying to maximize the availability of attributes in the clear and to minimize the fragmentation enforced. Also, additional criteria could be taken into account such as the query workload or possible visibility requirements.

Fragmentation approaches assume fragments to not be linkable (and therefore associations to be protected) when they have no common attributes. In other words, attributes are assumed to be independent. However, often dependencies may exist among attributes introducing inferences from some attributes over others that indirectly expose otherwise not visible attributes or enable linking among fragments [11]. To illustrate, consider the set of attributes and constraints in Figure 3(a), also represented as a graph with one node per attribute and constraint and with multi-arcs connecting attributes to constraints. A fragmentation reporting, Birth, Zip and Disease in one fragment (light gray in the graph) and Treatment, Premium, and Insurance in the other (dark gray in the graph) appears to satisfy the constraints (note that attributes appearing dotted

R(SSN, Birthdate, Zip, Name, Treatment, Disease, Job, Premium, Insurance)

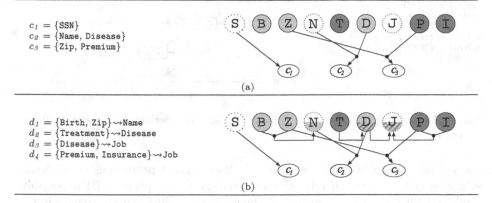

$c_1 = \{\text{SSN}\}$
$c_2 = \{\text{Name, Disease}\}$
$c_3 = \{\text{Zip, Premium}\}$

(a)

$d_1 = \{\text{Birth, Zip}\} \rightsquigarrow \text{Name}$
$d_2 = \{\text{Treatment}\} \rightsquigarrow \text{Disease}$
$d_3 = \{\text{Disease}\} \rightsquigarrow \text{Job}$
$d_4 = \{\text{Premium, Insurance}\} \rightsquigarrow \text{Job}$

(b)

Fig. 3. An example of exposure of sensitive associations due to data dependencies

in the graph are not represented in the clear in any of the fragments). In fact, no sensitive information is exposed in the fragments and not having attributes in common the fragments cannot be linked. This reasoning would be perfectly fine if attributes where independent. However, dependencies might exist and some information be inferable from other, allowing an observer to: from the Birthdate and Zip reduce uncertainty over the Name; from the Treatment infer the Disease; from the Disease reduce uncertainty over the Job; and from the Premium and the Insurance infer the Job. Such derivations due to dependencies can indirectly expose information and leak sensitive information or enable linking. Figure 3(b) extends the graph with multi-arcs representing dependencies (from the premises to the consequence) and illustrates such inferences by propagating colors from the premises to the consequence. More precisely, if a given color appears in all the attributes of a premise, it is propagated to the attribute in the consequence (in the graphical representation, propagated colors are reported in the bottom half of the nodes). Multi colored attributes represent (indirect) violations of the constraints.

2.2 Access Control Enforcement

In many scenarios access to data is *selective*, meaning that different users, or groups of them, should have different views/access on the data. With data outsourced to external servers, the problem therefore arises of how to enforce access control. In fact, the data owner cannot mediate every access request, as the advantages of delegating the management of data to an external server would be lost. On the other hand, the server storing the data may not be trusted for the enforcement of the access control policy, which could also be sensitive and should be protected from the server' eyes.

A possible solution to have access control enforced without requiring the data owner intervention at every access consists in combining access control with

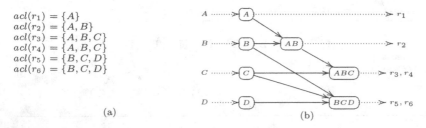

$acl(r_1) = \{A\}$
$acl(r_2) = \{A, B\}$
$acl(r_3) = \{A, B, C\}$
$acl(r_4) = \{A, B, C\}$
$acl(r_5) = \{B, C, D\}$
$acl(r_6) = \{B, C, D\}$

(a)   (b)

Fig. 4. An example of access control policy (a) and key derivation hierarchy (b) enforcing it

encryption, wrapping the data with a (self-enforcing) protecting layer. Some solutions in this direction rely on attribute-based encryption (ABE), possibly combined with other cryptographic techniques (e.g., [30]). An alternative interesting approach combines access control with encryption by selectively encrypting resources based on the authorizations on them [12]. Intuitively, data are encrypted with different keys and users are given only the keys for data which they are authorized to access. This solution introduces some challenges related to key management: users would like to have a single key (regardless of the number of resources for which they have access), and data should be encrypted at most once (i.e., different replicas with different keys should be avoided). These requirements can be satisfied by adopting a *key derivation* approach [2], by which users can derive keys from a single key assigned to them and public tokens. Access control can then be enforced by properly organizing the keys with which resources are encrypted in a hierarchy reflecting the authorizations on the resources, or better their access control lists (ACLs), where the key corresponding to an ACL allows deriving, via one or more tokens, the keys associated with all ACLs that are superset of it. This way a user is able to derive, from her key and public tokens, all (and only) the keys that are needed to access resources that she is authorized to access according to the access control policy. Figure 4(a) reports an example of access control policy involving four users (A, B, C, and D) and six resources ($r_1, r_2, r_3, r_4, r_5, r_6$). Figure 4(b) reports a corresponding hierarchy for keys, including one key for each user and one key for each non singleton ACL appearing in the policy. Dotted lines connect users to their keys, and keys to resources encrypted with them. Tokens, represented as continuous line, allow users to derive from their own key the keys of all and only resources for which they are authorized. This hierarchy-based approach can also be extended to support write privileges [9], and subscription-based scenarios [8].

As the key with which resources are encrypted depends on their ACL, in principle any change to the authorization policy would require downloading, decrypting, re-encrypting, and re-uploading the involved resources. This process can be avoided assuming some cooperation of the server in enforcing authorization changes by over-encrypting resources to make them not accessible to non-authorized users who know the key with which resources have been encrypted by the owner. Intuitively, every resource is subject to two layers of encryption [12]: a *base encryption layer* (BEL) applied by the data owner reflects the access control policy at initialization time; a *surface encryption layer* (SEL) applied on top of the BEL by the server takes into account possible changes in the access control policy. A user will be able to access a resource only if she can pass both layers of encryption.

2.3 Private Access

In some scenarios what can be sensitive might be not (or not only) the data stored at the external server but (also) the accesses that users make on such data. In particular, the fact that an access aims at specific data (*access confidentiality*) or that different accesses aim at the same data (*pattern confidentiality*) should be maintained confidential, even to the server providing access itself. Traditional approaches addressing these issues are based on *private information retrieval* (PIR) techniques, which however assume that data are stored in the clear, and suffer from high computation costs, thus limiting their applicability (e.g., [32]). Alternative solutions are based on the Oblivious RAM structure (ORAM) [21] and on dynamic data allocation techniques (e.g., [17,18,35]). These solutions provide access and pattern confidentiality by encrypting data and changing their physical allocation at every access so to destroy the, otherwise static, correspondence between data and physical blocks where they are stored. In particular, *Path ORAM* [35] maintains some data in a local cache (called *stash*) and some data in an external tree structure where nodes contain, in addition to actual blocks, also dummy blocks (to provide uniformity of the size of all nodes). Every access entails reading a path of the tree (containing the searched block) and bringing the nodes in the path in the stash. Then, the nodes in the tree path read are rewritten back (possibly moving out from the stash nodes mapping to leaves intersecting the path).

The *shuffle* index also assumes a local cache but maintains at the external storage the complete data structure (so providing also more resilience in case of failures and accommodating concurrent accesses or distributed scenarios [18,19]). The data stored externally are organized with a B+-tree whose nodes are encrypted and that has no pointer between leaves (to avoid leaking to the server information on the order of values stored). The advantage of a key-based hierarchical organization is that it allows supporting range queries. To protect pattern confidentiality, for every search operation, the client asks retrieval of more values: the actual target and some covers (which provide uncertainty for the server on the block to which the client actually aims). Also, the client performs a *shuffling* among nodes in the cache and those retrieved by the search, then rewriting the involved blocks (whose content have been changed by the re-allocation enforced by the shuffling) on the server. Figure 5(a) illustrates an example of nodes for a shuffle index where, for readability, we have omitted the pointers from a node to its children; the parent-child relationship is however understandable from the label assigned to nodes in the figure, as leaf nodes have as prefix the label of their parent. The figure shows a sample execution with target *c1* and cover *b2*, assuming *a1* (and then the path to it) be in cache. The dotted arrows in Figure 5(a) illustrate a possible shuffling that changes the data allocated to blocks

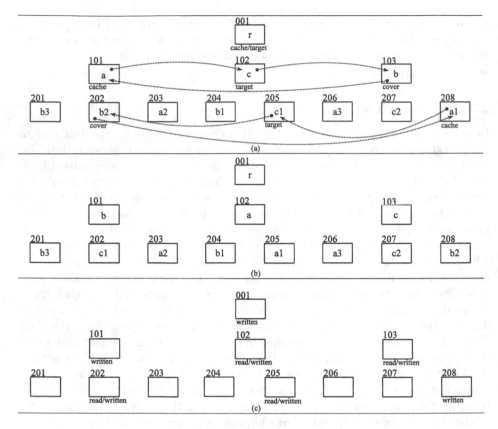

Fig. 5. An example of logical shuffle index with cache/target/cover and shuffling operations due to an access (a), logical shuffle index at the end of the access (b), and server's view on the access (c)

as in Figure 5(b). Figure 5(c) illustrates instead the view of the server on the access.

3   Data and Computation Integrity

Another issue that needs to be considered when storing – or processing – data at external servers is the ability to assess the correct behavior of the servers. This implies verifying that data are maintained correctly and that queries performed on them are correctly executed.

As for data storage, typical solutions are based on hashing and *digital signature schemas* (e.g., [23,31]). Signature-based approaches provide a *deterministic* guarantee of data integrity but impose an overhead not always acceptable in cloud scenarios. Alternative solutions, which provide *probabilistic* (i.e., not certain) guarantees of data integrity, are *Proof of Retrievability* (POR) approaches (e.g., [28]), which apply to encrypted data, or *Provable Data Possession* (PDP)

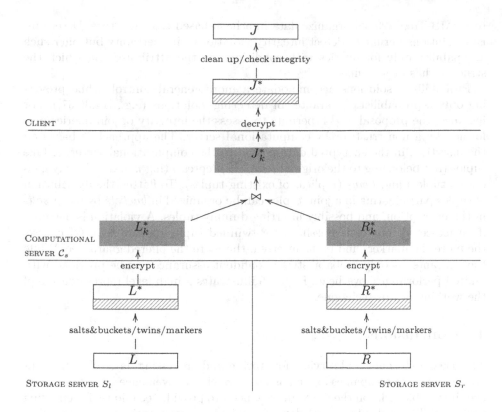

Fig. 6. Join execution and integrity controls

approaches (e.g., [3]), which apply to generic datasets. They are based on control sentinels hidden among the encrypted data (for POR) or on homomorphic verifiable tags (for PDP) whose presence and correctness can be verified by the owner or other trusted parties.

As for query computation, guaranteeing integrity requires to provide users with mechanisms to verify the *correctness*, *completeness*, and *freshness* of computations. Correctness means that the result has been performed on the original data and the computation performed correctly. Completeness means that no data is missing from the result. Freshness means that the computation has been performed on the most recent version of the data. Similarly to data storage solutions, also solutions assessing integrity of computations can be distinguished in *deterministic* and *probabilistic*. Deterministic solutions are based on the use of *authenticated data structures* and allow assessing integrity of query results based on a *verification object* which the server should return together with the results. Different approaches can different with respect to how data are organized and the verification object computed. For instance, signature chaining schemas (e.g., [33]) organize tuples in a chain while Merkle tree and its variation (e.g., MB-Tree) [29,38] organize data in a hash-based tree structure. Deterministic solutions permit to detect integrity violations with certainty but offer such a capability only for queries with conditions on the attribute/s on which the structure has been defined.

Probabilistic solutions accommodate a more general control, while providing only a probabilistic guarantee of detecting violations (e.g., [14,36,37]). For instance, the proposal in [14] permits to assess the integrity of join queries performed by a non trustworthy computational server. The approach is based on the insertion, in the encrypted data passed to the computational server, of fake tuples (not belonging to the original relations) representing *markers* (newly generated tuples) and *twins* (replicas of existing tuples). To flatten the distribution of tuples participating in a join, tuples can be organized in *buckets* by using *salts* in the encryption, and possibly inserting dummy tuples. A violation is detected if an expected marker is missing or a twinned tuple appears solo. Of course, the more the markers and twins inserted, the more the offered guarantee. While the guarantee is only probabilistic, a confident assurance can be provided with limited performance overhead. Figure 6 illustrates a high level representation of the working of this technique.

4   Conclusions

The use of external cloud services for storing and processing data offers tremendous benefits to companies as well as users. Such a convenience introduces however inevitable risks on the data, and the need to provide techniques for ensuring confidentiality and integrity of data as well as of computations on them. This paper discussed these needs and some solutions addressing them.

Acknowledgments. I would like to thank Sabrina De Capitani di Vimercati for suggestions and comments. This paper is based on joint work with Sabrina De Capitani di Vimercati, Sara Foresti, Giovanni Livraga, Sushil Jajodia, Stefano Paraboschi, and Gerardo Pelosi. The work was supported in part by Italian MIUR PRIN project "GenData 2020" and EC 7FP project ABC4EU (312797).

References

1. Aggarwal, G., Bawa, M., Ganesan, P., Garcia-Molina, H., Kenthapadi, K., Motwani, R., Srivastava, U., Thomas, D., Xu, Y.: Two can keep a secret: A distributed architecture for secure database services. In: Proc. of the 2nd Biennial Conference on Innovative Data Systems Research, CIDR 2005, Asilomar, CA, USA (January 2005)
2. Atallah, M., Blanton, M., Fazio, N., Frikken, K.: Dynamic and efficient key management for access hierarchies. ACM Transactions on Information and System Security 12(3), 18:1–18:43 (2009)
3. Ateniese, G., Burns, R., Curtmola, R., Herring, J., Kissner, L., Peterson, Z., Song, D.: Provable data possession at untrusted stores. In: Proc. of the 14th ACM Conference on Computer and Communications Security (CCS 2007), Alexandria, VA, USA (October-November 2007)

4. Ciriani, V., De Capitani di Vimercati, S., Foresti, S., Jajodia, S., Paraboschi, S., Samarati, P.: Fragmentation and encryption to enforce privacy in data storage. In: Biskup, J., López, J. (eds.) ESORICS 2007. LNCS, vol. 4734, pp. 171–186. Springer, Heidelberg (2007)
5. Ciriani, V., De Capitani di Vimercati, S., Foresti, S., Jajodia, S., Paraboschi, S., Samarati, P.: Keep a few: Outsourcing data while maintaining confidentiality. In: Backes, M., Ning, P. (eds.) ESORICS 2009. LNCS, vol. 5789, pp. 440–455. Springer, Heidelberg (2009)
6. Ciriani, V., De Capitani di Vimercati, S., Foresti, S., Jajodia, S., Paraboschi, S., Samarati, P.: Combining fragmentation and encryption to protect privacy in data storage. ACM Transactions on Information and System Security (TISSEC) 13(3), 22:1–22:33 (2010)
7. Damiani, E., De Capitani di Vimercati, S., Jajodia, S., Paraboschi, S., Samarati, P.: Balancing confidentiality and efficiency in untrusted relational DBMSs. In: Proc. of the 10th ACM Conference on Computer and Communications Security (CCS 2003), Washington, DC, USA (October 2003)
8. De Capitani di Vimercati, S., Foresti, S., Jajodia, S., Livraga, G.: Enforcing subscription-based authorization policies in cloud scenarios. In: Cuppens-Boulahia, N., Cuppens, F., Garcia-Alfaro, J. (eds.) DBSec 2012. LNCS, vol. 7371, pp. 314–329. Springer, Heidelberg (2012)
9. De Capitani di Vimercati, S., Foresti, S., Jajodia, S., Livraga, G., Paraboschi, S., Samarati, P.: Enforcing dynamic write privileges in data outsourcing. Computers & Security (COSE) 39, 47–63 (2013)
10. De Capitani di Vimercati, S., Foresti, S., Jajodia, S., Livraga, G., Paraboschi, S., Samarati, P.: Extending loose associations to multiple fragments. In: Wang, L., Shafiq, B. (eds.) DBSec 2013. LNCS, vol. 7964, pp. 1–16. Springer, Heidelberg (2013)
11. De Capitani di Vimercati, S., Foresti, S., Jajodia, S., Livraga, G., Paraboschi, S., Samarati, P.: Fragmentation in presence of data dependencies. IEEE Transactions on Dependable and Secure Computing (TDSC) (2014)
12. De Capitani di Vimercati, S., Foresti, S., Jajodia, S., Paraboschi, S., Samarati, P.: Encryption policies for regulating access to outsourced data. ACM Transactions on Database Systems (TODS) 35(2), 12:1–12:46 (2010)
13. De Capitani di Vimercati, S., Foresti, S., Jajodia, S., Paraboschi, S., Samarati, P.: Fragments and loose associations: Respecting privacy in data publishing. Proc. of the VLDB Endowment 3(1), 1370–1381 (2010)
14. De Capitani di Vimercati, S., Foresti, S., Jajodia, S., Paraboschi, S., Samarati, P.: Integrity for join queries in the cloud. IEEE Transactions on Cloud Computing (TCC) 1(2), 187–200 (2013)
15. De Capitani di Vimercati, S., Foresti, S., Jajodia, S., Paraboschi, S., Samarati, P.: On information leakage by indexes over data fragments. In: Proc. of the 1st International Workshop on Privacy-Preserving Data Publication and Analysis (PrivDB 2013), Brisbane, Australia (April 2013)
16. De Capitani di Vimercati, S., Foresti, S., Livraga, G., Samarati, P.: Data privacy: Definitions and techniques. International Journal of Uncertainty, Fuzziness and Knowledge-Based Systems 20(6), 793–817 (2012)
17. De Capitani di Vimercati, S., Foresti, S., Paraboschi, S., Pelosi, G., Samarati, P.: Efficient and private access to outsourced data. In: Proc. of the 31st International Conference on Distributed Computing Systems (ICDCS 2011), Minneapolis, Minnesota, USA (June 2011)

18. De Capitani di Vimercati, S., Foresti, S., Paraboschi, S., Pelosi, G., Samarati, P.: Distributed shuffling for preserving access confidentiality. In: Crampton, J., Jajodia, S., Mayes, K. (eds.) ESORICS 2013. LNCS, vol. 8134, pp. 628–645. Springer, Heidelberg (2013)

19. De Capitani di Vimercati, S., Foresti, S., Paraboschi, S., Pelosi, G., Samarati, P.: Supporting concurrency and multiple indexes in private access to outsourced data. Journal of Computer Security (JCS) 21(3), 425–461 (2013)

20. De Capitani di Vimercati, S., Foresti, S., Samarati, P.: Managing and accessing data in the cloud: Privacy risks and approaches. In: Proc. of the 7th International Conference on Risks and Security of Internet and Systems (CRiSIS 2012), Cork, Ireland (October 2012)

21. Goldreich, O., Ostrovsky, R.: Software protection and simulation on Oblivious RAMs. Journal of the ACM 43(3), 431–473 (1996)

22. Hacigümüş, H., Iyer, B., Li, C., Mehrotra, S.: Executing SQL over encrypted data in the database-service-provider model. In: Proc. of the ACM SIGMOD International Conference on Management of Data (SIGMOD 2002), Madison, Wisconsin, USA (June 2002)

23. Hacigümüş, H., Iyer, B., Mehrotra, S.: Ensuring integrity of encrypted databases in database as a service model. In: De Capitani di Vimercati, S., Ray, I., Ray, I. (eds.) Data and Applications Security XVII. IFIP, vol. 142, pp. 61–74. Springer, Heidelberg (2004)

24. Jhawar, R., Piuri, V.: Adaptive resource management for balancing availability and performance in cloud computing. In: Proc. of the 10th International Conference on Security and Cryptography (SECRYPT 2013), Reykjavik, Iceland (July 2013)

25. Jhawar, R., Piuri, V., Samarati, P.: Supporting security requirements for resource management in cloud computing. In: Proc. of the 15th IEEE International Conference on Computational Science and Engineering (CSE 2012), Paphos, Cyprus (December 2012)

26. Jhawar, R., Piuri, V., Santambrogio, M.: A comprehensive conceptual system-level approach to fault tolerance in cloud computing. In: Proc. of the 2012 IEEE International Systems Conference (SysCon 2012), Vancouver, BC, Canada (March 2012)

27. Jhawar, R., Piuri, V., Santambrogio, M.: Fault tolerance management in cloud computing: A system-level perspective. IEEE Systems Journal 7(2), 288–297 (2013)

28. Juels, A., Kaliski, B.: PORs: Proofs of retrievability for large files. In: Proc. of the 14th ACM Conference on Computer and Communications Security (CCS 2007), Alexandria, VA, USA (October-November 2007)

29. Li, F., Hadjieleftheriou, M., Kollios, G., Reyzin, L.: Authenticated index structures for aggregation queries. ACM Transactions on Information and System Security (TISSEC) 13(4), 32:1–32:35 (2010)

30. Li, J., Chen, X., Li, J., Jia, C., Ma, J., Lou, W.: Fine-grained access control system based on outsourced attribute-based encryption. In: Crampton, J., Jajodia, S., Mayes, K. (eds.) ESORICS 2013. LNCS, vol. 8134, pp. 592–609. Springer, Heidelberg (2013)

31. Mykletun, E., Narasimha, M., Tsudik, G.: Authentication and integrity in outsourced databases. ACM Transactions on Storage (TOS) 2(2), 107–138 (2006)

32. Ostrovsky, R., Skeith III, W.E.: A survey of single-database private information retrieval: Techniques and applications. In: Okamoto, T., Wang, X. (eds.) PKC 2007. LNCS, vol. 4450, pp. 393–411. Springer, Heidelberg (2007)

33. Pang, H., Jain, A., Ramamritham, K., Tan, K.: Verifying completeness of relational query results in data publishing. In: Proc. of the ACM SIGMOD International Conference on Management of Data (SIGMOD 2005), Baltimore, MA, USA (June 2005)
34. Samarati, P., De Capitani di Vimercati, S.: Data protection in outsourcing scenarios: Issues and directions. In: Proc. of the 5th ACM Symposium on Information, Computer and Communications Security (ASIACCS 2010), Beijing, China (April 2010)
35. Stefanov, E., van Dijk, M., Shi, E., Fletcher, C., Ren, L., Yu, X., Devadas, S.: Path ORAM: An extremely simple Oblivious RAM protocol. In: Proc. of the 20th ACM Conference on Computer and Communications Security (CCS 2013), Berlin, Germany (November 2013)
36. Wang, H., Yin, J., Perng, C., Yu, P.: Dual encryption for query integrity assurance. In: Proc. of the 2008 ACM International Conference on Information and Knowledge Management (CIKM 2008), Napa Valley, CA (October 2008)
37. Xie, M., Wang, H., Yin, J., Meng, X.: Integrity auditing of outsourced data. In: Proc. of the 33rd International Conference on Very Large Data Bases (VLDB 2007), Vienna, Austria (September 2007)
38. Yang, Z., Gao, S., Xu, J., Choi, B.: Authentication of range query results in MapReduce environments. In: Proc. of the 3rd International Workshop on Cloud Data Management (CloudDB 2011), Glasgow, U.K. (October 2011)

Forbidden City Model – Towards a Practice Relevant Framework for Designing Cryptographic Protocols*

Mirosław Kutyłowski, Lucjan Hanzlik, Kamil Kluczniak,
Przemysław Kubiak, and Łukasz Krzywiecki

Faculty of Fundamental Problems of Technology, Wrocław University of Technology
{firstname.secondname}@pwr.wroc.pl

Abstract. Designing a cryptographic protocol for practical applications is a challenging task even for relatively simple scenarios. The usual approach is to design a protocol having in mind some simple attack scenarios. This produces clean designs but many security problems might be ignored. Repeatedly, the development in this area was a sequence of steps: many protocols have been proposed and subsequently broken by presenting realistic attack situations not covered by the original security model. The resulting situation is an abundance of models, which are less and less intuitive, hard to compare and to understand.

Our goal is to provide a simple and intuitive framework that would help us to capture the key properties of the real world architectures and attack scenarios. Motivated by the smart card design, the main idea is to build the system architecture in the way that resembles the courts of the Emperor's Palace in the ancient China. There are many internal courts and strict rules how to cross the boundaries between these separate areas. The crucial part of the model is specifying what the adversary can do in each part of the system.

Keywords: cryptographic device, security model, adversary, attack, PACE, active authentication.

1 Introduction

One of the major components of cryptography in practice are the cryptographic devices that implement somehow the crucial components of the cryptographic protocols. In fact, there is no way other than special purpose devices to enforce the following rules:

- the keys are protected so that their secrecy is guaranteed,
- the protocol is executed according to its specification.

The standard operating systems <u>do not guarantee</u> these properties. One can try to solve this problem by redesigning the operating system (e.g. Chinese project Kylin), or by securing isolated components by hardware means. The last approach resulted in a number of practical solutions and massive deployment of cryptographic protocols. The most spectacular solutions are: SIM cards used for cellular telecommunication, biometric passports and other electronic identity documents, signature smart cards, TPM modules, HSM devices, and general purpose smart cards such as Java Card.

---

* Partially supported by grant S30028/I-18 from the Institute of Mathematics and Computer Science of the Wrocław University of Technology.

X. Huang and J. Zhou (Eds.): ISPEC 2014, LNCS 8434, pp. 42–59, 2014.

These examples show that the deployment of cryptography is far away from the initial stage. On the other hand, we can see that there are quite clear design tendencies. In all cases the cryptographic suite is built from small components, with strictly defined functionalities and hardware level protection. Almost always, they are single purpose devices; they may serve as secure components of general purpose and programmable systems.

On the other hand, it turns out that even for such devices, very simple in principle, formal security analysis comes quite late or is incomplete and presented for bureaucratic reasons only. Nevertheless, there are many excellent designs of cryptographic devices constructed by security engineers. On the other hand, there are examples of painful mistakes. May be the most spectacular case are the early electronic voting machines, designed and deployed rapidly due to political pressure, ignoring the warnings of security specialists.

In out opinion, the common lack of systematic approach and realistic security analysis is not due to negligent attitude of system designers, but rather to a gap between system design problem and realistic threats on one hand, and theoretical models for security that became to live their own life in the academic community.

Paper Contents. The goal of this paper is to present a different view on the protocol design methodology. We think that it might be much easier to address the practical security questions, if the model becomes closer to the technical reality.

This paper presents only a sketch of the approach. It does not present new proof techniques but rather tries to organize the proof steps. This is quite important since the number of details even for a very simple protocol might be abundant and it is easy to overlook some issues.

The second important twist in our approach are the adversary models. In the cryptographic literature there is a tendency to either underestimate the adversary and make idealistic assumptions that cannot be fulfilled in practice, or to overestimate the adversary and create too complicated algorithms to meet unrealistic threats.

More details will be presented in the forthcoming journal version of this paper.

2   Traditional Methodology

Standard Approach. Typically a party running a protocol is regarded as a universal computing machine such a Turing Machine. It runs a program performing internal computation on available data: static secrets, ephemeral secrets, and data received from other participants. When terminated correctly it usually has to be in an accepting state. In case of AKE protocols it results with a session key shared with the peer party device. The attacks on the protocol functionalities may affect:

Authentication: each party identifies and checks its peer within the session;

Consistency: if two parties A and B, establish a common session key K, then A believes it communicates with B, and B believes it communicates with A;

Secrecy: if a session is established between two honest peers, then no adversary should learns any information about the resultant session key and the messages encrypted with this key.

In case of other functionalities, like creating electronic signatures, attacks may be targeted at a simple *forgery*. In case of more sophisticated schemes like group signatures the attack may aim violating *anonymity* of the signatory.

Abstract models of adversary measure its strength as the probability of breaking the required functionality of the device. Usually the adversary is given the power:

- to control communication between devices
    - intercept messages
    - change/generate messages
- get the internal data stored on the device (long term static secrets – *LongTermReveal*, ephemeral secrets – *EphemeralReveal*).

The ability to learn the party's data by the adversary is modelled by abstract oracles. There are oracles associated with each party running an instance of the protocol, called a *session*. The adversary can query the party's oracle in a given session to get the required data. The most widely accepted models Canetti-Krawczyk (CK), extended Canetti-Krawczyk (eCK), strengthen extended Canetti-Krawczyk (seCK) differ by details how the adversary may learn the internal state of the protocol parties. As an example we provide below a chart with some oracles available for these protocols:

CK	eCK	seCK (model 1)	seCK (model 2)
Send sends a message to party P_j on behalf of P_j. The oracle returns P_j's response to the message.	**Send** sends a message to party P_j on behalf of P_j. The oracle returns P_j's response to the message.	**Send** sends a message to party P_j on behalf of P_j. The oracle returns P_j's response to the message.	
State-Reveal returns the ephemeral session key, but not the long-term secret state.	**Ephemeral Key Reveal** reveals an ephemeral key of a party	**Ephemeral Key Reveal** reveals an ephemeral key of a party	**intermediate results** reveals intermediate results of computation (which may involve using secret values)
	Long-Term Key Reveal reveals static secret key of a party	**Corrupt**$_{SC}$ returns the entire internal state including long-term secrets.	**Corrupt**$_{SC}$ returns the entire internal state including long-term secrets.
Corrupt returns the entire internal state including long-term secrets.	realized by *Long-Term Key Reveal, Ephemeral Key Reveal, Reveal*		
Session-Key-Reveal reveals a session key of a completed session.	**Reveal** reveals a session key of a completed session	**SessionKeyReveal** reveals a session key of a completed session.	**SessionKeyReveal** reveals a session key of a completed session.

Of course if too many informations are revealed, then trivially security of a session may disappear. So the authors introduce the concept of *fresh sessions*. A session is fresh if it is not exposed, i.e. if secret data, which would trivially be used by the adversary to break the security of the protocol, is not leaked. Therefore in the above-mentioned models, to provide the freshness of the session in the security game, the adversary is not allowed to query the following oracles:

CK	eCK	seCK (model 1)	seCK (model 2)
Session-Key-Reveal	**Reveal**	**SessionKeyReveal**	**SessionKeyReveal**
Corrupt	**Long-Term Key Reveal, Ephemeral Key Reveal** of one party	**Corrupt**$_{SC}$, **Ephemeral Key Reveal** of one party	**intermediate results** on **Corrupt**$_{SC}$, and **Ephemeral Key Reveal** of one party

The protocol under attack is modelled by a sequence of executions of oracles. So the approach is adversary-centric and at very high level of abstraction. In order to define a uniform framework and comparable results the number of different kinds of oracles should be kept low. This is hard, as there are different requirements for different protocols may and the framework built for one occasion is not suitable for the other one. Even for a quite focused problem of AKE our experience is that there is an abundance of models, oracles and their relations are at least unclear for the laymen.

Attacks Not Covered. Unfortunately, the general models still may not reflect all attack possibilities. So we have to deal with adding new models all the times. For instance, we believe that in certain cases the adversary can execute *AlterData* oracle: he can change the internal data of a protocol participant or even replace it by the chosen value without knowing the value changed. The possibilities what can be changed and how may differ very much from case to case.

2.1   Demonstration of the Attacks

Signature Based Attacks. Consider the smart-card device realizing of the signature functionality based on the Schnorr's scheme:

1. choose $k \in [1, q-1]$ uniformly at random,
2. $r := g^k$,
3. $e := H(M||r)$,
4. $s := k - x \cdot e \mod q$,
5. return (r, s).

Obviously, the adversary that queries the oracle *Ephemeral Key Reveal* (and thereby gets k) can derive the static secret x from the signature (r, s). However, a similar attack can be mounted without the use of *Ephemeral Key Reveal* oracle. We consider the malicious card implementation that can mount the following attack in two subsequent functionality executions (say E1, E2) with the *AlterData* oracle: In E1 the value k is not erased after Step 2. In E2 Step 1 is not executed - instead the stored value k from execution E1 is used. Now the secret static key can be derived from signatures: (e_1, s_1) over the message M_1, and (e_2, s_2) over the message M_2, obtained from E1 and E2 respectively: $x := (s_1 - s_2)/(H(M_1||r) - H(M_1||r))$.

The attack might be feasible due to a wrong implementation of the PRNG component that executes Step 1 (it produces two the same outputs in subsequent runs), or due to the wrong implementation of the control flow (not erasing the previous k, and skipping Step 1 in the next execution).

The attack discussed above can be used not only for signature functionality itself, but for any protocol that uses that signature scheme as a building block.

Password Based Attacks. We just mention a single simple example. Password authentication protocols aim to protect against unauthorized usage of a device - the attacker should not be able to use the device without knowing the password. Now consider the malicious implementation that would store the password internally on the device during the first protocol run in a secure memory section, and use that stored value since then. Now after stealing a device the adversary can use it for authentication. Again the attacked value - the password in this case - is not learned by the attacker, but the functionality of the protocol implemented on the device is affected in a substantial way.

3 Forbidden City Model

The main problem with the traditional approach is that it separates the algorithm design from the security proof. The other problem is that the algorithm design may disregard crucial elements of the protocol implementation. In this section we present the methodology of co-design of a cryptographic scheme with it security model.

3.1 Model Components

Component. The component is the fundamental concept of the Forbidden City model. A basic component C consists of

- the main subcomponent containing the code executed by the component and logic necessary to perform the input and output operations,
- component's input and output gates,
- optionally: a subcomponent as memory of the component.

A component may contain more subcomponents inside – we shall discuss it later.

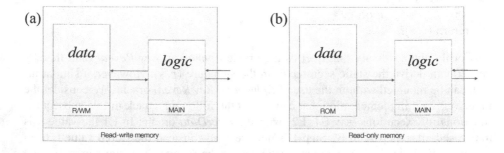

Fig. 1. A basic component: (a) with *read/write* memory, (b) with *read-only* data

Component's Code. When activated, a component C executes the code from its MAIN component. Each component executing code may communicate with other components using MPI mechanisms – sending and receiving data via output and input gates.

Thereby, we regard a cryptographic protocol as a distributed algorithm, where each container is one of the (independent) protocol participants. As always for distributed algorithms, we do not assume that there is a priori synchronization between different components, their executions might be inconsistent. In most cases, the code executed by a component is a simple sequential program with a very straightforward control flow.

Nesting. The idea of nesting the components is the central concept of the Forbidden City model. Each component may contain any number of subcomponents. In turn, an internal component may contain its own subcomponents, and so on.

For instance, we may concern a smart card with the operating system on a ROM memory which directly operates the input and output of the smart card. The smart card may have another components, like a cryptographic coprocessor and a (pseudo)random number generator inside the cryptographic coprocessor. The main memory is the part that is open for uploading and running user's applications.

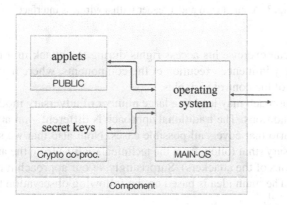

Fig. 2. An example of a nested component architecture – a smart card with the operating system on ROM, a cryptographic coprocessor and an area for uploading and running applets

Examples: A Communication Channel. Fig. 3 describes a situation of a smart card and a card reader with the user entering a PIN on the keyboard of the computer connected to the smart card reader via a wireless channel. In order to model the system behavior the wireless channel is a separate component where the MAIN subcomponent may be used to describe physical properties of the communication channel.

3.2   Adversary Model

An adversary is defined by the access methods to the data and code separately for each component. The examples of access rights are: erase, replace by a fixed content, replace by a content of choice, read, ...

Note that erasing and replacing need not to come together with the read access. Each operation might by a partial one – instead of erasing a given block of memory the adversary may erase each bit of this block with some probability. Similarly, a read operation for D may return the value $f(D)$, where f is a (randomized) operation corresponding to the technical reality.

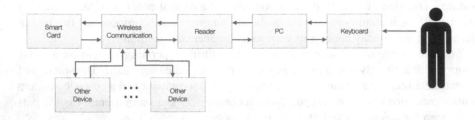

Fig. 3. A smart card and a reader with a wireless interface

The adversary can exercise his access rights during the attack in a malicious way. In particular, he may influence execution of the components, where he can change the code or the values of the control variables.

Note that our approach may lead to a large number of adversary models, describing different attack conditions. The traditional approach is different – an attempt to find a single attack scenario that covers all possible cases. Note also that we separate access rights of the adversary (that follow from the technical reality) from the attack strategies (which are inventions of the attackers). Surprisingly, in our approach it might be easier to cover all cases. The main idea is based on the following observation that holds for a wide range of attacks[1]:

> If in some adversary model the attack is infeasible, then it is infeasible in all cases when the adversary has weaker access rights.

So, it suffices to consider only maximal elements in the partial order of access rights in the set of access right that should not lead to a successful attack.

4 Examples

In this section we discuss two specific applications: creation of Schnorr signatures and the issues of authentication for an electronic identity document establishing communication with a reader.

4.1 Secure Signature Creation Device

Architecture for Schnorr Signatures. Let us consider the Schnorr signature scheme recalled in Sect. 2.1. While this is a complete description concerning algebraic operations, it leaves crucial details necessary to evaluate the protocol's security. There are problems with two parts of the specification: the first is realization of "choose k uniformly at random". The second one is computing the hash value $\text{Hash}(M||r)$.

Choosing a number at random is a nice abstract step, but it cannot be executed directly by a standard circuitry. For computing $\text{Hash}(M||r)$, the problem might be the

---

[1] Surprisingly, this is not always the case, see the discussion on the privacy issues in [8].

size of M. So, it seems that the signing algorithm is executed by a signing component consisting of at least three components: RNG responsible for generating random element k, HASH responsible for hashing $(M\|r)$, and the SIGN component implementing the operations involving the secret key x. Moreover, the communication between RNG and SIGN has to be well protected, since leaking k reveals immediately the signing key. In order to simplify the communication, one can use block hashing for computing Hash$(M\|r)$, and prepare the intermediate result for M outside the signing component and finalize the computation with r inside. Therefore, it seems to be reasonable to embed RNG inside SIGN, and two HASH components (see Fig. 4).

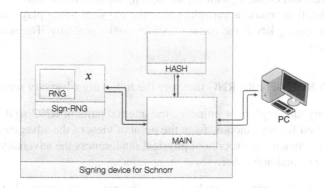

Fig. 4. Basic model of a device creating Schnorr signatures

Security Conditions. The basic conditions required for a signature scheme are *key secrecy* (meaning that it is impossible to derive the key from signatures created) and *unforgeability* (meaning that it is impossible to create valid signatures without the private key). These two properties can be viewed as abstract versions that have to guarantee the following concrete condition:

Definition 1. *Let C be a component implementing creation of electronic signatures. Then C guarantees <u>unforgeability</u> for the adversary model A, if with an overwhelming probability the adversary A cannot create a valid signature σ on a message M of his choice without running the SIGN subcomponent of C storing the signing key so that it delivers σ. Before attempting to create the signature σ, the adversary may run C many times, possibly performing the attacks according to the model A. In particular, the adversary may create signatures for arbitrary messages, but σ has to be different from all these signatures.*

Remark 1. Note that the above definition refers to a <u>successful termination</u> of the signature creation by the component SIGN that stores the signing key. So we can claim that in case of execution interruption no signature can be derived. This solves nicely many legal issues.

Remark 2. Definition 1 admits that unforgeability refers only to a given adversary model. In particular, the situation may be quite different in the case when the adversary may influence the protocol execution of the signing device – the standard definitions assume that the adversary can change the protocol execution only when acting as a different protocol participant.

Remark 3. The attack strategy might be to derive the secret signing key x. Once it succeeds, it is possible to use x outside SIGN in order to derive a new signature σ.

Note also that we do not necessarily demand that no data about the signing key x is leaked. The main point is that, as long as the holder of the device implementing SIGN is the only party that can create signatures, the signing scheme is considered to be secure. This is an application centric approach, where the physical token plays the main role and the private signing key is the mean to achieve unforgeability. The secrecy of x is not the goal itself.

Problems with RNG. For the RNG there are the following adversary scenarios:

- the adversary may replace or influence the internal parts of RNG so that its output is no more "uniformly random" from the point of view of the adversary,
- instead of influencing the source of physical randomness the adversary may attack the output gate and inject there some other values.

In this case when k is not uniformly random, it might become predictable by the adversary. This leads directly to the disclosure of the signing key via the equality $s = k - x \cdot e \bmod q$. Note that the standard tests (like the NIST suite) can detect the attacks only if RNG becomes severely and permanently damaged. So, the SIGN component cannot really test the output received allegedly from RNG.

There is a large variety of practical possibilities leading to such attack situations. The RNG has to be implemented by a separate hardware module embedded in the signing chip. So the manufacturers of the SIGN and RNG might be different and the manufacturer of RNG might be tempted to install a back-door via a hardware Trojan (like indicated in [2]). The problem is that proving non-existence of the back-door might be very hard or even impossible. On the other hand, we have to take into account physical attacks (like exposing the chip to extreme temperatures) that would change the physical properties of the RNG without switching off the electronic parts.

Due to the problems with the RNG sketched above one may consider to implement the Schnorr signatures in a slightly different way. Let us describe an idea based on distributed generation of Schnorr signatures [13]. We split the signing key x into two parts x_1, x_2, where $x = x_1 + x_2 \bmod q$ (the public key is still $y = g^x$, where g is the group generator). The algebraic description of the signing procedure takes now the following form:

1. choose $k_1 \in [1, q-1]$ uniformly at random
2. $r_1 := g^{k_1}$
3. $count := count + 1$
4. $k_2 := \mathrm{PRNG}(z, count) \bmod q$

5. $r_2 := g^{k_2}$
6. $r := r_1 \cdot r_2$
7. $e := \text{Hash}(M\|r)$
8. $s_1 := k_1 - x_1 \cdot e \bmod q$
9. $s_2 := k_1 - x_2 \cdot e \bmod q$
10. $s := s_1 + s_2 \bmod q$
11. return (e, s)

In the description above the parameter z is a secret key embedded in the signing device, *count* is an internal counter, and PRNG is a pseudorandom number generator.

From the external point of view, the result (e, s) is the Schnorr signature created with exactly the same probability distribution as the Schnorr signatures created in the traditional way. It can be implemented as described by Fig. 5 and in Table 1. The idea is that there are two parts of the execution: one of them is vulnerable to attacks on RNG. The other part is deterministic and is immune to physical attacks aimed to limit randomness of the k component. However, it might be vulnerable to an attack by a dishonest manufacturer retaining z.

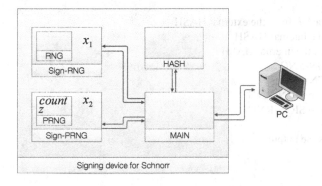

Fig. 5. A distributed implementation of Schnorr signatures

We may consider an adversary model that any physical random generator may be influenced so that the outcome of random number generators can be guessed. This has a dramatic impact on the RNG contained in C_1 but no impact on C_2. We may assume that the adversary knows k_1, but the attack fails: $s = k_1 + k_2 - x \cdot e \bmod q$, but still there are two unknowns k_2 and x. Moreover, if PRNG is well chosen, then we may assume that its output is indistinguishable from the output of a real random number generator. The Achilles Heel of C_2 is the secret z. If in turn the adversary can read the memory of PRNG or replace it in some way, then k_2 becomes exposed. So we see that the scheme does not protect against forgery if both C_1 and C_2 are exposed, but the attacks against C_1 and C_2 require different capabilities of the adversary.

Table 1. A modified realization of Schnorr signatures - the code executed by the components

code executed by SIGN-RNG:

activate upon request from MAIN
choose $k_1 \in [1, q$ uniformly at random
$r_1 := g^{k_1}$
send r_1 to MAIN
receive e from MAIN
$s_1 := k_1 - x_1 \cdot e \bmod q$
send s_1 to MAIN
reset

code executed by SIGN-PRNG:

activate upon request from MAIN
send a request to PRNG
receive k_2 from PRNG
$r_2 := g^{k_2}$
send r_2 to MAIN
receive e from MAIN
$s_2 := k_1 - x_2 \cdot e \bmod q$
send s_1 to MAIN
reset

code executed by MAIN:

send a request to SIGN-RNG
send a request to SIGN-PRNG
receive r_1 from SIGN-RNG
receive r_2 from SIGN-PRNG
$r := r_1 \cdot r_2$
receive pre-hash h from the external HASH
send h, r to the internal HASH
receive e from the internal HASH
send e to SIGN-RNG
send e to SIGN-PRNG
receive s_1 from SIGN-RNG
receive s_2 from SIGN-RNG
$s := s_1 + s_2$
send (s, e) as the output

code executed by PRNG:

receive request from SIGN-PRNG
$count := count + 1$
$k_2 := \mathrm{PRNG}(z, count) \bmod q$
send k_2 to SIGN-PRNG

Issues Related to Hashing. The main problem with the hashing operation is that the length of M may prevent performing the hash operation inside a well protected component. This may create a problem: if the hashing is performed directly by a PC, then the adversary may influence creation of the hash value e in an arbitrary way. Luckily, the hash functions are not monolithic – usually we have iterative constructions, each built upon some compression function. That is, the message to be hashed is divided into blocks, and the compression function is applied iteratively to the output of the last iteration and the current message block (as the initial „output", the initial vector defined in the specification of the hash function is utilized). Hence in case of Schnorr signatures all but the last message blocks could be compressed on a PC, and then the compression result and the last message block are transferred to the smart card. The smart card applies the last iteration of the compression function and obtains $\mathrm{Hash}(M\|r)$ (note that in this way manipulations on e are prevented). Then only at this point:

1. the exponent k is generated,
2. $r := g^k$ is calculated in the secure area,
3. the next compression function is applied to the compression result already obtained and to the value r, hence $e := \text{Hash}(M\|r)$ is calculated,
4. k, e, x are used to obtain s.

To sum up, the construction $e := \text{Hash}(M\|r)$ used in [14], [6, Sect.4.2.3] may be utilized to achieve a kind of atomic operation composed from the sequence of steps 1-4, all executed in the secure area of the smart card. Note that no output dependent on k leaves the smart card until the complete signature is generated, and the time between the first and the last step of the sequence above is minimized. Hence the time when k is exposed to changes (for example some changes made by loss of power or by a deliberate attack aimed e.g., at setting a fixed value) is minimized. See that in some way the ephemeral key k might be more precious for the adversary than the private key x! Indeed, knowledge of k is equivalent to the knowledge of x, but setting the value of x to the one known to the adversary would destroy the key, whereas setting the value of k may yield a successful attack. That is, existence of k may open new possibilities for the adversary. Consequently, the key k should be protected very carefully and its existence time frame should be minimized, and, before revealing the results of computations, a consistency check [4] should be performed in a reliable manner (by reliable we mean a check which does not accept a signature which is invalid). Note that sometimes a check could be bypassed by a powerful adversary – cf. the attack on a `checkcast` instruction when `ClassCastException` should be thrown [1, Subsect.4.1].

See that the atomic operation considered above is rather hard to achieve in the construction $e := \text{Hash}(r\|M)$ used in [12], [9], [10]. In the latter construction the exponent k is generated at first, $r = g^k$ is transferred to the PC, and then the smart card (which usually possesses no clock) waits for the response from the PC... What is more, a reliable signature verification (which is one of possible consistency checks) is infeasible for the smart card without an honest assistance from the PC (at least for large M)!

However, the construction $e := \text{Hash}(r\|M)$, due to the randomizer r put in front of the message, makes collision attacks on Hash more difficult [12]. Hence from purely theoretical point of view the construction seems to be more suitable than the version with $e := \text{Hash}(M\|r)$. But which construction should be implemented in practice? Is the optimal answer possible without considering the details above? Maybe advantages of both constructions could be combined? This seems to be an interesting problem of applied cryptography.

Security Model for the Main Component. The important thing that we learn from the Forking Lemma proof is that "freezing" the RNG by a physical attack or overwriting the value of k in SIGN by a fixed value makes it possible to derive the signing key and thereby break unforgeability. So we see that SIGN has to fulfill the property that its memory must be resistant not only against leaking k, but also against possibly a broader class of attacks against memory manipulations.

As we see, a big disadvantage of the Schnorr signatures (and many other signature schemes based on the Discrete Logarithm Problem) is that the computation of s involves k and x in a way such that any of them and s immediately reveal the other one. But can we do any better? It turns out that it is possible. For signatures like BLS [5], there are no values like k that might endanger the secret key x and the exponentiation operation with x can be performed in the innermost component. In such an architecture the component of the signing key is like the Emperor's Pavilion in the Forbidden City.

4.2   Authentication of Identity Documents

In this section we focus on two protocols executed when a wireless smart card reader starts communication with an identity document on a smart card, called from now on eID. The goal of these protocols is to protect the communication in the following sense:

Password Authentication: the eID admits to establish a session if it becomes convinced that the reader knows the password,

Active Authentication: the reader obtains a proof that the eID holds the secret key corresponding to the declared identity of the eID.

The protocol yields also a session key shared by the eID and the reader.

Security Model. The main objectives of the protocols presented above is as follows:

Definition 2 (Security of Password & Active Authentication). *Let I be a component modelling an eID. Let x be the private key installed in I and y be the corresponding public key. Let π be the password assigned to I.*

We say that a password and active authentication protocol is secure if upon the protocol termination:

- *if a reader R and an eID J share a session key, none of them has aborted the protocol, and R regards y as the public key associated with the session partner, then with a high probability $J = I$,*
- *if a reader R and the eID I share a session key, and none of them has aborted the protocol, then with a high probability R knows the password π.*

The above definition is closely related to the matching sessions concept and security of AKE. However, we define session ID as the private session key and adopt the definition to what we are supposed to achieve regarding the reader. Namely, we cannot believe that the reader connected with the eID is the same reader where the holder of eID has entered the password. Indeed, at exactly the same time another reader knowing π may start communication with the eID and may succeed to establish the connection.

For the sake of completeness let us mention that in case of the protocols discussed privacy protection is another crucial condition. It can be formulated as follows (this general definition consumes both privacy requirements stated in [8]):

Definition 3 (Privacy in Password & Active Authentication). *A protocol guarantees privacy if the adversary cannot decide if a given session has been executed by an eID component I, even if the reader presents to the adversary private data allegedly used during the protocol. The only exception from this situation is when the adversary runs the reader himself and the eID does not abort the protocol.*

The phrase "cannot decide" means here that the probability distribution to provide the correct answer cannot differ in a non-negligible way from the probability distribution where the adversary has no access to the data from the protocol execution concerned for the decision. Before the guessing phase starts, the adversary may observe the interactions and itself may execute the protocol with any eID. Some executions might be faulty and the adversary may take advantage of the access rights defined by the adversary model.

Example Protocols. Let us now recall protocols that merge password authentication (PACE) with an active authentication. We discuss PACE|AA [3] and SPACE|AA protocols [8] (also presented later as PACE|CA during INTRUST 2013 by J. Bender et al.). In both cases the eID holds a password π and a secret key x, for which $y = g^x$ is the public key (as before, the operations are executed in a group G of order q where Discrete Logarithm Problem is hard). The reader obtains π via an independent channel (read optically from the eID card surface or entered by the eID holder). Below we describe operations executed during the protocol execution (with some details skipped).

Operations executed by the eID:	Operations executed the reader:
reset	
$K_\pi := \mathrm{Hash}(0\|\pi)$	$K_\pi := \mathrm{Hash}(0\|\pi)$
choose $s < q$ uniformly at random	
$z := \mathrm{ENC}(K_\pi, s)$	
send z	receive z
	$s := \mathrm{DEC}(K_\pi, z)$
choose $y_A < q$ uniformly at random	choose $y_B < q$ uniformly at random
PACE|AA version	
$Y_A := g^{y_A}$	$Y_B := g^{y_B}$
SPACE|AA version	
$t := g^{y_A}$	$Y_B := g^{y_B}$
$Y_A := t^x$	
receive Y_B	send Y_B
send Y_A	receive Y_A
PACE|AA version	
$h := Y_B^{y_A}$	$h := Y_A^{y_B}$
SPACE|AA version	
$\tau := Y_B^{y_A}$	$h := Y_A^{y_B}$
$h := \tau^x$	
$\hat{g} := h \cdot g^s$	$\hat{g} := h \cdot g^s$
choose $y_A' < q$ uniformly at random	choose $y_B' < q$ uniformly at random
$Y_A' := \hat{g}^{y_A'}$	$Y_B' := \hat{g}^{y_B'}$
receive Y_B'	send Y_B'
send Y_A'	receive Y_A'
$K := Y_B'^{y_A'}$	$K := Y_A'^{y_B'}$
$K_{ENC} := \mathrm{Hash}(1\|K)$	$K_{ENC} := \mathrm{Hash}(1\|K)$
$K_{SC}' := \mathrm{Hash}(2\|K)$	$K_{SC}' := \mathrm{Hash}(2\|K)$
$K_{MAC} := \mathrm{Hash}(3\|K)$	$K_{MAC} := \mathrm{Hash}(3\|K)$

$K'_{MAC} := \text{Hash}(4||K)$

$T_A := \text{MAC}(K'_{MAC}, Y'_B))$

receive T_B

abort if T_B invalid

send T_A

$K'_{MAC} := \text{Hash}(4||K)$

$T_B := \text{MAC}(K'_{MAC}, Y'_A))$

send T_B

receive T_A

abort if T_A invalid

PACE|AA version

$\sigma := y_A + \text{Hash}(5||Y_A||Y'_A) \cdot x$

send $\text{ENC}(K'_{SC}, \sigma||cert(y))$

receive and decrypt $\text{ENC}(K'_{SC}, \sigma||cert(y))$

check certificate $cert(y)$

abort if $g^\sigma \neq Y_A \cdot y^{\text{Hash}(5||Y_A||Y'_A)}$

SPACE|AA version

$w := y_A$

send $\text{ENC}(K'_{SC}, w||cert(y))$

receive and decrypt with K'_{SC}

check certificate $cert(y)$

abort if $y^w \neq Y_A$

PACE|AA and SPACE|AA are relatively simple communication protocols, nevertheless it is quite difficult to track down all details. We do not aim to explain them but rather wish to illustrate some design decisions and security issues.

Architecture of PACE|AA and SPACE|AA. Below we discuss how to organize each protocol as an interaction of components. First observe that protecting π in a secure memory does not make sense. Indeed, an adversary holding an eID may try the passwords one by one attempting to establish communication. On the other hand, x has to be well protected, otherwise it would be possible to clone the eID component.

Definitely, we may implement random number generation via a separate component RNG. Upon request RNG generates an element in the range $[0, q - 1]$ uniformly at random.

In case of SPACE|AA one can implement x in a separate component EXP. Given an input γ the component responds with γ^x. There are no other operations available. In case of PACE|AA the situation is more complicated due to interaction between y_a, σ and x. In this case it is necessary to embed signature generation in a separate component SIGN-EXP which additionally may perform exponentiation. This is definitely a complication as this does not look as a standard component to be reused elsewhere.

Attacking Randomness. In order to show profound differences between PACE|AA and SPACE|AA we discuss the situation where the adversary may reduce the entropy of randomness by attacking the component responsible for choosing random exponents.

First consider PACE|AA. If the adversary guesses y_A, then from the public parameters Y_A, Y'_A and σ he can easily derive x by the equality $\sigma = y_A + \text{Hash}(5||Y_A||Y'_A) \cdot x$. If the adversary is not running the reader that interacts with the eID (and therefore does not receive σ directly), then the attack is slightly harder. First the adversary has to guess the exponent y'_A and computes the candidates for K, K'_{SC}, decrypt the ciphertext and checks if the result is of the form $\sigma||cert(y)$. Getting π requires more effort: having y'_A and Y'_A one can derive $\hat{g} = (Y'_A)^{y'^{-1}_A \bmod q}$. By guessing y_A we get candidates for

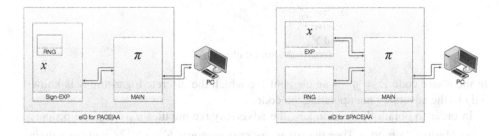

Fig. 6. eID of PACE|AA and SPACE|AA

$h = Y_B^{y_A}$ and then for $g^s = \hat{g}/h$. Then for each candidate password π is suffices to decrypt z and check whether the obtained plaintext s satisfies the equality $\hat{g} = h \cdot g^s$. Once the adversary gets π and x, he can create a clone of the eID and thereby the properties from Definition 2 are violated.

In case of SPACE|AA let us assume that the adversary has seized control over the whole eID component except for the component EXP. However, in this case all what the adversary can do is to run EXP as an oracle for raising to power x. Therefore, under standard assumptions the adversary cannot derive x. However, SPACE|AA is still insecure regarding Definition 2. Indeed, after guessing y_A' it is possible to derive K and thereby the session key. Afterwards it is possible to hijack the session.

Finally, let us note that the situation is the same for the model where the ephemeral keys are revealed, as already stated in [8].

Attacks by Manipulating the Code Component. The second adversary model concerned here is the situation that the adversary can manipulate the code in the MAIN eID component (e.g. the malicious manufacturer). Now we assume that the adversary cannot read any ephemeral data, but can eavesdrop the communication channel between the eID attacked and the reader.

Below we show that the adversary may gain the access to the session key and can hijack the session for PACE|AA. Thereby, the protocol is insecure regarding Definition 2, as the second condition is violated. The manipulated code executed by the manipulated eID component is as follows (the new code line is underlined):

$$K_\pi := \text{Hash}(0||\pi)$$
$$\text{choose } s < q \text{ uniformly at random}$$
$$z := \text{ENC}(K_\pi, s)$$
$$\text{send } z$$
$$\text{choose } y_A < q \text{ uniformly at random}$$
$$Y_A := g^{y_A}$$
$$\text{receive } Y_B$$
$$\text{send } Y_A$$
$$h := Y_B^{y_A}, \quad \hat{g} := h \cdot g^s$$
$$\text{~~choose } y_A' < q \text{ uniformly at random~~}$$
$$\underline{y_A' := \text{Hash}(Z^{y_A}) \bmod q}$$

$$Y'_A := \hat{g}^{y'_A}$$
receive Y'_B
send Y'_A
... (continue without changes)

In the above code $Z = g^\alpha$ is an element for which the discrete logarithm α is known only to the adversary manipulating the code.

In order to obtain the session key, the adversary recomputes y'_A using the property $y'_A = \text{Hash}(Y^\alpha_A) \bmod q$. Then the adversary may compute $K := Y'_B{}^{y'_A}$ and the remaining keys using exactly the same operations as the eID component.

Let us summarize the attack properties:

- The attack idea is in fact borrowed from [15]. It takes advantage of the fact that the PACE algorithm creates powers for randomly chosen exponents <u>twice</u>.
- Reverse engineering the code component may reveal the parameter Z to the third parties. However, Z does not suffice to perform the attack on the session keys.
- The attack does not require any non volatile memory to store some extra values. The attacker requires neither the private key x nor the password π.
- The manipulated values Y'_A cannot be distinguished from the values Y'_A produced by the original protocol. This follows from the fact that (Y_A, Z, Z^{y_A}) is a Diffie-Hellman triple and the last element cannot be distinguished from a random group element. Of course, we require also that it is infeasible to distinguish the random source of elements from $[0, \ldots, q-1]$ from a source that chooses a group element R at random and outputs $\text{Hash}(R) \bmod q$.

Finally note that

- The attack works without any change against the plain PACE protocol.
- For SPACE|AA the only modification in the attack to be done is that the adversary has to fix Z for which $Z = y^\beta$ and β is known to the adversary. As before, instead of generating y'_A at random the manipulated code takes $y'_A := \text{Hash}(Z^{y_A}) \bmod q$. The recovery of y'_A by the adversary is possible thanks to the equality $Z^{y_A} = Y^\beta_A$.

The lesson to be learnt is that it is hard to design a protocol without any potential implementation weakness. In case of PACE based protocols the problem is that after reset of the smart card the protocol executes Diffie-Hellman key exchange protocol twice and thereby has to use two randomly chosen exponents. This makes room for the SETUP technique from [15]. However, what we really need here is not randomness, but unpredictability for the adversary observing the protocol execution. This problem can be solved by using signatures instead of random exponents, as proposed in [7]. However, thereby we may fall back into some problems as the extended execution code may give rise to new security traps. Another strategy could be to abandon double Diffie-Hellman key exchange and return to the idea of SPEKE [11] despite patent problems.

References

1. Barbu, G., Thiebeauld, H., Guerin, V.: Attacks on Java Card 3.0 combining fault and logical attacks. In: Gollmann, D., Lanet, J.-L., Iguchi-Cartigny, J. (eds.) CARDIS 2010. LNCS, vol. 6035, pp. 148–163. Springer, Heidelberg (2010)

2. Becker, G.T., Regazzoni, F., Paar, C., Burleson, W.P.: Stealthy dopant-level hardware Trojans. In: Bertoni, G., Coron, J.-S. (eds.) CHES 2013. LNCS, vol. 8086, pp. 197–214. Springer, Heidelberg (2013)
3. Bender, J., Dagdelen, Ö., Fischlin, M., Kügler, D.: The PACE|AA protocol for machine readable travel documents, and its security. In: Keromytis, A.D. (ed.) FC 2012. LNCS, vol. 7397, pp. 344–358. Springer, Heidelberg (2012)
4. Boneh, D., DeMillo, R.A., Lipton, R.J.: On the importance of checking cryptographic protocols for faults. In: Fumy, W. (ed.) EUROCRYPT 1997. LNCS, vol. 1233, pp. 37–51. Springer, Heidelberg (1997)
5. Boneh, D., Lynn, B., Shacham, H.: Short signatures from the Weil pairing. J. Cryptology 17(4), 297–319 (2004)
6. Bundesamt für Sicherheit in der Informationstechnik: Elliptic Curve Cryptography. Technische Richtlinie TR-03111 v2.0 (June 2012)
7. Gołebiewski, Z., Kutyłowski, M., Zagórski, F.: Stealing secrets with SSL/TLS and SSH – kleptographic attacks. In: Pointcheval, D., Mu, Y., Chen, K. (eds.) CANS 2006. LNCS, vol. 4301, pp. 191–202. Springer, Heidelberg (2006)
8. Hanzlik, L., Krzywiecki, Ł., Kutyłowski, M.: Simplified PACE|AA protocol. In: Deng, R.H., Feng, T. (eds.) ISPEC 2013. LNCS, vol. 7863, pp. 218–232. Springer, Heidelberg (2013)
9. ISO/IEC 14888-3/Amd 1:2010: Information technology - Security techniques - Digital signatures with appendix - Part 3: Discrete logarithm based mechanisms, AMENDMENT 1 (2010)
10. ISO/IEC 14888-3/Amd 2:2012: Information technology - Security techniques - Digital signatures with appendix - Part 3: Discrete logarithm based mechanisms, AMENDMENT 2 (2012)
11. Jablon, D.P.: Extended password key exchange protocols immune to dictionary attacks. In: WETICE, pp. 248–255. IEEE Computer Society (1997)
12. Neven, G., Smart, N.P., Warinschi, B.: Hash function requirements for Schnorr signatures. J. Mathematical Cryptology 3(1), 69–87 (2009)
13. Nicolosi, A., Krohn, M.N., Dodis, Y., Mazières, D.: Proactive two-party signatures for user authentication. In: NDSS. The Internet Society (2003)
14. Schnorr, C.P.: Efficient signature generation by smart cards. J. Cryptology 4(3), 161–174 (1991)
15. Young, A., Yung, M.: The prevalence of kleptographic attacks on discrete-log based cryptosystems. In: Kaliski Jr., B.S. (ed.) CRYPTO 1997. LNCS, vol. 1294, pp. 264–276. Springer, Heidelberg (1997)

A CAPTCHA Scheme Based
on the Identification of Character Locations

Vu Duc Nguyen, Yang-Wai Chow, and Willy Susilo*

Centre for Computer and Information Security Research,
School of Computer Science and Software Engineering,
University of Wollongong, Australia
{vdn108,caseyc,wsusilo}@uow.edu.au

Abstract. CAPTCHAs are a standard security mechanism used on many websites to protect online services against abuse by automated programs, or bots. The purpose of a CAPTCHA is to distinguish whether an online transaction is being carried out by a human or a bot. Unfortunately, to date many existing CAPTCHA schemes have been found to be vulnerable to automated attacks. It is widely accepted that state-of-the-art in text-based CAPTCHA design requires that a CAPTCHA be resistant against segmentation. In this paper, we examine CAPTCHA usability issues and current segmentation techniques that have been used to attack various CAPTCHA schemes. We then introduce the design of a new CAPTCHA scheme that was designed based on these usability and segmentation considerations. Our goal was to also design a text-based CAPTCHA scheme that can easily be used on increasingly pervasive touch-screen devices, without the need for keyboard input. This paper also examines the usability and robustness of the proposed CAPTCHA scheme.

Keywords: Text-based CAPTCHA, segmentation resistance, optical character recognition.

1 Introduction

CAPTCHAs (Completely Automated Public Turing test to tell Computers and Humans Apart) are essentially automated reverse Turing tests that are commonly used by online services to distinguish whether an online transaction is being carried out by a human or an automated program, i.e. a bot [24]. Since its inception, many diverse CAPTCHA schemes have been proposed, and to date, CAPTCHAs have become a standard Internet security mechanism for deterring automated attacks by bots and other malicious programs. Of the different types of CAPTCHAs (e.g. text-based, image-based, audio-based) that are currently used in practice, text-based CAPTCHAs are the most prevalent form in use. Chellapilla et al. [12] attribute the popularity and pervasiveness of text-based

---

* This work is supported by ARC Future Fellowship FT0991397.

X. Huang and J. Zhou (Eds.): ISPEC 2014, LNCS 8434, pp. 60–74, 2014.
© Springer International Publishing Switzerland 2014

CAPTCHAs to its human friendliness, intuitiveness, ease of use, low implementation cost, etc. In general, a traditional text-based CAPTCHA challenge consists of a word or a random sequence of characters, which may consist of letters and/or digits, that are embedded within an image. The user's task is to solve the CAPTCHA challenge by entering the appropriate sequence of characters in the correct order.

Unfortunately, while there are numerous existing CAPTCHA schemes that are currently deployed on a vast number of websites, many of these schemes have been found to be insecure. The vulnerability of these schemes stem from various design flaws that can be exploited to break these CAPTCHAs. Over the years, researchers have documented many techniques that can be used to break a variety of CAPTCHA schemes at high success rates [1,3,4,7,13,16,19,21,20,28,29]. Furthermore, attacks against CAPTCHA schemes are not only limited to traditional text-based CAPTCHAs, as techniques to break other forms of CAPTCHAs have also been documented. These include techniques for breaking animated CAPTCHAs [23,27], 3D-based CAPTCHAs [22], image-based CAPTCHAs [31], audio-based CAPTCHAs [5], etc. As such, the design of a CAPTCHA scheme that is robust against automated attacks is an important and open research problem. In addition, the challenge of designing a secure CAPTCHA scheme is further complicated by the fact that not only must the resulting CAPTCHA be secure against automated attacks, it must also be easily usable by a human.

This paper presents the design of a new CAPTCHA scheme along with a discussion on the security and usability of the proposed scheme. It is widely accepted that state-of-the-art in CAPTCHA design requires that a CAPTCHA be segmentation-resistant [1,12], as once a CAPTCHA can be segmented into its constituting characters, the scheme is essentially deemed to be broken [11]. In this paper, we first examine CAPTCHA usability issues and current segmentation techniques that have been used to attack a variety of existing CAPTCHAs, in order to identify the various factors that must be considered when designing a robust CAPTCHA scheme. This will then be followed by a discussion on the design of our proposed scheme in relation to these usability and segmentation considerations. In addition, this paper presents the results of a user study that was conducted to ascertain the usability of the proposed CAPTCHA scheme, followed by an analysis on the robustness of the scheme.

Our Contributions. In this paper, we present and discuss the design of a new text-based CAPTCHA scheme that is robust against current segmentation techniques. The proposed CAPTCHA scheme is also usable on touch-screen interfaces, without the need to enter text via a physical or on-screen keyboard. Our proposed approach alters the traditional challenge posed by conventional text-based CAPTCHAs in which the user's task is to answer the question of "What is the text?", into a question of "Where is the text?". Hence, the user's task is to recognize and identify the locations of characters in the CAPTCHA challenge. Furthermore, this paper outlines and examines the various usability and security issues that must be considered in the design of a robust CAPTCHA scheme.

2 Background

2.1 Usability versus Security

The fundamental requirement of a practical CAPTCHA scheme necessitates that humans must be able to solve the CAPTCHA challenges with a high degree of success, while the likelihood that a computer program can correctly solve them must be very small. This tradeoff between the usability and security of a CAPTCHA scheme is a hard act to balance. Security considerations push designers to increase the difficulty of the CAPTCHA scheme, while usability requirements compel them to make the scheme only as difficult as they need to be, but still be effective in deterring automated abuse. These conflicting demands have resulted in the ongoing arms race between CAPTCHA designers and those who try to break them [10,15].

The design of a robust CAPTCHA must capitalize on the difference in natural human ability and the capabilities of current computer programs [10]. This is a challenging task because on one hand, computing technology and algorithms that can be used to solve CAPTCHAs are constantly evolving and improving (e.g. Optical Character Recognition (OCR) software), while on the other hand, humans must rely on their inherent abilities and are unlikely to get better at solving CAPTCHAs. In addition, it has been shown that several key features that are commonly employed to increase the usability of CAPTCHA schemes can easily be exploited by computer programs.

The use of color is a major factor that has to be considered in CAPTCHA design. Color is used in CAPTCHAs for a variety of reasons. From a usability perspective, color is a strong attention-getting mechanism, it is appealing and can make CAPTCHA challenges interesting, appropriate use of color can facilitate recognition and comprehension of a CAPTCHA, and so on [2]. However, it has been shown that the imprudent use of color can have a negative impact on both CAPTCHA usability and security [1,30].

To aid usability, text-based CAPTCHA challenges that are based on dictionary words are intuitive and easier for humans to solve because humans find familiar text easier to perceive and read [25]. However, CAPTCHA challenges that are based on language models are susceptible to dictionary attacks. Rather of trying to recognize individual characters, which may be difficult if the characters are overly distorted and/or overlapping, researchers have successfully used holistic approaches to recognize entire words for CAPTCHA schemes that are based on language models [4,21].

Instead of using actual dictionary words, it is possible to take advantage of text familiarity using "language-like" strings. Phonetic text or Markov dictionary strings are pronounceable strings that are not words of any language. Experiments have shown that humans perform better when solving CAPTCHAs with pronounceable strings in contrast to CAPTCHAs which contain purely random characters [25]. Nevertheless, the disadvantage of using this approach is that certain characters (i.e. vowels) will appear at higher frequencies in pronounceable strings compared to other characters. The higher frequencies of certain characters makes the resulting CAPTCHA more vulnerable to attacks.

In addition, for usability purposes text-based CAPTCHAs should avoid the use of confusing digits and letters like the digit '0' and the letter 'O', the digit '1' and the letter 'l', etc. Confusing character combinations like 'W' and 'VV', 'm' and 'rn', etc. should also be avoided. Furthermore, if letter case is important, then confusing characters include upper and lower case pairs like 'S' and 's', 'Z' and 'z', etc. [30].

2.2 Segmentation Resistance

Chellapilla et al. [11,13] demonstrated that machine learning algorithms can successfully be used to break a variety of different CAPTCHA schemes. In doing so, they also showed that computers can outperform humans at the task of recognizing individual characters. The task of solving a text-based CAPTCHA consists of two main challenges; namely, a segmentation challenge, followed by a recognition challenge. The segmentation challenge refers to the identification and separation of a sequence of characters into its constituting characters in the correct order, and the recognition challenge involves recognizing the individual characters. As such, it follows that once a computer program can adequately reduce a CAPTCHA to the problem of recognizing individual characters, the CAPTCHA is essentially broken. Hence, it is widely accepted that a secure CAPTCHA scheme must be designed to be segmentation-resistant [1,10].

Broad classifications of three of the mainstream segmentation-resistant methods that are currently employed by a number of CAPTCHA schemes to deter segmentation, as defined by Bursztein et al. [7], are described as follows:

- **Background Confusion**: CAPTCHA schemes that use this approach to prevent segmentation attempt to blend the CAPTCHA text with the background. There are three main ways of achieving this; namely, by using a complex background image, by using a background with very similar colors to the text, or by adding noise. Some CAPTCHA schemes employ a combination of these techniques.
- **Using Lines**: In this approach, random line(s) that cross over multiple characters are drawn over the CAPTCHA text. This is done to help prevent segmentation because characters in the CAPTCHA challenge are connected together by the lines.
- **Collapsing**: This approach typically involves removing the space between characters, tilting characters and/or overlapping them, which in effect crowds the characters together. The notion behind this approach is to make segmentation difficult because the characters are either very close or joined together. While this is considered to be the most secure anti-segmentation mechanism, often design flaws in the CAPTCHA scheme allow attackers to exploit these flaws in order to perform segmentation [7]. Some of these attacks are described in the next section.

2.3   CAPTCHA Segmentation Techniques

While it is widely accepted that a robust CAPTCHA scheme must be designed to be segmentation-resistant, many existing schemes that adopt anti-segmentation mechanisms have in fact been found to be insecure. This is mainly due to certain design flaws in the scheme that can be exploited by the attacker to segment the CAPTCHA. Over the years, researchers have documented a variety of different techniques that can be used to segment various CAPTCHA schemes. Among others, several key segmentation techniques are described as follows:

- **De-noising Algorithms**: De-noising techniques are mainly used to remove random noise from a CAPTCHA. Of the various de-noising techniques that have been proposed over the years, the Markov Random Field technique, a.k.a. Gibbs algorithm [18], has been found to be very effective [7]. The algorithm works by computing the energy of each pixel based on its surroundings and removing pixels that have an energy below a certain threshold. This is performed iteratively until there is no more pixels to remove.
- **Histogram-Based Segmentation**: Histogram-based segmentation is a popular CAPTCHA segmentation technique that projects a CAPTCHA's pixels to their respective X or Y coordinates [3,7,19,28,29]. By producing a histogram of the number of pixels in the X or Y dimension, in general, sections that contain a large pixel count contain characters, while sections with a low pixel count are potential positions that can be used to segment the characters. For CAPTCHAs where the characters are only joined slightly or connected using small lines, this method is effective in segmenting the CAPTCHA. In other CAPTCHA attacking methods, this technique is efficient in separating groups of characters or potential groups prior to the use of other segmentation techniques.
- **Color Filling Segmentation (CFS)**: The basic idea behind this technique is identify a foreground color pixel (i.e. a pixel with a color associated with the text) and to trace all the neighboring pixels with the same color which are connected to this pixel, in effect performing a flood fill algorithm, to identify a chunk of connected pixels. This process is repeated until all chunks in a CAPTCHA have been identified [3,29]. The end result of using this method is that an attacker can identify individual characters or groups of characters. This method is often used in conjunction with other segmentation techniques.
- **Opportunistic Segmentation**: This technique relies on making educated guesses based on prior knowledge about the CAPTCHA scheme. The technique exploits regular and predictable features of a CAPTCHA scheme in order to approximate where the segmentation cuts should be. For example, CAPTCHA schemes that use a fixed number of characters per challenge, where characters are usually placed at certain fixed locations, and all characters have roughly the same width, are susceptible to opportunistic segmentation. The reason for this is because it is easy to make an educated guess as to where the segmentation cuts are likely to occur [7,10].

- **Segmentation Based on Patterns and Shapes**: In this segmentation approach, attackers try to identify certain patterns and shapes that typically characterize some characters. For example, characters like 'a', 'b', 'd', 'e', 'g', 'o', 'p', 'q' all contain loops or circular regions, characters like 'i', 'j', 'l' typically consist of small vertical blocks of pixels, etc. [3,16]. Once these patterns are determined, these particular features can be identified in the CAPTCHA which in turn allows the attacker to ascertain appropriate locations to segment the text.

The techniques described here are some generic methods that have been adopted to attack a number of different CAPTCHA schemes. There are also other specialized segmentation methods that have been used to attack specific CAPTCHA schemes [1,28]. While to date there is no comprehensive segmentation solution that can be used to break all CAPTCHA schemes, many CAPTCHA segmentation attacks use a combination and/or variations of the techniques described above.

3   Design of the Proposed CAPTCHA Scheme

Many of the existing CAPTCHA schemes that adopt anti-segmentation mechanisms have actually been broken through the use of using various segmentation techniques, including those described in the previous section. As such, in designing a CAPTCHA scheme, it is imperative to examine the use of anti-segmentation mechanisms and to consider the resulting CAPTCHA's robustness against current segmentation techniques. Since a CAPTCHA scheme's robustness is determined by the cumulative effects of its design choices [10], we will discuss the reasons and security issues that were considered in the design of our proposed CAPTCHA scheme.

In general, the use of background confusion techniques as a security mechanism has been deemed to be insecure. For one thing, human usability considerations require that the text stand out from the rest of the background, otherwise a human will not be able to adequately solve the CAPTCHA, and for this reason it is likely that any background can be processed, filtered and removed. It has therefore been recommended that backgrounds only be used for cosmetic purposes [7]. In addition, using lines to connect characters as a segmentation-resistant technique has also been found to be inadequate in preventing the resulting CAPTCHA from being segmented. This is because there are a variety of techniques that can efficiently detect and/or remove lines, for example, through the use of line detection algorithms such as the Hough transform [17], erosion and dilation techniques [26], as well as histogram-based segmentation techniques.

Collapsing techniques such as crowding and overlapping characters together are considered to be the most secure anti-segmentation approach to date. However, an increasing number of CAPTCHA scheme that have been designed with these techniques have been successfully broken because attackers have managed to exploit design flaws in the various schemes [3,7]. One of the reasons for this is due to the fact that current text-based CAPTCHAs crowd and overlap characters in the horizontal dimension only. This has allowed attackers to identify predictable features in the CAPTCHA schemes and to approximate where the segmentation cuts should occur.

In this paper, we propose the design of a text-based CAPTCHA scheme that is robust against current segmentation techniques. One of our goals was to also design a scheme that can easily be used on the increasingly popular and pervasive touch-screen devices, without having to rely on the need to input text using a physical or on-screen keyboard. As such, unlike conventional text-based CAPTCHAs which deal with the question of "What is the text?", our approach alters this into the question of "Where is the text?". Examples of our proposed CAPTCHA scheme are depicted in Figure 1.

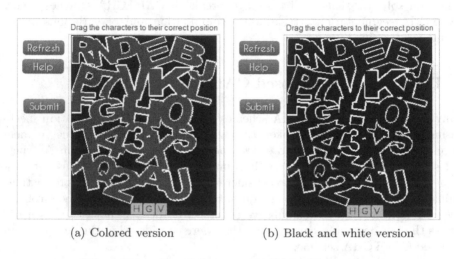

(a) Colored version   (b) Black and white version

Fig. 1. Examples of the proposed CAPTCHA scheme

There are two slightly different versions of our proposed scheme. Figure 1(a) shows an example of a colored version of the proposed CAPTCHA, while Figure 1(b) shows a black and white version. Note that the use of color in our scheme is not for any security reasons, but rather it is primarily used for reasons of usability. This is in line with recommendations that color be used in CAPTCHAs for usability rather than for security [2]. The colored version of our scheme was implemented to ascertain whether or not it would facilitate human visual perception, by making it easier for humans to distinguish characters from the background, instead of having to solely rely on the outlines of characters. To help answer this question, a user study was conducted and the findings of the experiment are discussed in Section 4.1.

For each CAPTCHA in our proposed scheme, a user is provided with a challenge character set (the list of characters at the bottom of the CAPTCHA) and an image that contains these specific characters, along with a whole lot of other non-relevant characters. To solve the CAPTCHA, the user's task is to find the locations of the characters provided in the challenge character set in the image, then drag-and-drop each challenge character onto the correct character in the image. This can easily be done using a mouse, a pointing device or on a touch-screen. Figure 2(a) and Figure 2(b) show examples of an incorrect answer and a correct answer respectively[1]. Note that the correct characters in the CAPTCHA are only highlighted after the solution has been submitted. Drag-and-drop CAPTCHAs are not new and have previously been proposed, for example, for identifying images of 3D text objects [9]. Others have proposed clickable CAPTCHAs for mobile devices [14].

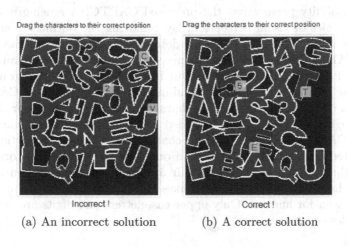

(a) An incorrect solution   (b) A correct solution

Fig. 2. Example answers

The design of the proposed CAPTCHA scheme mainly relies on the collapsing technique for preventing segmentation. However, unlike conventional text-based CAPTCHAs, it can be seen from the examples shown in Figures 1 and 2 that our approach not only crowds, tilts and overlaps characters in the horizontal dimension, it also does this in the vertical dimension. In addition, our approach uses many more characters than is actually contained in the challenge character set. For conventional CAPTCHAs that adopt the crowding characters together approach, each character only has a maximum of two neighboring left and right characters that it can overlap with. Our approach allows for center characters to overlap with a maximum of eight neighboring characters. Obviously, characters at the sides have less neighboring characters. As such, it can easily be seen that our approach effectively prevents segmentation techniques like histogram-based segmentation, color filling segmentation or methods that try to identify character patterns and shapes to determine where the text should be segmented, because the text cannot simply be segmented using single lines.

---

[1] Animated examples depicting user interaction with the proposed scheme can be found at: http://www.uow.edu.au/~wsusilo/CAPTCHA/newCAPTCHA.html

The challenge character set in the proposed scheme consists of random characters instead of dictionary words, and is therefore not affected by dictionary attacks. Rather than using a fixed number of characters per challenge, the number of characters in the challenge set can be randomized. Furthermore, for all characters in the image, their rotation angles, positions and sizes, as well as the number of characters, can all be randomized within a certain range of values. This prevents other segmentation techniques like opportunistic segmentation, because the randomization makes it difficult to predict where individual characters are located. Also, since color in our scheme is not used for security, attackers cannot use color filtering to identify the locations of individual characters in the image.

From a usability perspective, the proposed CAPTCHA scheme is based on Gestalt principles of visual perception. By removing the outlines of characters wherever they overlap in the image to deter segmentation, a human can still solve the CAPTCHA because humans perceive objects as a whole and the visual system fills in the missing areas. Our implementation was programmed to avoid the use of confusing character combinations within the same CAPTCHA challenge. In our scheme, each unique character only occurs once per challenge. Also, although the characters are crowded together, unlike many conventional text-based CAPTCHAs which rely on character warping or distortion to deter automated attacks, the characters in our approach are not distorted. This is because the security mechanism of our approach does not rely on character warping or distortion, which in turn makes the task of recognizing undistorted characters easier for humans. Only upper case letters and digits are used in the current implementation.

4   Results and Discussion

4.1   User Study

User studies with human participants are the best method of establishing the human-friendliness of a CAPTCHA scheme [10]. As such, a pilot user study was conducted to determine the usability of the proposed CAPTCHA scheme. The study was also done to ascertain whether the use of color in one of the CAPTCHA versions would make a significant difference for a human. A total of 42 volunteers, 33 male and 9 female, took part in the experiment. Participants were aged between 18 and 58 (average $\sim$32.9, standard deviation $\sim$1.05). None of the participants had ever seen or had any prior knowledge about the proposed CAPTCHA scheme.

Method. For the study, a total of 30 CAPTCHA challenges were generated. Of this, 15 were the colored version and the other 15 were the black and white version. For each version, the challenge character set consisted of 3 characters for 7 of the CAPTCHAs, while the challenge character set for the remaining 8 CAPTCHAs consisted of 4 characters. The order in which the CAPTCHAs were presented to the participants was randomized. In order to compare results, the same experimental conditions were maintained for all participants. Hence, each participant was required to solve the same set of 30 CAPTCHAs.

Before the experiment, each of the participants was given instructions about the experimental task and what they were required to do. Their task was simply to view each challenge and solve the CAPTCHA using a mouse. The duration of the experiment was designed to be short to avoid participants loosing concentration. The total time required by each participant to complete the experiment varied between individuals, but took no longer than 15 minutes. During the experiment, we recorded the time taken by each user to complete each CAPTCHA challenge as well as all their answers. Participants were not provided with any information regarding the correctness of their answers. At the end of the experiment, participants were also given a post-experiment questionnaire that contained questions about their subjective opinions in relation to the usability of the proposed CAPTCHA scheme.

Results. Table 1 shows the results of the experiment. It shows the difference in accuracy and average completion time between the colored version of the CAPTCHA and the black and white version. For good usability and to avoid users getting annoyed, Chellapilla et al. [10] state that the human success rate of a good CAPTCHA should approach 90%. It can be seen from the user study results that the success rate of both versions of our proposed CAPTCHA satisfies this benchmark.

Table 1. Average completion time and the success rates

	Accuracy (%)	Average Time (s)
Colored version	96.35	18.97
Black and white version	93.81	26.24

In addition, the experimental results suggest that the use of color has an effect on the overall usability of the CAPTCHA scheme. In Table 1, one can see that the accuracy for the colored version was higher than the black and white version. However, a Chi-square test did not reveal a significant difference. The results also show a difference in the average completion times. Upon further analysis, a t-test showed a significant difference in the average completion time for the black and white version ($M = 26.24$s, $SD = 18.26$s) and the colored version ($M = 18.97$s, $SD = 7.60$s); $t(841) = 9.22$, $p < 0.001$. This suggests that perceptually the use of color to distinguish characters from the background makes the CAPTCHA easier for a human to solve. Table 2 shows the breakdown of average completion times based on the number of characters per challenge. Not surprisingly, the more challenge characters in a CAPTCHA, the longer it took participants to solve the CAPTCHA.

Table 2. Average completion time based on the number of challenge characters

	Average Time (s)	
	3 characters	4 characters
Colored version	17.70	21.52
Black and white version	20.67	31.12

It should be noted that overall the time taken by participants to complete our proposed CAPTCHA scheme appears to be longer than that required to solve other image CAPTCHAs. In a large scale evaluation study by Bursztein et al. [6] where they tested a variety of CAPTCHA schemes, they reported an average solving time of 9.8 seconds for image CAPTCHAs and 28.4 seconds for audio CAPTCHAs. The lengthy duration required to solve our proposed CAPTCHA, especially the black and white version, is probably due to two factors. First, users have to search the image in order to identify the locations of the appropriate characters. A task that appears to be more difficult in the case of the black and white version. Second, users may spend more time when trying to accurately drag-and-drop characters to the appropriate locations in the image, compared to traditional text-based CAPTCHAs where they would simply input text via a keyboard. Figure 3 is an example of a plot which shows the locations of where the participants' "dropped" each of the individual challenge characters when attempting to solve the CAPTCHA.

In one of the questions on the post-experiment questionnaire, participants were asked to rate the ease of use of the proposed CAPTCHA scheme using a 7-point Likert scale, with 1 being very difficult to use and 7 being very easy to use.

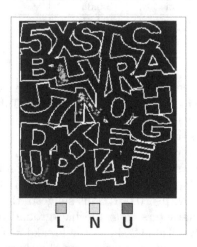

Fig. 3. Example showing the locations of where participants' "dropped" the respective challenge characters in the CAPTCHA

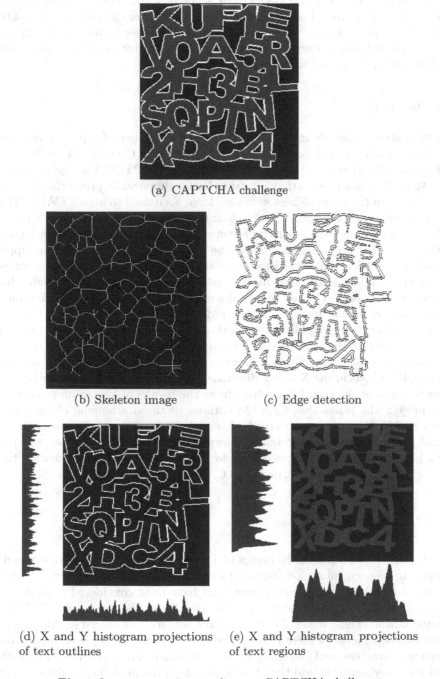

(a) CAPTCHA challenge

(b) Skeleton image

(c) Edge detection

(d) X and Y histogram projections of text outlines

(e) X and Y histogram projections of text regions

Fig. 4. Image processing results on a CAPTCHA challenge

The average participant response to this question was 5.14. When asked to rate the usability of the proposed CAPTCHA scheme as compared to other existing CAPTCHAs that they had used in the past, the average response was 4.65, where 1 was much harder to use and 7 was much easier to use. This indicates that in general, the majority of participants had a positive opinion about the usability of the proposed scheme.

4.2 Security

Figure 4 shows example images resulting from a number of typical techniques that are often used to attack CAPTCHA schemes. The CAPTCHA challenge itself is shown in Figure 4(a). Figure 4(b) shows the CAPTCHA image's skeleton. Skeletonization is a process that is used to thin a shape while preserving the general pattern of the shape. Skeleton images have been used to attack CAPTCHAs as the skeleton thins the characters to a single pixel thickness, which may potentially be used to identify geometric features of the characters [3]. It can be seen in the figure that because characters in the proposed CAPTCHA are overlapped in both the vertical and horizontal dimensions, the skeleton image does not result in useful information that can be used to segment or to identify individual characters. Figure 4(c) shows the results of processing the CAPTCHA using a Canny edge detection filter [8]. In the proposed CAPTCHA scheme, the edge detection filter merely highlights the outlines of the overlapping characters, but does not facilitate the task of separating the characters.

Histogram-based segmentation is a commonly used approach that projects CAPTCHA pixels in the X and Y dimensions in order to identify potential locations to segment the text. Figure 4(d) shows the results of histogram projections that project the pixels that form the outlines of the overlapping characters in the X and Y dimensions respectively. X and Y histogram projections of the internal regions of the characters are shown in Figure 4(e). It can be seen that both histogram projection approaches do not provide enough information that can be used to adequately segment the CAPTCHA challenge.

5   Conclusion

In this paper, we presented the design of a new CAPTCHA scheme that was developed to be segmentation-resistant. To achieve this, this paper first examined the various usability and security issues that have to be considered when designing a robust CAPTCHA scheme, then described how the proposed CAPTCHA scheme satisfied these issues. The CAPTCHA scheme introduced in this paper is based on the concept of identifying character locations, rather than merely recognizing characters, and can easily be used on touch-screen devices without the need for a keyboard. In addition, this paper also presented the results obtained from a user study that was conducted to ascertain the usability of the proposed CAPTCHA scheme.

References

1. Ahmad, A.S.E., Yan, J., Marshall, L.: The robustness of a new CAPTCHA. In: EUROSEC, pp. 36–41 (2010)
2. Ahmad, A.S.E., Yan, J., Ng, W.-Y.: CAPTCHA design: Color, usability, and security. IEEE Internet Computing 16(2), 44–51 (2012)
3. Ahmad, A.S.E., Yan, J., Tayara, M.: The robustness of Google CAPTCHAs. University of Newcastle, UK, Technical Report 1278, 1–15 (2011)
4. Baecher, P., Büscher, N., Fischlin, M., Milde, B.: Breaking reCAPTCHA: A holistic approach via shape recognition. In: Camenisch, J., Fischer-Hübner, S., Murayama, Y., Portmann, A., Rieder, C. (eds.) SEC 2011. IFIP AICT, vol. 354, pp. 56–67. Springer, Heidelberg (2011)
5. Bursztein, E., Beauxis, R., Paskov, H., Perito, D., Fabry, C., Mitchell, J.C.: The failure of noise-based non-continuous audio CAPTCHAs. In: IEEE Symposium on Security and Privacy, pp. 19–31. IEEE Computer Society (2011)
6. Bursztein, E., Bethard, S., Fabry, C., Mitchell, J.C., Jurafsky, D.: How good are humans at solving CAPTCHAs? a large scale evaluation. In: IEEE Symposium on Security and Privacy, pp. 399–413. IEEE Computer Society (2010)
7. Bursztein, E., Martin, M., Mitchell, J.C.: Text-based CAPTCHA strengths and weaknesses. In: Chen, Y., Danezis, G., Shmatikov, V. (eds.) ACM Conference on Computer and Communications Security, pp. 125–138. ACM (2011)
8. Canny, J.: A Computational Approach to Edge Detection. IEEE Transactions on Pattern Analysis and Machine Intelligence PAMI-8(6), 679–698 (1986)
9. Chaudhari, S.K., Deshpande, A.R., Bendale, S.B., Kotian, R.V.: 3D drag-n-drop CAPTCHA enhanced security through CAPTCHA. In: Mishra, B.K. (ed.) ICWET, pp. 598–601. ACM (2011)
10. Chellapilla, K., Larson, K., Simard, P.Y., Czerwinski, M.: Building segmentation based human-friendly Human Interaction Proofs (HIPs). In: Baird, H.S., Lopresti, D.P. (eds.) HIP 2005. LNCS, vol. 3517, pp. 1–26. Springer, Heidelberg (2005)
11. Chellapilla, K., Larson, K., Simard, P.Y., Czerwinski, M.: Computers beat humans at single character recognition in reading based Human Interaction Proofs (HIPs). In: CEAS (2005)
12. Chellapilla, K., Larson, K., Simard, P.Y., Czerwinski, M.: Designing human friendly Human Interaction Proofs (HIPs). In: van der Veer, G.C., Gale, C. (eds.) CHI, pp. 711–720. ACM (2005)
13. Chellapilla, K., Simard, P.Y.: Using machine learning to break visual Human Interaction Proofs (HIPs). In: NIPS (2004)
14. Chow, R., Golle, P., Jakobsson, M., Wang, L., Wang, X.: Making CAPTCHAs clickable. In: Spasojevic, M., Corner, M.D. (eds.) HotMobile, pp. 91–94. ACM (2008)
15. Chow, Y.-W., Susilo, W.: AniCAP: An animated 3D CAPTCHA scheme based on motion parallax. In: Lin, D., Tsudik, G., Wang, X. (eds.) CANS 2011. LNCS, vol. 7092, pp. 255–271. Springer, Heidelberg (2011)
16. Cruz-Perez, C., Starostenko, O., Uceda-Ponga, F., Alarcon-Aquino, V., Reyes-Cabrera, L.: Breaking reCAPTCHAs with unpredictable collapse: Heuristic character segmentation and recognition. In: Carrasco-Ochoa, J.A., Martínez-Trinidad, J.F., Olvera López, J.A., Boyer, K.L. (eds.) MCPR 2012. LNCS, vol. 7329, pp. 155–165. Springer, Heidelberg (2012)
17. Duda, R.O., Hart, P.E.: Use of the Hough transformation to detect lines and curves in pictures. Commun. ACM 15(1), 11–15 (1972)

18. Geman, S., Geman, D.: Stochastic relaxation, Gibbs distributions, and the Bayesian restoration of images. IEEE Transactions on Pattern Analysis and Machine Intelligence (6), 721–741 (1984)
19. Huang, S.-Y., Lee, Y.-K., Bell, G., Ou, Z.-H.: An efficient segmentation algorithm for CAPTCHAs with line cluttering and character warping. Multimedia Tools and Applications 48(2), 267–289 (2010)
20. Liu, P., Shi, J., Wang, L., Guo, L.: An efficient ellipse-shaped blobs detection algorithm for breaking Facebook CAPTCHA. In: Yuan, Y., Wu, X., Lu, Y. (eds.) ISCTCS 2012. CCIS, vol. 320, pp. 420–428. Springer, Heidelberg (2013)
21. Mori, G., Malik, J.: Recognizing objects in adversarial clutter: Breaking a visual CAPTCHA. In: CVPR (1), pp. 134–144 (2003)
22. Nguyen, V.D., Chow, Y.-W., Susilo, W.: Breaking a 3D-based CAPTCHA scheme. In: Kim, H. (ed.) ICISC 2011. LNCS, vol. 7259, pp. 391–405. Springer, Heidelberg (2012)
23. Nguyen, V.D., Chow, Y.-W., Susilo, W.: Breaking an animated CAPTCHA scheme. In: Bao, F., Samarati, P., Zhou, J. (eds.) ACNS 2012. LNCS, vol. 7341, pp. 12–29. Springer, Heidelberg (2012)
24. von Ahn, L., Blum, M., Hopper, N.J., Langford, J.: CAPTCHA: Using hard AI problems for security. In: Biham, E. (ed.) EUROCRYPT 2003. LNCS, vol. 2656, pp. 294–311. Springer, Heidelberg (2003)
25. Wang, S.-Y., Baird, H.S., Bentley, J.L.: CAPTCHA challenge tradeoffs: Familiarity of strings versus degradation of images. In: ICPR (3), pp. 164–167. IEEE Computer Society (2006)
26. Wilkins, J.: Strong CAPTCHA guidelines v1.2 (2009), http://www.bitland.net/captcha.pdf
27. Xu, Y., Reynaga, G., Chiasson, S., Frahm, J.-M., Monrose, F., Van Oorschot, P.: Security and usability challenges of moving-object CAPTCHAs: Decoding codewords in motion. In: Proceedings of the 21st USENIX Conference on Security Symposium, Security 2012, p. 4. USENIX Association, Berkeley (2012)
28. Yan, J., Ahmad, A.S.E.: Breaking visual CAPTCHAs with naive pattern recognition algorithms. In: ACSAC, pp. 279–291. IEEE Computer Society (2007)
29. Yan, J., Ahmad, A.S.E.: A low-cost attack on a Microsoft CAPTCHA. In: Ning, P., Syverson, P.F., Jha, S. (eds.) ACM Conference on Computer and Communications Security, pp. 543–554. ACM (2008)
30. Yan, J., Ahmad, A.S.E.: Usability of CAPTCHAs or usability issues in CAPTCHA design. In: Cranor, L.F. (ed.) SOUPS, ACM International Conference Proceeding Series, pp. 44–52. ACM (2008)
31. Zhu, B.B., Yan, J., Li, Q., Yang, C., Liu, J., Xu, N., Yi, M., Cai, K.: Attacks and design of image recognition CAPTCHAs. In: Al-Shaer, E., Keromytis, A.D., Shmatikov, V. (eds.) ACM Conference on Computer and Communications Security, pp. 187–200. ACM (2010)

A Mulitiprocess Mechanism of Evading Behavior-Based Bot Detection Approaches

Yuede Ji, Yukun He, Dewei Zhu, Qiang Li*, and Dong Guo

College of Computer Science and Technology, Jilin University,
Changchun China 130012
{jiyd12,heyk12,zhudw5509}@mails.jlu.edu.cn,
{li_qiang,guodong}@jlu.edu.cn

Abstract. Botnet has become one of the most serious threats to Internet security. According to detection location, existing approaches can be classified into two categories: host-based, and network-based. Among host-based approaches, behavior-based are more practical and effective because they can detect the specific malicious process. However, most of these approaches target on conventional single process bot. If a bot is separated into two or more processes, they will be less effective. In this paper, we propose a new evasion mechanism of bot, multiprocess mechanism. We first identify two specific features of multiprocess bot: separating C&C connection from malicious behaviors, and assigning malicious behaviors to several processes. Then we further theoretically analyze why behavior-based bot detection approaches are less effective with multiprocess bot. After that, we present two critical challenges of implementing multiprocess bot. Then we implement a single process and multiprocess bot, and use signature and behavior detection approaches to evaluate them. The results indicate that multiprocess bot can effectively decrease the detection probability compared with single process bot. Finally we propose the possible multiprocess bot architectures and extension rules, and expect they can cover most situations.

1 Introduction

Botnet has become one of the most serious threats to Internet security. A bot is a host compromised by malwares under the control of the botmaster through Command and Control (C&C) channel. A large scale of bots form a botnet. The botmaster can utilize botnets to conduct various cyber crimes such as spreading malwares, DDoS attacks, spamming, and phishing. Bots always try to hide themselves from detection tools to accomplish malicious behaviors.

According to detection location, existing approaches can be divided into two categories: host-based and network-based. (1) Host-based approaches mainly include signature- and behavior-based approaches [1]. Signature-based approaches mainly extract the feature information of the suspicious program to match with

---

* Corresponding Author.

X. Huang and J. Zhou (Eds.): ISPEC 2014, LNCS 8434, pp. 75–89, 2014.

a knowledge database [2]. Behavior-based detection approaches monitor the abnormal behaviors on hosts to detect bot [3–6]. (2) Network-based approaches mainly analyze network traffic to filter out bot host [7–9].

Among host-based detection approaches, behavior-based approaches are more practical and effective because they can detect the specific malicious process. However, most behavior-based approaches are based on single process or related family processes. If a bot is separated into two or more processes, these approaches will be less effective. Multiprocess bot has two specific features as we proposed in this paper: (1) It can separate C&C connection from malicious behaviors; (2) It can assign malicious behaviors to several processes. As we know, the biggest difference between bot and other malwares is the C&C infrastructure. If the C&C connection is separated from malicious behaviors, the detection approaches correlating network behaviors with malicious behaviors will be less effective. Similarly, if malicious behaviors are assigned to several processes and each process only performs a part of malicious behaviors, the suspicion level may drop to the same with benign process. Thus, malicious behaviors detection approaches will be less effective. If bot can successfully evade existing behavior-based detection approaches, it will cause more threats to Internet security.

Multiprocess malware has been analyzed by some researchers. Ramilli M *et al.* propose the idea of multiprocess malware and prove that the malware divided into several processes will effectively evade the detection of most anti-virus engines [10]. Lejun Fan *et al.* define three important architectures of multiprocess malwares, relay trace, master slave, and dual active mode [11]. Weiqin Ma *et al.* present a new attack, namely "shadow attacks", which divides a malware into multiple "shadow processes" [12]. Experiments indicate that multiprocess malwares can effectively evade the detection of behavior-based detection approaches. Multiprocess bots have been discovered [13], while they have not been studied in detail. If multiprocess bots really explodes, we know nothing about their architectures, communication mechanisms, and other critical knowledge, then they will cause great threats. Thus analyzing them will be very significant.

Our work makes the following contributions:

(1) We identify two specific features of multiprocess bot: separating C&C connection from malicious behaviors, and assigning malicious behaviors to several processes. Then we theoretically analyze why existing behavior-based bot detection approaches are less effective with multiprocess bot according to four categories of behavior-based approaches.

(2) We present two critical challenges of implementing multiprocess bot, and implement a single process and multiprocess bot from a simplified version of Zeus. We use signature and behavior based detection approaches to evaluate them. The results indicate that multiprocess bot can effectively decrease the detection probability. Then we propose other multiprocess bot architectures and extension rules, and expect they can cover most situations.

2 Evasion Mechanism of Multiprocess Bot

We first present the two specific features of multiprocess bots, then analyze why they are able to evade behavior bot detection approaches.

2.1 Specific Features of Multiprocess Bot

There are two specific differences between multiprocess and conventional bot: separating C&C connection from malicious behaviors, and assigning malicious behaviors to several processes. Lejun Fan *et al.* propose a typical multiprocess architecture *master slave mode* [11]. We rename it as *star architecture* using the terminology of network topology. In star network topology, each host is connected to a central hub with a point-to-point connection. Similarly, as shown in Figure 1, process P_1 acts as the central hub, connects with C&C server S and other malicious processes P_2, P_3, and P_4. In Figure 1, the circle denotes benign process, the hexagon denotes malicious process, S denotes C&C server, and P_i denotes different processes. We will analyze the two features using star architecture.

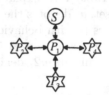

Fig. 1. Star Architecture of Multiprocess Bot

Feature 1: Separating C&C Connection from Malicious Behaviors. The first feature of multiprocess bot is separating C&C connection from malicious behaviors. It means that the process communicating with C&C server has no other malicious behaviors, and the malicious processes do not communicate with C&C server directly. We regard this specific process as server process. We will analyze this feature using the star architecture as shown in Figure 1.

In star architecture, P_1 is the server process that establishes C&C channel with server S. P_2, P_3, and P_4 are the malicious processes. Suppose the botmaster sends a command to the multiprocess bot and we will explore the whole execution procedure. C&C server S sends a command to P_1. In order to evade track techniques like taint analysis [14], the server process can transform data flow dependence into control flow dependence or other obfuscation techniques. After the transformation, the server process sends the command to a certain process using process communication mechanisms. This process performs malicious behaviors in accordance with the command. After execution, the malicious process sends the result data to the server process. The malicious process can also use obfuscation techniques to better evade track techniques. After receiving the result data, the server process sends them to the C&C server.

In this feature, the server process P_1 only has network behaviors, and the malicious processes P_1, P_2, and P_3 only perform a part of all malicious behaviors. Some behavior-based bot detection approaches detect the process which only has network behaviors as benign, and the process without network behaviors will be neglected. Through transforming data flow dependence into control flow dependence or other obfuscation mechanisms, the server process is separated from other malicious processes. Thus this feature is able to evade the detection approaches correlating network behaviors with malicious behaviors. However it may not be able to evade approaches which only detect host malicious behaviors.

Feature 2: Assigning Malicious Behaviors to Several Processes. The second feature is that malicious behaviors are assigned to several processes. Thus, each process only performs a small part of whole malicious behaviors. This feature can effectively evade malicious behavior detection approaches with well designed number of malicious behaviors each process has. Thus, the number becomes a critical challenge. We will use three phases to explain how to define the number and prove that multiprocess bot is able to evade behavior detection.

We utilize the notations in Table 1 to explain this feature. In Table 1, C denotes the critical system call set, a_i denotes the ith system call, and there are k system calls in total. f_i denotes the ith behavior which has $num(f_i)$ system calls, and each one of them is denoted as a_j^i. $num1_i$ denotes the number of critical system calls of each behavior f_i, and $num2_i$ denotes the number of behaviors that critical system call a_i is in.

Table 1. Notations of system calls and behaviors

Description	Set
critical system call set	$C = \{a_1, \ldots, a_i, \ldots, a_k\}$
system call set of each behavior	$f_i = \{a_1^i, \ldots, a_j^i, \ldots, a_{num(f_i)}^i\}$
number of critical system calls of each behavior f_i	$Num1 = \{num1_1, \ldots, num1_i, \ldots, num1_n\}$
number of behaviors that critical system call a_i is in	$Num2 = \{num2_1, \ldots, num2_i, \ldots, num2_k\}$

Phase 1: Suppose we extract the system calls of known malicious behaviors to build the system call set f_i of each behavior. We build the critical system call set C using the similar methods of building Common API in [15]. The system calls in the critical set are frequently called by these malicious behaviors.

Phase 2: We match every system call a_j^i of each set f_i with critical set C to generate $num1_i$, and after matching all we can get set $Num1$. It denotes the number of critical system calls of each behavior. We match every system call a_i of critical set C with each set f_i to generate $num2_i$, and then $Num2$. It denotes the number of behaviors that call a specific critical system call.

Phase 3: Based on set $Num1$ and $Num2$ we can get two assignment mechanisms: behavior level and system call level assignment mechanism. In behavior level assignment, we sort the behaviors in descending order in set $Num1$. The top behaviors represent the most frequent behaviors. We can separate the top behaviors with each other to average the critical behavior numbers of each process. In this way, we can decrease the malicious grain size of each process. We can assign the sorted set to the processes in S shape, and other assignment mechanisms like arithmetic, random walk, etc. can also be used. Set $Num2$ is about system call level assignment mechanism. We also sort the system calls in descending order. We assign top system calls to different processes or even a process only performing one critical system call. This assignment mechanism is more complicated than behavior level.

We summarized the whole procedure in Algorithm 1. A multiprocess bot using either of them will significantly improve the evasion probability. If a multiprocess bot uses both of them, it will be very difficult to detect. Thus this feature can effectively evade behaviors detection approaches.

Algorithm 1. Process Assignment Algorithm

---
1. build the system call set f_i for each malicious behavior
2. build the critical system call set C
3. match each system call set f_i with C to generate $Num1$
4. match critical set C with each system call set f_i to generate $Num2$
5. $t =$ number of processes
6. sort $Num1$ in descending order
7. **for** i from 1 to t **do**
8.   assign behavior $i, 2*t+1-i, 2*t+i, \ldots$ to process i
9. **end for**
10. sort $Num2$ in descending order
11. **for** i from 1 to t **do**
12.   assign system call $i, 2*t+1-i, 2*t+i, \ldots$ to process i
13. **end for**

2.2   Evading Behavior-Based Bot Detection Approaches

According to detection targets, we classify existing behavior-based bot detection approaches into 4 categories: detecting C&C connections, detecting malicious behaviors, detecting bot commands, and detecting bots (correlating C&C connection with malicious behaviors). Based on the two specific features, we utilize an example approach of each category to analyse why behavior-based bot detection approaches are less effective with multiprocess bot.

Detecting C&C Connections. In this category, detection approaches detect bots based on C&C connections on host and JACKSTRAWS [16] is a typical one. It associates with each network connection a behavior graph that captures the system calls that lead to the connection and operate on returned data.

We use star architecture in Figure 1 to present the evasion procedure. The server process P_1 establishes connection with C&C server S and it will be captured by JACKSTRAWS. P_1 can transform data flow dependence into control flow and distributes the corresponding data to appropriate processes using process communication mechanisms. The malicious processes P_2, P_3, and P_4 perform fine-grained malicious behaviors which have nothing to do with network connections. After finishing the malicious behaviors, they will send the result data to P_1. Then P_1 will upload them to C&C server. In this way, multiprocess bot can separate network connection from malicious behaviors.

According to JACKSTRAWS, the captured network connection alone is not enough for being detected as malicious C&C. What's more, if the connection is encrypted, the detection will be more difficult. They mention three failed detection cases and the first is that the bot process did not finish its malicious behaviors after receiving commands. In this way, multiprocess bot can evade this detection approach.

Detecting Malicious Behaviors. Approaches in this category detect bots based on host malicious behaviors. Martignoni *et al.* propose an typical approach using hierarchical behavior graphs to detect malicious behaviors.

This approach is less effective with multiprocess bot. First, it monitors the execution of one single process, while in multiprocess bot, there are several processes performing malicious behaviors. Specifically, multiprocess bot can evade taint analysis from transforming data flow dependence into control flow, thus this approach is not able to detect any relationship between processes.

Second, the first feature of multiprocess bot is separating C&C connection from malicious processes. As shown in star architecture, S only communicates with the server process P_1. Based on this feature, P_1 only has network behaviors, thus in behavior graphs it is similar with benign network processes. The other malicious processes perform a part of malicious behaviors without C&C connection, thus in behavior graphs they may not be the same with malicious behavior graphs. However, if a process still performs critical malicious behaviors, it can also be detected.

Third, the second feature is assigning malicious behaviors to several processes. As we discussed before, there are two separation mechanisms: behavior and system call level. A multiprocess bot using these two mechanisms can make the event sequence of each process different from any malicious behavior graph. Thus this approach is less effective with multiprocess bot.

Detecting Bot Commands. In this category, detection approaches detect bots based on bot commands. BotTee [15] is a typical approach of identifying bot commands by run time execution monitoring.

BotTee can effectively detect conventional bot commands. However, it has two obvious drawbacks: it monitors the execution of single process; it highly relies on network related system calls. The first drawback is opposite with the second feature of multiprocess bot which assigns malicious behaviors to several processes. BotTee detects bot commands in system call level thus behavior level assignment mechanism is ineffective, while system call level assignment is still effective. The second drawback is opposite with the first feature which separates C&C connection from malicious behaviors. This is a fatal blow to BotTee because they suppose bot command begins with recv or other network reception system calls and ends with send or other network sending system calls.

We use an example to present the evasion procedure. In star architecture, suppose S sends a command to P_1. After P_1 received the command, Deviare API [17] captures the recv command and begins to monitor process P_1. P_1 assigns the command to appropriate process, for example P_2. Then P_2 performs malicious behaviors and sends the result to P_1. Then P_1 sends the result to S, while Deviare API captures the command and triggers Bot Command Identifier. Then Bot Command Identifier analyses the system call sequences between recv and send. And then the sequence will be sent to other components. Thus the sequence of P_1 does not includes malicious behaviors and it will be detected as benign. In this way, multiprocess bot can evade BotTee.

Detecting Bots. Detecting bots means the detection approach correlates malicious behaviors with C&C connection. BotTracer detects bots through three phases: automatic startup, establishment of C&C channel, and information harvesting/dispersion [18].

BotTracer highly relies on the behaviors of a bot process, and multiprocess bot can effectively evade them. We will present the evasion mechanism using star architecture. After the bootstrap phase, P_1, P_2, P_3 and P_4 are flagged as suspicious processes. All the processes of multiprocess bot have to be started automatically, thus they are not able to evade this phase. In the C&C establishment phase, only the server process P_1 establishes C&C channel and other processes communicate with P_1. Thus only P_1 is regarded as suspicious and others can effectively evade this phase. In the last phase, the server process P_1 only communicates with other processes and the C&C server. Thus it can evade this phase because it does not perform malicious activities. In summary, the server process P_1 can evade BotTracer in the last phase, other malicious processes can evade in the C&C establishment phase. Thus multiprocess bots can effectively evade this kind of detection approaches.

3 Critical Challenges of Multiprocess Bot

Although multiprocess bot is able to evade behavior-based bot detection approaches, it still has many critical challenges. We will present two of them: bootstrap mechanism, and process communication mechanism.

Bootstrap Mechanisms. Conventional bots can be started automatically by modifying the bootstrap process list or Registry entries [18]. This is essential for bot to actively initialize C&C channel.Conventional bot which has one process only needs to start itself, while multiprocess bot need to start all the processes. Multiprocess bot may run in the hosts stealthily, while the bootstrap of all the processes is not easy to accomplish stealthily. If the bootstrap mechanism is not well designed, multiprocess bot may be detected at the startup stage. Thus the design of bootstrap mechanisms becomes a critical challenge of multiprocess bot.

Process Communication Mechanisms. Each process of multiprocess bot has to communicate with others to accomplish malicious behaviors together. The communication methods mainly include Interprocess Communications (IPC) and covert channel communication.

IPC mechanisms are common and mainly include clipboard, Component Object Model (COM), data copy, Dynamic Data Exchange (DDE), file mapping, mailslots, pipes, Remote Procedure Call (RPC), and Windows sockets. Covert channel is a computer security attack that can transfer information between processes that are illegal to communicate by the computer security policy. Covert channels are classified into storage and timing channels [19]. A variety of covert channels have been proposed. Aciiçmez *et al.* propose an attack named Simple Branch Prediction Analysis (SBPA) [20], which analyzes the CPU's Branch Predictor states through spying on a single quasi-parallel computation process. Percival demonstrates that shared access to memory caches provides not only an easily used high bandwidth covert channel between threads, but also permits a malicious thread to monitor the execution of another thread [21].

IPC data may be easy to capture, while it may not be easy to identify the suspicious data from the variety benign IPC data. Covert channels are difficult to detect and changeable. Thus the process communication mechanisms make the detection more difficult.

4   Experiments

In order to evaluate the above analyses, we develop a prototype of multiprocess bot from Zeus bot[22]. First, we develop a single process bot, named Mini_Zeus, which is a simplified version of Zeus. Then, we develop a multiprocess version of Mini_Zeus. We use signature and behavior analysis to evaluate them.

4.1   Prototype Architecture

Mini_Zeus is a simplified version of Zeus bot. It has 4 major behaviors: (1) It uses bootstrap mechanisms to make the bot process automatically started. (2) It establishes C&C channel. Thus it can receive commands, execute commands, and send information. (3) It captures http requests of Internet Explorer and sends them to C&C server. (4) It will copy itself to the directory of *system32*, and replace its time stamp with the time stamp of *ntdll.dll*.

The single process version of Mini_Zeus is shown in Figure 2(a). *Mini_Zeus.exe* is the bot infection process. Once started, it will modify Registry to make it automatically start. Then it will use remote thread injection to make *Explorer.exe*

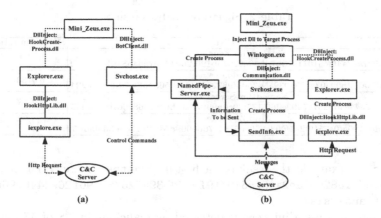

Fig. 2. Architecture of Mini_Zeus

load *HookCreateProcess.dll*, and *Svchost.exe* load *BotClient.dll*. When *HookCreateProcess.dll* is loaded, it will hook function *CreateProcess*. When users try to launch IE browser, *HookHttpLib.dll* will be injected to *iexplorer.exe*. This dll will inject function *HttpSendRequest*, thus the information of post operation will be injected and sent to C&C server. When *BotClient.dll* is loaded, *Svchost.exe* will create a thread to communicate with C&C server. In summary, *Mini_Zeus.exe* is the initial process and *Svchost.exe* is the running bot process.

Multiprocess version of Mini_Zeus is shown in Figure 2(b). *Mini_Zeus.exe* is the bot infection process. Once started, it will use remote thread injection to make *Winlogon.exe* load *Schedule.dll*. *Schedule.dll* firstly modify the Registry to make *Mini_Zeus.exe* automatically started. It has three other major behaviors: (1) It will create *NamedPipeServer.exe*. (2) It will inject *Communication.dll* into *Svchost.exe*. (3) It will inject *HookCreateProcess.dll* into *Explorer.exe*. After these three steps, *NamedPipeServer.exe* will establish a named pipe server and is responsible for receiving and sending information. *Svchost.exe* will create process *SendInfo.exe*. *SendInfo.exe* will establish a named pipe to connect with *NamedPipeServer.exe*. It also establishes C&C channel with C&C server. When *HookCreateProcess.dll* is loaded by *Explorer.exe*, it will hook function *CreateProcess*. Once users try to launch IE browser, *HookHttpLib.dll* will be injected to *iexplorer.exe*. This dll will inject function *HttpSendRequest* and establish a named pipe, thus the information of post operation will be injected and sent to *NamedPipeServer.exe*. In summary, *Mini_Zeus.exe* is the initial bot process, and *NamedPipeServer.exe*, *SendInfo.exe*, and the controlled *iexplore.exe* are the running bot processes.

4.2 Signature Analysis

We use VirusTotal to take a signature analysis of single process Mini_Zeus and multiprocess Mini_Zeus. The results are shown in Table 2, the URL in the table is the ID number and the real url is `https://www.virustotal.com/en/file/URL/`

Table 2. Signature analysis results

File / URL	Detection ratio
Single_Mini_Zeus.exe 71e82907ae2a45fc51071910b7db39a62675b190f26e444b796eb81dbdfad77f	28 / 47
SendInfo.exe 5d86d1fabefb094034e192039a5d75d5f982205b1149f5684bf3e74dc6e63224	6 / 33
NamedPipeServer.exe edb8897344e40b237c7d99ed6f5177f39c0b99f693a7b619e168c667058f0d55	2 / 47
Mini_Zeus.exe 0647dcd190af0e7519f2a4f003a6502e6186776be609c5494fe23cd6335fada5	13 / 47

analysis. For example, the result of the first url is https://www.virustotal.co
m/en/file/71e82907ae2a45fc51071910b7db39a62675b190f26e444b796eb81d
bdfad77f/analysis/.

The single process Mini_Zeus is detected as malicious by 28 of 47 antivirus engines, benign by 19 antivirus engines. Mini_Zeus is detected as benign because it has different signatures with Zeus bot, it is a simplified version and only has the basic functions, and we distribute some malicious behaviors into dll files. In Multiprocess Mini_Zeus, the main process *Mini_Zeus.exe* is detected as malicious by 13 of 47 antivirus engines, as benign by 34 antivirus engines. The other two processes are detected as malicious by 6 and 2. The main process is detected as malicious because it uses remote thread injection. This injection mechanism is a little obvious for antivirus engines, and we believe the number can further decrease if we use different injection mechanisms. These two analysis reports are able to indicate that multiprocess bot can effectively decrease the detection probability compared with single process bot.

4.3 Behavior Analysis

In behavior analysis, we use host-based behavior analysis tool ThreatFire.

ThreatFire is a host-based behavior detection tool, we use it to comparatively analyze our single process and multiprocess version of Mini_Zeus bot. The bot

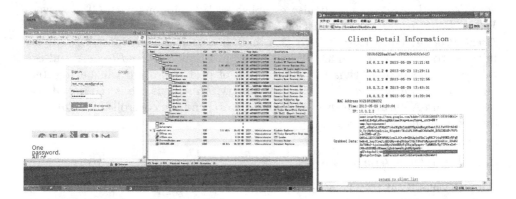

Fig. 3. Behavior analysis results

host has the following configurations: Intel Q6600 quad-core processor, 2.40GHz, 2GB RAM, and Windows XP SP3 operating system. ThreatFire and Process Hacker are installed. The server host has the same configurations, with XAMPP and Google Chrome installed. We perform the following experiments:

1. We ran ThreatFire and adjusted its sensitive level to 5 (highest) in the bot host. We ran our bot server program in the server host.

2. For each bot, we ran it to evaluate the kinds of alerts. We all click "Allow this process to continue" to make the bot started.

3. After the bot successfully started, we ran IE browser to test bot behaviors. The results of our experiments are as follows:

1. In single process Mini_Zeus, there are 5 alerts, one for registering itself in "Windows System Startup" list. The other four are for remote thread injection. Remote thread injection is not able to evade the detection because of its high risk. C&C connection behavior is not detected because we create a thread to connect with bot server.

2. In multiprocess Mini_Zeus, there are 2 alerts for *Mini_Zeus.exe* and they are both remote thread injection. There are no alerts for other processes. There are no alerts for register because we hook winlogon to make it register Mini_Zeus.

3. Both of these two bots can work well without alerts. Figure 3 shows multiprocess Mini_Zeus can successfully capture the post information.

The results indicate that multiprocess Mini_Zeus performs better than single process Mini_Zeus. It can successfully reduce the number of alerts and the risk level, however, there still exists some alerts. In summary, the experiments indicate that multiprocess bot can effectively decrease the detection probability compared with single process bot.

5   Extended Architectures of Multiprocess Bot

Besides star architecture, Lejun Fan *et al.* also present the relay race mode and dual active mode. The relay race mode is the same with the ring in network topology, thus we rename it as ring architecture. Since these two architectures are well suited with network topology, we analyse other network topology architectures and find that multiprocess bot can also adopt these architectures. Thus we present 6 more architectures and 4 extension rules as shown in Figure 4. We hope these architectures with the extension rules can cover most situations.

Architecture 1: Bus Architecture. In bus network, all nodes are connected to a single cable. Similarly, in the bus architecture of multiprocess bot all malicious processes are connected to C&C server. As shown in Figure 4(a), malicious processes P_1, P_2, and P_3 connect to C&C server S. Malicious behaviors are assigned to several processes and each one only performs a part of them.

Architecture 2: Ring Architecture. A ring network is set up in a circular architecture in which data travels around in one direction. Similarly, in the ring architecture of multiprocess bot as shown in Figure 4(b), all the processes form a one direction ring. The data travels along the ring and every process identifies whether the data is for it.

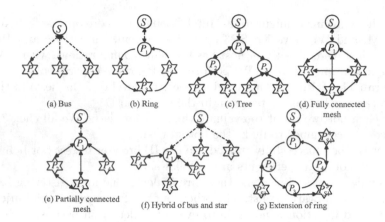

Fig. 4. Architectures of multiprocess bot

Architecture 3: Tree Architecture. Tree architecture is a hierarchical architecture as shown in Figure 4(c). The highest level of this tree is the root process P_1. It communicates with C&C server S. In this architecture, only the leaf processes perform malicious behaviors and other processes are the controller of their child nodes. The data are passed along the tree.

Architecture 4: Fully Connected Mesh Architecture. There are two mesh architectures, fully connected and partially connected. In fully connected mesh architecture, the processes can communicate with each other as shown in Figure 4(d). P_1 communicates with C&C server S and other processes. P_2, P_3, and P_4 perform malicious behaviors and they can communicate with each other.

Architecture 5: Partially Connected Mesh Architecture. In partially connected mesh architecture, some nodes connect with more than one. As shown in Figure 4(e), P_1, P_2, and P_3 connect with each other and P_4 only connects with P_1. This architecture is a subset of fully connected mesh with one specific condition that P_1 should connect with all other processes directly or indirectly.

Architecture 6: Hybrid Architecture. The above 5 architectures and star architecture are the basic architectures, while multiprocess bot can generate more complicated architectures through combining them. For example, we can combine bus with star architecture to generate a new architecture as shown in Figure 4(f). S, P_1, P_2, and P_3 forms the standard bus architecture, S, P_1, P_4, P_5, and P_6 forms the standard star architecture.

Extension Rules. Besides these architectures, we define four extension rules. The server process and malicious processes can create a child process, and we can get the following rules.

(1) Rule 1: The server process communicates with C&C server and its child process communicates with others. (2) Rule 2: The malicious process communicates with others and its child process communicates with C&C server. (3) Rule 3: The malicious process communicates with others and its child process performs malicious behaviors. (4) Rule 4: The malicious process performs malicious behaviors and its child process communicates with others.

Figure 4(g) is an extension architecture of ring using Rule 3. Each of the original malicious processes creates a child process to perform malicious behaviors. Through these rules, the behaviors of all the processes can be minimized and may cause great confusions to behavior-based bot detection approaches.

6   Related Work

Ramilli M *et at.* propose an attack mode named multiprocess malware [10]. If a malware is divided into multiple coordinated processes, no sequence of system calls executed by one process will match the behavioral signatures. Thus this attack mode can evade anti-virus detection tools. However, it also faces many problems, such as the division of malware, the communication of multiple processes, the bootstrp of multiple processes, and the execution sequence of multiple processes. Lejun Fan *et al.* use dynamic analysis approaches to detect privacy theft malware [11]. They also monitor the related processes of suspicious process to discover the collaborative behavior of multiprocess privacy theft malwares. They propose three important architectures of multiprocess malwares, relay trace mode, master slave mode, and dual active mode. Weiqin Ma *et al.* present a new generation of attacks, namely "shadow attacks", to evade current behavior-based malware detections by dividing a malware into multiple "shadow processes" [12]. They analyze the communication between different processes, and the division of a malware into multiple processes. They also develop a compiler-level prototype, AutoShadow, to automatically transform a malware to several shadow processes.

These works all target on multiprocess malwares, however, we target on the attack of multiprocess bot. Although bot is one category of malwares, it has different architectures and features and can cause more serious threat. The architectures are more complicated than others, especially the C&C infrastructure. We propose some specific features of multiprocess bot, and deeply analyze why existing behavior-based approaches are less effective with multiprocess bot.

Virtual machine based malware detection approaches, Holography, Anubis, and CWSandbox , *etc.* can track multiprocess malwares, while these approaches run malwares in an isolated environment. Many novel bots can detect whether they are running in a virtual machine before they perform malicious behaviors. Also, these approaches are not practical for protecting hosts of normal users.

7   Limitations and Future Work

There are several limitations in our work. (1) We theoretically analyzed behavior-based bot detection approaches and did not implement them. There are many challenges when we try to implement them, such as the large-scale data, and the unclear implementation details. If we can implement these approaches to evaluate multiprocess bot we can get a more convincing result. (2) Mini_Zeus is a simplified version of Zeus, and many malicious behaviors are not implemented.

However, the primary behaviors of Zeus are included and more than half anti-virus engines detect it as malicious. The experiment results are still clear. (3) In our experiment about behavior detection, we only use one detection engine to analyze. We will try to use more behavior-based detection approaches to evaluate multiprocess bot.

We are very interested in multiprocess bot and this is a primary work. We will perform the following further works: (1) We will try to implement some behavior-based bot detection approaches, and perform some systematic tests about the concrete reasons why existing behavior-based approaches are less effective with multiprocess bot. (2) We will try to find or implement more instances of multi-process bots to perform a large-scale experiments. (3) We will deeply analyze the advantages and disadvantages of multiprocess bot, and try to find the effective detection approaches about multiprocess bot.

8 Conclusion

In this paper we analyze multiprocess bot in detail. First, we identify two specific features of multiprocess bot, separating C&C connection from malicious behaviors and assigning malicious behaviors to several processes. Based on the two features, we theoretically analyze why existing behavior-based bot detection approaches are less effective with multiprocess bot. After that we present two critical challenges of implementing multiprocess bot. Then we implement a single process and a multiprocess bot. We use signature and behavior based detection approaches to evaluate them. The results indicate that multiprocess bot can effectively decrease the detection probability compared with single process bot. Finally we propose the possible multiprocess architectures and extension rules, and hope they can cover most situations of multiprocess bot.

Acknowledgment. This work is supported by the National Natural Science Foundation of China under Grant No. 61170265, Fundamental Research Fund of Jilin University under Grant No. 201103253.

References

1. Silva, S.S.C., Silva, R.M.P., Pinto, R.C.G., Salles, R.M.: Botnets: A survey. Computer Networks (2012)
2. Goebel, J., Holz, T.: Rishi: Identify bot contaminated hosts by irc nickname evaluation. In: Proceedings of the First Conference on First Workshop on Hot Topics in Understanding Botnets, Cambridge, MA, p. 8 (2007)
3. Stinson, E., Mitchell, J.C.: Characterizing bots remote control behavior. In: Hämmerli, B.M., Sommer, R. (eds.) DIMVA 2007. LNCS, vol. 4579, pp. 89–108. Springer, Heidelberg (2007)
4. Kolbitsch, C., Comparetti, P.M., Kruegel, C., Kirda, E., Zhou, X., Wang, X.: Effective and efficient malware detection at the end host. In: Proceedings of the 18th Conference on USENIX Security Symposium, pp. 351–366. USENIX Association (2009)

5. Shin, S., Xu, Z., Gu, G.: Effort: Efficient and effective bot malware detection. In: 2012 Proceedings of the IEEE INFOCOM, pp. 2846–2850 (2012)
6. Martignoni, L., Stinson, E., Fredrikson, M., Jha, S., Mitchell, J.C.: A layered architecture for detecting malicious behaviors. In: Lippmann, R., Kirda, E., Trachtenberg, A. (eds.) RAID 2008. LNCS, vol. 5230, pp. 78–97. Springer, Heidelberg (2008)
7. Gu, G., Porras, P., Yegneswaran, V., Fong, M., Lee, W.: Bothunter: Detecting malware infection through ids-driven dialog correlation. In: Proceedings of 16th USENIX Security Symposium on USENIX Security Symposium, p. 12. USENIX Association (2007)
8. Gu, G., Perdisci, R., Zhang, J., Lee, W., et al.: Botminer: Clustering analysis of network traffic for protocol-and structure-independent botnet detection. In: Proceedings of the 17th Conference on Security Symposium, pp. 139–154 (2008)
9. Gu, G., Zhang, J., Lee, W.: Botsniffer: Detecting botnet command and control channels in network traffic (2008)
10. Ramilli, M., Bishop, M., Sun, S.: Multiprocess malware. In: 2011 6th International Conference on Malicious and Unwanted Software (MALWARE), pp. 8–13. IEEE (2011)
11. Fan, L., Wang, Y., Cheng, X., Li, J., Jin, S.: Privacy theft malware multi-process collaboration analysis. In: Security and Communication Networks (2013)
12. Ma, W., Duan, P., Liu, S., Gu, G., Liu, J.-C.: Shadow attacks: Automatically evading system-call-behavior based malware detection. Journal in Computer Virology 8(1-2), 1–13 (2012)
13. Microsoft security intelligence report, http://www.microsoft.com/security/sir/story/default.aspx#!zbot (accessed November 2013)
14. Schwartz, E.J., Avgerinos, T., Brumley, D.: All you ever wanted to know about dynamic taint analysis and forward symbolic execution (but might have been afraid to ask). In: 2010 IEEE Symposium on Security and Privacy (SP), pp. 317–331. IEEE (2010)
15. Park, Y., Reeves, D.S.: Identification of bot commands by run-time execution monitoring. In: Annual Computer Security Applications Conference, ACSAC 2009, pp. 321–330. IEEE (2009)
16. Jacob, G., Hund, R., Kruegel, C., Holz, T.: Jackstraws: Picking command and control connections from bot traffic. In: USENIX Security Symposium (2011)
17. http://www.nektra.com/products/deviare-api-hook-windows/ (accessed November 2013)
18. Liu, L., Chen, S., Yan, G., Zhang, Z.: Bottracer: Execution-based bot-like malware detection. In: Wu, T.-C., Lei, C.-L., Rijmen, V., Lee, D.-T. (eds.) ISC 2008. LNCS, vol. 5222, pp. 97–113. Springer, Heidelberg (2008)
19. Zander, S., Armitage, G., Branch, P.: A survey of covert channels and countermeasures in computer network protocols. IEEE Communications Surveys and Tutorials 9(3), 44–57 (2007)
20. Aciiçmez, O., Koç, Ç.K., Seifert, J.-P.: On the power of simple branch prediction analysis. In: Proceedings of the 2nd ACM Symposium on Information, Computer and Communications Security, pp. 312–320. ACM (2007)
21. Percival, C.: Cache missing for fun and profit (2005)
22. Binsalleeh, H., Ormerod, T., Boukhtouta, A., Sinha, P., Youssef, A., Debbabi, M., Wang, L.: On the analysis of the zeus botnet crimeware toolkit. In: 2010 Eighth Annual International Conference on Privacy Security and Trust (PST), pp. 31–38. IEEE (2010)

Obfuscating Encrypted Web Traffic
with Combined Objects

Yi Tang[1,2], Piaoping Lin[1], and Zhaokai Luo[3]

[1] School of Mathematics and Information Science
Guangzhou University, Guangzhou 510006, China
[2] Key Laboratory of Mathematics and Interdisciplinary Sciences of Guangdong
Higher Education Institutes
Guangzhou University, Guangzhou 510006, China
[3] School of Computer Engineering and Science
Shanghai University, Shanghai 200072, China

Abstract. Web traffic demonstrates a sequence of request-response transactions during web page visiting. On one hand, the browser retrieves the basic HTML file and then issues requests in sequence for objects in HTML document. On the other hand, the server returns related objects in sequence as responses. This makes the traffic of a web page demonstrate pattern features different from other pages. Traffic analysis techniques can extract these features and identify web pages effectively even if the traffic is encrypted. In this paper, we propose a countermeasure method, CoOBJ, to defend against traffic analysis by obfuscating web traffic with combined objects. We compose some objects into a single object, the combined object, and force the object requests and responses on combined objects. By randomly composing objects with different objects, the traffic for a given web page is variable and exhibits different traffic patterns in different visits. We have implemented a proof of concept prototype and validate the CoOBJ countermeasure with some state of the art traffic analysis techniques.

Keywords: Encrypted Web Traffic, Web Page Identification, Traffic Analysis, Combined Object.

1 Introduction

Internet users are increasingly concerned with the private web browsing behaviors. They want to preserve the privacy of not only what content they have browsed but also which web site they have visited. Encryption is the popular method to ensure the privacy of data transferred in networks. The secure protocol suites, such as SSL, SSH, IPSec, and Tor, etc., are widely used in current web applications to ensure data privacy in flight. It seems that the user browsing privacy is preserved if the encryption method is perfect and the encryption key is not broken. However, encryption does not hide everything. The encrypted data streams are on web request-response sequences, the secure protocols do not alter the pattern of the traffic. Some basic traffic features, such as the order, number,

X. Huang and J. Zhou (Eds.): ISPEC 2014, LNCS 8434, pp. 90–104, 2014.

length, or timing of packets, are closely associated with the original web page and related objects. These explicit and implicit features can be extracted by traffic analysis (TA) and may lead to the disclosure of the web sites and the web pages user visited, or even the user private inputs [2][4][5][7][9][10].

Most of the proposals against TA attacks are on varying packet features on packet level. Padding extra bytes into transmitting data is the general method. The padding procedure is performed at server side before or after encryption [4][7]. An improved strategy on padding is traffic morphing which makes the web traffic similar to a predefined traffic distribution [12]. These efforts are on fine-grained single object analysis and they are not efficient against the coarse-grained aggregated statistics [5]. The BuFLO method intends to cut off the aggregated associations among packet sizes, packet directions, and time costs [5] by sending specified packets with a given rate during a given time period. Some other techniques on higher level, such as HTTPOS [8], try to influence the packet generation at server side by customizing specified HTTP requests or TCP headers at client side.

In this paper, we propose CoOBJ, a TA defence method on web application level. We try to make a web page with varying traffic features by introducing the notion of combined object. Our proposed method is on client-server cooperation. A combined object is an object combination which is composed by a set of original objects embedded in a web page. We translate a common web page into combined-object-enabled (CO-enabled) web page by introducing embedded scripts for combined objects and object identifiers within object tags. When the browser renders the CO-enabled web page, the embedded script is triggered and initiates requests for combined objects. Cooperatively, a script running on server will produce object combinations with random sizes and random chosen components. This kind of object generating and fetching procedure changes the traffic features of the original web page and hence may be used to defend against the traffic analysis.

The contribution of this paper can be enumerated as follows.

1. We introduce the notion of combined object to design a new defence method, CoOBJ, against traffic analysis.
2. We develop the CO-enabled web page structure to support the requests and responses for combined objects. By composing the combined objects with random number of random chosen component objects, the traffic features of CO-enabled web pages can be varied in different visits.
3. We have implemented a proof of concept prototype with data URI scheme and the AJAX technique, and we demonstrate the effectiveness of CoOBJ on defending against some typical TA attacks.

The rest of this paper is structured as follows. In Section 2, we overview some works on traffic analysis. In Section 3, we introduce the notion of combined objects. In Section 4, we discuss the method to construct the combined objects. In Section 5, we conduct some experiments to validate our proposed method. And finally, the conclusion is drawn in Section 6.

2   Traffic Analysis in Encrypted Web Flows

2.1   HTTP Traffic

A web page can be viewed as a set of document resources (objects) that can be accessed through a common web browser. When accessing a web page, the browser first fetches the basic HTML file from a destination server who hosts that file, and then, issues network requests to fetch other objects in sequence according to the order of corresponding objects in retrieved HTML document.

Table 1 demonstrates the numbers and sizes of objects related to two typical portal websites, *www.yahoo.com* and *www.sina.com.cn*. Note that many object requests are issued by the browser in order to render the required pages, and hence volumes of object downloading traffic are introduced. As illustrated in Table 1, at least 58 image files are needed to retrieve when visiting *www.yahoo.com* while the number is increased to 114 when visiting *www.sina.com.cn*. Correspondingly, the downloaded volumes of images are reached to $536k$ and $760k$, respectively. In total, the number and the volume of required objects for rendering these two pages are reached to 78, $883k$ and 227, $1,980k$, respectively. It implies that these two web pages can easily be distinguished on the number of requests and the volume of downloaded objects.

Table 1. Features of Some Web Pages on Nov. 15, 2013 (source: [13])

Object	www.yahoo.com		www.sina.com.cn	
	Number	Size (kB)	Number	Size (kB)
HTML	3	87	38	96
Script	11	214	57	209
CSS	3	45	1	2
Image	58	536	114	760
Flash	-	-	10	910
Others	3	1	7	3
Total	78	883	227	1,980

It is well known that HTTP is not a secure protocol which is faced with the leakage of message payloads. As shown in Fig. 1(a), the default HTTP payload is in plain. A simple man-in-the-middle (MITM) attack could easily eavesdrop and intercept the HTTP conversations. HTTPS is designed to resist such MITM attacks by providing bidirectional encrypted transmissions. As shown in Fig. 1(b), the HTTPS payloads are encrypted but the TCP and IP headers are preserved.

In some applications, we often require tunnel-based transmissions to hide real communicating IP address. The tunnel-based transmission means that the entire specified IP packet is encapsulated into a new IP packet, i.e., that specified packet is as the payload of that new packet. If the tunnel is encrypted, the

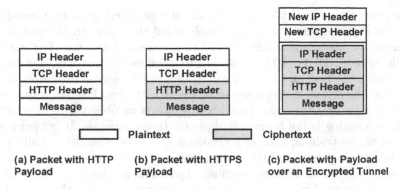

Fig. 1. IP packets without/with encrypted HTTP payloads

encapsulated packet is also encrypted. It implies that both the real IP addresses and port numbers are protected from any MITM attackers. As shown in Fig. 1(c), all the IP packet with HTTP payload is encrypted and is encapsulated into a packet with new header. A typical encrypted tunnel is the secure shell (SSH) tunnel. A SSH tunnel can be used to forward a given port on a local machine to HTTP port on a remote web server. It means a user may visit an external web server in private if he can connect to an external SSH server to create an SSH tunnel.

From the viewpoint of confidentiality, it seems that the privacy of the conversations on HTTPS or SSH tunnel is preserved because of the encryption of browsed web pages. However, some traffic features, such as the number of object requests, are consistent in the same way whether or not the traffic is encrypted. A traffic analysis attack can effectively use these features to identify the web page the user visited, or even the data that the user input. For example, when visiting the two portal websites in Table 1, counting the number of object requests can distinguish them easily.

2.2   Traffic Analysis

We view a web page *page* as an object set $\{obj_i\}$, i.e., $page = \{obj_i\}$, where each object obj_i is needed to retrieve from some hosted web servers. To render these objects, the src attribute is used to specify the URI for retrieving. With specified URIs, the browser will send a sequence of HTTP requests to servers, and the servers will reply those requests with response packets. It is noted that the order of objects retrieving requests are basically on the order of corresponding objects in *page*.

When the traffic is encrypted and the encryption is perfect, only the encrypted payload size and the packet direction can be taken. Consider that the popular encryption methods cannot largely enlarge the difference between the length of encrypted message and the length of corresponding plaintext version, we assume that the encryption is approximatively length-preserved. This implies that the size of an encryption object is similar to the size of object in plain. Considering the order of objects in transmitting, it implies that the aggregated size of packets between two requests is generally related to a certain object size. For example, the traffic vector $\langle(20,\uparrow),(100,\downarrow),(40,\downarrow),(30,\uparrow)\rangle$ denotes four sets of encrypted HTTP traffic, the first and the last are from client to server with sizes 20, 30, respectively, the others are from server to client with sizes 100, 40, respectively, and we can infer that the client possibly downloads an object with size 140.

Machine learning is the basic technique for traffic analysis. It is operated in two steps: model training and data classifying. Firstly, a model is built and is trained by training data, and then it is incorporated into a classifier to classify a data set. Supervised machine learning algorithms are used to construct TA classifiers. It means that a classifier is trained on sets of traces that are labeled with a set of web pages, and then it is used to determine whether or not a new trace set is from a given web page. Formally, the TA classifier is trained on a given labeled feature set $\{(F_1, page_1), (F_2, page_2), ..., (F_k, page_k)\}$, where each F_i is a feature vector and $page_i$ is a label. And then, a new feature F' is input and the classifier will decide which label $page_i$ that the F' is attached.

Table 2. Traffic Analysis Attack Instances

Method	Classifier	Features Considered
LL [7]	naïve Bayes	packet lengths
HWF [6]	multinomial naïve Bayes	packet lengths
DCRS [5]	naïve Bayes	total trace time
		bidirectional total bytes
		bytes in traffic bursts

We consider three typical TA techniques listed in Table 2.

Liberatore and Levine [7] developed a web page identification algorithm (LL) by using naïve Bayes (NB) classifier. NB classifier is the classical classifier. In traffic analysis, it is used to predict a label $page$: $page = \arg\max_i P(page_i|F')$ for a given feature vector F' using Bayes rule $P(page_i|F') = \frac{P(F'|page_i)P(page_i)}{P(F')}$, where $i \in \{1, 2, ..., k\}$ and k is the number of web pages. The LL method adopts the kernel density estimation to estimate the probability $P(F'|page_i)$ over the example vector during the training phase, and the $P(page_i)$ is set to k^{-1}. The normalization constant $P(F')$ is computed as $\sum_{i=1}^{k} P(F'|page_i) \cdot P(page_i)$. The feature vector used in this method is constituted by the packet direction and the packet length.

Herrmann, Wendolsky, and Federrath [6] proposed a web page identification algorithm (HWF) by using a multinomial naïve Bayes (MNB) classifier. Both LL and HWF methods use the same basic learning method with the same traffic features. The difference is in the computation of $P(F'|page_i)$. The HWF method determines the $P(F'|page_i)$ with normalized numbers of occurrences of features while the LL method determines with corresponding raw numbers.

Most of the works are on single fine-grained packet analysis. In [5], Dyer, Coull, Ristenpart, and Shrimpton proposed an identification method (DCRS) based on three coarse trace attributes. The three coarse features are total transmission time, total per-direction bandwidth, and traffic burstiness (total length of non acknowledgement packets sent in a direction between two packets sent in another direction). They use NB as the underlying machine learning algorithm and build the VNG++ classifier. Their results show that TA methods can reach a high identification accuracy against existed countermeasures without using individual packet lengths. It implies that the chosen feature attributes are more important in identifying web pages.

2.3 The Padding-Based Countermeasures

Visiting a web page means an HTTP session is introduced. This session is composed by a sequence of network request-response communications. As we discussed previously, the corresponding network packets, in both lengths and directions, are associated with the original web page and hence the web page could be identified even if the packets are transmitted in encrypted.

To change the profiles of communicated packets, a simple and effective method is padding extra bytes to packet payloads [10]. Note that the length of packet payload is limited by the length of maximum transmission unit (MTU). When no ambiguity is possible, we also denote the length of MTU as MTU. There exists many padding-based methods [5]. In this paper, we consider the following four padding-based methods.

1. **PadFixed** This method randomly chooses a number $r, r \in \{8, 16, ..., 248\}$, and pads some bytes data to each packet in session. In detail, let len be the original packet length, we pad r bytes data to packet if $r + len \leq$ MTU, otherwise, pad each packet to MTU.
2. **PadMTU** All packet lengths are increased to MTU.
3. **PadRand1** For each packet in session, randomly pick a number $r : r \in \{8, 16, ..., 248\}$ and increase packet length to $\min\{len + r, \text{MTU}\}$ for this packet where len is the original packet length.
4. **PadRand2** For each packet in session, randomly pick a number $r : r \in \{0, 8, ..., \text{MTU} - len\}$ and increase packet length to $len + r$ for this packet where len is the original packet length.

3 The Combined Object

In this section, we will introduce the notion of combined object and analyze the number scale of combined object sequences in a web page.

Suppose there is an object set S, $S = \{obj_1, obj_2, ..., obj_n\}$, where each obj_i is in a web page with $1 \leq i \leq n$.

Definition 1. *(Combined Object) A combined object with size m, CoObj, is an object combination which is constructed by m objects in object set S. The size of CoObj is denoted as $m = |CoObj|$ and CoObj is called as a m-object.*

A typical m-object, $CoObj$, can be denoted as $\langle obj_{i_1}, obj_{i_2}, ..., obj_{i_m} \rangle$, where $obj_{i_j} \in S$ with $j \in \{1, 2, ...m\}$, and $1 \le i_1 < i_2 < ... < i_m \le n$. The obj_{i_j} is called as the component object of $CoObj$. All the component objects in a combined object constructs the component object set, denoted by CO, for this combined object. We also denote the size of CO as $|CO|$. For the m-object $CoObj$, $CO_{CoObj} = \{obj_{i_1}, obj_{i_2}, ..., obj_{i_m}\}$, and $|CO_{CoObj}| = m$.

For example, let $ExampleS = \{obj_1, obj_2, ..., obj_8\}$ be an object set, the combined object $CoObj_1 = \langle obj_1, obj_2 \rangle$ is a 2-object, and $CoObj_2 = \langle obj_3, obj_4, obj_8 \rangle$ is a 3-object. And $CO_{CoObj_1} = \{obj_1, obj_2\}$, and $CO_{CoObj_2} = \{obj_3, obj_4, obj_8\}$.

Definition 2. *(k-Partition) Given an integer $k \ge 2$, a k-Partition in object set S is a set of object sets $\{CO_1, CO_2, ..., CO_N\}$, where $S = \cup_{i=1}^{N} CO_i$, $2 \le |CO_i| \le k$, and $CO_i \cap CO_j = \phi$ for any $i \ne j$.*

Definition 3. *(k-Partition sequence) Given a k-Partition in object set S $kP = \{CO_1, CO_2, ..., CO_N\}$, a k-partition sequence over kP is a an object set sequence, $CO_{s_1}, CO_{s_2}, ..., CO_{s_N}$, where $1 \le s_i \le N$ for each i with $1 \le i \le N$ and $s_i \ne s_j$ for any $i \ne j$.*

For the set $ExampleS$, if $CO_1 = \{obj_1, obj_2\}$, $CO_2 = \{obj_3, obj_4, obj_5\}$, and $CO_3 = \{obj_6, obj_7, obj_8\}$, the set $\{CO_1, CO_2, CO_3\}$ is a 3-partition in $ExampleS$. For this k-partition, there exists 6 k-partition sequences.

Another 3-partition example is $\{CO_1, CO_2', CO_3'\}$ where $CO_2' = \{obj_3, obj_4, obj_6\}$ and $CO_3' = \{obj_5, obj_7, obj_8\}$. For this 3-partition, there also exists 6 different sequences. If the granularity of each object request is on combined object, a k-partition sequence implies a sequence of traffic volumes.

Let $kP = \{CO_1, CO_2, ..., CO_N\}$ be a k-partition in S, let $COS_i = \{CO|CO \in kP \land |CO| = i\}$ be the set of i-objects in kP with $2 \le i \le k$ and $d_i = |COS_i|$. We are interested in how many sequences of different k-partitions are existed for a given k.

Lemma 1. *Given an object set with size n, if kP is a k-partition over it and d_i is the number of i-objects over kP, the number of k-partitions, with the same integer sequence d_i, we can construct is $\frac{n!}{\prod_{i=2}^{k}(i!)^{d_i}}$.*

Let $D = \{\mathbf{d}|(d_2, d_3, ..., d_k) : \forall i : 2 \le i \le k, d_i \ge 0 \land \sum_{i=2}^{k} i \cdot d_i = n\}$.

Theorem 1. *Given $k \ge 2$ and an object set with size n, the sequence number of different k-partitions we can construct is $\sum_{\mathbf{d} \in D} \frac{n!}{\prod_{i=2}^{k}(i!)^{d_i}}$.*

We define a rounding function

$$\delta(n, i) = \begin{cases} 0 & \text{if } n \mod i = 0 \\ 1 & \text{if } n \mod i \ne 0. \end{cases}$$

Note that the length of sequence depends on the size of each CO_j. The longest length of sequence is $\lfloor \frac{n}{2} \rfloor + \delta(n, 2)$.

In the next, we estimate the scale of sequences number of different k-partitions with Stirling's approximation in the case of n is even. According to the Stirling's approximation, $n!$ is bounded by $1 \leq \frac{n!}{\sqrt{2\pi n}(\frac{n}{e})^n} \leq \frac{e}{\sqrt{2\pi}}$, we have $\sum_{\mathbf{d} \in D} \frac{n!}{\prod_{i=2}^{k}(i!)^{d_i}} \geq \frac{n!}{2^{\frac{n}{2}}} \geq \frac{\sqrt{2\pi n}(\frac{n}{e})^n}{(\sqrt{2})^n} = \sqrt{2\pi n}(\frac{n}{\sqrt{2}\cdot e})^n$. It implies that the scale of sequence number of different k-partitions is at least $O(\sqrt{n}(\frac{n}{\sqrt{2}\cdot e})^n)$ when n is even. For the case that n is odd, we have similar results.

Theorem 2. *Given $k \geq 2$ and an object set with size n, the scale of sequence number of k-partitions is $O(\sqrt{n}(\frac{n}{\sqrt{2}\cdot e})^n)$.*

Theorem 2 implies when introducing k-partition for a web page with n objects, the number of different sequences of k-partitions can reach to $O(\sqrt{n}(\frac{n}{\sqrt{2}\cdot e})^n)$. As an example, when n is 10, the scale of sequence number reaches to 10^5, while n is 30, the scale reaches to 10^{27}. Considering that the machine learning based classifier needs training on enough number of traffic samples, the huge number of possible traffic traces may decrease the learning efficiency.

4 Constructing the Combined Objects

In this section, we will discuss how to represent combine objects in HTML document and how to retrieve those objects from server. We will present the structure of combined-object-enabled (CO-enabled) HTML document.

4.1 The CO-enabled HTML Document

The data URI scheme allows inclusion of small media type data as immediate data inline [14]. The data URIs are in the form of data:[<mediatype>][;base64],<encoded-data> where the mediatype part specifies the Internet media type and the ;base64 indicates that the data is encoded as base64. For example, the fragment <img src="data:image/png;base64,iVBORw0..."> could be used to define an inline image embedded in HTML document.

We extend the general data URI form to include multiple base64-encoded objects. The combined object in a k-partition can be described in pseudo regular expression form, data:{<mediatype>;base64,<encoded-data>|ObjID:}{2,k}, where each component object is identified by ObjID and separated by |ObjID:, and the notation {2,k} indicates that the number of component objects is between 2 and k.

In order to support retrieving combined objects, it needs to redefine the structure of traditional HTML document. We call the HTML document that can support accessing combined objects as the combined-object-enabled (CO-enabled) HTML document. The following demonstrates this kind of CO-enabled HTML document structure with img tags.

```
<html>
    <head> ...... </head>
    <script> ......
      function CombinedObject()
        ......
    </script>
    <body onload="CombinedObject()">
        ......
        <img id = ObjID1>
        ......
        <img id = ObjID2>
        ......
    </body>
</html>
```

To retrieve the combined objects, the scripts for combined objects must be included in HTML document and the URIs for extern objects are also needed to be changed. The fragment <body onload="CombinedObject()"> implies that when the basic HTML document has been loaded, the onload event triggers the embedded script for combined objects. Note that the contents within img tags are referred to the object identifier (ObjID), the browser does not request the single image file. When the script CombinedObject() is initiated, an XMLHttpRequest (XHR) object will be created. It means that some parts of the web page could be updated while not downloading the whole web page. We use this XHR object to download combined objects.

The open() and send() methods in XHR object are used to require combined objects. The server generates combined objects and translate them into base64 encoded texts and returns them to client. We also use the responseText attribute in the XHR object to read the response from server. When the browser receives the responses, it triggers the onreadystatechange event and the readyState attribute stores the state of XHR objects. Particularly, when readyState is 4 and the state is 200, it indicates that the response is success. We define the action when the server is ready and call the success method in callback object to deal the server response. The response string responseText contains the base64-encoded combined objects. We decompose the text and obtain renderable base64-encoded image files.

4.2   The Communications for Combined Objects

Fig. 2 demonstrates the communications between browser and web server for combined objects in CO-enabled HTML document. When the web browser initiates the request for basic HTML file, the server returns the CO-enabled HTML file. The browser renders this HTML file and requires combined objects corresponding to different objects. The returned base64-encoded combined objects are then decomposed and dispatched to the browser for rendering. The require-compose-decompose-dispatch procedure will be continue until all objects are downloaded.

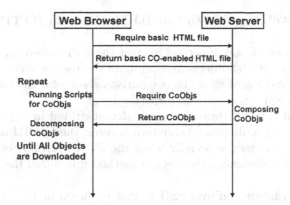

Fig. 2. Communications for Combined Objects

5 Experiments and Discussions

We have implemented a proof of concept prototype for combined objects. In this session, we will discuss the validation experiments for our proposed CoOBJ method.

5.1 The Experiment Setup

Our experiments are on artificial web pages with only image objects. We create an image library by picking some image files whose sizes are ranged from $5k$ to $25k$ from some websites. We then randomly select m image files to construct 200 combined-object-enabled web pages, respectively. The experimental web server is a PC running Apache-tomcat-6.0.33. We also construct 200 traditional web pages with the same number of images for comparison. For each artificial web page, we visit 100 times via HTTPS and SSH tunnel, respectively. We record the traces in each visit, strip packet payloads with TCPurify tool [16], and construct two types of traces set, $\texttt{CoDataHTTPS}_m$ and $\texttt{CoDataSSH}_m$. For comparing with other TA countermeasures, we also construct 200 traditional web pages with the same number of image and visit them via HTTPS and SSH tunnel. The datasets for comparison tests are $\texttt{TrDataHTTPS}_m$, and $\texttt{TrDataSSH}_m$. In our conducted experiments, we set m as 20, 60, and 100, respectively, and set the object partition as 4-partition.

To test the performances against the traffic analysis, we run the code from [15] with classifiers and countermeasures we discussed in Section 2 on our constructed test datasets. The size K of private traces are set to 2^i with $1 \leq i \leq 7$ and 200, respectively. This means that the identifying web page is limited in K web pages. We use the default parameters in original code configuration. For each K with different classifiers and countermeasures, we run the test 10 times and average the accuracy as the ratio of successful identification.

5.2   Visiting Web Pages with CoOBJ Method via HTTPS and SSH

We test our proposed CoOBJ method against the 3 discussed classifiers on the CO-enabled pages with 60 objects and compare the results with other countermeasures. Fig. 3 and Fig. 4 show the comparison results for the case of HTTPS transmission and SSH transmission, respectively.

For the case of HTTPS transmission, as demonstrated in Fig. 3, comparing with the other four padding-based countermeasures, the CoOBJ method lowers the identification accuracy, especially when the size of privacy sets exceeds 16. In the tests for all 3 classifiers, the CoOBJ method minimized the identification accuracy.

The case for transmission over SSH tunnel is shown in Fig. 4. The performances of the CoOBJ method are different in the 3 classifiers. It is the most effective countermeasure to defend against the HWF classifier, but for the LL classifier, the effectiveness is neither good nor bad. It is weak in defending against the DCRS classifier.

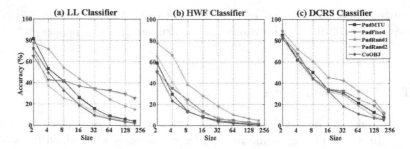

Fig. 3. Accuracy in HTTPS traffic: CoOBJ and other countermeasures

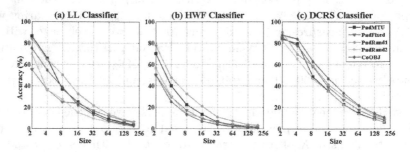

Fig. 4. Accuracy in SSH traffic: CoOBJ and other countermeasures

5.3   The CoOBJ Method against Different Classifiers

Fig. 5 and Fig. 6 demonstrate the identification accuracy of 3 classifiers on the trace sets for combined-object-enabled web pages with different objects. Both figures show that the DCRS classifier can obtain higher identification accuracy on the test dataset.

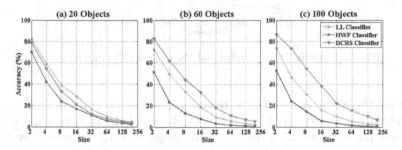

Fig. 5. Accuracy on visiting web pages with CoOBJ via HTTPS

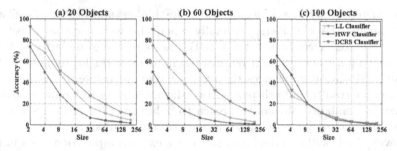

Fig. 6. Accuracy on visiting web pages with CoOBJ via SSH tunnel

5.4   Time Cost for the CoOBJ Method

To evaluate the time costs of the proposed CoOBJ method, we compare the time costs visiting CO-enabled web pages with visiting traditional web pages. We first construct 10 web pages with m images, and transform them into CO-enabled pages, respectively. Because we intend to evaluate extra computation cost introduced by CoOBJ, these pages will be visited in HTTP protocol. We visit each page 10 times, record the total time for loading objects, and then compute the average of time cost. We average the average values for two types of pages, respectively.

Fig. 7 demonstrates the comparison results in visiting two types of web pages, where m is set as 20, 40, 60, 80, and 100. It shows that as the number of objects

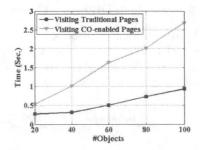

Fig. 7. Loading Time: Traditional Pages and CO-enabled Pages

increasing, the extra time cost is increased in much more. For example, visiting CO-enabled pages with 20 objects needs 0.53 seconds in average while visiting traditional pages needs 0.27 seconds. For the pages with 100 objects, it averagely needs 2.69 seconds to visit CO-enabled pages while needs 0.93 seconds to visit traditional pages.

5.5   Discussions

Our conducted experiments demonstrate the higher abilities of the CoOBJ method against TA classifiers, especially when the web pages are visited in HTTPS protocol. According to the CoOBJ method, the granularity of HTTP requests is on a set of objects. It reduces the number of HTTP requests at least in a half, and obviously changes the traffic volume of responses comparing to the volume of traditional web page. Also, the number of different appearance sequences of combined objects can reach to a larger scale. It lowers the page identification accuracy according to the experiment results.

However, the CoOBJ method may introduce extra computation costs in both server side and client side. Since the combined object is composed in base64-encode, it may increase the network traffic volumes.

Our POC implementation is immature. We do not consider the render order introduced by scripts. And also, we do not consider the case that the objects in page are from different web servers.

5.6   Related Work

Encrypting web traffic is a common strategy to preserve users' privacy while surfing the Web. However, the current encryption suites are focused on transmission content protection and some traffic features cannot be effectively protected. A traffic analysis attack could use these features to infer the users' web browsing habits and their network connections. Identifying web page on encrypted traffic is an important class of traffic analysis attacks.

Sun et al. [10] proposed a classifier based on the Jaccard coefficient similarity metric, and reliably identified a large number of web pages in 100,000 web pages.

They also proposed some countermeasures against TA attacks but our proposed method is not addressed. Bissias et al. [2] used cross-correlation to determine web page similarity with features of packet length and timing. Liberatore et al. [7] showed that it is possible to infer web pages with naïve Bayes classifier by observing only the lengths and the directions of packets. Herrmann et al. [6] suggested a multinomial naïve Bayes classifier for page identification that examines normalized packet counts.

Panchenko et al. [9] developed a Support Vector Machine(SVM) based classifier to identify web pages transmitted on onion routing anonymity networks (such as Tor). They used a variety of features, include some totaling data, based on volume, time, and direction of the traffic. Dyer et al. [5] provided a comprehensive analysis of general-purpose TA countermeasures. Their research showed that it is the chosen features, not the analysis tools, that mainly influence the accuracy of web page identification.

Some other attacks are not only depended on network packets. Wang et al. [11] proposed a new web page identifying technique on Tor tunnel. They interpreted the data by using the structure of Tor elements as a unit of data rather than network packets.

Padding extra bytes to packets is a standard countermeasure. Various padding strategies have been proposed to change encrypted web traffic [5]. However, this kind of countermeasures is on a single non-MTU packet, it is vulnerable when using coarse-grain traffic features [5][9]. Traffic morphing [12] tries to make a web page traffic similar to another given web page. This method is also focused on the fine-grain packets and is limited in changing coarse-grain features. Sending specified packets at fixed intervals [5] can reduce the correlation between the observed traffic and the hidden information and demonstrate more capabilities against the coarse-grain feature based analysis. However, it also introduces traffic overhead or delay in communication.

Some countermeasure proposals are on application-level. The browser-based obfuscation method, such as the HTTPOS method [8], takes the existing HTTP and TCP functionalities to generate randomized requests with different object data requirements at client. It changes the number of requests from clients and the distribution of response packet volumes from servers. The HTTPOS method is on splitting the response packets by introducing special HTTP requests or TCP packets. Although it is effective against some of existing classifiers, it increases the number of requests and the number of response packets.

6   Conclusion

We have proposed a countermeasure method, CoOBJ, to defend against web page identification based traffic analysis by introducing combined objects. We compose some web objects into an aggregated one with base64-encoded form. By composing different number of objects with randomly chosen objects, we can reduce the number of object requests and make web traffic different in different visits. We have implemented a proof of concept prototype and validated it with conducted experiments. Possible future work may include reducing the computation costs in client side and server side, and make it more compatible in current web applications.

Acknowledgments. We would like to thank Xuan Zhang, Zihao He, Yongjian Gu, and Shaohe Hong for their help in experiments. This paper was partially supported by the Science and Technology Project of Guangzhou Municipal Higher Education under grant 2012A022, and the Project of Creative Training of Guangzhou University for undergraduate students 2013.

References

1. Backes, M., Doychev, G., Köpf, B.: Preventing Side-Channel Leaks in Web Traffic: A Formal Approach. In: Proceedings of NDSS 2013 (2013)
2. Bissias, G.D., Liberatore, M., Jensen, D., Levine, B.N.: Privacy Vulnerabilities in Encrypted HTTP Streams. In: Danezis, G., Martin, D. (eds.) PET 2005. LNCS, vol. 3856, pp. 1–11. Springer, Heidelberg (2006)
3. Cai, X., Zhang, X., Joshi, B., Johnson, R.: Touching from a Distance: Website Fingerprinting Attacks and Defenses. In: Proceedings of ACM CCS 2012, pp. 605–616 (2012)
4. Chen, S., Wang, R., Wang, X., Zhang, K.: Side-channel Leaks in Web Applications: a Reality Today, A Challenge Tomorrow. In: Proceedings of IEEE S&P 2010, pp. 191–206 (2010)
5. Dyer, K., Coull, S., Ristenpart, T., Shrimpton, T.: Peek-a-Boo, I still see you: Why Traffic Analysis Countermeasures Fail. In: Proceedings of IEEE S&P 2012, pp. 332–346 (2012)
6. Herrmann, D., Wendolsky, R., Federrath, H.: Website Fingerprinting: Attacking Popular Privacy Enhancing Technologies with the Multinomial Naïve-bayes Classifier. In: Proceedings of CCSW 2009, pp. 31–42 (2009)
7. Liberatore, M., Levine, B.: Inferring the Source of Encrypted HTTP Connections. In: Proceedings of ACM CCS 2006, pp. 255–263 (2006)
8. Luo, X., Zhou, P., Chan, E., Lee, W., Chang, R.: HTTPOS: Sealing Information Leaks with Browserside Obfuscation of Encrypted Flows. In: Proceedings of NDSS 2011 (2011)
9. Panchenko, A., Niessen, L., Zinnen, A., Engel, T.: Website Fingerprinting in Onion Routing Based Anonymization Networks. In: Proceedings of ACM WPES 2011, pp. 103–114 (2011)
10. Sun, Q., Simon, D., Wang, Y., Russell, W., Padmanabhan, V., Qiu, L.: Statistical Identification of Encrypted Web Browsing Traffic. In: Proceedings of IEEE S&P 2002, pp. 19–30 (2002)
11. Wang, T., Goldberg, I.: Improved Website Fingerprinting on Tor. In: Proceedings of WPES 2013, pp. 201–212 (2013)
12. Wright, C., Coull, S., Monrose, F.: Traffic Morphing: An Efficient Defense Against Statistical Traffic Analysis. In: Proceedings of NDSS 2009, pp. 237–250 (2009)
13. HTTP Archive, http://httparchive.org
14. Masinter, L.: The "data" URL scheme, http://www.ietf.org/rfc/rfc2397.txt
15. https://github.com/kpdyer/traffic-analysis-framework
16. http://masaka.cs.ohiou.edu/eblanton/tcpurify/

A Website Credibility Assessment Scheme Based on Page Association

Pei Li[1], Jian Mao[1], Ruilong Wang[1], Lihua Zhang[2], and Tao Wei[3]

[1] School of Electronic and Information Engineering, BeiHang University, China
[2] Institute of Computer Science and Technology, Peking University, China
[3] FireEye Inc, United States

Abstract. The credibility of websites is an important factor to prevent malicious attacks such as phishing. These attacks cause huge economic losses, for example attacks to online transaction systems. Most of the existing page-rating solutions, such as PageRank and Alexa Rank, are not designed for detecting malicious websites. The main goal of these solutions is to reflect the popularity and relevance of the websites, which might be manipulated by attackers. Other security-oriented rating schemes, e.g., black/white listed based, voting-based and page-similarity-based mechanisms, are limited in the accuracy for new pages, bias in recommendation and low efficiency. To balance the user experience and detection accuracy, inspired by the basic idea of PageRank, we developed a website credibility assessment algorithm based on page association. We prototyped our algorithm and developed a website assessment extension for the Safari browser. The experiment results showed that our method is accurate and effective in assessing websites for threats from phishing with a low performance overhead.

Keywords: Website credibility, Page association, Page rating.

1 Introduction

The credibility of websites is an important factor to prevent malicous websites from attacking users. For example, phishing websites defraud users of their private information for attackers' financial benefits. The attacks from malicious websites have been increasing in the past a few years, which have become one of the main security threats to users.

To protect users from such websites, we need to recognize malicious websites and make users aware the threats from websites with low reputation. A common solution is to use a reputation system to help users identify malicious websites, such as blacklist/whitelist based detection and page-feature based detection. Blacklist/whitelist based detection uses blacklist/whitelist provided by trusted third parties to assess URLs and identify malicious pages. Unfortunately, it is challenging to update the list in time, while malicious pages typically exist only for a short period of time. Page-feature based detection [8,9] is another important technique to detect malicious websites, which extracts page features and checks

X. Huang and J. Zhou (Eds.): ISPEC 2014, LNCS 8434, pp. 105–118, 2014.

them for similarity to benign pages. These types of solutions usually achieve a lower false negative, but introduce more system overhead. Most of existing feature-based solutions focus on static page features that might be bypassed by attackers via simple modification on the malicious pages.

Another type of methods use page relationships to assess the credibility of websites, e.g., PageRank [15], Alexa Rank [3], etc. However, such solutions focus on the popularity and relevance with respect to page contents. They cannot be used to accurately access the credibility of websites. In addition, as running security solutions incurs computation and operation overhead to browsers, it inevitably brings delay of loading pages. Such overhead affects user experience, so it is important to reduce the computation of mechanisms. On the other hand, mechanisms using less computation tend to be less accurate. How to balance user experience and detection accuracy is a key challenge.

In this paper, we propose a website credibility assessment[1] algorithm. It uses page associations and user behaviors as the basis to determine the credibility of websites. We implemented the algorithm into a website assessment extension for the Safari browser. The experiment results confirmed that analyzing user behaviors is helpful to enhance efficiency of identifying malicious pages.

The paper is organized as follows. Section 2 discusses related work. Section 3 proposes our assessment algorithm based on page association. In Section 4, we describe the extension's system architecture. In Section 5, we analyze performance of extension and illustrate its accuracy. Section 6 concludes this paper.

2   Related Work

PageRank [15] is an algorithm developed by Google Inc. and used by Google Search to measure the importance of websites. It assumes that more important web pages are likely to receive more and better links from other pages. PageRank considers each link as a vote. For instance, page A has a link poiting to page B. This link is a support of website importance from A to B. The more important page A is, the more this link contributes to page B's rank. By counting the quantity and quality of links to a page, an integer scaled from 0 to 10 is given to estimate the importance of this page. PageRank is updated every few months, so a new website has to wait a relatively long time to get a promotion in PageRank. It results in a condition that newly created websites seem no difference in PageRank from malicious websites even if they have improved their outlinks and backlinks in the last weeks or months.

Alexa Rank [3] is a measure of how popular a site is. To calculate Alexa Rank of a site, it needs to estimate the average daily unique visitors to the site, as well as the number of pageviews on the site. The Alexa Rank for the site is calculated from the above two values over the past 3 months. Although PageRank and Alexa Rank are the most popular page rating algorithms, they are not suitable for the credibility assessment on web pages' trustworthiness. As they are not developed

---

[1] We use the term assessment and evaluation interchangeably in this paper.

for the website security evaluation, both of them concerned about the relevance or importance of the target page rather than the website trustworthiness.

Kim et al. [8] inquire Google PageRank, WHOIS database to get page features like the registration date, lifetime and ranks of websites. They give different weight to each feature, define different risk levels, and compute comprehensive risk index of pages to identify untrusted websites. This approach is effective for most malicious pages with short lifetime and low access frequency, but may cause false positive for newly created websites with low access frequency.

Blacklist/whitelist is a URL list of all the trusted/untrusted pages. By comparing URL with the lists, we can tell if it is a trusted or an untrusted page and give them corresponding ratings. Black/Whitelist based mechanism is easy to implement, but its accuracy depends on the correctness of the lists. Most lists applied today are updated by users' reports. Due to the short lifetime of malicious websites, it is difficult to maintain the accuracy of blacklist and whitelist. Many agencies depend on user reports to collect suspicious websites and share the list with all users using their service. Phishtank [19] allows users to report phishing websites to it, and shares the list with all the institution and individual users through open APIs after the URL is verified by user votes. WOT [14] relies on community members to report and get down untrusted pages. Blacklist/whitelist approaches are usually employed by browser extensions, like Netcraft [13], Trustwatch [5], Google safe Browsing [16], Microsoft Phishing Filter [6], and SpoofGuard [4]. Blacklist/whitelist based mechanisms have a high false negative because of the delay in update and incompleteness of the list. It is vulnerable to newly created malicious pages especially for those with a lifetime less than two hours [17].

Because of the limitation of blacklist/whitelist based methods, some researchers employ machine-learning mechanisms to develop new solutions based on the features of the web page. Their researches focus on how to characterize dangerous web pages and detect malicious pages effectively with lower false positive rate [21]. Some existing approaches are focused on analyzing websites trustworthiness by using page-elements' properties since the majority of attackers use page content to show their spoofing information. Intuitively, phishing pages not only copy the layout of real pages, but also include some redundant information that real pages do not have. Layton et al. [9] compute the difference of redundant information between phishing websites and real websites to detect the phishing sites aiming at branded websites, but this approach only works for specific phishing behaviors. Mao et al. [12] presented another page-feature based approach, BaitAlarm, which computes CSS similarity between two pages to identify phishing pages that imitate real pages based on the rating given by their algorithm. The conflict/tradeoff between false negative and performance overhead introduced is still the kernel problem of the content-based or layout-based approaches.

3 Page Association Based Website Credibility Assessment

From the analysis above, it can be concluded that the tradeoff between the accuracy and performance overhead is still an unsolved problem in these malicious page analysis approaches based on credibility assessment. According to our observation and experimental test [11] on the page association, we found that normally, few trustworthy websites may point to malicious ones, especially for the new generated malicious pages. So the quality and the quantity of a website's back-links might be used as a dominate feature to evaluate its trustworthiness. Based on this intuition, we developed our websites credibility assessment algorithm by using the page association properties.

In this section, we describe the algorithm we developed for website credibility assessment and our credibility assessment based website analysis scheme as well.

3.1 Assessment Features Extraction and Aggregation Analysis

Our method consists of three parts: page association property extraction; property analysis and aggregation; decision making based on aggregation result.

Back-links [18]of a page have a strong expression of how this page is associated with other pages. As mentioned above, the quality and the quantity of back-links are qualified to evaluate the credibility of the target page the back-links pointing to. So we consider back-links as the page association property applied in our assessment method. In order to reduce the computation of assessment, we select the most important 10 back-links to take part in the property analysis and aggregation. As Yahoo! search sorts back-links according to the order of importance of websites, we choose the top 10 back-links in the result list of Yahoo! search for further analysis and aggregation.

For a target page d, we consider each back-link b_i as a support to the target page in trustworthiness evaluation. The rating of back-link, represented as $R(b_i)$, is regarded as the amount of the support this page can contribute to other pages in total. These pages share the contribution of credibility support from the back-link equally. For example, the credibility value of page A is 0.8 and it has two links pointing to page B and page C. The credibility support that either B and C get from page A is 0.4. On the other hand, the higher the rank of back-link is, more credible the support from the back-link is. For a page with several back-links, the credibility support from high-rating back-links should be more trustworthy than others. We use a normalized coefficient W_i, to weight credibility support from different back-links.

We illustrate the notations required in our algorithm in Table 1. Let d be the target page. Suppose there are n links pointing to the page d, and $b_i(1 \leq i \leq n)$ is the page which contains a link pointing to the page d, d's credibility $R(d)$ is calculated by Formula(1),

$$R(d) = \sum_{i=1}^{n} W_i \frac{R(b_i)}{N(b_i)} \qquad (1)$$

Table 1. Notations Announcement

Symbol	Description
d	the target page that needs to be assessed.
$R(d)$	the credibility value of d.
b_i	a page which contains a link pointing to d. ($1 \leq i \leq n$, $i \in Z$)
n	the total number of links pointing to d.
$N(b_i)$	the total number of links in page b_i.
W_i	the weight of back-link b_i.
$R(b_i)$	the credibility value of b_i.

where $N(b_i)$ is the number of links in page b_i, and W_i is the weight of each back-link which is calculated by Formula (2):

$$W_i = \frac{R(b_i)}{\sqrt{\sum_{i=1}^{n} R^2(b_i)}} \qquad (2)$$

After receiving the credibility value of the target page, we compare it with a preset threshold to identify malicious pages which are defined as web pages with a credibility value lower than threshold.

3.2 Credibility Assessment Based Malicious Page Detection

In order to reduce further computation of our method, we use Alexa Rank to whitelist benign pages with high Alexa Rank. Malicious websites usually have a short lifetime and low access frequency. Because of these features, they cannot get the high rating during the Alexa's 3-month updating period.

We randomly choose 100 websites from Alexa as the seed set of benign websites T, 100 websites from PhishTank as the seed set of malicious websites P. Our approach inquires back-links and their credibility value in T and P after successfully extracting every back-link. We define the credibility value of links from T as 1, the credibility value of links from P as 0. Others take one-tenth of PageRank as their credibility value.

The operational process of our approach is described as below: 1) inquire Alexa Rank of the page to filter out high-rank benign pages; 2) assess credibility of the page if it did not pass the Alexa check; 3) return assessment result to users. We illustrate the process of our approach in Algorithm 1.

Our approach uses received URL to inquire the Alexa Rank of the page and compare it with the AR threshold. If the threshold is larger, then the page is classified as a safe one, otherwise our approach needs to compute the credibility value of the page to do further analysis. Credibility value is a decimal between 0 and 1. The larger the credibility value is, the more credible the page is. The scheme contains four URL lists: whitelist, blacklist, portal websites list, and history list. The whitelist contains all the websites whose credibility value is 1, while the blacklist holds all the zero-value pages. The credibility value of

---

Algorithm 1. Page Association Based Website Credibility Assessment

---

1 let d be a suspicious web page;
2 let $R(d)$ be the credibility value of d
3 let t_{AR} be a preset threshold of Alexa Rank
4 let t_{CV} be a preset threshold of Credibility Value
5 **Phase** I: Filter Out Suspicious Pages With Alexa Rank.
6 **Function** Alexa(d)is
    input : a suspicious page d
    output: whether d is benign or malicious
7   compute $A(d)$; /* inquire Alexa Rank of d online   */
8   **if** $A(d) < t_{AR}$ **then**
9   page d is benign;
10   display "Safe" and details of assessment;
11   **else**
12   perform the credibility assessment, Assess $\{d\}$;

13 **Phase** II: Compute Credibility Value.
14 **Function** Assess(d)is
    input : a suspicious page d
    output: credibility value of d, $R(d)$
15   **if** $R(d)$ *is recorded in local storage* **then**
16   get $R(d)$ from local sotrage;
17   **else**
18   search back-links of d; /* use Yahoo! to search back-links of d */
19   compute $S(d) = \{b_0, b_1...b_n\}(n < 10)$;
20   /* store at most 10 top back-links in $S(d)$ */
21   get credibility value of every link in $S(d)$;
22   compute the weight of every back-link W_i, $(0 \leq i \leq 9)$
23

$$W_i = \frac{R(b_i)}{\sqrt{\sum_{i=1}^{n} R^2(b_i)}}$$

      compute the credibility value of page d
24

$$R(d) = \sum_{i=1}^{n} W_i \frac{R(b_i)}{N(b_i)}$$

      Return $R(d)$;

25 **Phase** III: Make Decision.
26 **Function** Decision($R(d)$)is
    input : credibility value of d, $R(d)$
    output: the result of assessment
27   **if** $R(d) > t_{CV}$ **then**
28   page d is benign;
29   display "Safe" and details of assessment;
30   **else**
31   page d is malicious;
32   display "Warn" and details of assessment;

portal websites is defined as one-tenth of their PageRank. Our approach retrieves target URLs in the order of whitelist, blacklist, portal websites list, and history list. Once the existence of the target URL is confirmed, our approach returns assessment result directly to users. Otherwise, it searches for all the back-links of target page by Yahoo! search. To reduce the time overhead, we extract at most 10 back-links of the page as the back-link set $S(d)$ of the target page d. Then we inquire each link from $S(d)$ in T and P to get their credibility value. For those beyond T and P, we inquire their PageRank online to get credibility value. With every credibility value obtained, we will be able to calculate $R(d)$ and compare it with CV threshold (the threshold of credibility value). Websites with credibility value larger than CV threshold are classified as credible pages, the rest are classified as malicious pages.

Discussion. To solve the limitation that detection methods based on Alexa Rank and PageRank are easy to cause false positive for newly created and low-access-frequency benign sites, we adopt a user behavior analysis module. Our approach checks the way users open login pages. If a URL is manually typed in by users, it is familiar to users. We consider such pages as benign websites. On the contrary, if a new page was opened by clicking a link, there is no guarantee that its URL is exactly the same as the legitimate one. The possibility that such a page is a malicious page is relatively high. For other pages visited in some other ways like clicking links from history or favorite pages, their credibility have been announced the first time they were visited. As a result, our approach only needs to evaluate the login pages accessed by clicking links.

4   Implementation as Browser Extension

The architecture of our extension is illustrated in Fig. 1. It consists of three modules: a *page script*, a *global HTML page*, and a *menu*. In this section, we introduce these modules in the order of the operation process.

4.1   Page Script

The functional requirement of the page script is to judge whether the target page is a login page, report click behaviors to global HTML pages, and show assessment result.

Attackers usually induce users to input private information in a dangerous page to steal their accounts and passwords. In the case that the webpage is not a login page and users do not need to input their personal information, our scheme treats this kind of pages harmless pages that are unable to steal users' accounts related information. If a website asks users for password before launching the next page, this page should be treated as a suspicious page which need further credibility evaluation. To avoid possible impact on user experience, we use similar triggering condition as paper [20] that normal page-surfing will not be disturbed and only the login pages will trigger the credibility assessment.

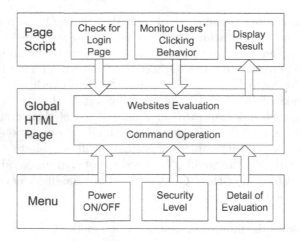

Fig. 1. The extension architecture

A login page must have input areas for account and password, so we identify a login page by checking input objects whose type is "password". We set the triggering condition of extension as "a login page opened by clicking a link". Once the new page matches the triggering condition, our approach starts to assess the credibility of it. Every time a user visits a new page, our approach launches a script to check if the new page is a login page and sends its URL to global HTML page immediately. If it is a login page, the page scripts will announce global HTML page to check how this page was accessed. Assessment can only be triggered if both checks above returned positive results, otherwise the extension will do nothing but refresh history list.

When Safari opens a new page, the first work of the page script is to define a `str` layer and a `detail` layer for displaying results, both of them are hidden at the moment. The next step is to judge if this new page is a login page by searching for `input` object whose `type` is `password`. If the existence of `password` object is confirmed, the page script will send a message named `newURL` to global HTML page in order to report URL of the target page. If there is not any `password` object, the URL of target page will be send in a `message` named `onload`.

When users click on an `href` object in the page, the page script reports this action and its location (URL of the page it happens) to the global HTML page in a `message` named `onclick`.

The page script modifies the content of `str` and `detail` layer according to assessment result. From now on, `str` and `detail` layer will turn up whenever the mouse enters an `input` area and be hidden when the mouse leaves or highlight the `input area`.

`Str` layer gives a one-word result display while `detail` layer presents the detail information of the assessment. `Str` turns up as a tiny tip at the right of mouse. "Warn" in red means the page is untrusted. "Safe" in orange stands for the

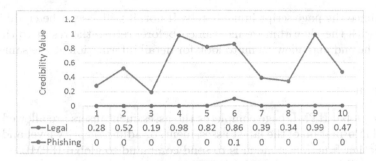

Fig. 2. Threshold Determination

page that has the Alexa Rank lower than AR threshold but the credibility value larger than CV threshold. "Safe" in green is on behalf of the pages with the Alexa Rank higher than AR threshold. Apart from str, our extension display details of the assessment in the same color of str on the top of the page as well. In this paper the AR threshold can be adjusted by changing security level of the extension.

The CV threshold is an empirical value. To determine the CV threshold, we randomly chose 10 legal login websites and 10 verified phishing websites from PhishTank to test their credibility value. The results are illustrated in Fig. 2. No legal websites have a credibility value less than 0.19 while all the phishing websites have a credibility value scaled from 0 to 0.1. So we choose 0.15 as the CV threshold.

4.2 Global HTML Page

The Global HTML page is the kernel of our extension. Nearly all the operations and computations are done in the global HTML page. In our extension, the global HTML page is in charge of operating messages from the page script and commands from menu.

Messages from the page script are classified as three types: onload message means the new page does not need to be assessed, in this case the global HTML page modifies few parameters to prevent detection; onclick message is an announcement of clicking behavior, the global HTML page extracts details of this action and gets ready for possible detections; newURL message informs global HTML page that the new page is a login page and reminds it to check the action which opens this page. If the action is a clicking behavior, detection is triggered, otherwise the global HTML page does nothing but refreshes history list.

Once detection is triggered, the global HTML page stores the new URL first and initializes related parameters to get ready for the next detection. Then the global HTML page inquires Alexa Rank of the target page online and compares it with AR threshold. If the target URL is identified as safe, the global HTML page will announce the page script immediately. If not, it will assess the credibility of the page with the algorithm we mentioned before, return the result to the page script at the end and allow menu to look for detail information at the same time.

4.3 Menu

When the global HTML page completes the assessment, users are allowed to see the detail information of the latest assessment, or adjust security level and on-off state. Another function of menu is to send command to global HTML page. All command will be executed in global HTML page.

5   Performance Analysis

We conducted an experiment to evaluate correctness, accuracy, and robustness of our extension in different login pages. The experiment environment is listed in Table 2. All the experiment is conducted in a virtual machine.

Table 2. The experiment environment

Mainboard	Intel GM45
CPU	Intel(R) Core(TM)2 Duo CPU P8400 @2.26GHz 2.27FHz
RAM	2.00GB
Operation System	Windows 7 Ultimate Service Pack 1
Virtual Machine	VirtualBox 4.1.10
Virtual OS	Windows 7 (32bits)
Virtual RAM	512M
Virtual Hard Disk	31.32G

We selected 20 login pages (9 shopping websites, 5 E-mail websites, 5 social websites and a file sharing website) to test whether our extension can function properly in different websites. The working condition of extension is illustrated in Fig. 3. The number of tested websites is colored in blue while the number of websites that our extension can function properly is colored in green. As showed in Fig. 3, our extension works for 90% (18 out of 20) websites. Some websites with high security protection do not allow strange scripts to be injected, and our extension relies on the page script to extract detection target and monitor user behavior, so we cannot perform our experiment on these pages currently.

Fig. 4 is the login page of Kaixin (`http://login.kaixin001.com/`) whose Alexa Rank is higher than AR threshold so its assessment result is exhibited in green. In Fig. 5, we show the login page of the website Manzuo (`http://www.man zuo.com/login`), whose Alexa Rank is lower than AR threshold but has a credibility value larger than CV threshold, so its result was exhibited in orange. Both Fig. 4 and Fig. 5 are benign websites while Fig. 6 is a verified malicious websites

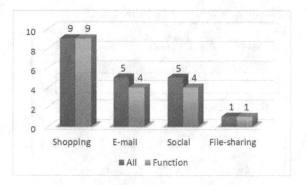

Fig. 3. Working condition of extension

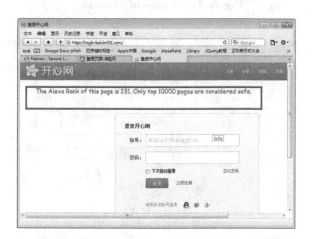

Fig. 4. Login page of Kaixin

from PhishTank (`http://cashexpr.com/sales/remax/index.htm`), which induces users to type in their E-mail accounts and passwords. This page has an Alexa Rank lower than AR threshold and a credibility value smaller than CV threshold so it was classified as a dangerous websites.

We also tested the robustness of our extension by calculating the extra time it brings when loading several websites. We chose login pages of four websites (Kaixin, Manzuo, 360yunpan and 55tuan), averaged 25 loading time of each website[2]. The results are shown in Table 3.

---

[2] The loading time of websites depends greatly on the network condition, so we tested the loading time of a page without the extension 25 times in a row, and tested the same page with our extension 25 times in a row immediately. The purpose of doing so is to keep the experiment environment as stillest as we can.

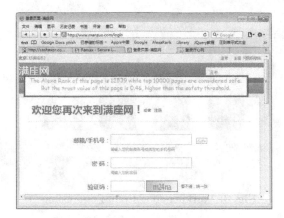

Fig. 5. Login page of Manzuo

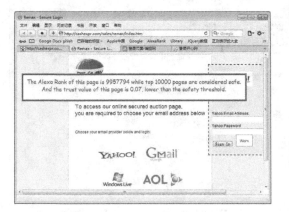

Fig. 6. Malicious websites

Table 3. Overhead on loading pages

Websites	Without Extension	With Extension	Delay(ms)	Delay Proportion
Kaixin [7]	1015.76	1147.56	131.8	12.98%
Manzuo [10]	1180.72	1212.52	31.8	2.69%
360yunpan [1]	1135.08	1259.48	124.4	10.96%
55tuan [2]	989.8	1083.6	93.8	9.48%
Average	1080.34	1175.79	75.45	9.03%

From the experiment results listed in Table 3, we can see that loading time of pages increases 95.45ms (9.03%) on average. This overhead is reasonable that will not affect the user experience. The experiment validates that our extension can assess most login pages effectively and alert users on time with little overhead.

6 Conclusion

In this paper, we propose a website credibility assessment algorithm based on page association and user behaviors, and develop a malicious site analysis scheme by using the credibility assessment algorithm. User behaviors are adopted in our scheme to achieve less false positive caused by less frequently accessed websites. We developed a Safari extension to implement the algorithm and deploy our solution. The experiment shows that our approach is effective in assessing credibility of most login websites with limited overhead, which does not affect user experience.

Acknowlegements. We thank the anonymous reviewers for their insightful comments. We thank Zhenkai Liang for discussions on the early draft of this paper. This work was supported in part by the Beijing Natural Science Foundation (No. 4132056), the National Key Basic Research Program (NKBRP) (973 Program) (No. 2012CB315905), the Beijing Natural Science Foundation (No.4122024), and the National Natural Science Foundation of China (No. 61370190, 61272501, 61173154, 61003214).

References

1. 360. 360 cloud drive, http://yunpan.360.cn/
2. 55tuan. 55tuan,
   http://user.55tuan.com/toLogin.no?service=
   http%3A%2F%2Fwww.55tuan.com%2F&casIsLogin=false&source=1
3. Alexa. What is alexa traffic rank,
   http://www.alexa.com/help/traffic-learn-more
4. Chou, N., Ledesma, R., Teraguchi, Y., Boneh, D., Mitchell, J.C.: Client-side defense against web-based identity theft. In: 11th Annual Network and Distributed System Security Symposium. Internet Society, San Diego (2004)
5. GeoTrust Corp. Geotrust introduces industry first secure consumer search service, http://www.geotrust.com/about/news_events/press/PR_TrustedSearch_092605s.pdf
6. Microsoft Corp. Microsoft phishing filter: A new approach to build trust in e-commerce, http://www.microsoft.com/downloads/
7. Kaixin. Kaixin, http://login.kaixin001.com/
8. Kim, Y.-G., Cho, S., Lee, J.-S., Lee, M.-S., Kim, I.H., Kim, S.H.: Method for evaluating the security risk of a website against phishing attacks. In: Yang, C.C., et al. (eds.) ISI Workshops 2008. LNCS, vol. 5075, pp. 21–31. Springer, Heidelberg (2008)
9. Layton, R., Brown, S., Watters, P.: Using differencing to increase distinctiveness for phishing website clustering. In: Ubiquitous, Autonomic and Trusted Computing, Symposia and Workshops, Brisbane, pp. 488–492. IEEE (2009)
10. Manzuo. Manzuo, http://www.manzuo.com/login.
11. Mao, J., Dong, X., Li, P., Wei, T., Liang, Z.: Rating web pages using page-transition evidence. In: Qing, S., Zhou, J., Liu, D. (eds.) ICICS 2013. LNCS, vol. 8233, pp. 49–58. Springer, Heidelberg (2013)

12. Mao, J., Li, P., Li, K., Wei, T., Liang, Z.K.: Baitalarm: Detecting phishing sites using similarity in fundamental visual features. In: 5th International Conference on Intelligent Networking and Collaborative Systems, Xi'an, pp. 790–795. IEEE (2013)
13. Netcraft. Netcraft anti-phishing toolbar, http://toolbar.netcraft.com/
14. Web of Trust. Web of trust (WOT) - crowdsourced web safety, https://www.mywot.com/en/aboutus
15. Page, L., Brin, S., Motwani, R., Winograd, T.: The pagerank citation ranking: Bringing order to the web. Technical report, Stanford InfoLab
16. Robichaux, P., Ganger, D.L.: Gone phishing: Evaluating anti-phishing tools for windows. 3Sharp Project Report (September 2006), http://3sharp.com/projects/antiphishing/gonePhishing.pdf
17. Sheng, S., Wardan, B., Warner, G., Granor, L., Hong, J., Zhang, C.: An empirical analysis of phishing blacklists. In: Sixth Conference on Email and Anti-Spam (2009)
18. Wikipedia. Back link, http://en.wikipedia.org/wiki/Backlink
19. Wikipedia. Phishtank, http://en.wikipedia.org/wiki/Phishtank
20. Zhang, L.H., Wei, T., Li, K., Mao, J., Zhang, C.: A phishing detection method depending on the pagerank. In: 5th Conference on Vulnerability Analysis and Risk Assessment, Shanghai (2012)
21. Zhuang, W., Ye, Y.F., Li, T., Jiang, Q.S.: Intelligent phishing website detection using classification ensemble. System Engineering - Theory/Practice 31, 2008–2020 (2011)

A Methodology for Hook-Based Kernel Level Rootkits

Chien-Ming Chen[1,2], Mu-En Wu[3], Bing-Zhe He[4], Xinying Zheng[1], Chieh Hsing[4], and Hung-Min Sun[4]

[1] School of Computer Science and Technology, Harbin Institute of Technology
Shenzhen Graduate School, Shenzhen, China
`dr.chien-ming.chen@ieee.org, xinying_15@163.com`
[2] Shenzhen Key Laboratory of Internet Information Collaboration, Shenzhen, China
[3] Department of Mathematics, Soochow University, Taipei, Taiwan, R.O.C.
`mnasia1@gmail.com`
[4] Department of Computer Sciences, National Tsing Hua University, Hsinchu,
Taiwan, R.O.C.
`{ckshjerho,jhsing}@is.cs.nthu.edu.tw,`
`hmsun@cs.nthu.edu.tw`

Abstract. It is easy to discover if there are hooks in the System Service Dispatch Table (SSDT). However, it is difficult to tell whether theses hooks are malicious or not after finding out the hooks in the SSDT. In this paper, we propose a scheme that evaluates the hooks by comparing the returned results before hooking and after hooking. If a malicious hook which hides itself by the way of modifying the parameters passed to the Native API, we can easily detect the difference. Furthermore, we use a runtime detour patching technique so that it will not perturb the normal operation of user-mode programs. Finally, we focus on the existing approaches of rootkits detection in both user-mode and kernel-mode. Our method effectively monitors the behavior of hooks and brings an accurate view point for users to examine their computers.

Keywords: Security, SSDT, Rootkits.

1 Introduction

With the rapidly growth of computer system, more and more issues have been concerned. One of the most concerned issue is security [15,1,3,12]. Rootkits is a technique used by a malicious program to hide itself. It has been widely used in software, even in embedded systems. The rootkits have became a serious threat to our computer. These rootkits can be classified into two primary classes: (1) User-mode rootkits and (2) Kernel-mode rootkits. User-mode rootkits may hide itself through High-Level API intercepting and filtering. This kind of rootkits can easily be detected by existing anti-rootkits software. In this paper, we focus on Kernel-mode rootkits which are harder to detect. Kernel-mode rootkits are extremely dangerous because they compromise the innermost of an operation system.

X. Huang and J. Zhou (Eds.): ISPEC 2014, LNCS 8434, pp. 119–128, 2014.

Kernel-mode rootkits often use SSDT (System Service Dispatch Table) Hooking, or DKOM (Direct Kernel Object Manipulation) to achieve information manipulation. Although there is a lot of existing anti-virus softwares that can detect malicious code, when deal with rootkits, they cannot determine if its behavior is suspicious. Besides, several methods for detecting kernel-mode rootkits have been proposed [6,9,10,11,14,16]. However, if a user employs these softwares (e.g., Rootkit Unhookers [2], Rootkit Hook Analyzer [13]) to do the analysis and find out a suspicious driver, he can remove the driver immediately. However, a wrong decision may disable the functionality of some programs, such as anti-virus software, or some on-line games.

In this paper, we propose a scheme to evaluate the hooks by comparing the returned results before hooking and after hooking. Through this comparison, if a malicious hook which hides itself by modifying the parameters passed to the Native API, we can easily detect the difference. Besides, we use a runtime detour patching technique to not to perturb the normal operation of user-mode programs.

2   System Overview

According to our observation of the behavior of a hooked SSDT-based rootkit, these kinds of rootkits usually hook the SSDT to achieve information manipulation. Normally, a hooked SSDT-based rootkit hooks the SSDT to achieve information manipulation. Even though existing tools are sufficient to detect hooks in SSDT; however, we have to make a decision with caution whether to remove the hook or not. The decision we made will influence the usability of the computer.

In this section, we first describe design goals and assumptions. Then, we explain advantages of our scheme.

2.1   Design Goals and Assumption

Since we target at hooked SSDT-based rootkits, user-mode rootkits and other parts of kernel-mode Rootkit (e.g., DKOM, Inline Function Patch) are beyond our scope. Our scheme focuses on a machine which is probably infected with rootkits. TAN [17] proposed a framework to defeat kernel Native API hookers by SSDT restoration. We are inspired by his idea. In our scheme, we assume that in the beginning, there is no other kind of rootkits running on this machine.

Our scheme has the following two design goals: (1) Effectively analyzing the situation in the state before SSDT restoration $SSDT_{<before>}$ and the state after SSDT restoration $SSDT_{<after>}$ [17]. (2) This program should not perturb the normal operation of the program.

First, the SSDT restoration scheme [17] does not mention how to compare these two states accurately, because after we executed the SSDT restoration. We cannot reconstruct exactly the same parameters in the stack for the further comparison. In other words, when a program executes a non-specific Native API

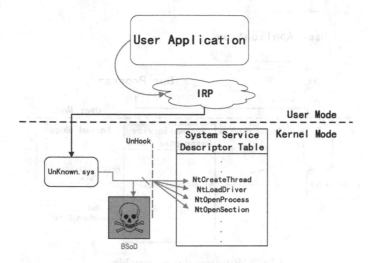

Fig. 1. Unhook an Unknown driver

calls, we are unable to compare the differences between these two states since we do not have any source code. When a Program A executes part of its code and calls *ZwCreateFile*, we cannot alter its control flow and roll back to compare the differences after SSDT restoration. To effectively analyze $SSDT_{<before>}$ and $SSDT_{<after>}$, the first way is to find some special programs that use the same Native API all the time. By calling the API twice, we can see the difference. For example, Windows Task Manager queries the job list by a single Native API and is a good candidate for us. Another way is to write our own program; that is, we can call the same API many times that do not affect our analysis. Toward these two considerations, we decide to write our own program.

Second, a normal program will send IRP request in order to communicate and exchange information with the driver. To obtain the analysis of the driver behavior, we must unload the driver. Under such circumstances, the functionality of the program which communicates with this driver will be incompleted. In Figure 1, if a user application communicates with an unknown driver (e.g., antivirus software, online gaming software driver), they will hook a part of the SSDT entries. During the time we desire to test the driver, it must be unloaded. However, such a move may cause Blue Screen of Death *BSoD*.

2.2 Advantages

Cross View Detection. We obtain the cross view detection ability by comparing $SSDT_{<before>}$ and $SSDT_{<after>}$. Since we write our own program by calling Native API directly for receiving the original message from the Native API; this has two advantages. First, user-mode rootkits have been defeated. Second, we can identify whether hooked SSDT-based rootkit exist or not by executing Windows Task Manager as well as our own programs at the same time.

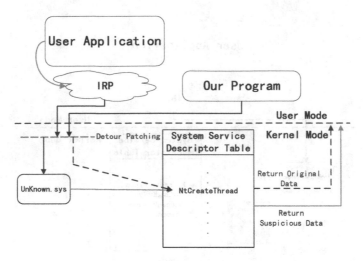

Fig. 2. Runtime detour patching

Runtime Detour Patching. The original idea is from the runtime detour patching rootkit [5] and the characteristic of this kind of rootkit is that it can modify the control flow of the system without awareness. In other words, the rootkit redirects the control flow to their code when a user calls a Native API from user-mode to kernel-mode. As the same mechanism, we modify its malicious behavior and make this kind of harmful action turn into an effective identification tool.

Since we should not affect the normal operation of program, we write a driver to hook SYSENTER. If we are making a comparison of $SSDT_{<before>}$ and $SSDT_{<after>}$ at the same time, the program can directly read the original address of each SSDT entries when calling up a Native API. In Figure 2, a normal program releases a called unknown driver. This driver hooks a part of or one of the SSDT entry, and the driver returns the suspicious information to the user. After our driver loads into kernel memory, we can directly read the original address of SSDT entry. Through our technique, we will be able to return the original SSDT address to the driver. Our scheme, to use the hooked SYSENTER technique, will enable us to make an immediate choice whether to read the original SSDT entry or not. If we wish to unhook the driver which is harmless, our scheme can reduce the impact on the system while unloading this driver may cause BSoD.

3 Our Scheme

Our systems shown in Figure 3 can be divided into two parts, originSSDTaddr function and *the detour driver*. The detailed processes are listed as follows.

1. **Preparation.** Our program must be called up before calling up Windows Task Manager.

2. **OriginSSDTaddr Function.** We use our program to check the hooked state, generate the original SSDT address, and send the address to the detour driver in the kernel-mode.
3. *The Detour Driver.* The detour driver enables the hook function which can redirect the call to the original SSDT address.
4. **Start Windows Task Manager.** Once the above processes done, Windows Task Manager is called up. The APIs in ToolHelp32 API are used.
5. **ToolHelp32 API.** ToolHelp32 API is located in kernel32.dll. Hence, the system starts to call up the ToolHelp32 API in kernel32.dll.
6. **NtQuerySystemInformation.** kernel32.dll calls NtQuerySystemInformation in the Native API. This action triggers SYSENTER and stores current EAX, EDX register. Then, SYSENTER is started.
7. *The Detour Driver.* Before switching to the kernel-mode, the control flow executes the detour driver in this step. It will enable the hook at KiFastCallEntry.
8. **KiFastCallEntry.** Once the detour driver is enabled, this step replaces the original SYSENTER address with our own code and reconstructs the information from user-mode.
9. **Original NtQuerySystemInformation.** Since the original KiFastCallEntry is already modified, the control flow executes the current EAX register with the original SSDT address.
10. **Reconstructed Information.** When the control flow returns to user mode, this message is already reconstructed.

If we desire to analyze a system whether it exists a malicious hook or not, the first step, our originSSDTaddr function generates the original SSDT to compare with the current SSDT address no matter there is any hook existed; if there is one, loads the driver of our program, the detour driver will hook SYSENTER. If an API has been hooked, the detour driver will replace the current address of SSDT in kernel-mode with the address which obtained from the originSSDTadd function. Finally, we call Windows Task Manager, and compare it with the function we detoured. Through the difference between $SSDT_{<before>}$ and $SSDT_{<after>}$, the cross view are presented.

4 Evaluation

The existing unhook mechanism directly removes all the possible malicious driver as usually; however, not all hooks are malicious. When unloaded a non-malicious driver, it may affect the normal operation of a single program, or even affects the whole system. To that end, we implement our scheme in compares with the original address of SSDT entry without unloading a driver, and we can gain the cross view detection ability by contrasting these two situations. As shown in Figure 4, NtQuerySystemInformation hook can directly affect the results of Windows Task Manager, while our system will be able to reach in the case of cross view detection ability without remove the driver.

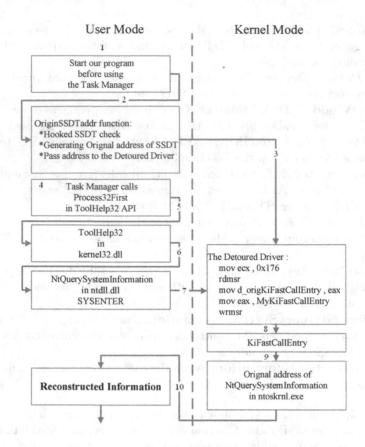

Fig. 3. The architecture of our system

In this section, we show: (1) Cross view detection ability effectively detects the hook-based kernel rootkits in our scheme,(2) to achieve runtime detour for comparison, and (3) we present current antivirus software measurement results.

4.1   Cross View Detection Ability

We tested the SSDT hook from [4], this driver hook NtQuerySystemInformation API, any process name started with _root_ will be hidden. The user executes Windows Task Manager and cannot detect the existence of this program. And we use Rootkit Hook Analyzer to confirm the existence of the hook at No.173 in the API, $0xAD$, the memory address is $0xF9DCC00E$. In Figure 4, we use a small program INSTDRV, this program is used to load drivers for a small instrument. We modified the name of this small program into the file name _root_INSTDRV.exe. When the driver loads into kernel module, we find there is no process called _root_INSTDRV.exe existed in Windows Task Manager(Fig. 5).

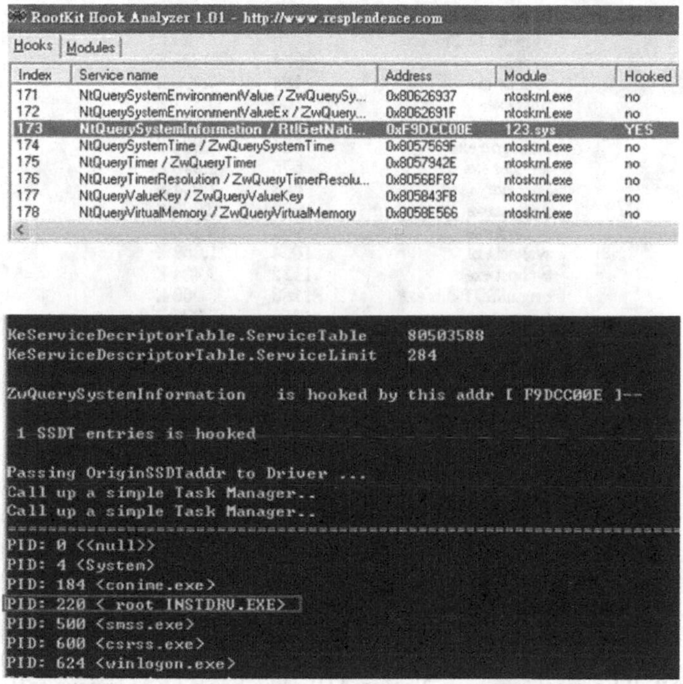

Fig. 4. The detection result from Rootkit Hook Analyzer & our program

4.2 Runtime Detour for Comparison

Since we use the communication from *the detour driver* and the originSSDTaddr function. It allows us to achieve the capacity in runtime detour. As shown in Figure 4, we first checked whether there is hook in the SSDT or not. The system detected an existing hook, and the address existed in the kernel memory. Second, we found out the location of the original SSDT address, and passed it to *the detour driver*. Last, we made a simple Task Manager, and communicated with *the detour driver* to allow our program directly calling the original Native API, and listed the process. With such runtime detour ability as well as the cross view comparison, we recognized whether the driver has malicious action or not.

Table 1. The statistics for the current antivirus software

Numbers of hooks	
Kasperskey antivirus	39 hooks
Norton AntiVirus	35 hooks
F-Secure Anti-Virus	14 hooks
Trend Micro	13 hooks
McAfee	0 hooks
Avira Anti-virus	5 hooks

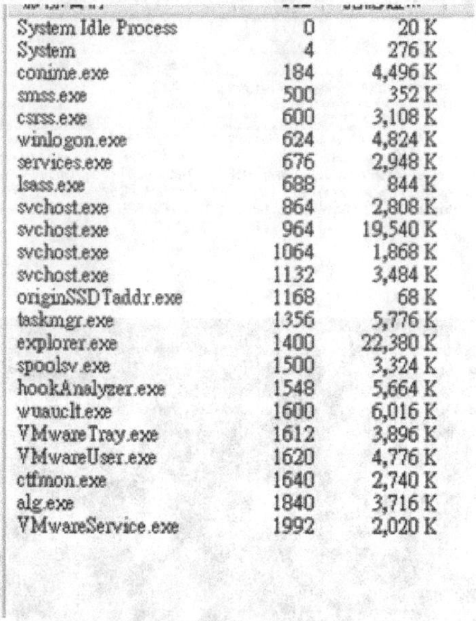

System Idle Process	0	20 K
System	4	276 K
conime.exe	184	4,496 K
smss.exe	500	352 K
csrss.exe	600	3,108 K
winlogon.exe	624	4,824 K
services.exe	676	2,948 K
lsass.exe	688	844 K
svchost.exe	864	2,808 K
svchost.exe	964	19,540 K
svchost.exe	1064	1,868 K
svchost.exe	1132	3,484 K
originSSDTaddr.exe	1168	68 K
taskmgr.exe	1356	5,776 K
explorer.exe	1400	22,380 K
spoolsv.exe	1500	3,324 K
hookAnalyzer.exe	1548	5,664 K
wuauclt.exe	1600	6,016 K
VMwareTray.exe	1612	3,896 K
VMwareUser.exe	1620	4,776 K
ctfmon.exe	1640	2,740 K
alg.exe	1840	3,716 K
VMwareService.exe	1992	2,020 K

Fig. 5. Process list in Windows Task Manager

Table 2. The most common Native API that hook by antivirus software

Results		
Native API name NtCreateThread	NtLoadDriver	NtOpenProcess
# of Hookers 5	4	4
API number 53	97	122
Native API name NtOpenSection	NtTerminateProcess	NtWriteVirtualMemory
# of Hookers 4	5	5
API number 125	257	277

4.3 Current Antivirus Software Measurement

As mentioned before, not only a malicious program will hook SSDT, but even an anti-virus software will hook specific Native APIs. From Table I, it is a common behavior that the current antivirus software will hook a part of SSDT entry. Through this kind of action, it increases the capability of antivirus software to detect malicious code and makes it more efficiency. It is worth mentioning that Kasperskey antivirus hooks 39 APIs to monitor the system information. However, McAfee and Avira Anti-virus hooks the SSDT no more than 5 APIs. Table II also shows the most common Native API that hook by antivirus software.

5 Related Work

In the rootkits detection mechanism, it is divided into *cross view detection* and *VMM-Based*. In the *cross view detection*, it mainly utilizes the difference between the two comparisons to find a suspicious process, file and registry. In VMM-Based, it mainly uses the Host machine to analyze the memory of the client to check out whether the malicious program exists or not. In the following, we discuss about the current scheme in rootkits detection.

– **Cross View Detection**
  Wang *et al.* [18] designed and implemented a quick scanner for user-mode hiding Trojans and rootkits. They compared the information which scanned from inside the host as "the lie" with "the truth"; "the truth" can be obtained from the lowest level of user-mode before invoking into kernel-mode. Thus, they hook a part of the Native API (e.g., NtEnumerateKey, NtQuerySystemInformation) to monitor the Registry and process enumeration API. After the hook obtained "the truth", it uses a regular Win32 API call to obtain "the lie".
  Rutkowska [7] mentioned that cross view based detectors, to be effective, need to implement extremely deep method to get the system information. And it is complex to support all hardwares. The author reminds us that compromise detection is very difficult, and we should not expect a single idea to revolutionize it.
– **VMM-Based** Jiang *et al.* [6,8] emphasized that the current technique of the anti-virus systems is limited and vulnerable because they are running inside the hosts where they are also been protected. Therefore, a new technique based on the Virtual Machine (VM) was born to solve this problem. Nevertheless, it leads to another problem, known as the semantic gap. For the reasons given above, they implemented an "Out-of-the-box" approach to overcome the semantic gap between the VM and the host machine.

6 Conclusions

To find a hook in the system is easy by checking the SSDT. Nevertheless, it is difficult to tell whetehr it is a malicious hook or not. In this paper, we had proposed a scheme to distinguish the malicious behavior by comparing the returned results of hooking before and after. In addition, we adopted a runtime detour patching technique to avoid perturbing the normal operation of user-mode programs.

Acknowledgement. The authors would like to thank anonymous reviewers for their valuable comments and suggestions, which certainly led to improvements of this paper. Chien-Ming Chen were partially supported by Shenzhen peacock project, China, under contract No. KQC201109020055A and Shenzhen Strategic Emerging Industries Program under Grants No. ZDSY20120613125016389. Hung-Min Sun was partially supported by the National Science Council, Taiwan, R.O.C., under the Grants NSC 100-2628-E-007-018-MY3. The corresponding author is Professor Hung-Min Sun.

128   C.-M. Chen et al.

References

1. Chen, C.-M., Wang, K.-H., Wu, T.-Y., Pan, J.-S., Sun, H.-M.: A scalable transitive human-verifiable authentication protocol for mobile devices. IEEE Transactions on Information Forensics and Security 8(8), 1318–1330 (2013)
2. DiabloNova. Rootkit Unhooker v3.8 (2007), http://www.rootkit.com/newsread.php?newsid=902
3. He, B.-Z., Chen, C.-M., Su, Y.-P., Sun, H.-M.: A defence scheme against identity theft attack based on multiple social networks. Expert Systems with Applications 41(5), 2345–2352 (2014)
4. Hoglund, G., Butler, J.: HideProcessHookMDL (2004), http://www.rootkit.com/
5. Hoglund, G., Butler, J.: Rootkits-Subverting the Windows Kernel. Addison-Wesley (2004)
6. Jiang, X., Wang, X., Xu, D.: Stealthy Malware Detection through VMM-Based "Out-of-the-Box" SemanticView Reconstruction. In: Proceedings of the 14th ACM Conference on Computer and Communications Security, pp. 128–138 (2007)
7. Joanna, R.: Thoughts about Cross-View Based Rootkit Detection (2005), http://invisiblethings.org
8. King, S.T., Chen, P.M., Wang, Y.-M., Verbowski, C., Wang, H.J., Lorch, J.R.: SubVirt: Implementing Malware with Virtual Machines. In: 2006 IEEE Symposium on Security and Privacy, pp. 314–327 (2006)
9. Kruegel, C., Robertson, W., Vigna, G.: Detecting Kernel-Level Rootkits through Binary Analysis. In: Proceedings of the 20th Annual Computer Security Applications Conference, pp. 91–100. IEEE Computer Society (2004)
10. Levine, J., Grizzard, J., Owen, H.: A Methodology to Detect and Characterize Kernel Level Rootkit Exploits Involving Redirection of the System Call Table. In: Proceedings of the Second IEEE International Information Assurance Workshop, pp. 107–125. IEEE (2004)
11. Levine, J., Grizzard, J., Phillip, H., Owen, H.: A Methodology to Characterize Kernel Level Rootkit Exploits that Overwrite the System Call Table. In: Proceedings of the IEEE SoutheastCon, pp. 25–31. IEEE (2004)
12. Lin, C.-W., Hong, T.-P., Chang, C.-C., Wang, S.-L.: A greedy-based approach for hiding sensitive itemsets by transaction insertion. Journal of Information Hiding and Multimedia Signal Processing 4(4), 201–227 (2013)
13. R. S. Projects. RootKit Hook Analyzer (2007), http://www.resplendence.com/hookanalyzer
14. Quynh, N.A., Takefuji, Y.: Towards a Tamper-Resistant Kernel Rootkit Detector. In: Proceedings of the 2007 ACM Symposium on Applied Computing, pp. 276–283. ACM (2007)
15. Sun, H.-M., Chen, C.-M., Shieh, C.-Z.: Flexible-pay-per-channel: A new model for content access control in pay-tv broadcasting systems. IEEE Transactions on Multimedia 10(6), 1109–1120 (2008)
16. Sun, H.-M., Wang, H., Wang, K.-H., Chen, C.-M.: A native apis protection mechanism in the kernel mode against malicious code. IEEE Transactions on Computers 60(6), 813–823 (2011)
17. Tan, C.K.: Defeating Kernel Native API Hookers by Direct Service Dispatch Table Restoration (2004), http://www.security.org.sg
18. Wang, Y.-M., Beck, D.: Fast User-Mode Rootkit Scanner for the Enterprise. In: Proceedings of the 19th Conference on Large Installation System Administration Conference, pp. 23–30. USENIX (2005)

Precise Instruction-Level Side Channel Profiling of Embedded Processors

Mehari Msgna, Konstantinos Markantonakis, and Keith Mayes

Smart Card Centre, Information Security Group,
Royal Holloway, University of London, Egham, Surrey, TW20 0EX, UK
{mehari.msgna.2011,k.markantonakis,k.mayes}@rhul.ac.uk

Abstract. Since the first publication, side channel leakage has been widely used for the purposes of extracting secret information, such as cryptographic keys, from embedded devices. However, in a few instances it has been utilised for extracting other information about the internal state of a computing device. In this paper, we show how to create a precise instruction-level side channel leakage profile of an embedded processor. Using the profile we show how to extract executed instructions from the device's leakage with high accuracy. In addition, we provide a comparison between several performance and recognition enhancement tools. Further, we also provide details of our lab setup and noise minimisation techniques, and suggest possible applications.

Keywords: Side Channel Leakage, Templates, Principal Components Analysis, Linear Discriminant Analysis, Multivariate Gaussian Distribution, k-Nearest Neighbors Algorithm, Reverse Engineering.

1 Introduction

In the last decade, several methods that use side channel leakage for cryptanalysis have been proposed [1,2,3,4,5,6]. Since then, virtually all efforts in side channel analysis have been focused into extracting data dependencies in the side channel leakage. Yet, other information can be extracted from the same leakage, such as executed instructions.

In [7], Novak presents a method to extract an A3/A8 substitution table from the devices side channel leakage. In his attack the secret key and one of the substitution tables must be known. Clavier [8] improved Novak's attack by proposing a method to extract both substitution tables and the key without any prior knowledge. In [9], Vermoen *et al.* show how to extract executed bytecode instructions from Java Cards. In their work they created a profile by averaging power traces of known bytecodes and then correlated it with averaged traces of unknown sequence bytecode instructions. In [10], Quisquater *et al.* presented a method that recognizes executed instructions from a single trace by means of self-organizing maps, which is a special form of neural network. In [11], Eisenbarth *et al.* presented a more advanced statistical analysis methods to extract executed instructions from PIC microcontrollers. In [12] Standaert *et al.* show

X. Huang and J. Zhou (Eds.): ISPEC 2014, LNCS 8434, pp. 129–143, 2014.

that a similar setup can be used to detect instructions from the device's electro-magnetic emission.

In this paper we present a precise instruction-level side channel profiling of an embedded processor. In the process we provide a detailed discussion of template construction, dimensionality reduction and classification techniques. In addition, we also provide a comparative discussion between several dimensionality reduction and classification algorithms. In our work we achieved a 100% recognition rate which is significantly higher than any of the previous work. Furthermore, we also provide a detailed explanation of our lab equipment setup and suggest possible applications.

The rest of the paper is structured as follows. Sections 2 and 3 discuss the template construction and dimensionality reduction techniques. Section 4 provides a detailed explanation and comparison of different classification techniques. Section 5 describes our lab equipment setup and experimental results. Section 6 shows the related works. Section 7 briefly explains some of the possible application areas. Finally, section 8 concludes the paper.

2   Template Construction

The first step in profiling an embedded processor is the collection of training (template) data. Here we make the assumptions that all legitimately manufac-tured devices of the same model have similar leakage characteristics. The training traces are collected by recording the power intake of a reference device while ex-ecuting the selected instructions repeatedly. This can be achieved by running simple training programs on a batch of reference devices. Now let us consider N L-dimensional observations of the device's power consumption $\{x_n\}$ where $1 \leq n \leq N$. Each of these N L-dimensional observations belongs to one of the K instructions I_k, where $1 \leq k \leq K$. The template for each instruction would now be the mean and covariance matrix of the N L-dimensional observations. The mean (μ_k) and covariance (σ_k) are calculated as follows:

$$\mu_k = \frac{1}{N_k} \sum_{\{x_n\} \in I_k} x_n \quad (1) \qquad \sigma_k = \frac{1}{N_k} \sum_{\{x_n\} \in I_k} (x_n - \mu_k)(x_n - \mu_k)^T \quad (2)$$

Thus, the template for each instruction is defined by the tuplets of (μ_k, σ_k). However, in practice the observations $\{x_n\}$ may have too many closely corre-lated points and the template construction process may be too time consuming. Therefore, to escape the curse of dimensionality we have to employ dimension-ality reduction techniques.

3   Dimensionality Reduction

Dimensionality reduction techniques are feature selection algorithms used to compress data while preserving as much variance of the original data as possible. In the literature, several dimensionality reduction methods have been proposed

[13,12]. In this paper we have implemented two of the most common techniques, the *Principal Components Analysis* and the *Fisher's Linear Discriminant Analysis*. In addition, we have also implemented three other methods, the Sum of Difference of Means, Means-PCA and Means-Variance.

3.1 Sum of Difference of Means

In the past differential power has been used for correlating information leakage with the power consumption of a device [1]. In [14] the same technique has been utilized to reduce the dimensionality of traces obtained from RC4 [15]. In our work we use this method to reduce the dimensionality of our instruction-level traces. To compute the new dimension ,D, from the original dimension, L, we performed, (a) compute the difference of each pair of mean vectors, (b) compute the summation of these differences, and (c) select the first D points among the highest peaks.

3.2 Means-Variance

The most important criterion when reducing the dimensions of a data is to retain as much variance of the original data as possible. So, it may be reasonable to take the feature points accounting for the maximum variance of the original data across the different classes. To identify these points we need the mean of each class μ_k, where $1 \leq k \leq K$. If we put these means, into a matrix (with k^{th} row being the mean of the kth class), we will have a $K \times L$ matrix where L is the dimension of the original data. The variance of each column is the inter-class variance of each feature point. Finally, we reduce the dimension by taking the first D columns with the highest variance.

3.3 Principal Components Analysis (PCA)

A Principal Components Analysis (PCA) [16] is a technique that reduces the dimensionality of a data while maximizing as much of its variance as possible. This is achieved by projecting the data orthogonally onto a lower dimensional subspace. A lower dimensional subspace can be defined by a D-dimensional unit vector $\vec{u_1}$. The projection of each observation, x_n, onto this subspace is given by $\vec{u_1}^T \cdot x_n$. Now if we stack up all the observations into a matrix the projection of each row of the matrix is represented as $U^T \cdot X$, where U is a matrix of *eigenvectors* of the covariance matrix σ. The projection of the observations into a D-dimensional subspace that maximises the projected variance is given by D *eigenvectors* [17] $\vec{u_1}, \ldots, \vec{u_d}$ with the D largest *eigenvalues* $\lambda_1, \ldots, \lambda_d$.

3.4 Means-PCA

PCA maximises the overall variance of class observations but does not consider other classes. Here our aim is achieving a higher classification rate it may be reasonable to maximise the variance of inter-class observations. The reason for this is moving the class means apart may result a higher classification rate. Let us consider the class means as instances and compute the projection coefficients using the techniques discussed in Section 3.3. Later on, these projection coefficients will be used to transform the observations.

3.5 Fisher's Linear Discriminant Analysis (F-LDA)

Fisher's Linear Discriminant Analysis (F-LDA) is a method used in pattern recognition and machine learning to find a linear combination of features which characterises two or more class observations [18,19,20]. The resulting combination may be used for dimensionality reduction before classification. However, instead of maximising the variance of the intra-class data like PCA, information regarding the covariance of different classes is taken into consideration. These are the "between-class" and "within-class" covariance matrices. Let us consider again the N L-dimensional observations for each class. Then the "within-class" covariance σ_W and the "between-class" covariance σ_B are computed as,

$$\sigma_W = \sum_{i=1}^{S} N_{q_i} \sigma_{q_i} \quad (3) \qquad \sigma_B = \sum_{i=1}^{S} (\mu_{q_i} - \mu)(\mu_{q_i} - \mu)^T \quad (4)$$

where, N_{q_i}, σ_{q_i}, μ_{q_i} and w are the number of observations, the covariance, the mean and the power traces of class q_i. Now, let us consider a D-dimensional unit vector $\vec{u_1}$ onto which the data is projected. This time the objective is to maximise both the projected "between-class" and the projected "within-class" covariance:

$$\mathcal{J}(\vec{u_1}) = \frac{\vec{u_1}^T \sigma_B \vec{u_1}}{\vec{u_1}^T \sigma_W \vec{u_1}} \quad (5)$$

The projected $\mathcal{J}$ is maximised if $\vec{u_1}$ is the *eigenvector* of $\sigma_W^{-1} \sigma_B$. The D-dimensional subspace is created by the first D *eigenvectors* $\vec{u_1}, \cdots, \vec{u_D}$ of $\sigma_W^{-1} \sigma_B$ with the largest *eigenvalues* $\lambda_1, \cdots, \lambda_D$.

4   Instruction Classification

After the templates are created, the next step is testing our classification observations. In this section we discuss two classification algorithms.

4.1 Multivariate Gaussian Probability Density Function

Given the μ_k and σ_k of each instruction, classification is performed as follows. Let W be the power consumption waveform captured at runtime and assume that its samples are drawn from a *Multivariate Gaussian Normal Distribution* model [21]. The noise introduced into the power waveform, W, is extracted by subtracting the mean value from the waveform as in equation (6).

$$n_k = \{(W[1] - \mu_k[1]), (W[2] - \mu_k[2]), ..., (W[p] - \mu_k[p])\} \quad (6)$$

where μ_k is the mean of instruction I_k and p is the selected feature points if the original dimensionality is reduced. The probability of observing the noise n_k in the device's power trace is then computed as shown in equation (7).

$$\mathcal{N}(n_k, (\mu_k, \sigma_k)) = \frac{1}{(2\pi)^{D/2}\sqrt{\sigma_k}} \exp(-\frac{1}{2}(n_k)\sigma_k^{-1}(n_k)^T) \qquad (7)$$

The instruction with the template that generates the highest probability of observing the noise n_k is chosen as the instruction executed by the processor.

4.2 k-Nearest Neighbors Algorithm (kNN)

The kNN is a non-parametric lazy supervised learning algorithm. The "non-parametric" means the learning algorithm does not make assumptions about the data and "lazy" means data generalization is not needed. In a supervised learning the training data is an ordered pair $\langle x, y \rangle$, where x is an instance and y is its class label. The goal of the algorithm is to assign a class for a given instance x'. In this algorithm, the training phase simply stores the training data along with their class labels. During classification, the classifier computes the distance between the instance x' and all training instances $x \in X$. It then keeps the k closest training instances, where $k \geq 1$. The class that is most common among these instances is then assigned to x'. In kNN there are two major design choices to be made; (a) the value of k, for example, if only 2 classes exist $k = 3$ is used to avoid ties and (b) the distance function. The most common distance function used in kNN is the *Euclidean distance function* [22,23]. Given two instances x and x' the Euclidean distance, d_e is computed as in equation (8).

$$d_e(x, x') = \|x - x'\| = \sqrt{(x_1 - x_1')^2 + \cdots + (x_p - x_p')^2} = \sqrt{\sum_{i=1}^{p}(x_i - x_i')^2} \quad (8)$$

where x and x' have p points and x_i and x_i' are the ith point. Some of the other distance functions that can be used in kNN are *Correlation* and *Cosine* learning distance functions.

5 Experimental Results

To implement the techniques discussed above we have selected an *ATMega163 + 24C256* based smart card. The ATMega163 is an 8-bit microcontroller based on an AVR architecture, and it has 130 instructions. To simplify our experiment we chose 39 instructions. During the instruction selection process we considered the following criteria; redundancy and usage of instructions. The redundancy refers to more than one instruction performing the same operation; for example in ATMega163 the instructions LD R_d, Z and LDD R_d, Z+q perform indirect load operation. So, in our experiment we only use LD. Besides the redundancy, we also tried to choose the most commonly used instructions by analyzing several source codes. We created a source code base by using publicly available source codes from various web sites [24,25]. We have also included our own implementation of cryptographic algorithms and general purpose applications in the analysis. The power traces are captured via a voltage drop across a shunt resistor connecting the ground pin of the smart card and the ground pin of the voltage source. The smart card is running at a clock frequency of 4MHz and is powered by a +5V supply from the reader. The measurements are recorded using a *LeCroy WaveRunner 6100A* [26] oscilloscope capable of measuring traces at a rate of 5 billion samples per second (5GS/s). The shunt resistor is connected with the oscilloscope using a special cable, a *probe*, which was a *Pomona 6069A* [27], a 1.2m co-axial cable with a 250MHz bandwidth, $10\text{M}\Omega$ input resistance and 10pf input capacitance. All measurements are sampled at a rate of 500 MS/s.

5.1   Template Construction

To generate the number of traces we needed for the templates construction we created several training code snippets. To construct the templates we attempted to remove all other factors that influence the power consumption apart from the instructions themselves. Such factors can be the initial values of source and destination registers/memory cells, data processed by the instruction and, intrinsic or ambient noise introduced by the measurement setup. To remove the influence of the source and destination registers/memory cells we selected a random source and destination before we executed the selected instructions and we initialised them with random values sent from the terminal over the Application Protocol Data Unit (APDU) channel. For the data processed, we have generated random data for each execution of the target instruction. To minimise the influence of the ambient noise introduced in the measurement, all equipment is properly warmed up beforehand so that it is all running at a uniform temperature throughout the power trace collection phase. This requires running a few test measurements to be discarded before the actual power trace collection begins.

To minimise the effect of measurement noise introduced by the reference card on the power traces we used 5 of the same model reference cards throughout the experiment. To reduce the influence of other random noise from our measurement we collected 3000 traces for each of the selected instructions (i.e. 600 traces from each of the reference cards). Out of these 3000 traces, we used 2500 of them to construct the templates. As part of the templates we took the average of recorded traces and this reduces the standard deviation of the random noise by a factor of $\sqrt{n}$, given that n is the number of traces used for calculating the averaged value.

For multiple clock cycle instructions, the clock cycles are treated as consecutive instructions. Hence, more than one template is created for them. For the conditional branching instructions, templates are created for both conditions. When the condition is false the branching instructions only need one clock cycle; however, when it is true they need two clock cycles. Therefore, for each conditional branching instruction we created three templates. Including the multiple

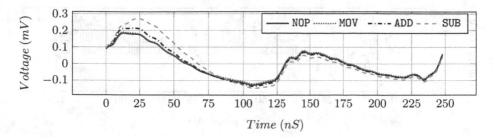

Fig. 1. Power consumption waveform of selected ATmega163's one clock cycle instructions (NOP, MOV, ADD and SUB)

templates for the multi-clock cycle instructions and conditional branching instructions we generated a total of 76 templates. In Fig. 1 and Fig. 2 we plot the average of the power consumption waveforms generated by one and two clock cycle instructions respectively for selected instructions.

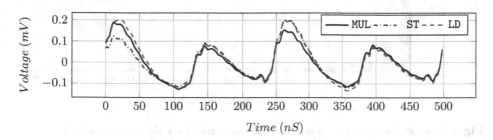

Fig. 2. Power consumption waveform of selected ATmega163's two clock cycle instructions (MUL, ST and LD)

As shown in both the plots, some instructions (for instance NOP and SUB) generate sufficiently different waveforms to recognise them successfully. However, others (for instance NOP and MOV) generate similar waveforms which makes it more difficult to recognise them from their power waveform. So, in order to recognise each instruction from a given waveform we have to create a well-conditioned template and for that we need several training traces.

5.2   Dimensionality Reduction

When using the *Sum of Difference of Means* to reduce the dimensionality we computed 2850 vector subtractions and additions. Fig. 3 illustrates the summation of these differences. The Means-Variance is a straight forward method and involves the computation of variance for 125 column vectors.

When using PCA, the new dimensionality D has to be chosen carefully. On the one hand, if D is too small, too much of variance of the original data may get lost

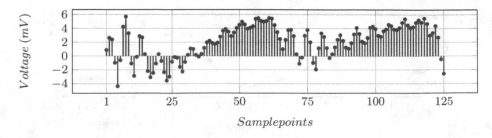

Fig. 3. Sum of Difference of Means

and with it important information about the observations. On the other hand, if D is too large, the templates cross-correlation increases and the classification becomes less reliable.

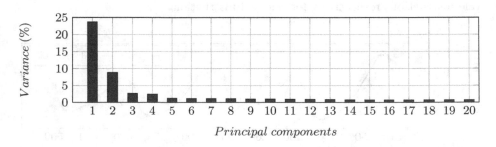

Fig. 4. Overall variance of the original data accounted for the first 20 principal components of the instruction MOV

As shown in Fig. 4, the first 4 components accounted for 37.598%, the first 10 for 44.163% and the first 15 for 48.3387% of the overall variance of the original data. So, when choosing the dimension, D, we have to decide how much variance of the original data that we are willing to lose. In addition, we also performed Means-PCA and LDA to reduce the dimensions of the original data to 50.

5.3   Instruction Classification

So far, we have selected 39 instructions out of the possible 130 and collected 3000 power consumption traces for each of the instructions. Out of these 3000 traces we used 2500 of them to train the templates. Now we discuss the classification result for the remaining 500 traces.

Multivariate Gaussian Probability Distribution Function (MVGPDF):
We have tested the MVGPDF classification both before and after the dimensionality reduction. Before reduction, we utilised the full space of the original data,

Table 1. Percentage of true (**bold**) and false positive recognition rate for a selected instructions using MVGPDF. The rows and columns represent executed and recognised instructions respectively.

Instruction	Recognised as [%]										
	NOP	MOV	ADD	ADC	MUL_1	MUL_2	CLR	CP	INC	SUB	SBC
NOP	**28.7**	0	2.8	5.2	0.8	14.3	0.2	10	1.2	0	0.6
MOV	0	**49.2**	5.2	0	0.4	0	3.2	0	10.2	0	0.6
ADD	9	4.6	**17.5**	0	0.4	0.6	0	0.2	7.2	0.6	0.2
ADC	0.6	0	0	**91.6**	0	1.6	0	5.2	0	0	0.2
MUL_1	2.6	0.4	1.2	0	**68.7**	0	9.2	0.8	0	0	0.6
MUL_2	20.7	0.8	1	1	0	**41.6**	0	0	9.4	0	0.2
CLR	4.8	2	0.6	0	7.2	0.6	**80.1**	0	1	0	1.2
CP	2.2	0	0.6	3.8	0	0	0	**89.8**	0	0	1.2
INC	7.8	4.8	7.8	0.2	0.2	0	0.4	0	**42**	0.2	0.6
SUB	0	0	0	0	0	0	0	0	0	**86.1**	0
SBC	0.6	0	0.8	3.6	1.2	0	1.6	3.6	0.2	0	**86.3**

the overall recognition rate was 64.97%. In Table 1, we present the recognition rate of 11 selected instructions using the full data space.

However, this computation is too time consuming. So, to find a good subspace for our dimensionality reduction, we tested MVGPDF for the first 50 dimensions of the original data.

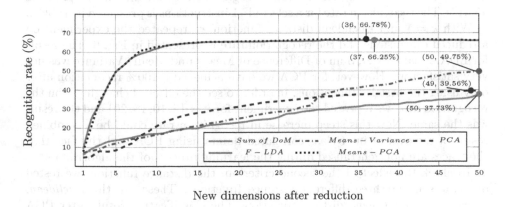

New dimensions after reduction

Fig. 5. Classification rate after dimensionality reduction using *MVGPDF* for all 39 instructions

In Fig. 5 we plotted the result of our classification rate after the dimensionality reduction techniques. In the graph, the first number within the bracket is the dimension and the second number is the maximum classification rate. Using MVGPDF, the maximum classification rate we could achieve was 66.78% after using Means-PCA for reducing the dimensions.

Table 2. Percentage of true (**bold**) and false positive recognition rate for a selected instructions using kNN. The rows and columns represent executed and recognised instructions respectively.

Instruction	Recognised as [%]										
	NOP	MOV	ADD	ADC	MUL_1	MUL_2	CLR	CP	INC	SUB	SBC
NOP	**25.9**	0.2	2.8	4.6	2.0	13.9	1.8	6.0	2.2	0	1.0
MOV	1.6	**31.1**	4.4	0	0.8	0.2	7.6	0	5.6	0	0.4
ADD	6.6	3.8	**10.2**	0.4	1.0	1.4	1.6	0.6	7.6	0.2	0.4
ADC	7.6	0	0.2	**43.4**	0.4	15.3	2.0	18.9	0.6	0	0.8
MUL_1	5.6	1.2	1.6	0.2	**33.5**	1.6	1.6	0.8	0.6	0	0
MUL_2	27.5	1.6	1.6	2.2	0.4	**51.2**	1.2	0	3.4	0	0
CLR	3.6	3.2	12.5	0.2	6.4	1.4	**36.4**	0	9.0	0	1.0
CP	10.6	0	5.0	7.0	1.0	0.6	0.4	**27.7**	0.4	0	3.8
INC	9.0	4.4	8.6	0	0.6	0.4	4.0	0.8	**11.3**	0	1.2
SUB	0	0	1.6	0	0	0	0	0	0	**89.8**	0
SBC	4.2	0.4	9.4	9.8	5.2	2.0	3.2	7.2	2.0	0.2	**23.3**

k-Nearest Neighbors Algorithm (kNN): In kNN there are two major design decisions that need to be made. One is the number of neighbors, k, participating in the decision making. The other is the distance function used to compute the closeness between the template data and the signal that need to be classified. First, we tested our traces with $k = 1$, Euclidean distance function and full dimension of the traces. The average recognition rate for all the templates is 45.31%. The recognition rate for a selected 11 instructions is presented in Table 2.

With $k = 1$ and Euclidean distance function we repeated the experiment on a reduced dimensions and the recognition rate is presented in Fig. 6. The result for LDA, Means-PCA, Sum of Difference of Means and Means-Variance was not very satisfactory. However, for PCA we have achieved a 100% recognition after only using the first 13 dimensions. In order to see the effect of changing k on the recognition rate, we repeated the experiment for $k = \{5, 10, 15, 20\}$ and the result was the same. Now this steep increase in recognition rate could be a combined result of removal of inter-class correlated points using PCA and the fact that the traces are not generalised during the learning process of the algorithm.

To check the effect of the second criterion, the distance function, we tested our traces using three different distance functions. These are the *Euclidean*, *Correlation* and *Cosine* distance function. The classification result after PCA using all three different distance functions is plotted in Fig. 7. As shown in the graph, apart from a minor difference for dimensions $1 \leq D \leq 12$, the recognition rates are the same. They all reached a 100% of recognition rate after the first $D \geq 13$ dimensions.

Finally, it may be worth noting that apart from the two classification techniques, we have also experimented with several others. These algorithms include Self-Organizing Maps [28], Support Vector Machines [29], Linear Vector Quantization [30] and Naive Bayes Classifiers [31]. However, their results were not satisfactory and we stopped pursuing them.

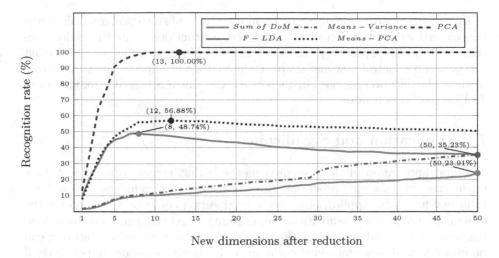

Fig. 6. Recognition rate for all 39 instructions using *kNN* for k=1 after applying dimensionality reduction techniques

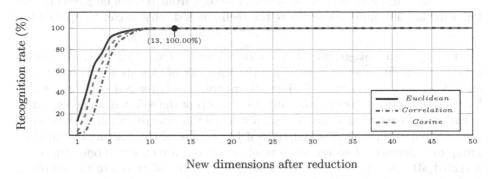

Fig. 7. Recognition rate for all 39 instructions using *K-Nearest Neighbours Algorithm* with different distance functions for k=1 after applying PCA

6   Related Work

In [9], Vermoen *et al.* shows how to extract information about executed byte-code instructions from Java Card smart cards. In his work he created a power consumption profile of the card by averaging several traces collected when the Java Card was executing known sequence of training bytecode instructions. Later on, he correlates the profile to averaged traces of the card's power consumption belonging to unknown sequence of bytecode instructions. In [10], Quisquater *et al.* presented a method that recognises executed instructions from a single trace using self-organizing maps [28], which is a special form of neural network. Both papers discuss the general idea and feasibility of extracting executed instructions from the device's power consumption without really quantifying their success rate.

In [11], Eisenbarth *et al.* presented a more advanced statistical analysis methods to extract information about executed instructions from PIC microcontrollers. In their paper they also used Hidden Markov Model to reconstruct the program's control flow and source code analysis to improve the success rate of their classification process. In their work they have achieved a maximum of 70.1% classification rate.

7   Application and Significance

The first application of the presented methods that comes to mind is reverse engineering of embedded programs. Reverse engineering techniques are well established methods. Applications reverse engineering could be to re-analyse the design of a program or ensure its interoperability with other programs by reverse engineering and studying it. Another application where reverse engineering can be useful is analysing embedded cryptographic algorithms, more importantly if the design of the algorithm is unknown. In such a case instruction-level side channel templates of the embedded device can be used to reverse engineer the crypto algorithm and analyse its security. Apart from reverse engineering the following are few applications where the techniques discussed can be applied to.

Verifying Code Integrity. One scenario where the technique discussed can be applied for useful analysis is verifying the integrity of executed instructions by embedded devices. Traditionally integrity of software is verified by computing a hash or digital signature over the immutable parts of the software and comparing it with a pre-computed value. In such a scheme the integrity value is computed over a group of instructions and verified before any of the instructions in that group are executed. However, since the instructions are executed one at a time, a skilled attacker may target them when they are transferred into the registers from the non-volatile memory. In such a case, the discussed techniques can be used to extract executed instructions from the power trace. Then the integrity value is computed over their immutable part and compared to the pre-computed value. This way any changes to the instructions can be detected; as they will be reflected on the power consumption.

Counterfeit Detection. Counterfeits can be designed to be hard to detect by only functional testing. Instruction-level side channel template can be used to detect a known sequence of instructions inserted by the genuine developer. This way if the known sequence is not detected the devices will be labelled as a counterfeit.

Malware Detection. Malware is a program that disturbs the operation of a computer system, gathers sensitive information or gains access into private data. Another program known as *Anti-Malware* is used to detect malware in PCs. In embedded systems, much emphasis is given into the installation of programs to avoid malware. If the attacker manages to install the malware into the embedded device it is very difficult to detect it. In such situation the methods that we discussed can be utilized to extract the executed instructions and analyse if malware exists or not.

Attack Preparation. Apart from the above applications the presented methods can also be used for attack preparation. Attacks on embedded devices have a higher impact if they are applied at the right time. Hence, the presented methods can be used to gather information on the target programs before applying the main attack on programs with a varying execution time or random shuffling of instructions.

In our experiment we have achieved a 100% classification rate which has never been achieved in previous works. So, our next work will be to test the methods on real-time algorithms such as DES [32] and AES[33]. One should remember that we did not target the data processed throughout our experiment, thus side channel protections such as masking [34], shuffling [35] or random delays [36] will not make any difference.

8   Conclusion

This paper has explored the idea of side channel profiling of a processor down to its instruction-level properties. The maximum classification success rate achieved prior to our work was 70.1%. In our experiment we discussed a four stage classification process; trace collection, pre-processing, template construction and classification. We tested several dimensionality reduction and classification algorithms some of which were not investigated previously in the context of side channel analysis. We experimented on the algorithms using traces collected from five AVR processors, *ATMega163*. We improved the previous classification success rate to a 100% using a specific combination of dimensionality reduction and classification algorithm. These are PCA and k-NN algorithm. Finally, we discussed few of the possible applications where the presented methods can be applied to. Even though, it requires further investigation we can say that instruction-level side channel templates could be used to detect hardware Trojans if the Trojan circuit is big enough to change the device's power consumption waveform.

References

1. Kocher, P., Jaffe, J., Jun, B.: Differential power analysis. In: Wiener, M. (ed.) CRYPTO 1999. LNCS, vol. 1666, pp. 388–397. Springer, Heidelberg (1999)
2. Oswald, D., Paar, C.: Breaking mifare DESFire MF3ICD40: Power analysis and templates in the real world. In: Preneel, B., Takagi, T. (eds.) CHES 2011. LNCS, vol. 6917, pp. 207–222. Springer, Heidelberg (2011)
3. Kocher, P.C.: Timing attacks on implementations of Diffie-Hellman, RSA, DSS, and other systems. In: Koblitz, N. (ed.) CRYPTO 1996. LNCS, vol. 1109, pp. 104–113. Springer, Heidelberg (1996)

4. Dhem, J.-F., Koeune, F., Leroux, P.-A., Mestré, P., Quisquater, J.-J., Willems, J.-L.: A practical implementation of the timing attack. In: Quisquater, J.-J., Schneier, B. (eds.) CARDIS 1998. LNCS, vol. 1820, pp. 167–182. Springer, Heidelberg (2000)
5. Heyszl, J., Mangard, S., Heinz, B., Stumpf, F., Sigl, G.: Localized electromagnetic analysis of cryptographic implementations. In: Dunkelman, O. (ed.) CT-RSA 2012. LNCS, vol. 7178, pp. 231–244. Springer, Heidelberg (2012)
6. Van Eck, W., Laborato, N.: Electromagnetic radiation from video display units: An eavesdropping risk? Computers & Security 4, 269–286 (1985)
7. Novak, R.: Side-channel attack on substitution blocks. In: Zhou, J., Yung, M., Han, Y. (eds.) ACNS 2003. LNCS, vol. 2846, pp. 307–318. Springer, Heidelberg (2003)
8. Clavier, C.: Side channel analysis for reverse engineering (SCARE) - An improved attack against a secret A3/A8 GSM algorithm. IACR Cryptology ePrint Archive 2004, 49 (2004)
9. Vermoen, D., Witteman, M., Gaydadjiev, G.N.: Reverse engineering Java Card applets using power analysis. In: Sauveron, D., Markantonakis, K., Bilas, A., Quisquater, J.-J. (eds.) WISTP 2007. LNCS, vol. 4462, pp. 138–149. Springer, Heidelberg (2007)
10. Quisquater, J.-J., Samyde, D.: Automatic code recognition for smartcards using a kohonen neural network. In: Proceedings of the Fifth Smart Card Research and Advanced Application Conference, CARDIS 2002, November 21-22. USENIX (2002)
11. Eisenbarth, T., Paar, C., Weghenkel, B.: Building a side channel based disassembler. In: Gavrilova, M.L., Tan, C.J.K., Moreno, E.D. (eds.) Transactions on Computational Science X. LNCS, vol. 6340, pp. 78–99. Springer, Heidelberg (2010)
12. Standaert, F.-X., Archambeau, C.: Using subspace-based template attacks to compare and combine power and electromagnetic information leakages. In: Oswald, E., Rohatgi, P. (eds.) CHES 2008. LNCS, vol. 5154, pp. 411–425. Springer, Heidelberg (2008)
13. Bishop, C.M., Nasrabadi, N.M.: Pattern recognition and machine learning. J. Electronic Imaging 16(4) (2007)
14. Rechberger, C., Oswald, E.: Practical template attacks. In: Lim, C.H., Yung, M. (eds.) WISA 2004. LNCS, vol. 3325, pp. 440–456. Springer, Heidelberg (2005)
15. Mousa, A., Hamad, A.: Evaluation of the RC4 algorithm for data encryption. IJCSA 3(2), 44–56 (2006)
16. Berrendero, J.R., Justel, A., Svarc, M.: Principal components for multivariate functional data. Computational Statistics & Data Analysis 55(9), 2619–2634 (2011)
17. Strang, G.: Introduction to Linear Algebra, 3rd edn. Wellesley-Cambridge Press, MA (2003)
18. Fisher, R.A.: The use of multiple measurements in taxonomic problems. Annals of Eugenics 7, 179–188 (1936)
19. Fukumi, M., Mitsukura, Y.: Feature generation by simple-FLDA for pattern recognition. In: CIMCA/IAWTIC, November 28-30, pp. 730–734. IEEE Computer Society (2005)
20. Zhang, L., Wang, D., Gao, S.: Application of improved Fisher Linear Discriminant Analysis approaches. In: International Conference on Management Science and Industrial Engineering (MSIE), pp. 1311–1314 (2011)
21. Gut, A.: An Intermediate Course In Probability, 2nd edn. Springer, Department of Mathematics, Uppsala University, Sweden (2009)
22. Wang, L., Zhang, Y., Feng, J.: On the Euclidean distance of images. IEEE Trans. Pattern Anal. Mach. Intell. 27(8), 1334–1339 (2005)
23. Deza, M.M., Deza, E.: Encyclopedia of Distances. Springer (2009)

24. Web site. Tutorial for learning assembly language for the AVR-Single-Chip-Processors, http://www.avr-asm-tutorial.net/avr_en/ (visited October 2013)
25. Web site. AVR freaks, http://www.avrfreaks.net/ (visited October 2013)
26. LeCroy, T.: Teledyne LeCroy website, http://www.teledynelecroy.com (visited February 2013)
27. Pomona Electronics. 6069A scope probe, website, www.pomonaelectronics.com/pdf/d4550b-sp150b_6_01.pdf (visited October 2012)
28. Kohenen, T.: Self-organized formation of topologically correct feature maps. Biological Cybernetics 43(1), 59–69 (1982)
29. Cortes, C., Vapnik, V.: Support-vector networks. Machine Learning 20(3), 273–297 (1995)
30. Kohenen, T.: Learning Vector Quantization. Springer (2001)
31. Rish, I.: An empirical study of the naive bayes classifier. In: IJCAI 2001 Workshop on Empirical Methods in Artificial Intelligence, vol. 3(22), pp. 41–46 (August 2001)
32. National Institute of Standards and Technology. Data encryption standard (DES), publication 46-3. Technical report, Department of Commerce (Reaffirmed October 1999), http://csrc.nist.gov/publications/fips/fips46-3/fips46-3.pdf
33. National Institute of Standards and Technology. Advanced encryption standard (AES), publication 197. Technical report, Department of Commerce (November 2001), http://csrc.nist.gov/publications/fips/fips197/fips-197.pdf
34. Coron, J.-S., Goubin, L.: On boolean and arithmetic masking against differential power analysis. In: Koç, Ç.K., Paar, C. (eds.) CHES 2000. LNCS, vol. 1965, pp. 231–237. Springer, Heidelberg (2000)
35. Yu, B., Li, X., Chen, C., Sun, Y., Wu, L., Zhang, X.: An AES chip with DPA resistance using hardware-based random order execution. Journal of Semiconductors 33(6) (2012)
36. Clavier, C., Coron, J.-S., Dabbous, N.: Differential power analysis in the presence of hardware countermeasures. In: Koç, Ç.K., Paar, C. (eds.) CHES 2000. LNCS, vol. 1965, pp. 252–263. Springer, Heidelberg (2000)

Automated Proof for Authorization Protocols of TPM 2.0 in Computational Model

Weijin Wang, Yu Qin, and Dengguo Feng

Trusted Computing and Information Assurance Laboratory,
Institute of Software, Chinese Academy of Sciences, Beijing, China
{wangweijin,qin_yu,feng}@tca.iscas.ac.cn

Abstract. We present the first automated proof of the authorization protocols in TPM 2.0 in the computational model. The Trusted Platform Module(TPM) is a chip that enables trust in computing platforms and achieves more security than software alone. The TPM interacts with a caller via a predefined set of commands. Many commands reference TPM-resident structures, and use of them may require authorization. The TPM will provide an acknowledgement once receiving an authorization. This interact ensure the authentication of TPM and the caller. In this paper, we present a computationally sound mechanized proof for authorization protocols in the TPM 2.0. We model the authorization protocols using a probabilistic polynomial-time calculus and prove authentication between the TPM and the caller with the aid of the tool CryptoVerif, which works in the computational model. In addition, the prover gives the upper bounds to break the authentication between them.

Keywords: TPM, Trusted Computing, formal methods, computational model, authorization.

1 Introduction

The Trusted Platform Module(TPM) is a chip that enables trust in computing platforms and achieves higher levels of security than software alone. Starting in 2006, many new laptop computers have been sold with a Trusted Platform Module chip built-in. Currently TPM is used by nearly all PC and notebook manufacturers and Microsoft has announced that all computers will have to be equipped with a TPM 2.0 module since January 1, 2015 in order to pass the Windows 8.1 hardware certification. Moreover, the TPM specification is an industry standard [20] and an ISO/IEC standard [14] coordinated by the Trusted Computing Group.

Many commands to the TPM reference TPM-resident structures, and use of them may require authorization. When an authorization is provided to a TPM, the TPM will provide an acknowledgement. As we know, several vulnerabilities of the authorization in the TPM 1.2 have been discovered [9,10,16,12]. Most of them are found by the formal analysis of the secrecy and authentication properties. These attacks highlight the necessity of formal analysis of the authorization in

X. Huang and J. Zhou (Eds.): ISPEC 2014, LNCS 8434, pp. 144–158, 2014.

the TPM 2.0. But as far as we know, there is not yet any analysis of authorization protocols in the TPM 2.0. Hence, we perform such an analysis in this paper.

There are two main approaches to the verification of cryptographic protocol. One approach, known as the computational model, is based on probability and complexity theory. Messages are bitstring and the adversary is a probability polynomial-time Turing machine. Security properties proved in this model give strong security guarantees. Another approach, known as the symbolic or Dalev-Yao model, can be viewed as an idealization of the former approach formulated using an algebra of terms. Messages are abstracted as terms and the adversary is restricted to use only the primitives. For the purpose of achieving stronger security guarantees, we provide the security proof of the authorization protocols in the computational model. Up to now, the work in the literatures are almost based on the symbolic model, our work is the first trial to formally analyze the authorization in the computation model.

Related Work and Contributes. Regarding previous work on analyzing the API or protocols of TPM, most of them are based on the TPM 1.2 specifications and analyses of the authorization are rare. Lin [16] described an analysis of various fragments of the TPM API using the theorem prover Ptter and the model finder Alloy. He modeled the OSPA and DSAP in a model which omits low level details. His results in the authorization included a key-handle switching attack in the OSAP and DSAP. Bruschi *et al.* [9] proved that OIAP is exposed to replay attack, which could be used for compromising the correct behavior of a Trusted Computing Platform. Chen *et.al* found that the attacks about authorization include offline dictionary attacks on the passwords or *authdata* used to secure access to keys [10], and attacks exploiting the fact that the same *authdata* can be shared between users [11]. Nevertheless, they did not get the aid of formal methods. Delaune *et.al.* [12] have analyzed a fragment of the TPM authentication using the ProVerif tool, yet ignoring PCRs and they subsequently analyzed the authorization protocols which rely on the PCRs [13]. Recently, Shao [18] *et.al.* have modeled the Protect Storage part of the TPM 2.0 specification and proved their security using type system.

In our work, we first present the automated proof of authorization protocols in the TPM 2.0 at the computational leval. To be specific, we model the authorization protocols in the TPM 2.0 using a probabilistic polynomial-time calculus inspired by pi calculus. Also, we propose correspondence properties as a more general security goal for the authorization protocols. Then we apply the tool CryptoVerif [4,5,6] proposed by Blanchet, which works in the computational model, to prove the correspondence properties of the authorization protocols in the TPM 2.0 automatically. As a result, we show that authorization protocols in the TPM 2.0 guarantee the authentication of the caller and the TPM and give the upper bounds to break the authentication.

Outline. We review the TPM 2.0 and the authorization sessions in the next section. Section 3 describes our authorization model and the definition of security properties, Section 4 illustrates its results using the prover CryptoVerif. We conclude in Section 5.

2 An Overview of the TPM Authorization

When a protected object is in the TPM, it is in a shielded location because the only access to the context of the object is with a Protected Capability (a TPM command). Each command has to be called inside an authorization session. To provide flexibility in how the authorizations are given to the TPM, the TPM 2.0 specification defines three authorization types:

1. Password-based authorization;
2. HMAC-based authorization;
3. Policy-based authorization.

We focus on the HMAC-based authorization. The commands that requires the caller to provide a proof of knowledge of the relevant *authValue* via the HMAC-based authorization sessions have an authorization HMAC as an argument.

2.1 Session

A session is a collection of TPM state that changes after each use of that session. There are three uses of a session:

1. *Authorization* – A session associated with a handle is used to authorize use of an object associated with a handle.
2. *Audit* – An audit session collects a digest of command/response parameters to provide proof that a certain sequence of events occurred.
3. *Encryption* – A session that is not used for authorization or audit may be present for the purpose of encrypting command or response parameters.

We pay attention to the authorization sessions. Both HMAC-based authorization sessions and Policy-based authorization sessions are initiated using the command **TPM2_StartAuthSession**. The structures of this command can be found in TPM 2.0 specification, Part 3 [20]. The parameters of this command may be chosen to produce different sessions. As mentioned before, we just consider the HMAC-based authorization sessions and set the *sessionType* =HMAC. The TPM 2.0 provides four kinds of HMAC sessions according to various combination of the parameters *tpmkey* and *bind*:

1. **Unbound and Unsalted Session.** In the version of session, *tpmkey* and *bind* are both null.
2. **Bound Session.** In this session type, *tpmkey* is null but *bind* is present and references some TPM entity with *authValue*.
3. **Salted Session.** For this type of session, *bind* is null but *tpmkey* is present, indicating a key used to encrypt the *salt* value.
4. **Salted and Bound Session.** In this session, both *bind* and *tpmkey* is present. The *bind* is used to provide an *authValue*, *tpmkey* encrypts the *salt* value and the *sessionkey* is computed using both of them.

A more detailed description of the sessions is given in [20].

2.2 Authorization Protocols

We start with modelling the authorization protocols constructed from an example command, named **TPM2_Example**, within some authorization sessions. **TPM2_Example** is a more generic command framework other than a specific command which can be found in TPM 2.0 specification, Part 1 [20]. This command has two handles (*handleA* and *handleB*) and use of the entity associated with *handleA* required authorization while *handleB* does not. Therefore, *handleB* does not necessarily appear in our protocol models.

We take the authorization protocol based on Salted and Bound Session as an example. The other three protocols will be presented in the full version [21].

Protocol Based on Salted and Bound Session. We omit some size parameters that will not be involved in computation, such as *commandSize*, *authorizationSize* and *nonceCallerSize*. The specification of the protocol is given in the Figure 1. For the protocol based on Salted and Bound Session, the **Caller** sends the command **TPM2_StartAuthSession** to the **TPM**, together with a handle of the bound entity, an encrypted salt value, a hash algorithm to use for the session and a nonce *nonCallerStart* which is not only a parameter for computing session key but also a initial nonce setting nonce size for the session. The response includes a session handle and a nonce *nonceTPM* for rolling nonce. Then the **Caller** and **TPM** both compute the session key as

$$sessionKey = \mathbf{KDFa}(sessionAlg, bind.authValue\|salt, \mathrm{ATH},$$
$$nonceTPM, nonceCallerStart, bits)$$

and save *nonceTPM* as *lastnonceTPM*, where **KDFa()** is a key derivation function (a hash-based function to generate keys for multiple purposes). After that, **TPM2_Example** within such a session will be executed. If the session is used to authorize use of the bound entity, i.e. *bind.Handle = key.Handle*, then

$$comAuth = \mathbf{HMAC}_{sessionAlg}(sessionKey,$$
$$(cpHash\|nonceCaller\|lastnonceTPM\|sessionAttributes)),$$

where $cpHash = H_{sessionAlg}(commandCode\|key.name\|comParam)$. Next the **TPM** will generate a new *nonceTPM* named *nextnonceTPM* for next rolling and send back an acknowledgment

$$resAuth = \mathbf{HMAC}_{sessionAlg}(sessionKey,$$
$$(rpHash\|nextnonceTPM\|nonceCaller\|sessionAttributes)),$$

where $rpHash = H_{sessionAlg}(responseCode\|commandCode\|resParam)$.

Else if the session is used to access a different entity, i.e. *bind.Handle $\neq$ key.Handle*, then

$$comAuth = \mathbf{HMAC}_{sessionAlg}(sessionKey\|key.authVaule,$$
$$(rpHash\|nonceCaller\|lastnonceTPM\|sessionAttributes)),$$

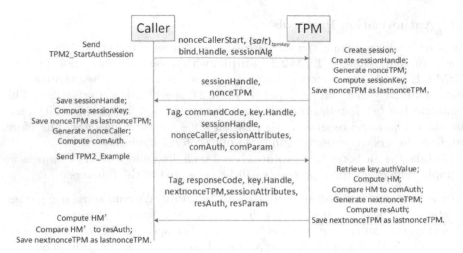

Fig. 1. Protocol based on Unbound and Unsalted Session

and

$$resAuth = \mathbf{HMAC}_{sessionAlg}(sessionKey||key.authValue,$$
$$(rpHash||nextnonceTPM||nonceCaller||sessionAttributes)).$$

When finalizing current session, Both **Caller** and **TPM** save $nextnonceTPM$ as $lastnonceTPM$.

3   Authorization Model and Security Properties

In the beginning of this section, we model the authorization protocols of TPM 2.0. Our model uses a probabilistic polynomial-time process calculus, which is inspired by the pi calculus and the calculi introduced in [17] and [15], to formalize the cryptographic protocols. In this calculus, messages are bitstrings and cryptographic primitives are functions operating on bitstrings. Then we define the security properties of the participants in our model.

3.1   Modelling the Authorization Protocols

To be more general, we present the **Caller**'s actions base on Salted and Bounded Session used to access the bound entity in the process calculus as an example. (The formalizations of the other sessions will be present in full version [21].)

We defined a process Q_C to show **Caller**'s actions, detailed in Figure 2. The replicated process $!^{i_C \leq N}P$ represents N copies of P, available simultaneously, where N is assumed to be polynomial in the security parameter η. Each copy starts with an input $c_4[i_C]$, means that the adversary gives the control to the process. Then the process chooses a random nonce N_C_Start, a $salt$ value for

$Q_C = !^{i_C \leqslant N} c_4[i_C]()$;

    new N_C_Start : $nonce$; **new** $salt$: $nonce$; **new** r_1 : $seed$;

    $\overline{c_5[i_C]}(handle_{bind}, N_C\_Start, \textbf{enc}(salt, tpmkey, r_1))$;

    $c_8[i_C](n_T : nonce)$;

    let $skseed = \textbf{hash}_1(\textbf{concat}_6(salt, \textbf{getAuth}(handle_{bind}, auth_{bind}))$,
                          $\textbf{concat}_5(ATH, n_T, N_C\_Start, bits))$ **in**

    let $sk_C = \textbf{mkgen}(skseed)$ **in**

    new N_C : $nonce$;

    let $cpHash = \textbf{hash}(hk, \textbf{concat}_3(comCode, \textbf{getName}(handle_{bind})$,
                       $comParam))$ **in**

    let $comAuth = \textbf{mac}(\textbf{concat}_1(cpHash, N_C, n_T, sAtt), sk_C)$ **in**

    even $CallerRequest(N_C, n_T, sAtt)$;

    $\overline{c_9[i_C]}(comCode, handle_{bind}, N_C, sAtt, comAuth, comParam)$;

    $c_{12}[i_C](= resCode, = handle_{bind}, n_T\_next : nonce, = sAtt,$
           $resHM$: $macres, = resParam)$;

    let $rpHa = \textbf{hash}(hk, \textbf{concat}_4(comCode, resCode, resParam)$ **in**

    if check$(\textbf{concat}_2(rpHa, n_T\_next, N_C, sAtt), sk_C, resHM)$ **then**

    event $CallerAccept(N_C, n_T\_next, sAtt)$.

Fig. 2. Formalization of Caller's actions

establishing a session key, and a random seed r_1 for encryption. The process then sends a message $handle_{bind}, NCStart, enc(salt, tpmkey, r_1)$ on the channel $c_5[i_C]$. The $handle_{bind}$ is the key handle of the bound entity. This message will be received by the adversary, and the adversary can do whatever he wants with it.

After sending this message, the control is returned to the adversary and the process waits for the message on the channel $c_8[i_C]$. The expected type of this message is $nonce$. Once receiving the message, the process will compute a session key sk_C and an authorization $comAuth$. The function $\textbf{concat}_i (1 \leq i \leq 6)$ are concatenations of some types of bitstrings. We also use the functions **getAuth** and **getName** to model the actions getting the authorization value and key name of the enitity from the key handle. $comCode, resCode, comParam$ and $resParam$ represent the command code, respond code, remaining command parameters and the response parameters respectively. $sAtt$ stands for the session attributes, which is a octet used to identify the session type. Since our analysis uses the same session type, we model it a fixed octet here.

When finalizing the computation, the process will execute the event **Caller-Request**$(N_C, n_T, sAtt)$ and send the authorization $comAuth$, together with $comCode, handle_{bind}, N_C, sAtt$ and $comParam$ on the channel $c_9[i_C]$. Then the process waits for the second message from the environment on the channel

$Q_T = !^{i_T \leqslant N} c_2[i_T](bdhandle : keyHandle, cCode : code, rCode : code,$
$\qquad\qquad\qquad cParam : parameter, rParam : parameter);$

$\overline{c_3[i_T]}();$

$c_6[i_T](= bdhandle, n_C\_Start : nonce, e : ciphertext);$

new $N_T : nonce;$

let $injbot(salt_T) = dec(e, tpmkey)$ **in**

let $skseed = \mathbf{hash}_1(\mathbf{concat}_6(salt_T, \mathbf{getAuth}(bdhandle, auth_{bind})),$
$\qquad\qquad\qquad \mathbf{concat}_5(ATH, N_T, n_C\_Start, bits))$ **in**

let $sk_T = \mathbf{mkgen}(skseed)$ **in**

$\overline{c_7[i_T]}(N_T);$

$c_{10}[i_T](= cCode, = bdhandle, n_C : nonce, sAttRec : flags,$
$\qquad comHM : macres, = cParam);$

if $\mathbf{getContinue}(sAttRec) = \mathbf{true}$ **then**

let $cpHa = \mathbf{hash}(hk, \mathbf{concat}_3(cCode, \mathbf{getName}(bdhandle), cParam))$ **in**

if $\mathbf{check}(\mathbf{concat}_1(cpHa, n_C, N_T, sAttRec), sk_T, comHM)$ **then**

even $TPMAccept(n_C, N_T, sAttRec);$

new $N_T\_next : nonce;$

let $rpHash = \mathbf{hash}(hk, \mathbf{concat}_4(cCode, rCode, rParam)$ **in**

let $resAuth = \mathbf{mac}(\mathbf{concat}_2(rpHash, N_T\_next, n_C, sAttRes), sk_T)$ **in**

event $TPMAcknowledgment(n_C, N_T\_next, sAttRec);$

$\overline{c_{11}[i_T]}(rCode, bdhandle, N_T\_next, sAttRec, recAuth, rParam).$

Fig. 3. Formalization of TPM's actions

$c_{12}[i_C]$. The expected message is $resCode, handle_{bind}, n_T\_next, sAtt, resHM$ and $resParam$. The process checks the first component of this message is $resCode$ by using the pattern $= resCode$, so do the $handle_{bind}, sAtt$ and $resParam$; the two other parts are stored in variables. The process will verify the received acknowledgment $resHM$. If the check succeeds, Q_C executes the event **CallerAccept**$(N_C, n_T\_next, sAtt)$.

In this calculus, executing these events does not affect the execution of the protocol, it just records that a certain program point is reached with certain values of the variables. Events are used for specifying authentication properties, as explained next session. We show the **TPM**'s action in the Figure 3, corresponding to the **Caller**'s action.

3.2   Security Properties

Definition of Authentication. The formal definitions can be found in [6]. The calculus use the correspondence properties to prove the authentication of the participants in the protocols. The correspondence properties are properties of the form if some event has been executed, then some other events also have been executed, with overwhelming probability. It distinguishes two kinds of correspondences, we employ the description from [8] below.

1. A process Q satisfies the non-injective correspondence $\mathbf{event}(e(M_1, ..., M_m))$ $\Rightarrow \bigwedge_{i=1}^{k} \mathbf{event}(e_i(M_{i1}, ..., M_{im_i}))$ if and only if, with overwhelming probability, for all values of the variables in $M_1, ..., M_m$, if the event $e(M_1, ..., M_m)$ has been executed, then the events $e_i(M_{i1}, ..., M_{im_i})$ for $i \leq k$ have also been executed for some values of the variables of $M_{ij}(i \leq k, j \leq m_i)$ not in $M_1, ..., M_m$.
2. A process Q satisfies the injective correspondence $\mathbf{inj\text{-}event}(e(M_1, ..., M_m))$ $\Rightarrow \bigwedge_{i=1}^{k} \mathbf{inj\text{-}event}(e_i(M_{i1}, ..., M_{im_i}))$ if and only if, with overwhelming probability, for all values of the variables in $M_1, ..., M_m$, for each execution of the event $e(M_1, ..., M_m)$, there exist distinct corresponding executions of the events $e_i(M_{i1}, ..., M_{im_i})$ for $i \leq k$ for some values of the variables of $M_{ij}(i \leq k, j \leq m_i)$ not in $M_1, ..., M_m$.

Security Properties of the Authorization. One of the design criterion of the authorization protocol is to allow for ownership authentication. We will formalize these security properties as correspondence properties. Firstly, we give the informal description of the security properties.

1. When the TPM receives a request to use some entity requiring authorization and the HMAC verification has succeeded, then a caller in possession of the relevant $authValue$ has really requested it before.
2. When a caller accepts the acknowledgment and believes that the TPM has executed the command he sent previously, then the TPM has exactly finished this command and sent an acknowledgment.

The first property expresses the authentication of the **Caller** and the second one expresses the authentication of the **TPM**. We can formalize the properties above as injective correspondence properties:

$$\mathbf{inj} : \mathbf{TPMAccept}(x, y, z) \Rightarrow \mathbf{inj} : \mathbf{CallerRequest}(x, y, z). \tag{1}$$

$$\mathbf{inj} : \mathbf{CallerAccept}(x, y, z) \Rightarrow \mathbf{inj} : \mathbf{TPMAcknowledgment}(x, y, z). \tag{2}$$

4   Authentication Results with CryptoVerif

In this section, we will take a brief introduction of CryptoVerif and the assumption used in our model. Then we present security properties directly proven by CryptoVerif under the assumptions in the computational model.

4.1 CryptoVerif

There are two main approaches to the verification of cryptographic protocols. One approach is known as the computational model and another approach, is known as the symbolic or Dalev-Yao model. The CryptoVerif, proposed by Blanchet[4,5,6,7], can directly prove security properties of cryptographic protocols in the computational model. This tool is available on line at:

http://prosecco.gforge.inria.fr/personal/bblanche/cryptoverif/

CryptoVerif builts proofs by sequences of games [19,3]. It starts from the initial game given as input, which represents the protocol to prove in interaction with an adversary (real mode). Then, it transforms this game step by step using a set of predefined game transformations, such that each game is indistinguishable from the previous one. More formally, we call two consecutive games Q and Q' are observationally equivalent when they are computationally indistinguishable for the adversary. CryptoVerif transforms one game into another by applying the security definition of a cryptographic primitive or by applying syntactic transformations. In the last game of a proof sequence the desired security properties should be obvious (ideal mode).

Given a security parameter η, CryptoVerif proofs are valid for a number of protocol sessions polynomial in η, in the presence of an active adversary. CryptoVerif is sound: whatever indications the user gives, when the prover shows a security property of the protocol, the property indeed holds assuming the given hypotheses on the cryptographic primitives.

4.2 Assumptions

We introduce the basic assumptions and cryptographic assumptions adopted by our model and the CryptoVerif as follow.

Basic Assumptions. One of the difficulties in reasoning about authorization such as that of the TPM is non-monotonic state. If the TPM is in a certain state s, and then a command is successfully executed, then typically the TPM ends up in a state $s' \neq s$. Suppose two commands use the same session, the latter must use the nonce generated by the former called $nextnonceTPM$ as the $lastnonceTPM$ when computing the authorization $comAuth$. In other words, the $lastnonceTPM$ in the latter is equal to the $nextnonceTPM$ in the former. CryptoVerif does not model such a state transition system.

We address these restrictions by introducing the assumption described by the S. Delaune $et.al$ [12], such that only one command is executed in each session.

Cryptographic Assumptions. In the analysis of the authorization protocols, the Message Authentication Code (MAC) scheme is assumed to be unforgeable under chosen message attacks (UF-CMA). Symmetric encryption is assumed to be indistinguishable under chosen plaintext attacks (IND-CPA) and to satisfy ciphertext integrity (INT-CTXT). These properties guarantee indistinguishability under adaptive chosen ciphertext attacks (IND-CCA2), as shown in [2].

We assume that the key derivation function is a pseudo-random function and use it to derive, from a key seed, a key for the message authentication code. The key seed is generated from a keying hash function. The keying hash function is assumed to be a message authentication code, weakly unforgeable under chosen message attacks, which is in accordance with [1]. To be specific, we compute the *sessionkey* in a more flexible way, the result of the keying hash function is a *keyseed* and the *sessionkey* is generated from this *keyseed* using a pseudo-random function.

4.3   Experiment Results

Here we present authentication results directly proven in the computational model by CryptoVerif 1.16 under assumptions mentioned above.

Experiment 1: Case of Unbound and Unsalted Session. In this case, we consider a protocol without session key. The attacker can obtain the key handle but cannot get the corresponding *authValue*. The **Caller** and **TPM** will compute the HMAC keyed by *authValue* directly.

But unfortunately, we cannot achieve the injective correspondences between the event **CallerAccept** and **TPMAcknowledgment** in (2) by CryptoVerif directly because of limitations of the prover: it crashes when proving this property. However, it succeeds in the non-injective case, hence we complete this proof by hand.

Lemma 1. *In the protocol based on Unbound and Unsalted Session, if the property:*

$$CallerAccept(NC, nextnT, sAtt) \Rightarrow$$
$$TPMAcknowledgment(nC, nextNT, sAttRec)$$

holds, then we have

$$inj{:}CallerAccept(NC, nextnT, sAtt) \Rightarrow$$
$$inj{:}TPMAcknowledgment(nC, nextNT, sAttRec).$$

Proof. Since the non-injective property succeeds, we can find $i_C \leq N$ such that $N_C[i_C] = n_C[u[i_C]]$, $n_T\_next[i_C] = N_T\_next[u[i_C]]$, $sAtt[i_C] = sAttRec[u[i_C]]$ and $i_T \leq N$ such that $u[i_C] = i_T$.

Suppose that there exists another i'_C and i'_T satisfy the property above, and $u[i'_C] = i'_T$. In order to prove injectivity, It remains to show that the probability of $\{i_T = i'_T, i_C \neq i'_C\}$ is negligible. The equality $i_T = i'_T$, i.e. $u[i_C] = u[i'_C]$, combined with $N_C[i_C] = n_C[u[i_C]]$ and $N_C[i'_C] = n_C[u[i'_C]]$ implies that $N_C[i_C] = n_C[u[i_C]] = n_C[u[i'_C]] = N_C[i'_C]$. Since N_C is defined by restrictions of the large type nonce, $N_C[i_C] = N_C[i'_C]$ implies $i_C = i'_C$ with over-whelming probability, by eliminating collisions. This implies that the probability of $\{i_T = i'_T, i_C \neq i'_C\}$ is negligible. □

With Lemma 1, we prove the injective correspondence properties in (1) and (2) under assumptions of UF-MAC in the MAC scheme and collision resistant in hash function using CryptoVerif.

Experiment 2: Case of Bound Session. We must compute the *sessionkey* bound to an entity in this protocol. According to the authorization entity, there are two kinds of protocols in this experiment. Firstly we consider the session is used to authorize use of the bound entity with an authorization value $authVaule_{bind}$, the HMAC is keyed by *sessionKey*. In another situation, we employ the bound session to access a different entity with an authorization value $authVaule_{entity}$. The *sessionKey* is still bound to the entity with authorization value $authValue_{bind}$ while the HMAC will take the concatenation of *sessionkey* and the $authVaule_{entity}$ as a key.

Providing the MAC scheme assumed to be UF-MAC and hash function in the random oracle model, we prove the injective correspondence properties of two kinds of protocols mentioned above using CryptoVerif.

Experiment 3: Case of Salted Session. This session can be treated as the enhanced version of unbound and unsalted session. Salting provides a mechanism to allow use of low entropy $authValue$ and still maintain confidentiality for the $authVaule$. If the $authValue$ used in an unsalted session has low entropy, the attacker will perform an off-line attack, which is detailed in the TPM 2.0 specification, Part 1 [20].

The *salt* value may be symmetrically or asymmetrically encrypted. In our analysis, We assume an IND-CPA and INT-CTXT probabilistic symmetric encryption scheme is adopted by the participants. We show that this protocol satisfies the injective correspondence properties in (1) and (2) under the assumption of IND-CPA, INT-CTXT and UF-MAC.

Experiment 4: Case of Salted and Bound Session. If the bound entity has a low entropy, it will still be under threat of the off-line attack. This session looks like the enhanced version of bound session. Unlike the bound session only using the authorization value of bound entity to compute the *sessionKey*, this session employs both the $authValue_{bind}$ and the *salt* value. The remaining computation is the same as the bound session and the session also exist two kinds of the protocols.

Nevertheless, we can still prove the injective correspondence properties of two kinds of protocols using CryptoVerif under the assumption of IND-CPA, INT-CTXT and UF-MAC.

As a result, We formalize the experiment results mentioned above as the following theorems. The authentication of **TPM** can be represented as the theorem 1.

Theorem 1. *In the all kinds of authorization protocols, if there is an instance of:*

1. *The TPM received a Caller's command with a request for authorization of some sensitive data,*
2. *The TPM executed this command and the HMAC check in this command has succeeded.*

Then with overwhelming probability, there exists a distinct corresponding instance of:

1. *The Caller is exactly in possession of the authValue of this sensitive data.*
2. *The Caller has exactly send this command with a request for authorization of this sensitive data.*

We formalize the authentication of **TPM** as the following theorem.

Theorem 2. *In the all kinds of authorization protocols, if there is an instance of:*

1. *The Caller received an acknowledgment from the TPM,*
2. *The HMAC check in the response has succeeded and the Caller accepted the acknowledgment.*

Then with overwhelming probability, there exists a distinct corresponding instance of:

1. *The TPM has precisely received the callers request and executed this command,*
2. *The TPM has really send an acknowledgment to the Caller.*

The proof for the Theorem 1 and Theorem 2 in the case of **Salted and Bound Session** used to access the bound entity has been presented in the full version [21] due to the page limitation. But the corresponding upper bounds to break the authentication between the **Caller** and **TPM** can be found in Appendix A. The other cases can be proved in a similar way, so we omit the details because of length constrains.

Note that in the case of **Unbound and Unsalted Session**, CryptoVerif is only able to prove the non-injective correspondence property between the even **CallerAccept** and **TPMAcknowledgment**, but thanks to Lemma 1, we can obtain the results of Theorem 2.

5 Conclusions

We have proved the security of authorization protocols in the TPM 2.0 using the tool CryptoVerif working in the computational model. Specifically, we presented a detailed modelling of the protocols in the probabilistic calculus inspired by the pi calculus. Additionally, we model security properties as correspondence properties. Then we have formalized and mechanically proved these security properties of authorization protocols in the TPM 2.0 using Cryional model.

As future work, we will find out the reason why the prover crashes when proving the injective correspondences between the event **CallerAccept** and event **TPMAcknowledgment** in the protocols based on the **Unbound and Unsalted Sessions** and try to improve the prover to fix it. We will extend our mode with the asymmetric case encrypting the *salt* value. Also, we argue that our model can be adapted to prove the confidentiality using CryptoVerif and it will be our future work.

Acknowledgments. The research presented in this paper is supported by the National Natural Science Foundation of China under Grant Nos. 91118006, 61202414 and the National Grand Fundamental Research 973 Program of China under Grant No. 2013CB338003. We also thank the anonymous reviewers for their comments.

References

1. Bellare, M., Canetti, R., Krawczyk, H.: Keying hash functions for message authentication. In: Koblitz, N. (ed.) CRYPTO 1996. LNCS, vol. 1109, pp. 1–15. Springer, Heidelberg (1996)
2. Bellare, M., Namprempre, C.: Authenticated encryption: Relations among notions and analysis of the generic composition paradigm. In: Okamoto, T. (ed.) ASIACRYPT 2000. LNCS, vol. 1976, pp. 531–545. Springer, Heidelberg (2000)
3. Bellare, M., Rogaway, P.: The security of triple encryption and a framework for code-based game-playing proofs. In: Vaudenay, S. (ed.) EUROCRYPT 2006. LNCS, vol. 4004, pp. 409–426. Springer, Heidelberg (2006)
4. Blanchet, B.: A computationally sound mechanized prover for security protocols. IEEE Transactions on Dependable and Secure Computing 5(4), 193–207 (2008)
5. Blanchet, B.: A Computationally Sound Mechanized Prover for Security Protocols. In: IEEE Symposium on Security and Privacy (SP 2006), pp. 140–154 (2006)
6. Blanchet, B.: Computationally sound mechanized proofs of correspondence assertions. In: CSF 2007, pp. 97–111 (2007)
7. Blanchet, B., Pointcheval, D.: Automated Security Proofs with Sequences of Games. In: Dwork, C. (ed.) CRYPTO 2006. LNCS, vol. 4117, pp. 537–554. Springer, Heidelberg (2006)
8. Blanchet, B., Jaggard, A.D., Scedrov, A., Tsay, J.-K.: Computationally Sound Mechanized Proofs for Basic and Public-Key Kerberos. In: Proceedings of the 2008 ACM Symposium on Information, Computer and Communications Security (ASIACCS 2008), pp. 87–99. ACM (2008)
9. Bruschi, D., Cavallaro, L., Lanzi, A., Monga, M.: Replay attack in TCG specification and solution. In: Proc. 21st Annual Computer Security Applications Conference (ACSAC 2005), pp. 127–137. IEEE Computer Society (2005)
10. Chen, L., Ryan, M.D.: Offine dictionary attack on TCG TPM weak authorisation data, and solution. In: Future of Trust in Computing. Vieweg & Teubner (2009)

11. Chen, L., Ryan, M.: Attack, solution and verification for shared authorisation data in TCG TPM. In: Degano, P., Guttman, J.D. (eds.) FAST 2009. LNCS, vol. 5983, pp. 201–216. Springer, Heidelberg (2010)
12. Delaune, S., Kremer, S., Ryan, M.D., Steel, G.: A formal analysis of authentication in the TPM. In: Degano, P., Etalle, S., Guttman, J. (eds.) FAST 2010. LNCS, vol. 6561, pp. 111–125. Springer, Heidelberg (2011)
13. Delaune, S., Kremer, S., Ryan, M.D., Steel, G.: Formal Analysis of Protocols Based on TPM State Registers. In: Proc. 24th IEEE Computer Security Foundations Symposium (CSF 2011), pp. 66–80 (2011)
14. ISO/IEC PAS DIS 11889: Information technology C security techniques C Trusted Platform Modules
15. Laud, P.: Secrecy Types for a Simulatable Cryptographic Library. In: Proceedings of the 12th ACM Conference on Computer and Communications Security (CCS 2005), pp. 26–35. ACM (2005)
16. Lin, A.H.: Automated Analysis of Security APIs. Masters thesis. MIT (2005), http://groups.csail.mit.edu/cis/theses/amerson-masters.pdf
17. Mitchell, J., Ramanathan, A., Scedrov, A., Teague, V.: A Probabilistic Polynomial-Time Process Calculus for the Analysis of Cryptographic Protocols. Theoretical Computer Science 353(1-3), 118–164 (2006)
18. Shao, J., Feng, D., Qin, Y.: Type-based analysis of protected storage in the TPM. In: Qing, S., Zhou, J., Liu, D. (eds.) ICICS 2013. LNCS, vol. 8233, pp. 135–150. Springer, Heidelberg (2013)
19. Shoup, V.: Sequences of games: a tool for taming complexity in security proofs. Cryptology ePrint Archive, Report 2004/332 (2004), http://eprint.iacr.org/2004/332
20. Trusted Computing Group. TPM Specification version 2.0. Parts 1-4, revision 00.99 (2013), http://www.trustedcomputinggroup.org/resources/tpm_library_specification
21. Wang, W.J., Qin, Y., Feng, D.G.: Automated Proof for Authorization Protocols of TPM 2.0 in Computational Model (full version). Cryptology ePrint Archive (2014), http://eprint.iacr.org/2014/120

A   Proof of Theorem 1 and Theorem 2

A.1   Proof of Theorem 1

Proof. Case of Salted and Bound Session used to access the bound entity: the security properties have proved by CryptoVerif automatically and we refer the readers to full version [21] for the details of proof procedure.

The probability $P(t)$ that an attacker running in time t breaks the correspondence

$$\textbf{inj} : \textbf{TPMAccept}(x,y,z) \Rightarrow \textbf{inj} : \textbf{CallerRequest}(x,y,z)$$

is bounded by CryptoVerif by $P(t) \leq \frac{42.5 \times N^2}{|nonce|} + N \times Pmac(t_{G31} + (N^2 + 2N - 3)t_{check} + (N^2 + 8N - 9)t_{mac} + (N-1)t_{mkgen}, N + 9, N + 3, l) + N \times Pmac(t_{G24} + t + (9N - 9)t_{check} + (3N - 3)t_{mac} + (N-1)t_{mkgen}, 3, 9, l) + Penc(t_{G14} + t, N) + Pencctxt(t_{G11} + t, N, N))$ where N is the maximum number of sessions of the protocol participants, $|nonce|$ is the cardinal of the set of nonces, $Pmac(t, N, N', l)$ is the probability of breaking the UF-CMA property in time t for one key, N MAC queries, N' verification queries for massages of length at most l, $Penc(t, N)$ is the probability of breaking the IND-CPA property in time t and N encryption queries, $Pencctxt(t, N, N')$ is the probability of breaking the INT-CTXT property in time t, N encryption queries, and N' decryption queries, and $t_{G_{11}}, t_{G_{14}}, t_{G_{24}}, t_{G_{31}}$ are bounds on the running time of the part of the transformed games not included in the UF-CMA or INT-CTXT or IND-CPA equivalence, which are therefore considered as part of the attacker against the UF-CMA or INT-CTXT or IND-CPA equivalence, and t_{check}, t_{mac} and t_{mkgen} are the maximal runtime of one call to functions, correspondingly, **check**, **mac** and **mkgen**. The first terms of $P(t)$ comes from elimination of collisions between nonces, while the other terms come from cryptographic transformations.   □

A.2   Proof of Theorem 2

Proof. Similar to the proof of theorem 1, and The probability $P(t)$ that an attacker running in time t breaks the correspondence

$$\text{inj} : \textbf{CallerAccept}(x, y, z) \Rightarrow \text{inj} : \textbf{TPMAcknowledgment}(x, y, z)$$

is bounded by CryptoVerif by $P(t) \leq \frac{6.5 \times N^2}{|nonce|} + N \times Pmac(t_{G_{31}} + (N^2 + 2N - 3)t_{check} + (N^2 + 8N - 9)t_{mac} + (N-1)t_{mkgen}, N+9, N+3, l) + N \times Pmac(t_{G_{24}} + t + (9N - 9)t_{check} + (3N - 3)t_{mac} + (N-1)t_{mkgen}, 3, 9, l) + Penc(t_{G_{14}} + t, N) + Pencctxt(t_{G_{11}} + t, N, N)).$ □

SBE — A Precise Shellcode Detection Engine Based on Emulation and Support Vector Machine

Yonggan Hou[1], J.W. Zhuge[2], Dan Xin[1], and Wenya Feng[1]

Institute for Network Science and Cyberspace, Tsinghua University, China
{yghouforsec,xindan53,pkuwenyafeng}@gmail.com,
zhugejw@cernet.edu.cn

Abstract. An important method of detecting zero-day attacks is to identify the shellcode which is usually taken as part of the attacks. However, the detection range is always restricted, for existent emulation based detection techniques only take several features that are observed when shellcode is emulated. In this paper, we propose a new shellcode detection algorithm based on emulation and Support Vector Machine(SVM). One of the most prominent advantages is that by means of emulating, we can get the real executed path which includes key features to identify shellcode e.g. loop, xor, GetPC etc. Moreover, by recording aforementioned features and training them with SVM, we can rely on general features to detect shellcode rather than on specific features. In addition, we build a complete shellcode data set so that other researchers can focus on detection algorithms. We have implemented a prototype system named SBE on Ubuntu/Amd-64 and tested our algorithm with various kinds of shellcode. Experiment shows that the proposed algorithm has a better detection rate than Libemu and could effectively detect all x86 shellcode with very few false positives.

1 Introduction

Code injection attack has become one of the most prevalent and pernicious attacking methods since it occurred. The detection of code injection attack mainly concentrates on detecting shellcode which serves as a crucial part of attack vector[5]. Moreover, shellcode detection is also an important way to defend against zero-day attack. Significant work that includes both static and dynamic methods have been proposed in recent years to identify shellcode in network traffic.

The existing static detection methods could be easily bypassed by polymorphism[10,14] and more complicated tricks such as metamorphism[20], and the common dynamic detection method such as GetPC Heuristic is not capable of identifying plain shellcode that does not change itself when being executed. In this paper, we first propose a new shellcode detection algorithm based on emulation, then record shellcode information when it is executed, and finally use our SVM engine to classify it. Emulation ensures that the detection is not hindered by shellcode polymorphism and metamorphism; and SVM engine guarantees us

X. Huang and J. Zhou (Eds.): ISPEC 2014, LNCS 8434, pp. 159–171, 2014.

of wide shellcode detection range, for it depends on general features rather than specific features. In addition, we generate a data set which is consisted of various polymorphic shellcode. These shellcodes are encrypted by twenty different shellcode engines[10,14,16,17]. We believe shellcode researchers will benefit a lot from it(Appendix A). The proposed approach is implemented and tested with thousands of polymorphic and plain shellcode. Results show that it could detect all x86 shellcode with an acceptable overhead.

Section 2 describes related work, in section 3, we introduce our new way to detect both plain shellcode and self-decrypting shellcode, and then present methods that could reduce the overhead caused by emulation. Our experiment and analysis are shown in section 4.

2   Related Work

Generally speaking, there are two kinds of shellcode: polymorphic shellcode which will decrypt itself when it is running, and plain shellcode that will never change itself in any case.

There are two common methods to detect shellcode: the static method and the dynamic method. The most widely used static shellcode detection tool is Snort[1], which uses generic signatures such as */bin/sh* string matching and NOP-SLED matching. It could be easily evaded by polymorphism. Stride[2] detects NOP-SLED, which is an important attack vector in code injection. However, in some special cases, NOP-SLED is not necessary. Buttercup[3] tries to detect possible return address ranges of known buffer overflow vulnerabilities, but it brings more false positives and usually is impossible to include all suspectable return addresses. Moreover, static detection method could not effectively handle shellcode that is highly obfuscated.

Zhang[4] proposed an efficient detection method that combines emulation and data flow analysis, but it can not detect shellcode that doesn't contain GetPC code[15]. Polychronaks[5] presented a new shellcode detection method that could identify non-self contained shellcode, but it could not detect shellcode that remain unchanged during the execution. Dynamic shellcode detection methods based on emulation could detect obfuscated shellcode effectively but they were unable to detect plain shellcode. Libemu[24] is an open source shellcode detector that could x86 shellcode using GetPC heuristics and binary backwards traversal(similar to Zhang[4]). However, GetPC heuristic method could detect obfuscated shellcode effectively, but can not detect most plain shellcode that do not contain GetPC coded.

Gene[6] took advantage of shellcode's behavior when resolving kernel32.dll address, Khodaverdi[23] and Feng[22] emphasized on monitoring suspicious system calls. Their methods works well on Windows platform, however, Linux shellcode is beyond their capabilities.

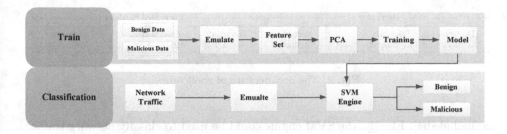

Fig. 1. Overview of the proposed architecture

3 The Proposed Method

In this section, we first present an overview of the method and then give a detailed introduction of data extraction and feature extraction. Feature selection and performance optimization is explained in the next two subsections.

To detect the shellcode effectively in the proposed method, two steps must be achieved efficiently. Firstly the shellcode must be emulated correctly, otherwise it will have a negative influence on the result of the next step. Then in the second step, features must be elaborately selected, for its result will have both high false positives and negatives unless the features are selected accurately.

3.1 Overview of the Proposed Method

Figure 1 illustrates the main parts of SBE architecture. The high level process comprises two stages: train and classification. A brief interpretation is given below and a more detailed description will be illustrated in the following sections.

In the train phrase, data(including both shellcode and benign data) is obtained and labeled first, then it is emulated and all features are recoded before triming redundant features with PCA algorithm, and finally a predictive model is achieved after training procedure. In the classification phrase, network traffic is emulated and classified by SVM engine with the model acquired before.

Network traffic packets will be emulated before further examination. As all static analysis could be bypassed or deceived by advanced polymorphic techniques, emulation is a reliable way to resist shellcode polymorphism or obfuscation[7,8]. According to some suitable modifications, our emulator is able to emulate hard-coded shellcode[6]which could not be emulated by most existing polymorphic shellcode emulators.

The more steps network traffic could be run with, the more shellcode information could be got. Normally, most benign network traffic has a low execution chain[9], it means that most harmless traffic will distinct from malicious traffic. In order to get enough features when shellcode is emulated, we choose all instructions and pick some typical features as initial SVM engine feature set at the beginning, then sufficient features will be chosen and redundant features will be trimmed. It is worth mentioning that some existing common features should

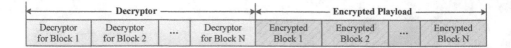

Fig. 2. The architecture of shellcode

be included[4]. Finally, the SVM engine could be used to classify network traffic data that are emulated after train stage.

The reason why we choose SVM instead of NN(Neural Network) is that SVM can achieve a decent detection accuracy while maintaining a better efficiency than NN[27]. Whats more, SVM is less prone to overfitting in practice. We make a comparison between RBF kernel and linear kernel(Appendix 2) to analyze which one we should choose in real deployment and we decide to choose RBF kernel SVM because it outperforms other kernels in practice.

3.2 Data Extraction

In order to achieve a better detection rate, data set should have a wide range and cover most popular shellcodes including plain shellcode and polymorphic shellcode. In this subsection, we introduce how to build our data set so that researchers can focus on algorithm design rather than data collection. The following methods are made for the sake of generating our ample and various shellcodes:

1. All primitive shellcodes are obtained from shell-storm[18] and exploit-db [19], both of which contain various shellcode provided by security researchers and ardent hackers. Besides, open source toolkits such as Metasploit is also adopted to generate shellcode data.

2. Owing to most of the data is plain shellcode, we use some popular shell-code polymorphic engines to encrypt shellcode that is obtained from the first step. These engines are the most popular shellcode engines such as AMDmu-tate[10,14,17] and other seventeen x86 shellcode encoders in Metasploit[16].

3. We make an agent with JSoup[22] to visit Alex Top 500 sites randomly and capture all the data responded by these sites. It makes sense because most of the data is frequently visited by common users. Other benign data is randomly generated, such as ascii data and printable data.

4. A part of the test data is achieved from our honeynet that is deployed in several Chinese universities. These data could guarantee the engines' reliability in real deployment. The other test data is generated from previous encoders by encrypting previous random picked captured data.

All these data(benign or malicious) will be used to generate network streams: malicious data will be used as the payload in a stimulated attack, benign data is going to be adopted in engendering normal network streams that are most likely to arise false positives.

```
00000000  31C9              xor ecx,ecx
00000002  6681E940FF        sub cx,0xff40
00000007  E8FFFFFFFF        call dword 0xb
0000000C  C05E8176          rcr byte [esi-0x7f],0x76
00000010  0E                push cs
00000011  C9                leave
00000012  CB                retf
00000013  EC                in al,dx
00000014  40                inc eax
00000015  83EEFC            sub esi,byte -0x4
00000018  E2F4              loop 0xe
0000001A  E6E1              out 0xe1,al
0000001C  E660              out 0x60,al
0000001E  E3EB              jecxz 0xb
......
```

Fig. 3. Static disassemble code

3.3   Features Extraction

Most plain shellcode do not have many features they are executable, but they still have some features similar to polymorphic shellcode. To be more specific, they would initialize registers and apply *call* or *int* instructions in the process of execution. All features which have been observed and analyzed in the training phrase are added in initial feature set, for the redundancy features will be eliminated by feature selecting procedure.

As illustrated in figure 2, polymorphic shellcode contains two main parts. The first part of the shellcode is a decryptor that could decrypt shellcode dynamically, then follows the encrypted payload of the shellcode. Polymorphic shellcode will decrypt the encrypted part first, then executes the decrypted payload to achieve certain purpose.

We analyze a typical polymorphic shellcode encrypted by *call4_dword_xor* engine in Metasploit, the disassembly code is shown in figure 3 and the real execution chain is illustrated in figure 4. The left column of figure 3 is instructions addresses in hex format, and the middle column shows the instruction codes, the third column shows the disassembled instructions. Figure 4 is the same as figure 3 except that the first column is the emulator's *eip* address.

The shellcode in figure 3, takes advantage of several special tricks which could be described as follows:
(1) Call in the middle of instruction. The disassemble code is altered because call dword 0xb instruction jumps into the middle of itself and instructs the CPU to reinterpret the machine code bytes starting with the call instruction.
(2) GetPC. GetPC is a simple way to get program counter[11]. In figure 4, call dword 0xb instruction will push the return address onto the stack and pop esi instruction will store the return address in *esi* register, this address could be used to compute the encrypted payload address later. Most polymorphic shellcodes contain GetPC code except some non-self-contained shellcodes, as argued by Polychronakis[5].

```
00471002  31C9                   xor ecx,ecx
00471007  6681E940FF             sub cx,0xff40
0047100b  E8FFFFFFFF             call dword 0xb
0047100d  FFC0                   inc eax
0047100e  5E                     pop esi
00471015  81760EC9CBEC40         xor dword [esi+0xe],0x40eccbc9
00471018  83EEFC                 sub esi,0xfffffffc
0047100e  E2F4                   loop 0xfffffff6
00471015  81760EACB5BAA1         xor dword [esi+0xe],0xa1bab5ac
00471018  83EEFC                 sub esi,0xfffffffc
```

Fig. 4. Real execution chain

(3) Loop and Self-decrypting. As the primary goal of polymorphism is to conceal its real code from Intrusion Detection Systems(IDS), self-modifying is an investable part of polymorphic shellcode and using loops is a suitable way to achieve this goal.

There are also some other techniques to encode a polymorphic shellcode[8], and all features of these techniques are applied in SBE feature extraction step. All instructions are added as well, to guarantee that ample runtime information is generated from emulation.

3.4   Feature Selection

As illustrated in figure 1, once initializing our feature set, next step is to filter the useless, and redundant features should be done next. Feature selection could boost SVM engines efficiency and speed. We use PCA algorithm[12] to select ultimate features of recorded information. Before applying PCA algorithm, feature scaling[13] must be done first.

Suppose the training set X is $x^{(1)}x^{(2)}(x^3)...x^{(n)}$. PCA algorithm could be described as below:

(1) Compute covariance matrix of XX^T using follow Eq1(Σ represents covariance , n is origin data dimension, m is translated data dimension):

$$\Sigma = \frac{1}{m} \sum_{n}^{i=1} \left(x^{(i)} \right) \left(x^{(i)} \right)^T \tag{1}$$

(2) Compute eigenvectors of matrix Σ, get a $m \times n$ matrix.
(3) Translate each training data from n dimensions to m dimensions by multiplying them separately.
Overall feature selection flow could be described as:
(1)Try PCA with $k = 4$.
(2)Compute $\Sigma, x^{(1)}, x^{(2)}, x^{(3)},...x^{(m)}$.
(3)If Eq2 is false, continue and add k, else return k value.

```
CommandReturn:
    pop ebx
    xor eax,eax
    push eax
    push ebx
    mov ebx,0x7c8615b5
    call ebx
    xor eax,eax
    push eax
    mov ebx, 0x7c81ca82
    call ebx
GetCommand: ;Define label for location of command string
    call CommandReturn
    db "cmd.exe /c net user PSUser PSPasswd /ADD && net localgroup Administrators /ADD PSUser"
    db 0x00
```

Fig. 5. Example of a hard-coded shellcode

$$\frac{\frac{1}{m}\sum_{i=1}^{m}\left\|x^{(i)} - x_{approx}^{(i)}\right\|^2}{\frac{1}{m}\sum_{i=1}^{m}\left\|x^{(i)}\right\|^2} \leqslant 0.01? \tag{2}$$

where denominator represents total variation in the data, numerator is average squared projection error.

3.5   Performance Optimization

(1)Enhance emulation ability

Some modifications are made to enable SBE to emulate some hard-coded address shellcode, as illustrated in figure 5, 0x7c8615b5 is the address of WinExec in Windows SP2, but the function's address is different in other versions of Windows. Gene[11] and other existing dynamic detector choose to ignore these kinds of shellcode because it is impossible to emulate.

In this paper, we enable the emulation of hard-coded address shellcode by initializing all Windows memory with 0x3c before loading any dlls. 0x3c is the operation code of *ret* instruction, if any shellcode accesses a wrong address of system function, the emulator will just simply call a *ret* instruction and the execution chain will not be interrupted. As is shown in figure 5, two direct address calling instruction will be simply returned.

(2) Trim impossible paths

Network traffic emulation could achieve a decent throughput because most benign traffic will terminate early when emulated. And common traffic often contains privileged instructions, which can't participate in a common shellcode.

Our way to skip illegal paths is quite similar to Polychronakis[5], the principle of which could be described as: if there is a privileged instruction in the execution path but it doesn't contain any control transfer and self-modifying instructions, the path could be skipped. As is illustrated in figure 6, the red path1,2,3,4,5,6 could be escaped because *outsb* is a privileged instruction and these paths do not contain any control transfer or self-modifying instructions.

4   Experiment Evaluation

In order to verify the proposed method, a large number of data including both malicious and benign samples are used to train and test the SVM engine. Since most shellcode detectors are not public available except Libemu, we make a comparison between SBE and Libemu in section 4.2. Result shows that the detection engine is able to detect all kinds of shellcode with few false negatives and zero false positives.

4.1   Data Set

Both benign and malicious data in our data set are uploaded to the internet, and are publicly available now. Moreover, some useful tools which could translate these data to specific format are also included. As there is no existing complete shellcode data set before, this data set will liberate shellcode security researchers from seeking experimental data. The format of the data is c style(looks like $\backslash xf1\backslash x3c$).

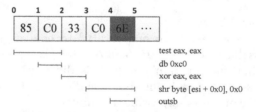

Fig. 6. Illegal instruction path

Name		Description	Size
Benign	Set 1	data that was captured from top 10 site ranked by Alex	1.2G
	Set 2	printable data that is randomly generated	1G
	Set 3	random ascii data	1.2G
	Set 4	Windows and Linux data	5.98G
Malicious	Set 1	plain shellcode obtained from shell-storm, exploit-db and Metasploit	74.3MB
	Set 2	Clet, ADMmuated Tapion encrypting shellcode	381.7MB
	Set 3	Metasploit(17 encoders) encrypting shellcode	906MB

Fig. 7. Data set composition

Name	SBE	Libemu
Clet	100%	99%
ADMmutate	100%	97.5%
Tapion	98.5%	93.5%
MSF Encoders(17)	97.5%	87%
Real	100%	85%
Plain	91.5%	30.2%

Fig. 8. Detection Rate Comparison of SBE and Libemu

Plain shellcode is obtained from shell-storm[18] ,exploit-db[19] and Metasploit[16] toolkit, various range of shellcodes are included, such as port-bind shellcode, connect back shellcode, add-user shellcode, egg-hunt shellcode etc. Then these shellcodes are encrypted by different shellcode encrypting engienes(20 in total).

Benign data could be divided into 4 categories: random ascii data, random printable data, benign network traffic data and Windows and Linux executable data is also included because it is most likely to arouse false positives.

One part of the test data is obtained from the honeynet deployed in TsingHua University and Northeastern University. The other part is achieved from mutated train data and the test data is randomly picked and encrypted by other shellcode engine. figure 7 illustrates the detailed information about data set covering both benign and malicious ones.

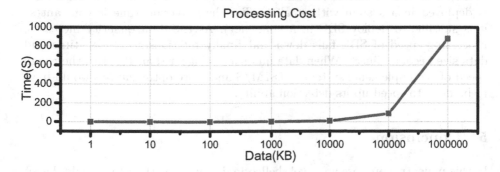

Fig. 9. Overhead caused by SBE

4.2   Detection Rate vs Libemu

We conducted several experiments with SBE and Libemu(an open source shell-code detection library), the results are shown in figure 8.

As it is shown in figure 8, SBE identifies all shellcode encrypted by Clet and ADMmuate while Libemu loses less than 2% of them. The abilities of detecting Tapion shellcode of both detectors are quite similar. The detection rate of Libemu is a little lower in MSF encrypted shellcode detection and we believe that some emulation bugs in Libemu emulator(could not emulate some assembly instructions such as 'movsb') are responsible for the declining after debugging Libemu.

SBE has a prominent advantage of detecting plain shellcode over Libemu, because most plain shellcode doesn't contain GetPC code, which is a basic detecting principle of Libemu.

All benign data that we generated were embedded in six million streams which contained various types such as TCP, UDP, FTP, etc. In both SBE and Libemu, zero false positive was found while detecting ASCII and printable data. Ten http packets and 50 windows binary packets were wrongly identified by Libemu while SBE only mistook zero http packet and one windows binary packet. As a matter of fact, SBE surpasses most of other existing detectors[4, 5, 11] in false positive.

The results prove that SBE is reliable shellcode detection engine which could sensitively discover attacks that contain shellcode and beats Libemu in all aspects.

4.3   Processing Cost

In this section, we evaluate the time cost of the proposed method. The time of loading one shellcode to memory is not included because in most cases, the loading time of network traffic data is negligible. SBE is run on a machine equipped with Ubuntu 12.10, Core i3 2.26GHz CPU and 4GB RAM. Figure 9 shows the speed of SBE dealing with various files.

We could observe that when the data quantity is smaller than 10MB, the overhead of SBE is almost constant(about 0.2s), it also means that when SBE is deployed in a system with small traffic, the detection time is constant(so it is suitable to deploy SBE in a honeynet). As the data quantity increases, processing speed of SBE falls down and finally relationship of cost time and data size becomes linear. When data quantity is bigger than 100MB , the rough speed of the implements system is 0.81M/S and more optimizations would have to be done to speed up its detection ability.

5   Conclusion

In this paper, we propose an novel shellcode detection method that could detect both polymorphic shellcode and plain shellcode and the proposed method is independent of specific shellcode features and more robust than other engines[4,6], and we have implemented a prototype system called SBE on Unbuntu/Amd64. In addtion, we make a complete data set that contains thousands of shellcode encrypted with 20 different public engines, 1.4G in total. We believe this data set will facilitate the data collection work of other security researchers.

The evaluation results have shown that our method is quite promising. SBE has a better detection rate than Libemu and could detect various kinds of shellcode with a considerably low false negatives and no false positives. In addition, the overhead SBE caused is roughly linear so it could achieve a decent performance compared with other methods[4,5].

Future work may focus on further performance optimization of SBE to enhance its data processing ability. In addition, we plan to extend our method to other system architectures which require more emulation supports.

Acknowledgement. This work is supported by National Science and Technology Major Project of China (2012ZX01039-004) and National Natural Science Foundation of China (61003127).

References

1. Roesch, M.: Snort-lightweight intrusion detection for networks. In: Proceedings of the 13th USENIX Conference on System Administration, pp. 229–238 (1999)
2. Akritidis, P., Markatos, E.P., Polychronakis, M., Anagnostakis, K.: Stride: Polymorphic sled detection through instruction sequence analysis. In: Sasaki, R., Qing, S., Okamoto, E., Yoshiura, H. (eds.) Security and Privacy in the Age of Ubiquitous Computing. IFIP AICT, vol. 181, pp. 375–391. Springer, Heidelberg (2005)
3. Pasupulati, A., Coit, J., Levitt, K., Wu, S.F., Li, S., Kuo, J., et al.: Buttercup: On network-based detection of polymorphic buffer overflow vulnerabilities. In: Network Operations and Management Symposium, NOMS 2004, pp. 235–248. IEEE/IFIP (2004)
4. Zhang, Q., Reeves, D.S., Ning, P., Iyer, S.P.: Analyzing network traffic to detect self-decrypting exploit code. In: Proceedings of the 2nd ACM Sympoium on Information, Computer and Communications Security, pp. 4–12 (2007)
5. Polychronakis, M., Anagnostakis, K.G., Markatos, E.P.: Emulation-based detection of non-self-contained polymorphic shellcode. In: Recent Advances in Intrusion Detection, pp. 87–106 (2007)
6. Polychronakis, M., Anagnostakis, K.G., Markatos, E.P.: Comprehensive shellcode detection using runtime heuristics. In: Proceedings of the 26th Annual Computer Security Applications Conference, pp. 287–296 (2010)
7. Song, Y., Locasto, M.E., Stavrou, A., Keromytis, A.D., Stolfo, S.J.: On the infeasibility of modeling polymorphic shellcode. In: Proceedings of the 14th ACM Conference on Computer and Communications Security, pp. 541–551 (2007)
8. Mason, J., Small, S., Monrose, F., MacManus, G.: English shellcode. In: Proceedings of the 16th ACM Conference on Computer and Communications Security, 2009, pp. 524–533 (2009)
9. Tóth, T., Kruegel, C.: Accurate buffer overflow detection via abstract payload execution. In: Wespi, A., Vigna, G., Deri, L. (eds.) RAID 2002. LNCS, vol. 2516, pp. 274–291. Springer, Heidelberg (2002)

10. Detristan, T., Ulenspiegel, T., Malcom, Y., Underduk, M.: Polymorphic shellcode engine using spectrum analysis (2003) Phrack, ed.
11. Polychronakis, M., Anagnostakis, K.G., Markatos, E.P.: Network Level polymorphic shellcode detection using emulation. In: Büschkes, R., Laskov, P. (eds.) DIMVA 2006. LNCS, vol. 4064, pp. 54–73. Springer, Heidelberg (2006)
12. Guyon, I., Elisseeff, A.: An introduction to variable and feature selection. The Journal of Machine Learning Research 3, 1157–1182 (2003)
13. Joachims, T.: Making large scale SVM learning practical (1999)
14. K2. ADMmutate, http://www.ktwo.ca/ADMmutate-0.8.4.tar.gz (2001)
15. Skape. Implementing a custom x86 encoder. Uninformed, 5 (September 2006)
16. Metasploit project (2006), http://www.metasploit.com/
17. Bania, P.: TAPiON (2005), http://pb.specialised.info/all/tapion/
18. Salwan, J.: Shell-storm, http://www.shell-storm.org/
19. Offensive Security. Exploit DB, http://www.exploit-db.com/
20. Szor, P.: The Art of Computer Virus Research and Defense. Addison-Wesley Professional (February 2005)
21. Hedley, J.: Jsoup: Java html parser, ed. (2010)
22. Feng, H.-A.: "Generic shellcode detection," ed: US Patent 8,307,432 (2012)
23. Khodaverdi, J.: Enhancing the Effectiveness of Shellcode Detection by New Runtime Heuristics. International Journal of Computer Science 3, 02–11 (2013)
24. Baecher, P., Koetter, M.: libemu (2009), http://libemu.carnivore.it/
25. Chang, C.-C., Lin, C.-J.: LIBSVM: A library for support vector machines. ACM Transactions on Intelligent Systems and Technology (TIST) 2, 27 (2011)
26. Fan, R.-E., Chang, K.-W., Hsieh, C.-J., Wang, X.-R., Lin, C.-J.: LIBLINEAR: A library for large linear classification. The Journal of Machine Learning Research 9, 1871–1874 (2008)
27. Andrs, P.: The equivalence of support vector machine and regularization neural networks. Neural Processing Letters 15, 97–104 (2002)

Appendix

A   Data Address

All data sets are transformed to C Style and are uploaded to Baidu Yun already, the addresses are listed below:

1.ADMmutate: http://pan.baidu.com/s/15TS7H
2.CLET: http://pan.baidu.com/s/1EHv3A
3.Shell-storm windows shellcode: http://pan.baidu.com/s/1f0ah
4.Shell-storm linux shellcode: http://pan.baidu.com/s/1LLJG
5.MSF Windows Shellcode: http://pan.baidu.com/s/1y2uEy
6.MSF Linux Shellcode: http://pan.baidu.com/s/1gl0u0
7.Alex Data: http://pan.baidu.com/s/1xMylf
8.ASCII Data: http://pan.baidu.com/s/1CF18w
9.Printable Data: http://pan.baidu.com/s/17VJW3

More data will be uploaded later after we finish the format transformation.

B   Kernel Selection

We made a comparison of linear SVM and nonlinear SVM with RBF kernel. We compared LIBSVM[25] and LIBLINEAR[26], the results are shown in table3.

As it is shown in Fig 10, parameters C andare automatically found by a tool called grid.py[25]. Data sets in the table contain same benign samples and different malicious for the reason that it is more intuitive for us to analyze the detection ability of SBE separately. It is clear that Linear SVM is more efficient that RBF-SVM, but it lacks of accuracy. In most cases, SBE will be trained first before it deployed in the real environment and be re-trained to cover new cases. So we choose RBF instead of linear with parameter $C=8$, $\gamma=0.5$.

Data Set	Linear (LIBLINEAR)			RBF (LIBSVM)			
	C	Time(s)	Accuracy	C	γ	Time(s)	Accuracy
Clet	30	0.2	99.1%	8	0.5	0.8	100%
ADMmutate	32	0.1	99.5%	8	0.5	0.4	100%
Tapion	30	1.1	97.6%	6	0.7	2.0	99%
MSF Encoders(17)	31	1.6	94%	10	0.6	4.0	98%
Captured Data	31	1.2	91%	7	0.4	2.2	93%
Plain	32	0.5	98%	8	0.5	1.3	100%

Fig. 10. Comparison between linear SVM and RBF SVM

HDROP: Detecting ROP Attacks
Using Performance Monitoring Counters

HongWei Zhou[1,2,3], Xin Wu[1,2], WenChang Shi[1,2],
JinHui Yuan[3], and Bin Liang[1,2]

[1] Key Laboratory of Data Engineering and Knowledge Engineering,
Ministry of Education, Beijing, China
[2] School of Information, Renmin University of China, Beijing, China
[3] Information Engineering University, Zhengzhou, China

Abstract. Combining short instruction sequences originated only from existing code pieces, Return Oriented Programming (ROP) attacks can bypass the code-integrity effort model. To defeat this kind of attacks, current approaches check every instruction executed on a processor, which results in heavy performance overheads. In this paper, we propose an innovative approach, called HDROP, to detecting the attacks. It utilizes the observation that ROP attacks often make branch predictor in modern processors fail to determine the accurate branch destination. With the support of PMC (Performance Monitoring Counters) that is capable of counting performance events, we catch the abnormal increase in branch mis-prediction and detect the existence of ROP attacks. In HDROP, each basic unit being checked consists of hundreds of instructions rather than a single one, which effectively avoids significant performance overheads. The prototype system we developed on commodity hardware shows that HDROP succeeds in detecting ROP attacks, and the performance tests demonstrate that our approach has acceptably lower overheads.

Keywords: ROP, misprediction, branch, performance monitoring counters.

1 Introduction

ROP(Return Oriented Programming) is a kind of code-reuse attack technique which constructs the exploits by combining short instruction sequences only originating from the existing binaries code. Without injecting any new component, it can circumvent the protection provided by current code-integrity efforts including W⊕X, NICKLE[1] and Secvisor[2], etc. Furthermore, the adversary is able to perform Turing-complete computation with ROP technology, and ROP has been a practical attack technique to subvert computer system.

The first ROP attack is proposed in 2007[3], it chains some gadgets together which are the short instruction sequences ending with *ret* instruction. Gadgets are the essential units for ROP attack. Therefore, a feasible prevention idea is to make it difficult to identify gadgets in the available code-bases. Following

X. Huang and J. Zhou (Eds.): ISPEC 2014, LNCS 8434, pp. 172–186, 2014.

this idea, an approach to build *ret*-less software is presented[4]. However, to avoid the reliance on *ret* instruction, JOP(Jump Oriented Programming)[6,7] is proposed which launches attack using gadgets ending with *jmp* instruction instead of *ret* instruction. Meanwhile, some improved ROP techniques that are able to automatically construct ROP exploits are presented[8,9].

ROP prevention solutions can be divided into two main categories. One is to defeat ROP attacks by eliminating the available gadgets in the code-base[4,5]. G-free[5] is a typical approach which focus on removing the gadgets from the intended and unintended code-base. It wipes off the unintended instructions by aligning the instructions with a code-rewriting technology and protects the existing *ret* and indirect *jmp/call* instruction with the another approach. Thus, the adversary fails to find the available gadgets in the new code-base to launch ROP attack.

The other is to detect ROP attacks on the abnormity introduced by its execution[13,14,15]. ROPdefender[13] checks the destination of every *ret* instruction, because ROP misuse *ret* instruction to transfer the control from one gadget to the next gadget. Other researches follow a similar method. However, these solutions are usually implemented on the binary instrumentation framework such as pin[19] or Valgrind[20]. With the support of binary instrumentations, they check each executing instruction to detect the special abnormity. As a consequence, they all incur a heavy performance overhead from 2x to 5.3x times slower.

In this paper, we focus on how to detect ROP attacks, and propose a novel solution called HDROP(Hardware-based solution to Detect ROP attack) which is capable of detecting ROP attacks without significant performance overheads. Unlike existing solutions, HDROP takes hundreds of instructions as a basic checking unit rather than a single one. Thus, the monitor is not necessary to be frequently trapped in. Consequently, it is able to reduce the performance overhead induced by the context-switches between monitoring objects and detecting mechanism.

Our approach is on the following observation. It is well known that modern processors utilize branch predictor to improve their performance. However, ROP attacks often make it fail to predict the right branch target. The cause is that ROP attacks break the normal execution for transferring the control from one gadget to the next, which makes branch targets sharply different from the original ones. Therefore, HDROP detects ROP attacks by our new idea that if there is an abnormal increase of misprediction on the given execution path, it maybe introduce a ROP attack.

To catch mispredictions and other interesting processor events, HDROP utilizes the capabilities supported by the hardware PMC(Performance Monitoring Counters) which is available on the Intel processor[16]. PMC holds some hardware counters to count the processor performance events including retired instruction, executed *ret* instruction and so on. With the support of PMC, we build a misprediction profile for the monitored execution path, and expose the abnormal increase of misprediction introduced by ROP attacks.

Our prototype system is developed on Fedora 5 with a 2.6.15-1 kernel. At first, HDROP collected the related data by inserting thousands of checkpoints into the kernel utilizing a compiler-based approach. Then, it catched the abnormal increase of misprediction and detected ROP attacks on the prepared data. To validate the effectiveness of HDROP, we have constructed a ROP rootkit with the approaches introduced by [3] and [7]. Our experiments show that HDROP is capable of detecting ROP attack. Furthermore, we have implemented the performance tests on commodity hardware and the results demonstrate that HDROP has acceptable lower performance overheads.

The rest of the paper is organized as follows. Section 2 and section 3 present our design and implementation of HDROP respectively, followed by the evaluation of HDROP in section 4. The discussion of our solution is detailed in section 5. Section6 surveys related work and section 7 concludes this paper.

2   Design

In our design, there are three main challenges to be overcome. First, what are our interesting performance events? PMC is capable of monitoring a variety of processor performance events, and we need to identify those which are closely helpful to detect ROP attack. Second, how to collect the data from the hardware counters(e.g. PMC) for the further detection? Ideally, they should be collected without the heavy overhead. Third, how to design detecting algorithm. In this paper, we construct the algorithm on a balance between the accuracy and the performance overhead. The solutions will be discussed in detail in the following subsections.

2.1   Interesting Performance Event

BR_RET_MISSP_EXEC[16] is our first interesting performance event. More specifically, BR_RET_MISSP_EXEC means that hardware counter records the number of mispredicted executed *ret* instructions[16]. By catching it, we are able to detect ROP attacks on an abnormal increase of mispredicted *ret* instructions. It is noted that HDROP is designed to detect ROP attacks that utilize the gadgets ending with *ret* instruction in this paper. If detecting JOP attacks[6,7], we should identify other processor performance events, and we consider it as our future work.

There is a distinction between executed instruction and retired instruction. An executed instruction may not be a retired instruction. In other words, more executed instructions are counted than actual retired instructions on the same execution. Ideally, BR_RET_MISSP_RETIRED should be our interesting event. However, we fail to identify the expected performance event. To resolve this issue, we utilize BR_RET_MISSP_EXEC as the alternative, but this does not weaken the capability of detecting ROP attacks.

The number of executed *ret* instruction is also our interesting data. It is considered as the necessary data for accurately detecting ROP attacks. With the different input, there are different execution paths on the same monitored instructions. To detect the abnormal increase of mispredicted *ret* instructions for the given monitored instructions, we have to generate the baseline for each path. In more serious cases, the baseline may be submerged by "noise". However, if we obtain the number of executed *ret* instructions at the same time, it is more easy to identify the execution path than before. Furthermore, it is feasible to detect ROP attacks with several baselines. Therefore, BR_RET_EXEC is another interesting performance events which counts the number of executed *ret* instructions[16].

At last, we pay close attention to the number of the retired instructions. As mentioned earlier, our solution takes hundreds of instructions as a basic checking unit. So we want to know the number of the retired instructions on the checked execution path. With the number, we are able to know the length of our monitoring execution path, and the frequency that HDROP trap in at the checking time. The performance event is denoted as INST_RETIRED.ANY_P[16].

2.2   Collecting Data

Figure 1 demonstrates our scheme collecting data for monitored instructions. To prepare the data for the detection, we insert some CPs(Checking Points) into the software. These CPs scatter in the software, and read the hardware counters for collecting their current values, and log the values for further detection. To the end, there are two CPs located around the monitored instructions. As shown in figure 1, CP_1 reports $reading_1$, and CP_2 reports $reading_2$. Thus, $reading_2$ minus $reading_1$ is the prepared data for checking the monitored instructions A.

In our design, reported reading of every CP can be utilized many times. As shown in figure 1, monitored instructions A are adjacent to monitored instructions B. Therefore, CP_2 is not only considered as the exit of monitored instructions A, but also the entry of monitored instructions B. Thus, $reading_2$ is used twice as $reading_2$ minus $reading_1$ and $reading_3$ minus $reading_2$. Note that not every reading is used many times because the monitored instructions are not always adjacent to each other.

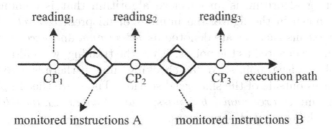

Fig. 1. An example of collecting data

Ideally, every entry and exit of the monitored instructions should be accompanied with one CP. With the above example, CP_1 and CP_2 should be located at the entry and exit of monitored instructions A respectively. However, it is impossible to accurately deploy CPs as we expect, because we often have not overall information of CFG(Control Flow Graph). Therefore, it maybe have some entries and exits of monitored instructions uncovered by CPs. We maybe fail to monitor some execution paths because no CPs collect the values of the hardware counters. To address the above problem, it seems as a feasible solution by reducing monitored instructions. However, there is a balance between the performance overhead and the length of monitored instructions. Let's imagine two extreme cases. First, the monitoring object only hold one or several instructions. However, the checker is trapped frequently, and this incurs a high performance slowdown as existing solutions. On the other hand, locating only several CPs in entire software is also not recommended because the introduced abnormity is easy to be submerged by "noise".

In our opinion, a function can be considered as the ideal basic monitoring unit. Suppose that we have known the number of mispredicted *ret* instructions of every subfunctions, the abnormity occurred in the parent function is easy to be captured. Two causes contribute to it. First, a function seldom has hundreds subfunctions. In other words, the sum of *ret* instructions is usually no more than one hundred. Second, not every *ret* instruction issues one BR_RET_MISSP_EXEC. Note that the proposed approach is recursive, we have to monitoring every subfunction before monitoring their parent. On the other hand, it is possible to take several functions as a monitoring unit if these functions incur few mispredictions. Thus, we can reduce the performance overhead further.

2.3   Detecting Algorithm

The goal of detecting algorithm is distinguishing the abnormality from "noise". To the end, the direct way is the classification algorithms. For example, we can use ANN(Artificial Neural Networks) as detecting algorithm. First, we define two categories including normality and abnormity to be classified. Then ANN is trained to recognize two classes at the training time, and output the likelihood of ROP attacks in the checking time. However, in this paper, we do not utilize it as our detecting algorithm because of its heavy performance overhead.

Our detecting algorithm is an effective algorithm that is demonstrated in figure 2. As shown in the figure, the number of mispredicted *ret* instructions and executed *ret* instructions are denoted as $missp\_num$ and $exec\_num$, and the prepared data are denoted as the points. After the training, we build a shadowed section to hold all legal points. At the checking time, if there is a ROP attack, the point locates outside of the shadowed section. There are the simple formula for the algorithm: $a * exec\_num + b < missp\_num < a * exec\_num + b + c$ where a, b and c are the computed parameters.

We first explain the parameter c. Usually, ROP attacks need about 5-10 gadgets[3,7,8]. Some existing detecting approaches consider that 3-5 gadgets contribute to ROP attacks[14,15]. In this paper, we regard the number as 5 which is denoted as c shown in figure 2. It means that most of ROP attacks increase the number of mispredicted *ret* instructions by 5. For example, assuming

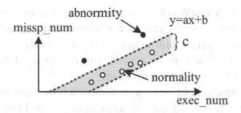

Fig. 2. An example of detecting algorithm

that the number of mispredicted *ret* instructions is 3 in the normal execution, there maybe a ROP attack if the number is more than 8 at the running time. In essence, our detecting algorithm is to identify a narrow-region to only hold all legal points whose width is less than parameter c.

We compute parameter a and parameter b on the training data. At the training time, we collect the number of mispredicted *ret* instructions and executed *ret* instructions. In this way, we get some legal points as shown in figure 2. Meanwhile, we know the possible illegal points since we have known the legal points. On the training data, we compute parameter a and b to build an expected section as shown in figure 2. The section must hold all legal points, but any illegal point. Note that the section does not always exist. In the scenario, the legal points and illegal points are mixed, and no section hold all legal points whose width is less than parameter c. To overcome it, we have to adjust the location of CPs, and reduce the length of monitored instructions. In an extreme case, we only monitor a function without any subfunctions by narrowing the length of monitored instructions, thus we absolutely obtain the section.

3 Implementation

We have implemented a prototype of HDROP on fedora 5 with a 2.6.15-1 kernel. Though most of ROP attacks are in the user space, [4] and [8] demonstrates the feasibility of developing ROP rootkit in the kernel-space. Moreover, [4] proposes a practicable defense technology to defeat ROP attacks. Like the above work, we have developed HDROP to check ROP attacks in the kernel-space in this paper. However, we believe that HDROP can be easily ported for detecting ROP attacks in the user-space.

HDROP consist of some CPs and a DU(Decision Unit). To collect data, we insert thousands of CPs into the kernel with a compiler-based approach, and every CP sends the readings of hardware counters to DU. DU is developed as a loadable module, and it activates the CPs in the kernel with a CP-map at the loading time. HDROP is capable of customizing the monitoring objects with the configured CP-map. At the training time, DU logs the collecting data to compute the parameters of the detecting algorithm. At the running time, it performs the final checking along the detecting algorithm.

In our implementation, the main challenge is to insert thousands of CPs into the kernel. Our solution is developing a *gcc* plug-in that dynamically inserts two CPs around each *call* instruction. More specifically, we rewrite the machine-described file that is used as the guider for generating assembly code, and ask *gcc* to insert the new instructions before and after each *call* instruction. The instruction call the CPs function to report the readings of hardware counters. Thus, we can monitor the execution of a function.

Figure 3 shows an example of our approach. Assume that we want to monitor function F_B, we insert two additional instructions around the *call* instruction in function F_A, which is shown as *call F_B* in figure 3. The inserted instruction is a five-byte call instruction which is shown as shadowed pane in the figure. Thus, CPs collect the readings of hardware counters before and after the execution of function F_B. We redirect the kernel control flow to our code for collecting readings of hardware counters.

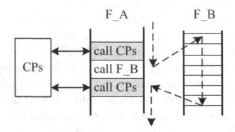

Fig. 3. An example of inserting CPs. The shadowed panes are the inserted instructions, and function F_B is the monitored object. The dashed line indicates original execution path, while the solid line shows appended execution path after CPs inserting into the kernel.

Some readers may wonder that why we place the CPs around each *call* instruction? Our original intention is to build a function-granularity monitoring framework. To the end, as shown in figure 3, one CP is inserted at the entry of the function, and the other is inserted at the exit. Before CPs are inserted, the execution path is shown by the dashed line in figure 3. After CPs are installed, two additional executions are introduced which are indicated by the solid line in figure 3. Moreover, with a configurable CP-map, it is flexible to monitor the different functions. In this way, HDROP is able to cover most of kernel execution path. Of course, there are some feasible solutions to insert CPs into the kernel with the same goal. For example, we can insert the CPs at the beginning and end of every function, which is considered it as an alternative scheme.

4   Evaluation

4.1   Effectiveness

To validate the effectiveness of our solution, we had constructed a ROP rootkit guided by the approaches introduced by [3] and [7]. The rootkit waved six gadgets together that ends with *ret* instruction. Moreover, it did not reach any malicious end, and only transfer the control from one gadget to next gadget for incrementing one word in the memory. We launched the rootkit in two ways. First, the kernel stack was overwritten to redirect kernel control flow to the rootkit. Second, kernel control data was modified for hijacking kernel control flow.

We had performed two experiments to show the effectiveness of HDROP. In the first test, we had built a tested module that listed the running processes in the kernel, and customized the CP-map to insert two CPs at the entry and exit of the monitored function, which scanned *task_struct* list to enumerate the running processes in the kernel. At the training time, we caught the data for computing the parameters of detecting algorithm. After that time, we launched the ROP rootkit, and HDROP is able to detect the attack with the abnormal increase on the number of mispredicted *ret* instructions.

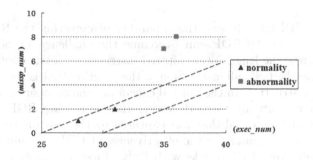

Fig. 4. The experiment monitoring a function in the module

Figure 4 shows the result of our first experiment. Every point in figure 4 means a two-tuples (missp_num,exec_num) where missp_num means the number of mispredicted *ret* instructions and exec_num is the number of executed *ret* instructions. For example, (1,28) means that normal execution took 1 mispredicted *ret* instruction and 28 executed *ret* instructions. If the ROP attack was launched, the number of mispredicted *ret* instructions was increased. As an example, the point (8,36) was abnormal which was denoted as a square in the figure. In the first test, the monitored execution path was simple, and HDROP was easy to detect the ROP rootkit.

In the second experiment, HDROP placed two CPs around an indirect call instruction in kernel function *real_lookup*. HDROP recorded the data when the ROP rootkit was or not loaded in the kernel by modifying the destination of the indirect call instruction. The data, including the number of mispredicted *ret* instruction and executed *ret* instruction, were also taken as a point in figure 5. Like figure 4, a legal point denotes as a triangle, while a illegal point as a square in figure 5. Moreover, figure 5 only shows the part of obtained data of HDROP for a better exhibition. As shown in figure 5, these points were mixed together, and we failed to identify a narrow-region to just hold all legal points. It meant HDROP failed to detect ROP rootkit with the deployed CPs.

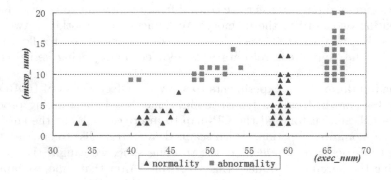

Fig. 5. The experiment monitoring a kernel function

Fortunately, HDROP still had the capability of detecting the ROP rootkit. As mentioned earlier, HDROP can overcome the challenge by adjusting the CP-map to narrow the length of monitored instructions. Thus another CP was implanted before the first call instruction in the function that is the target of the monitored call instruction. In the normal execution, the number of mispredicted *ret* instruction was usually zero. However, after launching ROP rootkit, the number abnormally increased that was captured by the new inserted CP.

The above tests demonstrator the effectiveness of HDROR, and indicate the feasibility of detecting ROP attacks with PMC. First, the rootkit is developed following by [3],[4] and [8]. Second, the monitored objects include a kernel function and a module function. At last, we launch the ROP rootkit by modifying kernel data which is a main way to subvert the kernel. In the future, we will perform more experiments to show its effectiveness. Since there are some existing ROP shellcodes in the user-space, to check further its effectiveness, we might improve HDROP for working in the user-space.

4.2 Performance

The second set of experiments is to measure the performance overhead of HDROP. The benchmark programs was UnixBench of version 4.1.0[17], and the tested OS was fedora 5 with 2.6.15-1 Linux kernel, and the hardware platform was Intel X200. We had implemented our tests as follows. First, UnixBench run with default setting in the clear kernel, and recorded the final score of UnixBench. Second, UnixBench run again while HDROP was installed in the kernel, and recorded the final score. At last, we computed the performance slowdown of HDROP.

Figure 6 shows the performance overhead of HDROP with 3000 CPs inserted into the kernel. To make our result precise, we repeated the test 5 times and took the average as the score. The performance overhead of eleven tasks of UnixBench are shown in figure 6. The task, called file read, incurred the maximal performance overhead that was about 38%. On the other hand, the runtime

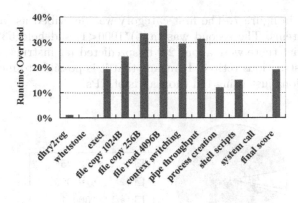

Fig. 6. Performance overhead of HDROP with 3000 CPs in the kernel

overhead of Dhrystone and Whetstone was almost zero. On the final score of UnixBench, the average slowdown of HDROP was about 19%.

How many CPs should be inserted into the kernel? In our opinion, the number is no more than ten thousands against one assumption. We suppose that the running kernel only hold several modules. To cover the dynamically loaded modules, it is inevitable to place more CPs in the kernel. Moreover, OS often loads different modules at the different time. So it is difficult to accurately estimate the number of CPs if we want to cover all loadable modules. To make the discussion clear, we optimistically suppose that the kernel only load few modules without introducing additional CPs.

With the above assumption, we had performed following experiments to show that several thousands CPs is able to cover the kernel. First, we caught the number of the retired instructions while HDROP was detecting ROP attack. We had performed our test based on the first experiment that was discussed in the above subsection. We reset the hardware counter, and made it count the number of retired instructions. What to be clarified was that the data was obtained after HDROP detecting the ROP rootkit. The cause was that our tested processor had only two hardware counters. At the detecting time, two counters were busy to catch BR_RET_MISSP_EXEC and BR_RET_EXEC. Therefore, the number of retired instructions was obtained by repeating the test without catching BR_RET_MISSP_EXEC. In the tests, we observed that HDROP monitored about four hundreds instructions with only two CPs. In other words, HDROP is able to take hundreds of instructions as the basic monitoring unit because BR_RET_MISSP_EXEC does not frequently occur.

To further validate our above idea, we had performed the other experiments that monitored the execution of system calls. We placed two CPs around the instruction *call *sys_call_table* to collect the number of retired instructions and executed mispredicted *ret* instructions. In the test, we had catched 35802 items. Every item can be denoted as $\{a,b\}$, where a was the number of executed mispredicted *ret* instructions and b was the number of retired instructions. According to the proportion of a to b, these items were divided into three categories that was shown in figure 7. The first category was described as (a/b)*1000>5, and held 2113 items. The second was (a/b)*1000<1, and held 532 items. The test indicated that there were about 2.9 mispredicted *ret* instructions while one thousand *ret* instructions retired. It means that it is possible to monitor several million instructions just using ten thousands of CPs.

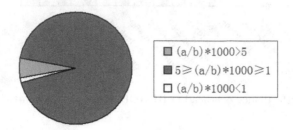

Fig. 7. Three categories divided against the proportion of *a* to *b* where a is the number of retired instructions and *b* is the number of executed mispredicted *ret* instructions

At last, we had performed another test to demonstrate the performance overhead of HDROP when different CPs are inserted into the kernel. In our opinion, there are some factors severely impacting on performance overhead of HDROP. First is the number of active CPs in the kernel, and second is the locality of active CPs. To make our result precise, we randomly built CP-map which indicated the number and locality of active CPs, and repeated the test with different number of CPs in the kernel. The number of inserted CPs was from 500 to 6000. As shown in figure 8, when 1000 CPs were inserted into the kernel, HDROP incurred a 7% slowdown. If there were 6000 active PCs in the kernel, HDROP introduced 31% performance overhead. Compared to existing solutions[13,14,15], the performance overhead of HDROP is acceptable.

5   Discussion

There are some security assumptions for HDROP. First, the kernel, including HDROP, is in the code-integrity. Otherwise, attackers can circumvent HDROP by tampering with the code. Since some security mechanisms are available[1,2], we believe this assumption is reasonable. Second, PMC is protected from malicious modifying. It is possible to tamper with the hardware counters to forge the readings. However, attackers have to do that with some crafting gadgets, and it make more difficult to identify the gadgets. Therefore, we optimistically suppose that PMC is immune to ROP attack. In this paper, we suppose a adversary is capable of modifying the kernel data to launch ROP attacks, which include return addresses, function pointers and so on.

Meanwhile, HDROP has some limitations. First, HDROP may send a false alarm. The parameters of detecting algorithm are computed on the training data.

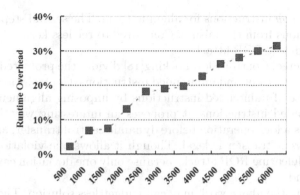

Fig. 8. Performance overhead of HDROP with different CPs in the kernel

So it is possible to take a legal execution as ROP attack for unfull coverage. Second, we fail to automatically generate the CP-map for covering the whole kernel. We are seeking a more appropriate detecting algorithm. At last, HDROP is not capable of detecting JOP. We believe it is easy to improve HDROP by identifying the new interesting performance events. To overcome the above limitations is our future work.

A novel contribution of our work is to demonstrate the feasibility of detecting ROP attacks with the support of PMC. More specifically, we not only propose a novel practical solution of checking ROP attacks, but also present a new usage of PMC. Furthermore, unlike existing software-based solutions, HDROP takes hundreds of instructions as a basic checking unit rather than a single one. Thus, HDROP does not incur a heavy performance overhead from 2x to 5.3x timer slower.

6   Related Work

In 2007, Hovav Shacham presents ROP attack[3], which is further generalized to a variety of platforms[10,12]. Meanwhile, there have been many efforts to defeat ROP attacks. As mentioned earlier, they are proposed in two categories, which are called gadget-less solution and abnormity-detecting solution. They are closely related to our work, and we introduce them as follows.

6.1   Gadget-Less Solution

ROP attacks depend on the crafted gadgets from the available code-base. Therefore, some solutions are proposed to kill the gadgets hiding in the code-base. A compiler-based way is presented to build a ret-less kernel[4]. They systematically replace *ret* instruction with other instructions while the kernel is recompiled. Thus, the gadgets is hard to be found in the patched kernel.

G-Free[5] proposes a novel two-step approach to build no-gadget software. The first step is to terminate all unintended *ret* and indirect *jmp* instructions by padding several *nop* instructions for aligning them. The second step is to protect aligned instructions from the misuse. Compared to ret-less kernel[4], G-Free is a generic way to defeat ROP attack.

Similar to G-Free, Control-Flow Locking[18] divides the protected instructions into intended instructions and unintended instructions. Control-Flow Locking removes the misuse of unintended instructions by imposing alignment artificially. To protect intended instructions, it proposes an interesting way. More specifically, it performs a lock operation before dynamic control transfer, and an unlock operation if current transfer is legal. Though it allows one violation of CFG, it still capable of defeating ROP attacks because only one deviation can not achieve the malicious end.

In our opinion, the above work may call gadget-less solution. Their main goal is generating a gadget-less code-base to eliminate ROP attacks. Beside that, they have presented the different ways to protect control transfer for defeating ROP attacks further. These work are considerable interesting, but our work is completely different from them for we detecting ROP attacks with the abnormity introduced by the attacks.

6.2   Abnormity-Detecting Solution

ROP attacks have some unique features. For example, ROP attacks often chain several gadgets ending with *ret* instruction[3]. Moreover, every gadget is a short instruction sequence, and it usually ranges from two to five instructions. Therefore, DynIMA[14] records the length of the instructions between two *ret* instructions. If it is a short instruction sequence, DynIMA[14] considers it as a "hit". DynIMA reports ROP attacks occurring if there are consecutively "hit". DynIMA is partly implemented with the support of the PIN[19].

DROP[15] is a binary instrument tool to detect ROP attack. DROP[15] shares the same observation with DynIMA[14]. However, it has developed a prototype system, and the experiments show its effectiveness. But it incurs a heavy performance overhead because it has to check every instruction for recording the length of instructions between two *ret* instructions. Moreover, the adversary may enlarge the length of the gadget, which makes them bypass DROP.

ROPDefender[13] detects ROP attacks on the side effect introduced by the execution. As mentioned earlier, some ROP attacks wave the gadgets together which end with *ret* instruction. Thus, the *call* and *ret* instruction are not paired. On the observation, ROPDefender[13] maintains a shadow stack to identify every *ret* instruction. More specifically, it monitors every executing instruction, and stores a copy of the return addresses in the shadow stack for identifying the misused *ret* instructions. Similar to DynIMA[14], ROPDefender is implemented on the binary instrumentation framework PIN[19].

kBouncer[21] presents an efficient ROP mitigation technology. It only monitors the last part of control transfers that lead to system call execution. In this way, it avoids monitoring all control transfer which may introduce a high performance overhead. It is on the observation that most of ROP attacks eventually perform a system call. Moreover, it considers that the control transfer on *ret* instruction is abnormal without paired *call* instruction. Furthermore, it is a hardware-based work with the support of LBR(Last Branch Recording)[16]. However, not all ROP attacks will perform a system call. Therefore, it is possible to be circumvented.

HDROP is proposed on the novel observation: ROP attacks induce an abnormal increase on the number of mispredicted *ret* instructions. Moreover, HDROP does not monitor each executing instruction, and it induces less performance overhead. Compared to some existing approaches, the performance overhead of HDROP is acceptable.

7 Conclusion

The HDROP we propose in this paper is a low-cost hardware-based approach to detecting ROP attacks. The observation behind our approach is straightforward and effective: ROP attacks lead to increase in mis-prediction. Unlike previous detection approaches, we take one or several functions as the basic monitoring unit, not every instruction. Furthermore, HDROP utilizes PMC to collect interested data to monitor a large body of instructions. Consequently, it greatly reduces performance overhead. We have developed a prototype system on fedora 5. Experiments show that our approach can effectively detect ROP attacks with an acceptable performance overhead.

Acknowledgment. The authors would like to thank the anonymous reviewers for their insightful comments that helped improve the presentation of this paper. The work is supported in part by the National Natural Science Foundation of China (61070192, 91018008, 61170240,61303074), National 863 High-Tech Research Development Program of China (2007AA01Z414), National Science and Technology Major Project of China (2012ZX01039-004), CNITSEC Program (CNITSEC-KY-2012-001/4), and Natural Science Foundation of Beijing (4122041).

References

1. Riley, R., Jiang, X., Xu, D.: Guest-Transparent Prevention of Kernel Rootkits with VMM-based Memory Shadowing. In: Proceedings of the 11th International Symposium on Recent Advances in Intrusion Detection (2008)
2. Seshadri, A., Luk, M., Qu, N., et al.: SecVisor: A Tiny Hypervisor to Provide Lifetime Kernel Code Integrity for Commodity OSes. In: Proceedings of the 21st ACM Symposium on Operating Systems Principles (October 2007)
3. Shacham, H.: The geometry of innocent flesh on the bone: Return-into-libc without function calls (on the x86). In: Proceedings of the 14th ACM Conference on Computer and Communications Security (2007)
4. Li, J., Wang, Z., Jiang, X., Grace, M., Bahram, S.: Defeating return-oriented rootkits with return-less kernels. In: Proceedings of the 5th ACM SIGOPS EuroSys Conference (2010)

5. Onarlioglu, K., Bilge, L., Lanzi, A., et al.: G-free: Defeating return-oriented programming through gadget-less binaries. In: Proceedings of the 26th ACSAC (2010)
6. Checkoway, S., Davi, L., Dmitrienko, A., et al.: Return-oriented programming without returns. In: Proceedings of the 17th CCS (2010)
7. Bletsch, T., Jiang, X., Freeh, V.W., et al.: Jump-oriented programming: A new class of code-reuse attack. In: Proceedings of the 6th ACM Symposium on Information, Computer and Communications Security (2011)
8. Hund, R., Holz, T., Freiling, F.: Return-oriented rootkits: Bypassing kernel code integrity protection mechanisms. In: Proceedings of USENIX Security 2009. USENIX (August 2009)
9. Chen, P., Xing, X., Mao, B., et al.: Automatic construction of jump-oriented programming shellcode (on the x86). In: Proceedings of 6th ASIACCS (2011)
10. Buchanan, E., Roemer, R., Shacham, H., et al.: When good instructions go bad: Generalizing return-oriented programming to RISC. In: Proceedings of the 15th ACM Conference on Computer and Communications Security (2008)
11. Checkoway, S., Feldman, A.J., Kantor, B., et al.: Can DREs provide long-lasting security? the case of return-oriented programming and the AVC Advantage. In: Proceedings of EVT/WOTE (2009)
12. Kornau, T.: Return oriented programming for the arm architecture. Technical report (2010)
13. Davi, L., Sadeghi, A.-R., Winandy, M.: ROPdefender: A detection tool to defend against return-oriented programming attacks. Technical Report HGI-TR-2010-001 (2010)
14. Davi, L., Sadeghi, A.R., Winandy, M.: Dynamic integrity measurement and attestation: Towards defense against return-oriented programming attacks. In: Proceedings of 4th STC (2009)
15. Chen, P., Xiao, H., Shen, X., Yin, X., Mao, B., Xie, L.: DROP: Detecting return-oriented programming malicious code. In: Prakash, A., Sen Gupta, I. (eds.) ICISS 2009. LNCS, vol. 5905, pp. 163–177. Springer, Heidelberg (2009)
16. Intel. Intel 64 and ia-32 architectures software developers manual, volume 3b: System programming guide, part 2
17. UnixBench (2012), http://ftp.tux.org/pub/benchmarks/system/unixbench
18. Bletsch, T., Jiang, X.: Mitigating Code-Reuse Attacks with Control-Flow Locking. In: Proceedings of the 27th Annual Computer Security Applications Conference, ACSAC (2011)
19. Luk, C.-K., Cohn, R., Muth, R., et al.: Pin: Building customized program analysis tools with dynamic instrumentation. In: Sarkar, V., Hall, M.W. (eds.) Proceedings of PLDI (2005)
20. Nethercote, N., Seward, J.: Valgrind: A framework for heavyweight dynamic binary instrumentation. SIGPLAN Not. 42(6), 89–100 (2007)
21. Pappas, V.: kBouncer: Efficient and transparent ROP mitigation. Technical report, Columbia University (2012)

Efficient Hardware Implementation of MQ Asymmetric Cipher PMI+ on FPGAs

Shaohua Tang*, Bo Lv**, Guomin Chen**, and Zhiniang Peng

School of Computer Science & Engineering,
South China University of Technology, Guangzhou, China
shtang@IEEE.org,
csshtang@scut.edu.cn

Abstract. PMI+ is a Multivariate Quadratic (MQ) public key algorithm used for encryption and decryption operations, and belongs to post quantum cryptography. We designs a hardware on FPGAs to efficiently implement PMI+ in this paper. Our main contributions are that, firstly, a hardware architecture of encryption and decryption of PMI+ is developed, and description of corresponding hardware algorithm is proposed; secondly, basic arithmetic units are implemented with higher efficiency that multiplication, squaring, vector dot product and power operation are implemented in full parallel; and thirdly, an optimized implementation for core module, including optimized large power operation, is achieved. The encryption and decryption hardware of PMI+ is efficiently realized on FPGA by the above optimization and improvement. It is verified by experiments that the designed hardware can complete an encryption operation within 497 clock cycles, and the clock frequency can be up to 145.6MHz, and the designed hardware can complete a decryption operation within 438 clock cycles wherein the clock frequency can be up to 37.04MHz.

Keywords: Multivariate Quadratic (MQ) Public Key Algorithm, PMI+ Encryption and Decryption, Hardware Implementation, FPGA, Optimized Large Power Operation.

1 Introduction

Public key cryptography has played an important role in modern communication and computer networks. The public key cryptography, which is used widely, mainly includes RSA based on integer factorization problem, ElGamal based on discrete logarithm problem and elliptic curve cryptography, etc. In order to adapt various occasions, many efficiently hardware implementations are proposed by researchers [22,18,25,19,23,14,8].

The quantum algorithm of P.Shor is able to solve the integer factorization and discrete logarithm problem in polynomial time, including a calculation problem in elliptic curve field, which directly threatens classical cryptosystems based on

---

* Corresponding Author.
** The authors Bo Lv and Guomin Chen contribute equally to this paper.

X. Huang and J. Zhou (Eds.): ISPEC 2014, LNCS 8434, pp. 187–201, 2014.

hard problems of number theory, and which helps to drive the development of post quantum cryptography. The post quantum cryptography can be divided into four categories: signature schemes based on hash function[17], lattice-based public key cryptosystem[13], public key cryptosystem based on error correcting code[16] and multivariate public key cryptosystem[7]. The research for post quantum cryptography is growing rapidly and many hardware and embedded system implementations of the post quantum cryptography appear in order to adapt various occasions[24,21,11,20,1,2,3,6].

PMI+ [5] is one kind of multivariate public key cryptosystem, and is a variant of MI[15]. Ding enhanced the security of MI by adding internal perturbation to the central map of MI in 2004, to produce a new variant of the MI cryptosystem which is called PMI cryptosystem[4]. However, the PMI cryptosystem has been broken by differential cryptanalysis by Fouque et al.[10] in 2005. Ding introduced new external perturbation to the central mapping of MI [5] in 2006, to produce PMI+ cryptosystem whose security has been greatly improved. Up to present, the PMI+ cryptosystem is still secure, and its hardware implementation is relatively less, so a hardware used to implement PMI+ is designed in this paper, which can be efficiently implemented in FPGA.

Our Contributions. The paper designs a hardware used to implement PMI+, which can be efficiently implemented on FPGA.

Firstly, a hardware architecture of encryption and decryption of PMI+ is developed, and description of corresponding hardware algorithm is proposed.

Secondly, basic arithmetic units are implemented with higher efficiency that multiplication, squaring, vector dot product and power operation are implemented in full parallel, wherein compared with a full parallel multiplier, a full parallel squarer takes up about one-twentieth of the logical unit and has shorter latency.

Thirdly, we implement an optimized large power operation, and compared with general power operation, it can reduce 4288 cycles at most in one process of decryption, with an obvious optimization. The encryption and decryption hardware of PMI+ is efficiently realized on FPGA by the above optimization and improvement.

Our experiments verify that if parameters are selected as $(n, q, \theta, r, a) = (84, 2, 4, 6, 14)$, the length of a plaintext block is 84 bits and the length of a ciphertext block is 98 bits, our designed hardware can complete an encryption operation within 497 clock cycles or $3.42us$, wherein the clock frequency can be up to 145.6MHz, and our designed hardware can complete an decryption operation within 438 clock cycles or $11.83us$, wherein the clock frequency can be up to 37.04MHz.

Organization. The structure of the rest of this paper goes as follows. Section 2 briefly introduces solution and theory of PMI+ encryption scheme, including the construction of algorithms, principles of encryption and decryption and the choice of parameters; Section 3 primarily focuses on hardware design and implementation of PMI+, including hardware structure design, algorithm description and implementation of basic arithmetic unit and hardware core module; Section 4 lists detailed experimental data, and makes performance contrast with other public key encryption schemes; and Section 5 is the conclusion of this paper, which summarizes the findings of this paper and proposes further research directions.

2   Preliminaries

We describes the basic theory of the encryption and decryption of PMI+ [5] in this section. The basic idea of PMI+ is adding internal perturbation and external perturbation to the central map of MI scheme to resist linearization equation attack and differential attack.

2.1   Notations for PMI+

Let k be a finite field of characteristic two and cardinality q, K be an extension of degree n over k. Let $\varphi : K \to k^n$ defined by $\varphi(a_0 + a_1 x + ... + a_{n-1} x^{n-1}) = (a_0, a_1, ..., a_{n-1})$.

Fix θ so that $\gcd(q^\theta + 1, q^n - 1) = 1$ and define $\tilde{F} : K \to K$ by $\tilde{F}(X) = X^{1+q^\theta}$. Then F is invertible and $\tilde{F}^{-1}(X) = X^t$, where $t(1 + q^\theta) \equiv 1 \bmod (q^n - 1)$.

Define the map $F' : k^n \to k^n$ by $F'(x_1, ..., x_n) = \varphi \circ \tilde{F} \circ \varphi^{-1}(x_1, ..., x_n)$.

Fix a small integer r and randomly choose r invertible affine linear functions $z_1, ..., z_r$, written as $z_j(x_1, ..., x_n) = \sum_{i=1}^{n} \alpha_{ij} x_i + \beta_j$, for $j = 1, ..., r$. This defines a map $Z : k^n \to k^r$ by $Z(x_1, ..., x_n) = (z_1, ..., z_r)$. The map Z is source of internal perturbation.

Randomly choose n quadratic polynomials $\hat{f}_1, ..., \hat{f}_n \in k[z_1, ..., z_r]$. The $\hat{f}_i$ define a map $\hat{F} : k^r \to k^n$ by $\hat{F}(z_1, ..., z_r) = (\hat{f}_1, ..., \hat{f}_n)$. Let P be the set consisting of the pairs (λ, μ), where λ is a point that belongs to the image of $\hat{F}$ and μ is the set of pre-images of λ under $\hat{F}$.

Define an internal perturbation map by $F^*(x_1, ..., x_n) = \hat{F} \circ Z(x_1, ..., x_n) = (f_1^*, ..., f_n^*)$. Define a map by $F(x_1, ..., x_n) = (F' + F^*)(x_1, ..., x_n)$.

Randomly choose a non-linear equations on $x_1, ..., x_n$ for the central map F as external perturbation. Randomly choose an invertible affine map L_1 in $n + a$ dimensional vector space k^{n+a}, randomly choose an invertible affine map L_2 in n dimensional vector space k^n, and $\bar{F}(x_1, ..., x_n) = L_1 \circ F \circ L_2(x_1, ..., x_n)$ is a public key of PMI+, and the private key includes the central map F', the map $\hat{F}$, Z, L_1^{-1} and L_2^{-1}.

2.2   PMI+ Encryption

For a given plaintext block $(x_1, ..., x_n)$, when encrypting the plaintext, it only needs to apply the plaintext into the public key polynomial

$$
\begin{aligned}
y_1 &= \bar{f}_1(x_1, x_2, ..., x_n), \\
&... \\
y_{n+a} &= \bar{f}_{n+a}(x_1, x_2, ..., x_n),
\end{aligned}
\tag{1}
$$

to calculate the evaluation of $n + a$ quadratic polynomials that a ciphertext $(y_1, ..., y_{n+a})$ can be acquired.

2.3 PMI+ Decryption

We can decrypt the ciphertext $(y_1, ..., y_{n+a})$ by computing

$$X = (x_1, ..., x_n) = L_2^{-1} \circ F^{-1} \circ L_1^{-1}(y_1, ..., y_{n+a}). \tag{2}$$

The process is:

(1) calculating $Y' = L_1^{-1}(Y) = (y_1', ..., y_{n+a}')$;

(2) removing a external perturbation polynomials from Y' to obtain $\bar{Y} = (\bar{y}_1, ..., \bar{y}_n)$;

(3) calculating $(y_{\lambda 1}, ..., y_{\lambda n}) = F^{-1}((\bar{y}_1, ..., \bar{y}_n) + \lambda)$ for each $(\lambda, \mu) \in P$, and checking if $\mu = Z(y_{\lambda 1}, ..., y_{\lambda n})$, if not, continuing this step, otherwise, moving on to the next step;

(4) applying $(y_{\lambda 1}, ..., y_{\lambda n})$ into a external perturbation polynomials, if the verification is successful, moving on to the next step, otherwise, returning to the previous step; and

(5) calculating $X = L_2^{-1}(y_{\lambda 1}, ..., y_{\lambda n}) = (x_1, ..., x_n)$, and X is a decrypted plaintext.

2.4 Security and Parameter Selection of PMI+

The obtained PMI+ instance can reach a corresponding security level after associated parameters are set. For example, Ding [5] has shown two sets of relatively practical PMI+ parameters in his paper that the security level can be up to over 2^{80}, and the following table shows the two sets of parameters.

Table 1. Parameters for PMI+

n	q	r	a	θ
84	2	4	6	14
136	2	8	6	18

The parameters for PMI+ encryption and decryption hardware implemented in this paper is as the first set of parameters shown in Table 1, and the security level can be up to over 2^{80}.

3   Design and Implementation of PMI+ Hardware

3.1 Hardware Structure Design and Algorithm Process

Design of PMI+ Encryption. The hardware structure of PMI+ encryption is as shown in Fig. 1.

It can be shown from (1) in Section 2.2, the operation process of PMI+ encryption is equivalent to applying the plaintext into the polynomial to calculate, and its hardware structure is illustrated in Fig. 1.

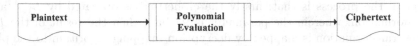

Fig. 1. The Hardware Structure of PMI+ Encryption

If parameters are selected as $(n, q, \theta, r, a) = (84, 2, 4, 6, 14)$, the length of the plaintext block is 84 bits and the length of the ciphertext block is 98 bits, it needs to add 14 external perturbations, the public key is 358,190 (3,655*98) bits, i.e. 44,774 bytes.

Design of PMI+ Decryption. The hardware structure of PMI+ Decryption is shown in Fig. 2.

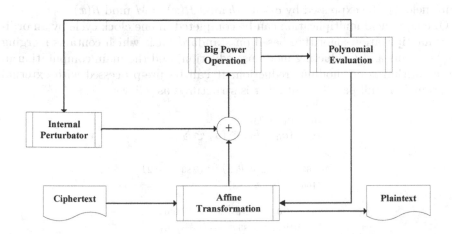

Fig. 2. The hardware structure of PMI+ Decryption

From Section 2.3, the process of decryption is equivalent to calculating Eq. (2) in Section 2.3. The process of PMI+ decryption is divided into four modules based on the process of calculating Eq. (2): affine transformation, internal perturbator, large power operation and polynomial calculation, as shown in Fig. 2. Wherein, the input of large power operation is a result of the affine transformed result adding the internal perturbator. The role of the polynomial calculation is to verify external perturbator, if the verification is successful, the result will be calculated in the affine transformation module again to obtain the plaintext block, otherwise, to select another element from the internal perturbator for large power operation after addition.

Based on Eq. (2), the process of PMI+ decryption can be abstracted into two parts: affine transformation and decryption mapping. In the parameters we selected, the process is that: firstly the ciphertext is operated by L_1^{-1} affine transformation, wherein the parameter is 98 bits; then the result of the L_1^{-1} affine transformation is mapped by decryption mapping algorithm to the plaintext space, and the result is 84 bits; finally the result of the PMI+ decryption mapping is operated by L_2^{-1} affine transformation, and a 84-bit plaintext block is obtained.

3.2 Basic Arithmetic Unit

Firstly, the basic arithmetic unit throughout the process of PMI+ encryption and decryption is described here.

Full Parallel Multiplier. Elements in the finite field K can be expressed by a polynomial as $a = \sum_{i=0}^{83} a_i x^i$, where $a_i \in \{0,1\}$. And a multiplication over the finite field can be expressed by $c = a \otimes b \bmod R(x) = M \bmod R(x)$.

One large field multiplication can be completed in one clock cycle by an ordinary multiplication algorithm based on standard basis which contains merging similar items and conducting modulus reduction, and the main computation in the algorithm is on modulus reduction. It can be pre-processed with external program. The full parallel multiplier is structured as follows.

$$m_0 = a_0 \otimes b_0,$$
$$m_1 = (a_0 \otimes b_1) \oplus (a_1 \otimes b_0),$$
$$\dots$$
$$m_{165} = (a_{82} \otimes b_{83}) \oplus (a_{83} \otimes b_{82}),$$
$$m_{166} = a_{83} \otimes b_{83};$$

$$c_0 = m_0 \oplus m_{84} \oplus \dots \oplus m_{166},$$
$$c_1 = m_1 \oplus m_{85} \oplus \dots \oplus m_{166},$$
$$\dots$$
$$c_{83} = m_{83} \oplus m_{110} \oplus \dots \oplus m_{165}.$$

The full parallel multiplier can complete one multiplication over the finite field K in one clock cycle, which uses 7,056 AND gate circuits and 9,997 XOR gate circuits. It was unrealistic to implement a direct look-up table over finite field $GF(2^{84})$ (the storage space of the table can be up to 2^{168} bits), in comparison the full parallel multiplier over the finite field K implemented in this paper should be the better.

Full Parallel Vector Dot Product. In the process of PMI+ decryption, the affine transformation is used twice, where in the first time, n is 98, and in the second time, n is 84. It needs to implement two vector dot products: a 98 dimensional vector dot product and a 84 dimensional vector dot product. The scalar value in the vector is 0 or 1, so for scalar value in the vector, the addition uses a XOR gate circuit, and the multiplication uses a AND gate circuit.

Set $a = (a_0, ..., a_{n-1})$, $b = (b_0, ..., b_{n-1})$, where $a_i, b_i \in \{0, 1\}$, $i = 0, ..., n-1$, and the dot product of vectors is $c \in \{0, 1\} : c = (a_0 \otimes b_0) \oplus ... \oplus (a_{n-1} \otimes b_{n-1})$.

The vector dot product operation can be completed in one clock cycle, which uses n AND gate circuits and $n-1$ XOR gate circuits.

Full Parallel Squarer. There is a very useful property in Frobenius mapping that for a map $T_i(X) = X^{q^i}$ over the finite field K, X is represented as a polynomial basis $a_0 + a_1 x + ... + a_{83} x^{83}$, and then the following equation holds: $T_i(X) = X^{q^i} = a_0 + a_1 x^{q^i} + ... + a_{83} x^{83 * q^i}$.

While in the finite field K, $q = 2$, set $a = \sum_{i=0}^{83} a_i x^i$ as any element in K, then: $a^2 = a_0 + a_1 x^2 + ... + a_{83} x^{83 * 2}$. It can be pre-processed with external program. The full parallel squarer has the following hardware structure.

$$c_0 = a_0 \oplus a_{42} \oplus ... \oplus a_{83},$$
$$c_1 = a_{56} \oplus a_{61} \oplus ... \oplus a_{83},$$
$$...$$
$$c_{83} = a_{55} \oplus a_{60} \oplus ... \oplus a_{82}.$$

The full parallel squarer can complete one squaring operation over the finite field K in one clock cycle, which uses 1,525 XOR gate circuits. Compared with a full parallel multiplier, the full parallel squarer uses about one in twenty logical units, and has a shorter latency, so it seems worthwhile to implement the full parallel squarer.

Full Parallel Power Operator. In order to implement the large power operation efficiently and reuse public arithmetic unit at the most extent, two power operators are implemented, where one is a full parallel power 16 operator and the other is a full parallel power 256 operator. Based on the nature of Frobenius mapping, set a as any element in K, and then:

$$a^{16} = a_0 + a_1 x^{16} + ... + a_{83} x^{83*16},$$
$$a^{256} = a_0 + a_1 x^{256} + ... + a_{83} x^{83*256}.$$

It can be pre-processed with external program. The full parallel power 16 operator has the following hardware structure:

$$c_0 = a_0 \oplus a_9 \oplus ... \oplus a_{81},$$
$$c_1 = a_1 \oplus a_7 \oplus ... \oplus a_{83},$$
$$...$$
$$c_{83} = a_8 \oplus a_{10} \oplus ... \oplus a_{83}.$$

The full parallel power 256 operator has the following hardware structure:

$$d_0 = a_0 \oplus a_4 \oplus ... \oplus a_{83},$$
$$d_1 = a_1 \oplus a_2 \oplus ... \oplus a_{83},$$
$$...$$
$$d_{83} = a_2 \oplus a_3 \oplus ... \oplus a_{83}.$$

The full parallel power operator that we implemented can complete one exponentiation over the finite field K in one clock cycle. Compared with a full parallel multiplier, the full parallel squarer uses about one in tenth logical units, and has a shorter latency.

3.3   Implementation of Hardware Core Modules

Implementation of Polynomial Calculation. The calculation of polynomial can be an addition or multiplication over finite field $GF(2)$, which can be implemented by XOR operation and AND operation respectively. The polynomial calculation module is used in both PMI+ encryption and decryption. Wherein, in PMI+ encryption, the input of the polynomial calculation module is a plaintext block of PMI+ and a public key polynomial, the output Y of the polynomial calculation module is a ciphertext block, and the role of the polynomial calculation module is to implement PMI+ encryption; in PMI+ decryption, the input of the polynomial calculation module is a result of the large power operation and a external perturbation polynomials of PMI+, the output of the polynomial calculation module is a result of PMI+ decryption mapping, and the role of the polynomial calculation module is to verify a external perturbation polynomials.

Implementation of Affine Transformation. The affine transformation includes a vector addition and a vector dot product. The vector addition can be implemented by XOR operation directly. The vector dot product can be implemented by the full parallel vector dot product defined by us. In the PMI+ decryption, two affine transformations are used, respectively before and after decryption mapping, the first uses a 98 dimensional vector dot product, and the second uses a 84 dimensional vector dot product.

Implementation of Internal Perturbator. When we implement the PMI+ decryption, it needs to abstract a component to complete a transformation for mapping from $r = 6$ dimensional vector to 84 dimensional vector, which is called as internal perturbator. The expression of the map is calculated by a external program off-line, and the arithmetic unit is implemented by 1,078 XOR gates and 627 AND gates.

Implementation of Large Power Operation. In one PMI+ decryption, it needs 64 large power operations at most, so optimized large power operation can improve the performance of the PMI+ decryption hardware at a large extent. If the parameter t is selected as 10240312824970976538687608, it is unrealistic to find the solution of power by multiplication over the finite field K.

Conventional Large Power Operation. The large power operation is implemented by a "square-multiplication" method. The binary equivalent for t is 10000111 10000111 10000111 10000111 10000111 10000111 10000111 10000111 10000111

10000111 1000, X^t can be expressed as $B^t = B^{2^3} \otimes B^{2^4} \otimes ... \otimes B^{2^{83}}$, so one large power operation can be completed by 83 squaring operations and 40 multiplications.

Optimal Implementation of Large Power Operation. The basic idea to implement large power operation is reusing public arithmetic unit at the most extent, so as to reduce clock cycles of the large power operation. The software implementation of PMI+ has been completed in a 8051 microcontroller by Chen [26] in his master dissertation, where the large power operation uses a similar idea. The differences between the above paper and this paper are that the size of t used in this paper is different (methods for optimization are different), and the implementation of PMI+ in this paper is based on FPGA hardware platform.

We find that fragment $S = 10000111$ appears 10 times in the binary string, so X^t can be expressed as $X^t = X^{2^3} \otimes (X^S)^{16} \otimes ((X^S)^{16})^{256} \otimes ... \otimes ((X^S)^{16}...)^{256}$.

In the optimized large power operation, $X^S = X^{10000111}$ is firstly calculated, and we implement it for optimization that X^S can be calculated in 5 cycles. Then, the operation of X^t can be quickly completed by adding new arithmetic unit, and the rest of the operation can be completed in 11 clock cycles.

Algorithm 1. Optimal Implementation of Large Power Operation

	Input: X;
	Output: Y;
	Procedure:
1	**begin**
2	$B2 := \text{square}(X)$;
3	$B4 := \text{square}(B2)$; $Y :=\text{multiply}(X, B2)$;
4	$B8 := \text{square}(B4)$; $Y :=\text{multiply}(Y, B4)$;
5	$B128 := \text{power16}(B8)$; $B16 := \text{square}(B8)$;
6	$B135 := \text{multiply}(B128, Y)$;
7	$tmp := \text{power16}(B135)$;
8	$Y := \text{multiply}(B16, tmp)$; $tmp = \text{power256}(tmp)$;
9	$i = 8$;
10	**while** $i >= 0$ **do**
11	$\quad Y := \text{multiply}(Y, tmp)$; $tmp = \text{power256}(tmp)$;
12	$\quad i--$;
13	**end**
14	$Y := \text{multiply}(Y, tmp)$;
15	**return** Y;
16	**end**

Algorithm 1 describes the process of the optimized large power operation. The input X is a 84 dimensional vector, the output Y is also a 84 dimensional vector, the arithmetic units of **square** and **multiply** are a full parallel squarer and a full parallel multiplier respectively, and the arithmetic units of **power16** and **power256** are a full parallel power 16 operator and a full parallel power 256 operator respectively.

Our new proposed large power operation can complete a large power operation in 16 clock cycles which are less than one-sixth of those for "square-multiplication" method, and only the logical units taken up by the arithmetic units of **power16** and **power256** increases for its area, so the operational performance is greatly enhanced.

4   Experiment Results and Analyses

The algorithm of PMI+ encryption and decryption is implemented in *Quartas II* 8.0 environment by VHDL with the idea of high speed and parallelization, its hardware simulation is implemented in *EP2S130F102014* of the family of *StratixII*, and the area of PMI+ encryption and decryption hardware is evaluated by *SynopsysDC*, where the process library is 0.18 *nm* process library of TSMC and the working voltage is 1.62 *volt*. The following results come from the real experimental data and compared with current implemented hardware in performance.

4.1   PMI+ Basic Arithmetic Unit

Some basic arithmetic units of PMI+ are implemented in Section 3.2, including a full parallel multiplier, a full parallel vector dot product, a full parallel squarer and a full parallel power operator, and the performance data of these basic arithmetic units is shown in Table 2.

Table 2. The Performance of PMI+'s Basic Arithmetic Units

Arithmetic Units	Area (um^2)	Number of Equivalent Gate	Logical Unit (ALUT)	Maximum Latency	Clock Cycles
Full Parallel Multiplier	277997.2	27800	4823	27.000	1
Full Parallel Vector Dot Product	3559.25	356	57	23.948	1
Full Parallel Squarer	19546	1955	289	17.483	1
Full Parallel Power 16 Operator	37115.8	3712	510	18.641	1
Full Parallel Power 256 Operator	39045	3905	538	19.191	1

It can be seen from the data in Table 2 that the basic arithmetic unit in PMI+ decryption hardware can complete one basic operation in one cycle, where the full parallel multiplier takes up the maximum area, and compared with the multiplier, the squarer and power operator complete an operation with lower latency while take up less area.

4.2   Large Power Operation in PMI+

A comparison of the number of logical units and the number of clock cycles between two different large power operations is listed in Table 3.

Table 3. Performance Comparison between two Large Power Operation Methods

Arithmetic Units	Area/ (um^2)	Number of Equivalent Gate	Logical Unit (ALUT)	Clock Cycles
Implementation Based on "Square - Multiplication"	334715	33472	5176	84
Our Optimal Implementation of Large Power Operation	435941	43595	6367	16

These results show that the performance of the optimized large power operation has a significant improvement that clock cycles of the optimized large power operation reduce by 80.9% and the area adds about 30.2% for one large power operation. In PMI+ decryption, it needs 64 large power operations at most, so it can save up to 4,416 clock cycle at most for a period of decryption.

4.3   PMI+ Encryption and Decryption

We implement the first PMI+ encryption and decryption hardware on FPGA. Compared with other public key encryption and decryption hardware, our hardware implementation of PMI+ possesses of advantages such as small space, fast speed of encryption and decryption, and practical security level.

The whole PMI+ decryption needs at least 207 clock cycles (excepting cycles of reading ROM) to complete a signature operation, and it takes up a total of 11,005 logical units with a area of 680,302 um^2 .

Table 5 lists performance data of the PMI+ encryption and decryption hardware. Using experiment data, it's easy to see the number of cycles of the PMI+ decryption is mutable, where 438 cycles for least and 2,915 cycles for most, and the running speed of the PMI+ encryption hardware is far faster than that of the PMI+ decryption hardware and the area of it is far less than the PMI+ decryption hardware.

4.4   Performance Comparison

The performances of the PMI+ decryption hardware is compared with other public key cryptosystem hardware in this section. Table 6 lists the results after comparing the implementation of the PMI+ decryption hardware with other public key cryptosystems.

Table 4. Cycles Required by Arithmetic Units in PMI+ Encryption

Step	Main Arithmetic Units	Clock Cycles
1	Calculate the Invertible Affine Map Function of L_1^{-1}	85
2	Sum of the Affine Transformed Result and the Enternal Perturbator	1 - 64
3	Large Power Operation	16 - 1024
4	Calculate the Map of Z	6 - 384
5	Calculate the Invertible Affine Map Function of L_2^{-1}	85
6	Check Extra Polynomial	14 - 56

Table 5. Performance of our PMI+ Encryption and Decryption

Hardware Implementation	Area (um^2)	Number of Equivalent Gate	Logical Unit (ALUT)	Clock Frequency (MHz)	Period (ns)	Clock Cycles	Total Time (us)
PMI+ Encryption	160385	16039	3468	145.60	6.868	497	3.42
PMI+ Decryption	680302	68031	11005	37.04	27.000	438 - 2915	11.83 - 78.71

Table 6. Performance Comparison among some Public Key Crypto Hardwares

The Hardware Implementation Scheme	Number of Equivalent Gate	Clock Cycles	Frequency (MHz)	Total time (us)	Area*time
RSA1024-PSS[12]	250000	357142	200	1785.71	554.70
ECC128[9]	183000	592976	204	2910	661.69
EN-TTS[27]	21000	60000	67	895.53	23.37
Our Parallelized PMI+ Decryption	68031	438 - 2915	37.04	11.83 - 78.71	1 - 6.66

The data in the table shows that compared with RSA and ECC, parallelization PMI+ decryption hardware that we implemented has a higher performance advantage, such as small product of area and time, and high operating efficiency.

5   Conclusion

We design a hardware on FPGAs used to efficiently implement PMI+. It is verified by experiments that our designed hardware can complete an encryption operation within 497 clock cycles, and the clock frequency can be up to 145.6MHz, and the designed hardware can complete a decryption operation within 438 clock cycles wherein the clock frequency can be up to 37.04MHz. Our main contributions are to develop hardware architecture of encryption and decryption of PMI+ and describe corresponding hardware algorithms. Meanwhile, basic arithmetic units are implemented in this paper with higher efficiency which can complete the operation with lesser latency. Thirdly, an optimized large power operation is implemented which needs only 16 cycles to complete one exponentiation, and compared with general power operation, it can reduce 4288 cycles at most in one process of decryption, with an obvious optimization.

Future studies will include: 1) using registers in hardware more accurately to reduce the area and power consumption of hardware; and 2) reducing the number of logical units of multiplier and latency on the premise that the clock cycles do not increase.

Acknowledgment. This work is supported by the National Natural Science Foundation of China under Grant No. U1135004 and 61170080, Guangdong Province Universities and Colleges Pearl River Scholar Funded Scheme (2011), and High-level Talents Project of Guangdong Institutions of Higher Education (2012).

References

1. Balasubramanian, S., Carter, H., Bogdanov, A., Rupp, A., Ding, J.: Fast Multivariate Signature Generation in Hardware: The Case of Rainbow. In: Application-Specific Systems, Architectures and Processors, pp. 25–30 (July 2008)
2. Bogdanov, A., Eisenbarth, T., Rupp, A., Wolf, C.: Time-Area Optimized Public-Key Engines: MQ-Cryptosystems as Replacement for Elliptic Curves? In: Oswald, E., Rohatgi, P. (eds.) CHES 2008. LNCS, vol. 5154, pp. 45–61. Springer, Heidelberg (2008)
3. Czypek, P., Heyse, S., Thomae, E.: Efficient Implementations of MQPKS on Constrained Devices. In: Prouff, E., Schaumont, P. (eds.) CHES 2012. LNCS, vol. 7428, pp. 374–389. Springer, Heidelberg (2012)
4. Ding, J.: A New Variant of the Matsumoto-Imai Cryptosystem through Perturbation. In: Bao, F., Deng, R., Zhou, J. (eds.) PKC 2004. LNCS, vol. 2947, pp. 305–318. Springer, Heidelberg (2004)
5. Ding, J., Gower, J.E.: Inoculating Multivariate Schemes Against Differential Attacks. In: Yung, M., Dodis, Y., Kiayias, A., Malkin, T. (eds.) PKC 2006. LNCS, vol. 3958, pp. 290–301. Springer, Heidelberg (2006)
6. Ding, J., Schmidt, D., Yin, Z.: Cryptanalysis of the New TTS Scheme in CHES 2004. International Journal of Information Security 5(4), 231–240 (2006)
7. Ding, J., Yang, B.Y.: Multivariate Public Key Cryptography. In: Bernstein, D., Buchmann, J., Dahmen, E. (eds.) Post-Quantum Cryptography, pp. 193–241. Springer, Heidelberg (2009)
8. Fan, J., Vercauteren, F., Verbauwhede, I.: Efficient Hardware Implementation of Fp-Arithmetic for Pairing-Friendly Curves. IEEE Transactions on Computers 61(5), 676–685 (2012)

9. Fan, J., Vercauteren, F., Verbauwhede, I.: Faster Fp-arithmetic for Cryptographic Pairings on Barreto-Naehrig Curves. In: Clavier, C., Gaj, K. (eds.) CHES 2009. LNCS, vol. 5747, pp. 240–253. Springer, Heidelberg (2009)

10. Fouque, P.-A., Granboulan, L., Stern, J.: Differential Cryptanalysis for Multivariate Schemes. In: Cramer, R. (ed.) EUROCRYPT 2005. LNCS, vol. 3494, pp. 341–353. Springer, Heidelberg (2005)

11. Ghosh, S., Verbauwhede, I.: BLAKE-512 Based 128-bit CCA2 Secure Timing Attack Resistant McEliece Cryptoprocessor. IEEE Transactions on Computers PP(99), 1 (2012)

12. Großschädl, J.: High-Speed RSA Hardware Based on Barrets Modular Reduction Method. In: Koç, Ç.K., Paar, C. (eds.) CHES 2000. LNCS, vol. 1965, pp. 191–203. Springer, Heidelberg (2000)

13. Hoffstein, J., Pipher, J., Silverman, J.H.: NTRU: A Ring-Based Public Key Cryptosystem. In: Buhler, J.P. (ed.) ANTS 1998. LNCS, vol. 1423, pp. 267–288. Springer, Heidelberg (1998)

14. Mahdizadeh, H., Masoumi, M.: Novel Architecture for Efficient FPGA Implementation of Elliptic Curve Cryptographic Processor Over $GF(2^{163})$. IEEE Transactions on Very Large Scale Integration (VLSI) Systems 21(12), 2330–2333 (2013)

15. Matsumoto, T., Imai, H.: Public Quadratic Polynomial-Tuples for Efficient Signature-Verification and Message-Encryption. In: Günther, C.G. (ed.) EUROCRYPT 1988. LNCS, vol. 330, pp. 419–453. Springer, Heidelberg (1988)

16. McEliece, R.J.: A Public-Key Cryptosystem Based on Algebraic Coding Theory. DSN Progress Report 42(44), 114–116 (1978)

17. Merkle, R.C.: Secrecy, Authentication, and Public Key Systems. Ph.D. thesis, Stanford University (1979)

18. Miyamoto, A., Homma, N., Aoki, T., Satoh, A.: Systematic Design of RSA Processors Based on High-Radix Montgomery Multipliers. IEEE Transactions on Very Large Scale Integration (VLSI) Systems 19(7), 1136–1146 (2011)

19. Rebeiro, C., Roy, S.S., Mukhopadhyay, D.: Pushing the Limits of High-Speed $GF(2^m)$ Elliptic Curve Scalar Multiplication on FPGAs. In: Prouff, E., Schaumont, P. (eds.) CHES 2012. LNCS, vol. 7428, pp. 494–511. Springer, Heidelberg (2012)

20. Shih, J.R., Hu, Y., Hsiao, M.C., Chen, M.S., Shen, W.C., Yang, B.Y., Wu, A.Y., Cheng, C.M.: Securing M2M With Post-Quantum Public-Key Cryptography. IEEE Journal on Emerging and Selected Topics in Circuits and Systems 3(1), 106–116 (2013)

21. Shoufan, A., Wink, T., Molter, H., Huss, S., Kohnert, E.: A Novel Cryptoprocessor Architecture for the McEliece Public-Key Cryptosystem. IEEE Transactions on Computers 59(11), 1533–1546 (2010)

22. Sutter, G., Deschamps, J., Imana, J.: Modular Multiplication and Exponentiation Architectures for Fast RSA Cryptosystem Based on Digit Serial Computation. IEEE Transactions on Industrial Electronics 58(7), 3101–3109 (2011)

23. Sutter, G., Deschamps, J., Imana, J.: Efficient Elliptic Curve Point Multiplication Using Digit-Serial Binary Field Operations. IEEE Transactions on Industrial Electronics 60(1), 217–225 (2013)

24. Tang, S., Yi, H., Ding, J., Chen, H., Chen, G.: High-Speed Hardware Implementation of Rainbow Signature on FPGAs. In: Yang, B.-Y. (ed.) PQCrypto 2011. LNCS, vol. 7071, pp. 228–243. Springer, Heidelberg (2011)

25. Wang, D., Ding, Y., Zhang, J., Hu, J., Tan, H.: Area-Efficient and Ultra-Low-Power Architecture of RSA Processor for RFID. Electronics Letters 48(19), 1185–1187 (2012)
26. Chen, Y.: An Implementation of PMI+ on Low-Cost SmartCard. Master's thesis, National Taiwan University (2006)
27. Yang, B.-Y., Cheng, C.-M., Chen, B.-R., Chen, J.-M.: Implementing Minimized Multivariate PKC on Low-Resource Embedded Systems. In: Clark, J.A., Paige, R.F., Polack, F.A.C., Brooke, P.J. (eds.) SPC 2006. LNCS, vol. 3934, pp. 73–88. Springer, Heidelberg (2006)

High-Speed Elliptic Curve Cryptography on the NVIDIA GT200 Graphics Processing Unit

Shujie Cui[1,2], Johann Großschädl[2], Zhe Liu[2,*], and Qiuliang Xu[1]

[1] Shandong University,
School of Computer Science and Technology,
Shunhua Road 1500, Jinan 250101, Shandong, P.R. China
shujiecui1@gmail.com, xql@sdu.edu.cn
[2] University of Luxembourg,
Laboratory of Algorithmics, Cryptology and Security,
6, rue Richard Coudenhove-Kalergi, L–1359 Luxembourg
{johann.groszschaedl,zhe.liu}@uni.lu

Abstract. This paper describes a high-speed software implementation of Elliptic Curve Cryptography (ECC) for GeForce GTX graphics cards equipped with an NVIDIA GT200 Graphics Processing Unit (GPU). In order to maximize throughput, our ECC software allocates just a single thread per scalar multiplication and aims to launch as many threads in parallel as possible. We adopt elliptic curves in Montgomery as well as twisted Edwards form, both defined over a special family of finite fields known as Optimal Prime Fields (OPFs). All field-arithmetic operations use a radix-2^{24} representation for the operands (i.e. 24 operand bits are contained in a 32-bit word) to comply with the native (24×24)-bit integer multiply instruction of the GT200 platform. We implemented the OPF arithmetic without conditional statements (e.g. if-then clauses) to prevent thread divergence and unrolled the loops to minimize execution time. The scalar multiplication on the twisted Edwards curve employs a comb approach if the base point is fixed and uses extended projective coordinates so that a point addition requires only seven multiplications in the underlying OPF. Our software currently supports elliptic curves over 160-bit and 224-bit OPFs. After a detailed evaluation of numerous implementation options and configurations, we managed to launch 2880 threads on the 30 multiprocessors of the GT200 when the elliptic curve has Montgomery form and is defined over a 224-bit OPF. The resulting throughput is 115k scalar multiplications per second (for arbitrary base points) and we achieved a minimum latency of 19.2 ms. In a fixed-base setting with 256 precomputed points, the throughput increases to some 345k scalar multiplications and the latency drops to 4.52 ms.

1   Introduction

Driven by the requirements of 3D computer games, Graphics Processing Units (GPUs) have evolved into massively parallel processors consisting of hundreds

---

* Co-first author, supported by the FNR Luxembourg (AFR grant 1359142).

X. Huang and J. Zhou (Eds.): ISPEC 2014, LNCS 8434, pp. 202–216, 2014.
© Springer International Publishing Switzerland 2014

of cores that are capable of running thousands of threads concurrently [14]. In contrast, recent general-purpose CPUs feature a maximum of 12 cores and can handle only few threads per core. They dedicate a large portion of their silicon area to support a hierarchical memory organization (i.e. multi-level cache) and sophisticated flow control mechanisms (e.g. branch prediction, out-of-order execution). In a modern GPU, on the other hand, the vast majority of transistors (more than 80% according to [19]) is devoted to data processing (i.e. numerical computations) rather than data caching and flow control. Over the past couple of years, the performance of CPUs doubled roughly every 18 months, whereas the computational power of GPUs increased significantly faster with an average doubling rate of just about six months ("Moore's law cubed") [13]. Today, the floating-point performance of contemporary GPUs exceeds that of CPUs of the same or similar price by more than an order of magnitude. The unprecedented computational power and relatively low cost of modern GPUs has made them an attractive platform for various "number-crunching" applications outside the graphics domain, e.g. in cryptography [4,6] and cryptanalysis [5].

The recent literature contains several case studies that demonstrate the use of a GPU as "accelerator" for cryptographic workloads; a well-known example is SSLShader [12], a GPU-based reverse proxy for SSL servers. SSL, along with its successor TLS, is the current de-facto standard protocol for enabling secure communication over an insecure network like the Internet. The most expensive part of SSL/TLS is the handshake sub-protocol, whose task is to authenticate the server to the client[1] and establish a so-called pre-master secret [12]. When an RSA-based cipher suite is used for the handshake, the server has to execute computation-intensive modular exponentiations, which causes excessive delays and hampers throughput. SSLShader tackles this problem by "off-loading" the modular exponentiations to one or more GPUs, thereby alleviating the burden of the server's CPU. Practical experiments in [12] show that GPU acceleration of the handshake increases the number of SSL transactions per second by a factor of 2.5 (1024-bit RSA) and 6.0 (2048-bit RSA) compared to a configuration where the CPU performs the exponentiations. Even though [12] only considers RSA-based cipher suites, the idea of accelerating SSL via one or more GPUs is also applicable to handshakes using Elliptic Curve Cryptography (ECC).

In this paper, we present an efficient implementation of ECC (or, more precisely, of scalar multiplication in an elliptic curve group) for NVIDIA graphics cards featuring a Tesla GPU [14]. Our implementation is specifically optimized for high throughput, which means we aimed at maximizing the number of scalar multiplications the GPU can execute per second. The basic idea we pursue is to employ just one single thread for each scalar multiplication, but launch as many threads in parallel as possible. This contrasts with the bulk of previous work, which followed a relatively "fine-grained" approach to parallel processing by invoking several threads to cooperatively compute one scalar multiplication [2]. Avenues for exploiting thread-level parallelism to speed up ECC on GPUs

---

[1] Client authentication is optional in SSL. Web applications usually authenticate the client (i.e. user) through a higher-level protocol, e.g. by entering a password.

exist in both the field arithmetic (i.e. modular multiplication and squaring, see e.g. [1,4]) and the group arithmetic (i.e. point addition and point doubling, see e.g. [6,11]). A major challenge of such a "many-threads-per-task" strategy is to partition the task (scalar multiplication in our case) into independent subtasks that can be executed in parallel with little communication and synchronization overhead. The goal is to find a partitioning that keeps all threads busy all the time so that no resources are wasted by idling threads, which is difficult due to the iterative (i.e. sequential) nature of scalar multiplication algorithms. On the other hand, a "one-thread-per-task" strategy avoids these issues and is easy to implement because all involved operations are executed sequentially by a single thread. Therefore, this approach has the virtue of (potentially) better resource utilization when launching a large number of threads. However, the problem is that the threads, even though they are independent of each other, share certain resources such as registers or fast memory, which are sparse. The more threads are active at a time, the fewer resources are available per task.

This paper seeks to shed new light on the question of how to "unleash" the full performance of GPUs to achieve maximum throughput for scalar multiplication. To this end, we combine the state-of-the-art in terms of implementation options for ECC with advanced techniques for parallel processing on GPUs, in particular the NVIDIA GT200 [14,19]. Our implementation currently supports elliptic curves in Montgomery [18] and twisted Edwards form [3], both defined over a special type of prime field known as Optimal Prime Field (OPF) [9]. In order to ensure a fair comparison with previous work (most notably [1,6]), we benchmarked our ECC software on a GeForce GTX285 graphics card equipped with a GT200 processor. Even though the GT200 is already five years old and has a (by today's standards) rather modest compute capability of 1.3 [20], its integer performance is still "remarkably good," as was recently noted by Bos in [6, Section 5]. This is not surprising since, in the past few years, NVIDIA has focused primarily on cranking up the performance of single-precision floating-point operations, whereas integer performance improved at a rather slow pace from one GPU generation to the next. A peculiarity of the GT200 GPU are its integer multipliers, which "natively" support only (24×24)-bit multiplications and MAC operations, even though the integer units, including registers, have a 32-bit datapath. (32×32)-bit multiplications can be executed, but they need to be composed of several `mul24` instructions and are, therefore, slow.

2   Preliminaries

In this section, we first discuss some basic properties and features of NVIDIA's GT200 platform (Subsection 2.1) and then recap the used elliptic curve models as well as the underlying prime field (Subsection 2.2).

2.1   Graphics Processing Units (GPUs)

A large number of multi-core GPU platforms exist today, e.g. the Tesla, Fermi and Kepler families from NVIDIA, or the Radeon series from AMD. We use an

NVIDIA GeForce GTX285 card for our implementation due to its attractive price-performance ratio and easy programmability. The main component of an NVIDIA GPU is a scalable array of multi-threaded Streaming Multiprocessors (SMs), in which the actual computations are carried out. A GT200 is composed of exactly 30 SMs, each coming with its own control units, registers, execution pipelines and caches. The main components of an SM are Streaming Processors (SPs), which are essentially just ALUs, referred to as "cores" in NVIDIA jargon [20]. Each SM contains eight cores and two Special Function Units (SFUs). The SMs are designed to create, manage, schedule, and execute a large number of threads concurrently following the SIMT (Single-Instruction, Multiple-Thread) principle. A batch of 32 threads executed physically in parallel is called a *warp*. At each cycle, the SM thread scheduler chooses a warp to execute. We should note that a warp executes one common instruction at a time. If there is a data-dependent conditional branch, divergent paths will be executed serially. So, in order to obtain full performance, all the threads of a warp should have the same execution path, i.e. conditional statements should be avoided.

The so-called Compute Unified Device Architecture (CUDA) is a parallel programming model introduced by NVIDIA to simplify software development for GPUs, including software for general-purpose processing on GPUs (GPGPU). It provides both a low-level and high-level API and also defines the memory hierarchy. The parallel portion of an application is executed on GPUs as kernels (a *kernel* is a grid of thread blocks). A *block* is a group of threads, whereby all threads in one block can cooperate with each other. A thread is the smallest unit of parallelism and only threads with the same instructions can be executed synchronously. Our implementation launches thousands of threads to compute thousands of scalar multiplications in parallel on the GT200.

CUDA provides a hierarchical memory model, including registers, shared memory, global memory, and constant memory [20]. Registers are on-chip memories, which are private to individual threads. Variables that reside in registers can be accessed at the highest speed in a highly parallel manner. On a GT200, each SM has 16384 registers of a width of 32 bits. However, registers can not be addressed. Shared memory is also located on chip and can, therefore, be accessed at a high speed. Shared memory is allocated to a thread block. All the threads in one block can cooperate by sharing their input data and intermediate results through shared memory. In the GT200 series, each SM has 16 kB shared memory. Global memory and constant memory are off-chip memories. Global memory is the only one that can be accessed by the host processor, so it is normally used to exchange data with host memory. Constant memory can only be read and is optimized for one-dimensional locality of accesses. One can achieve optimal performance by carefully considering the advantages of the different variants of memory. As registers and shared memory are the fastest memory spaces, we mainly use them in our implementation. In order to get the best performance, it is vital to balance the number of parallel threads per block with the utilization of the limited registers and shared memory. Furthermore, one has to be careful to prevent bank conflicts [20] when accessing shared memory.

2.2   Elliptic Curve Cryptography (ECC)

Twisted Edwards Curve. Twisted Edwards curves were presented by Bernstein et al [3] and are widely considered to be one of the most efficient models for implementers. Let K be a field with char$(K) \neq 2$. A twisted Edwards curve over K can be defined as

$$E_{T,a,d} : ax^2 + y^2 = 1 + dx^2 y^2 \tag{1}$$

where a and d are distinct non-zero elements of K, i.e. $ad(a - d) \neq 0$.

Our implementation adopts the idea of extended coordinates from [11] to perform a point addition and point doubling. A point in extended projective coordinates can be represented as $(X : Y : T : Z)$ whereby the corresponding extended affine coordinates have the form $(X/Z, Y/Z, T/Z)$ with $Z \neq 0$. The auxiliary coordinate T has the property $T = XY/Z$. Fixing the parameter a to -1 allows for a further reduction of the cost of point operations as described in [11]. We follow the approach from [7] and use a quintuple with two variables E and H instead of T to represent a point, whereby $E \cdot H = T$. In this case, a point doubling can be performed with three multiplications and four squarings (i.e. 3M + 4S), while the point addition costs seven multiplications (7M).

To reach high throughput, our implementation adopts a comb method [10] for scalar multiplication, which can only be used in scenarios where the base point is fixed. Given the amount of constant memory the GTX285 provides, we chose a window width of $w = 8$ for the comb method. Consequently, 256 points (one of which is the neutral element) have to be pre-computed off-line and then transferred to constant memory before the actual execution of the scalar multiplication. To prevent thread divergence and protect our implementation against timing-based side-channel attacks, we simply exploit the completeness of the Edwards addition law (i.e. we add the neutral element when an 8-bit digit of the scalar is zero) to achieve a branchless execution path.

Montgomery Curve. Peter Montgomery introduced in 1997 a special family of elliptic curves with outstanding implementation properties [18]. A Montgomery curve E_M with coefficients A and B over $\mathbb{F}_p$ is defined as

$$E_{M,A,B} : By^2 = x^3 + Ax^2 + x \tag{2}$$

Montgomery curves allow a special ladder technique to perform a scalar multiplication, which is generally referred to as "Montgomery ladder". Instead of using conventional (x, y) coordinates, the scalar multiplication on a Montgomery-form curve can be computed using only the x coordinate of the base point. Due to this feature, all point additions and doublings can be executed in an efficient way since they never involve a y coordinate. Therefore, the point addition has an operation count of of only 3M + 2S, where M represents a field multiplication and S a squaring operation. Doubling a point costs 2M + 2S + 1C, where C stands for a multiplication of a field element by the constant $(A + 2)/4$. In our implementation, the parameter A is chosen such that this constant is small.

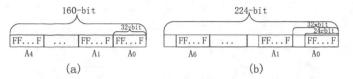

Fig. 1. Radix-2^{24} representation of a 160-bit integer using 32-bit words

Optimal Prime Fields (OPFs). We use a special class of finite field, known as *Optimal Prime Field* (OPF) [15]. OPFs are defined via a prime of the form $p = u \cdot 2^k + v$, whereby u and v are small in relation to 2^k. It is obvious that there exist many such primes for a given bitlength. In our implementation, v is always 1 and u is a 16-bit integer. A concrete example for a 160-bit prime is $p = 65356 \cdot 2^{144} + 1 = \text{0xff4c000000000000000000000000000000000001}$. Primes of such form have a low Hamming weight, i.e. they contain many zero words [15]. Generic modular reduction algorithms, e.g. Montgomery reduction, can be optimized for these primes as only the non-zero words must be processed.

3 Implementation

This section describes our implementation in detail. First, we demonstrate the advantage of using a radix-2^{24} representation for the field elements in Section 3.1, and then describe the field arithmetic operations in Section 3.2 and finally the group arithmetic along with the scalar multiplication in Section 3.3.

3.1 Integer Representation

One of the fundamental questions when implementing multi-precision arithmetic for a given architecture is how to represent the operands so as to take best advantage of its computational resources. In general, multiplication and carry propagation are of primary concern.

Multiplication plays an important role in ECC implementations, especially when projective coordinates are used. The GT200 series is based on the Tesla architecture, which means the native integer multiply instruction calculates a (24×24)-bit product. A 32-bit integer multiplication is actually performed via a combination of several 24-bit multiplications, shifts and additions. According to the CUDA C programming guide [20], eight 24-bit integer multiplications can be executed per clock cycle on each SM, which is more efficient than the integer multiplication using a straightforward 32-bit representation. Thus, we adopt a 24-bit representation for the field elements in our work.

Multi-precision operands are typically represented by arrays of w-bit words whereby w is determined by the word-size of the target processor. When using a straightforward 32-bit-per-word representation, a 160-bit operand X can be stored in an array of five 32-bit words. On the other hand, a radix-2^{24} representation (i.e. 24 bits per word) requires seven 32-bit words as shown in

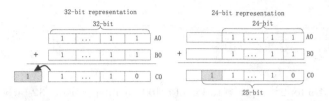

Fig. 2. Comparison of multi-precision addition (radix-2^{32} vs radix-2^{24})

Figure 1. The most significant byte is 0 in every word and the most significant word of a 160-bit integer contains only 16 bits. Even though this representation takes two additional 32-bit words (namely seven in total instead of five), it yields significantly better field-multiplication performance on a GT200.

2^{24} Addition vs 2^{32} Addition. As shown in the left side of Figure 2, when using the radix-2^{32} representation, the sum of two words may overflow, and the resulting carry bit has to be added to the next-higher word. This can be performed efficiently in PTX assembly language using the add.cc instruction [21]. On the other hand, the radix-2^{24} representation provides enough space in the unused most significant byte to hold the carry. However, there are extra instructions necessary to extract the carry bit and then add it to the next-higher pair of words. Thus, the radix-2^{24} representation makes multi-precision addition slightly slower, but this is more than compensated by a significant gain in multiplication performance as will be described below.

2^{24} Multiplication vs 2^{32} Multiplication. We use the product-scanning method [10], which can be optimized to take advantage our 24-bit integer representation. Figure 3 shows an example of its implementation. As mentioned before, CUDA provides the [u]mul24.lo/hi instructions, whereby the former multiplies the 24 Least Significant Bits (LSBs) of the operands and returns the 32 LSBs of the 48-bit product. On the other hand, [u]mul24.hi also multiplies the 24 LSBs of the operands, but returns the 32 Most Significant Bits (MSBs) of the product [21, p. 60]. Therefore, the 48-bit product is written to two 32-bit registers. In the inner loop of the product-scanning method, the partial products of the same column are added together. Due to the 24-bit representation, we have 8 unused bits, which allows the carries to be added as part of the operands (we only need to extract the carries at the end of the inner loop). Hence, only two 32-bit additions are needed in each iteration of the inner loop.

The inner loop is much slower when using a 32-bit representation, which has two main reasons. First, a 32-bit integer multiplication takes much longer than the native 24-bit multiply instruction. Second, the processing of the carry bits requires additional effort because both a 32-bit addition (to accumulate the lower part) and a 64-bit addition (to accumulate the higher part) has to be executed per loop iteration. A further disadvantage is the need for extra registers. Figure 4 compares the execution time of the multiplication using a radix-2^{24} and

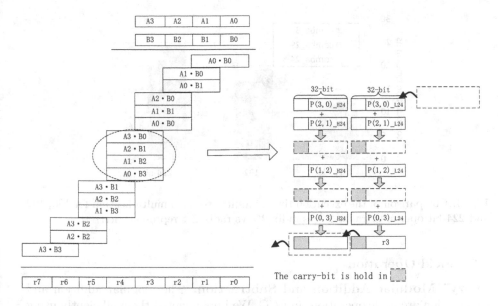

Fig. 3. Product-scanning method for multi-precision multiplication

a radix-2^{32} representation. The figure also includes a radix-2^{29} representation, which uses 32-bit multiply instructions to get the partial products, but handles the carries in the same way as the radix-2^{24} representation. Our results show that the 24-bit representation outperforms the other two approaches by far.

Besides addition and multiplication, the proposed radix-2^{24} representation is also beneficial for modular reduction. The reason is twofold:

- **No Reduction Operation:** The idea of incomplete modular reduction was described in detail by Yanik et al [23]. This technique allows the result of an operation to be greater than the prime p, but it must have the same bit length (denoted as s). Normally, if $p < 2^s < 2p - 1$, we require the result of a field arithmetic operation to be in the range $[0, 2^s - 1]$, but it does not necessarily need to be smaller than p. Consequently, the reduction operation can be avoided when this condition is met, which means incompletely reduced results can save execution time. However, if the result does not fit into s bits, we need to reduce it until it is in the range $[0, 2^s - 1]$. Our implementation does not need to perform the reduction operation for every field operation since the excess bits can be held in the unused bits without additional memory or register usage.
- **No Conditional Branches:** Addition and Montgomery reduction may require a final subtraction of p, which can cause thread divergence and leak side-channel information if implemented in a naive way. As we pointed out before, the radix-2^{24} representation does not have this problem.

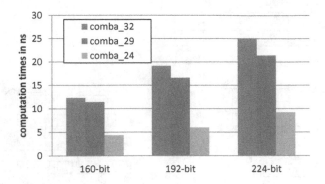

Fig. 4. Comparison of the execution time of multi-precision multiplication for 160, 192 and 224-bit operands (radix-2^{24} vs radix-2^{29} vs radix-2^{32} representation)

3.2 Field Operations

"Lazy" Modular Addition and Subtraction. The modular addition and subtraction are basic operations in ECC. We implemented them efficiently using our special integer representation. For modular addition, we replace the field addition $a + b \bmod p$ by an ordinary integer addition $a + b$ without reduction operation. Since the unused bits in the most significant word can hold excess bits (i.e. carries), the conditional subtraction can be eliminated. In a modular subtraction, it is not possible to get a negative result due to the final reduction operation (i.e. addition of p). However, this is not true for an ordinary subtraction. In our work, we compute $kp + a - b$ instead of $a - b$ to avoid to get negative results, which is more efficient than doing a reduction since we just need to add two 24-bit words before subtracting. The problem is to decide how many p have to be added, which of course depends on the operands a and b. If $a > b$ is always true then we could just compute $a - b$. Unfortunately, there is no guarantee that this is the case. In our implementation, the field-arithmetic operations are invoked by the point addition and point doubling. In these two operations, the inputs of a modular subtraction are generally the outputs of addition, modular multiplication or squaring. The outputs of modular multiplication and squaring are always in $[0, 2p)$. On the other hand, the output of an addition is in the range of $[0, 4p)$. Therefore, we can avoid a negative result when $k = 4$, which means we can simply replace $a - b \bmod p$ by $4p + a - b$.

Efficient Field Multiplication and Squaring. Modular multiplication and modular squaring are the two most performance-critical arithmetic operations in ECC. In our implementation, they are realized through Montgomery's modular reduction technique introduced in [17]. We use a special variant of the so-called Montgomery multiplication, the so-called Finely Integrated Product Scanning (FIPS) method. The OPF primes we use have a very low Hamming weight so that only the most significant and the least significant 24-bit word needs to be considered in the reduction. We implemented both modular multiplication and squaring on basis of Liu et al's OPF-FIPS algorithm introduced in [15], which simply ignores all the zero-words and, in this way, achieves very high performance. We refer to [15] for a detailed description of the implementation. Some further optimizations are possible when using a radix-2^{24} representation and following the approach of incomplete modular reduction. In this way, the final subtraction in both the Montgomery multiplication and squaring does not need to be carried out. However, the result of a modular multiplication/squaring is now in the range of $[0, 2p - 1]$. Note that, since the FIPS method is based on the product-scanning approach, we can process carries efficiently as described before. All loops are fully unrolled for performance reasons. The operands are loaded into registers and then we perform the computation in a word by word fashion. Finally, the result is written back to memory.

3.3   Group Operations and Scalar Multiplication

Point Addition and Doubling. The most efficient way to represent a point $P = (x, y)$ on a twisted Edwards curve is to use extended projective coordinates of the form $(X : Y : T : Z)$ as proposed by Hisil et al in [11]. However, in order to further optimize the point arithmetic, our implementation omits the multiplication that produces the auxiliary coordinate T and outputs the two factors E, H it is composed of instead (see [7] for details). In this way, one can obtain more efficient point addition formulae, especially when the curve parameter $a = -1$. By applying these optimizations, the cost of addition and doubling amounts to 7M and 3M + 4S, respectively.

We implemented the point addition/doubling on the Montgomery curve in a straightforward way using exactly the formulae given in [18].

Scalar Multiplication. We benchmark our GPU implementation with two different scalar multiplication techniques. In the case of an arbitrary point (i.e. a base point that that neither constant or known in advance), we use the standard Montgomery ladder on the Montgomery curve. In this way, we have to always execute exactly one point addition and one point doubling for each bit of the scalar, which amounts to $5M + 4S$ per bit. On the other hand, if the base point is fixed, our implementation uses a regular version of the *comb method* with 256 pre-computed points, similar as described in [16]. The idea of the regular comb method is as follows: Since the base point P is fixed, we can do an off-line pre-computation of multiples $d \cdot P$ of P and store them in a table. Then, during the actual scalar multiplication, we process 8 bits of the scalar at a time, and add the corresponding entry from the table to the previous intermediate result. In this way, the number of point doublings is reduced by a factor of 8 compared to the straightforward double-and-add method. The number of point additions is exactly the same as the number of doublings since we exploit the completeness of the Edwards addition law and add the neutral element $\mathcal{O} = (0, 1)$ when an 8-bit block of the scalar is 0. The overall cost of our comb method with 256 pre-computed points amounts to $\frac{10}{8}nM + \frac{4}{8}nS$ for an n-bit scalar.

4   Experimental Results

Our experimental platform is an NVIDIA GTX285 graphics card; it contains a GT200 GPU clocked at a frequency of 1476 MHz. The GT200 is nowadays considered a low-end GPU with a compute capability of 1.3.

4.1   Throughput and Latency

The number of blocks per grid and the number of threads per block are two essential parameters of an execution configuration since they directly impact the utilization of the GPU. Furthermore, these two parameters interplay with the memory and register usage. In our evaluation, we focus on three parameters, namely the number of blocks running on each SM, the number of threads per block, and the usage of on-chip memory.

The threads are assigned to an SM in a group of blocks. A block of threads gets scheduled to one available multiprocessor. We can use more than one block to expand the throughput by taking advantages of the 30 SMs. In [1], the best performance was achieved by launching 30 blocks on the GT200. However, the GT200 allows for up to 512 threads per SM, provided that there is sufficient on-chip memory and registers available for each thread. Unfortunately, both is severely limited, which requires to carefully balance the number of threads per block with register and shared memory usage. Furthermore, the performance also varies depending on what kind of memory is used. There are three basic implementation options; we briefly describe them below taking variable-base scalar multiplication on the 160-bit Montgomery curve as example.

- Shared memory can be accessed very fast, but is small. We can achieve the lowest latency when all operands are held in shared memory. However, due to its limited capacity of 16 kB per SM, only up to 80 threads per block can be launched. We call this number of threads the *threads limit point*.
- Global memory is large. Thus, we can move some operands that are not frequently used into global memory. In this case, the threads limit point increases to 144. However, due to slower access time, the latency rises.
- To launch even more threads, we can put all operands into global memory. In this case, the threads limit point is 160 threads per block, determined by the register restriction. Unfortunately, the latency becomes very high.

The resulting throughput and latency of all three cases are illustrated in Figure 5. We can see that the blue line representing the latency is flat until the first threads limit point of 80. Thereafter (i.e. from 96 onwards), the latency rises slightly since now global memory is used to hold parts of operands. After passing the second threads limit point (i.e. 144), only global memory is used, and therefore the latency increases sharply. In our work, throughput refers to the number of point multiplications that can be executed per second, which is an important performance metric. Figure 5 shows that the green bars representing this metric keep increasing until the second thread limit point of 144, where the

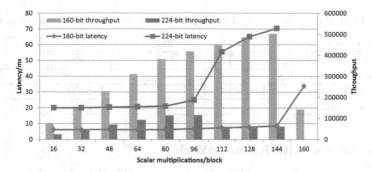

Fig. 5. Throughput and latency for a different number of variable-base scalar multiplications per block (using the Montgomery ladder on a Montgomery curve)

peak is reached. After this point, the throughput declines sharply. Hence, we achieve the highest throughput, namely 502k scalar multiplications per second, with 4320 threads (i.e. 144 threads per block). This shows that one can increase throughput by sacrificing latency; we did this by using both shared memory and global memory for storing operands. For the 224-bit Montgomery ladder, the highest throughput of 115k scalar multiplications per second is achieved when 96 threads per block are launched (i.e. 2880 threads altogether).

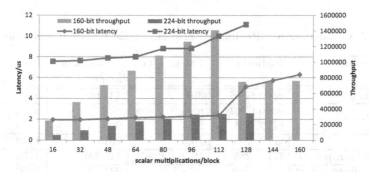

Fig. 6. Throughput and latency for a different number of fixed-base scalar multiplications per block (using a comb method with 256 points on a twisted Edwards curve)

Our implementation of the comb method stores the pre-computed points in constant memory. Figure 6 shows the latency and throughput for a twisted Edwards curves over a 160 and 224-bit OPF, respectively. Table 1 summarizes the maximum performance of the four implementations. The throughput of the comb method is about 1412k and 345k in the 160 and 224-bit case, respectively. The performance is highly dependent on choosing the proper number of scalar multiplications per block. Our results show that 112 and 128 are the best choices for 160 and 224-bit curves, respectively, if one aims for high throughput.

Table 1. Minimum latency and maximum throughput of scalar multiplication

Implementation	Latency [ms]	Throughput [op/s]
160-bit Montgomery ladder	5.9	502326
160-bit Comb method	1.84	1411756
224-bit Montgomery ladder	19.2	115200
224-bit Comb method	4.52	345417

4.2 Comparison with Related Work

In recent years, numerous ECC implementations for GPUs have been reported in the literature. In [1], Antão et al introduced a parallel algorithm for point multiplication using a Residue Number System (RNS) to expose parallelism in the multi-precision integer arithmetic. Their results on the GTX285 platform suggest a maximum throughput of 9990 scalar multiplications per second and a latency of 24.3 ms if the underlying field has a size of 224 bits. Szerwinski and Güneysu [22] presented an implementation on an NVIDIA 8800GTS based on the operand-scanning method for multi-precision multiplication. Their results indicate a throughput of 1412 scalar multiplications per second using the NIST P-224 curve. In [8], Giorgi et al did a comprehensive evaluation of both prime-field arithmetic and point arithmetic (including scalar multiplication) on the NVIDIA 9800 GX2 GPU for operands of different length. When using a 224-bit field, they achieved throughput of 1972 scalar multiplications per second.

Table 2. Comparison of GPU implementations of 224-bit scalar multiplication

Implementation	Platform	Latency [ms]	Throughput [op/s]	Processor clock [MHz]
Szerwinski [22]	8800 GTS	305	1412.6	n./a.
Giorgi [8]	9800 GX2	n./a.	1972	n./a.
Antão [1]	GTX 285	24.3	9990	1476
Bos [6]	GTX 295	10.6	79198	1242
Our work (var. point)	GTX 285	19.2	115200	1476
Our work (fixed point)	GTX 285	4.52	345417	1476

To our knowledge, Bos reported in [6] the best previous result for ECC over a 224-bit prime field on the GT200, even though he optimized latency instead of throughput. He used a Montgomery ladder on a Weierstrass curve for scalar multiplication, which is implemented with 8 threads so as to exploit parallelism in the point operations. As shown in Table 2, he reached a throughput of 79198 scalar multiplications per second, but one has to consider that the GTX295 he used for benchmarking contains two GT200 GPUs, which are clocked with a slightly lower frequency than in our GTX285. Taking these differences into account, our throughput in the variable-base setting is 2.45 times higher than that of Bos. On the other hand, the latency differs by a factor of 2.15.

5 Conclusions

In order to push the performance envelope of ECC on GPUs, we combined the state-of-the-art in terms of efficient group arithmetic (namely Montgomery and twisted Edwards curves) with fast finite-field arithmetic (enabled by using an OPF) and implemented both to match the characteristics of the NVIDIA Tesla microarchitecture. We measured throughput and latency of our implementation on the GT200, a Tesla GPU with compute capability 1.3. To optimize the field arithmetic with respect to 24-bit integer multipliers of the GT200, we adopted a radix-2^{24} representation (i.e. we placed only 24 bits in a 32-bit word) for the field elements. Our results indicate that this approach, even though it increases the number of words, improves the performance of a 224-bit multiplication by a factor of 2.75 compared to a straightforward radix-2^{32} representation. Since we aimed to maximize throughput (i.e. to carry out as many scalar multiplications per second as possible), we used only one thread for each scalar multiplication and tried to launch as many threads in parallel as possible. We found that the main bottleneck of such a "one-thread-per-task" strategy is the relatively small amount of shared memory (16 kB per SM). To work around this limitation, we scarified latency for throughput and moved some less-frequently used operands from shared memory to un-cached global memory. In this way, we managed to launch 2,880 threads and achieved a throughput of 115k scalar multiplications per second on a Montgomery curve over a 224-bit OPF.

Acknowledgements. The research described in this paper was supported, in part, by the National Science Foundation of China (61173139), the Specialized Research Fund for the Doctoral Program of Higher Education of China (20110131110027), and the Key Program of the Natural Science Foundation of Shandong Province (ZR2011FZ005).

References

1. Antão, S., Bajard, J.-C., Sousa, L.: Elliptic curve point multiplication on GPUs. In: Proceedings of the 21st IEEE International Conference on Application-Specific Systems, Architectures and Processors (ASAP 2010), pp. 192–199. IEEE Computer Society Press (2010)
2. Antão, S., Bajard, J.-C., Sousa, L.: RNS-based elliptic curve point multiplication for massive parallel architectures. Computer Journal 55(5), 629–647 (2012)
3. Bernstein, D.J., Birkner, P., Joye, M., Lange, T., Peters, C.: Twisted Edwards curves. In: Vaudenay, S. (ed.) AFRICACRYPT 2008. LNCS, vol. 5023, pp. 389–405. Springer, Heidelberg (2008)
4. Bernstein, D.J., Chen, H.-C., Chen, M.-S., Cheng, C.-M., Hsiao, C.-H., Lange, T., Lin, Z.-C., Yang, B.-Y.: The billion-mulmod-per-second PC. In: Proceedings of the 4th Workshop on Special-Purpose Hardware for Attacking Cryptographic Systems (SHARCS 2009), Lausanne, Switzerland, pp. 131–144 (September 2009)
5. Bernstein, D.J., Chen, T.-R., Cheng, C.-M., Lange, T., Yang, B.-Y.: ECM on graphics cards. In: Joux, A. (ed.) EUROCRYPT 2009. LNCS, vol. 5479, pp. 483–501. Springer, Heidelberg (2009)

6. Bos, J.W.: Low-latency elliptic curve scalar multiplication. International Journal of Parallel Programming 40(5), 532–550 (2012)
7. Chu, D., Großschädl, J., Liu, Z., Müller, V., Zhang, Y.: Twisted Edwards-form elliptic curve cryptography for 8-bit AVR-based sensor nodes. In: Proceedings of the 1st ACM Workshop on Asia Public-Key Cryptography (AsiaPKC 2013), pp. 39–44. ACM Press (2013)
8. Giorgi, P., Izard, T., Tisserand, A.: Comparison of modular arithmetic algorithms on GPUs. In: Parallel Computing: From Multicores and GPU's to Petascale. Advances in Parallel Computing, vol. 19, pp. 315–322. IOS Press (2010)
9. Großschädl, J.: TinySA: A security architecture for wireless sensor networks. In: Proceedings of the 2nd International Conference on Emerging Networking Experiments and Technologies (CoNEXT 2006), pp. 288–289. ACM Press (2006)
10. Hankerson, D.R., Menezes, A.J., Vanstone, S.A.: Guide to Elliptic Curve Cryptography. Springer (2004)
11. Hisil, H., Wong, K.K.-H., Carter, G., Dawson, E.: Twisted Edwards curves revisited. In: Pieprzyk, J. (ed.) ASIACRYPT 2008. LNCS, vol. 5350, pp. 326–343. Springer, Heidelberg (2008)
12. Jang, K., Han, S., Han, S., Moon, S., Park, K.: SSLShader: Cheap SSL acceleration with commodity processors. In: Andersen, D.G., Ratnasamy, S. (eds.) Proceedings of the 8th USENIX Symposium on Networked Systems Design and Implementation (NSDI 2011). USENIX Organization (2011)
13. Khan, F.G.: General Purpose Computation on Graphics Processing Units using OpenCL. Ph.D. Thesis, Politecnico di Torino, Torino, Italy (March 2013)
14. Lindholm, E., Nickolls, J., Oberman, S., Montrym, J.: NVIDIA Tesla: A unified graphics and computing architecture. IEEE Micro 28(2), 39–55 (2008)
15. Liu, Z., Großschädl, J., Wong, D.S.: Low-weight primes for lightweight elliptic curve cryptography on 8-bit AVR processors. In: Lin, D., Xu, S., Yung, M. (eds.) INSCRYPT 2013. LNCS. Springer, Heidelberg (to appear)
16. Liu, Z., Großschädl, J., Wenger, E.: MoTE-ECC: Energy-scalable elliptic curve cryptography for wireless sensor networks. In: Boureanu, I., Owezarski, P., Vaudenay, S. (eds.) ACNS 2014. LNCS. Springer, Heidelberg (to appear)
17. Montgomery, P.L.: Modular multiplication without trial division. Mathematics of Computation 44(170), 519–521 (1985)
18. Montgomery, P.L.: Speeding the Pollard and elliptic curve methods of factorization. Mathematics of Computation 48(177), 243–264 (1987)
19. NVIDIA Corporation. NVIDIA GeForce® GTX 200 GPU Architectural Overview. Technical brief (2008),
   http://www.nvidia.com/docs/IO/55506/
   GeForce_GTX_200_GPU_Technical_Brief.pdf
20. NVIDIA Corporation. CUDA C Programming Guide. Design guide (2013),
   http://docs.nvidia.com/cuda/pdf/CUDA_C_Programming_Guide.pdf
21. NVIDIA Corporation. Parallel Thread Execution ISA. Application guide (2013),
   http://docs.nvidia.com/cuda/pdf/ptx_isa_3.2.pdf
22. Szerwinski, R., Güneysu, T.: Exploiting the power of GPUs for asymmetric cryptography. In: Oswald, E., Rohatgi, P. (eds.) CHES 2008. LNCS, vol. 5154, pp. 79–99. Springer, Heidelberg (2008)
23. Yanık, T., Savaş, E., Koç, Ç.K.: Incomplete reduction in modular arithmetic. IEE Proceedings – Computers and Digital Techniques 149(2), 46–52 (2002)

A Progressive Dual-Rail Routing Repair Approach for FPGA Implementation of Crypto Algorithm

Chenyang Tu[1,3,4,*], Wei He[2], Neng Gao[1,3,**], Eduardo de la Torre[2], Zeyi Liu[1,3,4], and Limin Liu[1,3]

[1] State Key Laboratory of Information Security,
Institute of Information Engineering, CAS,
Beijing, China
[2] Centro de Electronica Industrial, Universidad Politecnica de Madrid,
Jose Gutierrez Abascal. 2, 28006 Madrid, Spain
[3] Data Assurance and Communication Security Research Center, CAS,
Beijing, China
[4] University of Chinese Academy of Sciences, Beijing, China
{chytu,gaoneng,liuzeyi,lmliu}@lois.cn,
{wei.he,eduardo.delatorre}@upm.es

Abstract. Side Channel Analysis (SCA), which has gained wide attentions during the past decade, has arisen as one of the most critical metrics for the cryptographic algorithm security evaluation. Typical SCA analyzes the data-dependent variations inspected from side channel leakages, such as power and electromagnetism (EM), to disclose intra secrets from cryptographic implementations on varying platforms, like microprocessor, FPGA, etc. Dual-rail Precharge Logic (DPL) has proven to be an effective logic-level countermeasure against classic correlation analysis by means of dual-rail compensation protocol. However, the DPL design is hard to be automated on FPGA, and the only published approach is subject to a simplified and partial AES core. In this paper, we present a novel implementation approach applied to a complete AES-128 crypto algorithm. This proposal bases on a partition mechanism which splits the whole algorithm to submodules and transform individuals to DPL format respectively. The main flavor lies within its highly symmetric dual-rail routing networks inside each block, which significantly reduces the routing bias between each routing pair in DPL. This paper describes the overall repair strategy and technical details. The experimental result shows a greatly elevated success rate during the routing repair phase, from lower than 60% to over 84% for Xilinx Virtex-5 FPGA in SASEBO-GII evaluation board.

Keywords: Side Channel Analysis, Dual-rail Precharge Logic (DPL), routing repair, Design Automation, Xilinx FPGA.

* This work is supported by a grant from the National High Technology Research and Development Program of China (863 Program, No. 2013AA01A214) and the National Basic Research Program of China(973 Program, No. 2013CB338001).
** Corresponding Author.

X. Huang and J. Zhou (Eds.): ISPEC 2014, LNCS 8434, pp. 217–231, 2014.
© Springer International Publishing Switzerland 2014

1   Introduction

Side Channel Analysis (SCA) has evolved as a crucial security issue when building a sound cryptographic circuit since Paul Kocher et al's innovative discovery in [1]. This attack typically observes the power consumption or EM emanation from a running crypto device to infer internal circuit behaviors or processed date, particularly as the secret key. Differing from traditional cryptanalysis techniques, SCA can be seen as a non-intrusive attack since it theoretically doesn't interrupt the algorithmic functions, which makes it difficult to be detected and defended with passive counter strategies.

The countermeasure research towards SCA is a complex issue which needs to be scrutinized from the design bring-up, which involves the target algorithm, required security level and performance, implementation platform, cost (e.g. power, chip area) and computation capability of adversaries. Two major popular methods, *masking* and *hiding*, have been proposed for removing or alleviating SCA threats. Precisely, masking applies to the algorithmic level, to alter the sensitive intermediate values with a mask in reversible ways. Unlike the linear masking, non-linear operations that widely exist in modern cryptography are difficult to be masked. Approved to be an effective countermeasure, the hiding method mainly refers to a compensation strategy that is specially devised for smoothening the data-dependent leakage in power or EM signature. While, none of them can be extensively secure mainly being stunted from their implementations. In this paper, we focus on the Dual-rail Precharge Logic (DPL) - one solution from hiding approach - to introduce the technical proposals.

For dynamically compensating the intermediates, DPL is equipped with an original (True/T) rail and a complementary (False/F) rail, which should be a counterpart of the T rail [4]. In this way, the side-channel fluctuation in power or EM signatures can be theoretically flattened. What's more, timing achieves a highly precise compensation manner between the two rails, the symmetry routing paths are essential in the DPL solution. In practice it is pretty hard to have the rigorous requirements using vendor provided tools, especially when implementing a DPL design upon FPGA. This is mainly due to the weird logic structure of DPL logic which requires strict physical symmetry between the two logic rails that cannot be properly satisfied using generic FPGA design flow. A series of novel packed techniques were introduced in [7][9] which depict a dual-rail creation technique for FPGA implemented DPL, supported by low-layer element manipulations from third-party APIs. This approach relies on two consecutive execution procedures, namely "dual-rail transformation and routing repair" to (a) highly expedite the logic realization; and (b) automatically heal the problematic routings.

However, the described proposal is only validated with a very tiny design - a simplified 8-bit AES core module [3]. To be concrete, the tool doesn't work efficiently upon complex designs, because it is severely retarded by its low computation efficiency during the reentrant repair process. In a sizable cryptographic algorithm, all components of cryptographic circuits should be repaired as an unity. The result is influenced by two aspects: firstly, the number of the conflict complementary routing pairs is increasing due to the drastic routing resource competition on the routing channels while the number of circuit components is increasing; secondly, the security of DPL implementation is decreased with non-identical complementary routing pairs.

To mitigate the implementation trouble, a progressive repair approach is proposed, which relies on a partition strategy to progressively process each submodule. The main challenges for this technique are described from the following three parts:

1) Split the complex cryptographic design to numerous functional blocks. In the FPGA environment, the block is defined as a local territory to implement one logic cluster, such as buffer, RAM, CLB and pin. The conventional concept of block is not applicable to our cryptographic functional block. Therefore, a new definition of cryptographic functional block is required.
2) Map the circuit components into each block. All circuit components should be relocated as close as possible with a conventional mapping approach. It might lead to more non-identical complementary routing pairs, which cripple the global network symmetry.
3) Take different executions over each block because it is unnecessary to transform some blocks to DPL format in consideration of cost/security tradeoff.

Our contribution mainly lies within a logic division tactic, and a progressive repair mechanism supported by previously presented third-party auto repair toolkit. The described work splits the whole algorithm to several functional submodules and deal with them sequentially. Our approach is appropriate for complex cryptographic design scenario. Experiments show that the routing repair success rate of an AES-128 implementation is higher than 84% after the automatic routing repair. However, the mechanism increases the repair success rate while slightly weakens certain performance, like design density and maximal frequency. Note that the proposal is valuable for proof-of-concept in security-critical applications, instead of being a globally-adaptive closed system. A meticulous tradeoff between security and cost sufficiently before project bring-up is still mandatory.

The rest of the paper is organized as follows. In Section 2, the prior relevant work is briefly described. Section 3 discusses the barriers on automatic DPL generation of a sizable algorithm by the existing techniques. Section 4 elaborates the proposed progressive repair mechanism for achieving identical net pairs in an FPGA application. Section 5 validates the achieved conflict rate and repair success rate from the improved approach, the security grade from practical comparison attacks and the expenses of extra performance overhead. Finally, Section 6 draws conclusions and perspectives for future work.

2   Related Work

From generic sense of Side channel attacks, interesting leakages come from the lower physical (transistor, gate) level instead of higher level layer (logic algorithmic level). Accordingly, most countermeasures are deployed at low-level logic layers, i.e., gate level (or equivalent LUT level in FPGA) for reducing or concealing the exploitable signatures. DPL consists of an original (True/T) rail and a complementary (False/F) rail, which should be a counterpart of the T rail[4]. In this logic, dual rails work simultaneously in complementary behaviors. Two phases, precharge and evaluation, are alternatively switched by this protocol. The value $a_{(T)}$ in T rail and $a_{(F)}$ in F rail compensate with each other (i.e., '$a_{(T)}$: $a_{(F)}$' is always in state of '1:0' or '0:1') during the evaluation phase. Likewise, $a_{(T)}$ and $a_{(T)}$ both are reset to a fixed state (typically '0', or in a few cases '1').As a typical DPL, Simple Dynamic Differential Logic (SDDL) is first introduced in [4]. In [5], same authors have proposed a new technique to implement SDDL on FPGA with higher slice utilization.

In [3], the technique of automatic generation of identical routing pairs for FPGA implemented DPL is presented. It is based on the copy-paste and conflict-repair method, which makes use of a file format called Xilinx Design Language (XDL) and a series of java-based third-party tools from RapidSmith [6] to carry on the XDL format to include significant LUT-level modifications. XDL is a human-readable equivalent version of the Xilinx NCD file, which is a proprietary binary format to describe designs internally either after mapping or place and route steps used by Xilinx commercial FPGA tools. The technique transforms the normal algorithm design NCD design file to XDL format. Then it performs the copy-paste execution to create the complementary F rail on XDL manner. Next, the technique, relying on RapidSmith toolkit, analyses and modifies the XDL design file to repair conflict routing pairs and complete the PA-DPL logic. Finally, it transforms the new XDL design file to NCD version and generate bit file to complete the whole automatic DPL generation process. And a PA-DPL AES core implementation on a FPGA chip soldered on SASEBO-GII SCA-evaluation board is generated automatically as a case study in this paper.

3   DPL Implementation Difficulties for Sizable Algorithm

The technique proposed in [3] about automatic generation of identical routing pairs for FPGA implemented DPL employs an incorporated two phases mechanism known as copy-paste and conflict-repair, to realize rail transformation and routing repair work. A brief design flow is diagrammed in Fig 1. To obtain concurrent dual-rail behavior precisely, complete T/F compensation, and the two rails must be maintained identical [2]. Meanwhile, the DPL in row-cross interleaved placement can protect design against EM analysis which makes use of the long distance between the complementary rails. Hence, the complementary routing pairs in circuit translate one unit (a slice) on FPGA chip, and their shapes are identical.

However, the existing technique is not suitable to the design of a complex cryptographic algorithm, since it suffers from a low repair success rate due to severe local resource congestion and the slow repair speed when a direct global execution has been performed.

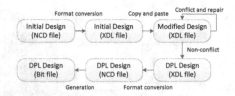

Fig. 1. The process of the existing technique

3.1   Serious Routing Congestion with Large Numbers of Components

The interleaved format of the routing pair would result in very close routing channels with each other [7][10]; the reuses of routing conflicts are likely to occur in local parts, which might result in circuit electrical failures. There is a set of competitions on the routing channels from particular passed territories once a number of routing pairs span through those regions. We note that the routing conflicts are inherently avoided from single-rail circuit, since vendor router algorithm never allows this to happen. However, in dual-rail duplication, the back-end created F network is relocated, which is possible to reuse some used routing resources in practise.

When the Xilinx commercial FPGA tools load a design, the circuit will be concentrated in a certain local area instead of being placed dispersedly over the entire FPGA fabric. To simplicity, the density of the used components in particular region is much higher than that from other regions and the densities of nets vary greatly in different regions. For instance, the density of nets in the left clock region is much lower than that in the right part, as seen in Fig 2. The routing resource competition of the routing channels is severe and the conflict of routing pairs would take place with a high probability in the region with congested wires, especially after the copy-paste process. Furthermore, the success rate of routing repair work would descend while the number of wires is exceeding the resource threshold of the routing channel. Therefore, the region with a high logic density (i.e., all components in the region are used) is exceeding, the conflict rate of the routing channel rises after the copy-paste process and the routing repair success rate get lower as a domino effect.

In addition, the routing repair algorithms presented in [11][12][13] employ a greedy brute force mechanism to thoroughly find-and-test all the possible identical paths for both T/F nets. In some cases, the local optimization is hard to realize. It means that some conflict routings would be repaired successfully by the global optimization algorithm. The repair success rate is likely to be decreased when that case takes place at a real repair process.

3.2   Unacceptable Time-Consuming Path Selection

As previously mentioned, the routing repair algorithm developed based on Rapid-Smith is an exhaustive search. It is worthy to note that this process basically

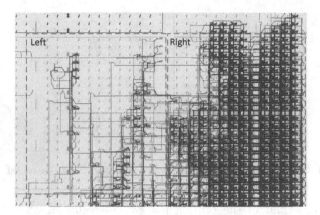

Fig. 2. Different densities of nets in different local region

doesn't touch other logic paths when it is amending a certain pair of nets. It leads to local rather than global optimization. In other words, a case would take place with a high possibility that some routing pairs at the top of the conflict nets list are easy to be repaired and other routing pairs at the bottom of the list are getting retardant to be healed (success with several times of modification or failure after many times of modification). This congestion would exacerbate if the design scale is large.

We perform an experiment that directly implements AES-128 coprocessor over Xilinx Virtex-5 FPGA. The experiment shows that the repair process has run more than 100 hours without an outcome on DELL Server (PowerEdge R610). There are 1032 non-identical routing pairs existing, and the repair success rate is no more than 60% in the completed portion. It is hence hard to directly apply the existing technique to a complex algorithm implementation by the experimental result. Even using a more powerful computer, this retarded process rate makes the technique not attractive in practice. Hence, some optimization techniques must be replied on to achieve a viable way to mitigate this problem.

4   Progressive Repair Mechanism

4.1   The Overview of Progressive Repair Mechanism

To expedite the repair process of identical routing pairs for a whole crypto algorithm, a progressive repair mechanism based on the logic division is developed to expand the existing technique to a broader range of real-world applications. The new approach splits the whole cryptographic circuit to functional blocks, maps each block individually to the corresponding local region, and takes different executions to individual functional block. The functional block has balanced logic density in each individual. This strategy brings higher repair success rate for the sake of an eased routing competition.

The process for generating dual-rail pairs of a whole cryptographic design by our improved approach is shown in Fig 3. Firstly, the program loads an original single rail design, and splits the whole design to different cryptographic functional blocks. Then, the program find out a block that requires DPL transformation, and converts it to a dual-rail format by directly cloning the original T rail to a reserved new fabric, performing as the complementary F rail. All the conflicts are found out afterwards, and then to be repaired. The executable repair procedure consists of three steps: (a) The first step is to unroute both T/F nets by removing all the "nodes" for the nets; (b) The second step aims to find a new routable path for the T net. It is stressed that only T net is routed by the custom router, and the F net is completely copied from the new T net and be pasted to the new location; (c) The third step dedicates to review the newly generated F net, to find the existing conflict nodes. A judgment is inserted here: once new conflict exists, the repair process would jump to the next pending net pairs, and otherwise, the process would start again from the first step. When no pending net pair exists in the block, the program would deal with other blocks sequentially until all blocks that need DPL are processed. Finally, the program would process the nets between blocks and generate the whole DPL design.

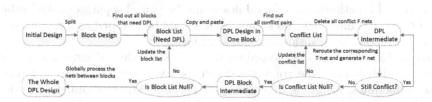

Fig. 3. The process flow of the improved approach

The testbed in our experiment is a complete AES-128 coprocessor which performs one round of an AES encryption in one single clock cycle, and generates 128 bits encrypted data in total after 10 rounds, as diagrammed in Fig 4. Even though the use of Block RAM significantly reduces the leakages [8], this test still implements the S-box by logic elements (slice in Xilinx FPGA, rather than Block RAM) in order to have a closely deployed dual-rail format.

4.2 FPGA Block Division Relevant to Algorithm Structure

In FPGA scenario, the block is defined as a local region to house one functional module, such as buffer, RAM, CLB and pin. The conventional conception is not applicable to this cryptography; hence, a new definition of cryptographic functional block is necessary.

The new definition of block should be proposed from the perspective of cryptographic algorithms. The cryptographic functional block is defined as a local region to realize one special cryptographic function, such as S-box, key expansion and controller. The new block definition corresponds to the function or

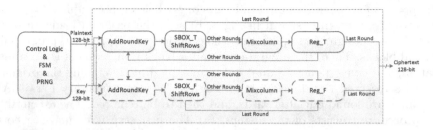

Fig. 4. DPL implementation of the whole AES

module in cryptographic algorithm. It puts the signals generated from one function or module into the same block. Due to the same DPL security requirement of all signals from the same function or module, it is reasonable that the corresponding components and nets are placed into the same block region. Yet different cryptographic modules do not uniformly desire the same security grade in consideration of overall resource expense. Take a wrapped AES in use as an example, the wrapper block which provisions execution commands to the crypto core is not necessary to be protected. The encryption module enclosing all special encrypted functions and submodules would be placed separately. And other special encrypted functions and submodules should be mapped as a row-crossed interleaved placement transform to dual-rail format.

Looking into an AES-128, according to the relationship of modules in Verilog source description, the complete design is divided into diversity of functional submodules, including S-box, Key-Expansion, Mix-Column, Encryption packaging all special encrypted functions and Control. For these functional submodules, several blocks are divided over FPGA chip as follows: four functional blocks called SB0, SB1, SB2 and SB3 to enclose 4 responsible S-box respectively; a functional block called SBK to execute Key-Expansion; two function blocks called Mxor and MX to realize Mix-Column; a functional block named Enc for encapsulating all blocks described above; as well as a functional block Cont to supply clock signal, control I/O and be the top package. The functional blocks are mapped on the FPGA chip as described in Fig 5(a) and Fig 5(b).

4.3 Different DPL Realization for a Single Block

To those functional blocks with interleaved placement, the density of the used components in these regions should be reduced in order to relieve the resource competition in routing channels. Thus, the possibility of the routing conflicts is decreased, and the repair success rate arises, which favorably reduces the time spent on the whole repair process.

For those blocks that need to be transformed into interleaved format, it's necessary to set aside the same number of the components as in the original circuit in order to implement the duplications. We hereafter name the mapping way as "2VS1" placement, which divides the block regions consisting of functional modules into a number of $2 * 1$ slice arrays. We only utilize the bottom slice with the upper one forbidden, as illustrated in Fig 5(a). Then, Xilinx XST tool grants optimized paths for all the T-rail nets. However, the DPL circuit using 2VS1 placement has higher routing density in each block region.

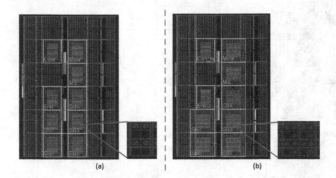

Fig. 5. Different mapping in 2VS1 placement and 4VS1 placement leading to different densities of the used components

We further reduced the logic density by employing a "4VS1" placement approach. Unlike the 2VS1 solution, each block in clock region is divided into a series of $2 * 2$ slice arrays, and only the slice in the lower left corner is used with the other three forbidden ones, as depicted in Fig 5(b). As well, Xilinx router is adopted to route all the T nets. The motivation here is to leave a more relaxed routing conditions for facilitating (i) to provide sufficient routing resource for T nets, which, in this way, can result in comparatively shorter routing paths, and (ii) give higher routability for each duplicated F net with a less number of repair iteration, so as to increase the success rate and speed up the repair process.

When the 4VS1 placement is completed, the duplication execution is performed into each 4VS1 block and then all the conflict routings are to be processed by the provided repair tool. The global routing pairs on FPGA chip and the repaired complementary routing pairs inside each block are illustrated in Fig 6. The difference between 2VS1 and 4VS1 placement method influences the number of the occurred conflicts and observed repair success rates.

4.4 Global Process about the Nets between Blocks

Compared to the prior approach of direct global repair, the proposal discussed in this paper achieves a feasible repair task to a whole cryptographic algorithm with regionally identical routing networks at the expense of sacrificing dual-rail protection to a portion of nets. The difference here is that some security-sensitive nets are not guaranteed in duplicated F rails, as those feedback signals that are deleted in block approach, as given in Fig 7. However, this sacrifice can be minimized by meticulously scheming the partition tactics, to ensure that the

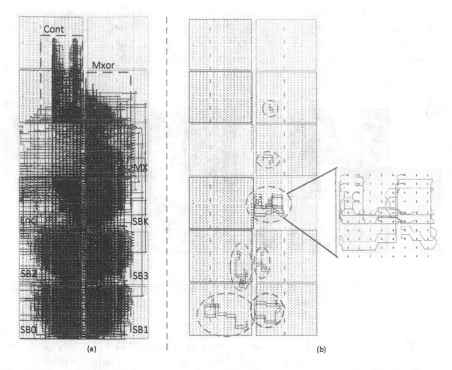

Fig. 6. The global DPL routing result on FPGA chip and several highlighted complementary routing pairs inside each block

sources of each pair of security-critical nets are exclusively deployed inside each single module. Another effort to mitigate this pitfall is to optimize the routing repair efficiency to be able to rapidly find a routing paths for each high-fanout pending nets, thus a global repair can be yielded.

5   Validation on AES-128

We implemented PA-DPL dual-rail style with row-crossed placement format on a Virtex-5 Xilinx FPGA on SASEBO-GII board. Pearson Correlation Coefficient based ElectroMagnetic Analysis (CEMA) is applied during the security analysis. The objective is to attack the AES-128 which was diagrammed in Fig 4. The testbed core (xc5vlx50ff324) owes 12 independent clock regions that are sufficient for housing 9 partitioned submodules.

5.1   Estimation of Conflict Rate and Repair Success Rate

In contrary to the direct routing repair approach of which the repair objective is to globally repair a whole circuit in only one process, the progressive repair process places the global circuit components into a set of sub-regions by partitioning

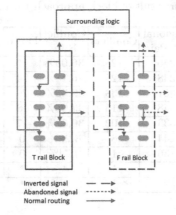

Fig. 7. Feedback signals sacrificed in duplicated F rails

the algorithm according to its functions and hierarchies using 4vs1 placement scheme. Thus the density of the used components in each 4VS1 block is greatly reduced.

Placing each submodule into a single clock region helps to reduce the intra routings. More importantly, this solution also prevents the massive use of long routings, which in practice bring in extra routing delay. However, the long wires between neighboring partitions still exist and remain unprotected. Owing to the small size of each block, the net number within each region is relatively small, and the lengths of them are short. All of these lead to less conflicts among routing pairs, and the velocity and success rate of repair process are relatively high.

Table 1. The repair result of original approach with 4VS1 placement

Part	Format	Regional Net Pairs	Conflicts	Conflict Rate	Repair Time	Repair Complete
Enc	Transformed	2803	1032	36.82%	More than 100 hours	no
Cont	Uncharged	*	*	*	*	*

We launched two experiments over AES-128 on the same FPGA in parallel. The first experiment uses the original and the improved dividing scheme with 4VS1 placement respectively, and the other one employs the proposed progressive partition scheme with 2VS1 and 4VS1 placements. Then the outcomes are illustrated in Table 1, Table 2 and Table 3.

The counted problematic (conflict) routing pairs are 1032 and the conflict rate during the repair process in the original approach is 36.82%. Contrarily, the total number of the conflict routing pairs in original scheme where the dividing method processed with 2VS1 and 4VS1 placements is decreased to 620 and 502,

Table 2. The repair result of block approach with 2VS1 placement

Part	Format	Regional Net Pairs	Conflicts	Conflict Rate	Failed	Exeecd Threshold	Success Rate
SB0	Transformed	355	128	36.06%	15	20	72.66%
SB1	Transformed	348	128	36.78%	24	4	78.13%
SB2	Transformed	351	138	39.32%	29	1	78.26%
SB3	Transformed	348	115	33.05%	18	1	83.48%
SBK	Transformed	333	102	30.63%	17	4	79.41%
MX	Transformed	244	8	3.28%	0	0	100.00%
Mxor	Transformed	136	1	0.74%	0	0	100.00%
Enc	Single-Rail	*	*	*	*	*	*
Cont	Single-Rail	*	*	*	*	*	*

and the conflict rates are reduced to 29.31% and 23.74% respectively. Besides the proposed progressive partition, the repair process has been concluded in several hours while the original one has not yet been completed within several days. The repair success rate of the completed section with the original scheme is lower than 60%. In the case of 2VS1, repair success rate rises up to higher than 72%. Furthermore, repair success rate rises up to higher than 84% in the 4VS1 partition approach (Actually, all the blocks, except one, favors success rate more than 90% in this case study).

Table 3. The repair result of block approach with 4VS1 placement

Part	Format	Regional Net Pairs	Conflicts	Conflict Rate	Failed	Exeecd Threshold	Success Rate
SB0	Transformed	355	108	30.42%	10	7	84.26%
SB1	Transformed	348	95	27.30%	1	6	92.63%
SB2	Transformed	351	104	29.63%	3	0	97.12%
SB3	Transformed	348	100	28.74%	5	5	90.00%
SBK	Transformed	333	87	26.13%	3	1	95.40%
MX	Transformed	244	8	3.28%	0	0	100.00%
Mxor	Transformed	136	0	*	0	0	*
Enc	Single-Rail	*	*	*	*	*	*
Cont	Single-Rail	*	*	*	*	*	*

5.2 Attack Results

A series of comparison attacks have been launched to validate the achieved security level among three circuits. (a) In the first circuit, the same 128 bit AES algorithm is implemented using default settings, except I/O pin configurations; (b) In the second circuit, 4VS1 placement is applied to security-critical partitions, however it is kept as single-rail without introducing the transformation;

(c) The third circuit is transformed from the second circuit, being processed by the proposed progressive repair strategy as aforementioned. For the two single-rail (SR) circuits, equally 10,000 EM traces are inspected from the last encryption rounds with a same sampling rate. For the first circuit, correlation EM analysis successfully recovered all the 16 subkey bytes (See Table 4). For the attack to the second SR circuit, 15 out of the 16 subkey bytes are recovered, with exception of the 15th subkey, where a hexadecimal value 18 is differentiated in contrast to the real subkey 77 (See Table 5). For the attack to the third exported dual-rail (DR) AES-128, correlation analysis over 300,000 traces have not yet disclosed any of the real subkey(See Table 6). The "rank" parameter in Table 4, 5 and 6 represents the correlation coefficient rank of the found key among the 256 kinds of the assumed keys.

Table 4. The attack result of unconstrained SR scheme by 10,000 EM traces

Key	16 last round subkeybytes (hex)															
	0	1	2	3	4	5	6	7	8	9	10	11	12	13	14	15
real	F3	AC	78	29	F0	77	E7	4E	3D	CD	7A	D4	81	C8	99	E1
found	F3	AC	78	29	F0	77	E7	4E	3D	CD	7A	D4	81	C8	99	E1
rank	1	1	1	1	1	1	1	1	1	1	1	1	1	1	1	1

Table 5. The attack result of placement constrained SR scheme by 10,000 EM traces

Key	16 last round subkeybytes (hex)															
	0	1	2	3	4	5	6	7	8	9	10	11	12	13	14	15
real	F3	AC	78	29	F0	77	E7	4E	3D	CD	7A	D4	81	C8	99	E1
found	F3	AC	78	29	F0	18	E7	4E	3D	CD	7A	D4	81	C8	99	E1
rank	1	1	1	1	1	2	1	1	1	1	1	1	1	1	1	1

Table 6. The attack result of progressively repaired DR scheme by 300,000 EM traces

Key	16 last round subkeybytes (hex)															
	0	1	2	3	4	5	6	7	8	9	10	11	12	13	14	15
real	F3	AC	78	29	F0	77	E7	4E	3D	CD	7A	D4	81	C8	99	E1
found	37	18	CF	7B	F4	66	6E	3C	4C	13	8A	59	55	B2	72	F2
rank	124	66	45	252	186	191	226	5	212	110	206	99	253	110	242	241

Observing from the first two circuitries, they merely have slight difference from the attack results upon the analyzed 10,000 traces. However, it is not safe to claim identical security levels for the two parties. As just stated, unconstrained circuit doesn't employ user placement constrained, hence the default map tool would place the components "seemingly" randomly across the FPGA fabric. In this case, the security-critical routings might traverse a large territory, which would practically result in longer routing path (Assuming that the timing closure is not violated). Comparatively, the placement constrained circuit has been meticulously partitioned by logic function and hierarchy. The security-sensitive routings are more likely to be restricted inside a local territory. By this way, the local routing paths for those nets are shorter compared to the prior approach. Therefore, the routing relevant leakage from placement constrained one would be less than that from the placement unconstrained one. This conceptually grants higher security level to the second circuit, where in this case study, one subkey byte is failed to be recovered.

The third produced dual-rail circuit has demonstrated profound safety in contrast to the previous two counterparts, where none of the 16 key bytes is cracked by analyzing up to 300,000 traces. The key rank index also foresees that most real subkeys are not likely to be differentiated if not to substantially increase the analysis samples or to employ more suitable analysis models. Note that the attack to the last round of AES-128 makes sense unless all the subkeys have been retrieved. A failure to any bit of the last round key crumbles the initial key recovery.

5.3   The Expense of Extra Performance Overhead

Furthermore, the main expense of extra performance overhead is the utilization of occupied slices on the FPGA chip. The number of used slices is 977 and the utilization rate is 13% at both unconstrained and constrained single-rail circuits. The total number of 4VS1 dual-rail circuit is 2614 (i.e., the utilization rate is 36.3%), which is less than 3 times of the corresponding single-rail circuit due to some blocks without 4VS1 placement, such as Cont.

6   Conclusion and Future Work

The routing pairs between T and F rails in DPL logic are unbalanced, which is generated by commercial FPGA design tools. And the original dual-rail creation technique for FPGA implemented DPL is only validated with a very tiny design. In this paper, we proposed a progressive repair strategy based on a partition solution to expedite the auto routing technique. In our approach, we splitted the complex cryptographic design to several functional blocks, afterwards to map the circuit components into each block and took different executions to individual blocks. Several different mapping ways are investigated including 2VS1 and 4VS1 placements. Experimental result shows that the 4VS1 solution performs better in terms of the conflict rate and the repair success rate.

We applied this technique to a row-crossed interleaved PA-DPL and carried comparison EM attacks to validate the increased resistance of this approach. Attack results show that the produced dual-rail circuit on FPGA is resistant against classical correlation analysis. What's more, the elevated security with more identical routing pairs and the acceleration of entire process are achieved at the expense of resource and area.

In future work, we plan to improve the routing algorithm to obtain globally optimized paths to decrease the expenses from logic partition. Meanwhile, applying the technique to other dual-rail logics will be another direction of the future work.

References

1. Kocher, P.C., Jaffe, J., Jun, B.: Differential Power Analysis. In: Wiener, M. (ed.) CRYPTO 1999. LNCS, vol. 1666, pp. 388–397. Springer, Heidelberg (1999)
2. Clarke, J.A., Constantinides, G.A., Cheung, P.Y.K.: On the feasibility of early routing capacitance estimation for FPGAs. In: FPL, pp. 234–239. IEEE Press, New York (2007)
3. He, W., Otero, A., de la Torre, E., et al.: Automatic generation of identical routing pairs for FPGA implemented DPL logic. In: International Conference on Reconfigurable Computing and FPGAs, pp. 1–6. IEEE Press, New York (2012)
4. Tiri, K., Verbauwhede, I.: A logic level design methodology for a secure DPA resistant ASIC or FPGA implementation. In: Proceedings of the Conference on Design, Automation and Test in Europe, vol. 1, pp. 246–251. IEEE Computer Society (2004)
5. Tiri, K., Verbauwhede, I.: Synthesis of Secure FPGA Implementations. In: The Proceedings of the International Workshop on Logic and Synthesis (IWLS 2004), pp. 224–231 (June 2004)
6. Lavin, C., Padilla, M., Lundrigan, P., et al.: Rapid prototyping tools for FPGA designs: RapidSmith. In: International Conference on Field-Programmable Technology, pp. 353–356. IEEE Press, New York (2010)
7. Velegalati, R., Kaps, J.-P.: Improving Security of SDDL Designs Through Interleaved Placement on Xilinx FPGAs. In: 21st IEEE International Conference on Field Programmable Logic and Applications, Crete, Greece, pp. 506–511. IEEE Press, New York (2011)
8. Shah, S., Velegalati, R., Kaps, J.-P., Hwang, D.: Investigation of DPA Resistance of Block RAMs in Cryptographic Implementations on FPGAs. In: Prasanna, V.K., Becker, J., Cumplido, R. (eds.) ReConFig, pp. 274–279. IEEE Computer Society (2010)
9. Tiri, K., Verbauwhede, I.: Secure Logic Synthesis. In: Becker, J., Platzner, M., Vernalde, S. (eds.) FPL 2004. LNCS, vol. 3203, pp. 1052–1056. Springer, Heidelberg (2004)
10. He, W., de la Torre, E., Riesgo, T.: An interleaved EPE-immune PA-DPL structure for resisting concentrated EM side channel attacks on FPGA implementation. In: Schindler, W., Huss, S.A. (eds.) COSADE 2012. LNCS, vol. 7275, pp. 39–53. Springer, Heidelberg (2012)
11. Lavin, C., Padilla, M., Lamprecht, J., et al.: RapidSmith: Do-It-Yourself CAD Tools for Xilinx FPGAs. In: 21st IEEE International Conference on Field Programmable Logic and Applications, pp. 349–355. IEEE Press, New York (2011)
12. Lavin, C., Padilla, M., Lamprecht, J., et al.: HMFlow: Accelerating FPGA Compilation with Hard Macros for Rapid Prototyping. In: IEEE 19th Annual International Symposium on Field-Programmable Custom Computing Machines, pp. 117–124. IEEE Press, New York (2011)
13. RAPIDSMITH: A Library for Low-level Manipulation of Partially Placed-and-Routed FPGA Designs. Technical Report and Documentation (November 2013), http://rapidsmith.sourceforge.net/doc/TechReportAndDocumentation.pdf

Fault-Tolerant Linear Collision Attack: A Combination with Correlation Power Analysis

Danhui Wang[1], An Wang[2,*], and Xuexin Zheng[1]

[1] Key Lab of Cryptologic Technology and Information Security,
Ministry of Education, Shandong University, Jinan 250100, China
{wangdanhui,zhxuexin}@mail.sdu.edu.cn
[2] Institute of Microelectronics, Tsinghua University, Beijing 100084, China
wangan1@tsinghua.edu.cn

Abstract. The framework of test of chain was presented by Bogdanov et al. in 2012, which combines collision attack with divide-and-conquer side-channel attacks. Its success rate highly depends on the correctness of the chain established from collision attack. In this paper, we construct a fault-tolerant chain which consists of 15 paths, and each path includes only one step. In order to decrease the misjudgments, we combine this chain with correlation power analysis, linear collision attack and search. So the fault-tolerant linear collision attack is proposed. Our experiments show that the new attack is more efficient than the method of Bogdanov et al. Furthermore, we give a fault-identification mechanism to find the positions of wrong key bytes, and thus the subsequent search space can be reduced a great deal. Finally, the choice of threshold in correlation power analysis is discussed in order to optimize our attack.

Keywords: power analysis attack, correlation power analysis, test of chain, linear collision attack.

1 Introduction

Differential power analysis was proposed at CRYPTO 1999 by Kocher et al. [1]. This method can recover key by analyzing the information of intermediate value which is obtained from the instantaneous power consumption of the cryptographic chip [2]. In 2002, Chari et al. proposed template attack for distinguishing the different intermediate values corresponding to the different keys [3]. Two years later, Brier et al. put forward correlation power analysis (CPA) which uses the correlation coefficient model to recovery key [4]. In 2008, Gierlichs et al. gave mutual information analysis attack based on the information theory [5]. Masking is usually employed against the first-order power analysis attacks [6,7,8,9,10]. However, it can only increase the difficulty of attacks instead of providing absolute security.

Collision attack was proposed in 2003 [11,12], which broke the cipher device by looking for the internal collisions of specific intermediate values. In 2007, Bogdanov proposed linear collision attack [13], which established the relationships

---

* Corresponding Author.

X. Huang and J. Zhou (Eds.): ISPEC 2014, LNCS 8434, pp. 232–246, 2014.

among several key bytes based on the collisions between different S-boxes. Subsequently, he presented multiple-differential side-channel collision attacks based on the voting method [14]. In 2010, Moradi et al. proposed correlation-enhanced collision attack which can be regarded as a tool of linear collision detection [15]. Their attack was improved by Clavier et al. in CHES 2011 [16].

In 2012, according to the new concept of test of chain, Bogdanov et al. combined CPA with collision attack [1,17], which can recover key more efficiently than both stand-alone CPA and collision attacks. Although the test of chain discussed the high efficiency of their combined attack, they did not give a practical attack scheme. On the other hand, their method can only correct the errors in CPA, but can not in the part of collision attack. In other words, once a step error occurs in a path of the chain, it will lead to consecutive errors. And the errors will take place in the entire path, which will result a failed attack. Indeed, the efficiency of typical collision attack is much lower than CPA, which may lead to the unavailability of Bogdanov's method.

Our Contribution. In this paper, we propose a fault-tolerant combination between CPA and collision attack. Specifically,

- A concept of fault-tolerant chain is presented, which significantly improve the success rate of the collision attack part.
- A new framework of practical combination between correlation power analysis and correlation-enhanced collision attack is proposed.
- The step where error occurred can be identified with high probability according to a specific threshold. Thus, the search space of the key is greatly reduced.

Organization. The remainder of this paper is organized as follows. In Section 2, we briefly describe CPA , correlation-enhanced collision attack, and Bogdanov's attack. Section 3 introduces our fault-tolerant attack followed by the experiments and discussions of efficiency. In Section 4, We propose the fault-identification mechanism, and then discuss the threshold value of CPA based on experiments. Finally, we conclude the whole paper in Section 5.

2   Preliminary

2.1   Notations

This article focuses on AES algorithm. We use the following notations to represent the variables. $K = \{k_i | i = 1, 2, \ldots, 16\}$ is the 16-byte user-supplied key. $P^j = \{p_i^j | i = 1, 2, \ldots, 16\}$ denotes an 16-byte AES plaintext, where $j = 1, 2, \ldots, N$ is the number of an AES execution. For the jth plaintext P^j, let $\{T_i^j | i = 1, 2, \ldots, 16\}$ denote 16 sections of the power trace corresponding to 16 S-boxes. Each trace section consists of l interesting points. We use $\{x_i | i = 1, 2, \ldots, 16\}$ to denote the input bytes of S-boxes in the first round. The output bytes of S-boxes are expressed by $\{S(x_i) | i = 1, 2, \ldots, 16\}$. Th_{CPA} is the threshold in CPA, and Th_{CA} is the threshold in collision attack.

2.2 Bogdanov's Combined Side-Channel Collision Attack

A combined collision attack was proposed by Bogdanov et al. in 2012 [17], which combines linear collision attack with side-channel attacks such as CPA [1]. For simplicity, their work is built on AES-128, and uses the key-recovery technique based on linear collisions. Notably, all the techniques of their work may extend to other ciphers which can be broken by collisions.

2.2.1 Correlation Power Analysis

In this section we describe CPA [4] which is used in Bogdanov's attack and our work. The algorithm is described as follows (an example of the first S-box is given).

Algorithm 1. Correlation Power Analysis on S-box 1

Online Stage:
  1: $P = (P^1, P^2, \ldots, P^N) \leftarrow$ **RandomPlaintexts()**
  2: $\{T_1^j | j = 1, 2, \ldots, N\} \leftarrow$ **AcquireTraces**(P)
Key-recovery Stage:
  1: **for** each guess $k_1 \in \{0, 1, \ldots, 255\}$ **do**
  2:      $\{HW^j(x_1) | j = 1, 2, \ldots, N\} \leftarrow$ **ComputeValue**$(\{p_1^j | j = 1, 2, \ldots, N\}, k_1)$
  3:      $\rho_{k_1} \leftarrow$ **CorrelationCoefficient**$(\{HW^j(x_1)\}, \{T_1^j\})$
  4: **end for**
  5: **return** $k_1 \leftarrow \arg\max_{k_1} \rho_{k_1}$

In the online stage, the attacker randomly chooses N 16-byte plaintexts $\{P^j | j = 1, 2, \ldots, N\}$ (**RandomPlaintexts**), and then records the relevant sections of traces $\{T_1^j | j = 1, 2, \ldots, N\}$ for the first AES S-box (**AcquireTraces**). Furthermore, 16 sets of trace sections can be extracted corresponding to 16 S-boxes.

In the key-recovery stage, the attacker guesses the first key byte k_1 from 0 to 255, and then for each k_1 computes the hamming weights of $\{p_1^j \oplus k_1 | j = 1, 2, \ldots, N\}$ (**ComputeValue**). Subsequently, the 256 correlation coefficients ρ_{k_1} (**CorrelationCoefficient**) of the hamming weights and power traces can be computed. Then these correlation coefficients are sorted to obtain a corresponding rank ξ which consists of the 256 candidates of k_1. The candidate of k_1 which corresponds to the max ρ_{k_1} is returned as the recovered key byte. The attacker may repeat **Algorithm 1** for the other 15 key bytes until all the key bytes are recovered.

Suppose that each of the trace sections $\{T_1^j | j = 1, 2, \ldots, N\}$ consists of l interesting points which are aligned as abscissas, for each abscissa, the attacker looks up the N corresponding points of trace sections. A vector is constructed by these N points. Then the correlation coefficient between this vector and

$\{HW^j(x_1)|j = 1, 2, \dots, N\}$ for a fixed k_1 is computed. Attacker will get l correlation coefficients for the l abscissas. The average value of these l correlation coefficients is ρ_{k_1} which is the output of **CorrelationCoefficient**().

Remark. In order to decrease the misjudgements, the attacker may choose the largest Th_{CPA} correlation coefficients from $\{\rho_0, \rho_1, \dots, \rho_{255}\}$, and then find out their corresponding key-byte candidates, where Th_{CPA} is the threshold in CPA. Let γ_1 denote this set of survived key-byte candidates for the first S-box. After using **Algorithm 1** to the other S-boxes, 16 sets γ_1, γ_2, ..., γ_{16} can be gotten. Each of these sets consists of Th_{CPA} survived key-byte candidates. They contain the user-supplied key with an extremely high probability.

2.2.2   Linear Collision Attack

In 2007, Bogdanov proposed the concept of linear collision attack [13] : If a collision between two S-boxes can be detected by some methods (as described in **Fig.1**), i.e.

$$S(p_1 \oplus k_1) = S(p_2 \oplus k_2),$$

then we will obtain a linear equation concerning key-bytes k_1 and k_2

$$k_1 \oplus k_2 = p_1 \oplus p_2 = \Delta_{1,2}.$$

If attacker finds M collisions by a collision detection method, a system of M

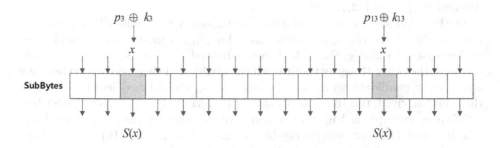

Fig. 1. A linear collision between two AES S-boxes

linear equations can be obtained:

$$\begin{cases} k_{i_1} \oplus k_{i_2} & = \Delta_{i_1,i_2} \\ k_{i_3} \oplus k_{i_4} & = \Delta_{i_3,i_4} \\ \quad \vdots \\ k_{i_{2M-1}} \oplus k_{i_{2M}} & = \Delta_{i_{2M-1},i_{2M}}. \end{cases}$$

It is worth noting that some of these equations have no correlation. Thus they can be divided into h_0 independent subsystems with respect to the parts of the key [17], of which each may have one free variable and one or more equations. Let h_1 denotes the number of all missing variables which are not in those subsystems. Each of the subsystems or missing variables is called a **chain**. And one equation is defined as a **step** of a chain. Hence the number of chains is $h = h_0 + h_1$.

For instance, a classic chain is expressed as follows:

$$\begin{cases} k_1 \oplus k_2 & = \Delta_{1,2} \\ k_2 \oplus k_3 & = \Delta_{2,3} \\ \quad\vdots \\ k_{15} \oplus k_{16} = \Delta_{15,16}. \end{cases} \tag{1}$$

2.2.3   Framework of Combined Side-Channel Collision Attack

There are three stages in the framework of Bogdanov's attack: online stage, process stage and key-recovery stage [17]. For an example, we use the classic chain (1) to describe the attack.

In the online stage, the attacker randomly chooses N plaintexts $\{P^j | j = 1, 2, \ldots, N\}$. Through the AES device, the attacker obtains N power traces, of which each contains 16 sections $\{T_i^j | i = 1, 2, \ldots, 16\}$ for 16 S-boxes.

In the process stage, collision detection method is used to obtain linear collisions. On the other hand, for each S-box, the attacker sorts the correlation cofficientsto obtain a rank of 256 key-byte candidates in CPA. The 16 ranks are denoted by $\{\xi_i | i = 1, 2, \ldots, 16\}$.

In the key-recovery stage, attacker determines a threshold Th_{CPA} and the free variable of the chain, and then picks the Th_{CPA} most possible candidates of the key-byte variable. For each of these survived candidates, the attacker may compute the other 15 key bytes through the chain, and then verify whether they are in their candidate sets (each set has Th_{CPA} candidates) in turn. If all of them are survived, the 16 key bytes should be returned as a correct 128-bit key.

With an example in **Fig.2**, the chain is represented by the solid arrow lines. The 16 vertical lines express the key-byte ranks $\{\xi_i | i = 1, 2, \ldots, 16\}$, and the horizontal line stands for the threshold line of CPA. Only the sets $\{\gamma_i | i = 1, 2, \ldots, 16\}$ of survived key-byte candidates are over the threshold line. For each of the Th_{CPA} candidates of k_1, we compute $k_2, k_3, \ldots, k_{16}$ according to the chain. If the computed $\{k_i | i = 1, 2, \ldots, 16\}$ are all over the threshold line, we conclude that the 16 key bytes are correct, else they are wrong. Bogdanov called this method test of chain.

Remark. This framework can only tolerate faults in CPA, but faults in collision attack will cause a failed attack. The reason is as follow: In order to recover the key efficiently, attacker usually hopes that a chain includes 15 steps. For a chain, one of the common cases is that there are several steps in the path from the free variable to the end. If an error takes place in one of these steps (e.g. the step

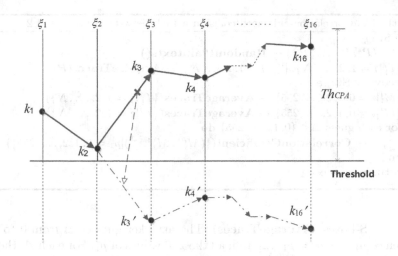

Fig. 2. Test of chain from Bogdanov et al.

from k_2 to k_3 described by the dotted line in **Fig. 2**), the key bytes computed from the following steps will be wrong in the key-recovery stage, which will result the failure of the whole attack. Unfortunately, this kind of errors happens with non-negligible probability. It leads to low efficiency of Bogdanov's attack.

2.3 Correlation-Enhanced Collision Attack

Due to lacking a practical scheme in Bogdanov's work, we use correlation-enhanced collision attack [15] for collision detection.

As mentioned in Section 2.2.2, if a collision is occurred between two S-boxes (e.g. S-box 1 and S-box 2), they have equal outputs

$$S(x_1) = S(x_2).$$

Moreover, they also have equal inputs

$$k_1 \oplus p_1 = k_2 \oplus p_2.$$

Therefore, there is a linear relationship between the two key bytes k_1 and k_2. What is more,

$$\Delta = k_1 \oplus k_2 = p_1 \oplus p_2$$

is a constant. The attack algorithm is given in **Algorithm 2**.

In the online stage, the attacker chooses plaintexts $\{P^j | j = 1, 2, \ldots, N\}$ (**RandomPlaintexts**), then records the corresponding trace sections $\{T_1^j | j = 1, 2, \ldots, N\}$ and $\{T_2^j | j = 1, 2, \ldots, N\}$ for the first two S-boxes (**AcquireTraces**).

In the key-recovery stage, the attacker sorts the traces corresponding to the plaintext byte which equals a certain value from 0 to 255, and then averages the trace sections to obtain $\{M_1^a | a = 0, 1, 2, \ldots, 255\}$ and $\{M_2^a | a = 0, 1, 2, \ldots, 255\}$

Algorithm 2. Correlation-enhanced collision attack between S-box 1 and 2

Online Stage:
  1: $P = (P^1, P^2, \ldots, P^N) \leftarrow$ **RandomPlaintexts()**
  2: $\{T_1^j | j = 1, 2, \ldots, N\}, \{T_2^j | j = 1, 2, \ldots, N\} \leftarrow$ **AcquireTraces**(P)
Key-recovery Stage:
  1: $\{M_1^i | i = 0, 1, 2, \ldots, 255\} \leftarrow$ **AverageTraces**$(\{T_1^j | j = 1, 2, \ldots, N\})$
  2: $\{M_2^i | i = 0, 1, 2, \ldots, 255\} \leftarrow$ **AverageTraces**$(\{T_2^j | j = 1, 2, \ldots, N\})$
  3: **for** each guess $\Delta \in \{0, 1, \cdots, 255\}$ **do**
  4:      $\rho_\Delta \leftarrow$ **CorrelationCoefficient**$(\{(M_1^{p_1}, M_2^{p_1 \oplus \Delta}) | p_1 = 0, 1, 2, \ldots, 255\})$
  5: **end**
  6: **return** $\arg\max\limits_{\Delta} \rho_\Delta$

---

for the two S-boxes (**AverageTraces**). The attacker guesses Δ from 0 to 255, and then computes $p_2 = p_1 \oplus \Delta$ from all the 256 values of p_1. For each Δ, the 256 average power traces $M_2^{p_1 \oplus \Delta}$ are found to calculate the correlation coefficient ρ_Δ of $M_1^{p_1}$ and $M_2^{p_1 \oplus \Delta}$ (**CorrelationCoefficient**). Finally, 256 correlation coefficients are gotten. If Δ is correct, ρ_Δ should be the maximum. As a result, Δ is given by

$$\arg\max_{\Delta} \rho(M_1^{p_1}, M_2^{p_1 \oplus \Delta}).$$

3 Fault-Tolerant Linear Collision Attack

Because of the limits of Bogdanov's attack described in Section 2.2.3, we propose a more efficient work which can tolerant faults in both CPA and collision attack.

3.1 Fault-Tolerant Chain

In this section, we construct a new system of chain, which is more integrated and powerful. First, we regard k_1 as the origin of the chain, i.e. k_1 is the only free variable in this chain. Then we detect collisions between S-box 1 and the others.

$$S(p_1 \oplus k_1) = S(p_i \oplus k_i), \quad \text{for } i \geq 2.$$

Thus, 15 equations with respect to k_1 can be gotten:

$$\begin{cases} k_1 \oplus k_2 = \Delta_{1,2} \\ k_1 \oplus k_3 = \Delta_{1,3} \\ \quad \vdots \\ k_1 \oplus k_{16} = \Delta_{1,16}. \end{cases}$$

From these equations, we construct a new chain named **fault-tolerant chain**. In this system, $k_i (i \geq 2)$ only depends on k_1 instead of the other 14 key bytes. There are 15 paths which begin from k_1 to the ends in one chain (as shown

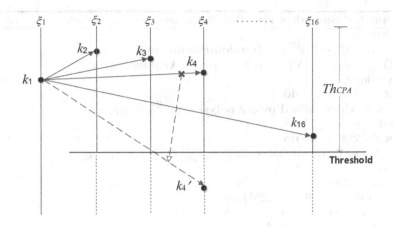

Fig. 3. Fault-tolerant chain

in **Fig.3**). If one k_i is wrong (under the threshold line), we can still attempt to recover others. So we may take a threshold Th_{CA} in collision attack. For example if $Th_{CA} = 1$, i.e. no less than 14 $k_i(i \geq 2)$ survived (at most one k_i is under the threshold line), we can deduce that one path in the chain may be wrong. Subsequently, a practical exhaust search can find the correct key.

3.2 Framework of Fault-Tolerant Linear Collision Attack

Based on the fault-tolerant chain, our work is named fault-tolerant linear collision attack. The detailed process is outlined in **Algorithm 3**.

In the online stage, we encrypt random plaintexts $\{P^j | j = 1, 2, \ldots, N\}$ (**RandomPlaintexts**), then record the power traces and extract the sections for AES S-boxes (**AcquireTraces**).

In the process stage, CPA is employed to get the sets $\{\gamma_i | i = 1, 2, \ldots, 16\}$ of key-byte candidates (**CorrelationPowerAnalysis**). Each set has Th_{CPA} candidates. Meanwhile, the correlation-enhanced collision attack is adopted for collision detection. Then we construct a fault-tolerant chain, and obtain $\{\Delta_{1,i} | i = 2, 3, \ldots, 16\}$ from the collisions (**CollisionDetection**).

In the test of chain stage, for each $k_1 \in \{0, 1, \ldots, 255\}$, we compute the other 15 key bytes by $k_i = k_1 \oplus \Delta_{1,i}$, and denote *error* as the number of key bytes those are not in $\{\gamma_i | i = 2, 3, \ldots, 16\}$. For convenience, **Algorithm 3** describes the case of tolerating one wrong key byte. If finally *error* ≤ 1 (here $Th_{CA} = 1$), the recorded key bytes are user-supplied with high probability. Otherwise this attack fails. Usually, the test of chain stage does not return more than one 128-bit key candidate. In this paper, we did not consider the case of two or more key candidates temporarily.

In the key-recovery stage, we verify the 16 key bytes which are returned from the test of chain stage through an AES encryption (**VerifyKey**). If we get a wrong AES output, there are one or more wrong key bytes. In **Algorithm 3**, only one

---

Algorithm 3. Framework of Fault-Tolerant Linear Collision Attack

Online Stage:
1: $P = (P^1, P^2, \cdots, P^N) \leftarrow$ **RandomPlaintexts()**
2: $\{\{T_i^j | j = 1, 2, \ldots, N\} | i = 1, 2, \ldots, 16\} \leftarrow$ **AcquireTraces**(P)

Process Stage:
1: **for** $i = 1, 2, \ldots, 16$ **do**
2:    $\gamma_i \leftarrow$ **CorrelationPowerAnalysis**$(P, \{T_i^j\}, Th_{CPA})$
3: **end**
4: **for** $i = 2, 3, \ldots, 16$ **do**
5:    $\Delta_{1,i} \leftarrow$ **CollisionDetection**$(P, \{T_1^j\}, \{T_i^j\}, Th_{CA})$
6: **end**

Test of Chain Stage:
1: **for each** $k_1 \in \{0, 1, \ldots, 255\}$ **do**
2:    $error = 0$
3:    **for** $i = 2, 3, \ldots, 16$ **do**
4:       $k_i \leftarrow k_1 \oplus \Delta_{1,i}$
5:       **if** $k_i \notin \gamma_i$
6:          $error \leftarrow error + 1$
7:          **if** $error > 1$ $(Th_{CA} = 1)$
8:             **break for**   (Exit the current loop)
9:          **end if**
10:       **end if**
11:       **if** $i == 16$ (More than 14 k_i survived)
12:          **Record**$(\{k_i | i = 1, 2, \ldots, 16\})$
13:       **end if**
14:    **end for**
15: **end for**

Key-Recovery Stage:
1: **if** no $\{k_i | i = 1, 2, \ldots, 16\}$ is recorded
2:    **return** failure
3: **else**
4:    **if VerifyKey** $(\{k_i | i = 1, 2, \ldots, 16\}) == 1$
5:       **Return** $\{k_i | i = 1, 2, \ldots, 16\}$
6:    **else**
7:       **for each** $\{k_i^* | i = 1, 2, \ldots, 16\} \in$ **SearchKeyByte**$(\{k_i | i = 1, 2, \ldots, 16\})$
8:          **if VerifyKey**$(\{k_i^* | i = 1, 2, \ldots, 16\}) == 1$
9:             **Return** $\{k_i^* | i = 1, 2, \ldots, 16\}$
10:          **end if**
11:       **end for**
12:    **end if**
13: **end if**

---

wrong key byte is tolerated, otherwise this attack fails. The key bytes $k_2, k_3, \ldots, k_{16}$ are searched (**SearchKeyByte**), and the key candidates are verified in turn. As a result, we recover the full key $\{k_i^* | i = 1, 2, \ldots, 16\}$.

Search Complexity. We can not control the correctness of the first key byte. So once error occurs, the first key byte must be exhaustively searched. If there is one wrong key byte in $\{k_2, k_3, \ldots, k_{16}\}$, we may need to search at most

$$2^8 \cdot 2^8 \cdot \binom{15}{1} \approx 2^{20}$$

times. furthermore, if there are two wrong key bytes, the maximum number of search times is

$$2^8 \cdot (2^8)^2 \cdot \binom{15}{2} \approx 2^{31}.$$

Thereupon, the number is $2^8 \cdot (2^8)^n \cdot \binom{15}{n}$ for n wrong key bytes.

Remark. In this work, we use correlation-enhanced collision attack to detect collisions for two reasons:

- During the collision detection stage, we must find the relationships between k_1 and the other 15 key bytes. The correlation-enhanced collision attack can finish it in parallel after acquiring enough power traces.
- We hope that the same set of power traces can be reused to mount both CPA and collision attack. The SNR (Signal-to-Noise Ratio) of correlation-enhanced collision attack is close to that of CPA.

3.3   Experiments and Efficiency

In order to evaluate our attack, we made some simulations in MATLAB. In an experiment, we generated lots of power traces to mount **Algorithm 3**. If in the test of chain stage, the recorded key candidate differs from the user-supplied key just in no more than one byte except k_1, this experiment is regarded as a successful one (The correct key can be subsequently searched). Let the standard deviation of noise $\sigma = 2.7$, the experiment was repeated 100 times to compute a success rate.

We fixed $Th_{CPA} = 10$. With the number of power traces picked from 256 to 1792, a relation curve between success rate and the trace number could be gotten (as described in **Fig.4**). The vertical axis stands for the success rate, and the horizontal axis represents the trace number. The solid line signifies the success rate of our fault-tolerant collision attack, and the dotted line corresponds to the success rate of Bogdanov's attack.

It is clear that the solid line is approaching 1 faster than the dotted line. For example, when the success rates are both about 92%, the trace number of our attack is 1024, while that of Bogdanov's attack is 1408.

Then we selected $\sigma = 4$ to obtain another group of experimental data, and the trace number was chosen from 1024 to 3328. This result is shown in **Fig.5**. Similarly, the solid line is also higher than the dotted line. It is obviously that our framework improved the success rate greatly. The experimental data confirm the theoretical conjecture.

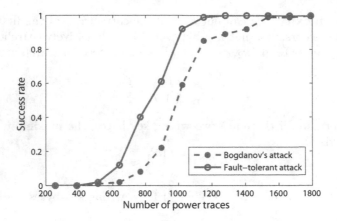

Fig. 4. The comparison between the success rates of two frameworks when $\sigma = 2.7$

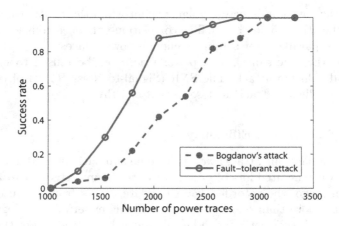

Fig. 5. The comparison between the success rates of two frameworks when $\sigma = 4$

4 Fault-Identification Mechanism

In this section, we try to identify the position of wrong key byte with high probability so that the search space may be reduced greatly.

4.1 Procedure and Effectiveness

In the test of chain stage of **Algorithm 3**, for a specific key byte $k_i (i \geq 2)$, if $k_i \notin \gamma_i$, it is likely a wrong key byte. We add a step

$$\mathbf{Record}(k_1, i)$$

between step 6 and 7. If this 128-bit key is not recorded in step 12 at last, the previously recorded (k_1, i) should be dropped. At last, a 128-bit key candidate and the position where error mostly occurred are recorded.

Subsequently in the key-recovery stage, if the 128-bit key candidate $\{k_i | i = 1, 2, \ldots, 16\}$ is verified as a wrong key, we record i as the position of the wrong key byte. Then we search k_i and verify it.

Search Complexity. If $Th_{CA} = 1$, we only need to search one key byte. The number of search times will be reduced to $2^8 \cdot 2^8 = 2^{16}$. If there are two wrong key bytes, we may search $2^8 \cdot (2^8)^2 = 2^{24}$ times, which is also easy to finish. And so on, n wrong key bytes will be searched $2^8 \cdot (2^8)^n$ times.

Effectiveness. The errors which lead to wrong key bytes may occur in collision attack or in CPA. In other words, the steps of the chain or the key-byte candidate sets may be wrong. If the threshold in CPA is chosen as small as possible, and the wrong key bytes are under the threshold line, it indicates that the errors occurred in collision attack. Thus the fault-identification mechanism can be used to record the wrong positions, and then reduce the search space.

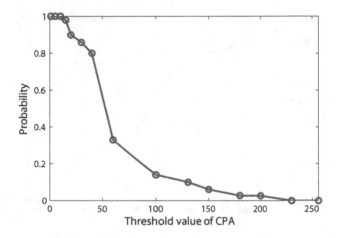

Fig. 6. The relation between the probability of the case that the two wrong key bytes are all under the threshold line and Th_{CPA}

First, we discuss it in the case of one wrong key byte ($Th_{CA} = 1$). It consists of two cases:

1. The wrong key byte is over the threshold line.
2. The wrong key byte is under the threshold line.

Obviously that the probability of case 2 is extremely high when Th_{CPA} is small, so the fault-identification mechanism is efficient.

Second, if there are two wrong key bytes ($Th_{CA} = 2$), we discuss the probability of the case that the two wrong key bytes are all under the threshold line. Here, we also made a simulation experiments. We chose $\sigma = 2.7$, and the number of power traces was 1024. For different Th_{CPA}, we could get the corresponding probability with which the two wrong key bytes are all under the threshold line. The relation curve between this probability and Th_{CPA} is described in **Fig.6**. As a result, the probability is over 90%, while Th_{CPA} is about less than 30.

   If Th_{CPA} is too large, we can not use fault-identification mechanism to confirm the positions. Then the search times are tended to exhaustive search.

4.2   Choice of Threshold in CPA

We discussed the choice of threshold in CPA for the effectiveness of fault-identification mechanism in Section 4.1. The result is in a wide range. For example in **Fig.6**, Th_{CPA} is picked from 1 to 30, when $Th_{CA} = 2$.

   Actually, the success rate is also determined by Th_{CPA}. We wish to give a more precise value range of Th_{CPA} on further experiments. Supposed that $Th_{CA} = 2$, we have made 100 experiments for each Th_{CPA}.

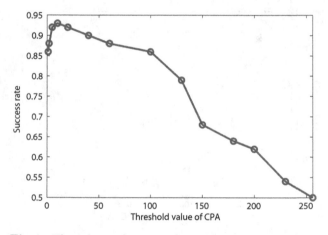

Fig. 7. The relation between the success rate and Th_{CPA}

Fig.7 shows the success rate curve with respect to Th_{CPA}. In this experiment, the number of power traces was also fixed 1024, and $\sigma = 2.7$. We note that the success rate reaches the maximum when Th_{CPA} is from 5 to 20.

   We hope the number of search times is as small as possible, while the success rate is high enough. So, we suggest that Th_{CPA} is chosen as 10, which corresponds to the maximum success rate in this experiment.

5   Conclusion

In this paper, we present fault-tolerant linear collision attack which enhances collision attack with fault-tolerant chain. We use correlation-enhanced collision attack to construct fault-tolerant chain. The key-byte candidates are ranked by CPA and filtered with a threshold. We indicate the fact that our attack is more powerful and practicable than Bogdanov's basic test of chain. On the basis of experimental data, simulation results show the feasibility of our algorithm and the range of threshold in CPA. The techniques used in our work may be extended to the cryptographic symmetric algorithms which can be attacked by the collision method.

Acknowledgments. This work is supported by the National Natural Science Foundation of China (No. 61133013), the 973 Program (No.2013CB834205), and the Foundation of Science and Technology on Information Assurance Laboratory (No. KJ-13-101).

References

1. Kocher, P.C., Jaffe, J., Jun, B.: Differential Power Analysis. In: Wiener, M. (ed.) CRYPTO 1999. LNCS, vol. 1666, pp. 388–397. Springer, Heidelberg (1999)
2. Mangard, S., Oswald, E., Popp, T.: Power Analysis Attacks: Revealing the Secrets of Smart Cards. Springer, Heidelberg (2007)
3. Chari, S., Rao, J.R., Rohatgi, P.: Template Attacks. In: Kaliski Jr., B.S., Koç, Ç.K., Paar, C. (eds.) CHES 2002. LNCS, vol. 2523, pp. 13–28. Springer, Heidelberg (2003)
4. Brier, E., Clavier, C., Olivier, F.: Correlation Power Analysis with a Leakage Model. In: Joye, M., Quisquater, J.-J. (eds.) CHES 2004. LNCS, vol. 3156, pp. 16–29. Springer, Heidelberg (2004)
5. Gierlichs, B., Batina, L., Tuyls, P., Preneel, B.: Mutual Information Analysis. In: Oswald, E., Rohatgi, P. (eds.) CHES 2008. LNCS, vol. 5154, pp. 426–442. Springer, Heidelberg (2008)
6. Bilgin, B., Nikova, S., Nikov, V., Rijmen, V., Stütz, G.: Threshold Implementations of All 33 and 44 S-Boxes. In: Prouff, E., Schaumont, P. (eds.) CHES 2012. LNCS, vol. 7428, pp. 76–91. Springer, Heidelberg (2012)
7. Canright, D., Batina, L.: A Very Compact "Perfectly Masked" S-Box for AES. In: Bellovin, S.M., Gennaro, R., Keromytis, A.D., Yung, M. (eds.) ACNS 2008. LNCS, vol. 5037, pp. 446–459. Springer, Heidelberg (2008)
8. Carlet, C., Goubin, L., Prouff, E., Quisquater, M., Rivain, M.: Higher-Order Masking Schemes for S-Boxes. In: Canteaut, A. (ed.) FSE 2012. LNCS, vol. 7549, pp. 366–384. Springer, Heidelberg (2012)
9. Genelle, L., Prouff, E., Quisquater, M.: Thwarting Higher-Order Side Channel Analysis with Additive and Multiplicative Maskings. In: Preneel, B., Takagi, T. (eds.) CHES 2011. LNCS, vol. 6917, pp. 240–255. Springer, Heidelberg (2011)
10. Roy, A., Vivek, S.: Analysis and Improvement of the Generic Higher-Order Masking Scheme of FSE 2012. In: Bertoni, G., Coron, J.-S. (eds.) CHES 2013. LNCS, vol. 8086, pp. 417–434. Springer, Heidelberg (2013)
11. Schramm, K., Leander, G., Felke, P., Paar, C.: A Collision-Attack on AES Combining Side Channel- and Differential- Attack. In: Joye, M., Quisquater, J.-J. (eds.) CHES 2004. LNCS, vol. 3156, pp. 163–175. Springer, Heidelberg (2004)
12. Schramm, K., Wollinger, T., Paar, C.: A New Class of Collision Attacks and Its Application to DES. In: Johansson, T. (ed.) FSE 2003. LNCS, vol. 2887, pp. 206–222. Springer, Heidelberg (2003)

13. Bogdanov, A.: Improved side-channel collision attacks on AES. In: Adams, C., Miri, A., Wiener, M. (eds.) SAC 2007. LNCS, vol. 4876, pp. 84–95. Springer, Heidelberg (2007)
14. Bogdanov, A.: Multiple-Differential Side-Channel Collision Attacks on AES. In: Oswald, E., Rohatgi, P. (eds.) CHES 2008. LNCS, vol. 5154, pp. 30–44. Springer, Heidelberg (2008)
15. Moradi, A., Mischke, O., Eisenbarth, T.: Correlation-enhanced power analysis collision attack. In: Mangard, S., Standaert, F.-X. (eds.) CHES 2010. LNCS, vol. 6225, pp. 125–139. Springer, Heidelberg (2010)
16. Clavier, C., Feix, B., Gagnerot, G., Roussellet, M., Verneuil, V.: Improved Collision-Correlation Power Analysis on First Order Protected AES. In: Preneel, B., Takagi, T. (eds.) CHES 2011. LNCS, vol. 6917, pp. 49–62. Springer, Heidelberg (2011)
17. Bogdanov, A., Kizhvatov, I.: Beyond the Limits of DPA: Combined Side-Channel Collision Attacks. IEEE Trans. Computers 61(8), 1153–1164 (2012)

Implementing a Covert Timing Channel Based on Mimic Function

Jing Wang[1,2,3], Le Guan[1,2,3], Limin Liu[1,2,*], and Daren Zha[3]

[1] Data Assurance and Communication Security Research Center, CAS,
Beijing, China
[2] State Key Laboratory of Information Security, Institute of Information
Engineering, CAS, Beijing, China
[3] University of Chinese Academy of Sciences, Beijing, China
{jwang,lguan,lmliu}@lois.cn,
zhadaren@ucas.ac.cn

Abstract. Covert timing channel is a mechanism that can be exploited
by an attacker to conceal secrets in timing intervals of transmitted packets. With the development of detection techniques against such channel,
it has become increasingly difficult to exploit a practical covert timing
channel that is both detection-resistant and of high capacity. In this
paper, we introduce a new type of covert timing channel. Our novel encoding technique uses mimic functions as the basis to accomplish the
mimicry of legitimate traffic behaviors. We also design and implement
a mimicry framework for automatically creating this new type of covert
timing channel. In the end, we utilize the state-of-the-art detection tests
to validate the effectiveness of our mimicry approach. The experimental results show that the created covert timing channel can successfully
evade the detection tests while achieving a considerable channel capacity.

Keywords: network security, covert timing channel, mimic function,
detection resistance.

1 Introduction

Covert channel was first introduced by Lampson [15], and originally, studied in
the context of multi-level secure systems. Ever since Girling started the study
of covert channel in the network scenario [10], the security threat posed by network covert channel has attracted increasing attention. Network covert channel
involves in a wide range of attacks, e.g., data exfiltration [18], DDoS attacks [12],
privacy enhancement [13], and packet traceback [20].

Traditionally, network covert channel is classified into storage channel and
timing channel. The former exploits the redundancy of network protocols, i.e.,
random/unused bits in packet header, while the latter manipulates inter-packet
delays (IPDs) of network traffic. Storage channels can be discovered by observing
the anomalies in the patterns of packet header fields. The detection of timing

---

* Corresponding Author.

X. Huang and J. Zhou (Eds.): ISPEC 2014, LNCS 8434, pp. 247–261, 2014.

channels is usually based on statistical analysis of shape and regularity in packet timing intervals. Compared with storage channels, it is more difficult to detect timing channels due to the high variation in timing intervals. To thwart such channels, researchers have proposed substantial detection techniques [2,16,8], the focus among which is on using entropy-based method [8]. This promising method has been proven an effective way for detecting various covert timing channels.

In recent years, in order to evade detection, several works propose to create covert timing channels by mimicking the statistical properties of legitimate traffic [9,19,14]. In particular, Walls et al. [19] first revealed the entropy-based detection method can be defeated. Their approach uses a half of packets to smooth out the anomalies caused by covert traffic. As a consequence, the detection resistance results in a significant reduction in channel capacity. By far, it remains a challenge work to implement a covert timing channel that is both detection-resistant and of high capacity.

In this paper, we propose a new type of detection-resistant covert timing channel with a considerable channel capacity. Leveraging a stenographic technique—mimic function in the encoding method, covert traffic generated has the similar statistical properties with legitimate traffic. The statistical properties include the first-order and high-order statistics, which actually correspond to the shape of distribution and inter-packet dependencies in network traffic, respectively.

To construct practical covert timing channels, we also develop and implement a mimicry framework, which is intended for automatically mimicking, encoding, and transmitting. More specifically, the framework includes five phases: filtering, symbolization, modeling, encoding, and transmission. Through these phases, covert traffic which is statistically approximate to legitimate traffic is generated, and finally is transmitted to the Internet. The covert timing channel constructed by the framework can also be adjusted by certain parameters in line with different requirements in undetectability, error rate, and capacity.

In the end, we conduct a series of experiments to validate the effectiveness of our mimicry approach. Experimental results show that the covert timing channel built from the mimicry framework can successfully evade the entropy-based tests while achieving almost 3-6 times the throughput of Liquid [19].

The rest of this paper is organized as follows. Section 2 introduces the related work in covert timing channel. Section 3 describes mimic functions and our mimicry framework. Section 4 shows the experiment results on the effectiveness of our mimicry approach. Finally, Section 5 concludes this paper.

2   Related Work

The timing of network packets can be utilized to leak secret information. In [2], Cabuk et al. presented IPCTC, the first IP covert timing channel. IPCTC employs a simple on/off encoding scheme. During a specific timing interval, the sender transmits a 1-bit by sending a packet and a 0-bit by not sending a packet. Gianvecchio et al. [9] explored a model-based covert timing channel, which is named

MBCTC in short. MBCTC models distribution functions for legitimate traffic, and mimics its first-order statistics. In [18], Shah et al. proposed a novel passive covert timing channel, which can leak typed passwords over the network without compromising the host or creating additional traffic. Sellke et al. [17] proposed the "L-bits to N-packets" encoding scheme for building a high-capacity covert timing channel, and quantified the data rate of that scheme. Walls et al. [19] presented a detection-resistant covert timing channel relying on the idea of Jitterbug. The main idea is to insert shaping IPDs into covert traffic, so as to smooth out shape distortion generated by Jitterbug.

On the other hand, researchers have proposed various disruption and detection techniques to defend against those channels. Compared with disruption techniques, channel detection has two major advantages: 1) it has no effect on network performance; 2) it has an additional benefit that the hosts transmitting covert information can be located. Detection techniques are based on the fact that the creation of covert timing channels causes shape or regularity distortion in traffic's timing characteristics. The Kolmogorov-Smirnov test [16] is a nonparametric test that is used to determine whether a sample comes from a reference distribution or tell the difference between two samples. It has been experimentally proven that this test is able to sniff out abnormal traffic which distorts in shape. Cabuk et al. [2] investigated two detection tests, namely ϵ-similarity and regularity test. However, they are only effective to a minority of covert timing channels, because they are over-sensitive to the variation of traffic. Gianvecchio et al. [8] introduced a fruitful detection method using the combination of entropy and corrected conditional entropy, which is effective in finding out the anomalies in the shape and regularity, respectively. In the literature, this detection method has the best performance on detecting a wide variety of covert timing channels.

To evade the detection tests, the technology of mimicking legitimate traffic has been used in intelligent channel design [9,19,14]. In [9], the distribution of covert traffic is very close to that of legitimate traffic. However, owing to the lack of inter-packet dependencies, this kind of channel fails to evade the entropy-based detection method [8]. In [19], the goal of channel design is to defeat the entropy-based detection method. Its encoding method is based on that proposed by Shah et al. [18] but sacrifices a half of IPDs to evade detection tests, therefore, it has a low channel capacity, which is nearly 0.5 bit/packet. Kothari et al. [14] proposed an undetectable timing channel that uses a mechanism of Regularity Tree to mimic the irregularity of legitimate traffic. This channel maintains throughput of 1 bit/packet.

3   Our Scheme

In this section, we first introduce mimic functions, the basis of our encoding scheme. Then, we describe the mimicry framework that is designed to automatically create the new type of detection-resistant covert timing channel.

3.1   Mimic Functions

Mimic functions [21], which were introduced by Peter Wayner, are used to transmit hidden information as a subliminal technique. A mimic function changes input data so it assumes the statistical properties of another type of data, and consequently accomplishes the mimicry of identity. This technique has been applied in various scenarios, e.g., text steganography [1], digital watermarking [5], and code obfuscation [22]. Nevertheless, to the best of our knowledge, this technique has not yet been employed in the field of covert timing channel.

Regular Mimic Functions. Regular mimic functions use Huffman coding algorithm as the base. In Huffman coding, a table of occurrence frequency for each symbol in the input is required to build a variable-length code table, according to which a binary tree of nodes, namely a huffman tree, is generated. As a result, the symbols which occur frequently reside at the top, that is, they are given short representations, while the rare symbols are represented as long codes and located at the deep.

The inverse of Huffman coding can be used as mimic functions if the input is a random bit stream. The mimic process consists of two parts: compression phase and expansion phase. In the compression phase, the frequency table of each symbol in a data set A is estimated and the corresponding huffman tree is constructed. In the second phase, a data set B of random bits is expanded, specifically, variable length blocks are converted into fixed length blocks due to the huffman decoding operation, which is based on the huffman tree of A.

However, there is a problem that symbols occur in regular mimic functions output with different probabilities from the original ones. In fact, the regular model limits all symbols to have a probability which is a negative power of two, e.g., .5, .25, .125, and so on. The following technique can be used to solve this problem.

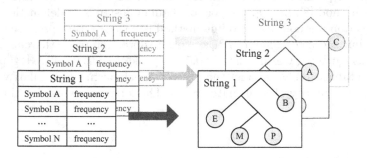

Fig. 1. The huffman forest

High-order Mimic Functions. Compared with regular mimic functions, high-order mimic functions capture more detailed statistical profile of data. In order

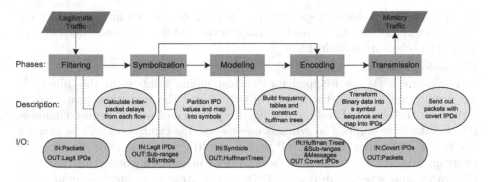

Fig. 2. The mimicry framework

to maintain regularity in the data, high-order mimic functions extract the inter-symbol dependencies by estimating the frequency of each symbol that follows a specific string of length $n - 1$. High-order mimic functions build a huffman tree for each occurred string of length $n - 1$, which results in a forest of huffman trees, as shown in Figure 1.

As a start, the encoding of high-order mimic functions requires one possible string as a seed. Given the seed, the encoding program locates the right huffman tree with the prefix of that selected string in the forest, and then uses the huffman decoding operation to determine the symbol that will follow the string. The resulting symbol and its preceding string of length $n - 2$ form a new prefix of length $n - 1$. The encoding program will take iterations in this order and output one by one. As the order n increases, the results become more and more approximate to the original data.

3.2 The Mimicry Framework

Given the advantage of high-order mimic functions, we decide to use their encoding technique as the basis for our scheme. To construct practical covert timing channels, we design a mimicry framework for mimicking, encoding, and transmitting. This framework includes five phases: filtering, symbolization, modeling, encoding, and transmission. Figure 2 gives an overview of our framework and a concise description of each phase. Details are expanded in the following paragraphs.

I. Filtering

In this phase, the packet sniffer captures packets from legitimate network connections. The packets are then classified into individual flows according to protocols, and source and destination IP addresses and ports. Generally, different types of traffic have different statistical properties. For example, HTTP and SSH protocols are both based on TCP/IP, but the difference between their traffic behaviors also exists and has been revealed by statistical tests [8]. Furthermore, the more specific traffic we filter out, the more precise statistical properties we can mimic.

For this reason, we choose a specific application protocol as a filtering condition. After trace classification, the packet analyzer calculates timing intervals between adjacent packets from each trace.

II. Symbolization

The input IPDs are mapped into corresponding symbols in this phase. In our application scenario, the objective is to mimic the statistical properties of legitimate traffic and thereby cover up the presence of covert timing channels. If IPD values are mapped to symbols one-to-one, the symbol set will be oversize due to the high variation in HTTP traffic, resulting in overload of the encoding program. To solve this problem, we sort all IPDs in ascending order, and partition IPD range into several sub-ranges. IPDs in the same sub-range are mapped to the same symbol.

The partitioning approach is of vital importance to the effectiveness of mimicking. Our approach is based on the observation that the IPD data is intensive in some ranges and rare in the other ones, and hence, the parameter of probability density provides a critical basis for partitioning. Specifically, the principle of our approach is that data has nearly uniform density within each sub-range. To achieve this, we firstly calculate the cumulative distribution function for IPD data. If data is uniformly distributed within a certain range, this part of the cumulative distribution curve exhibits a straight line. An inflection point is likely to exist between a high-density area and a low-density area on the cumulative distribution curve. Due to finite samples, the obtained cumulative distribution curve is very rough, and actually, composed of many line segments. In consideration of the objective and analysis described hereinbefore, we choose to use Douglas-Peucker algorithm [7] as the appropriate method of locating inflection points.

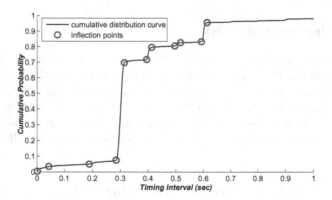

Fig. 3. Inflection points located by Douglas-Peucker algorithm ($\varepsilon = 0.01$)

The Douglas-Peucker algorithm is also known as the line simplification algorithm. The purpose of the algorithm is to produce a simplified polyline that approximates the original one within a specified tolerance ε. Figure 3 shows the effect of Douglas-Peucker algorithm on locating inflection points in a cumulative distribution curve. According to these points, sub-ranges are determined and then legitimate IPDs are mapped to corresponding symbols.

III. Modeling

The modeling phase is a phase of extracting statistical properties of legitimate IPDs by constructing huffman trees. This phase takes the sequence of symbolized IPDs as the modeling object and mimicry target.

The first step is building frequency tables for all occurred strings of length $n-1$ in order to extract the nth order statistics. The modeling function processes the input sequence in a sequential manner. When moving onto a string of length $n-1$, the function determines whether this pattern has already occurred. If so, the function gets the symbol that follows the string, and increments the corresponding frequency counter in the table appended to this pattern. If it is absent, then a new table is created and appended to it. These operations are repeatedly conducted until the search is completed. If the input sequence has a total of 2000 symbols, $2001-n$ strings of length $n-1$ can be collected, some of which may have the same pattern. The strings of length $n-1$, acting as the "prefixes" in mimic functions, are the indexes of their frequency tables. At the end of modeling phase, each frequency table is converted into a huffman tree. All the huffman trees with corresponding indexes are output to the next phase.

IV. Encoding

Based upon the modeling results, the encoding phase converts an arbitrary binary stream into a sequence of symbols, which has similar statistics with the mimicry target. The encoding function has three components: randomization, mimic encoding process, and inverse mapping.

Covert messages are mostly encoded into binary sequences with ASCII scheme [3], and each letter is represented as a code with length of 8 bits. Due to different occurrence frequency of letters [6], these binary sequences are non-random, whereas the input of mimic functions is required to be random. To solve this problem, each binary sequence is randomized by XORing with a pseudo-random bit stream. This stream is assumed to be known by the sender and receiver of the covert timing channel.

After randomization, the input of mimic encoding process is an arbitrary binary stream. To start the encoding of nth order mimic functions, the first string of length $n-1$ is chosen as a seed. The right huffman tree of the specific string is located according to its index. Then the process performs the operation of walking the tree. From the root node, the process selects left or right branches according to the input bit, until it arrives at a leaf node, which represents a symbol. The most recently generated symbol and its preceding string of length $n-2$ forms a new string of length $n-1$. The encoding program will take iterations in this order and output one by one. In the end, a sequence of symbols is obtained.

Inverse mapping refers to an operation of inversely mapping symbols to IPD values. First, one symbol is mapped into the corresponding sub-range. Then, an IPD value is randomly selected from the sub-range.

V. Transmission

In this phase, the sender of the covert timing channel modulates the timing of packets corresponding to the sequence of IPDs, and then forwards the packets to the Internet.

3.3 Design Details

Prior Agreement: In this channel, there is a prerequisite that the sender and receiver should share the same mimicry target and have the same modeling results. One choice is to transmit the modeling results from the sender to the receiver. However, this solution requires a large amount of communication traffic before the covert channel is built up. The other choice is to collect the same legitimate traffic as the mimicry target by the two parties. They agree in advance on a particular period and a particular network trace. For instance, they single out the given trace during 8:00 AM and 8:05 AM. Even if several packets are lost or effected by network jitters, the modeling results will stay the same. This is because our partitioning method is based on the cumulative distribution function of IPDs, and thus slight changes during the transmission almost have no effect on the overall distribution. Moreover, slight changes have little influence on the generated huffman trees.

Decreasing Error Rate: In the symbolization phase, the distribution of IPDs in each sub-range is treated as the uniform distribution approximately. Accordingly, an IPD value is uniformly selected from the corresponding sub-range in the inverse mapping operation. When the selected IPD value is close to the cut-off point between the adjacent sub-ranges, a transmission error will probably arise due to network jitters. One solution is adding error correcting bits to covert data. In addition, the areas with a certain distance apart from cut-off points can be removed from the selection ranges, but this solution theoretically has a little influence on the mimicry effectiveness.

Parameter Selection: The tolerance ε in the Douglas-Peucker algorithm has dual influence on the practicality of our scheme. If ε is large, then the number of inflection points is small and sub-ranges are wide, thus the approximation to legitimate traffic is inaccurate. In contrast, if ε is small, then sub-ranges are narrow, causing a relatively high decoding error rate. Moreover, increasing the number of sub-ranges will increase the number of huffman trees. A large number of huffman trees will result in low efficiency of modeling and encoding. After comprehensive consideration, we choose $\varepsilon = 0.01$ in the following experiments.

4 Experimental Evaluation

We conducted a series of experiments to validate the effectiveness of our mimicry approach. The emphasis of our experiments is on determining if the covert timing channel exploited from the mimicry framework can evade the state-of-the-art detection tests. In addition, we examined the capacity of this new type of covert timing channel.

4.1 Experimental Setup

The detection tests are based on statistical analysis, therefore a large volume of network data is necessary in order to perform these tests. The selection of test data is detailed in the following paragraphs.

Legitimate Data Collection. In our experiments, we selected HTTP traffic as our mimicry target. The reasons include: 1) HTTP is the most widely used protocol on the Internet, thus the defensive perimeter of a network commonly allows HTTP packets to pass through. 2) The large volume of HTTP traffic makes it an ideal medium for covert communication. The HTTP traffic used in our experiments was extracted from publicly available data sets named NZIX-II [11]. The data sets contain the mixed traces of diverse network protocols. To filter out only HTTP traces, we used the destination port number 80 as the filtering condition. After that, HTTP streams were grouped into individual flows according to the source and destination IP addresses. IPDs calculated from each individual flow were jointed together to be our legitimate data set.

For different purposes, the legitimate data set is divided into two subsets: training set and test set. The training set, composed of 10,000,000 IPDs, is intended to initialize detection tests. The test set is used as the mimicry target for generating covert traffic, as well as the comparison object for the detection tests. This set contains 100 samples, each of which has 2000 IPDs.

Covert Data Generation. To automatically create the new type of covert timing channel, referred to as MFCTC hereinafter, we implemented each function of the framework on our testing machine, and integrated each into a complete pipeline for generating covert traffic. We then input legitimate data as the mimicry target. In the experiments, we set the tolerance ε in the Douglas-Peucker algorithm to be 0.01. The order of mimic functions was tuned to create different MFCTC data sets.

For the comparison purpose, we also implemented two existing covert timing channels: MBCTC [9] and IPCTC [2]. For MBCTC, each 100 packets of the test set are fitted to a model, which is used to generate covert traffic. For IPCTC, the timing interval is rotated among 0.04, 0.06, and 0.08 seconds after each 100 packets as suggested by Cabuk et al. [2].

4.2 Detection Resistance

The detection resistance is the objective of our mimicry approach. It can be estimated from two aspects: the *shape* and *regularity* of network traffic. The shape of traffic is described by first-order statistics, e.g., distribution. The regularity of traffic is described by high-order statistics, e.g., correction. In the experiments, we utilized the most advanced detection method—the entropy-based method [8], which uses the combination of entropy and corrected conditional entropy to examine the shape and regularity respectively. To our knowledge, the entropy-based detection method has the best performance on detecting various covert timing channels. In this section, we detail this detection method and show the detection results.

The Entropy-based Detection Method. This detection method is based on the observation that the creation of a covert timing channel changes the entropy of the original traffic in a certain extent. In information theory, entropy is used as a measure of the uncertainty in a random variable [4].

This detection method utilizes two metrics: entropy (EN) and corrected conditional entropy (CCE). The definition of entropy of a random variable X is given as:

$$EN(X) = -\sum_X P(x)logP(x)$$

The entropy describes the first-order statistics of traffic and can be used as a shape test. In addition, the corrected conditional entropy that is used to estimate the entropy rate can be used as a regularity test:

$$CCE(X_m|X_1, ..., X_{m-1}) = CE(X_m|X_1, ..., X_{m-1}) + perc(X_m) * EN(X_1)$$

Where $CE(X_m|X_1, ..., X_{m-1})$ is the conditional entropy of a random process $X = X_i$, $perc(X_m)$ is the percentage of unique sequence patterns of length m, and $EN(X_1)$ is the first-order entropy.

The detection method requires a large number of legitimate IPDs for training. For maximum effectiveness, this method divides the training data into Q equiprobable bins. When the Q bins have the same number of IPDs, the entropy reaches a maximum. Abnormal traffic, which has a different distribution, usually gets a low entropy score. Gianvecchio et al. chose $Q = 65536$ for EN test while $Q = 5$ for CCE test.

Dataset. In our experiments, we used seven data sets, including:
  ▷ HTTP training set: 10,000,000 HTTP IPDs
  ▷ HTTP test set: 200,000 HTTP IPDs
  ▷ IPCTC test set: 200,000 HTTP IPDs
  ▷ MBCTC test set: 200,000 HTTP IPDs
  ▷ 3rd-MFCTC test set: 200,000 HTTP IPDs
  ▷ 4th-MFCTC test set: 200,000 HTTP IPDs
  ▷ 5th-MFCTC test set: 200,000 HTTP IPDs

To initialize the detection tests, we used the HTTP training set to determine the bin ranges for EN and CCE tests, respectively. MBCTC and MFCTC test sets are both generated by mimicking the HTTP test set. The three MFCTC test sets are based on third-order, forth-order, and fifth-order mimic functions, respectively.

Detection Results. Our *first* set of experiments is to investigate the effect of the order of mimic functions on approximation. Theoretically, mimic functions with higher order capture more detailed statistical profile of data. Therefore, the statistics of the corresponding MFCTC traffic are more similar to those of original traffic. However, it is impractical to employ a mimic function with a very high order. Increasing n will increase the number of huffman trees exponentially. This means the order has the direct effect on the performance of data processing. In our experiments, we chose $n = 3, 4, 5$ for generating covert traffic, respectively.

In order to investigate the effect in reality, we ran EN and CCE test 100 times against HTTP test set and three MFCTC test sets, respectively. A sample of 2000 IPDs was used in each time. To compare the results, we calculate the difference between the test score for each sample of covert data and that for the corresponding sample of legitimate data. The mean of the test scores and the comparative scores are shown in Table 1. The test scores for the three MFCTC test sets are all higher on average than those of legitimate test set. Whereas, with the increasing of the order, the comparative scores are decreasing gradually. This indicates that the higher order results in the more accurate approximation.

Table 1. The mean of the test scores and the comparative scores

test	LEGIT	3rd-MFCTC		4th-MFCTC		5th-MFCTC	
	Mean	Mean	Diff	Mean	Diff	Mean	Diff
EN	16.214	19.566	3.894	19.416	3.666	19.340	3.565
CCE	1.949	2.016	0.117	1.996	0.106	1.987	0.098

Our *second* set of experiments is to determine if MFCTC traffic created from our mimicry framework can evade the entropy-based detection method. We ran each detection test 100 times against legitimate, 4th-MFCTC, IPCTC, and MBCTC traffic, respectively. A sample of 2000 IPDs was used in each time. The mean of EN and CCE test scores are shown in Figure 4 and Figure 5, respectively. In theory, a low EN test score indicates the first-order probability of the test traffic is distinct from that of training data, and hence suggests this traffic is abnormal. In turn, the higher EN test score the traffic gets, the more similar to legitimate data it is. Analyzing in the same way, when the CCE test score is very high, the traffic lacks regularity. When the CCE test score is very low, the traffic is too regular. Our test results show that the mean EN test score of MFCTC is much higher than that of legitimate traffic, while the mean CCE test score is very close to that of legitimate traffic. The EN and CCE test scores of IPCTC are both too low. For MBCTC, the EN test score is higher than that of legitimate traffic, however, the CCE test score is too much higher.

In order to estimate the detection rates, we introduce a criterion called *false positive rate*, which was also used by Gianvecchio et al [8]. The false positive rate refers to the rate of legitimate samples that are incorrectly classified as covert. We calculate the *cutoff* scores for both tests to achieve a false positive rate of 1%. Any sample with a test score beyond the normal range, partitioned by the cutoff, would be identified as covert. The detection rates for MFCTC, IPCTC, and MBCTC samples are shown in Table 2.

The EN and CCE tests are both able to detect the presence of IPCTC. Although the EN detection rate for MBCTC is 0%, the CCE detection rate reaches up to 90%. This reveals that MBCTC only exploits the first-order statistics of legitimate traffic, but ignores the regularity. The EN detection rate for MFCTC is 0%, while the CCE detection rate is very low, only 6%.

We also investigate the distributions of the CCE test scores for legitimate and MFCTC samples, which are illustrated in Figure 6. Most scores for both fall between 1.8 and 2.2. There is a heavy overlap between the distributions. Moreover, with the increasing of the order of mimic functions, the overlap becomes

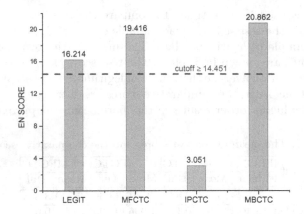

Fig. 4. EN test scores for legitimate, MFCTC, IPCTC, and MBCTC IPDs

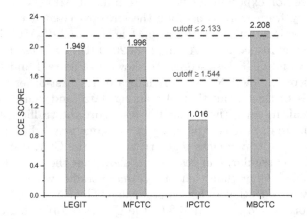

Fig. 5. CCE test scores for legitimate, MFCTC, IPCTC, and MBCTC IPDs

Table 2. The detection rates for MFCTC, IPCTC, and MBCTC samples

Test	LEGIT	MFCTC	IPCTC	MBCTC
	False Positive	Detection Rate	Detection Rate	Detection Rate
$EN \leq 14.451$	1%	0%	100%	0%
$CCE \leq 1.544$	1%	0%	100%	0%
$CCE \geq 2.133$	1%	6%	0%	90%

heavier. This implies that the detection rate can be reduced by increasing the order. In conclusion, the detection results indicate that our new type of covert timing channel is undetectable by the entropy-based detection tests.

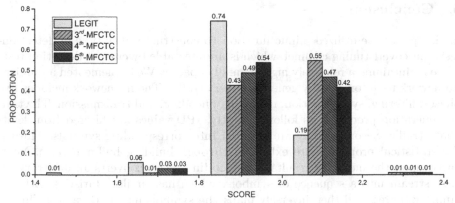

Fig. 6. The proportion of CCE test scores

Other Detection Tests. To be more convincing, we also ran Kolmogorov-Smirnov test [16] and regularity test [2] against MFCTC. The Kolmogorov-Smirnov test quantifies the maximum distance between two empirical distribution functions, so it can be used to examine the shape of traffic. If the test score is small, it implies that the sample is close to the legitimate behavior. For the regularity test, network traffic is separated to several windows with the same size, and the standard deviation is computed for each window. In general, the regularity score of legitimate traffic is high, because legitimate traffic changes over time. This test can be used to examine the regularity of traffic. Our results showed that the two detection tests both get 0% detection rate for MFCTC when the false positive rate is 1%.

4.3 Capacity

The channel capacity of MFCTC depends on the sizes and heights of huffman trees. Due to different mimicry targets and modeling results, the capacity of MFCTC is indefinite. To estimate the channel capacity, we count up the number of sub-ranges for 100 samples. When the tolerance $\varepsilon = 0.01$, these samples have 1044 sub-ranges in total, that is, there is nearly 10 sub-ranges on average. Consequently, for the first-order mimic function, each huffman tree has approximately 10 leaf nodes, thus the corresponding channel capacity is between 2 and 3.25 bits/packet in theory. Whereas, owing to the limited size of the mimicry target, only 2000 IPDs in each sample, huffman trees of high-order mimic functions have much fewer leaf nodes. For these 100 samples of 4th-MFCTC, the mean of bit transmission rate is 1.5 bits/packet. When we enlarge the size to be 20000 and 200000 IPDs in each sample, the transmission rate increases to be 1.7 and 1.9 bits/packet, respectively. On the whole, the capacity of our encoding scheme is much higher than that of Liquid [19] and Mimic [14], which delivery 0.5 and 1 bit per packet respectively.

5   Conclusion

In this paper, we utilized mimic function to construct a new type of detection-resistant covert timing channel, which is undetectable by current detection tests while maintaining a relatively high channel capacity. We implemented a mimicry framework to automatically generate covert traffic. The framework includes five phases: filtering, symbolization, modeling, encoding, and transmission. The traffic generation process is as follows. Firstly, IPD values are filtered from legitimate traffic. Secondly, they are mapped into corresponding symbols. Thirdly, the statistical properties are extracted through building huffman trees. Next, based upon the modeling results, the encoding phase converts an arbitrary binary stream into a sequence of symbols, which has similar statistics with the mimicry target, and then inversely maps the symbols into IPD values. Finally, network packets with the mimicry IPDs are forwarded to the Internet.

In order to validate the effectiveness of the mimicry approach, we performed the state-of-the-art detection tests against our new type of channel (MFCTC) and known channels (IPCTC and MBCTC). The results show that only MFCTC can successfully evade the detection tests. Moreover, MFCTC is able to maintain a considerable capacity, which is much higher than existing undetectable channels, i.e., Liquid and Mimic.

Acknowledgement. This work was supported by the National Basic Research Program (973 Program) of China (No. 2013CB338001) and the Strategy Pilot Project of Chinese Academy of Sciences Sub-Project XDA06010702.

References

1. Atallah, M.J., Raskin, V., Hempelmann, C.F., Karahan, M., Sion, R., Topkara, U., Triezenberg, K.E.: Natural language watermarking and tamperproofing. In: Petitcolas, F.A.P. (ed.) IH 2002. LNCS, vol. 2578, pp. 196–212. Springer, Heidelberg (2003)
2. Cabuk, S., Brodley, C., Shields, C.: IP covert timing channels: Design and detection. In: Proceedings of the 11th ACM Conference on Computer and Communications Security, pp. 178–187 (2004)
3. Cabuk, S., Brodley, C., Shields, C.: IP covert channel detection. ACM Transactions on Information and System Security (TISSEC) 12(4), 22 (2009)
4. Cover, T., Thomas, J.: Elements of information theory. Wiley-interscience (2006)
5. Cox, I., Miller, M., Bloom, J., Fridrich, J., Kalker, T.: Digital watermarking and steganography. Morgan Kaufmann (2007)
6. Dewey, G.: Relative frequency of English spellings. Teachers College Press, New York (1970)
7. Douglas, D.H., Peucker, T.K.: Algorithms for the reduction of the number of points required to represent a digitized line or its caricature. Cartographica: The International Journal for Geographic Information and Geovisualization 10(2), 112–122 (1973)
8. Gianvecchio, S., Wang, H.: Detecting covert timing channels: An entropy-based approach. In: Proceedings of the 14th ACM Conference on Computer and Communications Security, pp. 307–316 (2007)

9. Gianvecchio, S., Wang, H., Wijesekera, D., Jajodia, S.: Model-based covert timing channels: Automated modeling and evasion. In: Proceedings of the 11th International Symposium on Recent Advances in Intrusion Detection, pp. 211–230 (2008)
10. Girling, C.: Covert channels in LAN's. IEEE Transactions on Software Engineering, 292–296 (1987)
11. WAND Research Group. Waikato internet traffic storage, http://wand.net.nz/wits/nzix/2/
12. Henry, P.A.: Covert channels provided hackers the opportunity and the means for the current distributed denial of service attacks. CyberGuard Corporation (2000)
13. Houmansadr, A., Nguyen, G.T., Caesar, M., Borisov, N.: Cirripede: Circumvention infrastructure using router redirection with plausible deniability. In: Proceedings of the 18th ACM Conference on Computer and Communications Security, pp. 187–200 (2011)
14. Kothari, K., Wright, M.: Mimic: An active covert channel that evades regularity-based detection. Computer Networks (2012)
15. Lampson, B.: A note on the confinement problem. Communications of the ACM 16(10), 613–615 (1973)
16. Peng, P., Ning, P., Reeves, D.: On the secrecy of timing-based active watermarking trace-back techniques. In: IEEE Symposium on Security and Privacy, pp. 334–349 (2006)
17. Sellke, S., Wang, C., Bagchi, S., Shroff, N.: TCP/IP timing channels: Theory to implementation. In: INFOCOM, pp. 2204–2212 (2009)
18. Shah, G., Molina, A., Blaze, M.: Keyboards and covert channels. In: Proceedings of the 15th Conference on USENIX Security Symposium, vol. 15 (2006)
19. Walls, R., Kothari, K., Wright, M.: Liquid: A detection-resistant covert timing channel based on IPD shaping. Computer Networks 55(6), 1217–1228 (2011)
20. Wang, X., Reeves, D.S.: Robust correlation of encrypted attack traffic through stepping stones by manipulation of interpacket delays. In: Proceedings of the 10th ACM Conference on Computer and Communications Security, pp. 20–29 (2003)
21. Wayner, P.: Mimic functions. Cryptologia 16(3), 193–214 (1992)
22. Wu, Z., Gianvecchio, S., Xie, M., Wang, H.: Mimimorphism: A new approach to binary code obfuscation. In: Proceedings of the 17th ACM Conference on Computer and Communications Security, pp. 536–546 (2010)

Detecting Frame Deletion in H.264 Video

Hongmei Liu, Songtao Li, and Shan Bian

School of Information Science and Technology, Sun Yat-sen University,
Higher Education Mega Center, Guangzhou, China
isslhm@mail.sysu.edu.cn, lisongt@mail2.sysu.edu.cn
bianshan.sysu@gmail.com

Abstract. Frame deletion is one of the common video tampering operations. The existing schemes in detecting frame deletion all focus on MPEG. This paper proposes a novel method to detect frame deletion in H.264. We introduce the sequence of average residual of P-frames (SARP) and use its time- and frequency- domain features to classify the tampered videos and original videos. Specifically, in the time domain, we analyze the periodicity of the SARP of videos with frame deleted and define a position vector to describe this feature. In the frequency domain, we demonstrate that the periodicity of SARP results in spikes (frequency-domain feature) at certain positions in the DTFT(Discrete Time Fourier Transform) spectrum. The time- and frequency- domain features of tampered videos are different from that of original videos and thus can be used to separate these videos apart. Experimental results show that the proposed method is very effective with the detection rate as high as 92%.

1 Introduction

Digital videos are almost ubiquitous now. With ever-developing video editing methods, people can tamper the video with ease. Tampered videos may convey inaccurate messages which tend to mislead the mass media. When used in court, tampered video may cause severe effects. Thus it is imperative to authenticate the integrity of digital videos.

The existing methods that aim to authenticate videos fall into two groups: active authentication and passive authentication. An example of active authentication is using digital watermark. In most cases, however, videos do not contain such watermark. In contrast, passive authentication that does not need previously embedded data is gaining strength. Some passive authentication methods leverage noise features introduced by cameras during video formation[1-2]. Many other passive authentication methods employ artifacts introduced during video compression [3-8].

The methods to detect double video compression are proposed in [3-5] while methods that aim to detect frame deletion are proposed in [6-8]. In [6], block artifacts are used to form a feature curve whose change indicates frame deletion. In [7], the authors propose a method based on Motion-Compensation Edge Artifact to detect frame deletion. In [8], the authors analyze the periodicity of motion error sequence which is

X. Huang and J. Zhou (Eds.): ISPEC 2014, LNCS 8434, pp. 262–270, 2014.
© Springer International Publishing Switzerland 2014

transformed into the frequency domain. Spikes on both sides in the frequency domain which are peculiar to tampered videos suggest frame deletion.

The methods in [6-8] are performed in MPEG. However, there is little method that aims to detect frame deletion in H.264 which is more complicated than MPEG. The methods that work well in MPEG may fail in H.264. For example, method in [6] using block artifact to detect frame deletion in MPEG may not work well in H.264 because there is a de-blocking filter in H.264 which largely attenuates the block artifact. The method in [8] fails to yield ideal results in H.264 either. This will be illustrated later in Section 2.

In this paper, we propose a novel method by using the sequence of average residual of P-frames (SARP) both in the time and frequency domain to detect frame deletion. Many videos with different content are tested and experiments show that our method is quite effective. The rest of this paper is organized as follows. Section 2 analyzes the statistical features of frame deletion in H.264 video. Section 3 is our proposed method to detect frame deletion. Section 4 shows experimental results. Section 5 is the conclusion.

2   Statistical Features of Frame Deletion in H.264 Video

H.264 is a new video compression standard. Compared with early standards like MPEG, the main changes in H.264 are details of each part. For example, intra prediction in H.264 is used in the pixel domain to produce the residual. Inter prediction in H.264 may use multiple reference frames. H.264 also supports a range of block sizes and subsample motion vectors and the de-blocking filter is also peculiar to H.264 [9].

Frame (I, B, P) and GOP are also general terms in H.264 as in MPEG. In this paper, of our particular interest is P-frame. With original P-frame and its reference frames, we can get the predicted frame via motion estimation and compensation. P-frame residual is acquired by subtracting the predicted frame from the original frame. GOP is short for a group of pictures that refers to frames between two adjacent I-frames.

A video forger needs to decode a video (encoded bit streams) to the pixel domain before deleting some frames. After frame deletion this video should be encoded again and thus a tampered video is usually encoded twice. We now analyze the effects of frame deletion in H.264 video. Let matrix $\mathbf{Y}_k$ be the kth frame, $\mathbf{Y}_t$ ' be the tth reconstructed frame, thus we have

$$\mathbf{r}_k = \mathbf{Y}_k - C\left(\mathbf{Y}_t'\right) \tag{1}$$

where matrix $\mathbf{r}_k$ is the residual of the kth frame, C is the motion compensation operator, $\mathbf{Y}_t$ ' serves as the reference frame of $\mathbf{Y}_k$. Thus we get the following equation in the decoding process

$$\mathbf{Y}_k' = F\left(\mathbf{r}_k' + C\left(\mathbf{Y}_t'\right)\right) \tag{2}$$

where matrix $\mathbf{Y}_k$ ' is the kth reconstructed frame, F is the de-blocking operator which will not be considered from now on just for simplicity, $\mathbf{r}_k$ ' is the kth decoded residual.   The compression noise of the kth frame is defined as

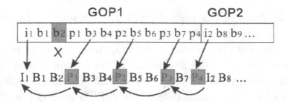

Fig. 1. The upper and lower rows stand for the original H.264 video and tampered H.264 video respectively

$$\mathbf{n}_k = \mathbf{Y}'_k - \mathbf{Y}_k \qquad (3)$$

and thus $\mathbf{r}_k{}'$ can be expressed as

$$\mathbf{r}'_k = \mathbf{Y}_k - C(\mathbf{Y}_t) + \mathbf{n}_k - C(\mathbf{n}_t) \qquad (4)$$

where matrix $\mathbf{n}_t$ is compression noise of the tth frame. The SARP of a video is defined as

$$r(n) = \frac{1}{N} \sum_i \sum_j |\mathbf{r}'_n(i,\ j)| \qquad (5)$$

where N is the number of pixels in one frame, $\mathbf{r}'_n(i,\ j)$ is the residual of the nth P-frame at pixel location (i, j).

In one GOP, the P-frames are strongly correlated because they refer to the initial I-frame directly or indirectly. Therefore the correlation between $\mathbf{n}_k$ and $\mathbf{n}_t$ is relatively strong if if the kth and t^{th} frames belong to the same GOP during the first compression. So the term $\mathbf{n}_k - C(\mathbf{n}_t)$ in (4) can be approximately cancelled and $\mathbf{r}_k{}'$ can be expressed as

$$\mathbf{r}'_k = \mathbf{Y}_k - C(\mathbf{Y}_t) \qquad (6)$$

and thus the corresponding $r(k)$ is small. However, if the kth and t^{th} frames belong to different GOPs, the term $\mathbf{n}_k - C(\mathbf{n}_t)$ cannot be cancelled and thus the corresponding $r(k)$ is likely to be large. In summary, if the kth P-frame and its reference frame belong to the same GOP, $r(k)$ is likely to be small, otherwise $r(k)$ is likely to be large. Thus there is a sign of periodicity in the SARP. We will give examples to illustrate this periodicity in more details.

Without loss of generality, we set the GOP to be I B B P B B P B B P B P(12 frames) which contains 4 P-frames. In our paper, 20 GOPs are considered. Fig.1 illustrates the case of deleting the frame b_2 from an original H.264 video. When b_2 is deleted, b_3, b_5, b_7, i_2 are re-encoded to be P_1, P_2, P_3, P_4 whose reference frames are I_1, P_1, P_2, P_3 respectively.

Please refer to Fig.1, the upper and lower rows stand for the first and second compression respectively. It can be seen that $P_j (j= 1, 2, 3)$ and its reference frame

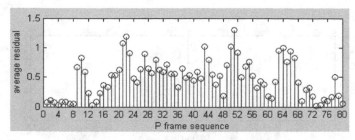

Fig. 2. (a) SARP for the original H.264 video

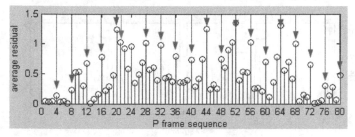

Fig. 2. (b) SARP for the tampered H.264 video

belong to the same GOP(GOP$_1$) during the first compression while P$_4$ and its reference frame belong to different GOPs(GOP$_1$ and GOP$_2$) during the first compression. From the above analysis, we know that r(1), r(2) and r(3) are likely to be small while r(4) is likely to be large in the first GOP. The same phenomena also exist in other GOPs. Fig.2(a) and Fig.2(b) show the SARPs for original and tampered videos respectively. In each GOP, '*l*' is used to denote the P-frame whose average residual is the largest and '*s*' denotes the other P-frames. Thus the SARP in Fig.2(b) can be denoted as "*s s s l; s s s l; s s s l; s s s l; s s s l...*" which shows signs of periodicity. In contrast, the SARP in Fig.2(a) does not show this periodicity. To distinguish the tampered videos from original videos, we will extract useful features in the time domain from the SARP in Section 3.

In order to analyze SARP more thoroughly, we transform the SARPs in Fig.2(a) and Fig.2(b) into the frequency domain by DTFT. The DTFT curves are shown in Fig.3(a) and Fig.3(b) respectively. In [8], the authors state that spikes in the frequency domain suggest frame deletion. However, Fig.3(a) shows that there may also exist spikes in the frequency domain for original H.264 video. This is mainly because the H.264 mechanism differs from MPEG. We have tested many other original H.264 videos and found out that they possess such spikes too. So the spikes in the frequency domain do not necessarily suggest tampering in H.264 any longer. To tackle this problem, we will extract new and useful features in the frequency domain in Section 3.

3 Proposed Method

In this section, we address the problems stated in Section 2 and propose our method to detect frame deletion.

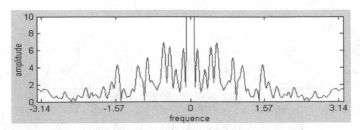

Fig. 3. (a) DTFT curve of Fig.2(a)   (Original)

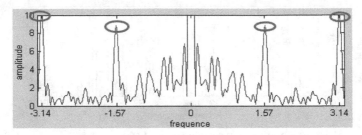

Fig. 3. (b) DTFT curve of Fig.2(b)   (Tampered)

Let T be number of P-frames in one GOP and G be the number of GOPs, so the periodicity of the SARP after deleting some frames is also T. In the ith GOP, let $\varphi(i)$ be the position of the P-frame whose average residual is the largest among the T P-frames. The position vector of SARP is defined as

$$V(i) = \begin{cases} T & \text{if } \varphi(i) \text{ is a multiple of } T \\ \varphi(i) \bmod T & \text{if } \varphi(i) \text{ is not a multiple of } T \end{cases} \tag{7}$$

where $i = 1, 2, \ldots, G$, $1 \leq V(i) \leq T$. Thus the position vectors for Fig.2(a) and Fig.2(b) are [2,1,2,4,4,2,3,2,1,1,3,1,3,3,2,4,2,3,3,2] and [4,4,4,4,4,1,4,4,4,4,4,4,4,4,4,4,4,4,4,4] respectively. Let $S(j)$ be the times that value j occurs in $V(i)$, μ be the mean value of S and σ^2 be the variance of S. Therefore we get the following equations

$$\sigma^2 = \frac{\sum_{j=1}^{T}(S(j) - \mu)^2}{T - 1} \tag{8}$$

$$\mu = \frac{\sum_{j=1}^{T} S(j)}{T} = G / T \tag{9}$$

$$\sigma^2_{\max} = \frac{(G - G / T)^2 + (T - 1)(G / T)^2}{T - 1} \tag{10}$$

We know that the sum of all elements in S is G, so σ^2 achieves its largest value when one element in S is G and all the other elements are 0. Therefore $\sigma^2_{\max}$ is

$$Q_t = \frac{\sigma^2}{\sigma_{\max}^2} = \frac{T \sum_{j=1}^{T} (S(j) - G/T)^2}{(T-1)G^2} \tag{11}$$

We use the normalized σ^2 to define the time domain feature ratio Q_t by

It is clear that S is relatively scattered for the tampered video and results in larger variance. Therefore Q_t is relatively small for the original video. This is the time-domain feature.

We use DTFT to transform the SARP($i.e.$ $r(n)$) into the frequency domain. The DTFT of SARP is denoted as $R(e^{j\omega})$. It is obvious that the periodicity of $|R(e^{j\omega})|$ is 2π and is symmetric with respect to the vertical axis, so we only have to consider the interval $[0, \pi]$. $|R(e^{j\omega})|$ achieves largest value when ω is 0. We have shown that the SARP is T when some frames are deleted. We can demonstrate the following equation if $r(n)$ is strictly periodic

$$R(e^{j(\omega+2\pi/T)}) = R(e^{j\omega}) \tag{12}$$

In such situation, there is also a large value when ω is a multiple of $2\pi/T$. In our actual experiment, $r(n)$ shows signs of periodicity but it is not strictly periodic for the tampered video. Therefore there also exist a spike at $2k\pi/T(k$ is a nonzero integer) but this spike is not as strong as the spike at 0(largest value). We define $h_{\min}$ to be

$$h_{\min} = |R(e^{j2m\pi/T})|_{\min} \tag{13}$$

where $m \in K$, K is the set of all integers in $(0, T/2]$. Thus $h_{\min}$ is likely to be smaller for the original video. This phenomenon can also be seen from Fig.3(a) and Fig.3(b).

We know that $|R(e^{j\omega})|$ achieves its largest value at 0, namely

$$|R(e^{j\omega})|_{\max} = |R(e^{j\omega})|_{\omega=0} = \sum_{n=1}^{N} r(n) \tag{14}$$

Compared with Fig.2(a), some values in Fig.2(b) become smaller and some become larger. We assume that the sum of all values in SARP is relatively stable after deleting some frames. Therefore, $|R(e^{j\omega})|_{\max}$ is relatively stable. This assumption is confirmed by our actual experiments that $|R(e^{j\omega})|_{\max}$ changes little when some frames are deleted. The frequency domain feature ratio Q_f is then defined as

$$Q_f = \frac{h_{\min}}{|R(e^{j\omega})|_{\max}} \tag{15}$$

From the analysis above, we know that Q_f is likely to be smaller for the original video. This is our proposed frequency-domain feature. Incidentally, the larger the $r(n)$, the larger the $|R(e^{j\omega})|$ will be, yet Q_f can counteract this effect and thus robust to different video content whether the SARP of which is large or small.

Let the time- and frequency- domain thresholds be τ_t and τ_f. Based on the analysis above, an H.264 video is considered as an original video if $Q_t < \tau_t$ and $Q_f < \tau_f$. If either of these two conditions is violated, the H.264 video is then considered as a tampered video.

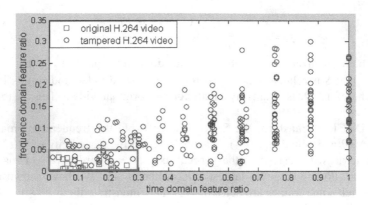

Fig. 4. Time- and frequency-domain feature ratios

4   Experiments

In our experiments, 20 YUV videos[10-11] are used. Each YUV video has 300 frames and the resolution is 176×144. We choose x264[12] as the encoder and H.264 Joint Model (JM)[13] as the decoder. The encoding GOP is I B B P B B P B B P B P.

The 20 original YUV videos are encoded to generate 20 original H.264 videos which are then decoded back into the pixel domain. For each decoded YUV video, we delete 1 to 11 frames to generate 11 tampered YUV videos. Thus we get 220 (20×11) tampered YUV videos in total. The 20 original YUV videos and 220 tampered YUV videos are then encoded and decoded again. We extract the SARPs in the decoding process, so the time-domain feature ratio Q_t and the frequency-domain feature ratio Q_f are acquired from the SARPs.

Fig.4 shows the Q_t and Q_f for 240 videos (20+220). The small rectangles stand for 20 original H.264 videos and the small circles stand for 220 tampered H.264 videos. For a video to be tested, we can get a (Q_t, Q_f) pair. With a certain (τ_t, τ_f) pair, we are able to tell whether this video has undergone frame deletion or not by using our method in Section 3. It can be seen from Fig.4 that the original videos and tampered videos can be roughly separated by a large rectangle whose location is related to the (τ_t, τ_f) pair.

For all the videos to be tested, a certain (τ_t, τ_f) pair determines a (*fp*, *tp*) pair in which *fp* denotes false positive rate and *tp* denotes true positive rate. With different (τ_t, τ_f) pairs, we are able to get their corresponding (*fp*, *tp*) pairs which together form a ROC curve shown in Fig.5.

According to Fig.4, we finally set the (τ_t, τ_f) pair to be (0.30, 0.05) for reference. The false positive rate is 5% and the true positive rate is 91.82%. The average detection accuracy is 92.08%. It can be seen from Fig.4 that if we only consider the time- or frequency- domain feature ratio solely, the average detection accuracy is not

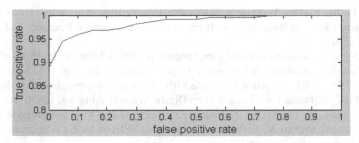

Fig. 5. ROC curve

very good (79.60% or 82.50% respectively). Therefore, higher accuracy can be achieved by combining both the time- and frequency- domain features.

Existing methods in literature[6-8] to detect frame deletion are almost based on MPEG. Authors in [6] detect frame deletion by visually checking the change of the feature curve and the final detection accuracy is not given. Their method fails to work when the number of deleted frames is a multiple of 3 and may not work in H.264 owing to the de-blocking filter. Authors in [8] only consider the frequency-domain characteristics and distinguish tampered videos from original videos by visually checking frequency-domain spikes. The positions of the spikes to be checked are not stated and the final detection accuracy is not presented. Their method may not work quite effectively in H.264 as illustrated in part II. Compared with methods in [6] and [8], our method combine both the time- and frequency- domain features to detect frame deletion in H.264 and the average detection accuracy is 92.08%. Our method can remedy the above-stated limitations in [6] and [8]. Compared with the method in [7], our method works well for videos with low motion, such as 'akiyo', 'mother' and so on.

5   Conclusion and Future Works

In this paper, we have proposed a novel method to detect frame deletion in H.264. Tampered videos are distinguished from original videos by using the SARP both in the time and frequency domain. A large number of videos are tested in our experiments and the detection results show that our method is fairly effective in H.264.

The tampered videos and original videos are separated by setting hard thresholds in this paper. Our future work is to set the thresholds adaptively or introduce machine learning methods in the decision stage. Moreover, new features in H.264 should be considered in our future work.

References

1. Kobayashi, M., Okabe, T., Sato, Y.: Detecting video forgeries based on noise characteristics. In: Proc. of the 3rd Pacific-Rim Symposium on Image and Video Technology, Tokyo, Japan, pp. 306–317 (2009)

2. Kobayashi, M., Okabe, T., Sato, Y.: Detecting forgery from static-scene video based on inconsistency in noise level function. IEEE Trans. on Information Forensics and Security, 883–892 (2010)
3. Su, Y., Xu, J.: Detection of double-compression in MPEG-2 videos. In: Proc. of International Workshop on Intelligent Systems and Applications, Wuhan, pp. 1–4 (2010)
4. Chen, W., Shi, Y.-Q.: Detection of double MPEG compression based on first digit statistics. In: Proc. of International Workshop on Digital Watermarking, pp. 16–30 (2010)
5. Liao, D., Yang, R., Liu, H., Li, J., Huang, J.: Double H.264/AVC compression detection using quantized nonzero AC coefficients. In: Proc. of SPIE on Media Watermarking, Security, and Forensics III, 7880 (2011)
6. Luo, W., Wu, M., Huang, J.: MPEG recompression detection based on block artifacts. In: Proc. of SPIE on Security, Forensics, Steganography, and Watermarking of Multimedia Contents 6819 (2008)
7. Su, Y., Zhang, J., Liu, J.: Exposing digital video forgery by detecting motion-compensated edge artifact. In: Proc. of Inter. Conf. on Computational Intelligence and Software Engineering, pp. 1–4 (2009)
8. Wang, W., Farid, H.: Exposing digital forgeries in video by detecting double MPEG compression. In: Proc. of the 8th Workshop on Multimedia and Security, pp. 37–47 (2006)
9. Richardson Iain, E.G.: H.264 and MPEG-4 Video Compression. John Wiley & Sons, New York (2003)
10. YUV Video Sequences, http://trace.eas.asu.edu/yuv/
11. The Consumer Digital Video Library, http://www.cdvl.org/
12. x264, http://www.videolan.org/developers/x264.html
13. JM, http://iphome.hhi.de/suehring/tml/download/old_jm

Efficient Adaptive Oblivious Transfer in UC Framework

Vandana Guleria and Ratna Dutta

Indian Institute of Technology, Kharagpur, India
vandana.math@gmail.com, ratna@maths.iitkgp.ernet.in

Abstract. We propose an efficient universally composable (UC) *adaptive k-out-of-n* ($\mathsf{OT}_k^{n\times1}$) protocol. Our scheme is proven to be secure in the presence of malicious adversary in static corruption model under the Decision Linear (DLIN) and q-Strong Diffie-Hellman (SDH) assumptions. We use Groth-Sahai proofs and trapdoor commitments of Fischlin *et al*. The proposed protocol outperforms the existing similar schemes in terms of both communication and computation. More interestingly, our construction guarantees the receiver that he has learnt the correct information at the end of each transfer phase.

Keywords: Oblivious transfer, universally composable security, Groth-Sahai proofs.

1 Introduction

Adaptive oblivious transfer (OT) protocol is a widely used primitive in cryptography and is useful in adaptive oblivious search of large database such as patent database and medical database where the database holder does not want to reveal the entire database to the recipient. OT protocols have been extensively used in many cryptographic applications including fair exchange in e-commerce and secure multi-party computation. A typical OT protocol is a two party protocol with a sender S and a receiver R. At the beginning of the protocol, S has the database $m_1, m_2, \ldots, m_n$ and R has index $\sigma \in \{1, 2, \ldots, n\}$. The receiver R interacts with S in such a way that at the end of the protocol, R learns only m_σ and S is unable to get any knowledge about the index σ. This is 1-out-of-n OT protocol which has been extended to *non-adaptive k-out-of-n* (OT_k^n) [1] and *adaptive k-out-of-n* ($\mathsf{OT}_k^{n\times1}$) [9], [15]. In the non-adaptive setting, R simultaneously learns all the k messages $m_{\sigma_1}, m_{\sigma_2}, \ldots, m_{\sigma_k}, \sigma_j \in \{1, 2, \ldots, n\}, j = 1, 2, \ldots, k$, whereas in adaptive setting, R learns one message at a time. In adaptive setting, R may learn $m_{\sigma_{i-1}}$ before deciding on σ_i.

The first oblivious transfer protocol was introduced by Rabin [20] which was later generalized in [6], [13] to construct secure protocols for multiparty computation. Since then many OT schemes have been proposed and studied. The security of the OT protocols [6], [9], [13], [18], [20] are in simulation-based-model where the simulator uses adversarial rewinding. Although the aforementioned OT protocols satisfy both sender's security and receiver's security, they become

X. Huang and J. Zhou (Eds.): ISPEC 2014, LNCS 8434, pp. 271–286, 2014.

insecure under concurrent execution when composed with arbitrary protocols. To address this, Canetti and Fischlin [11] introduced ideal functionality for OT protocol in *universal composable* (UC) framework [11]. The UC secure [11] OT protocols can be securely composed with arbitrary protocols even under concurrent execution. Peikert *et al.* [19] introduced first efficient, UC secure 1-out-of-2 OT protocols under the Decisional Diffie-Hellman (DDH), quadratic residuosity and worst-case lattice assumptions. Later, Choi *et al.* [12] proposed UC-secure 1-out-of-2 OT protocols based on Decision Linear (DLIN), Symmetric External Diffie-Hellman (SXDH), DDH and Decision composite residuosity (DCR) assumption. Very recently, Abdalla *et al.* [1] designed an 1-out-of-n OT protocol using smooth projective hash framework. Green and Hohenberger [15] introduced UC secure $\mathsf{OT}_k^{n \times 1}$ protocol. It combines Boneh, Boyen and Shacham (BBS) [5] encryption, Camenisch-Lysyanskaya (CL) signature [8] and Boneh-Boyen signature [3]. Later, Rial *et al.* [21] proposed an efficient UC secure priced $\mathsf{OT}_k^{n \times 1}$ protocol by employing BBS [5] encryption and P-signatures [2].

Our Contribution. We construct an UC secure, efficient adaptive $\mathsf{OT}_k^{n \times 1}$ protocol inspired by $\mathsf{OT}_k^{n \times 1}$ of [15], [21]. Our scheme couples BBS [5] encryption and batch Boneh and Boyen (BB) [4] signature with Groth-sahai proofs [16] and exploits trapdoor commitments of Fischlin *et al.* [14]. Unlike the construction in [15], [21], we rely on batch BB [4] signature, instead of CL signature [8], Boneh-Boyen signature [3] and P-signatures [2]. Besides, Fischlin *et al.* [14] trapdoor commitment is used to commit the sender's input database $m_1, m_2, \ldots, m_n$, in our scheme. It enables the receiver to verify that he has learnt the correct message at the end of each transfer phase. This feature is not achievable in [15], [21]. The verification of pairing product equations is done in non-interactive way using Groth-Sahai proofs [16]. The UC security holds against malicious adversary which can deviate from its protocol specification under DLIN and q-Strong Diffie-Hellman (SDH) assumptions. We consider static corruption model in which adversary pre-decides the corrupted parties before the execution of the protocol. Corrupted parties remain corrupted and honest parties remain honest throughout the protocol execution.

The proposed adaptive $\mathsf{OT}_k^{n \times 1}$ protocol is computationally efficient with low communication overhead. The computation overhead is measured by counting the number of pairing and exponentiation operations which are the most expensive operations as compared to addition and multiplication. The initialization phase of our $\mathsf{OT}_k^{n \times 1}$ protocol requires $5n+1$ pairings and $17n+5$ exponentiations whereas k transfer phases need a total $147k$ pairings and $150k$ exponentiations. In addition, 18 exponentiation operations are performed to generate common reference string. The communication overhead is $12n + 5$ group elements in initialization phase and $47k + 28k = 75k$ group elements in k transfer phases. As illustrated in table 1, our protocol outperforms the best known schemes so far [15], [21] with similar security levels.

Table 1. Comparison Summary (PO stands for number of pairing operations, EXP for number of exponentiation operations, IP for initialization phase, TP for transfer phase, CRSG for crs generation, T for a ciphertext database, PK for public key, $\alpha X + \beta Y$ for α elements from the group X and β elements from the group Y)

$OT_k^{n \times 1}$	Pairing PO		Exponentiation EXP			Communication		Storage	
	TP	IP	TP	IP	CRSG	Request	Response	crs-Size	(T + PK)Size
[15]	$\geq 207k$	$24n + 1$	$249k$	$20n + 13$	18	$(68\mathbb{G}_1 + 38\mathbb{G}_2)k$	$(20\mathbb{G}_1 + 18\mathbb{G}_2)k$	$7\mathbb{G}_1 + 7\mathbb{G}_2$	$(15n + 5)\mathbb{G}_1 + (3n + 6)\mathbb{G}_2$
[21]	$> 450k$	$15n + 1$	$223k$	$12n + 9$	15	$(65\mathbb{G})k$	$(28\mathbb{G})k$	$23\mathbb{G}$	$(12n + 7)\mathbb{G}$
Ours	$147k$	$5n + 1$	$150k$	$17n + 5$	18	$(47\mathbb{G})k$	$(28\mathbb{G})k$	$16\mathbb{G}$	$(12n + 5)\mathbb{G}$

2   Preliminaries

Notations: Throughout, we use ρ as the security parameter, $x \overset{\$}{\leftarrow} A$ means sample an element x uniformly at random from the set A, $y \leftarrow B$ indicates y is the output of algorithm B and $\mathbb{N}$ denotes the set of natural numbers. A function $f(n)$ is *negligible* if $f = o(n^{-c})$ for every fixed positive constant c.

Definition 1. *Two probability distributions $X = \{X_r\}_{r \in \mathbb{N}}$ and $Y = \{Y_r\}_{r \in \mathbb{N}}$ are said to be computationally indistinguishable, denoted by $X \overset{c}{\approx} Y$, if for every probabilistic polynomial time (PPT) distinguisher $\mathcal{D}$, there exists a negligible function $\epsilon(r)$ such that $\left| Pr\left[\mathcal{D}(X_r, 1^r) = 1\right] - Pr\left[\mathcal{D}(Y_r, 1^r) = 1\right] \right| \leq \epsilon(r)$, $\forall\, r \in \mathbb{N}$.*

2.1   Bilinear Pairing and Complexity Assumptions

Bilinear Pairing: Let $\mathbb{G}_1, \mathbb{G}_2$ be two multiplicative cyclic groups of prime order p, g_1 a generator for G_1 and g_2 for G_2. Then the map $e : \mathbb{G}_1 \times \mathbb{G}_2 \to \mathbb{G}_T$ is bilinear if it satisfies the following conditions: (i) (Bilinear) $e(x^a, y^b) = e(x, y)^{ab}$ $\forall\, x \in \mathbb{G}_1, y \in \mathbb{G}_2, a, b \in \mathbb{Z}_p$, (ii) (Non-Degenerate) $e(x, y)$ generates $\mathbb{G}_T$ $\forall\, x \in \mathbb{G}_1, y \in \mathbb{G}_2, x \neq 1, y \neq 1$ and (iii) (Computable) the pairing $e(x, y)$ is computable efficiently $\forall\, x \in \mathbb{G}_1, y \in \mathbb{G}_2$.
If $\mathbb{G}_1 = \mathbb{G}_2$, then e is *symmetric* bilinear pairing. Otherwise, e is *asymmetric* bilinear pairing. Throughout the paper, we use symmetric bilinear pairing.

q-Strong Diffie-Hellman (SDH) Assumption [4]: Let $\mathbb{G}$ be a multiplicative cyclic group of prime order p with generator g. The q-SDH assumption in $\mathbb{G}$ states that given $(q+1)$-tuple $(g, g^x, g^{x^2}, \ldots, g^{x^q})$, $x \in \mathbb{Z}_p$ as input, it is hard to output a pair $(c, g^{\frac{1}{x+c}})$, $c \in \mathbb{Z}_p$.
The q-SDH is proven to be true in generic group model [4].

Decision Linear (DLIN) Assumption [5]: Let $\mathbb{G}$ be a multiplicative cyclic group of prime order p with generator g. Let $g_1 = g^a, g_2 = g^b \in \mathbb{G}, a, b \in \mathbb{Z}_p$. The DLIN assumption in $\mathbb{G}$ states that given g_1, g_2, g and $g_1^r, g_2^s, g^t, r, s, t \overset{\$}{\leftarrow} \mathbb{Z}_p$, it is hard to distinguish $r + s$ from t.
If DLIN problem is easy, then decisional Diffie-Hellman (DDH) problem is easy. In generic group model DLIN is proven to be hard even if DDH is easy [22].

2.2 Groth-Sahai Proofs [16]

We discuss non-interactive zero-knowledge (NIZK) proofs and non-interactive witness indistinguishable (NIWI) proofs by Groth and Sahai [16] under the DLIN assumption. These proofs are used in our protocol construction. Let us first briefly explain Groth-Sahai commitments. Depending on the public parameters, there are two types of settings in Groth-Sahai proofs - *perfectly sound* setting and *witness indistinguishability* setting. We discuss below how to commit a group element $X \in \mathbb{G}$ in both the settings for Groth-Sahai proofs. The product of two vectors is defined component wise, i.e, $(a_1, a_2, a_3)(b_1, b_2, b_3) = (a_1 b_1, a_2 b_2, a_3 b_3)$ for $(a_1, a_2, a_3), (b_1, b_2, b_3) \in \mathbb{G}^3$ for a finite order group $\mathbb{G}$.

Commitment in Perfectly Sound Setting: Generate public parameters $\mathsf{params} = (p, \mathbb{G}, \mathbb{G}_T, e, g) \leftarrow \mathsf{BilinearSetup}(1^\rho)$, where $\mathsf{BilinearSetup}$ is an algorithm which on input security parameter ρ generates $\mathsf{params} = (p, \mathbb{G}, \mathbb{G}_T, e, g)$, where $e : \mathbb{G} \times \mathbb{G} \rightarrow \mathbb{G}_T$, g is a generator of group $\mathbb{G}$ and p, the order of the groups $\mathbb{G}$ and $\mathbb{G}_T$, is prime. In this setting, the common reference string is $\mathsf{GS} = (\mathsf{params}, u_1, u_2, u_3)$, where $u_1 = (g_1, 1, g), u_2 = (1, g_2, g)$, $u_3 = u_1^{\xi_1} u_2^{\xi_2} = (g_1^{\xi_1}, g_2^{\xi_2}, g^{\xi_1 + \xi_2}) \in \mathbb{G}^3$, $\xi_1, \xi_2 \xleftarrow{\$} \mathbb{Z}_p$, $g_1 = g^a, g_2 = g^b$, $a, b \xleftarrow{\$} \mathbb{Z}_p$. To commit $X \in \mathbb{G}$, one picks $r_1, r_2, r_3 \xleftarrow{\$} \mathbb{Z}_p$ and sets $\mathsf{Com}(X) = (1, 1, X)u_1^{r_1} u_2^{r_2} u_3^{r_3} = (g_1^{r_1 + \xi_1 r_3}, g_2^{r_2 + \xi_2 r_3}, X \cdot g^{r_1 + r_2 + r_3(\xi_1 + \xi_2)})$. Note that $\mathsf{Com}(X)$ forms a BBS ciphertext [5] which is *fully extractable* as it can be decrypted using $a = \log_g(g_1), b = \log_g(g_2)$.

Commitment in Witness Indistinguishability Setting: Generate public parameters $\mathsf{params} = (p, \mathbb{G}, \mathbb{G}_T, e, g) \leftarrow \mathsf{BilinearSetup}(1^\rho)$. In this setting, the common reference string is $\mathsf{GS}' = (\mathsf{params}, u_1, u_2, u_3)$, where $u_1 = (g_1, 1, g) \in \mathbb{G}^3, u_2 = (1, g_2, g) \in \mathbb{G}^3$, $u_3 = u_1^{\xi_1} u_2^{\xi_2}(1, 1, g) = (g_1^{\xi_1}, g_2^{\xi_2}, g^{\xi_1 + \xi_2 + 1})$, $\xi_1, \xi_2 \xleftarrow{\$} \mathbb{Z}_p$, $g_1 = g^a, g_2 = g^b$, $a, b \xleftarrow{\$} \mathbb{Z}_p$. To commit $X \in \mathbb{G}$, one picks $r_1, r_2, r_3 \xleftarrow{\$} \mathbb{Z}_p$ and sets $\mathsf{Com}(X) = (1, 1, X)u_1^{r_1} u_2^{r_2} u_3^{r_3} = (g_1^{r_1 + \xi_1 r_3}, g_2^{r_2 + \xi_2 r_3}, X \cdot g^{r_1 + r_2 + r_3(\xi_1 + \xi_2 + 1)})$. One can note that $\mathsf{Com}(X)$ perfectly hides the message X which cannot be decrypted using $a = \log_g(g_1), b = \log_g(g_2)$.

> Let Commit be an algorithm which on input $X \in \mathbb{G}$ and GS, generates $\mathsf{Com}(X)$, i.e, $\mathsf{Com}(X) \leftarrow \mathsf{Commit}(\mathsf{GS}, X)$.

The commitments in both the setting are computationally indistinguishable by the following theorem.

Theorem 1. *[16] The common reference string in perfectly sound setting and witness indistinguishability setting is computationally indistinguishable under the DLIN assumption.*

Non-interactive Verification of Pairing Product Equation: Groth-Sahai proofs verify the pairing product equation

$$\prod_{i=1}^{n} e(\mathcal{A}_i, \mathcal{Y}_i) \prod_{i=1}^{m} e(\mathcal{X}_i, \mathcal{B}_i) \prod_{i=1}^{m} \prod_{j=1}^{n} e(\mathcal{X}_i, \mathcal{Y}_i)^{a_{i,j}} = t_T, \qquad (1)$$

in a non-interactive way, where the variables $\mathcal{X}_{i=1,2,\ldots,m} \in \mathbb{G}_1, \mathcal{Y}_{j=1,2,\ldots,n} \in \mathbb{G}_2$, constants $\mathcal{A}_{i=1,2,\ldots,n} \in \mathbb{G}_1, \mathcal{B}_{j=1,2,\ldots,m} \in \mathbb{G}_2$, $a_{i,j} \in \mathbb{Z}_p$ and $t_T \in \mathbb{G}_T$. The Groth-Sahai proofs are two party protocols with the prover and the verifier. The Groth-Sahai proofs consist of three PPT algorithms AGSSetup, AGSProve and AGSVerify described in Algorithms 1-3 respectively. In our construction, we will use following type of pairing product equations for a symmetric bilinear pairing e.

$$e(x,g)e(y,w) = e(g,g), \tag{2}$$

$$e(x,y) = e(g,g), \tag{3}$$

where, $x, y \in \mathbb{G}$ are secret values and $g, w \in \mathbb{G}, e(g,g) \in \mathbb{G}_T$ are public. Let us illustrate how the prover and the verifier use Algorithms 1-3 to verify the pairing product equations 2 and 3. The equation 2 is linear and 3 non-linear. The prover wants to convince the verifier in a non-interactive way that he knows the solution x, y to equations 2 and 3 without revealing anything about x and y to the verifier. Let $\mathcal{E}$ be the set of all equations which the prover wishes to prove in non-interactive way to the verifier and $\mathcal{W}$ be the set of all secret values in $\mathcal{E}$. The set $\mathcal{W}$ is referred as witnesses of statement $\mathcal{E}$. We follow the notation of [10] for writing equations in statement. In reference to equations 2 and 3, $\mathcal{E} = \{e(x,g)e(y,w) = e(g,g) \wedge e(x,y) = e(g,g)\}$ and $\mathcal{W} = (x,y)$. Let params $= (p, \mathbb{G}, \mathbb{G}_T, e, g) \leftarrow$ BilinearSetup(1^ρ).

Algorithm 1. AGSSetup
Input: params $= (p, \mathbb{G}, \mathbb{G}_T, e, g)$.
Output: GS $= (u_1, u_2, u_3)$,
$\qquad\qquad u_1, u_2, u_3 \in \mathbb{G}^3$.

1: $a, b, \xi_1, \xi_2 \xleftarrow{\$} \mathbb{Z}_p$;
2: $g_1 = g^a, g_2 = g^b$;
3: $u_1 = (g_1, 1, g), u_2 = (1, g_2, g)$;
4: $u_3 = u_1^{\xi_1} u_2^{\xi_2} = (g_1^{\xi_1}, g_2^{\xi_2}, g^{\xi_1 + \xi_2})$;
5: GS $= (u_1, u_2, u_3)$;

Algorithm 2. AGSProve
Input: GS $= (u_1, u_2, u_3), \mathcal{E} = (\text{eq}_1, \text{eq}_2, \ldots, \text{eq}_m)$,
$\qquad\qquad \mathcal{W} = (h_1, h_2, \ldots, h_l)$.
Output: π.

1: **for** $(i = 1, 2, \ldots, l)$ **do**
2: $\quad$ Com(h_i) $\leftarrow$ Commit(GS, h_i);
3: **for** $(i = 1, 2, \ldots, m)$ **do**
4: $\quad$ Generate P_i for equation $\text{eq}_i \in \mathcal{E}$;
5: $\pi = (\text{Com}(h_1), \text{Com}(h_2), \ldots, \text{Com}(h_l), P_1, P_2, \ldots, P_m)$;

The algorithm AGSSetup is run by a trusted party which on input params generates the common reference string GS in perfectly sound setting so that $\langle g_1, g_2, g, u_3^{(1)}, u_3^{(2)}, u_3^{(3)}\rangle$ forms a DLIN instance, where $u_3 = (u_3^{(1)}, u_3^{(2)}, u_3^{(3)})$. The trusted party makes GS public.

The prover runs AGSProve and generates commitments to x and y in perfectly sound setting using algorithm Commit. The proof components P_1 and P_2 for equations 2 and 3 are also generated by the prover using random values which were used to generate Com(x) and Com(y), where $P_1 = (P_1^{(1)}, P_1^{(2)}, P_1^{(3)})$ consists of 3 group elements and $P_2 = (P_2^{(1)}, P_2^{(2)}, P_2^{(3)}, P_2^{(4)}, P_2^{(5)}, P_2^{(6)}, P_2^{(7)}, P_2^{(8)}, P_2^{(9)})$ consists of 9 group elements as equation 2 is linear and equation 3 is non-linear respectively. The prover sets the proof $\pi = (\text{Com}(x), \text{Com}(y), P_1, P_2) \leftarrow$ AGSProve(GS, $\mathcal{E}, \mathcal{W}$) and gives π to the verifier.

Algorithm 3. AGSVerify
Input: GS $= (u_1, u_2, u_3), \pi = (\text{Com}(h_1), \text{Com}(h_2), \ldots, \text{Com}(h_l), P_1, P_2, \ldots, P_m)$.
Output: Either ACCEPT or REJECT.
1: **for** $(i = 1, 2, \ldots, m)$ **do**
2: $\quad$ Replace the variables in eq_i by their commitments;
3: $\quad$ Use proof components P_i of eq_i to check the validity of eq_i;

```
4:  if (All eq_i, i = 1, 2, ..., m are valid) then
5:      return ACCEPT;
6:  else
7:      return REJECT;
```

The algorithm AGSVerify is run by the verifier. The verifier checks whether $\mathsf{Com}(x)$, $\mathsf{Com}(y)$, and proof components P_1, P_2 satisfy

$$F(\mathsf{Com}(x), g)F(\mathsf{Com}(y), w) = (1, 1, e(g, g))F(u_1, \mathsf{P}_1^{(1)})F(u_2, \mathsf{P}_1^{(2)})F(u_3, \mathsf{P}_1^{(3)}), \quad (4)$$

$$F'(\mathsf{Com}(x), \mathsf{Com}(y)) = \begin{pmatrix} 1 & 1 & 1 \\ 1 & 1 & 1 \\ 1 & 1 & e(g, g) \end{pmatrix} F'(u_1, (\mathsf{P}_2^{(1)}, \mathsf{P}_2^{(2)}, \mathsf{P}_2^{(3)}))$$

$$F'(u_2, (\mathsf{P}_2^{(4)}, \mathsf{P}_2^{(5)}, \mathsf{P}_2^{(6)}))F'(u_3, (\mathsf{P}_2^{(7)}, \mathsf{P}_2^{(8)}, \mathsf{P}_2^{(9)})), \quad (5)$$

where $F : \mathbb{G}^3 \times \mathbb{G} \to \mathbb{G}_T^3$ and $F' : \mathbb{G}^3 \times \mathbb{G}^3 \to \mathbb{G}_T^9$ are respectively defined as
$$F((A, B, C), D) = (e(A, D), e(B, D), e(C, D)),$$

$$F'((x_1, x_2, x_3), (y_1, y_2, y_3)) = \begin{pmatrix} e(x_1, y_1) & e(x_1, y_2)e(x_2, y_1) & e(x_1, y_3)e(x_3, y_1) \\ 0 & e(x_2, y_2) & e(x_2, y_3)e(x_3, y_2) \\ 0 & 0 & e(x_3, y_3) \end{pmatrix}.$$

If equations 4 and 5 hold, the verifier outputs ACCEPT, otherwise, REJECT. Note that equations 4 and 5 hold if and only if equations 2 and 3 hold. For more details, we refer to [17].

2.3   Security Model

Universally Composable (UC) Framework [11]: This framework consists of a environment machine $\mathcal{Z}$, a real world adversary $\mathcal{A}$, an ideal world adversary $\mathcal{A}'$, an ideal functionality $\mathcal{F}$, parties $P_1, P_2, \ldots, P_N$ running the protocol Π in the real world and dummy parties $\widetilde{P_1}, \widetilde{P_2}, \ldots, \widetilde{P_N}$ interacting with $\mathcal{F}$ in the ideal world. The *environment machine* $\mathcal{Z}$ is always activated first. It interacts freely with $\mathcal{A}$ throughout the execution of the protocol Π in the real world and with $\mathcal{A}'$ throughout the execution of $\mathcal{F}$ in the ideal world. It oversees the execution of $\mathcal{F}$ in the ideal world and the execution of Π in the real world. The task of $\mathcal{Z}$ is to distinguish with non-negligible probability between the execution of Π in the real world and the execution of $\mathcal{F}$ in the ideal world.

$\mathcal{F}_{\mathsf{CRS}}^{\mathcal{D}}$ **Hybrid Model:** As OT protocol can be UC-realized only in the presence of common reference string (CRS) model, let us describe the $\mathcal{F}_{\mathsf{CRS}}^{\mathcal{D}}$-hybrid model [11] that UC realizes a protocol parameterized by some specific distribution $\mathcal{D}$. Upon receiving a message $(\mathsf{sid}, P_i), i = 1, 2, \ldots, N$, from the party P_i, where sid is session identity, $\mathcal{F}_{\mathsf{CRS}}^{\mathcal{D}}$ first checks if there is a recorded value crs. If not, $\mathcal{F}_{\mathsf{CRS}}^{\mathcal{D}}$ generates $\mathsf{crs} \xleftarrow{\$} \mathcal{D}(1^\rho)$ and records it. Finally, $\mathcal{F}_{\mathsf{CRS}}^{\mathcal{D}}$ sends $(\mathsf{sid}, \mathsf{crs})$ to the party P_i and the adversary.

Functionality of Oblivious Transfer: In the ideal world, the parties give their inputs to the ideal functionality $\mathcal{F}_{\mathsf{OT}}^{n \times 1}$ and get back their respective outputs.

These requirements are shown in Fig. 1 by the oblivious transfer functionality $\mathcal{F}_{\mathsf{OT}}^{n \times 1}$ following [11].

Definition 2. *Let* $\mathcal{F}_{\mathsf{OT}}^{n \times 1}$ *be the oblivious transfer functionality described in Fig. 1. A protocol* Π *securely realizes the ideal functionality* $\mathcal{F}_{\mathsf{OT}}^{n \times 1}$ *if for any real world adversary* $\mathcal{A}$*, there exists an ideal world adversary* $\mathcal{A}'$ *such that for any environment machine* $\mathcal{Z}$*,* $\mathsf{IDEAL}_{\mathcal{F}_{\mathsf{OT}}^{n \times 1}, \mathcal{A}', \mathcal{Z}} \overset{c}{\approx} \mathsf{REAL}_{\Pi, \mathcal{A}, \mathcal{Z}}$*, where* $\mathsf{IDEAL}_{\mathcal{F}_{\mathsf{OT}}^{n \times 1}, \mathcal{A}', \mathcal{Z}}$ *is the output of* $\mathcal{Z}$ *after interacting with* $\mathcal{A}'$ *and dummy parties interacting with* $\mathcal{F}_{\mathsf{OT}}^{n \times 1}$ *in the ideal world and* $\mathsf{REAL}_{\Pi, \mathcal{A}, \mathcal{Z}}$ *is the output of* $\mathcal{Z}$ *after interacting with* $\mathcal{A}$ *and the parties running the protocol* Π *in the real world.*

The functionality $\mathcal{F}_{\mathsf{OT}}^{n \times 1}$ interacts with S and R as follows:

1. Upon receiving a message $(\mathsf{sid}, \mathsf{S}, \langle m_1, m_2, \ldots, m_n \rangle)$ from S, $\mathcal{F}_{\mathsf{OT}}^{n \times 1}$ stores $\langle m_1, m_2, \ldots, m_n \rangle$, where $m_i \in \{0,1\}^l$, $i = 1, 2, \ldots, n$ and l is the fixed length of m_i which is known to both the parties.

2. Upon receiving a message $(\mathsf{sid}, \mathsf{R}, \sigma)$ from R, $\mathcal{F}_{\mathsf{OT}}^{n \times 1}$ checks if a message $(\mathsf{sid}, \mathsf{S}, \langle m_1, m_2, \ldots, m_n \rangle)$ was previously recorded.

- If no, $\mathcal{F}_{\mathsf{OT}}^{n \times 1}$ sends nothing to R.

- Otherwise, $\mathcal{F}_{\mathsf{OT}}^{n \times 1}$ sends $(\mathsf{sid}, \mathsf{request})$ to S. The sender S sends $(\mathsf{sid}, \mathsf{S}, b), b \in \{0,1\}$ in response to the request by $\mathcal{F}_{\mathsf{OT}}^{n \times 1}$. Also, S sends $(\mathsf{sid}, \mathsf{S}, b)$ to the adversary. If $b = 0$, $\mathcal{F}_{\mathsf{OT}}^{n \times 1}$ sends $(\mathsf{sid}, \perp)$ to R. Otherwise, $\mathcal{F}_{\mathsf{OT}}^{n \times 1}$ returns (sid, m_σ) to R.

Fig. 1. Functionality for adaptive oblivious transfer

3   Protocol

The communication flow in our adaptive k-out-of-n OT protocol is given in Figure 2 with five randomized algorithms, namely, AOTCrsGen, AOTInitialize, AOTInitializeVerify, AOTRequest, AOTRespond and a deterministic algorithm AOTComplete as described below in Algorithms 4-9 respectively. We will use algorithms AGSSetup, AGSProve and AGSVerify discussed in section 2.2.

Algorithm 4. AOTCrsGen
Input: Security parameter ρ.
Output: crs $=$ (params, FC, $\mathsf{GS_S}$, $\mathsf{GS_R}$).
1: params $= (p, \mathbb{G}, \mathbb{G}_T, e, g) \leftarrow$ BilinearSetup(1^ρ);
2: FC $= (u_1, u_2, u_3) \leftarrow$ AGSSetup(params);
3: $\mathsf{GS_S} \leftarrow$ AGSSetup(params);
4: $\mathsf{GS_R} \leftarrow$ AGSSetup(params);

The algorithm AOTCrsGen is run by the trusted party $\mathcal{F}_{\mathsf{CRS}}^{\mathcal{D}}$ which on input the security parameter ρ generates the common reference string crs consisting of params, FC, $\mathsf{GS_S}$ and $\mathsf{GS_R}$ in perfectly sound setting. The sender S uses Groth-Sahai common reference string $\mathsf{GS_S}$ to create non-interactive zero-knowledge (NIZK) proof and R uses Groth-Sahai common reference string $\mathsf{GS_R}$ for the creation of non-interactive witness indistinguishable (NIWI) proof. The common reference string crs is made public.

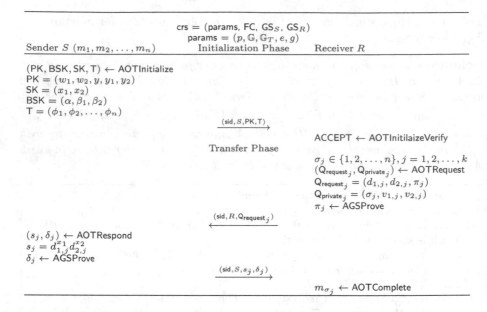

$$\mathsf{crs} = (\mathsf{params}, \mathsf{FC}, \mathsf{GS}_S, \mathsf{GS}_R)$$
$$\mathsf{params} = (p, \mathbb{G}, \mathbb{G}_T, e, g)$$

Sender S $(m_1, m_2, \ldots, m_n)$	Initialization Phase	Receiver R

$(\mathsf{PK}, \mathsf{BSK}, \mathsf{SK}, \mathsf{T}) \leftarrow \mathsf{AOTInitialize}$
$\mathsf{PK} = (w_1, w_2, y, y_1, y_2)$
$\mathsf{SK} = (x_1, x_2)$
$\mathsf{BSK} = (\alpha, \beta_1, \beta_2)$
$\mathsf{T} = (\phi_1, \phi_2, \ldots, \phi_n)$

$\xrightarrow{\;(sid, S, \mathsf{PK}, \mathsf{T})\;}$

$\mathsf{ACCEPT} \leftarrow \mathsf{AOTInitilaizeVerify}$

Transfer Phase

$\sigma_j \in \{1, 2, \ldots, n\}, j = 1, 2, \ldots, k$
$(\mathsf{Q}_{\mathsf{request}\,j}, \mathsf{Q}_{\mathsf{private}\,j}) \leftarrow \mathsf{AOTRequest}$
$\mathsf{Q}_{\mathsf{request}\,j} = (d_{1,j}, d_{2,j}, \pi_j)$
$\mathsf{Q}_{\mathsf{private}\,j} = (\sigma_j, v_{1,j}, v_{2,j})$
$\pi_j \leftarrow \mathsf{AGSProve}$

$\xleftarrow{\;(sid, R, \mathsf{Q}_{\mathsf{request}\,j})\;}$

$(s_j, \delta_j) \leftarrow \mathsf{AOTRespond}$
$s_j = d_{1,j}^{x_1} d_{2,j}^{x_2}$
$\delta_j \leftarrow \mathsf{AGSProve}$

$\xrightarrow{\;(sid, S, s_j, \delta_j)\;}$

$m_{\sigma_j} \leftarrow \mathsf{AOTComplete}$

Fig. 2. Communication flow for the jth transfer phase, $j = 1, 2, \ldots, k$

Algorithm 5. AOTInitialize

Input: $\mathsf{crs} = (\mathsf{params}, \mathsf{FC}, \mathsf{GS}_S, \mathsf{GS}_R), m_1, m_2, \ldots, m_n \in \mathbb{G}$.
Output: $(\mathsf{PK}, \mathsf{BSK}, \mathsf{SK}, \mathsf{T})$.

1: $x_1, x_2, \alpha, \beta_1, \beta_2 \xleftarrow{\$} \mathbb{Z}_p$;
2: $w_1 = g^{\frac{1}{x_1}}, w_2 = g^{\frac{1}{x_2}}, y = g^\alpha, y_1 = g^{\beta_1}, y_2 = g^{\beta_2}$;
3: $\mathsf{PK} = (w_1, w_2, y, y_1, y_2), \mathsf{SK} = (x_1, x_2), \mathsf{BSK} = (\alpha, \beta_1, \beta_2)$;
4: Parse FC as (u_1, u_2, u_3), where $u_1 = (g_1, 1, g), u_2 = (1, g_2, g), u_3 = u_1^{\xi_1} u_2^{\xi_2} = (u_3^{(1)}, u_3^{(2)}, u_3^{(3)})$,
   $\quad g_1 = g^a, g_2 = g^b, u_3^{(1)} = g_1^{\xi_1}, u_3^{(2)} = g_2^{\xi_2}, u_3^{(3)} = g^{\xi_1 + \xi_2}, a, b, \xi_1, \xi_2 \xleftarrow{\$} \mathbb{Z}_p$;
5: **for** $(i = 1, 2, \ldots, n)$ **do**
6: $\quad r_{1i}, r_{2i}, r_{3i}, r_i, s_i \xleftarrow{\$} \mathbb{Z}_p$;
7: $\quad \mathsf{Com}(m_i) = (1, 1, m_i) u_1^{r_{1i}} u_2^{r_{2i}} u_3^{r_{3i}} = (g_1^{r_{1i}} (u_3^{(1)})^{r_{3i}}, g_2^{r_{2i}} (u_3^{(2)})^{r_{3i}}, m_i g^{r_{1i} + r_{2i}} (u_3^{(3)})^{r_{3i}})$;
8: $\quad$ Batch BB signature on (i, r_i, s_i) is $\mathsf{sig}_i = g^{\frac{1}{\alpha + i + r_i \beta_1 + s_i \beta_2}}$;
9: $\quad$ Ciphertext $\phi_i = (\mathsf{Com}(m_i), g^{r_{1i}}, g^{r_{2i}}, g^{r_{3i}}, w_1^{r_i}, w_2^{s_i}, m_i g^{r_i + s_i}, y_1^{r_i}, y_2^{s_i}, \mathsf{sig}_i)$;
10: $\mathsf{T} = (\phi_1, \phi_2, \ldots, \phi_n)$;

The algorithm AOTInitialize is run by S. On input crs, n messages $(m_1, m_2, \ldots, m_n)$, AOTInitialize generates public key PK, signature secret key BSK, secret key SK and ciphertext T of n messages for R. The sender S gives $(\mathsf{PK}, \mathsf{T})$ to R and keeps $(\mathsf{BSK}, \mathsf{SK})$ secret to itself. In each $\phi_i = (c_i^{(1)}, c_i^{(2)}, c_i^{(3)}, c_i^{(4)}, c_i^{(5)}, c_i^{(6)}, c_i^{(7)}, c_i^{(8)}, c_i^{(9)}, c_i^{(10)}, c_i^{(11)}, c_i^{(12)}), i = 1, 2, \ldots, n,, (c_i^{(1)}, c_i^{(2)}, c_i^{(3)}) = (g_1^{r_{1i}} (u_3^{(1)})^{r_{3i}}, g_2^{r_{2i}} (u_3^{(2)})^{r_{3i}}, m_i g^{r_{1i} + r_{2i}} (u_3^{(3)})^{r_{3i}})$ is $\mathsf{Com}(m_i)$, $(c_i^{(4)}, c_i^{(5)}, c_i^{(6)}) = (g^{r_{1i}}, g^{r_{2i}}, g^{r_{3i}})$ are the opening values to $\mathsf{Com}(m_i)$ used by R to verify that he got the correct message from S at the end of each transfer phase. The opening values to these commitments are generated following [14]. Also, $(c_i^{(7)}, c_i^{(8)}, c_i^{(9)}) = (w_1^{r_i}, w_2^{s_i}, m_i g^{r_i + s_i})$ is a BBS ciphertext [5] of m_i, $(c_i^{(10)}, c_i^{(11)}) = (y_1^{r_i}, y_2^{s_i})$ is for signature verification and $c_i^{(12)} = \mathsf{sig}_i = g^{\frac{1}{\alpha + i + r_i \beta_1 + s_i \beta_2}}$ is a batch BB signature [7].

Algorithm 6. AOTInitializeVerify

Input: $\mathsf{PK} = (w_1, w_2, y, y_1, y_2), \mathsf{T} = (\phi_1, \phi_2, \ldots, \phi_n)$.
Output: (Either ACCEPT or REJECT).
1: **for** $(i = 1, 2, \ldots, n)$ **do**
2:     Parse ϕ_i as $(c_i^{(1)}, c_i^{(2)}, c_i^{(3)}, c_i^{(4)}, c_i^{(5)}, c_i^{(6)}, c_i^{(7)}, c_i^{(8)}, c_i^{(9)}, c_i^{(10)}, c_i^{(11)}, c_i^{(12)})$;
3:     **if** $\left(e(c_i^{(12)}, y \cdot g^i \cdot c_i^{(10)} \cdot c_i^{(11)}) = e(g,g) \wedge e(w_1, c_i^{(10)}) = e(c_i^{(7)}, y_1) \wedge e(w_2, c_i^{(11)}) = e(c_i^{(8)}, y_2) \right)$
4: **then**
5:     ϕ_i is correct
6:     **else**
7:        return REJECT;
8:        **break**;
9: return ACCEPT;

The algorithm AOTInitializeVerify is run by R in the initialization phase. If all the ciphertext are valid, the transfer phase will take place, otherwise the execution will be aborted by R. The validity of the ciphertext $\phi_i, i = 1, 2, \ldots, n$, is checked in line 3 of Algorithm 6.

Algorithm 7. AOTRequest

Input: $\mathsf{crs} = (\mathsf{params}, \mathsf{FC}, \mathsf{GS_S}, \mathsf{GS_R}), \mathsf{PK} = (w_1, w_2, y, y_1, y_2), \mathsf{T} = (\phi_1, \phi_2, \ldots, \phi_n), \sigma_j \in \{1, 2, \ldots, n\}$.
Output: $(\mathsf{Q}_{\mathsf{request}\,j}, \mathsf{Q}_{\mathsf{private}\,j}), j = 1, 2, \ldots, k$.
1: Parse ϕ_{σ_j} as $(c_{\sigma_j}^{(1)}, c_{\sigma_j}^{(2)}, c_{\sigma_j}^{(3)}, c_{\sigma_j}^{(4)}, c_{\sigma_j}^{(5)}, c_{\sigma_j}^{(6)}, c_{\sigma_j}^{(7)}, c_{\sigma_j}^{(8)}, c_{\sigma_j}^{(9)}, c_{\sigma_j}^{(10)}, c_{\sigma_j}^{(11)}, c_{\sigma_j}^{(12)})$;
2: $v_{1,j}, v_{2,j} \xleftarrow{\$} \mathbb{Z}_p$;
3: $d_{1,j} = c_{\sigma_j}^{(7)} \cdot w_1^{v_{1,j}}, d_{2,j} = c_{\sigma_j}^{(8)} \cdot w_2^{v_{2,j}}, t_{1,j} = g^{v_{1,j}}, t_{2,j} = g^{v_{2,j}}$;
4: $\mathcal{E}_{1,j} = \{e(c_{\sigma_j}^{(7)}, g)e(t_{1,j}, w_1) = e(d_{1,j}, g) \wedge e(c_{\sigma_j}^{(8)}, g)e(t_{2,j}, w_2) = e(d_{2,j}, g) \wedge$
    $e(c_{\sigma_j}^{(12)}, y \cdot g^{\sigma_j} \cdot c_{\sigma_j}^{(10)} \cdot c_{\sigma_j}^{(11)}) = e(g,g) \wedge e(w_1, c_{\sigma_j}^{(10)}) = e(c_{\sigma_j}^{(7)}, y_1) \wedge e(w_2, c_{\sigma_j}^{(11)}) = e(c_{\sigma_j}^{(8)}, y_2)\}$;
5: $\mathcal{W}_{1,j} = (c_{\sigma_j}^{(7)}, c_{\sigma_j}^{(8)}, t_{1,j}, t_{2,j}, c_{\sigma_j}^{(10)}, c_{\sigma_j}^{(11)}, c_{\sigma_j}^{(12)}, g^{\sigma_j})$;
6: $\pi_j \leftarrow \mathsf{AGSProve}(\mathsf{GS_R}, \mathcal{E}_{1,j}, \mathcal{W}_{1,j})$;
7: $\mathsf{Q}_{\mathsf{request}\,j} = (d_{1,j}, d_{2,j}, \pi_j), \mathsf{Q}_{\mathsf{private}\,j} = (\sigma_j, v_{1,j}, v_{2,j})$;

The algorithm AOTRequest is run by R. On input crs, T and R's choice of σ_j for jth transfer phase, AOTRequest generates $(\mathsf{Q}_{\mathsf{request}\,j}, \mathsf{Q}_{\mathsf{private}\,j})$ using $\mathsf{GS_R}$ for S, where $j = 1, 2, \ldots, k$. The receiver R sends $\mathsf{Q}_{\mathsf{request}\,j}$ to S and keeps $\mathsf{Q}_{\mathsf{private}\,j}$ secret to itself. In $\mathsf{Q}_{\mathsf{request}\,j}$, the values $d_{1,j}, d_{2,j}$ correspond to the masked versions of $c_{\sigma_j}^{(7)}, c_{\sigma_j}^{(8)}$ respectively and NIWI proof π_j generated by AGSProve in Algorithm 2 consists of commitments to witnesses in $\mathcal{W}_{1,j}$ and proof components for verifications of equations in statement $\mathcal{E}_{1,j}$. The proof generations for 1st, 2nd, 4th and 5th equation in $\mathcal{E}_{1,j}$ are similar to equation 2 and that for 3rd equation in $\mathcal{E}_{1,j}$ is similar to equation 3. Following the notation of [10] for writing equations in $\mathcal{E}_{1,j}$, the first two equations guarantee the masked versions of $c_{\sigma_j}^{(7)}, c_{\sigma_j}^{(8)}$ and remaining three equations correspond to valid signature held by R. These checks enable one to detect whether R deviates from the protocol execution. Thus $\mathcal{E}_{1,j}$ in line 4 of Algorithm 7 is a statement set by R to convince S that $\mathsf{Q}_{\mathsf{request}\,j}$ is framed correctly.

Algorithm 8. AOTRespond

Input: $\mathsf{crs} = (\mathsf{params}, \mathsf{FC}, \mathsf{GS_S}, \mathsf{GS_R}), \mathsf{PK} = (w_1, w_2, y, y_1, y_2), \mathsf{SK} = (x_1, x_2), \mathsf{Q}_{\mathsf{request}\,j} = (d_{1,j}, d_{2,j}, \pi_j)$.
Output: (s_j, δ_j).
1: **if** $(\mathsf{AGSVerify}(\mathsf{GS_R}, \pi_j) == \mathsf{ACCEPT})$ **then**
2:     Extract g from params;
3:     $a_1 = d_{1,j}^{x_1}, a_2 = d_{2,j}^{x_2}, s_j = a_1 \cdot a_2$;
4:     $\mathcal{E}_{2,j} = \{e(a_1, w_1)e(d_{1,j}^{-1}, a_3) = 1 \wedge e(a_2, w_2)e(d_{2,j}^{-1}, a_3) = 1 \wedge e(a_1 a_2, a_3)e(s_j^{-1}, g) = 1 \wedge$
       $e(w_1, a_3) = e(w_1, g)\}$;
5:     $\mathcal{W}_{2,j} = (a_1, a_2, a_3)$;

6: $\delta_j \leftarrow$ AGSProve(GS$_S$, $\mathcal{E}_{2,j}$, $\mathcal{W}_{2,j}$);
7: **else**
8:   abort the execution;

On input crs, PK, SK and Q$_{\text{request}_j}$, S runs the algorithm AOTRespond which first verifies the NIWI proof π_j using GS$_R$. If the proof π_j is valid, AOTRespond generates s_j using secret key SK and NIZK proof δ_j using GS$_S$. The proof δ_j consists of commitments to elements in $\mathcal{W}_{2,j}$ and proof components for equations in statement $\mathcal{E}_{2,j}$. The proof generations for 1st, 2nd and 4th equation in statement $\mathcal{E}_{2,j}$ are similar to equation 2 and that for 3rd equation in statement $\mathcal{E}_{2,j}$ is similar to equation 3. The first two equations in statement $\mathcal{E}_{2,j}$ guarantee that a_1, a_2 are generated using SK. The third equation corresponds to $s_j = a_1 \cdot a_2$ and the fourth equation indicates that a_3 is equal to g. Thus $\mathcal{E}_{2,j}$ in line 4 of Algorithm 8 is a statement framed by S in order to convince R that the response s_j is correctly framed.

Algorithm 9. AOTComplete
Input: crs = (params, FC, GS$_S$, GS$_R$), T = $(\phi_1, \phi_2, \ldots, \phi_n)$, s_j, δ_j, Q$_{\text{private}_j}$ = $(\sigma_j, v_{1,j}, v_{2,j})$.
Output: m_{σ_j}.
1: **if** (AGSVerify(GS$_S$, δ_j) == ACCEPT) **then**
2:   Extract g from params and $u_3 = (u_3^{(1)}, u_3^{(2)}, u_3^{(3)})$ from FC = (u_1, u_2, u_3);
3:   Parse Q$_{\text{private}_j}$ as $\sigma_j, v_{1,j}, v_{2,j}$;
4:   Parse ϕ_{σ_j} as $(c_{\sigma_j}^{(1)}, c_{\sigma_j}^{(2)}, c_{\sigma_j}^{(3)}, c_{\sigma_j}^{(4)}, c_{\sigma_j}^{(5)}, c_{\sigma_j}^{(6)}, c_{\sigma_j}^{(7)}, c_{\sigma_j}^{(8)}, c_{\sigma_j}^{(9)}, c_{\sigma_j}^{(10)}, c_{\sigma_j}^{(11)}, c_{\sigma_j}^{(12)})$;
5: $m_{\sigma_j} = c_{\sigma_j}^{(9)} \cdot g^{v_{1,j}} \cdot g^{v_{2,j}} / s_j$;
6: $\mathcal{E}_{3,j} = \{e(c_{\sigma_j}^{(1)}, g) = e(g_1, c_{\sigma_j}^{(4)})e(u_3^{(1)}, c_{\sigma_j}^{(6)}) \wedge e(c_{\sigma_j}^{(2)}, g) = e(g_2, c_{\sigma_j}^{(5)})e(u_3^{(2)}, c_{\sigma_j}^{(6)}) \wedge$
        $e(c_{\sigma_j}^{(3)}, g) = e(m_{\sigma_j} c_{\sigma_j}^{(4)} c_{\sigma_j}^{(5)}, g)e(u_3^{(3)}, c_{\sigma_j}^{(6)})\}$;
7:   **if** ($\mathcal{E}_{3,j}$ is valid) **then**
8:   return m_{σ_j};
9:   **else**
10:   abort the execution;
11: **else**
12:   abort the execution;

The algorithm AOTComplete is run by R which on input crs, T, s_j, δ_j and Q$_{\text{private}_j}$ first checks the validity of NIZK proof δ_j using GS$_S$ following AGSVerify in Algorithm 3. If the proof δ_j is valid, AOTComplete computes m_{σ_j} using s_j, Q$_{\text{private}_j}$ and checks the correctness of message m_{σ_j} by verifying the equations in statement $\mathcal{E}_{3,j}$ which is given in line 6 of Algorithm 9. If all checks hold, AOTComplete outputs m_{σ_j} for R. The algorithm correctly recovers the message m_{σ_j} in line 5 of Algorithm 9 as follows:

$$\frac{c_{\sigma_j}^{(9)} \cdot g^{v_{1,j}} \cdot g^{v_{2,j}}}{s_j} = \frac{m_{\sigma_j} g^{r_{\sigma_j} + s_{\sigma_j}} g^{v_{1,j}} \cdot g^{v_{2,j}}}{(w_1^{r_{\sigma_j}})^{x_1}(w_2^{s_{\sigma_j}})^{x_2}(w_1^{v_{1,j}})^{x_1}(w_2^{v_{2,j}})^{x_2}} = m_{\sigma_j} \quad \text{as} \quad w_1^{x_1} = w_2^{x_2} = g.$$

4   Security Analysis

Theorem 2. *The adaptive oblivious transfer protocol Π presented in section 3 securely realizes the ideal functionality $\mathcal{F}_{OT}^{n \times 1}$ in the $\mathcal{F}_{CRS}^{\mathcal{D}}$-hybrid model described in section 2.3 under the DLIN and q-SDH assumption.*

Proof. Let $\mathcal{A}$ be a static adversary in the real world interacting with the protocol Π. We construct an ideal world adversary $\mathcal{A}'$ also called simulator interacting with the ideal functionality $\mathcal{F}_{OT}^{n \times 1}$ in the ideal world such that no environment machine $\mathcal{Z}$ can distinguish with non-negligible probability whether it is interacting with Π and $\mathcal{A}$ in the real world or with $\mathcal{F}_{OT}^{n \times 1}$ and $\mathcal{A}'$ in the ideal world. Let $\text{IDEAL}_{\mathcal{F}_{OT}^{n \times 1}, \mathcal{A}', \mathcal{Z}}$ and $\text{REAL}_{\Pi, \mathcal{A}, \mathcal{Z}}$ are as defined in section 2.3. We will show $\text{IDEAL}_{\mathcal{F}_{OT}^{n \times 1}, \mathcal{A}', \mathcal{Z}} \overset{c}{\approx} \text{REAL}_{\Pi, \mathcal{A}, \mathcal{Z}}$ in each of the cases: (a) simulation when R is corrupted and S is honest, (b) simulation when S is corrupted and R is honest. We do not discuss the cases when both the parties are honest and when both the parties are corrupt.

We present the security proof using sequence of hybrid games. Let $\Pr[\text{Game } i]$ be the probability that $\mathcal{Z}$ distinguishes the transcript of Game i from the real execution. Let us start with describing four PPT algorithms namely AGSExtractSetup, AGSExtract, AGSSimSetup and AGSSimProve in Algorithms 10-13 respectively which are used in these games by $\mathcal{A}'$ to simulate Groth-Sahai proofs. Let params $= (p, \mathbb{G}, \mathbb{G}_T, e, g) \leftarrow \text{BilinearSetup}(1^\rho)$.

Algorithm 10. AGSExtractSetup

Input: params $= (p, \mathbb{G}, \mathbb{G}_T, e, g)$.
Output: $\text{GS}' = (u_1, u_2, u_3), u_1, u_2, u_3 \in \mathbb{G}^3$, trapdoor $t_{ext} = (a, b, \xi_1, \xi_2)$.

1: $a, b, \xi_1, \xi_2 \xleftarrow{\$} \mathbb{Z}_p$;
2: $g_1 = g^a, g_2 = g^b$;
3: $u_1 = (g_1, 1, g), u_2 = (1, g_2, g)$;
4: $u_3 = u_1^{\xi_1} u_2^{\xi_2} = (g_1^{\xi_1}, g_2^{\xi_2}, g^{\xi_1 + \xi_2})$;
5: $\text{GS}' = (u_1, u_2, u_3)$;
6: $t_{ext} = (a, b, \xi_1, \xi_2)$;

The simulator $\mathcal{A}'$ runs the algorithm AGSExtractSetup which has same distribution as AGSSetup and generates the common reference string GS' and trapdoor t_{ext} in perfectly sound setting. The simulator $\mathcal{A}'$ makes GS' public and keeps the trapdoor t_{ext} secret to itself.

The algorithm AGSExtract given below enables $\mathcal{A}'$ to extract the witnesses from the commitments embedded in a proof π generated using GS' and t_{ext}.

The algorithm AGSSimSetup given below run by $\mathcal{A}'$ generates the common reference string $\text{GS}'' = (u_1, u_2, u_3)$ and trapdoor $t_{sim} = (a, b, \xi_1, \xi_2)$ in witness indistinguishability setting. The common reference string GS'' in AGSSimSetup is such that $\langle g_1, g_2, g, u_3^{(1)}, u_3^{(2)}, u_3^{(3)} \rangle$ is not a DLIN instance whereas the common

---

Algorithm 11. AGSExtract

Input: $\text{GS}' = (u_1, u_2, u_3)$,
$\qquad t_{ext} = (a, b, \xi_1, \xi_2), \pi$.
Output: Witnesses $\mathcal{W}$.

1: $\mathcal{W} = \phi$;
2: for (each $\text{Com}(X)$ embedded in π) do
3: $\quad$ Parse $\text{Com}(X)$ as (A_1, A_2, A_3);
4: $\quad X = A_3 / (A_1^{\frac{1}{a}} A_2^{\frac{1}{b}})$;
5: $\quad \mathcal{W} = \mathcal{W} \bigcup \{X\}$;

Algorithm 12. AGSSimSetup

Input: params $= (p, \mathbb{G}, \mathbb{G}_T, e, g)$.
Output: $\text{GS}'' = (u_1, u_2, u_3), u_1, u_2, u_3 \in \mathbb{G}^3$,
$\qquad t_{sim} = (a, b, \xi_1, \xi_2)$.

1: $a, b, \xi_1, \xi_2 \xleftarrow{\$} \mathbb{Z}_p$;
2: $g_1 = g^a, g_2 = g^b$;
3: $u_1 = (g_1, 1, g), u_2 = (1, g_2, g)$;
4: $u_3 = u_1^{\xi_1} u_2^{\xi_2} (1, 1, g) = (g_1^{\xi_1}, g_2^{\xi_2}, g^{\xi_1 + \xi_2 + 1})$;
5: $\text{GS}'' = (u_1, u_2, u_3)$;
6: $t_{sim} = (a, b, \xi_1, \xi_2)$;

reference string GS′ in AGSExtractSetup is such that $\langle g_1, g_2, g, u_3^{(1)}, u_3^{(2)}, u_3^{(3)} \rangle$ is a DLIN instance, where $u_3 = (u_3^{(1)}, u_3^{(2)}, u_3^{(3)})$. Thus the output GS″ of AGSSimSetup is computationally indistinguishable from the output GS′ of AGSExtractSetup and the output GS of AGSSetup under the DLIN assumption by Theorem 1.

Algorithm 13. AGSSimProve
Input: GS″, $t_{sim} = (a, b, \xi_1, \xi_2)$, $\mathcal{E}' = (eq_1, eq_2, \ldots, eq_m)$, $\mathcal{W}' = (h_1, h_2, \ldots, h_l)$.
Output: δ'.
1: for $(i = 1, 2, \ldots, l)$ do
2:      Generate commitment to each element in $\mathcal{W}'$ by randomly picking $b_1, b_2, b_3 \xleftarrow{\$} \mathbb{Z}_p$ such that
        $Com(h_i) = (g^{b_1}, g^{b_2}, g^{b_3})'$;
3: for $(i = 1, 2, \ldots, m)$ do
4:      **if** (eq_i is linear equation) **then**
5:          Generate proof component P_i for equation eq_i by randomly picking 3 group elements;
6:      **else**
7:          Generate proof component P_i for equation eq_i by randomly picking 9 group elements;
8: Open the commitment of each element in $\mathcal{W}'$ to any value g^γ by using the trapdoor t_{sim}
        such that all equations in $\mathcal{E}'$ are satisfied;
9: $\delta' = (Com(h_1), Com(h_2), \ldots, Com(h_l), P_1, P_2, \ldots, P_m)$;

The algorithm AGSSimProve enables $\mathcal{A}'$ to generate the proof δ' using GS″ and t_{sim} such that AGSVerify(GS″, δ') = ACCEPT. We have the following Claim established by Groth-Sahai in [16].

Claim 1. *Groth-Sahai proofs are composable NIWI and NIZK for satisfiability of a set of equations over a bilinear group under the DLIN assumption.*

(a) Simulation when R is corrupted and S is honest.

Game 0: This game corresponds to the real world protocol interaction in which R interacts with honest S. So, $\Pr[\text{Game 0}] = 0$.

Game 1: This game is the same as Game 0 except that crs is generated by $\mathcal{A}'$. Let params $= (p, \mathbb{G}, \mathbb{G}_T, e, g) \leftarrow$ BilinearSetup(1^ρ). The adversary $\mathcal{A}'$ generates (FC′, t) $\leftarrow$ AGSSimSetup(params), (GS′$_S$, t_{sim}) $\leftarrow$ AGSSimsSetup(params) and (GS′$_R$, t_{ext}) $\leftarrow$ AGSExtractSetup(params) and sets crs = (params, FC′, GS′$_S$, GS′$_R$). The adversary $\mathcal{A}'$ makes params, FC′, GS′$_S$, GS′$_R$ public and keeps the trapdoors t, t_{sim}, t_{ext} secret to itself. The part GS′$_R$ of crs generated by $\mathcal{A}'$ is distributed identically to the output GS$_R$ of AGSSetup whereas FC′ and GS′$_S$ are not based on DLIN instances. By Theorem 1 in section 2.2, crs generated by $\mathcal{A}'$ and AOTCrsGen in actual protocol run are computationally indistinguishable. Therefore, there exists a negligible function $\epsilon_1(\rho)$ such that $|\Pr[\text{Game 1}] - \Pr[\text{Game 0}]| \leq \epsilon_1(\rho)$.

Game 2: This game is exactly the same as Game 1 except that for each request by $\mathcal{A}$, the adversary $\mathcal{A}'$ extracts the index σ_j as follows for transfer phase $j = 1, 2, \ldots, k$. It parses $Q_{request_j}$ as $(d_{1,j}, d_{2,j}, \pi_j)$ and extracts π_j. Note that $d_{1,j} = c_{\sigma_j}^{(7)} \cdot w_1^{v_{1,j}}$, $d_{2,j} = c_{\sigma_j}^{(8)} \cdot w_2^{v_{2,j}}$, $v_{1,j}, v_{2,j} \xleftarrow{\$} \mathbb{Z}_p$ in $Q_{request_j}$ according to the real protocol AOTRequest in Algorithm 7. As the proof π_j is generated by using GS′$_R$, the adversary $\mathcal{A}'$ runs AGSVerify(GS′$_R$, π_j) to check the validity of π_j. If REJECT, $\mathcal{A}'$ aborts the execution. So, $\Pr[\text{Game 2}] = \Pr[\text{Game 1}]$. Otherwise, $\mathcal{A}'$ extracts the witness $\mathcal{W}' = (\gamma_1, \gamma_2, \gamma_3, \gamma_4, \gamma_5, \gamma_6, \gamma_7, \gamma_8) \leftarrow$ AGSExtract(GS′$_R$, t_{ext}, π_j) using t_{ext}. The adversary $\mathcal{A}'$ parses T as $(\phi_1, \phi_2, \ldots, \phi_n)$ and for each $\phi_i = (c_i^{(1)}, c_i^{(2)}, c_i^{(3)}, c_i^{(4)}, c_i^{(5)}, c_i^{(6)}, c_i^{(7)}, c_i^{(8)}, c_i^{(9)}, c_i^{(10)}, c_i^{(11)}, c_i^{(12)})$, $i = 1, 2, \ldots, n$, checks if $(\gamma_1, \gamma_2) =$

$(c_i^{(7)}, c_i^{(8)})$. Let σ_j be the matching index. The adversary $\mathcal{A}'$ checks if $g^{\sigma_j} = \gamma_8$. If check holds then $\mathcal{W}' = (c_{\sigma_j}^{(7)}, c_{\sigma_j}^{(8)}, t_{1,j}, t_{2,j}, c_{\sigma_j}^{(10)}, c_{\sigma_j}^{(11)}, c_{\sigma_j}^{(12)}, g^{\sigma_j}), t_{1,j} = g^{v_{1,j}}, t_{2,j} = g^{v_{2,j}}$ in the witnesses $\mathcal{W}'$ extracted by $\mathcal{A}'$. The adversary $\mathcal{A}'$ queries $\mathcal{F}_{\mathsf{OT}}^{n \times 1}$ with the message $(\mathsf{sid}, \mathsf{R}, \sigma_j)$. The ideal functionality $\mathcal{F}_{\mathsf{OT}}^{n \times 1}$ gives m_{σ_j} to $\mathcal{A}'$. If no matching ciphertext found, it aborts the execution. However, this event occurs with negligible probability under the q-SDH assumption. If no matching index found, i.e, $\sigma_j \notin \{1, 2, \ldots, n\}$, then $\mathcal{A}$ has to construct a valid proof π_j for the ciphertext $\phi_{\sigma_j} \notin \mathsf{T} = (\phi_1, \phi_2, \ldots, \phi_n)$ to generate $\mathsf{Q}_{\mathsf{request}\,j}$. This eventually means that $\mathcal{A}$ has framed the ciphertext $\phi_{\sigma_j} = (c_{\sigma_j}^{(1)}, c_{\sigma_j}^{(2)}, c_{\sigma_j}^{(3)}, c_{\sigma_j}^{(4)}, c_{\sigma_j}^{(5)}, c_{\sigma_j}^{(6)}, c_{\sigma_j}^{(7)}, c_{\sigma_j}^{(8)}, c_{\sigma_j}^{(9)}, c_{\sigma_j}^{(10)}, c_{\sigma_j}^{(11)}, c_{\sigma_j}^{(12)})$ on its own which must be a correct ciphertext as the proof π_j generated by $\mathcal{A}$ for ϕ_{σ_j} is valid. This in turn indicates that $\mathcal{A}$ is able to come up with a valid batch BB signature $c_{\sigma_j}^{(12)}$, thereby $\mathcal{A}$ outputs $(c_{\sigma_j}^{(10)}, c_{\sigma_j}^{(11)}, c_{\sigma_j}^{(12)})$ as a forgery contradicting the fact that the batch BB signature is unforgeable under chosen-message attack assuming q-SDH problem is hard [4]. Therefore, there exists a negligible function $\epsilon_2(\rho)$ such that $|\Pr[\mathsf{Game}\ 2] - \Pr[\mathsf{Game}\ 1]| \leq \epsilon_2(\rho)$.

Game 3: This game is the same as Game 2 except that $\mathcal{A}'$ simulates the response s_j and proof δ_j for each transfer phase $j = 1, 2, \ldots, k$. The adversary $\mathcal{A}'$ parses the ciphertext ϕ_{σ_j} as $(c_{\sigma_j}^{(1)}, c_{\sigma_j}^{(2)}, c_{\sigma_j}^{(3)}, c_{\sigma_j}^{(4)}, c_{\sigma_j}^{(5)}, c_{\sigma_j}^{(6)}, c_{\sigma_j}^{(7)}, c_{\sigma_j}^{(8)}, c_{\sigma_j}^{(9)}, c_{\sigma_j}^{(10)}, c_{\sigma_j}^{(11)}, c_{\sigma_j}^{(12)})$, extracts γ_3, γ_4 from the witnesses $\mathcal{W}' = (\gamma_1, \gamma_2, \gamma_3, \gamma_4, \gamma_5, \gamma_6, \gamma_7, \gamma_8) = (c_{\sigma_j}^{(7)}, c_{\sigma_j}^{(8)}, t_{1,j}, t_{2,j}, c_{\sigma_j}^{(10)}, c_{\sigma_j}^{(11)}, c_{\sigma_j}^{(12)}, g^{\sigma_j})$, computes the simulated response $s_j' = c_{\sigma_j}^{(9)} \gamma_3 \gamma_4 / m_{\sigma_j}$, $\gamma_3 = t_{1,j} = g^{v_{1,j}}$, $\gamma_4 = t_{2,j} = g^{v_{2,j}}$ and proof $\delta_j' \leftarrow \mathsf{AGSSimProve}(\mathsf{GS's}, \mathsf{t}_{\mathsf{sim}}, \mathcal{E}_{2,j})$, where $\mathcal{E}_{2,j}$ is a statement set by the sender S to convince the receiver R that response s_j is correctly formed. The adversary $\mathcal{A}'$ thus simulates the proof δ_j' for the statement $\mathcal{E}_{2,j}$ such that s_j' is correctly framed. By Claim 2 provided below, there exists a negligible function $\epsilon_3(\rho)$ such that $|\Pr[\mathsf{Game}\ 3] - \Pr[\mathsf{Game}\ 2]| \leq \epsilon_3(\rho)$.

Claim 2. *Under the DLIN assumption, the response s_j and the proof δ_j in the real protocol honestly generated by the sender S are computationally indistinguishable from the response s_j' and proof δ_j' simulated by the simulator $\mathcal{A}'$.*

Proof of Claim 2. The simulated response by $\mathcal{A}'$ in Game 3 is $s_j' = c_{\sigma_j}^{(9)} \gamma_3 \gamma_4 / m_{\sigma_j} = (c_{\sigma_j}^{(7)})^{x_1} (c_{\sigma_j}^{(8)})^{x_2} \cdot m_{\sigma_j} \cdot g^{v_{1,j}} \cdot g^{v_{2,j}} / m_{\sigma_j}$ and the honestly generated response s_j in Game 2 is $s_j = (d_{1,j})^{x_1} (d_{2,j})^{x_2}$, $d_{1,j} = c_{\sigma_j}^{(7)} \cdot g^{\frac{v_{1,j}}{x_1}}$, $d_{2,j} = c_{\sigma_j}^{(8)} \cdot g^{\frac{v_{2,j}}{x_2}}$ which shows that s_j' is distributed identically to s_j. Now consider the proof δ_j of statement $\mathcal{E}_{2,j} = \{e(a_1, w_1)e((d_{1,j})^{-1}, a_3) = 1 \wedge e(a_2, w_2)e((d_{2,j})^{-1}, a_3) = 1 \wedge e(a_1 a_2, a_3)e(s_j^{-1}, g) = 1 \wedge e(w_1, a_3) = e(w_1, g)\}$ and witnesses $\mathcal{W}_{2,j} = (a_1, a_2, a_3)$. The proof δ_j consists of commitments to secret values a_1, a_2, a_3 and proof components to equations in statement $\mathcal{E}_{2,j}$. For simulation, $\mathcal{A}'$ generates commitments to a_1, a_2, a_3 and proof components such that each equation in statement $\mathcal{E}_{2,j}$ is satisfied. With the help of trapdoor $\mathsf{t}_{\mathsf{sim}}$, $\mathcal{A}'$ can open the commitment differently to any value of its choice in each equation of statement $\mathcal{E}_{2,j}$. To simulate the proof δ_j', $\mathcal{A}'$ sets $a_1 = a_2 = a_3 = g^0$ in first three equations of statement $\mathcal{E}_{2,j}$ and generate commitments to these values. The adversary $\mathcal{A}'$ opens the commitment of a_3 to g^0 in first three equations and a_3 to g^1 in fourth equation using $\mathsf{t}_{\mathsf{sim}}$.

As Groth-Sahai proofs are composable NIZK by Claim 1, the simulated proof $\delta_j' \leftarrow \mathsf{AGSSimProve}(\mathsf{GS}'_S, \mathsf{t}_{\mathsf{sim}}, \mathcal{E}_{2,j})$ is computationally indistinguishable from the honestly generated proof $\delta_j \leftarrow \mathsf{AGSProve}(\mathsf{GS}_S, \mathcal{E}_{2,j}, \mathcal{W}_{2,j})$ under the DLIN assumption.

<u>Game 4</u>: This game is the same as Game 3 except that the messages $m_1, m_2, \ldots,$ m_n are replaced by the random messages $\widehat{m}_1, \widehat{m}_2, \ldots, \widehat{m}_n \in \mathbb{G}$. The adversary $\mathcal{A}'$ replaces the sender S's first message $(\mathsf{sid}, S, \mathsf{PK}, \mathsf{T})$ by $(\mathsf{sid}, S, \mathsf{PK}, \mathsf{T}')$, where $\mathsf{T}' \leftarrow \mathsf{AOTInitialize}(\mathsf{crs}, \widehat{m}_1, \widehat{m}_2, \ldots, \widehat{m}_n)$. In each transfer phase, the response $(\mathsf{sid}, S, s_j, \delta_j)$ is replaced by the simulated response $(\mathsf{sid}, S, s_j', \delta_j')$ as in above game, but here the simulated response is computed on invalid statement. The only difference between Game 4 and Game 3 is in the generation of ciphertexts. In Game 4, $(\mathsf{sid}, S, \mathsf{PK}, \mathsf{T})$ is replaced by $(\mathsf{sid}, S, \mathsf{PK}, \mathsf{T}')$, where $\mathsf{T}' \leftarrow \mathsf{AOTInitialize}(\mathsf{crs}, \widehat{m}_1, \widehat{m}_2, \ldots, \widehat{m}_n)$. While T is BBS encryptions of perfect messages, T' is that of random messages. By the semantic security of BBS encryption scheme under the DLIN assumption, Game 3 and Game 4 are computationally indistinguishable. Therefore, $|\mathsf{Pr}[\mathsf{Game}\ 4] - \mathsf{Pr}[\mathsf{Game}\ 3]| \leq \epsilon_4(\rho)$, where $\epsilon_4(\rho)$ is a negligible function.

Thus Game 4 is the ideal world interaction whereas Game 0 is the real world interaction. Now $|\mathsf{Pr}[\mathsf{Game}\ 4] - [\mathsf{Game}\ 0]| \leq |\mathsf{Pr}[\mathsf{Game}\ 4] - [\mathsf{Game}\ 3]| + |\mathsf{Pr}[\mathsf{Game}\ 3] - [\mathsf{Game}\ 2]| + |\mathsf{Pr}[\mathsf{Game}\ 2] - [\mathsf{Game}\ 1]| + |\mathsf{Pr}[\mathsf{Game}\ 1] - [\mathsf{Game}\ 0]| \leq \epsilon_5(\rho)$, where $\epsilon_5(\rho) = \epsilon_4(\rho) + \epsilon_3(\rho) + \epsilon_2(\rho) + \epsilon_1(\rho)$ is a negligible function. Hence, $\mathsf{IDEAL}_{\mathcal{F}_{\mathsf{OT}}^{n \times 1}, \mathcal{A}', \mathcal{Z}} \overset{c}{\approx} \mathsf{REAL}_{\Pi, \mathcal{A}, \mathcal{Z}}$.

(b) Simulation when S is corrupted and R is honest.

<u>Game 0</u>: This game corresponds to the real world protocol interaction in which S interacts with honest R. So, $\mathsf{Pr}[\mathsf{Game}\ 0] = 0$.

<u>Game 1</u>: This game is the same as Game 0 except that the crs is generated by $\mathcal{A}'$. Let params $= (p, \mathbb{G}, \mathbb{G}_T, e, g) \leftarrow \mathsf{BilinearSetup}(1^\rho)$. The adversary $\mathcal{A}'$ generates $(\mathsf{FC}, \mathsf{t}) \leftarrow \mathsf{AGSExtractSetup}(\mathsf{params})$, $\mathsf{GS}_S \leftarrow \mathsf{AGSSetup}(\mathsf{params})$, $\mathsf{GS}_R \leftarrow \mathsf{AGSSetup}(\mathsf{params})$. The adversary $\mathcal{A}'$ makes params, $\mathsf{FC}, \mathsf{GS}_S, \mathsf{GS}_R$ public and keeps the trapdoor t secret to itself. In this Game, $\mathsf{FC}, \mathsf{GS}_S, \mathsf{GS}_R$, all are based on DLIN instance as in Game 0. Therefore, crs generated in Game 1 has the same distribution as in Game 0. Hence, $|\mathsf{Pr}[\mathsf{Game}\ 1] - \mathsf{Pr}[\mathsf{Game}\ 0]| = 0$.

<u>Game 2</u>: For each transfer phase, $j = 1, 2, \ldots, k$, $\mathcal{A}'$ parses T to get ϕ_1. The adversary $\mathcal{A}'$ generates $(\mathsf{Q}'_{\mathsf{request}_1}, \mathsf{Q}'_{\mathsf{private}_1}) \leftarrow \mathsf{AOTRequest}(\mathsf{crs}, \mathsf{PK}, \mathsf{T}, 1)$ and replaces R's request $\mathsf{Q}_{\mathsf{request}_j}$ in each transfer phase by simulated request $\mathsf{Q}'_{\mathsf{request}_1} = (d_{1,1}, d_{2,1}, \pi_1)$, $d_{1,1} = c_1^{(7)} w_1^{v_{1,1}}$, $d_{2,1} = c_1^{(8)} w_2^{v_{2,1}}$, where $v_{1,1}, v_{2,1} \in \mathbb{Z}_p$. For each ϕ_i, there exists witnesses $(c_i^{(7)}, c_i^{(8)}, t_{1,i}, t_{2,i}, c_i^{(10)}, c_i^{(11)}, c_i^{(12)}, g^i)$ which satisfy the equations in statement $\mathcal{E}_{1,i} = \{e(c_i^{(7)}, g) e(t_{1,i}, w_1) = e(d_{1,i}, g) \wedge e(c_i^{(8)}, g) e(t_{2,i}, w_2) = e(d_{2,i}, g) \wedge e(c_i^{(12)}, y \cdot g^i \cdot c_i^{(10)} \cdot c_i^{(11)}) = e(g, g) \wedge e(w_1, c_i^{(10)}) = e(c_i^{(7)}, y_1) \wedge e(w_2, c_i^{(11)}) = e(c_i^{(8)}, y_2)\}$. In each transfer phase, $\mathcal{A}'$ replaces $\mathsf{Q}_{\mathsf{request}_j}$ by $\mathsf{Q}'_{\mathsf{request}_1} = (d_{1,1}, d_{2,1}, \pi_1)$ which also satisfy all the equations in statement $\mathcal{E}_{1,1} = \{e(c_1^{(7)}, g) e(t_{1,1}, w_1) = e(d_{1,1}, g) \wedge e(c_1^{(8)}, g) e(t_{2,1}, w_2) = e(d_{2,1}, g) \wedge e(c_1^{(12)}, y \cdot g^1 \cdot c_1^{(10)} \cdot c_1^{(11)}) = e(g, g) \wedge e(w_1, c_1^{(10)}) = e(c_1^{(7)}, y_1) \wedge e(w_2, c_1^{(11)}) = e(c_1^{(8)}, y_2)\}$. As Groth-Sahai

proofs are composable NIWI by Claim 1, the simulated request $Q'_{request\,1}$ is computationally indistinguishable from the honestly generated request $Q_{request\,j}$. Therefore, we have $|\Pr[\text{Game 2}] - \Pr[\text{Game 1}]| \leq \epsilon_1(\rho)$, where $\epsilon_1(\rho)$ is a negligible function.

Thus Game 2 is the ideal world interaction whereas Game 0 is the real world interaction. Now $|\Pr[\text{Game 2}] - [\text{Game 0}]| \leq |\Pr[\text{Game 2}] - [\text{Game 1}]| + |\Pr[\text{Game 1}] - [\text{Game 0}]| \leq \epsilon_1(\rho)$, where $\epsilon_1(\rho)$ is a negligible function. Hence, $\text{IDEAL}_{\mathcal{F}_{OT}^{n\times 1}, \mathcal{A}', \mathcal{Z}} \overset{c}{\approx} \text{REAL}_{\Pi, \mathcal{A}, \mathcal{Z}}$.

It remains to show that the output of the honest R running the protocol with S and output of the ideal R interacting with the $\mathcal{F}_{OT}^{n\times 1}$ is the same. The ciphertext $\phi_i = (c_i^{(1)} = g_1^{r_{1i}}(u_3^{(1)})^{r_{3i}}, c_i^{(2)} = g_2^{r_{2i}}(u_3^{(2)})^{r_{3i}}, c_i^{(3)} = m_i g^{r_{1i}+r_{2i}}(u_3^{(3)})^{r_{3i}}, c_i^{(4)}, c_i^{(5)}, c_i^{(6)}, c_i^{(7)} = w_1^{r_i}, c_i^{(8)} = w_2^{s_i}, c_i^{(9)} = m_i g^{r_i+s_i}, c_i^{(10)}, c_i^{(11)}, c_i^{(12)})$, where $w_1 = g^{\frac{1}{x_1}}, w_2 = g^{\frac{1}{x_2}}, g_1 = g^a, g_2 = g^b, u_3^{(1)} = g_1^{\xi_1}, u_3^{(2)} = g_2^{\xi_2}, u_3^{(3)} = g^{\xi_1+\xi_2}$.

The message obtained by the real R using s_i generated with sender's secret key $SK = (x_1, x_2)$ in the real protocol is $\frac{c_i^{(9)}}{s_i g^{-v_{1,i}} g^{-v_{2,i}}} = \frac{m_i g^{r_i+s_i}}{(d_{1,i})^{x_1}(d_{2,i})^{x_2} g^{-v_{1,i}} g^{-v_{2,i}}} = \frac{m_i g^{r_i+s_i}}{(w_1^{r_i})^{x_1}(w_2^{s_i})^{x_2}} = m_i$, as the receiver R has $v_{1,i}, v_{2,i}$ and receives $c_i^{(9)}, s_i$ from the sender S. The adversary $\mathcal{A}'$ parses the trapdoor t, extracts (a, b) and computes

$$\frac{c_i^{(3)}}{(c_i^{(1)})^{1/a}(c_i^{(2)})^{1/b}} = \frac{m_i g^{r_{1i}+r_{2i}}(u_3^{(3)})^{r_{3i}}}{(g_1^{r_{1i}}(u_3^{(1)})^{r_{3i}})^{\frac{1}{a}}(g_2^{r_{2i}}(u_3^{(2)})^{r_{3i}})^{\frac{1}{b}}} = \frac{m_i g^{r_{1i}+r_{2i}}(g^{\xi_1+\xi_2})^{r_{3i}}}{(g_1^{r_{1i}}(g_1^{\xi_1})^{r_{3i}})^{\frac{1}{a}}(g_2^{r_{2i}}(g_2^{\xi_2})^{r_{3i}})^{\frac{1}{b}}} =$$

m_i, as $\mathcal{A}'$ receives the BBS ciphertext $(c_i^{(1)}, c_i^{(2)}, c_i^{(3)})$ from the sender S and $g_1 = g^a, g_2 = g^b$. The adversary $\mathcal{A}'$ gives m_i to $\mathcal{F}_{OT}^{n\times 1}$ for each $i = 1, 2, \ldots, n$. The ideal receiver R gets m_i when it asks $\mathcal{F}_{OT}^{n\times 1}$ for index i. Hence the output of the receiver of the ideal world is same as the output of the the real world receiver. Therefore, $\text{IDEAL}_{\mathcal{F}_{OT}^{n\times 1}, \mathcal{A}', \mathcal{Z}} \overset{c}{\approx} \text{REAL}_{\Pi, \mathcal{A}, \mathcal{Z}}$.

□

References

1. Abdalla, M., Benhamouda, F., Blazy, O., Chevalier, C., Pointcheval, D.: Sphf-friendly non-interactive commitments. Tech. rep., Cryptology ePrint Archive, Report 2013/588 (2013), http://eprint.iacr.org

2. Belenkiy, M., Chase, M., Kohlweiss, M., Lysyanskaya, A.: P-signatures and noninteractive anonymous credentials. In: Canetti, R. (ed.) TCC 2008. LNCS, vol. 4948, pp. 356–374. Springer, Heidelberg (2008)

3. Boneh, D., Boyen, X.: Efficient selective-id secure identity-based encryption without random oracles. In: Cachin, C., Camenisch, J.L. (eds.) EUROCRYPT 2004. LNCS, vol. 3027, pp. 223–238. Springer, Heidelberg (2004)

4. Boneh, D., Boyen, X.: Short signatures without random oracles. In: Cachin, C., Camenisch, J.L. (eds.) EUROCRYPT 2004. LNCS, vol. 3027, pp. 56–73. Springer, Heidelberg (2004)

5. Boneh, D., Boyen, X., Shacham, H.: Short group signatures. In: Franklin, M. (ed.) CRYPTO 2004. LNCS, vol. 3152, pp. 41–55. Springer, Heidelberg (2004)

6. Brassard, G., Crépeau, C., Robert, J.M.: All-or-nothing disclosure of secrets. In: Odlyzko, A.M. (ed.) CRYPTO 1986. LNCS, vol. 263, pp. 234–238. Springer, Heidelberg (1987)

7. Camenisch, J., Dubovitskaya, M., Neven, G.: Oblivious transfer with access control. In: ACM 2009, pp. 131–140 (2009)
8. Camenisch, J.L., Lysyanskaya, A.: Signature schemes and anonymous credentials from bilinear maps. In: Franklin, M. (ed.) CRYPTO 2004. LNCS, vol. 3152, pp. 56–72. Springer, Heidelberg (2004)
9. Camenisch, J.L., Neven, G., Shelat, A.: Simulatable adaptive oblivious transfer. In: Naor, M. (ed.) EUROCRYPT 2007. LNCS, vol. 4515, pp. 573–590. Springer, Heidelberg (2007)
10. Camenisch, J., Stadler, M.: Efficient group signature schemes for large groups. In: Kaliski Jr., B.S. (ed.) CRYPTO 1997. LNCS, vol. 1294, pp. 410–424. Springer, Heidelberg (1997)
11. Canetti, R., Lindell, Y., Ostrovsky, R., Sahai, A.: Universally composable two-party and multi-party secure computation. In: ACM 2002, pp. 494–503 (2002)
12. Choi, S.G., Katz, J., Wee, H., Zhou, H.-S.: Efficient, adaptively secure, and composable oblivious transfer with a single, global crs. In: Kurosawa, K., Hanaoka, G. (eds.) PKC 2013. LNCS, vol. 7778, pp. 73–88. Springer, Heidelberg (2013)
13. Even, S., Goldreich, O., Lempel, A.: A randomized protocol for signing contracts. Communications of the ACM 28(6), 637–647 (1985)
14. Fischlin, M., Libert, B., Manulis, M.: Non-interactive and re-usable universally composable string commitments with adaptive security. In: Lee, D.H., Wang, X. (eds.) ASIACRYPT 2011. LNCS, vol. 7073, pp. 468–485. Springer, Heidelberg (2011)
15. Green, M., Hohenberger, S.: Universally composable adaptive oblivious transfer. In: Pieprzyk, J. (ed.) ASIACRYPT 2008. LNCS, vol. 5350, pp. 179–197. Springer, Heidelberg (2008)
16. Groth, J., Sahai, A.: Efficient non-interactive proof systems for bilinear groups. In: Smart, N.P. (ed.) EUROCRYPT 2008. LNCS, vol. 4965, pp. 415–432. Springer, Heidelberg (2008)
17. Haralambiev, K.: Efficient cryptographic primitives for noninteractive zero-knowledge proofs and applications. Ph.D. thesis, New York University (2011)
18. Naor, M., Pinkas, B.: Oblivious transfer with adaptive queries. In: Wiener, M. (ed.) CRYPTO 1999. LNCS, vol. 1666, pp. 573–590. Springer, Heidelberg (1999)
19. Peikert, C., Vaikuntanathan, V., Waters, B.: A framework for efficient and composable oblivious transfer. In: Wagner, D. (ed.) CRYPTO 2008. LNCS, vol. 5157, pp. 554–571. Springer, Heidelberg (2008)
20. Rabin, M.O.: How to exchange secrets by oblivious transfer. Tech. rep., Technical Report TR-81, Harvard Aiken Computation Laboratory (1981)
21. Rial, A., Kohlweiss, M., Preneel, B.: Universally composable adaptive priced oblivious transfer. In: Shacham, H., Waters, B. (eds.) Pairing 2009. LNCS, vol. 5671, pp. 231–247. Springer, Heidelberg (2009)
22. Shacham, H.: A cramer-shoup encryption scheme from the linear assumption and from progressively weaker linear variants. IACR Cryptology ePrint Archive 2007, 74 (2007)

Multi-receiver Authentication Scheme for Multiple Messages Based on Linear Codes[*]

Jun Zhang[1], Xinran Li[1,2], and Fang-Wei Fu[1]

[1] Chern Institute of Mathematics and LPMC,
Nankai University, Tianjin, 300071, China
{zhangjun04,xinranli}@mail.nankai.edu.cn,
fwfu@nankai.edu.cn
[2] Cryptography Engineering Institute,
Information Engineering University,
Zhengzhou 450004, China

Abstract. In this paper, we construct an authentication scheme for multi-receivers and multiple messages based on a linear code C. This construction can be regarded as a generalization of the authentication scheme given by Safavi-Naini and Wang [1]. Actually, we notice that the scheme of Safavi-Naini and Wang is constructed with Reed-Solomon codes. The generalization to linear codes has the similar advantages as generalizing Shamir's secret sharing scheme to linear secret sharing sceme based on linear codes [2–6]. For a fixed message base field $\mathbb{F}_q$, our scheme allows arbitrarily many receivers to check the integrity of their own messages, while the scheme of Safavi-Naini and Wang has a constraint on the number of verifying receivers $V \leqslant q$. We further introduce access structure in our scheme. Massey [4] characterized the access structure of linear secret sharing scheme by minimal codewords in the dual code whose first component is 1. We slightly modify the definition of minimal codewords in [4]. Let C be a $[V, k]$ linear code. For any coordinate $i \in \{1, 2, \cdots, V\}$, a codeword c in C is called *minimal respect to i* if the codeword c has component 1 at the i-th coordinate and there is no other codeword whose i-th component is 1 with support strictly contained in that of c. Then the security of receiver R_i in our authentication scheme is characterized by the minimal codewords respect to i in the dual code $C^{\perp}$. Finally, we illustrate our authentication scheme based on the elliptic curve codes, a special class of algebraic geometry codes. We use the group of rational points on the elliptic curve to determine all the malicious groups that can successfully make a substitution attack to any fixed receiver.

Keywords: Authentication scheme, linear codes, secret sharing, minimal codewords, substitution attack.

1 Introduction

One of the important goals of cryptographic scheme is authentication, which is concerned with the approaches of providing data integrity and data origin validation

[*] This paper is supported by the National Key Basic Research Program of China (973 Program Grant No. 2013CB834204), and the National Natural Science Foundation of China (No. 61171082).

between two communication entities in computer network. Traditionally, it simply deals with the data authentication problem from a single sender to a single receiver. With the rapid progress of network communication, the urgent need for providing data authentication has escalated to multi-receiver and/or multi-sender scenarios. However, the original point-to-point authentication techniques are not suitable for multi-point communication. In [7], the authors considered a sender group and one receiver authentication model which was introduced by Boyd [8] and by Desmedt and Frankel [9]. In that paper, they studied unconditionally secure group authentication schemes based on linear perfect secret sharing and authentication schemes, and gave a construction based on maximum rank distance codes. In this paper, we discuss the multi-receiver authentication model where a sender broadcasts an authenticated message such that all the receivers can independently verify the authenticity of the message with their own private keys. It requires a security that malicious groups of up to a given size of receivers can not successfully impersonate the transmitter, or substitute a transmitted message. Desmedt et al. [10] gave an authentication scheme of single message for multi-receivers. Safavi-Naini and Wang [1] extended the DFY scheme [10] to be an authentication scheme of multiple messages for multi-receivers.

The receivers independently verify the authenticity of the message using each own private key. So multi-receiver authentication scheme involves a procedure of secret sharing. To introduce the linear secret sharing scheme based on linear codes, we recall some definitions in coding theory.

Let $\mathbb{F}_q^V$ be the V-dimensional vector space over the finite field $\mathbb{F}_q$ with q elements. For any vector $x = (x_1, x_2, \cdots, x_V) \in \mathbb{F}_q^V$, the *Hamming weight* $\mathrm{Wt}(x)$ of x is defined to be the number of non-zero coordinates, i.e., $\mathrm{Wt}(x) = \#\{i \mid 1 \leqslant i \leqslant V, x_i \neq 0\}$. A *linear* $[V, k]$ *code* C is a k-dimensional linear subspace of $\mathbb{F}_q^V$. The *minimum distance* $d(C)$ of C is the minimum Hamming weight of all non-zero vectors in C, i.e., $d(C) = \min\{\mathrm{Wt}(c) \mid c \in C \setminus \{0\}\}$. A linear $[V, k]$ code $C \subseteq \mathbb{F}_q^V$ is called a $[V, k, d]$ *linear code* if C has minimum distance d. A vector in C is called a *codeword* of C. A matrix $G \in \mathbb{F}_q^{k \times V}$ is called a *generator matrix* of C if the rows of G form a basis for C. A well known trade-off between the parameters of a linear $[V, k, d]$ code is the Singleton bound which states that

$$d \leqslant V - k + 1 .$$

A $[V, k, d]$ linear code is called a *maximum distance separable* (MDS) code if $d = V - k + 1$. The *dual code* $C^\perp$ of C is defined as the set $\{x \in \mathbb{F}_q^V \mid x \cdot c = 0 \text{ for all } c \in C\}$, where $x \cdot c$ is the inner product of vectors x and c, i.e., $x \cdot c = x_1 c_1 + x_2 c_2 + \cdots + x_V c_V$.

The secret sharing scheme provides security of a secret key by "splitting" it to several parts which are kept by different persons. In this way, it might need many persons to recover the original key. It can achieve to resist the attack of malicious groups of persons. Shamir [2] used polynomials over finite fields to give an (S, T) threshold secret sharing scheme such that any T persons of the S shares can uniquely determine the secret key but any $T - 1$ persons can not get any information of the key. A linear secret sharing scheme based on a linear code [4] is constructed as follows: encrypt the secret to be the first coordinate of a codeword and distribute the rest of the codeword (except the first secret coordinate) to the group of shares. McEliece and Sarwate [3] pointed out that the Shamir's construction is essentially a linear secret sharing scheme based on

Reed-Solomon codes. Also as a natural generalization of Shamir's construction and a specialization of Massey's construction [4, 5], Chen and Cramer [6] constructed a linear secret sharing scheme based on algebraic geometric codes.

The *qualified subset* of a linear secret sharing scheme is a subset of shares such that the shares in the subset can recover the secret key. A qualified subset is called *minimal* if any share is removed from the qualified subset, the rests cannot recover the secret key. The *access structure* of a linear secret sharing scheme consists of all the minimal qualified subsets. A codeword v in a linear code C is said to be *minimal* if v is a non-zero codeword whose leftmost nonzero component is 1 and no other codeword v' whose leftmost nonzero component is 1 has support strictly contained in the support of v. Massey [4, 5] showed that the access structure of a linear secret sharing scheme based on a linear code are completely determined by the minimal codewords in the dual code whose first component is 1.

Proposition 1 ([4]). *The access structure of the linear secret-sharing scheme corresponding to the linear code C is specified by those minimal codewords in the dual code $C^{\perp}$ whose first component is 1. In the manner that the set of shares specified by a minimal codeword whose first component is 1 in the dual code is the set of shares corresponding to those locations after the first in the support of this minimal codeword.*

In both schemes of Desmedt et al. [10] and Safavi-Naini and Wang [1], the key distribution is similar to that in Shamir's secret sharing scheme [2], using polynomials. Both schemes are (V, k) threshold authentication scheme, i.e., any malicious groups of up to $k - 1$ receivers can not successfully (unconditionally secure in the meaning of information theory) impersonate the transmitter, or substitute a transmitted message to any other receiver, while any k receivers or more receivers can successfully impersonate the transmitter, or substitute a transmitted message to any other receiver. Actually, in the proof of security of the authentication scheme of Safavi-Naini and Wang, the security is equivalent to the difficulty to recover the private key of other receivers. So the security essentially depends on the security of key distribution.

In this paper, we use general linear codes to generalize the scheme of Safavi-Naini and Wang. Our scheme is an unconditionally secure authentication scheme and has all the same advantages as the generalization of Shamir's secret sharing scheme to linear secret sharing sceme based on linear codes [4, 5]. Similarly as [4, 5], we introduce the concept of minimal codeword respect to each coordinate, which helps to characterize the capability of resisting substitution attack in our authentication scheme, similarly to the linear secret sharing scheme. It guarantees higher security for some important receivers.

The rest of this paper is organized as follows. In Section 2, we present our construction and main results about the security of our scheme. In Section 3, we give the security analysis of our scheme. In Section 4, we show the relationship between the security of our scheme and parameters of the linear code. Finally, in Section 5, the example of authentication schemes based on elliptic curve codes is given, and we use the group of rational points on the elliptic curve to characterize all malicious groups that can make a substitution attack to some other receiver.

2   Our Construction and Main Results

In a multi-receiver authentication model for multiple messages, a trusted authority chooses random parameters as the secret key and generates shares of private keys secretly. Then the trusted authority transmits a private key to each receiver and secret parameters to the source. For each fixed message, the source computes the authentication tag using the secret parameters and sends the message adding with the tag. In the verification phase, the receiver verifies the integrity of each tagged message using his private key. Groups of malicious receivers are considered in the model those who collude to perform an impersonation attack by constructing a fake message, or a substitution attack by altering the message content such that the new tagged message can be accepted by some other receiver or specific receiver.

In this section, we present our construction of an authentication scheme based on a linear code for multi-receivers and multiple messages. It will be shown that the ability of our scheme to resist the attack of the malicious receivers is measured by the minimum distance of the dual code and minimal codewords respect to specific coordinate in the dual code.

Let $C \subseteq \mathbb{F}_q^V$ be a linear code with minimum distance $d(C) \geq 2$. Assume that the minimum distance of the dual code $C^\perp$ is $d(C^\perp) \geq 2$. Fix a generator matrix G of C

$$G = \begin{pmatrix} g_{1,1} & g_{1,2} & \cdots & g_{1,V} \\ g_{2,1} & g_{2,2} & \cdots & g_{2,V} \\ \vdots & \vdots & \ddots & \vdots \\ g_{k,1} & g_{k,2} & \cdots & g_{k,V} \end{pmatrix}.$$

Then make G public. Our scheme is as follows.

– **Key Generation:** A trusted authority randomly chooses parameters

$$A = \begin{pmatrix} a_{0,1} & a_{0,2} & \cdots & a_{0,k} \\ a_{1,1} & a_{1,2} & \cdots & a_{1,k} \\ \vdots & \vdots & \ddots & \vdots \\ a_{M,1} & a_{M,2} & \cdots & a_{M,k} \end{pmatrix} \in \mathbb{F}_q^{(M+1) \times k}.$$

– **Key Distribution:** The trusted authority computes

$$B = A \cdot G = \begin{pmatrix} b_{0,1} & b_{0,2} & \cdots & b_{0,V} \\ b_{1,1} & b_{1,2} & \cdots & b_{1,V} \\ \vdots & \vdots & \ddots & \vdots \\ b_{M,1} & b_{M,2} & \cdots & b_{M,V} \end{pmatrix}.$$

Then the trusted authority distributes each receiver R_i the i-th column of B as his private key, for $i = 1, 2, \cdots, V$. Note that in this step, we can use public key cryptography method to complete the key distribution process. We don't expand it here since in this paper we only focus on the main authentication scheme.

- **Authentication Tag:** For message $s \in \mathbb{F}_q$, the source computes the tag map

$$L = [L_1, L_2, \cdots, L_k] : \mathbb{F}_q \to \mathbb{F}_q^k$$
$$s \mapsto [L_1(s), L_2(s), \cdots, L_k(s)],$$

where the map L_i $(i = 1, 2, \cdots, k)$ is defined by

$$L_i(s) = \sum_{j=0}^{M} a_{j,i} s^j .$$

Instead of sending the message $s \in \mathbb{F}_q$, the source actually sends the authenticated message x of the form

$$x = [s, L(s)] \in \mathbb{F}_q^{1+k} .$$

- **Verification:** The receiver R_i accepts the message $[s, L(s)]$ if $\sum_{t=0}^{M} s^t b_{t,i} = \sum_{j=1}^{k} L_j(s) g_{j,i}$. Under the integrity of the tagged message, one can easily verify the following

$$\sum_{t=0}^{M} s^t b_{t,i} = \sum_{t=0}^{M} s^t \sum_{j=1}^{k} a_{t,j} g_{j,i} = \sum_{j=1}^{k} (\sum_{t=0}^{M} a_{t,j} s^t) g_{j,i} = \sum_{j=1}^{k} L_j(s) g_{j,i} .$$

Here, we call the result $\sum_{t=0}^{M} s^t b_{t,i}$ the *label* of R_i for message s.

If we take C to be the Reed-Solomon code, i.e., the generator matrix G is of the form

$$G = \begin{pmatrix} 1 & 1 & \cdots & 1 \\ x_1 & x_2 & \cdots & x_V \\ x_1^2 & x_2^2 & \cdots & x_V^2 \\ \vdots & \vdots & \ddots & \vdots \\ x_1^{k-1} & x_2^{k-1} & \cdots & x_V^{k-1} \end{pmatrix}, \tag{2.1}$$

for pairwise distinct $x_1, x_2, \cdots, x_V \in \mathbb{F}_q$, then the scheme is the scheme of Safavi-Naini and Wang [1].

The security of the above authentication scheme is summarized in the following two theorems. The proofs of the two theorems will be given in Sections 3 and 4.

Theorem 2. *The scheme we constructed above is a unconditionally secure multi-receiver authentication code against a coalition of up to $(d(C^{\perp}) - 2)$ malicious receivers in which every key can be used to authentication up to M messages.*

More specifically, we consider what a coalition of malicious receivers can successfully make a substitution attack to one fixed receiver R_i. To characterize this malicious group, we slightly modify the definition of minimal codeword in [4].

Definition 1. Let C be a $[V, k]$ linear code. For any $i \in \{1, 2, \cdots, V\}$, a codeword c in C is called *minimal respect to i* if the codeword c has component 1 at the i-th location and there is no other codeword whose i-th component is 1 with support strictly contained in that of c.

Then we have

Theorem 3. *For the authentication scheme we constructed, we have*

(i) *The set of all minimal malicious groups that can successfully make a substitution attack to the receiver R_i is determined completely by all the minimal codewords respect to i in the dual code $C^\perp$.*

(ii) *All malicious groups that can not produce a fake authenticated message which can be accepted by the receiver R_i are one-to-one corresponding to subsets of $[V] \setminus \{i\}$ such that each of them together with i does not contain any support of minimal codeword respect to i in the dual code $C^\perp$, where $[V] = \{1, 2, \cdots, V\}$.*

Compared with Safavi-Naini and Wang's scheme, our scheme has all the advantages as the generalization of secret sharing scheme based on polynomials [2, 3] to that based on linear codes [4, 5]. The scheme of Safavi-Naini and Wang is a (V, k) threshold authentication scheme, so any coalition of k malicious receivers can easily make a substitution attack to any other receiver. While in our scheme, by Theorem 3, sometimes it can withstand the attack of coalitions of k or more malicious receivers to R_i. Indeed, it is in general **NP**-hard to list all coalitions of malicious receivers that can make a substitution attack to the receiver R_i. So our scheme has better security than the previous one.

3   Security Analysis of Our Authentication Scheme

In this section, we present the security analysis of our scheme. From the verification step, we notice that a tagged message $[s, v_1, v_2, \cdots, v_k]$ can be accepted by the receiver R_i if and only if $\sum_{t=0}^{M} s^t b_{t,i} = \sum_{j=1}^{k} v_j g_{j,i}$. So in order to make a substitution attack to R_i, it suffices to know the label $\sum_{t=0}^{M} s^t b_{t,i}$ for some $s \in \mathbb{F}_q$ not sent by the transmitter, then it is trivial to construct a tag $(v_1, v_2, \cdots, v_k)$ such that $\sum_{t=0}^{M} s^t b_{t,i} = \sum_{j=1}^{k} v_j g_{j,i}$.

Indeed, we will find that the security of the above authentication scheme depends on the hardness of finding the key matrix A from a system of linear equations. Suppose a group of K malicious receivers collaborate to recover A and make a substitution attack. Without loss of generality, we assume that the malicious receivers are $R_1, R_2, \cdots, R_K$. Suppose $s_1, s_2, \cdots, s_M$ have been sent. Each R_i has some information about the key A:

$$\begin{pmatrix} 1 & s_1 & s_1^2 & \cdots & s_1^M \\ 1 & s_2 & s_2^2 & \cdots & s_2^M \\ \vdots & \vdots & \vdots & \ddots & \vdots \\ 1 & s_M & s_M^2 & \cdots & s_M^M \end{pmatrix} \cdot A = \begin{pmatrix} L_1(s_1) & L_2(s_1) & \cdots & L_k(s_1) \\ L_1(s_2) & L_2(s_2) & \cdots & L_k(s_2) \\ \vdots & \vdots & \ddots & \vdots \\ L_1(s_M) & L_2(s_M) & \cdots & L_k(s_M) \end{pmatrix}$$

and

$$A \cdot \begin{pmatrix} g_{1,i} \\ g_{2,i} \\ \vdots \\ g_{k,i} \end{pmatrix} = \begin{pmatrix} b_{0,i} \\ b_{1,i} \\ \vdots \\ b_{M,i} \end{pmatrix}.$$

The group of malicious receivers combines their equations, and they get a system of linear equations

$$
\begin{cases}
S_M \cdot A = \begin{pmatrix} 1 & s_1 & s_1^2 & \cdots & s_1^M \\ 1 & s_2 & s_2^2 & \cdots & s_2^M \\ \vdots & \vdots & \vdots & \ddots & \vdots \\ 1 & s_M & s_M^2 & \cdots & s_M^M \end{pmatrix} \cdot A = \begin{pmatrix} L_1(s_1) & L_2(s_1) & \cdots & L_k(s_1) \\ L_1(s_2) & L_2(s_2) & \cdots & L_k(s_2) \\ \vdots & \vdots & \ddots & \vdots \\ L_1(s_M) & L_2(s_M) & \cdots & L_k(s_M) \end{pmatrix}, \\[4mm]
A \cdot \begin{pmatrix} g_{1,1} & g_{1,2} & \cdots & g_{1,K} \\ g_{2,1} & g_{2,2} & \cdots & g_{2,K} \\ \vdots & \vdots & \ddots & \vdots \\ g_{k,1} & g_{k,2} & \cdots & g_{k,K} \end{pmatrix} = \begin{pmatrix} b_{0,1} & b_{0,2} & \cdots & b_{0,K} \\ b_{1,1} & b_{1,2} & \cdots & b_{1,K} \\ \vdots & \vdots & \ddots & \vdots \\ b_{M,1} & b_{M,2} & \cdots & b_{M,K} \end{pmatrix}.
\end{cases}
\tag{3.1}
$$

Lemma 4. *Let P be the subspace of $\mathbb{F}_q^k$ generated by $\{g_j \mid j = 1, 2, \cdots, K\}$, where g_j represents the j-th column of the generator matrix G. Suppose $K_0 = \dim P \leqslant k - 1$. Then there exist exact q^{k-K_0} matrices A satisfying the system of equations (3.1).*

Proof. Rewrite the matrix A of variables $a_{i,j}$ as a single column of $k(M + 1)$ variables. Then System (3.1) becomes

$$
\begin{pmatrix} S_M & & & \\ & S_M & & \\ & & \ddots & \\ & & & S_M \\ g_{1,1}I_{M+1} & g_{2,1}I_{M+1} & \cdots & g_{k,1}I_{M+1} \\ g_{1,2}I_{M+1} & g_{2,2}I_{M+1} & \cdots & g_{k,2}I_{M+1} \\ \vdots & \vdots & \ddots & \vdots \\ g_{1,K}I_{M+1} & g_{2,K}I_{M+1} & \cdots & g_{k,K}I_{M+1} \end{pmatrix} \cdot \begin{pmatrix} a_{0,1} \\ a_{1,1} \\ \vdots \\ a_{M,1} \\ a_{0,2} \\ a_{1,2} \\ \vdots \\ a_{M,2} \\ \vdots \\ a_{0,k} \\ a_{1,k} \\ \vdots \\ a_{M,k} \end{pmatrix} = T
\tag{3.2}
$$

where I_{M+1} is the identity matrix with rank $(M + 1)$ and T is the column vector of constants in System (3.1) with proper order. Notice that the space generated by rows of S_M is contained in the space $\mathbb{F}_q^{M+1}$ generated by $g_{i,j}I_{M+1}$ if $g_{i,j} \neq 0$. So the rank of the big matrix of coefficients in System (3.2) equals to

$$
M \cdot k + K_0
$$

which is less than $k(M+1)$, the number of variables. So System (3.2) has $q^{k(M+1)-kM-K_0} = q^{k-K_0}$ solutions, i.e., System (3.1) has q^{k-K_0} solutions. $\qquad \square$

Note that if C is a $[V, k, d = V - k + 1]$ MDS code, e.g., Reed-Solomon code, then whenever $K \leqslant k - 1$ the vectors in any K-subset of columns of G are linearly independent.

By Lemma 4, part of the security of our authentication scheme follows.

Theorem 5. *The scheme we constructed above is an unconditionally secure multi-receiver authentication scheme against a coalition of up to $(d(C^{\perp}) - 2)$ malicious receivers in which every key can be used to authentication up to M messages.*

Proof. Suppose the source receiver has sent messages $s_1, s_2, \cdots, s_M$. It is enough to consider the case that $K = d(C^{\perp}) - 2$ malicious receivers $R_1, \cdots, R_K$ have received the M messages, since in this case they know the most information about the key matrix A.

What they try to do is to guess the label $b_{0,K+1} + b_{1,K+1}s_{M+1} + b_{2,K+1}s_{M+1}^2 + \cdots + b_{M,K+1}s_{M+1}^M$ for some $s_{M+1} \notin \{s_1, s_2, \cdots, s_M\}$ and construct a vector $(v_1, v_2, \cdots, v_k)$ such that

$$\sum_{i=1}^{k} v_i g_{i,K+1} = b_{0,K+1} + b_{1,K+1}s_{M+1} + b_{2,K+1}s_{M+1}^2 + \cdots + b_{M,K+1}s_{M+1}^M .$$

Then the fake message $[s_{M+1}, v_1, v_2, \cdots, v_k]$ can be accepted by R_{K+1}.

It is easy to see that any $K = d(C^{\perp}) - 2$ columns of the generator matrix G is linearly independent over $\mathbb{F}_q$. Otherwise there exist $x_1, \cdots, x_K \in \mathbb{F}_q$, not all zeros, such that $\sum_{j=1}^{K} x_j g_j = 0$ where g_j is the j-th column of G, then the dual code $C^{\perp}$ will have a codeword $(x_1, \cdots, x_K, 0, \cdots, 0)$ with Hamming weight $\leqslant d(C^{\perp}) - 2$ which is a contradiction. By Lemma 4, there exist $q^{k-d(C^{\perp})+2}$ matrices A satisfying the system of equations (3.1).

For any $s_{M+1} \notin \{s_1, s_2, \cdots, s_M\}$, we define the label map

$$\varphi_{s_{M+1}} : \{\text{Solutions of System (3.1)}\} \longrightarrow \mathbb{F}_q$$

$$A \mapsto (1, s_{M+1}, s_{M+1}^2, \cdots, s_{M+1}^M)A \begin{pmatrix} g_{1,K+1} \\ g_{2,K+1} \\ \vdots \\ g_{k,K+1} \end{pmatrix} .$$

By Lemma 4 and knowledge of linear algebra, one can prove the following two statements (due to the restriction of the length of the paper, the proof is omitted here):

(1) $\varphi_{s_{M+1}}$ is surjective.
(2) for any $y \in \mathbb{F}_q$, the number of the inverse image of y is $|\varphi_{s_{M+1}}^{-1}(y)| = q^{k-d(C^{\perp})+1}$.

So the information held by the colluders allows them to calculate q equally likely different labels for s_{M+1} and hence the probability of success is $1/q$ which is equal to that of guessing a label $b_{0,K+1} + b_{1,K+1}s_{M+1} + b_{2,K+1}s_{M+1}^2 + \cdots + b_{M,K+1}s_{M+1}^M$ for s_{M+1} randomly from $\mathbb{F}_q$. Hence we finish the proof of the theorem. $\square$

Remark 1. From the proofs of Lemma 4 and Theorem 5, the coalition of malicious receivers B can successfully make a substitution attack to the receiver R_i if and only if g_i is contained in the subspace of $\mathbb{F}_q^k$ generated by $\{g_j \mid j \in B\}$, where g_j represents the j-th column of the generator matrix G. In this case, they can recover the private key of R_i. This is the motivation of the next section.

4 Code-Based Authentication Scheme and Minimal Codewords

In the previous section, we considered that any coalition of K malicious receivers can not obtain any information about any other receiver's label to make a substitution attack.

To consider a weak point, we propose that for a fixed receiver R_i, what a coalition of malicious receivers that can not get any information of the label of R_i. By Theorem 5, we have seen that any coalition of up to $(d(C^\perp)-2)$ malicious receivers can not generate a valid codeword $[s, L(s)]$ for R_i in a probability better than guessing a label from $\mathbb{F}_q$ randomly for the fake message s.

Denote $[V] = \{1, 2, \cdots, V\}$ and $\mathcal{P} = \{R_1, R_2, \cdots, R_V\}$ as the index set and the receiver set respectively.

Definition 2. A subset of $\mathcal{P} \setminus \{R_i\}$ is called an *adversary group* to R_i if their coalition can not obtain any information of the label of R_i when they want to make a substitution attack to R_i. Define $t_i(C)$ to be the largest integer τ_i such that any subset $A \subseteq \mathcal{P} \setminus \{R_i\}$ with cardinality τ_i is an adversary group to R_i.

Definition 3. A subset of $\mathcal{P} \setminus \{R_i\}$ that can successfully make a substitution attack to R_i is called a *substitution group* to R_i. Moreover, a substitution group is called *minimal* if any one receiver is removed from the group, then the rests can not obtain any information of the label of R_i. Define $r_i(C)$ to be the smallest integer ρ_i such that any subset $B \subseteq \mathcal{P} \setminus \{R_i\}$ with cardinality ρ_i is a substitution group to R_i.

For any $A \subseteq [V]$, π_A is the projection of $\mathbb{F}_q^V$ to $\mathbb{F}_q^{|A|}$ defined by

$$\pi_A((x_1, x_2, \cdots, x_V)) = (x_j)_{j \in A},$$

for any $(x_1, x_2, \cdots, x_V) \in \mathbb{F}_q^V$. Denote by $\pi_i = \pi_{\{i\}}$ for short. For any receiver R_i, the substitution groups to R_i are completely characterized as follows.

Proposition 6. *For any receiver R_i, the following conditions are equivalent:*

(i) $B \subseteq \mathcal{P} \setminus \{R_i\}$ *is a substitution group to R_i;*
(ii) g_i *is contained in the subspace of $\mathbb{F}_q^k$ generated by $\{g_j \mid j \in B\}$, where g_j represents the j-th column of the generator matrix G;*
(iii) *there exists a codeword $c \in C^\perp$ such that*

$$\pi_i(c) = 1 \quad and \quad \pi_{B^c}(c) = 0,$$

where $B^c = (\mathcal{P} \setminus \{R_i\}) \setminus B$ is the complement of B in $\mathcal{P} \setminus \{R_i\}$;
(iv) *there is an $\mathbb{F}_q$-linear map*
$$f_{B,i} : \pi_B(C) \longrightarrow \mathbb{F}_q$$

such that $f_{B,i}(\pi_B(c)) = \pi_i(c)$ for all $c \in C$;
(v) *there is no codeword $c \in C$ such that*

$$\pi_i(c) = 1 \quad and \quad \pi_B(c) = 0.$$

Proof. By Remark 1, conditions (i) and (ii) are equivalent.

First, we show that there exists a codeword $c \in C^\perp$ such that $\pi_i(c) \neq 0$. If not, that is, for any codeword $c \in C^\perp$, it holds $\pi_i(c) = 0$. Then the unit vector with the unique nonzero component 1 at the i-th coordinate belongs to C, which contradicts to the assumption that $d(C) \geqslant 2$.

So there exists a codeword $c \in C^{\perp}$ such that $\pi_i(c) = 1$ by the linearity of C. The rest of the proof that conditions (ii) and (iii) are equivalent is clear.

(iii)$\Longrightarrow$(iv). For any codeword $y \in C^{\perp}$ with $\pi_i(y) = 1$ and $\pi_{B^c}(y) = \mathbf{0}$, and for any codeword $c \in C$, we have

$$\sum_{j \in B} \pi_j(y)\pi_j(c) + \pi_i(c) = 0.$$

So define $f_{B,i} : \pi_B(C) \to \mathbb{F}_q$ by setting

$$f_{B,i}(\pi_B(c)) = -\sum_{j \in B} \pi_j(y)\pi_j(c),$$

for all $c \in C$. Then $f_{B,i}$ satisfies the condition.

(iv)$\Longrightarrow$(iii). From the proof of "(iii)$\Longrightarrow$(iv)", we see that the required codeword in $C^{\perp}$ is actually the coefficients of the map

$$\phi_{B,i} = \pi_i - f_{B,i}.$$

(iv)$\Longrightarrow$(v). If the statement (v) does not hold, then there exists a codeword $c \in C$ such that $\pi_i(c) = 1$ and $\pi_B(c) = \mathbf{0}$. This contradicts to the fact that $f_{B,i}(\pi_B(c)) = \pi_i(c)$.

(v)$\Longrightarrow$(iv). A map $f_{B,i} : \pi_B(C) \longrightarrow \mathbb{F}_q$ satisfying $f_{B,i}(\pi_B(c)) = \pi_i(c)$ for all $c \in C$ is always linear over $\mathbb{F}_q$ by the linearity of C. So if the map $f_{B,i} : \pi_B(C) \longrightarrow \mathbb{F}_q$ satisfying $f_{B,i}(\pi_B(c)) = \pi_i(c)$ for all $c \in C$ does not exist, then there exist two different codewords $c, c' \in C$ such that $\pi_i(c) \neq \pi_i(c')$ and $\pi_B(c) = \pi_B(c')$. That is, the codeword $x = c - c' \in C$ satisfies $\pi_i(x) = \pi_i(c - c') \neq 0$ and $\pi_B(x) = \pi_B(c - c') = \mathbf{0}$. This contradicts to (v). $\square$

By Proposition 6, adversary groups to R_i can be completely characterized by

Proposition 7. *For any receiver R_i, the following conditions are equivalent:*

(i) $A \subseteq \mathcal{P} \setminus \{R_i\}$ *is an adversary group to R_i;*
(ii) g_i *is not contained in the subspace of $\mathbb{F}_q^k$ generated by $\{g_j \mid j \in A\}$;*
(iii) *there is no codeword $c \in C^{\perp}$ such that*

$$\pi_i(c) = 1 \quad \text{and} \quad \pi_{A^c}(c) = \mathbf{0} ;$$

(iv) *there exists a codeword $c \in C$ such that*

$$\pi_i(c) = 1 \quad \text{and} \quad \pi_A(c) = \mathbf{0} .$$

Corollary 8. (i) *For any $i = 1, 2, \cdots, V$, we have*

$$d(C^{\perp}) - 1 \leqslant r_i(C) \leqslant V - d(C) + 1 ,$$

and

$$\max\{r_i(C) \mid i = 1, 2, \cdots, V\} = V - d(C) + 1, \quad \min\{r_i(C) \mid i = 1, 2, \cdots, V\} = d(C^{\perp}) - 1 .$$

(ii) *For any* $i = 1, 2, \cdots, V$, *we have*

$$d(C^{\perp}) - 2 \leqslant t_i(C) \leqslant r_i(C) - 1 \,,$$

and

$$\min\{t_i(C) \mid i = 1, 2, \cdots, V\} = d(C^{\perp}) - 2 \,.$$

Proof. (i) Suppose $B \subseteq \mathcal{P} \setminus \{R_i\}$ is any substitution group to R_i. By Proposition 6 (iii), there is a codeword $c \in C^{\perp}$ such that $\pi_i(c) = 1$ and $\pi_{B^c}(c) = \mathbf{0}$. Then we have

$$d(C^{\perp}) \leqslant \mathrm{Wt}(c) \leqslant |B| + 1 \,.$$

So

$$r_i(C) \geqslant |B| \geqslant d(C^{\perp}) - 1 \,.$$

For any $B \subseteq \mathcal{P} \setminus \{R_i\}$ with cardinality $\geqslant V - d(C) + 1$, it is obvious that any codeword $c \in C$ with $\pi_i(c) = 1$ (in the proof of Proposition 6, we have seen that such a codeword does exist.) has $\pi_B(c) \neq \mathbf{0}$. Otherwise, the minimum distance $d(C) \leqslant V - (V - d(C) + 1) = d(C) - 1$. So by Proposition 6 (v), it follows

$$r_i(C) \leqslant V - d(C) + 1 \,.$$

Let c be a codeword in C with minimum Hamming weight. Denote by S the support of c. Let $B = [V] \setminus S$. Then by Proposition 6 (v), B is not a substitution group to R_i for any $i \in S$. So

$$\max\{r_i(C) \mid i = 1, 2, \cdots, V\} \geqslant \max\{r_i(C) \mid i \in S\} \geqslant |B| + 1 = V - d(C) + 1 \,.$$

Hence

$$\max\{r_i(C) \mid i = 1, 2, \cdots, V\} = V - d(C) + 1 \,.$$

To prove $\min\{r_i(C) \mid i = 1, 2, \cdots, V\} - 1 = d(C^{\perp}) - 1$, it suffices to show

$$r_i(C) = d(C^{\perp}) - 1$$

for some $i = 1, 2, \cdots, V$. Let y be a codeword in $C^{\perp}$ with minimum Hamming weight. Denote by T the support of y. For any $i \in T$, $T \setminus \{i\}$ is a substitution group to R_i with cardinality $d(C^{\perp}) - 1$. On the other hand, by Proposition 6 (ii), any subset of $\mathcal{P} \setminus \{R_i\}$ with cardinality $\leqslant d(C^{\perp}) - 2$ could not be a substitution group to R_i. So

$$r_i(C) = d(C^{\perp}) - 1$$

for any $i \in T$.

(ii) Notw that $t_i(C) \leqslant r_i(C) - 1$ by the definition. For any $B \subseteq \mathcal{P} \setminus \{R_i\}$ with cardinality $\leqslant d(C^{\perp}) - 2$, there is no codeword $c \in C^{\perp}$ such that $\pi_i(c) = 1$ and $\pi_{B^c}(c) = \mathbf{0}$. If not, then there is a codeword $c \in C^{\perp}$ such that $\pi_i(c) = 1$ and $\pi_{B^c}(c) = \mathbf{0}$. Then $C^{\perp}$ has a codeword c with Hamming weight $\leqslant |B| + 1 (\leqslant d(C^{\perp}) - 1)$ which is impossible. So by Proposition 7, B is an adversary group to R_i. Hence

$$d(C^{\perp}) - 2 \leqslant t_i(C) \,.$$

Since $d(C^{\perp}) - 2 \leqslant t_i(C) \leqslant r_i(C) - 1$, we have

$$d(C^{\perp}) - 2 \leqslant \min\{t_i(C) \mid i = 1, 2, \cdots, V\} \leqslant \min\{r_i(C) \mid i = 1, 2, \cdots, V\} - 1 = d(C^{\perp}) - 2.$$

So

$$\min\{t_i(C) \mid i = 1, 2, \cdots, V\} = d(C^{\perp}) - 2.$$

$\square$

By Corollary 8, it is natural to get

Corollary 9. *For any receiver R_i, we have*

(i) *Subsets of $\mathcal{P} \setminus \{R_i\}$ with cardinality $\geqslant (V - d(C) + 1)$ are substitution groups to R_i.*
(ii) *Subsets of $\mathcal{P} \setminus \{R_i\}$ with cardinality $\leqslant (d(C^{\perp}) - 2)$ are adversary groups to R_i.*
(iii) *For MDS codes C, subsets of $\mathcal{P} \setminus \{R_i\}$ with cardinality $\leqslant (d(C^{\perp}) - 2)$ are all the adversary groups to R_i.*

There is a gap in Corollary 9 in general that we do not known whether a subset of size in the gap is a substitution group to R_i or not for general code-based authentication scheme. Actually, it is **NP**-hard to list all substitution groups to R_i in general. Even for authentication scheme based on algebraic geometric codes from elliptic curves, it is already **NP**-hard (under **RP**-reduction) to list all substitution groups to R_i which we will see later in Section 5.

By Proposition 6, we obtain the main result of this section, a generalization of Proposition 1:

Theorem 10. *For the authentication scheme we constructed, we have*

(i) *The set of all minimal substitution groups to the receiver R_i is determined completely by all the minimal codewords respect to i in $C^{\perp}$.*
(ii) *All adversary groups to the receiver R_i are one-to-one corresponding to subsets of $[V] \setminus \{i\}$ such that each of them together with i does not contain any support of minimal codewords respect to i in $C^{\perp}$.*

5   The Authentication Scheme Based on Algebraic Geometry Codes

In this section, we give examples of our authentication schemes based on some explicit linear codes, algebraic geometry (AG) codes from elliptic curves. First, recall the definition of AG codes.

Let $X/\mathbb{F}_q$ be a geometrically irreducible smooth projective curve of genus g over the finite field $\mathbb{F}_q$ with function field $\mathbb{F}_q(X)$. Denote by $X(\mathbb{F}_q)$ the set of all $\mathbb{F}_q$-rational points on X. Let $D = \{R_1, R_2, \cdots, R_n\}$ be a proper subset of rational points $X(\mathbb{F}_q)$. Also write $D = R_1 + R_2 + \cdots + R_n$. Let G be a divisor of degree k $(2g - 2 < k < n)$ with $\operatorname{Supp}(G) \cap D = \emptyset$.

Let V be a divisor on X. Denote by $\mathscr{L}(V)$ the $\mathbb{F}_q$-vector space of all rational functions $f \in \mathbb{F}_q(X)$ with the principal divisor $\operatorname{div}(f) \geqslant -V$, together with the zero function.

Denote by $\Omega(V)$ the $\mathbb{F}_q$-vector space of all Weil differentials ω with divisor $\operatorname{div}(\omega) \geqslant V$, together with the zero differential (cf. [11]).

The residue AG code $C_\Omega(D, G)$ is defined to be the image of the following residue map:

$$res : \Omega(G - D) \to \mathbb{F}_q^n; \ \omega \mapsto (res_{R_1}(\omega), res_{R_2}(\omega), \cdots, res_{R_n}(\omega)) \ .$$

Its dual code, the functional AG code $C_{\mathscr{L}}(D, G)$, is defined to be the image of the following evaluation map:

$$ev : \mathscr{L}(G) \to \mathbb{F}_q^n; \ f \mapsto (f(R_1), f(R_2), \cdots, f(R_n)) \ .$$

They have the code parameters $[n, n-k+g-1, d \geqslant k-2g+2]$ and $[n, k-g+1, d \geqslant n-k]$, respectively. Moreover, we have the following isomorphism

$$C_\Omega(D, G) \cong C_{\mathscr{L}}(D, D - G + (\eta))$$

for some Weil differential η satisfying $\upsilon_{P_i}(\eta) = -1$ and $\eta_{P_i}(1) = 1$ for all $i = 0, 1, 2, \cdots, n$ ([11, Proposition 2.2.10]).

For the authentication scheme based on the simplest AG codes, i.e., generalized Reed-Solomon codes, we have determined all the malicious groups that can make a substitution attack to any (not necessarily all) other in Corollary 9. Next, we consider the authentication scheme based on AG codes $C_\Omega(D, G)$ from elliptic curves. The following theorem is a generalization of the main result in [12]. Using the Riemann-Roch theorem, the malicious groups who together are able to make a substitution attack to any (not necessarily all) other or not can be characterized completely as follows.

Theorem 11. *Let $X = E$ be an elliptic curve over $\mathbb{F}_q$ with a rational point O, $D = \{R_1, R_2, \cdots, R_n\}$ a subset of $E(\mathbb{F}_q)$ such that $O \notin D$ and let divisor $G = kO$ ($0 < k < n$). Endow $E(\mathbb{F}_q)$ a group structure [13] with the zero element O. Then for the authentication scheme based on the $[n, n - k]$ AG code $C_\Omega(D, G)$, we have*

(i) *Any coalition of up to $(n - k - 2)$ malicious receivers can not make a substitution attack to any other receiver.*

(ii) *A malicious group $A \subseteq D$, $|A| = n - k - 1$, can successfully make a substitution attack to the receiver $R_j \in D \setminus A$ if and only if*

$$\sum_{P \in D \setminus A} P = R_j$$

in the group $E(\mathbb{F}_q)$. Moreover, we note that they can only successfully make a substitution attack to the receiver $\sum_{P \in D \setminus A} P$ if $\sum_{P \in D \setminus A} P \in D \setminus A$.

(iii) *A malicious group $A \subseteq D$, $|A| = n - k$, can successfully make a substitution attack to the receiver $R_j \in D \setminus A$ if and only if there exists some $Q \in E(\mathbb{F}_q) \setminus \{R_j\}$ such that the sum*

$$Q + \sum_{P \in D \setminus A} P = R_j$$

in the group $E(\mathbb{F}_q)$, which is equivalent to that in the group $E(\mathbb{F}_q)$, we have

$$\sum_{P \in D \setminus A} P \neq O \ .$$

Note that the latter condition is independent of R_j, and hence, such a malicious group can successfully make a substitution attack to any other receiver.

(iv) *A malicious group with at least $(n - k + 1)$ members can successfully make a substitution attack to any other receiver.*

Proof. The statement (i) follows from Theorem 5 as the minimum distance

$$d^{\perp}(C_{\Omega}(D, G)) = d(C_{\mathscr{L}}(D, G)) \geq n - k .$$

For the statement (ii), if the malicious group $A \subseteq D$, $|A| = n - k - 1$, can successfully make a substitution attack to the receiver $R_j \in D \setminus A$, then there exists some non-zero function in the dual code $f \in \mathscr{L}(kO - \sum_{R \in D \setminus A} R + R_j)$, i.e., $\mathrm{div}(f) \geq \sum_{R \in D \setminus A} R - R_j - kO$. Both sides of the above inequality have degree 0, so it forces $\mathrm{div}(f) = \sum_{R \in D \setminus A} R - R_j - kO$. That is, in the group $E(\mathbb{F}_q)$, we have

$$\sum_{R \in D \setminus A} R = R_j .$$

Similarly for the statement (iii), if a malicious group $A \subseteq D$, $|A| = n - k$, can successfully make a substitution attack to the receiver $R_j \in D \setminus A$, there exists some non-zero function $f \in \mathscr{L}(kO - \sum_{R \in D \setminus A} R + R_j) \setminus \mathscr{L}(kO - \sum_{R \in D \setminus A} R)$, i.e., $f(R_j) \neq 0$ and $\mathrm{div}(f) \geq \sum_{R \in D \setminus A} R - R_j - kO$. So there is an extra zero $Q \in E(\mathbb{F}_q) \setminus \{R_j\}$ of f such that $\mathrm{div}(f) = \sum_{R \in D \setminus A} R - R_j + Q - kO$. That is,

$$\sum_{R \in A} R + Q = R_j .$$

The rest of (iii) is obvious.

We prove the statement (iv) by contradiction. A malicious group A can not successfully make a substitution attack to the receiver R_j if and only if there exists a linear function $f \in \mathscr{L}(D - G + (\eta))$ such that $f(R_j) = 1$, and $f(R) = 0 \; \forall R \in A$. As $f \in \mathscr{L}(D - G + (\eta))$, f has at most $\deg(D - G + (\eta)) = n - k$ zeros. So if $|A| \geq n - k + 1$, the malicious group A can successfully make a substitution attack to any other receiver.
□

Remark 2. (1) From the statements (ii) and (iii) in the above theorem and the result in [14], it is in general an **NP**-hard problem (under **RP**-reduction) to list all the substitution groups of size $n - k + 1$ and $n - k$ to any receiver.

(2) Comparing with the scheme of Safavi-Naini and Wang, from the statement (iii), there are groups of $n - k$ malicious receivers which can not make an efficient substitution attack to any other receiver. But in their scheme, any group of $n - k$ malicious receivers which can easily make a substitution attack to any other receiver.

6   Conclusion

In this paper, we construct an authentication scheme for multi-receivers and multiple messages based on linear code $C [V, k, d]$. Compared with schemes based on MACs or digital signatures which depend on computational security, our scheme is an unconditionally secure authentication scheme, which can offer robustness against a coalition of up to $(d(C^\perp) - 2)$ malicious receivers. Our scheme has all the same advantages as the generalization of Shamir's secret sharing scheme to linear secret sharing sceme based on linear codes [4, 5]. Compared with the scheme of Safavi-Naini and Wang [1] which has a constraint on the number of verifying receivers that can not be larger than the size of the finite field, our scheme allows arbitrary receivers for a fixed message base field. Moreover, for some important receiver, coalitions of k or more malicious receivers might not make a substitution attack on the receiver more efficiently than randomly guessing a label from the finite field for a fake message. While the authentication scheme of Safavi-Naini and Wang is a (V, k) threshold authentication scheme, any k of the V receivers can easily produce a fake message that can be accepted by the receiver. In general, it is very hard to list all the malicious groups respect to a fixed receiver. If we choose elliptic curve codes for the linear codes in our authentication scheme, then we can use the group of rational points on the elliptic curve to give a complete description of all the substitution groups to each receiver.

References

1. Safavi-Naini, R., Wang, H.: New results on multi-receiver authentication codes. In: Nyberg, K. (ed.) EUROCRYPT 1998. LNCS, vol. 1403, pp. 527–541. Springer, Heidelberg (1998)
2. Shamir, A.: How to share a secret. Commun. ACM 22, 612–613 (1979)
3. McEliece, R.J., Sarwate, D.V.: On sharing secrets and Reed-Solomon codes. Commun. ACM 24, 583–584 (1981)
4. Massey, J.L.: Minimal codewords and secret sharing. In: Proceedings of the 6th Joint Swedish-Russian International Workshop on Information Theory, pp. 276–279 (1993)
5. Massey, J.L.: Some applications of coding theory in cryptography. In: Codes and Ciphers: Cryptography and Coding IV, pp. 33–47 (1995)
6. Chen, H., Cramer, R.: Algebraic geometric secret sharing schemes and secure multi-party computation over small fields. In: Dwork, C. (ed.) CRYPTO 2006. LNCS, vol. 4117, pp. 521–536. Springer, Heidelberg (2006)
7. Van Dijk, M., Gehrmann, C., Smeets, B.: Unconditionally secure group authentication. Designs, Codes and Cryptography 14, 281–296 (1998)
8. Boyd, C.: Digital multisignatures. In: Beker, H., Piper, F. (eds.) Cryptography and Coding, pp. 241–246. Clarendon Press (1986)
9. Desmedt, Y.G., Frankel, Y.: Shared generation of authenticators and signatures. In: Feigenbaum, J. (ed.) CRYPTO 1991. LNCS, vol. 576, pp. 457–469. Springer, Heidelberg (1992)
10. Desmedt, Y., Frankel, Y., Yung, M.: Multi-receiver/multi-sender network security: efficient authenticated multicast/feedback. In: IEEE INFOCOM 1992, Eleventh Annual Joint Conference of the IEEE Computer and Communications Societies, pp. 2045–2054 (1992)
11. Stichtenoth, H.: Recent Advances in Nonlinear Dynamics and Synchronization, 2nd edn. Graduate Texts in Mathematics, vol. 254. Springer, Berlin (2009)
12. Chen, H., Ling, S., Xing, C.: Access structures of elliptic secret sharing schemes. IEEE Transactions on Information Theory 54, 850–852 (2008)
13. Silverman, J.H.: The arithmetic of elliptic curves, 2nd edn. Graduate Texts in Mathematics, vol. 106. Springer, Dordrecht (2009)
14. Cheng, Q.: Hard problems of algebraic geometry codes. IEEE Transactions on Information Theory 54, 402–406 (2008)

Efficient Sealed-Bid Auction Protocols Using Verifiable Secret Sharing

Mehrdad Nojoumian[1] and Douglas R. Stinson[2]

[1] Department of Computer Science
Southern Illinois University, Carbondale, Illinois, USA
nojoumian@cs.siu.edu
[2] David R. Cheriton School of Computer Science
University of Waterloo, Waterloo, Ontario, Canada
dstinson@math.uwaterloo.ca

Abstract. This article proposes efficient solutions for the construction of sealed-bid second-price and combinatorial auction protocols in an active adversary setting. The main reason for constructing secure auction protocols is that the losing bids can be used in the future auctions as well as negotiations if they are not kept private. Our motivation is to apply *verifiable secret sharing* in order to construct various kinds of sealed-bid auctions. We initially propose two *secure second-price auction* protocols with different masking methods. Subsequently, we provide two *secure combinatorial auction* protocols based on our second masking approach. In the first scheme, we apply an existing *dynamic programming* method. In the second protocol, we use inter-agent negotiation as an approximate solution in the *multiple traveling salesman problem* to determine auction outcomes. It is worth mentioning that our protocols are independent of the secret sharing scheme that is being used.

Keywords: Applied cryptography, security and privacy in auctions.

1 Introduction

The growth of e-commerce technologies has created a remarkable opportunity for *secure auctions* where bidders submit sealed-bids to auctioneers and then the auctioneers define outcomes without revealing the losing bids. The main motivation for protection of the losing bids is that the bidders' valuations can be used in the future auctions and negotiations by different parties, say auctioneers to maximize their revenues or competitors to win the auction. This problem can be resolved by constructing privacy-preserving auction protocols.

In fact, *secure comparison*, as the main building block of sealed-bid auctions, is first motivated by the *millionaires' problem* [38]. In this problem, the goal is to determine whether $x > y$, where both x and y are private secrets of two players. The answer to this question becomes known to the parties only after the execution of the protocol. The millionaires' problem ultimately leaded to the introduction of *secure multiparty computation* MPC, where n players cooperate to perform a computation task based on the private data they each provide.

X. Huang and J. Zhou (Eds.): ISPEC 2014, LNCS 8434, pp. 302–317, 2014.
© Springer International Publishing Switzerland 2014

Other methods were later proposed in order to construct protocols for *secure comparison, interval test* and *equality test*. For instance, [9] proposes multiparty computation techniques to implement these operations. The main building block of this construction is a protocol, named *bit-decomposition*, that converts a polynomial sharing of a secret into shares of its bits. This protocol is simplified in [22]. As a counterpart, [11] implements these operations by homomorphic encryption in a computationally secure setting. We later clarify why these operations are too expensive to build practical sealed-bid auctions, as shown in Table 2.

There exist many sealed-bid auctions in both *passive* and *active* adversary models. In the former, players follow protocols correctly but are curious to learn private bids. In the latter, players may also deviate from protocols. The majority of the sealed-bid auction protocols either are secure only in the passive adversary model or they apply costly bitwise approaches, e.g., using *verifiable secret sharing* VSS for every single bit of each bid rather than a single VSS for the entire bid.

1.1 Literature Review

All the following protocols utilize "secret sharing" as their main building block. In the initial construction of the first-price sealed-bid auction protocols, the authors in [10] implement a secure auction service by using verifiable secret sharing as well as verifiable signature sharing. At the end of the bidding time, auctioneers open bids to define outcomes, therefore, they learn the losing bids.

The authors in [12] illustrate a set of protocols for sealed-bid auctions by using secure distributed computation. The bidders' valuations are never revealed to any party even when the auction is completed. Their constructions support the first-price and second-price auctions. The general idea of their approach is to compare bids digit-by-digit by applying secret sharing techniques. This protocol is computationally very expensive.

The proposed first-price construction in [14] (modified in [15]) demonstrates a multi-round secure auction protocol in which winners from an auction round take part in a subsequent tie-breaking second auction round. The authors use the addition operation of secure multiparty computation in a passive adversary model. Later, the authors in [27] detected some shortcomings in this scheme such as the lack of verifiability. They then resolved those problems.

The authors in [13] present a protocol for the $(M + 1)$st-price auction. They illustrate a new method where bidders' valuations are encoded by the degree of distributed polynomials. The proposed construction requires only two rounds of computations; one round for bidders and one round for auctioneers. The proposed scheme in [6] is a fully private $(M + 1)$st-price auction protocol in which only the winning bidders and the seller learn the selling price. It has two main shortcomings. First, the scheme is not able to handle ties among multiple winners. Second, it is not an efficient construction in the computational setting.

Finally, the authors in [26] design a new first-price secure auction protocol based on a homomorphic secret sharing scheme. Their construction relies on hard computation problems and does not depend on any trust. They also show that the proposed protocol is secure against different kinds of attacks.

1.2 Motivation and Contributions

Our motivation is to propose efficient solutions for the construction of secure second-price as well as combinatorial auction protocols where losing bids are kept private in an active adversary model. We would like to use secret sharing techniques to define auction outcomes without using costly bitwise operations. This helps us to design approximate secure solutions for the general combinatorial auction that is expensive even without using sealed-bids. Even by having unlimited computational power, one can significantly reduce the communication cost by avoiding the use of bitwise operations, that is, sharing each bid as a single field element is more efficient compared to sharing every single bit/digit of that element, for an example of such a scheme, see [12]. Our constructions consist of an initializer $\mathcal{I}$, n bidders and m auctioneers. Here are our contributions:

- Our first solution is proposed for the second-price auction by using VSS. In this protocol, all bids are masked by using + operation, consequently, bids are sealed but their differences are revealed only to auctioneers. Although the general idea is similar to the comparison protocol in [22], our protocol works in an active adversary setting without using any bitwise operation. In that article, the authors use bitwise operations in a passive adversary model.

- We then improve our previous solution in order to prevent the revelation of the difference between each pair of bids. We propose another sealed-bid second-price auction protocol where all bids are masked by using + and × operations. As a result, both bids and their differences are sealed, however, the ratio of the bids are revealed only to auctioneers. We should stress that this protocol can be simply extended to the secure $(M + 1)$st-price auction.

- Finally, we provide two secure combinatorial auction protocols based on our second masking approach: (a) we use an existing *dynamic programming* method [33] to define auction outcomes. In that paper, the authors encode bids as the degree of secret sharing polynomials. As a result, their protocol only works in the passive adversary model whereas our construction works in an active adversary setting, (b) we apply the inter-agent negotiation approach, introduced in [16], as an approximate solution in a *multiple traveling salesman problem* in order to determine auction outcomes.

2 Preliminaries

2.1 Auction Protocols

In an auction, winner is a bidder who has submitted the highest bid. To define the selling price, there are two main approaches: *first-price* and *second-price* auctions. In the former, the winner pays the amount that he has proposed, i.e., highest bid. In the latter, the winner pays the amount of the second-highest bid. There exist other types of auctions such as $(M + 1)$st-price and *combinatorial auctions*. In the former, the highest M bidders win the auction and pay a uniform price defined by $(M+1)$-price. In the latter, multiple items with interdependent values are sold while bidders can bid on any combination of items.

In the first-price auction, a bidder potentially is able to define the winner as well as the selling price at the same time. On the other hand, in the second-price auction, a bidder potentially is able to define either the winner or the selling price for the winner. As a result, he proposes the actual highest value, say κ, he can afford to pay, which is also a profitable price for him [35]. Suppose the proposed bid is less than κ. In this case, the bidder decreases his chance of winning. If the proposed bid is bigger than κ, the bidder might win with an unprofitable price. This property forces the bidders to propose their true valuations.

2.2 Secret Sharing

In *secret sharing schemes*, a secret is divided into various shares in order to be distributed among participants, then a subset of players cooperate to reveal the secret [31,5]. In a (t,n)-*secret sharing scheme* where $t < n$, the secret is divided into n shares such that any $t+1$ players can combine their shares to reveal the secret, but any subset of t parties cannot learn anything about the secret.

In *verifiable secret sharing* VSS [8], players can verify the consistency of their shares with other players' shares. There are various techniques for performing the verification procedure, such as using zero knowledge proof with small probability of error, or applying bivariate polynomials without any probability of errors [4]; the latter construction works under the assumption that $n \geq 3t+1$ by considering secure pairwise channels among players. The proposed scheme in [29] applies the same communication model along with a broadcast channel to construct a new scheme with $n \geq 2t+1$. The authors in [32] construct a VSS protocol based on symmetric bivariate polynomials. This construction is simple and uses both pairwise channels and a broadcast channel under the assumption that $n \geq 4t+1$.

3 Our Constructions

Our model, Figure 1, consists of n bidders $\mathcal{B}_1 \dots \mathcal{B}_n$, m auctioneers $\mathcal{A}_1 \dots \mathcal{A}_m$ and a seller. We consider communication model of VSS that is being used [32].

In addition, a trusted initializer $\mathcal{I}$ distributes some information and then leaves the scheme before our protocols start. This is preferable to a trusted party who remains in the scheme. In the literature, trusted authorities are assumed in many secure auction protocols, for instance, semi-trusted third party [7,2],

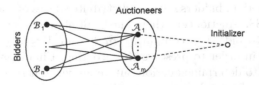

Fig. 1. Proposed Secure Auction Model

trusted third party [37,21], trusted centers [30], trusted authority [1,34], trustee [36]. It is worth mentioning that by paying an extra computational cost, a trusted party or initializer can be removed from any scheme to be replaced by MPC. Since each bidder acts as an independent dealer and the auctioneers perform the computation, our protocols have the following properties and assumptions:

- They can tolerate colluding auctioneers ∇ where $m \geq 4t + 1$ and $t \geq |\nabla|$ due to VSS of [32]. If the complicated VSS of [29] is used, our protocols can tolerate $m \geq 2t + 1$ since these protocols are independent of their VSS.

- They can tolerate dishonest bidders who submit inconsistent shares. Note that we assume the majority of the bidders are honest.

- We assume bidders do not collude with auctioneers similar to [25], and multi-auctioneer and multi-bidder protocols in [10,14].

There also exist other kinds of collusion assumptions in the literature, e.g., [20] assumes auctioneers do not collude with the auction issuer, [18] assumes the seller does not collude with the auction authority, etc. In Table 1, we have listed some protocols that have an assumption similar to our constructions.

Table 1. Protocols Where the Auctioneers Cannot Collude With the Bidders

Protocol	Cryptographic Technique	Adversary Model
Here	Verifiable Secret Sharing	Active
[25]	Homomorphic Encryption	Active
[14,15]	Secret Sharing	Passive
[10]	Verifiable Secret and Signature Sharing	Active

To construct our sealed-bid auction protocols, we use (1) + operation for adding two shared secrets, (2) × operation for multiplying two shared secrets. Although any arbitrary VSS can be used in our constructions, we apply the verifiable secret sharing scheme proposed in [32] due to its simplicity. This means our protocols would tolerate more dishonest auctioneers if the VSS of [4,29] were used. All computations are performed in a large enough finite field $\mathbb{Z}_q$.

3.1 Sealed-Bid Second-Price Auction Protocol Using +

In our first construction, bidders initially distribute shares of their bids β_i among auctioneers by VSS. Auctioneers then mask all shared secrets by adding an unknown value δ to bids, i.e., computing $\beta_i + \delta$ for $1 \leq i \leq n$: this increases valuations equally in order to preserve the ordering. Finally, auctioneers reveal the masked values to determine auction outcomes without revealing actual bids.

We assume that the total number of colluding auctioneers is limited to our secret sharing threshold, i.e., $|\nabla| \leq t$. We also select a large enough finite field to prevent the modular reduction after using the addition operation. Our first solution is shown in Figures 2 and 3. The first phase is repeated n times, i.e., it is used for each bidder $\mathcal{B}_k$ where $1 \leq k \leq n$.

Initialization

1. $\mathcal{I}$ initiates a secret sharing scheme by a symmetric polynomial, that is, he generates $h(x, y) \in \mathbb{Z}_q[x, y]$ of degree t in which $h(0, 0) = \delta$, where $q > \kappa + \delta$ to prevent the modular reduction and κ denotes the maximum possible price.

2. He then sends shares of auctioneers $\mathcal{A}_i$ for $1 \leq i \leq m$ accordingly and leaves the scheme, i.e., $h_i(x) = h(x, \omega^i)$ where ω is a primitive element in the field. Now, each auctioneer has a share of an unknown value δ.

Bid Submission

1. Each bidder $\mathcal{B}_k$ chooses a random symmetric polynomial $g_k(x, y) \in \mathbb{Z}_q[x, y]$ of degree t to send shares $g_{ki}(x) = g_k(x, \omega^i)$ to $\mathcal{A}_i$ for $1 \leq i \leq m$ through a private channel where $g_k(0, 0) = \beta_k$.

2. To verify distributed shares, auctioneers $\mathcal{A}_i$ and $\mathcal{A}_j$ perform pairwise checks, i.e., they verify that $g_{ki}(\omega^j) = g_{kj}(\omega^i)$, similar to VSS of [32]. They will either accept shares of β_k or disqualify $\mathcal{B}_k$.

Fig. 2. A. Secure Auction Protocol Using Addition Operation

Outcome Computation

1. Each auctioneer $\mathcal{A}_i$ **locally** adds $h_i(x)$ to the share that he has received from each bidder $\mathcal{B}_k$, that is, $\psi_{ki}(x) = g_{ki}(x) + h_i(x)$ for $1 \leq k \leq n$. In fact, $\psi_{ki}(x)$ are shares of $\beta_k + \delta$ for $1 \leq k \leq n$ where δ is unknown to everyone.

2. Each $\mathcal{A}_i$ then sends $\psi_{ki}(0)$ to a selected auctioneer $\mathcal{A}_j$ where $i, j \in \Gamma$, i.e., the set of good auctioneers. All computations performed by $\mathcal{A}_j$ are **only** visible to the auctioneers. $\mathcal{A}_j$ computes $\varphi_k(0, y)$ such that $\varphi_k(0, \omega^i) = \psi_{ki}(0)$ for at least $m - 2|\nabla|$ values of i.

3. In fact, $\varphi_k(x, y) = g_k + h$. $\mathcal{A}_j$ computes masked values $\varphi_k(0, 0) = \beta_k + \delta$ and then sorts them in decreasing order, i.e., $\varphi_w^1(0, 0), \varphi_s^2(0, 0), \ldots, \varphi_*^n(0, 0)$, where w is the index of the winner and s is the index of the second highest bid.

4. Auctioneers send the winner's index along with shares $g_{si}(x)$-s to all bidders through private channels. Each bidder **locally** computes the selling price by $g_s(0, 0) = \beta_s$. They can agree on β_s due to the honest majority assumption.

Fig. 3. B. Secure Auction Protocol Using Addition Operation

Since equal bids have equal masked values, ties among multiple winners can be detected and handled by assigning priority to bidders or by a random selection.

Theorem 1. *The proposed protocol defines auction outcomes correctly and only reveals the difference between each pair of bids to the auctioneers in an active adversary setting. We require $m \geq 4t+1$ even if one bidder is dishonest, otherwise, we require $m \geq 3t + 1$ when we use VSS of [32].*

Proof. The security of the verifiable secret sharing scheme that we use is proven in [32]. We provide further clarifications on the condition of this construction. Dishonest auctioneers have two possibilities: (a) they either collude to recover secret bids or (b) they send incorrect shares to disrupt the protocol.

(a) t-**privacy:** If all colluding auctioneers $|\nabla| \leq t$ collect their shares, they are not able to recover secret bids β_k since all secret sharing polynomials $g_k(x, y)$'s are of degree t and each of which requires $t + 1$ shares to be interpolated.

(b) t-**resilience:** On the other hand, dishonest auctioneers cannot disrupt the protocol. In the worst case scenario, if a dishonest bidder sends incorrect shares (i.e., less than $\frac{1}{4}$ of shares can be corrupted for an acceptable bid submission) to honest auctioneers during *bid submission* and also colluding auctioneers send incorrect shares (i.e., less than $\frac{1}{4}$ of the remaining $\frac{3}{4}$ shares) to the selected auctioneer $\mathcal{A}_j$ for the reconstruction of $\varphi_k(0,0)$ in the *outcome computation* phase, $\mathcal{A}_j$ can then use an error correction technique, such as the Reed-Solomon Codes [19], to interpolate $\varphi_k(0,y)$. Finally, if dishonest auctioneers $|\nabla| \leq t$ send incorrect shares to bidders in the step-4 of the *outcome computation* phase, they can each use error correction to recover β_s. If all bidders are honest, $m \geq 3t + 1$ satisfies the required condition of error correction.

Note that the dishonest bidders cannot disrupt the protocol if they collude with each others because they are only involved in two tasks. (a) Bid submission by VSS: either honest auctioneers receive consistent shares with respect to a secret bid and accept secret sharing, or the bidder is disqualified. In the former case, the bidder cannot repudiate his bid since those consistent shares are a strong commitment. (b) Selling price reconstruction: each bidder receives the winner's index along with shares of the selling price from auctioneers in order to compute the outcome, therefore, colluding bidders cannot disrupt the protocol since majority of bidders are honest and they are able to agree on the winner's index and a correct selling price.

At the end of the protocol, all bidders only know auction outcomes. Assuming bidders do not collude with auctioneers, all losing bids are kept secret from all parties because δ is an anonymous constant term only known to $\mathcal{I}$. It is worth mentioning that revealing $\varphi_k(0,0)$'s only discloses the masked values $\beta_k + \delta$ and the difference of each pair of bids to auctioneers, but not the actual bids β_k. □

3.2   Sealed-Bid Second-Price Auction Protocol Using $\times$ and $+$

We now apply a practical approach to hide bids as well as their exact distances. Similar to the previous approach, bidders initially distribute shares of their bids among auctioneers by VSS. Then, auctioneers mask shared secrets to define outcomes. They start by comparing each pair of consecutive bids from β_1 all the way to β_n to find the maximum element and repeat this process to define the second maximum element, i.e., $(n-1) + (n-2) = 2n - 3$ comparisons in total.

For each comparison, they multiply two bids by a new unknown secret $1 < \alpha_l$ and then add two new random secrets δ_{l1} and δ_{l2} (as noise) to the resulting values such that the order of two bids are maintained, i.e., $\alpha_l \beta_k + \delta_{l1}$ and $\alpha_l \beta_{k+1} + \delta_{l2}$ where $1 \le \delta_{l1} \ne \delta_{l2} < \alpha_l$, shown in Figures 4 and 5. Each time, after executing $\times$ operation, the degree reduction protocol in [24] is used to adjust the threshold.

Initialization

1. Initializer $\mathcal{I}$ generates symmetric polynomials $f_l, h_{l1}, h_{l2} \in \mathbb{Z}_q[x, y]$ of degree t for $1 \le l \le (2n - 3)$ with constant terms $\alpha_l, \delta_{l1}, \delta_{l2}$, where $q > \alpha_l(\kappa + 1)$ to prevent the modular reduction. In fact, we use different l for each comparison.

2. He then sends shares of f_l, h_{l1}, h_{l2} to $\mathcal{A}_i$ for $1 \le i \le m$ and leaves the scheme. That is, $f_l^i(x) = f_l(x, \omega^i)$, $h_{l1}^i(x) = h_{l1}(x, \omega^i)$ and $h_{l2}^i(x) = h_{l2}(x, \omega^i)$ where ω is a primitive element.

Bid Submission

- We apply the *bid submission* protocol of the previous construction, that is, each bidder $\mathcal{B}_k$ chooses a random symmetric polynomial $g_k(x, y)$ of degree t to send $g_{ki}(x) = g_k(x, \omega^i)$ to $\mathcal{A}_i$ for $1 \le i \le m$ through private channels such that $g_k(0, 0) = \beta_k$. Auctioneers also verify shares similar to that protocol.

Fig. 4. Secure Auction Using Addition and Multiplication Operations

In this protocol, equal bids are not distinguished due to the random noise δ_{l1} and δ_{l2}. Therefore, auctioneers can execute a secure equality test on β_w and β_k to detect potential ties between them, i.e., compute $\gamma_l(\beta_w - \beta_k)$ where γ_l is unknown. If it is zero, two bids are equal, otherwise, they are different.

Theorem 2. *The proposed protocol defines auction outcomes correctly and only reveals the ratio of bids to the auctioneers in an active adversary setting. We require $m \ge 4t + 1$ even if a single bidder is dishonest, otherwise, we only require $m \ge 3t + 1$ when we use VSS of [32].*

Proof. We provide a short clarification since the security proof is straightforward and the same as the previous theorem. In this protocol, the actual difference of each pair of bids are kept private due to the additive factors δ_{l1} and δ_{l2}, where $1 \le \delta_{l1} \ne \delta_{l2} < \alpha_l$. In other words, considering two consequtive bids $\beta_k < \beta_{k+1}$ where $\beta_{k+1} - \beta_k = 1$, their corresponding masked values have the same ordering, that is, $\alpha_l \beta_k + \delta_{l1} < \alpha_l \beta_{k+1} + \delta_{l2}$ even if $\delta_{l1} = \alpha_l - 1$ and $\delta_{l2} = 1$. However, upper and lower bounds of the bids' ratios are revealed only to auctioneers:

$$ratio = \frac{\alpha_l \beta_k + \delta_{l1}}{\alpha_l \beta_{k+1} + \delta_{l2}} < \frac{\alpha_l \beta_k + \alpha_l}{\alpha_l \beta_{k+1}} < \frac{\beta_k + 1}{\beta_{k+1}}$$

$$ratio = \frac{\alpha_l \beta_k + \delta_{l1}}{\alpha_l \beta_{k+1} + \delta_{l2}} > \frac{\alpha_l \beta_k}{\alpha_l \beta_{k+1} + \alpha_l} > \frac{\beta_k}{\beta_{k+1} + 1}$$

Outcome Computation

1. Auctioneers select shares of a pair of bids β_k and $\beta_{k'}$. Each $\mathcal{A}_i$ **locally** computes $\psi_{ki}(x) = f_l^i(x) \times g_{ki}(x)$ and $\psi_{k'i}(x) = f_l^i(x) \times g_{k'i}(x)$, that is, shares of new symmetric polynomials. They execute a degree reduction protocol for threshold adjustment [24]. After that, each $\mathcal{A}_i$ adds shares $h_{l1}^i(x)$ and $h_{l2}^i(x)$ to the previous shares, i.e., $\psi_{ki}(x) \leftarrow \psi_{ki}(x) + h_{l1}^i(x)$ and $\psi_{k'i}(x) \leftarrow \psi_{k'i}(x) + h_{l2}^i(x)$.

2. Each $\mathcal{A}_i$ then sends $\psi_{ki}(0)$ and $\psi_{k'i}(0)$ to a selected $\mathcal{A}_j$ where $i, j \in \Gamma$, i.e., the set of good auctioneers. Computations performed by $\mathcal{A}_j$ are **only** visible to the auctioneers. $\mathcal{A}_j$ computes polynomials $\varphi_k(0, y)$ and $\varphi_{k'}(0, y)$ such that $\varphi_k(0, \omega^i) = \psi_{ki}(0)$ and $\varphi_{k'}(0, \omega^i) = \psi_{k'i}(0)$ for at least $m - 2|\nabla|$ values of i.

3. In fact, $\varphi_k(x, y) = f_l \times g_k + h_{l1}$ and $\varphi_{k'}(x, y) = f_l \times g_{k'} + h_{l2}$. Therefore, $\mathcal{A}_j$ reveals $\varphi_k(0, 0) = \alpha_l \beta_k + \delta_{l1}$ and $\varphi_{k'}(0, 0) = \alpha_l \beta_{k'} + \delta_{l2}$. Now, auctioneers can define which bid is larger by comparing masked values $\alpha_l \beta_k + \delta_{l1}$ and $\alpha_l \beta_{k'} + \delta_{l2}$, where $\alpha_l, \delta_{l1}, \delta_{l2}$ are unknown to everyone.

4. Auctioneers repeat steps $1-3$ to determine two highest bids β_w and β_s accordingly. The winner's *id* along with shares $g_{si}(x)$-s are sent to all bidders through private channels. Each $\mathcal{B}_k$ **locally** computes the selling price by $g_s(0, 0) = \beta_s$. They can agree on β_s due to the honest majority assumption.

Fig. 5. Secure Auction Using Addition and Multiplication Operations

It is now easy to observe that the ratio of two bids are bounded as follows:

$$\frac{\beta_k}{\beta_{k+1} + 1} < ratio < \frac{\beta_k + 1}{\beta_{k+1}}$$

During the *outcome computation* phase and the execution of a degree reduction protocol, auctioneers can verify all computations by means of pairwise checks (similar to VSS of [32]) to make sure everyone is following the protocols correctly since all polynomials remain symmetric. We should mention that the degree reduction is avoidable in some other settings, e.g., having honest bidders under $m \geq 4t+1$ assumption, auctioneers can interpolate a polynomial of degree $2t$ in the existence of t malicious parties by using error correction [19].   □

3.3 Sealed-Bid Combinatorial Auction Protocol by Dynamic Programming

The first unconditionally secure combinatorial auction protocol was proposed in [33]. (For other type of unconditionally secure auction protocols see [23,17], i.e., sealed-bid Dutch-style auctions.) [33] applies a *dynamic programming* DP technique to determine auction outcomes. This solution is secure only in the passive adversary model and it is not verifiable. In addition, the number of auctioneers must be larger than the maximum possible revenue.

In this construction, weight publishers (bidders) submit their valuations as the degree of secret sharing polynomials. Then, evaluators (auctioneers) use $deg(g_k) + deg(g_l) = deg(g_k \times g_l)$ and $\max\{deg(g_k), deg(g_l)\} = deg(g_k + g_l)$ to implement *addition* and *max* operations accordingly. They also use mask publishers (trusted third parties) to execute these operations securely. The authors later propose the counterpart construction of this scheme in a computational setting based on the homomorphic encryption [39].

We first provide an example to show a combinatorial auction model based on a directed graph, Figure 6. We then illustrate the *dynamic programming* method in order to define auction outcomes. Finally, we explain our secure solution to this problem in an active adversary setting.

Example 1. Suppose six bidders $\mathcal{B}_1, \ldots, \mathcal{B}_6$ propose their evaluations on various subsets of three items $\{a, b, c\}$. For instance, $\beta_5 = \$5$ for all three items, $\beta_2 = \$3$ for $\{a\}$, and so on. As you can see, auctioneers earn the maximum revenue if they sell $\{b\}$ to the first bidder for \$1 and $\{a, c\}$ to the last bidder for \$5.

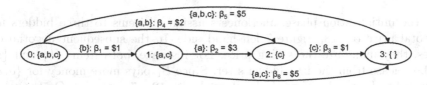

Fig. 6. Directed Graph to Model Combinatorial Auctions

$r = 3 : f(3) = 0$ destination function

$r = 2 : f(2) = \max\{w_{23} + f(3)\} = \max\{1\} = 1$

$r = 1 : f(1) = \max\{w_{12} + f(2), w_{13} + f(3)\} = \max\{4, 5\} = 5$

$r = 0 : f(0) = \max\{w_{01} + f(1), w_{02} + f(2), w_{03} + f(3)\} = \max\{6, 3, 5\} = 6$

More generally, $f(r) = \overset{link:r \to s}{\max}\{w_{rs} + f(s)\}$, where the value of the destination function is zero and w_{rs} is the weight of the link between two subsequent nodes r and s. Therefore, we need two operations *addition* and *max* in order to implement a sealed-bid combinatorial auction protocol in the active adversary setting.

Similar to the previous construction, $\mathcal{I}$ first distributes some multiplicative and additive factors based on the size of the directed graph. Bidders $\mathcal{B}_1, \ldots, \mathcal{B}_n$ then distribute their bids by symmetric bivariate polynomials of degree t. In the computation stage, auctioneers $\mathcal{A}_1, \ldots, \mathcal{A}_m$ use the same addition operation to execute $w_{rs} + f(s) = \beta_k + f(s)$. They also apply the previous comparison approach to implement the *max* operation. Finally, they define auction outcomes.

3.4   Sealed-Bid Combinatorial Auction Protocol by Multiple-TSP

In our last construction, we design an approximate secure solution in order to solve the combinatorial auction problem through a *multiple traveling salesman problem* MTSP, where more than one salesman is allowed to be used for finding the solution. In the fixed destination version of this problem, each salesman returns to his original depot after completing the tour. Similar to the traveling salesman problem, each city is visited exactly once and the total cost of visiting cities is minimized [3]. We first illustrate how to model a combinatorial auction based on the multiple traveling salesman problem and then we demonstrate an *inter-agent negotiation approach* [16] to solve this problem, Figure 7.

Example 2. Suppose three bidders $\mathcal{B}_1, \mathcal{B}_2, \mathcal{B}_3$ propose their bids on various subsets of seven items $\{a, b, c, d, e, f, g\}$, as shown below.

$$\mathcal{B}_1 \rightarrow \{a, b, c\} : \$12 \quad or \quad \{a, b\} : \$5 \quad or \quad \{a, c\} : \$7$$
$$\mathcal{B}_2 \rightarrow \{d, e\} : \$7 \quad or \quad \{b, d, e\} : \$13 \quad or \quad \{c, d, e\} : \$11$$
$$\mathcal{B}_3 \rightarrow \{f, g\} : \$9 \quad or \quad \{b, f, g\} : \$16 \quad or \quad \{c, f, g\} : \$14$$

In the initialization phase, auctioneers assign all items to three bidders for the total price of $28, Figure 7 left-hand side. In the subsequent negotiation stages, they maximize the selling price. For instance, both items $\{b\}$ and $\{c\}$ can be release from the first bidder's set. Since $\mathcal{B}_1$ pays more money for $\{a, c\}$ compared to $\{a, b\}$, therefore $\{b\}$ is released with $12 - 7 = \$5$ cost. On the other hand, $\mathcal{B}_2$ pays extra $13 - 7 = \$6 > \$5$ for $\{b\}$ while $\mathcal{B}_3$ pays extra $16 - 9 = \$7 > \$5$ for that. Therefore, $\{b\}$ is assigned to the last bidder and the total selling price is increased to $30 through one round of negotiation, Figure 7 right-hand side.

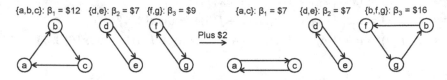

Fig. 7. Multiple Traveling Salesman Problem for Modeling Combinatorial Auctions

Similar to our previous construction, we require *addition* (minus is the same) and *max* (or comparison) operations to implement the negotiation protocol in a secure setting. We can also define a time interval for the entire protocol in order to limit the number of negotiation rounds for an approximate solution.

4   Complexity and Properties

We now clarify why the existing bitwise operations are too expensive to construct sealed-bid auction protocols. As we stated earlier, these protocols use VSS for every single bit of each bid rather than a single VSS for each bid. Let $\ell = \lceil \log_2 q \rceil$ denotes the number of bits of each bid, i.e., the size of each finite field's element.

The *round complexity* is measured by the number of rounds in which players execute the multiplication protocol and the *communication complexity* is measured by the number of invocations of the multiplication protocol. For instance, to compute $\alpha_1\alpha_2\alpha_3\alpha_4$, $\alpha_1\alpha_2$ and $(\alpha_1\alpha_2)\alpha_3$ and $(\alpha_1\alpha_2\alpha_3)\alpha_4$ can be computed sequentially, or $\alpha_1\alpha_2$ and $\alpha_3\alpha_4$ can be computed in parallel in order to compute $(\alpha_1\alpha_2)(\alpha_3\alpha_4)$. The former method takes 3 rounds with 3 invocations whereas the later method takes 2 rounds with 3 invocations. In all complexity analyses, the goal is to perform parallel multiplications as much as possible.

To construct bitwise operations, *Bit-Decomposition* BD protocol is proposed in [9] to convert a polynomial sharing of a secret into shares of its bits. This protocol takes 114 rounds and $118\ell + 110\,\ell\log\ell$ invocations. The authors also provide a protocol, named *Bitwise Less-Than* BIT-LT, to compare two decomposed elements in 19 rounds with 22ℓ invocations. Therefore, to compare two elements, they must be decomposed in parallel and then they can be compared, i.e., $(114 + 19)$ rounds and $(2 * (118\ell + 110\,\ell\log\ell) + 22\ell)$ invocations.

The authors in [22] show that the comparison protocol can be simplified by using simpler subprotocols, i.e., $(38 + 6)$ rounds and $(2 * (93\ell + 94\,\ell\log\ell) + 19\ell)$ invocations. They also show that the BD protocol itself can be simplified to achieve even a better result, i.e., $(25 + 6)$ rounds and $(2 * (93\ell + 47\,\ell\log\ell) + 19\ell)$ invocations. Finally, they propose a new comparison protocol without applying the DB protocol while using other bitwise operations. This construction takes $(13 + 2)$ rounds and $(3 * (93\ell + 1) + 2)$ invocations. Note that our comparison protocol only takes 1 round for two multiplications in parallel and 2 invocations.

The summary of these analyses are presented in Table 2. Even by using elements with $\ell = 128$ bits, it is impractical to use any of these bitwise operations. For instance, in the best case scenario, it requires $35,717$ secure multiplications in order to perform one single comparison. Having only 10 bids, it requires $350,717$ secure multiplications to find the highest bid whereas our protocol only requires 20 multiplications. This implies that avoiding bitwise operations is better than revealing partial information like ratio of bids.

Table 2. Single *Comparison*'s Cost in Terms of the Number of Multiplications

Secure Comparison Protocol	Number of Rounds	Communication Complexity	$\ell = 128$: Number of Secure Multiplications
Our 2nd Protocol	1	2	2
[22] not using BD	15	$279\ell + 5$	$35,717$
[22] using BD	31	$205\ell + 94\,\ell\log\ell$	$110,464$
[22] simplifying [9]	44	$205\ell + 188\,\ell\log\ell$	$194,688$
[9]	133	$258\ell + 220\,\ell\log\ell$	$230,144$

In general, sealed-bid auction protocols have some essential properties [28] as listed below. (a) *Correctness*: determining auction outcomes correctly, i.e., the winners and the selling price. (b) *Privacy*: preserving privacy of the losing bids. (c) *Verifiability*: parties who exchange money such as bidders and the seller (if applicable) must be able to verify auction outcomes. (d) *Fairness*: bidders must not be able to modify and/or deny (a.k.a non-repudiation) the submitted bids.

(e) *Robustness*: none of the active parties are assumed to be honest and malicious behavior must be tolerated. (f) *Anonymity*: the identities of the losers must be kept secret. Excluding property (f), our protocols have all the above features.

We also would like to highlight some important points regarding our protocols. Although partial information like the ratio of the bids might be revealed to auctioneers, our protocols keep the actual values of the losing bids secret. This is much better than using impractical bitwise approach to fully hide the losing bids. Moreover, revealing the ratio of the bids is better than revealing the exact difference between two bids, i.e., saying the 2nd-highest bid is 3/4 of the winning bid or saying the 2nd-highest bid is exactly \$10 less than the winning bid. In our schemes, auctioneers perform similar to an intermediate computation engine. In other words, bidders determine the actual value of the selling price themselves by outsourcing part of the computation, as in the client-server MPC model. Finally, our initializer, who can be replaced by MPC, is not an active party when the auction starts.

5   Concluding Remarks

We initially illustrated the lack of efficient solutions for the sealed-bid auction protocols that are secure in an active adversary setting (without using costly bitwise operations). We therefore proposed four secure constructions with different properties and applications. The summary of our contributions are presented in Table 3. Note that $m \geq 2t + 1$ can be tolerated using complicated VSS of [29].

Table 3. Sealed-Bid Auction Protocols Using VSS of [32]

Protocol	Adv.	$\mathcal{A}_{1..m}$	$\mathcal{B}_{1..n}$	Assumption	Opt.	Reveal
2nd-price					+	bids'
			honest	$m \geq 3t + 1$		differences
2nd-price	active	dishonest	or	or		ratio
combinatorial DP			dishonest	$m \geq 4t + 1$	$+, \times$	of
combinatorial MTSP						bids

It is quite challenging to construct sealed-bid auction protocols in an active adversary model without using a trusted party. In other words, if one relaxes these assumptions, he can decrease the computation and communication complexities. For instance, constructing the proposed schemes by considering the simple passive adversary model or using a trusted authority who remains in the scheme while the protocol is being executed. In addition, the winner determination problem of a general combinatorial auction is NP-complete and implementing this problem in a secure fashion adds extra computational cost to the protocol. Therefore, it is reasonable to apply simpler protocols (compared to bitwise approach where every single bit of bids is shared) along with approximate solutions to define auction outcomes. In this case, even by having unlimited computational power, we can significantly improve the communication cost.

References

1. Abe, M., Suzuki, K.: $M+1$-st price auction using homomorphic encryption. In: Naccache, D., Paillier, P. (eds.) PKC 2002. LNCS, vol. 2274, pp. 115–124. Springer, Heidelberg (2002)
2. Baudron, O., Stern, J.: Non-interactive private auctions. In: Syverson, P.F. (ed.) FC 2001. LNCS, vol. 2339, pp. 354–377. Springer, Heidelberg (2002)
3. Bektas, T.: The multiple traveling salesman problem: an overview of formulations and solution procedures. Omega 34(3), 209–219 (2006)
4. Ben-Or, M., Goldwasser, S., Wigderson, A.: Completeness theorems for non-cryptographic fault-tolerant distributed computation. In: 20th Annual ACM Symposium on Theory of Computing, STOC, pp. 1–10 (1988)
5. Blakley, G.R.: Safeguarding cryptographic keys. In: National Computer Conference, vol. 48, pp. 313–317. AFIPS Press (1979)
6. Brandt, F.: A verifiable, bidder-resolved auction protocol. In: 5th Int. Workshop on Deception, Fraud and Trust in Agent Societies, Special Track on Privacy and Protection with Multi-Agent Systems, pp. 18–25 (2002)
7. Cachin, C.: Efficient private bidding and auctions with an oblivious third party. In: ACM Conference on Computer and Communications Security, pp. 120–127 (1999)
8. Chor, B., Goldwasser, S., Micali, S., Awerbuch, B.: Verifiable secret sharing and achieving simultaneity in the presence of faults. In: 26th IEEE Annual Symposium on Foundations of Computer Science, FOCS, pp. 383–395 (1985)
9. Damgård, I.B., Fitzi, M., Kiltz, E., Nielsen, J.B., Toft, T.: Unconditionally secure constant-rounds multi-party computation for equality, comparison, bits and exponentiation. In: Halevi, S., Rabin, T. (eds.) TCC 2006. LNCS, vol. 3876, pp. 285–304. Springer, Heidelberg (2006)
10. Franklin, M.K., Reiter, M.K.: The design and implementation of a secure auction service. IEEE Transactions on Software Eng. 22(5), 302–312 (1996)
11. Garay, J.A., Schoenmakers, B., Villegas, J.: Practical and secure solutions for integer comparison. In: Okamoto, T., Wang, X. (eds.) PKC 2007. LNCS, vol. 4450, pp. 330–342. Springer, Heidelberg (2007)
12. Harkavy, M., Tygar, J.D., Kikuchi, H.: Electronic auctions with private bids. In: 3rd Workshop on E-Commerce, pp. 61–74. USENIX Association (1998)
13. Kikuchi, H.: (M+1)st-price auction protocol. In: Syverson, P.F. (ed.) FC 2001. LNCS, vol. 2339, pp. 341–363. Springer, Heidelberg (2002)
14. Kikuchi, H., Harkavy, M., Tygar, J.D.: Multi-round anonymous auction protocols. IEICE Transaction on Information and Systems 82, 769–777 (1999)
15. Kikuchi, H., Hotta, S., Abe, K., Nakanishi, S.: Distributed auction servers resolving winner and winning bid without revealing privacy of bids. In: 7th Int. Conference on Parallel and Distributed Systems, pp. 307–312. IEEE (2000)
16. Kim, I.C.: Task reallocation in multiagent systems based on vickrey auctioning. In: International Conference on Knowledge-Based and Intelligent Information and Engineering Systems, pp. 40–44. IOS Press (2002)
17. Krishnamachari, S., Nojoumian, M., Akkaya, K.: Implementation and analysis of dutch-style sealed-bid auctions: Computational vs unconditional security (2014) (Under Review Manuscript)
18. Lipmaa, H., Asokan, N., Niemi, V.: Secure vickrey auctions without threshold trust. In: Blaze, M. (ed.) FC 2002. LNCS, vol. 2357, pp. 87–101. Springer, Heidelberg (2003)

19. MacWilliams, F., Sloane, N.: The theory of error-correcting codes. North-Holland Amsterdam (1978)

20. Naor, M., Pinkas, B., Sumner, R.: Privacy preserving auctions and mechanism design. In: ACM Conference on Electronic Commerce, pp. 129–139 (1999)

21. Nguyen, K.Q., Traoré, J.: An online public auction protocol protecting bidder privacy. In: Clark, A., Boyd, C., Dawson, E.P. (eds.) ACISP 2000. LNCS, vol. 1841, pp. 427–442. Springer, Heidelberg (2000)

22. Nishide, T., Ohta, K.: Multiparty computation for interval, equality, and comparison without bit-decomposition protocol. In: Okamoto, T., Wang, X. (eds.) PKC 2007. LNCS, vol. 4450, pp. 343–360. Springer, Heidelberg (2007)

23. Nojoumian, M., Stinson, D.R.: Unconditionally secure first-price auction protocols using a multicomponent commitment scheme. In: Soriano, M., Qing, S., López, J. (eds.) ICICS 2010. LNCS, vol. 6476, pp. 266–280. Springer, Heidelberg (2010)

24. Nojoumian, M., Stinson, D.R.: On dealer-free dynamic threshold schemes. Advances in Mathematics of Communications, AMC 7(1), 39–56 (2013)

25. Parkes, D.C., Rabin, M.O., Shieber, S.M., Thorpe, C.: Practical secrecy-preserving, verifiably correct and trustworthy auctions. Electronic Commerce Research and Applications 7(3), 294–312 (2008)

26. Peng, K., Boyd, C., Dawson, E.: Optimization of electronic first-bid sealed-bid auction based on homomorphic secret sharing. In: Dawson, E., Vaudenay, S. (eds.) Mycrypt 2005. LNCS, vol. 3715, pp. 84–98. Springer, Heidelberg (2005)

27. Peng, K., Boyd, C., Dawson, E., Viswanathan, K.: Robust, privacy protecting and publicly verifiable sealed-bid auction. In: Deng, R.H., Qing, S., Bao, F., Zhou, J. (eds.) ICICS 2002. LNCS, vol. 2513, pp. 147–159. Springer, Heidelberg (2002)

28. Peng, K., Boyd, C., Dawson, E., Viswanathan, K.: Five sealed-bid auction models. In: Australasian Information Security Workshop Conference, pp. 77–86. Australian Computer Society (2003)

29. Rabin, T., Ben-Or, M.: Verifiable secret sharing and multiparty protocols with honest majority. In: 21th Annual ACM Symposium on Theory of Computing, STOC, pp. 73–85 (1989)

30. Sako, K.: An auction protocol which hides bids of losers. In: Imai, H., Zheng, Y. (eds.) PKC 2000. LNCS, vol. 1751, pp. 422–432. Springer, Heidelberg (2000)

31. Shamir, A.: How to share a secret. Comm. of the ACM 22(11), 612–613 (1979)

32. Stinson, D.R., Wei, R.: Unconditionally secure proactive secret sharing scheme with combinatorial structures. In: Heys, H.M., Adams, C.M. (eds.) SAC 1999. LNCS, vol. 1758, pp. 200–214. Springer, Heidelberg (2000)

33. Suzuki, K., Yokoo, M.: Secure combinatorial auctions by dynamic programming with polynomial secret sharing. In: Blaze, M. (ed.) FC 2002. LNCS, vol. 2357, pp. 44–56. Springer, Heidelberg (2003)

34. Suzuki, K., Yokoo, M.: Secure multi-attribute procurement auction. In: Song, J.-S., Kwon, T., Yung, M. (eds.) WISA 2005. LNCS, vol. 3786, pp. 306–317. Springer, Heidelberg (2006)

35. Vickrey, W.: Counterspeculation, auctions, and competitive sealed tenders. Journal of Finance 16(1), 8–37 (1961)

36. Viswanathan, K., Boyd, C., Dawson, E.: A three phased schema for sealed bid auction system design. In: Clark, A., Boyd, C., Dawson, E.P. (eds.) ACISP 2000. LNCS, vol. 1841, pp. 412–426. Springer, Heidelberg (2000)

37. Watanabe, Y., Imai, H.: Reducing the round complexity of a sealed-bid auction protocol with an off-line ttp. In: ACM Conference on Computer and Communications Security, CCS, pp. 80–86 (2000)
38. Yao, A.C.-C.: Protocols for secure computations. In: 23rd IEEE Annual Symposium on Foundations of Computer Science, FOCS, pp. 160–164 (1982)
39. Yokoo, M., Suzuki, K.: Secure multi-agent dynamic programming based on homomorphic encryption and its application to combinatorial auctions. In: 1st International Joint Conference on AAMAS, pp. 112–119. ACM (2002)

Information-Theoretical Secure Verifiable Secret Sharing with Vector Space Access Structures over Bilinear Groups

Jie Zhang[1] and Futai Zhang[1,2]

[1] School of Computer Science and Technology, Nanjing Normal University
[2] Jiangsu engineering research center on information security and privacy protection Technology
210097, Nanjing, China

Abstract. Verifiable secret sharing (VSS) is a fundamental tool of threshold cryptography and distributed computing. A number of VSS schemes for sharing a secret that is an element of a finite field, either on threshold access structures or on general access structures have been available. In this paper, we study the verifiably sharing of a random element of a bilinear group on vector space access structures. We propose such two information-theoretical secure schemes: a basic scheme and a modified one with improved efficiency. The basic one is more general for applications while the modified one has a smaller computational cost compared with the basic one. The computational cost as well as the security analysis for the proposed schemes are presented.

Keywords: Secret sharing, Verifiable secret sharing, Information-theoretical secure, Vector space access structure, Bilinear pairing.

1 Introduction

Secret sharing [1] is a method of distributing shares of a secret among a set P of participants in such a way that only qualified subsets of P can reconstruct the secret from their shares. The earliest and most common secret sharing schemes are threshold ones. In a (t, n) threshold secret sharing scheme, the dealer uses a probabilistic polynomial time algorithm to split the secret into n shares and sends them secretly to the n participants (or share-holders) such that using t (the threshold) or more shares can reconstruct the secret, while using less than t shares can not recover or even reveal any information of the secret. In real applications, the traditional threshold secret sharing schemes have some limitations: the first limit is that the dealer should always be honest, and the second is it requires all participants possess exactly the equal position, power and reliability.

To over the first limitation, the concept of Verifiable secret sharing (VSS) [2] was introduced. a VSS scheme is a secret sharing scheme with the special property that every participant is able to verify whether the share distributed to him

X. Huang and J. Zhou (Eds.): ISPEC 2014, LNCS 8434, pp. 318–329, 2014.

by a dealer is correct. Its emergence comes from the reasonable distrust to the dealer. In order to deal with the second limitation, general secret sharing schemes have been studied, which can be used to share a secret on any access structures as needed and do not have to assume the same position of share-holders. By now, a number of VSS schemes for sharing secrets from a finite field, both on threshold access structures[3, 4] and on general access structures[5–9], have been available.

The vector space construction[10, 11], with good algebraic properties, is a method to implement secret sharing schemes for a family of access structures called vector space access structures that includes threshold access structures as a particular case. F.Zhang et al. specially studied VSS for sharing a secret from a finite field on vector space access structures and proposed two schemes: the efficient one in [8] and the information-theoretical secure one in [9]. Recently, the bilinear pairing-based cryptography has received much attention from cryptographic researchers and many bilinear pairing-based schemes and protocols have been proposed[12–16]. In many of the pairing based cryptosystems, the private key of a user is an element (or elements) of a bilinear group. To the secure management of such privates, verifiably sharing of secrets from a bilinear group is needed. However, few VSS schemes for sharing secrets from a bilinear group on vector space access structures can be found in the literature. For the good properties of vector space access structures and the prosperous of pairing based cryptosystems, in this paper we investigate VSS on vector space access structures that shares secrets from bilinear groups. We present a basic VSS scheme with detailed description and particularly analyze its security and computational cost. Then we give a modified one with improved efficiency while enjoy the same level of security with the first one.

Organization:

In Section 2 we briefly describe the concepts of bilinear pairing and access structure and some related mathematical operations. Then in Section 3 we present a basic VSS scheme for sharing a random secret of a bilinear group on vector space access structures with detailed description. We also analyze the security and computational cost of our basic scheme. After that in Section 4 we give a modified VSS scheme with a brief analysis of its security and computational cost. At last we conclude our paper in Section 5.

2   Preliminaries and Definitions

We briefly review the concepts of bilinear pairing and access structure. Then we give two mathematical operations on vector space and bilinear group which will be used in the construction of our VSS schemes.

2.1   Bilinear Pairings

Let G_1 and G_2 be two groups with the same order q, where q is a large prime. Here, we assume that G_1 is an additive cyclic group, and G_2 is a multiplicative cyclic group. A map $\hat{e}: G_1 \times G_1 \longrightarrow G_2$ is called a bilinear pairing (or bilinear map) if it satisfies the following three conditions:

1. Bilinear: For all $P, Q \in G_1$ and $a, b \in Z_q^*$, $\hat{e}(aP, bQ) = \hat{e}(P, Q)^{ab}$.
2. Non-degenerate: There exist $P, Q \in G_1$ such that $\hat{e}(P, Q) \neq 1$.
3. Computable: For all $P, Q \in G_1$, there exists an efficient algorithm to compute $\hat{e}(P, Q)$.

We say that G_1 is a bilinear group if there exists a group G_2 and a bilinear pairing $\hat{e}: G \times G_1 \longrightarrow G_2$ as above, where $\hat{e}$ and the group action in G_1 and G_2 can be computed efficiently.

2.2   Access Structure

A secret sharing scheme involves of a dealer D who holds the secret and a set $H = \{H_1, ..., H_n\}$ of participants (share-holders) who receive shares of a secret from the dealer. An access structure Γ on H specifies a family of qualified subsets of H that are allowed to reconstruct the shared secret using their secret shares. We denote by $\Gamma_0 = \{A_1, ..., A_m\}$ the basis of Γ, that is the set of minimal elements of Γ under inclusion. Here we briefly describe the notion of the most common threshold access structure and the more general vector space one which actually involves the threshold one.

- **Threshold Access Structure:** A (k, n) threshold access structure consists of all those subsets of H containing at least t of the n share-holders.
- **Vector Space Access Structure:** Let the secret space $K = GF(q)$ be a finite field and $L = K^t$ the vector space over K with dimension t. An access structure Γ is said to be a vector space access structure if there exists a function

$$\psi : \{D\} \cup H \to L \tag{1}$$

such that $A \in \Gamma$ if and only if the vector $\psi(D)$ can be expressed as a linear combination of the vectors in the set $\{\psi(P)|P \in A\}$.

The vector space construction is a method to implement secret sharing schemes for vector space access structures that includes threshold access structures as a particular case. Obviously the Shamir's threshold scheme[17] can be seen as a vector space secret sharing scheme by taking $\psi(D) = (1, 0, ..., 0)$ and $\psi(H_i) = (1, x_i, ..., x_i^{t-1})$, where $x_1, x_2..., x_n$ are n distinct, nonzero elements of K[18].

2.3   Notations for Two Mathematical Operations

Let G_1, q be the same as specified in section 2.1. Denote by $K = GF(q)$ the finite field with q elements. Assume $\alpha = (a_1, ..., a_t)$, $\nu = (v_1, ..., v_t)$, $V = (V_1, ..., V_t)$, where $a_1, ..., a_t, v_1, ..., v_t$ are elements of finite field K and $V_1, ..., V_t$ are elements of the additive group G_1. In our construction, we will use the operation of inner product in K^t, and an operation of an element of K^t with an element in G_1^t. They are defined as follows.

- $\alpha \bullet \nu = a_1 v_1 + \cdots + a_t v_t$
- $\alpha \circ V = a_1 V_1 + \cdots + a_t V_t$

Obviously the result of the first operation is an element in K and the second belongs to G_1.

3 Verifiable Secret Sharing on Vector Space Access Structures over Bilinear Groups

In this section, firstly we show a technique of sharing a secret that is a random element of a bilinear group on vector space access structures. Then we present the corresponding information-theoretical secure VSS scheme. After that we demonstrate the correctness and analyze the security and the computational cost of our scheme.

3.1 Secret Sharing on Vector Space Access Structures over Bilinear Groups

Let D be dealer and $H = \{H_1, ..., H_n\}$ a set of n players (share-holders). Suppose Γ is the vector space access structure with basis Γ_0 defined on H. Both the secret space and the share space are G_1 which is an additive bilinear group with order q as specified in section 2.

To share a random secret $S \in G_1$, the dealer D firstly publishes a map ψ: $\{D\} \cup H \to Z_q^t$. Then D randomly chooses a secret vector $V = (V_1, ..., V_t)$ from G_1^t such that $\psi(D) \circ V = a_1 V_1 + \cdots + a_t V_t = S$. Denote by $\alpha = \psi(D) = (a_1, ..., a_t)$, $\alpha_j = \psi(H_j) = (a_{j1}, ..., a_{jt})$. The share distributed to H_j by D is $S_j = \psi(H_j) \circ V = a_{j1} V_1 + \cdots + a_{jt} V_t$.

When a qualified subset $A = \{H_{i1}, ..., H_{il}\}$ of Γ intends to reconstruct the secret, members of A firstly compute χ from $\chi \circ \psi(A) = \psi(D)$, where χ is a vector belongs to Z_q^l and $\psi(A)$ is a matrix with row vectors $\psi(H_{j1}), ..., \psi(H_{jl})$. And then the secret can be calculated from $S = \chi \circ S_A$ with $S_A = (S_{j1}, ..., S_{jl})$, where S_{ji} is the share held by player H_{ji}.

3.2 Verifiable Secret Sharing on Vector Space Access Structures over Bilinear Groups

- **Parameters:**
  Assume G_1, G_2 are two groups with the same order q and $\hat{e} : G_1 \times G_1 \longrightarrow G_2$ is the bilinear map as we refer previously in Section 2. Let P, Q be two different generators of G_1 and nobody knows $\log_P Q$. The elements P, Q can either be chosen by a trusted center when the system is initialized, or by (some of) the participants using a coin-flipping protocol. The secret space and the share space are G_1 and G_1^2 respectively and $G_1^t = \{(W_1, W_2, ..., W_t) : W_i \in G_1, i = 1, 2, ..., t\}$. The access structure Γ is a vector space access structure with basis Γ_0. Assume S is the secret randomly chosen from G_1 to be shared and t is the maximum cardinal number of the minimum qualified subsets.

- **Algorithm of Sharing:**
  - The dealer D publishes map ψ: $\{D\} \cup H \to Z_q^t$. Assume that $\psi(D) = (a_1, ..., a_t) = \alpha$ and $\psi(H_j) = (a_{j1}, ..., a_{jt}) = \alpha_j$.
  - D randomly chooses two secret vectors $V = (V_1, ..., V_t)$ and $B = (B_1, ..., B_t)$ from G_1^t such that $\psi(D) \circ V = a_1 V_1 + \cdots + a_t V_t = S$. Let $R = \psi(D) \circ B = a_1 B_1 + \cdots + a_t B_t$.
  - D computes and broadcasts $E_0 = E(S, R) = \hat{e}(S, P)\hat{e}(R, Q)$ and $E_k = E(V_k, B_k) = \hat{e}(V_k, P)\hat{e}(B_k, Q)$ for $k = 1, ..., t$, which are generally known as commitments of the secret S and the vector V.
  - D computes

$$S_j = \psi(H_j) \circ V = a_{j1} V_1 + \cdots + a_{jt} V_t, \tag{2}$$

$$R_j = \psi(H_j) \circ B = a_{j1} B_1 + \cdots + a_{jt} B_t \tag{3}$$

  and sends (S_j, R_j) secretly to H_j for $j = 1, ..., n$.
- **Algorithm of Verification:**
  When H_j has received his share (S_j, R_j) he checks if

$$E_0 = \prod_{k=1}^{t} E_k{}^{a_k} \tag{4}$$

$$E(S_j, R_j) = \hat{e}(S_j, P)\hat{e}(R_j, Q) = \prod_{k=1}^{t} E_k{}^{a_{jk}} \tag{5}$$

- **Algorithm of Reconstruction:**
  Suppose $A = \{H_{i1}, ..., H_{il}\} \in \Gamma$ is a qualified subset of H. And the players in A cooperate to reconstruct the shared secret. Each player $H_j (j = i1, ..., il)$ broadcasts his secret share (S_j, R_j) to others in A. Every one can verify the validity of shares provided by the others through Eq.(5).
  After receiving all the valid shares of players in A, they firstly computes χ from $\chi \circ \psi(A) = \psi(D)$ where χ is a vector belongs to Z_q^l and $\psi(A)$ is a matrix with row vectors $\psi(H_{j1}), ..., \psi(H_{jl})$. And then the secret can be calculated from $S = \chi \circ S_A$, where $S_A = (S_{j1}, ..., S_{jl})$ and S_{ji} comes from the secret share (S_{ji}, R_{ji}) of the share-holder H_{ji}. Actually, as long as they obtain the shares whose holders are enough to determine a minimum qualified subset of A, the secret can be reconstructed effectively.

3.3   Correctness

In this subsection we show the correctness of the newly proposed VSS scheme from two aspects: correctness of the verification algorithm and correctness of the reconstruction algorithm.

- **Correctness of the Verification Algorithm:**

  Theorem 1. *Verification is successful if and only if the dealer follows the protocol correctly.*

Proof. On one hand, if the dealer D follows the protocol correctly, then we can obtain the following equations:

$$S = \psi(D) \circ V = a_1 V_1 + \cdots + a_t V_t, R = \psi(D) \circ B = a_1 B_1 + \cdots + a_t B_t \quad (6)$$

$$S_j = \psi(H_j) \circ V = a_{j1} V_1 + \cdots + a_{jt} V_t, R_j = \psi(H_j) \circ B = a_{j1} B_1 + \cdots + a_{jt} B_t \quad (7)$$

So we have

$$\begin{aligned}
E_0 &= \hat{e}(S, P)\hat{e}(R, Q) \\
&= \hat{e}(a_1 V_1 + \cdots + a_t V_t, P)\hat{e}(a_1 B_1 + \cdots + a_t B_t, Q) \\
&= (\hat{e}(V_1, P)\hat{e}(B_1, Q))^{a_1} \cdots (\hat{e}(V_t, P)\hat{e}(B_t, Q))^{a_t} \\
&= \prod_{k=1}^{t} (\hat{e}(V_k, P)\hat{e}(B_k, Q))^{a_k} = \prod_{k=1}^{t} E_k{}^{a_k}
\end{aligned}$$

and

$$\begin{aligned}
E(S_j, R_j) &= \hat{e}(S_j, P)\hat{e}(R_j, Q) \\
&= \hat{e}(a_{j1} V_1 + \cdots + a_{jt} V_t, P)\hat{e}(a_{j1} B_1 + \cdots + a_{jt} B_t, Q) \\
&= (\hat{e}(V_1, P)\hat{e}(B_1, Q))^{a_{j1}} \cdots (\hat{e}(V_t, P)\hat{e}(B_t, Q))^{a_{jt}} \\
&= \prod_{k=1}^{t} (\hat{e}(V_k, P)\hat{e}(R_k, Q))^{a_{jk}} = \prod_{k=1}^{t} E_k{}^{a_{jk}}
\end{aligned}$$

On they other hand, if $E_0 = \prod_{k=1}^{t} E_k{}^{a_k}$ and $E(S_j, R_j) = \prod_{k=1}^{t} E_k{}^{a_{jk}}$, then

$$\begin{aligned}
\hat{e}(S, P)\hat{e}(R, Q) &= E(S, R) = \prod_{k=1}^{t} E_k{}^{a_k} \\
&= \prod_{k=1}^{t} (\hat{e}(V_k, P)\hat{e}(B_k, Q))^{a_k} \\
&= \prod_{k=1}^{t} (\hat{e}(V_k, P)^{a_k} \hat{e}(B_k, Q)^{a_k}) \\
&= \prod_{k=1}^{t} \hat{e}(V_k, P)^{a_k} \prod_{k=1}^{t} \hat{e}(B_k, Q)^{a_k} \\
&= \hat{e}(\sum_{k=1}^{t} a_k V_k, P)\hat{e}(\sum_{k=1}^{t} a_k B_k, Q)
\end{aligned}$$

$$\hat{e}(S_j, P)\hat{e}(R_j, Q) = E(S_j, R_j) = \prod_{k=1}^{t} E_k{}^{a_{jk}}$$

$$= \prod_{k=1}^{t} (\hat{e}(V_k, P)\hat{e}(B_k, Q))^{a_{jk}}$$

$$= \prod_{k=1}^{t} (\hat{e}(V_k, P) \prod_{k=1}^{t} \hat{e}(B_k, Q))^{a_j k}$$

$$= \prod_{k=1}^{t} \hat{e}(V_k, P)^{a_{jk}} \prod_{k=1}^{t} \hat{e}(B_k, Q)^{a_{jk}}$$

$$= \hat{e}(\sum_{k=1}^{t} a_{jk} V_k, P)\hat{e}(\sum_{k=1}^{t} a_{jk} B_k, Q)$$

So we have $S = \sum_{k=1}^{t} a_k V_k = \psi(D) \circ V$ and $S_j = \sum_{k=1}^{t} a_{jk} V_k = \psi(H_j) \circ V$ which means that the vector V has been properly chosen and the share S_j sent to H_j is valid.

- **Correctness of the Reconstruction Algorithm:**
  From the distribution algorithm we know that $S = \psi(D) \circ V = \alpha \circ V = a_1 V_1 + \cdots + a_t V_t$ and $S_j = \psi(H_j) \circ V = \alpha_j \circ V = a_{j1} V_1 + \cdots + a_{jt} V_t$ for $j = 1, ..., n$. For a qualified subset $A \in \Gamma$, without loss of generality we assume $A = \{H_1, ..., H_k\}$, the vector $\psi(D)$ can be expressed as a linear combination of the vectors $\psi(H_1), ..., \psi(H_k)$. That is, there must be a vector $\chi = (x_1, ..., x_k) \in Z_q^k$ such that $x_1 \alpha_1 + \cdots + x_k \alpha_k = \alpha$. So we have $a_i = x_1 a_{1i} + \cdots + x_k a_{ki}$ for $i = 1, ..., t$. Hence

$$\begin{aligned} S &= a_1 V_1 + \cdots + a_t V_t \\ &= (x_1 a_{11} + \cdots + x_k a_{k1}) V_1 + \cdots + (x_1 a_{1t} + \cdots + x_k a_{kt}) V_t \\ &= x_1 (a_{11} V_1 + \cdots + a_{1t} V_t) + \cdots + x_k (a_{k1} V_1 + \cdots + a_{kt} V_t) \\ &= x_1 S_1 + \cdots + x_k S_k = \chi \circ (S_1, ..., S_k) = \chi \circ S_A. \end{aligned}$$

3.4   Security Analysis

Consider a static and strong admissible adversary[19], i.e. the adversary has determined which share-holders to corrupt before the protocol being implemented, and can corrupt all but one player in an authorized subset. The only constraint on this adversary is that at least one authorized subset must remain pure i.e. composed of all uncorrupted players. The security of a VSS scheme involves the following three aspects.

- The public information reveals no information about the secret and the shares.
- Adversary cannot calculate the secret from the shares of those corrupted players.
- There must be at lest one qualified subset whose members are all uncorrupted, and adversary can not prevent such a qualified subset from reconstructing the secret.

We analyze our scheme's security including the three aspects above and present the following theorems with proofs.

Theorem 2. *The adversary can not get any information about the secret S and the shares (S_j, R_j) from the open information, i.e. the commitments of the secret S and the vectors V do not reveal any information about the secret and the shares.*

Proof. The public commitments are $E_0 = E(S, R) = \hat{e}(S, P)\hat{e}(R, Q)$ and $E_k = E(V_k, B_k) = \hat{e}(V_k, P)\hat{e}(B_k, Q)$ for $k = 1, ..., t$. As R is randomly chosen from G_1 and B is a random vector in G_1^t, $\hat{e}(R, Q)$ and $\hat{e}(B_k, Q)$ are uniformly distributed in G_2. Consequently, $E_0 = \hat{e}(S, P)\hat{e}(R, Q)$ and $E_k = \hat{e}(V_k, P)\hat{e}(B_k, Q)$ are uniformly distributed in G_2. This means that the public commitment E_0 reveals no information about S and those commitments E_k do not reveal any information about V_k, B_k and thus reveals no information about V, B.

According to the distribution algorithm, for each $j = 1, ..., n$, the share (S_j, R_j) of H_j is calculated from $S_j = \psi(H_j) \circ V$ and $R_j = \psi(H_j) \circ B$. As the public commitments reveal no information about V and B, the adversary can not acquire any information about (S_j, R_j) from the public commitments either.

Theorem 3. *With the shares of those corrupted participants, the static and strong admissible adversary can derive no information about the share kept by any honest one and consequently the secret S.*

Proof. We learn that the adversary can not get any information about the secret vectors V and B from Theorem 2. Nevertheless according to the distribution algorithm, to acquire the shares of honest players, the adversary has no choice but compute V and B merely using the shares of corrupted ones. Suppose that the corrupted players are $H_1, ..., H_k$. The adversary has to compute V from the following set of equations:

$$\begin{cases} \psi(H_1) \circ V = \alpha_1 \circ V = a_{11}V_1 + a_{12}V_2 + \cdots + a_{1t}V_t = S_1 \\ \psi(H_2) \circ V = \alpha_2 \circ V = a_{21}V_1 + a_{22}V_2 + \cdots + a_{2t}V_t = S_2 \\ \qquad\qquad\qquad\qquad \vdots \\ \psi(H_k) \circ V = \alpha_k \circ V = a_{k1}V_1 + a_{k2}V_2 + \cdots + a_{kt}V_t = S_k \end{cases} \tag{8}$$

i.e.

$$\begin{bmatrix} a_{11} & a_{12} & \cdots & a_{1t} \\ a_{21} & a_{22} & \cdots & a_{2t} \\ \vdots & & & \vdots \\ a_{k1} & a_{k2} & \cdots & a_{kt} \end{bmatrix} \begin{bmatrix} V_1 \\ V_2 \\ \vdots \\ V_t \end{bmatrix} = \begin{bmatrix} S_1 \\ S_2 \\ \vdots \\ S_k \end{bmatrix} \tag{9}$$

Since $\{H_1, ..., H_k\} \notin \Gamma$, the vector collection $\{\psi(H_1), ..., \psi(H_k)\}$ can not linearly express $\psi(D)$, i.e. there does not exist any vector $(x_1, ..., x_k)$ such that

$$(x_1, \cdots, x_k) \begin{bmatrix} \psi(H_1) \\ \psi(H_2) \\ \vdots \\ \psi(H_k) \end{bmatrix} = (a_1, \cdots, a_t) \tag{10}$$

Thus the rank of vector collection $\{\psi(H_1), \cdots, \psi(H_k)\}$ must be no more than k, which means that Eq.(8) has at least q answers and the probability for the adversary to dope out the genuine V is not more than $\frac{1}{q}$. Accordingly the probability to calculate the correct share of any uncorrupted player is not more than $\frac{1}{q}$. As q is a large primer, this probability can be ignored.

Theorem 4. *The adversary can not prevent uncorrupted players from reconstructing the secret*

Proof. From the definition of the adversary we know that there is at least one qualified subset must remain pure, i.e. all its members are uncorrupted. The distribution and reconstruction algorithms imply that the adversary cannot prevent such a qualified subsect from recovering the secret.

3.5 Computational Cost

We just count those time-consuming operations in distribution phase, verification phase and reconstruction phase. Let $\mathcal{P}$, $\mathcal{S}$ and $\mathcal{E}$ denote the operation of bilinear pairing from G_1 to G_2, scalar multiplication in G_1 and exponentiation in G_2 respectively. Assume there are t participants and the cost of verification is not included in the reconstruction phase. The result is list in the following table.

	$\mathcal{P}$	$\mathcal{S}$	$\mathcal{E}$
distribution phase	$2t + 2$	$2t + 2nt$	0
verification phase	$2n$	0	$nt + t$
reconstruction phase	0	t	0

Our reconstruction algorithm requires no pairing operations and no exponentiations in G_2, so it is very efficient.

4   A Modified Scheme with Improved Efficiency

In this section we propose a modified scheme with higher efficiency. The only constraint on the modified scheme is that the dealer knows the discrete logarithm of the secret, i.e. the secret can be generated by the dealer as his wish. We just describe the procedure of the new scheme and analyze its efficiency comparing with the former one. The correctness and security are similar as what we have described for the basic scheme thus we omit them here.

4.1 Description of the Scheme

- **Parameters:** Let D be the dealer, $H = \{H_1, ..., H_n\}$ the set of share-holders. The common parameters $(G_1, G_2, \hat{e}, P, Q, q)$, and the access structure Γ are defined the same as in the former scheme. The only difference is that before distribution, D firstly chooses a random $s \in Z_q$ and set $S = sP$ as the secret to be shared.

- **Algorithm of Sharing:**
  - D publishes map $\psi: \{D\} \cup H \to Z_q^t$. Assume that $\psi(D) = (a_1, ..., a_t) = \alpha$ and $\psi(H_j) = (a_{j1}, ..., a_{jt}) = \alpha_j$.
  - D randomly chooses two secret vectors $\nu = (v_1, ..., v_t)$ and $\beta = (b_1, ..., b_t)$ from Z_q^t such that $\psi(D) \bullet \nu = a_1 v_1 + \cdots + a_t v_t = s$. Set $r = \psi(D) \bullet \beta = a_1 b_1 + \cdots + a_t b_t$.
  - Compute and broadcast $E_0 = \hat{e}(P, P)^s \hat{e}(P, Q)^r$ and $E_k = \hat{e}(P, P)^{v_k} \hat{e}(P, Q)^{b_k}$ for $k = 1, ..., t$.
  - D computes

$$S_j = (\psi(H_j) \bullet \nu)P = (a_{j1}v_1 + \cdots + a_{jt}v_t)P, \qquad (11)$$

$$R_j = (\psi(H_j) \bullet \beta)P = (a_{j1}b_1 + \cdots + a_{jt}b_t)P \qquad (12)$$

  and sends (S_j, R_j) secretly to H_j for $j = 1, ..., n$.

- **Algorithm of Verification:**
  When H_j has received his share (S_j, R_j) he checks if

$$E_0 = \prod_{k=1}^{t} E_k^{a_k} \qquad (13)$$

$$E(S_j, R_j) = \hat{e}(S_j, P)\hat{e}(R_j, Q) = \prod_{k=1}^{t} E_k^{a_{jk}} \qquad (14)$$

- **Algorithm of Reconstruction:**
  Let $A = \{H_{i1}, ..., H_{il}\} \in \Gamma$ be a qualified subset of H to reconstruct the shared secret. Each player $H_j (j = i1, ..., il)$ broadcasts his secret share (S_j, R_j) to others in A. Every one can verify the validity of shares provided by others through Eq.(14).

  After receiving all the valid shares of a qualified subset, they firstly computes χ from $\chi\psi(A) = \psi(D)$ where χ is a vector belongs to Z_q^l and $\psi(A)$ is a matrix with row vectors $\psi(H_{j1}), ..., \psi(H_{jl})$. And then the secret can be calculated from $S = \chi \circ S_A$ with $S_A = (S_{j1}, ..., S_{jl})$. Actually as long as they obtain the shares whose holders are enough to determine a minimum qualified subset of A, the secret can be reconstructed effectively.

4.2 Computational Cost

To compare the computational cost of the modified scheme with the former one, we count those time-consuming operations in different phases and list them in the following table. The notation is defined the same as in Section 4.

	scheme in Section 3	scheme in Section 4
distribution phase	$(2t + 2)\mathcal{P} + (2nt + t)\mathcal{S}$	$2\mathcal{P} + 2n\mathcal{S} + (2t + 2)\mathcal{E}$
verification phase	$2n\mathcal{P} + (nt + t)\mathcal{E}$	$2n\mathcal{P} + (nt + t)\mathcal{E}$
reconstruction phase	$t\mathcal{S}$	$t\mathcal{S}$

Although exponentiation in G_2 increases in the modified scheme, bilinear pairing and scalar multiplication in G_1 are reduced. As computing bilinear pairings is the most time-consuming operation, it is reasonable to say that the modified scheme has a smaller computational cost.

5   Conclusion

General VSS is widely used in cryptography and the pairing-based cryptography is a very active research field recent years. In this paper, we have investigated the VSS on vector space access structures over bilinear groups. We have presented two unconditionally secure VSS schemes on vector space access structures for sharing secrets in a bilinear group which may be private keys of some pairing based cryptosystems. In addition to analyze the the correctness and computational cost of the proposed schemes, we also present security proofs to show the information-theoretic security of the basic scheme. Our newly proposed schemes are efficient and may have practical applications in multiparty computations involving bilinear pairings, safeguarding the private keys of some pairing based cryptosystems.

Acknowledgments. This work is supported by National Natural Science Foundation of China (No.61170298), Natural Science Fund for Colleges and Universities in Jiangsu Province (No. 12KJD520007), NSF of Jiangsu Province of China (No. BK20130908).

References

1. Shamir, A.: How to share a secret. Comm. ACM 22, 612–613 (1979)
2. Chor, B., Goldwasser, S., Micall, S., Awerbuch, B.: Verifiable secret sharing and achieving simultaneity in the presence of faults, FOCS (1985)
3. Feldman, P.: A practical scheme for non-interactive verifiable secret sharing. In: The 28th IEEE Symposium on the Foundations of Computer Science, pp. 427–437 (1987)
4. Pedersen, T.P.: Non-interactive and information-theoretic secure verifiable secret sharing. In: Feigenbaum, J. (ed.) CRYPTO 1991. LNCS, vol. 576, pp. 129–140. Springer, Heidelberg (1992)
5. Zhang, F., Wang, Y.: Construction of secret sharing schemes on access structure with transfer property. Acta Electronica Sinica 29, 1582–1584 (2001)
6. Zhang, F., Wang, Y.: An unconditional secure general verifiable secret sharing protocol. Jouranl of Computer Research and Development 39, 1199–1204 (2002)
7. Zhang, F., Zhang, F., Wang, Y.: A secure and efficient general VSS protocol. Journal of Software 13, 1187–1192 (2002)

8. Zhang, F., Gou, X., Wang, Y.: Efficient verifiable secret sharing on vector space access structures. Computer Engineering and Applications (2002)
9. Zhang, F., Shi, J., Wang, Y.: Information-theoretical secure verifiable secret sharing on vector space access structures. Journal of Electronics and Information Technology (8), 1288–1293 (2004)
10. Brickell, E.F.: Some ideal secret sharing schemes. J. Combin. Math. and Combin. Comput. 9, 105–113 (1989)
11. Padro, C., Sáez, G., Villar, J.L.: Detection of cheaters in vector space secret sharing schemes. Designs, Codes and cryptography (1999)
12. Baek, J., Zheng, Y.: Identity-based threshold signature scheme from the bilinear pairings. In: Proceedings of the international Conference on Information and Technology: Coding and Computing (2004)
13. Wu, T.Y., Tseng, Y.M.: A paring-based publicly verifiable secret sharing scheme. Journal of Systems Science and Complexity (2011)
14. Kiltz, E., Pietrzak, K.: Leakage resilient elGamal encryption. In: Abe, M. (ed.) ASIACRYPT 2010. LNCS, vol. 6477, pp. 595–612. Springer, Heidelberg (2010)
15. Boneh, D., Franklin, M.: Identity-based encryption from the weil pairing. SIAM J. Computing 32(3), 586–615 (2003)
16. Gentry, C.: Practical identity-based encryption without random oracles. In: Vaudenay, S. (ed.) EUROCRYPT 2006. LNCS, vol. 4004, pp. 445–464. Springer, Heidelberg (2006)
17. Shamir, A.: How to share a secret. Comm. ACM 22, 612–613 (1979)
18. Stinson, D.R.: An explication of secret sharing schemes. Designs, Codes and Cryptography 2, 357–390 (1992)
19. Gennaro, R.: Theory and practice of verifiable secret sharing. [Ph.D.Thesis]. MIT, pp. 51–107 (1996)

Proofs of Retrievability Based on MRD Codes*

Shuai Han[1], Shengli Liu[1], Kefei Chen[2], and Dawu Gu[1]

[1] Department of Computer Science and Engineering, Shanghai Jiao Tong University,
Shanghai 200240, China
[2] School of Science, Hangzhou Normal University, Hangzhou 310036, China
{dalen17,slliu,kfchen,dwgu}@sjtu.edu.cn

Abstract. Proofs of Data Possession (PoDP) scheme is essential to data outsourcing. It provides an efficient audit to convince a client that his/her file is available at the storage server, ready for retrieval when needed. An updated version of PoDP is Proofs of Retrievability (PoR), which proves the client's file can be recovered by interactions with the storage server. We propose a PoR scheme based on Maximum Rank Distance (MRD) codes. The client file is encoded block-wise to generate homomorphic tags with help of an MRD code. In an audit, the storage provider is able to aggregate the blocks and tags into one block and one tag, due to the homomorphic property of tags. The algebraic structure of MRD codewords enables the aggregation to be operated over a binary field, which simplifies the computation of storage provider to be the most efficient XOR operation. With properties of MRD codes, we also prove an important security notion, namely *soundness* of PoR.

Keywords: Proofs of retrievability, MRD codes, data integrity, cloud storage.

1 Introduction

Data outsourcing to cloud storage reduces the storage cost and makes the data maintenance easier at both personal and business level. When clients move their data to a service provider for storage, they can enjoy the convenience of out-sourcing storage with a relative low fee. However, they may also worry about the security of their data, as their data is out of their hands, and can be manipulated by the untrustworthy storage provider.

An efficient way is that a client performs an audit of the storage provider. A successful audit verifies that the provider stores the data, without the retrieval and transfer of all the data from the provider to the client. The ability of a storage system to generate proofs of possession of client's data, without having to retrieve the whole file, is called *Proofs of Data Possession*(PoDP). PoDP only

---

* Corresponding Author: Shengli Liu. Funded by NSFC Nos.61170229, 61133014, 61373153, Innovation Project (No.12ZZ021) of Shanghai Municipal Education Commission, and Specialized Research Fund (No.20110073110016) for the Doctoral Program of Higher Education, Major State Basic Research Development Program (973 Plan)(No.2013CB338004).

X. Huang and J. Zhou (Eds.): ISPEC 2014, LNCS 8434, pp. 330–345, 2014.

concerns the provider's proof of data possession. An improved version of PoDP is known as *Proof of Retrievability* (PoR), which enables the provider to convince the client that the original data could be recovered through enough interactions between the client and provider.

Related Works. It was Juels and Kaliski [8] (2007) who first formulated the concept of Proof of Retrievability and defined the corresponding security model. Dodis, Vadhan and Wichs [6] (2009) presented Proof of Retrievability Codes (PoR codes) for PoR schemes. More constructions of PoR schemes are given by Ateniese et al. [5] (2007), Shacham and Waters [11] (2008), or Schwarz and Miller [10] (2006). Oggier and Fathi [14] (2011) proposed an unconditionally secure authentication scheme that deals with multiple receivers.

Among all the PoDP/PoR schemes, the most charming ones are those with homomorphic authenticators. These schemes were identified as *homomorphic linear authenticator schemes* in [6]. Ateniese et al. [5] (2007) proposed constructions of PoDP scheme with homomorphic verifiable authenticator based on the RSA assumption. The PoDP security model was further extended to be against arbitrary adaptive PPT adversaries by Shacham and Waters [11](2008), who presented PoR schemes (called the SW scheme), and their security was given in the full security model. The file of a client is divided into blocks, and an authenticator (tag) is computed for each block. In the audit, the client samples blocks/authenticators (tags). The authenticator (tag) helps the owner of the file to check the integrity of the block with an authentication key. Because of the homomorphic property, multiple file blocks resp. authenticators can be combined into a single aggregated block/authenticator pair. And the verification is simplified to integrity check of the aggregated block. Therefore, both the computational complexity and communication complexity of an audit are greatly reduced, due to the homomorphic property of authenticators.

Our Contributions. In this paper, we proposed a PoR scheme based on MRD codes.

The linearity of the MRD code results in homomorphic authenticators (tag), just like the scheme by Shacham and Waters (the SW scheme). However, our proposal has different features from the SW scheme.

- **Efficient Computation by the Service Provider.** The MRD encoding plants algebraic structure in blocks so that the generation of tags and aggregation of messages and tags can be computed over a small field $\mathbb{F}_q$. As to the instantiation of $\mathbb{F}_2$, the challenge vector can be taken as a random binary sequence of length w, where w is the number of blocks of a storage file, and the computation of the storage server for the response is simply XOR. This is the most efficient operation for the storage server. For comparison, the SW scheme is based on a large prime field $\mathbb{F}_p$ with p at least 80 bits. To reduce the communication band and the computational overhead of the storage provider, the SW scheme suggests that only l $(l \leq w)$ random locations in the challenge vector are chosen to take values from a small set

$B \subseteq \mathbb{F}_p$. If $B = \{1\}$, the computation for the response is reduced to addition over the prime field $\mathbb{F}_p$. Unfortunately, $B = \{1\}$ is vulnerable to an attack, hence compromising the security of the SW scheme, as shown in [11]. Therefore, it is inevitable for the storage provider to use multiplications over $\mathbb{F}_p$ to prepare the aggregated response in the SW scheme.

- **Mild Amount of Pre-computation by the Client.** The MRD encoding is applied block-wise. If we take a file as a matrix, then each row, as a block, is encoded into an MRD codeword. The file encoding involves w MRD encoding, so the encoding computational complexity is of $O(w)$ in terms of MRD encoding. When parameters of the MRD code are fixed, the MRD encoding consumes a constant amount of computation. While in the SW scheme, each column of the file is encoded into an Erasure Correction Codeword, and such an encoding needs at least $O(w^2)$ multiplications over the prime field $\mathbb{F}_p$. This imposes a great computational burden for the client to encode the file.

- **Our Proposal Considers PoR with the Security Notion ϵ-Soundness, Which Justify the Sufficiency of the Audit Strategy.** We define the security notion served for the sufficiency of the audit strategy, namely ϵ-soundness. ϵ-soundness considers the proof of retrievability, which suggests that if the provider answers challenges with consistent responses with probability at least ϵ, it is possible for an extractor to retrieve the original file. The security proof strongly relies on the property of MRD codewords. The algebraic property of MRD codewords makes an adversary impossible to forge a response, which passes client's verification but is not computed as it is supposed to be. This helps to prove the ϵ-soundness of the scheme and justify the rationality of the audit strategy.

Performance Comparison.   Below gives a comparison among the SW[11] and our schemes. For a 1GB file, the block size is 1KB(the SW scheme [11]), 4KB(as suggested in Section 5, our proposal). The block number is $w = 2^{20}$, 2^{18} respectively.

Suppose the multiplication in $\mathbb{F}_p$ has computational complexity $O((\log p)^2)$ and exponentiation in $\mathbb{F}_p$ has computational complexity $O((\log p)^3)$ in terms of bit-XOR. The SW scheme takes a 80-bit p for $\mathbb{F}_p$. Our proposal takes a binary field as suggested in Section 5.

With the same sampling strategy as our scheme, namely, each block is sampled with probability $1/2$, we show the computation complexity and communication complexity of the two schemes in Table 1. The table includes precomputation, computation of the client in one interaction, computation of the server in one interaction, length of challenge in one interaction, and length of response in one interaction. Length of response of our scheme is larger than that of the SW scheme, but it is still affordable. A response in one interaction is an aggregated block/tag pair, thus length of response is mainly determined by the block size.

Table 1. Computational and Communication Complexity of the SW and Our Schemes

Scheme	Precomput. (bit-XOR)	Client Comput. (bit-XOR)	Server Comput. (bit-XOR)	Length of Challenge (KB)	Length of Response (KB)
SW	$O(2^{59})$	$O(2^{31})$	$O(2^{38})$	$O(2^{10})$	≈ 1
Ours	$O(2^{49})$	$O(2^{31})$	$O(2^{33})$	2^5	≈ 8

2 PoR Scheme: Definition and Security Model

2.1 Notations and Assumptions

We use the following notations throughout the paper. Let λ denote the security parameter, which is an integer tending to infinity. The current security standard requires that $\lambda \geq 80$.

Let $\mathbb{F}_q$ be a finite field with q elements, i.e., $GF(q)$. Let k denote a column vector of dimension t over $\mathbb{F}_q$, or an element in $\mathbb{F}_{q^t}$, and k^T denote transpose of the vector k. The notation $(C_1, \cdots, C_n)^\mathsf{T}$ represents $\begin{pmatrix} C_1 \\ \vdots \\ C_n \end{pmatrix}$ instead of $\begin{pmatrix} C_1^T \\ \vdots \\ C_n^T \end{pmatrix}$,

where $C_1, \cdots, C_n$ are matrices. Let "$\circ$" denote scalar multiplication over $\mathbb{F}_q$. For example, $\mathsf{k} = \left(k^{(1)}, k^{(2)}, \cdots, k^{(n)} \right)^T \in (\mathbb{F}_q)^n$ and $v \in \mathbb{F}_q$, then $v \circ \mathsf{k} = \left(v \cdot k^{(1)}, v \cdot k^{(2)}, \cdots, v \cdot k^{(n)} \right)^T$, where $\cdot$ is the multiplication over $\mathbb{F}_q$. Let a denote a row vector of column vectors, i.e., $\mathsf{a} = (\mathsf{a}_1, \mathsf{a}_2, \ldots, \mathsf{a}_n)$, where a_i is a column vector over $\mathbb{F}_q$. It can also be regarded as a matrix over $\mathbb{F}_q$. Then $v \circ \mathsf{a} = (v \circ \mathsf{a}_1, v \circ \mathsf{a}_2, \cdots, v \circ \mathsf{a}_n)$.

Let $A\|B$ denote the concatenation of A and B. Let $|S|$ denote the cardinality of set S, and $|s|$ denote the bit length of string s. The notation $s \leftarrow S$ indicates that s is chosen uniformly at random from set S. The notation $a \leftarrow \mathsf{Alg}(x)$ means that run the algorithm Alg with input x and obtain a as an output, which is distributed according to the internal randomness of the algorithm.

A function $f(\lambda)$ is *negligible* if for every $c > 0$ there exists a λ_c such that $f(\lambda) < 1/\lambda^c$ for all $\lambda > \lambda_c$. If the running time of probabilistic algorithm Alg is polynomial in λ, then Alg is a probabilistic polynomial time (PPT) algorithm.

Pseudo-Random Functions. Let l_1 and l_2 be two positive integers, which are polynomially bounded functions in security parameter λ. Let $\mathsf{PRF} = \{F_s\}_{s \in S}$ be a family of functions indexed by s, and $F_s : \{0,1\}^{l_1} \to \{0,1\}^{l_2}$. Function $F_s(\cdot)$ can also be represented by $F(s, \cdot)$. Let Γ_{l_1, l_2} be the set of all functions from $\{0,1\}^{l_1}$ to $\{0,1\}^{l_2}$.

Definition 1. *[9] Given an adversary $\mathcal{A}$ which has oracle access to a function in Γ_{l_1, l_2}, suppose that $\mathcal{A}$ always outputs a bit. The advantage of $\mathcal{A}$ over PRF is* *defined as*

$$Adv_{PRF}^{A}(1^{\lambda}) = \left| Pr\left[\mathcal{A}^{F_s}(1^{\lambda}) = 1 \mid s \leftarrow S\right] - Pr\left[\mathcal{A}^{f}(1^{\lambda}) = 1 \mid f \leftarrow \varGamma_{l_1,l_2}\right] \right|.$$

Define the advantage of PRF as $Adv_{PRF}(\lambda) = \max\limits_{PPT\mathcal{A}} Adv_{PRF}^{A}(1^{\lambda})$. *PRF is called pseudo-random if* $Adv_{PRF}(\lambda)$ *is negligible.*

Obviously, the output of a pseudo-random function is a pseudo-random sequence, which is indistinguishable from a real random sequence to any PPT adversary.

2.2 PoR Scheme

A PoR scheme consists of seven PPT algorithms KeyGen, Encode, Decode, Challenge, Response, Verification and an audit algorithm Audit, where the algorithms Challenge, Response and Verification constitute an interaction protocol. A PoR system associates a data storage service provider($\mathcal{P}$) with clients($\mathcal{V}$). The algorithms in a PoR scheme work as follows.

Key Generation: $(sk, pp) \leftarrow$ **KeyGen**(1^{λ}). Each client $\mathcal{V}$ calls $(sk, pp) \leftarrow$ KeyGen(1^{λ}) to get his own private key sk and a public parameter pp. $\mathcal{V}$ keeps the private key sk secret and stores (sk, pp) locally.

Storage Encoding: $M^* \leftarrow$ **Encode**(sk, pp, M). When a client $\mathcal{V}$ prepares a file M for outsourced storage, he/she will call $M^* \leftarrow$ Encode(sk, pp, M) to encode M to M^*. The client $\mathcal{V}$ submits M^* to the storage provider.

Storage Recovery: $\{M, \perp\} \leftarrow$ **Decode**(sk, pp, M^*). When a client $\mathcal{V}$ gets back the out-sourced file M^*, he/she will call $\{M, \perp\} \leftarrow$ Decode(sk, pp, M^*) to recover the original file M or $\perp$ indicating that M^* is too corrupted to recover M.

Storage. The storage provider $\mathcal{P}$ stores M^* submitted by the client $\mathcal{V}$.

Audit: $\beta \leftarrow$ **Audit** $(u, $**Interaction**$(\mathcal{P}(M^*, pp) \leftrightarrows \mathcal{V}(sk, pp)))$. A client $\mathcal{V}$ can run the interactive protocol Interaction$(\mathcal{P}(M^*, pp) \leftrightarrows \mathcal{V}(sk, pp))$ with the storage provider $\mathcal{P}$ for u times, which is polynomial in λ. The storage provider $\mathcal{P}$ possesses M^* and the client $\mathcal{V}$ keeps secret key sk. The protocol consists of the following three algorithms.

Interaction $(\mathcal{P}(M^*, pp) \leftrightarrows \mathcal{V}(sk, pp))$

(1) $ch \leftarrow$ **Challenge**(1^{λ}): This is a PPT algorithm run by the verifier $\mathcal{V}$. On input the security parameter λ, it outputs a challenge ch.

(2) $re \leftarrow$ **Response**(pp, M^*, ch): This is a deterministic algorithm run by the prover $\mathcal{P}$. On input the public parameter pp, the encoded file M^* and the challenge ch, the algorithm returns a corresponding response re.

(3) $b \leftarrow$ **Verification**(pp, sk, ch, re): This is a deterministic algorithm run by the verifier $\mathcal{V}$. On input the public parameter pp, the secret key sk, the challenge/response pair (ch, re), the algorithm returns a bit $b \in \{0, 1\}$, indicating acceptance with 1 or rejection with 0.

If $b = 0$, the interaction protocol outputs $\perp$; otherwise the protocol outputs (ch, re), and we call (ch, re) a *consistent* pair and the execution of the protocol *successful*.

After u executions of the interaction protocol in the audit, the client will output a bit β according to some audit strategy. If $\beta = 1$, the audit succeeds and the client will be convinced that the storage provider is still storing the file M^*. If $\beta = 0$, the audit fails, and the client will consider that his/her file M^* has been corrupted or lost.

Correctness of a PoR scheme requires that for all (sk, pp, M^*) such that $(sk, pp) \leftarrow \mathsf{KeyGen}(1^\lambda)$ and $M^* \leftarrow \mathsf{Encode}(sk, pp, M)$, the following two statements hold with probability 1.

- The original file M is always recovered from the correctly encoded file M^*, i.e., $M = \mathsf{Decode}(sk, pp, M^*)$ if $M^* \leftarrow \mathsf{Encode}(sk, pp, M)$.
- For honest $\mathcal{P}$ and $\mathcal{V}$, algorithm $\mathsf{Verification}(pp, sk, ch, re)$ always outputs 1 in the interaction protocol, hence the interaction protocol outputs a challenge/response, i.e, $(ch, re) \leftarrow \mathsf{Interaction}(\mathcal{P}(M^*, pp) \leftrightarrows \mathcal{V}(sk, pp))$.

Security of a PoR scheme is characterized by the following security notion.

Soundness for PoR. Each successful execution of $\mathsf{Interaction}$ protocol brings some confidence to the client that his/her file is still stored by the storage provider. Successful executions of $\mathsf{Interaction}$ protocol provide consistent challenge/response (ch_i, re_i) pairs and each pair may provide some information about the original M. The soundness of the PoR scheme suggests that the original file M can be extracted from those consistent challenge/response (ch_i, re_i) pairs collected from successful interactions as long as the number (polynomial in λ) of executions of $\mathsf{Interaction}$ protocol is big enough.

2.3   Soundness of PoR Scheme

Even a truthful storage provider may malfunction in an audit, due to temporary system failure, and that does not imply that the provider does not possess the audited data. To be more robust, it is desirable that the PoR system supports an ϵ-admissible storage prover, where the storage prover convincingly answers an ϵ fraction of the challenges in an audit. We want to prove that it is still possible to distill the original file M, as long as ϵ is larger than some threshold and the number of executions of $\mathsf{Interaction}$ protocol in the audit is big enough. This can be characterized by the *soundness of Proof of Retrievability (PoR)*.

A (cheating) prover $\tilde{\mathcal{P}}_\epsilon$ is ϵ-*admissible*, if it convincingly answers a challenge with probability at least ϵ, i.e.,

$$\Pr\left[\mathsf{Verification}(pp, sk, ch, re') = 1 \;\middle|\; ch \leftarrow \mathsf{Challenge}(1^\lambda), re' \leftarrow \tilde{\mathcal{P}}_\epsilon(pp, ch)\right] \geq \epsilon.$$

The PoR system is ϵ-sound if there exists a PPT algorithm $\mathsf{Extractor}$, which recovers M on input the public parameter pp, the secret key sk and the output of the interactive protocol $\mathsf{Interaction}(\tilde{\mathcal{P}}_\epsilon(pp, \cdot) \leftrightarrows \mathcal{V}(sk, pp))$, i.e.,

$$\mathsf{Extractor}\big(pp, sk, \mathsf{Interaction}(\tilde{\mathcal{P}}_\epsilon(pp, \cdot) \leftrightarrows \mathcal{V}(sk, pp))\big) = M,$$

with overwhelming probability.

The formal definition of soundness of PoR scheme has been presented in [6], [11]. Here we give a refined description.

Given a PoR scheme (KeyGen, Encode, Decode, Challenge, Response, Verification, Audit), we define the following soundness game $\mathsf{Sound}_{\mathcal{A}}^{PoR}(\lambda)$ between an adversary $\mathcal{A}$ and a challenger $\mathcal{V}$. $\mathcal{A}$ is going to create an adversarial prover $\tilde{\mathcal{P}}_\epsilon$, and a PPT Extractor aims to extract the original file from interactions with $\tilde{\mathcal{P}}_\epsilon$.

$\mathsf{Sound}_{\mathcal{A}}^{PoR}(\lambda)$

1. The challenger $\mathcal{V}$ obtains a secret key and a public parameter by $(sk, pp) \leftarrow \mathsf{KeyGen}(1^\lambda)$, and sends pp to the adversary $\mathcal{A}$.
2. $\mathcal{A}$ chooses a message M from the message space $\mathcal{M}$, and sends M to $\mathcal{V}$.
3. $\mathcal{V}$ encodes M to M^* with $M^* \leftarrow \mathsf{Encode}(sk, pp, M)$, and sends M^* to $\mathcal{A}$.
4. Test stage. The adversary $\mathcal{A}$ gets protocol access to $\mathcal{V}(sk, pp)$ and can interact with $\mathcal{V}$ for a polynomial times. Then the adversary $\mathcal{A}$ outputs an ϵ-admissible prover $\tilde{\mathcal{P}}_\epsilon$. This ϵ-admissible prover $\tilde{\mathcal{P}}_\epsilon$ functions as an oracle, which will output a consistent re for a proper query (challenge) ch with probability at least ϵ.
5. A PPT Extractor is given the public parameter pp, the secret key sk and oracle access to the ϵ-admissible prover $\tilde{\mathcal{P}}_\epsilon$. After querying $\tilde{\mathcal{P}}_\epsilon$ for a polynomial times, the Extractor outputs a file M'.

Definition 2. *[6] A PoR scheme (KeyGen, Encode, Decode, Challenge, Response, Verification, Audit) is ϵ-sound, if there exists a PPT Extractor, such that for any PPT adversary $\mathcal{A}$ which outputs an ϵ-admissible $\tilde{\mathcal{P}}_\epsilon$ through interacting with $\mathcal{V}$ in the above game $\mathsf{Sound}_{\mathcal{A}}^{PoR}(\lambda)$, Extractor is able to recover the original file M by querying $\tilde{\mathcal{P}}_\epsilon$ except with negligible probability. In formula,*

$$\Pr\left[M' \neq M \,\middle|\, \begin{array}{l} (sk, pp) \leftarrow \mathsf{KeyGen}(1^\lambda), M \leftarrow \mathcal{A}(pp), \\ M^* \leftarrow \mathsf{Encode}(sk, pp, M), \\ \tilde{\mathcal{P}}_\epsilon \leftarrow \mathcal{A}(pp, M, M^*, access\ to\ \mathcal{V}(sk, pp)), \\ M' \leftarrow \mathsf{Extractor}(pp, sk, \tilde{\mathcal{P}}_\epsilon) \end{array}\right]$$

is negligible.

3 Maximum Rank Distance Codes and Gabidulin Codes

Rank distance was first considered for error-correcting codes by Delsarte [4], and lots of work has been devoted to rank distance properties, code construction, and efficient decoding. In [4], [3], [2], a Singleton bound on the minimum rank distance of codes was established, and a class of codes achieving the bound with equality was constructed, e.g. MRD codes. Gabidulin codes is one of MRD codes, which can be considered as the rank metric analogues of Reed-Solomon codes.

3.1   Rank Distance Codes

Let $\mathbb{F}_q$ be a finite field, and $\mathbb{F}_{q^t}$ be an extended field of degree t. Let $(\mathbb{F}_{q^t})^n$ be the n-dimensional vector space over $\mathbb{F}_{q^t}$. Given a vector $\mathbf{a} = (\mathsf{a}_1, \mathsf{a}_2, \ldots, \mathsf{a}_n) \in (\mathbb{F}_{q^t})^n$, each entry $\mathsf{a}_i \in \mathbb{F}_{q^t}$ can be expressed as a t-dimensional column vector over $\mathbb{F}_q$, i.e., $\mathsf{a}_i = \left(a_i^{(1)}, a_i^{(2)}, \cdots, a_i^{(t)}\right)^T$. Consequently, vector $\mathbf{a}$ can be expressed as a $t \times n$ matrix over $\mathbb{F}_q$ by expanding all the entries of $\mathbf{a}$.

Definition 3. *[1] A rank distance code $\mathcal{C}_R$ over finite field $\mathbb{F}_{q^t}$ is a subspace of $(\mathbb{F}_{q^t})^n$, satisfying the following properties.*

(a) *For each codeword $c \in \mathcal{C}_R$, the rank weight (over $\mathbb{F}_q$) of c, denoted as $rank(c|\mathbb{F}_q)$, is defined as the rank of the corresponding $t \times n$ matrix over $\mathbb{F}_q$ when c is expressed as a matrix over $\mathbb{F}_q$.*
(b) *For any two codewords $a, b \in \mathcal{C}_R$, the rank distance (over $\mathbb{F}_q$) of a and b is defined as $d_R(a, b) = rank(a - b|\mathbb{F}_q)$.*
(c) *The minimum rank distance of the code $\mathcal{C}_R$, denoted as $d_R(\mathcal{C}_R)$, is the minimum rank distance of all possible pairs of distinct codewords in $\mathcal{C}_R$, i.e., $d_R(\mathcal{C}_R) = \min\limits_{a \neq b \in \mathcal{C}_R} d_R(a, b)$.*

We call $\mathcal{C}_R$ a $[q, c, n, t, d]$ rank distance code, if each codeword consists of n elements in $\mathbb{F}_{q^t}$, $c = |\mathcal{C}_R|$ is the number of codewords, $d = d_R(\mathcal{C}_R)$ is the minimum rank distance.

3.2   Maximum Rank Distance Codes and Gabidulin Code

For a $[q, c, n, t, d]$ rank distance code $\mathcal{C}_R$ with $t \geq n$, it was shown that $d_R \leq d_H$ in [3], where d_H denotes the minimum Hamming distance of $\mathcal{C}_R$. With the Singleton Bound for block codes, we have the minimum rank distance of $\mathcal{C}_R$ satisfies $d = d_R \leq n - k + 1$, where $k = \log_{q^t} c$.

Definition 4. *A $[q, c, n, t, d]$ rank distance code $\mathcal{C}_R$ with $t \geq n$ is called the maximum-rank-distance code(MRD code), if $\mathcal{C}_R$ achieves the bound $d = n - k + 1$, where $k = \log_{q^t} c$.*

Definition 5. *A $[q, k, n, t]$ Gabidulin code $\mathcal{C}_R$ with $t \geq n$ consists of a generation matrix $G_{k \times n}$, a parity check matrix $H_{n \times (n-k)}$ over $\mathbb{F}_{q^t}$ and two algorithms (GabiEncode, GabiDecode).*

Generation Matrix $G_{k \times n}$/Parity Check Matrix $H_{n \times (n-k)}$. *The generation matrix $G_{k \times n}$ is determined by n elements $(g_1, g_2, \ldots, g_n)$, with $g_i \in \mathbb{F}_{q^t}$, $i = 1, 2, \cdots, n$, and all the n elements are linearly independent over $\mathbb{F}_q$. The parity check matrix $H_{n \times (n-k)}$ is determined by the generation matrix $G_{k \times n}$ satisfying $G_{k \times n} \cdot H_{n \times (n-k)} = 0$. In [12], a fast algorithm was shown to find $h_i \in \mathbb{F}_{q^t}$, $i = 1, 2, \cdots, n$ such that*

$$G_{k \times n} = \begin{pmatrix} g_1 & g_2 & \cdots & g_n \\ g_1^q & g_2^q & \cdots & g_n^q \\ \vdots & \vdots & & \vdots \\ g_1^{q^{k-1}} & g_2^{q^{k-1}} & \cdots & g_n^{q^{k-1}} \end{pmatrix}, \quad H_{n \times (n-k)} = \begin{pmatrix} h_1 & h_1^q & \cdots & h_1^{q^{n-k-1}} \\ h_2 & h_2^q & \cdots & h_2^{q^{n-k-1}} \\ \vdots & \vdots & & \vdots \\ h_n & h_n^q & \cdots & h_n^{q^{n-k-1}} \end{pmatrix}.$$

$$(1)$$

GabiEncode($m, G_{k \times n}$). *Taking as input the generation matrix $G_{k \times n}$ and the message vector $m = (m_1, m_2, \cdots, m_k) \in (\mathbb{F}_{q^t})^k$, it computes $c = m \cdot G_{k \times n}$, and outputs the codeword $c = (c_1, c_2, \cdots, c_n)$.*

GabiDecode($r, H_{n \times (n-k)}$). *Taking as input the parity check matrix $H_{n \times (n-k)}$ and a vector $r = (r_1, r_2, \cdots, r_n) \in (\mathbb{F}_{q^t})^n$, it outputs $m = (m_1, m_2, \cdots, m_k)$. Refer to [7] for the specific decoding algorithm.*

A $[q, k, n, t]$ Gabidulin code $\mathcal{C}_R$ is a $[q, q^{tk}, n, t, n-k+1]$ MRD code and $\mathcal{C}_R = \{c \mid c = m \cdot G_{k \times n}, m = (m_1, m_2, \cdots, m_k), m_i \in \mathbb{F}_{q^t}, i = 1, 2, \cdots, k\} \subseteq (\mathbb{F}_{q^t})^n$.

The *correctness* of Gabidulin Code requires that $m = $ **GabiDecode**($c, H_{n \times (n-k)}$) if $c \leftarrow$ **GabiEncode**($m, G_{k \times n}$) for all $m \in (\mathbb{F}_{q^t})^k$.

Lots of work has been done on the efficient decoding of Gabidulin and other MRD Codes. Decoding algorithms have been proposed to decode erasures or errors or both of them simultaneously.

4   PoR Scheme from MRD Codes

We will use Gabidulin Code as an instantiation of MRD code. The only reason to use Gabidulin Code instead of a general MRD code is that Gabidulin Code has explicit generation matrix and parity check matrix, which helps us to analyze the performance of our proposal.

The primitives involved in the PoR scheme are

- a Pseudo-Random Function PRF : $\mathcal{K}_{prf} \times \{0,1\}^* \to \mathbb{F}_{q^t}$, which uses a seed k', randomly chosen from space $\mathcal{K}_{prf}$, to generate pseudo-random keys with PRF(k', i) for $i = 1, 2, \cdots$. The length of the seed k' is determined by the security parameter λ.
- A $[q, k, n, t]$ Gabidulin code $\mathcal{C}_R$ with $t \geq n$, which is associated with ($G_{k \times n}$, $H_{n \times (n-k)}$, GabiEncode, GabiDecode) defined in Definition 5.

The PoR scheme constructed from Gabidulin codes consists of the following algorithms.

- $(sk, pp) \leftarrow$ **KeyGen(1^λ):** The key generation algorithm takes as input the security parameter λ, chooses random elements $k \in \mathbb{F}_{q^n}$ and $k' \in \mathcal{K}_{prf}$. Choose a Pseudo-Random Function (PRF) PRF : $\mathcal{K}_{prf} \times \{0,1\}^* \to \mathbb{F}_{q^t}$ and a $[q, k, n, t]$ Gabidulin code $\mathcal{C}_R$. Output the public parameter $pp = (\mathsf{PRF}, \mathcal{C}_R)$ and the secret key $sk = (k, k')$.

- $M^* \leftarrow$ **Encode**(sk, pp, M): The storage encoding algorithm takes as input the secret key sk, the public parameter pp and the original file M. It will compute an encoded file M^* as follows.

  (1) **Block Division:** The original file M is divided into w blocks, denoted by $(M_1, M_2, \cdots, M_w)^\mathsf{T}$, each block $M_i = (\mathsf{m}_{i1}, \mathsf{m}_{i2}, \cdots, \mathsf{m}_{ik}) \in (\mathbb{F}_{q^t})^k$ consisting of k elements of $\mathbb{F}_{q^t}$.

  (2) **Gabidulin Encoding:** The original file M is encoded into Gabidulin codewords block by block with $C_i \leftarrow$ **GabiEncode**$(M_i, \mathsf{G}_{k \times n})$, $i = 1, 2, \cdots, w$. More precisely, given block $M_i = (\mathsf{m}_{i1}, \mathsf{m}_{i2}, \cdots, \mathsf{m}_{ik}) \in (\mathbb{F}_{q^t})^k$, the codeword $C_i = (\mathsf{c}_{i1}, \mathsf{c}_{i2}, \cdots, \mathsf{c}_{in}) \in (\mathbb{F}_{q^t})^n$ is computed as $C_i = (\mathsf{c}_{i1}, \mathsf{c}_{i2}, \cdots, \mathsf{c}_{in}) = (\mathsf{m}_{i1}, \mathsf{m}_{i2}, \cdots, \mathsf{m}_{ik}) \cdot \mathsf{G}_{k \times n}$. It should be noted that the encoding is a matrix multiplication over finite field $\mathbb{F}_{q^t}$. Express each c_{ij} as a column vector of dimension t over $\mathbb{F}_q$, i.e., $\mathsf{c}_{ij} = \left(c_{ij}^{(1)}, c_{ij}^{(2)}, \cdots, c_{ij}^{(t)} \right)^\mathsf{T}$. Then each codeword C_i can be expressed as a $t \times n$ matrix over $\mathbb{F}_q$.

  (3) **Tag Generation:** Compute a tag $\boldsymbol{\sigma}_i$ for each codeword C_i with the secret key $sk = (\mathsf{k}, k')$.

  (i) Express $\mathsf{k} \in \mathbb{F}_{q^n}$ as a vector of dimension n over $\mathbb{F}_q$, i.e., $\mathsf{k} = \left(k^{(1)}, k^{(2)}, \cdots, k^{(n)} \right)^\mathsf{T}$.

  (ii) Compute $\mathsf{k}_i = \mathsf{PRF}(k', i)$ for $i = 1, 2, \cdots, w$. Express $\mathsf{k}_i \in \mathbb{F}_{q^t}$ as a vector of dimension t over $\mathbb{F}_q$, i.e., $\mathsf{k}_i = \left(k_i^{(1)}, k_i^{(2)}, \cdots, k_i^{(t)} \right)^\mathsf{T}$.

  (iii) For each codeword C_i, a tag $\boldsymbol{\sigma}_i \in \mathbb{F}_{q^t}$ is computed with

  $$\boldsymbol{\sigma}_i = C_i \cdot \mathsf{k} + \mathsf{k}_i = \begin{pmatrix} c_{i1}^{(1)} & c_{i2}^{(1)} & \cdots & c_{in}^{(1)} \\ c_{i1}^{(2)} & c_{i2}^{(2)} & \cdots & c_{in}^{(2)} \\ \vdots & \vdots & & \vdots \\ c_{i1}^{(t)} & c_{i2}^{(t)} & \cdots & c_{in}^{(t)} \end{pmatrix} \cdot \begin{pmatrix} k^{(1)} \\ k^{(2)} \\ \vdots \\ k^{(n)} \end{pmatrix} + \begin{pmatrix} k_i^{(1)} \\ k_i^{(2)} \\ \vdots \\ k_i^{(t)} \end{pmatrix}, \quad (2)$$

  where all the operations are in the basic field $\mathbb{F}_q$.

  (4) **Storage File M^*** : Each block M_i is encoded as $(C_i || \boldsymbol{\sigma}_i) = (\mathsf{c}_{i1}, \mathsf{c}_{i2}, \cdots, \mathsf{c}_{in}, \boldsymbol{\sigma}_i)$. The final encoded file M^* consists of blocks attached with tags:

  $$M^* = (C_1 || \boldsymbol{\sigma}_1, C_2 || \boldsymbol{\sigma}_2, \cdots, C_w || \boldsymbol{\sigma}_w)^\mathsf{T} = \begin{pmatrix} \mathsf{c}_{11} & \mathsf{c}_{12} & \cdots & \mathsf{c}_{1n} & \boldsymbol{\sigma}_1 \\ \mathsf{c}_{21} & \mathsf{c}_{22} & \cdots & \mathsf{c}_{2n} & \boldsymbol{\sigma}_2 \\ \vdots & \vdots & & \vdots & \vdots \\ \mathsf{c}_{w1} & \mathsf{c}_{w2} & \cdots & \mathsf{c}_{wn} & \boldsymbol{\sigma}_w \end{pmatrix},$$

  where each entry in the matrix is an element from $\mathbb{F}_{q^t}$.

- $\{M, \perp\} \leftarrow$ **Decode**(sk, pp, M^*): Parse M^* as $M^* = (C_1' || \boldsymbol{\sigma}_1', C_2' || \boldsymbol{\sigma}_2', \cdots, C_w' || \boldsymbol{\sigma}_w')^\mathsf{T}$.

  for $i = 1, 2, \cdots, w$ **do**

  If $C_i' \cdot \mathsf{H}_{n \times (n-k)} \neq 0$ return "$\perp$".

  If $\boldsymbol{\sigma}_i' \neq C_i' \cdot \mathsf{k} + \mathsf{k}_i$ return "$\perp$".

$$M_i' \leftarrow \mathsf{GabiDecode}(C_i', \mathsf{H}_{n \times (n-k)}).$$

end for

Return $M = (M_1', M_2', \cdots, M_w')^{\mathsf{T}}$.

- $\{(ch, re), \bot\} \leftarrow \mathbf{Interaction}(\mathcal{P}(M^*, pp) \leftrightharpoons \mathcal{V}(sk, pp))$: The interactive protocol consists of three algorithms.

  ◆ $ch \leftarrow \mathbf{Challenge}(1^\lambda)$: The challenge $ch = (v_1, v_2, \cdots, v_w)$ is chosen uniformly at random from $(\mathbb{F}_q)^w$.

  ◆ $re \leftarrow \mathbf{Response}(pp, M^*, ch)$: **(i)** First the encoded file M^* is segmented into w blocks. Let $M^* = (C_1\|\boldsymbol{\sigma}_1, C_2\|\boldsymbol{\sigma}_2, \cdots, C_w\|\boldsymbol{\sigma}_w)^{\mathsf{T}}$.
  (ii) Then the response re is computed with aggregation.

$$re = ch \circ M^* = (v_1, v_2, \cdots, v_w) \circ \begin{pmatrix} \mathsf{c}_{11} & \cdots & \mathsf{c}_{1n} & \boldsymbol{\sigma}_1 \\ \mathsf{c}_{21} & \cdots & \mathsf{c}_{2n} & \boldsymbol{\sigma}_2 \\ \vdots & & \vdots & \vdots \\ \mathsf{c}_{w1} & \cdots & \mathsf{c}_{wn} & \boldsymbol{\sigma}_w \end{pmatrix}$$

$$= \left(\sum_{i=1}^{w} v_i \circ \mathsf{c}_{i1}, \cdots, \sum_{i=1}^{w} v_i \circ \mathsf{c}_{in}, \sum_{i=1}^{w} v_i \circ \boldsymbol{\sigma}_i \right),$$

where "$\circ$" is scalar multiplication over vector space on $\mathbb{F}_q$. More precisely, express $\mathsf{c}_{ij} = \left(c_{ij}^{(1)}, c_{ij}^{(2)}, \cdots, c_{ij}^{(t)} \right)^{T}$ as a t-dimentional vector over $\mathbb{F}_q$. Then $v_i \circ \mathsf{c}_{ij} = \left(v_i \cdot c_{ij}^{(1)}, v_i \cdot c_{ij}^{(2)}, \cdots, v_i \cdot c_{ij}^{(t)} \right)^{T}$.

  ◆ $b \leftarrow \mathbf{Verification}(pp, sk, ch, re)$: The input is given by the public parameter $pp = (\mathsf{PRF}, \mathcal{C}_R)$, where $\mathcal{C}_R$ is associated with the generation matrix $\mathsf{G}_{k \times n}$ and parity check matrix $\mathsf{H}_{n \times (n-k)}$, the secret key $sk = (\mathsf{k}, k') \in \mathbb{F}_{q^n} \times \mathcal{K}_{prf}$, the challenge $ch = (v_1, v_2, \cdots, v_w) \in (\mathbb{F}_q)^w$, and response $re = (\bar{\mathsf{c}}_1, \bar{\mathsf{c}}_2, \cdots, \bar{\mathsf{c}}_n, \bar{\boldsymbol{\sigma}}) \in (\mathbb{F}_{q^t})^{n+1}$.

  (i) Parse re as $(\bar{C}, \bar{\boldsymbol{\sigma}})$, where $\bar{C} = (\bar{\mathsf{c}}_1, \bar{\mathsf{c}}_2, \cdots, \bar{\mathsf{c}}_n)$. Check whether $\bar{C}$ is an MRD codeword by testing $\bar{C} \cdot \mathsf{H}_{n \times (n-k)} = 0$. If not, output $b = 0$.

  (ii) Express $\mathsf{k} \in \mathbb{F}_{q^n}$ as a vector of dimension n over $\mathbb{F}_q$, i.e., $\mathsf{k} = \left(k^{(1)}, k^{(2)}, \cdots, k^{(n)} \right)^{T}$. Compute $\mathsf{k}_i = \mathsf{PRF}(k', i) \in \mathbb{F}_{q^t}$ for $i = 1, 2, \cdots, w$. Express k_i as a vector of dimension t over $\mathbb{F}_q$, i.e., $\mathsf{k}_i = \left(k_i^{(1)}, k_i^{(2)}, \cdots, k_i^{(t)} \right)^{T}$.

  (iii) Express $\bar{C}$ as a matrix over $\mathbb{F}_q$, i.e., $\bar{C} = \begin{pmatrix} \bar{c}_1^{(1)} & \bar{c}_2^{(1)} & \cdots & \bar{c}_n^{(1)} \\ \bar{c}_1^{(2)} & \bar{c}_2^{(2)} & \cdots & \bar{c}_n^{(2)} \\ \vdots & \vdots & & \vdots \\ \bar{c}_1^{(t)} & \bar{c}_2^{(t)} & \cdots & \bar{c}_n^{(t)} \end{pmatrix}$ and

$\bar{\boldsymbol{\sigma}} = \left(\bar{\sigma}^{(1)}, \bar{\sigma}^{(2)}, \cdots, \bar{\sigma}^{(t)} \right)^{T}$.

(iv) Check

$$
\bar{\sigma} = \begin{pmatrix} \bar{c}_1^{(1)} & \bar{c}_2^{(1)} & \cdots & \bar{c}_n^{(1)} \\ \bar{c}_1^{(2)} & \bar{c}_2^{(2)} & \cdots & \bar{c}_n^{(2)} \\ \vdots & \vdots & \vdots & \vdots \\ \bar{c}_1^{(t)} & \bar{c}_2^{(t)} & \cdots & \bar{c}_n^{(t)} \end{pmatrix} \cdot \begin{pmatrix} k^{(1)} \\ k^{(2)} \\ \vdots \\ k^{(n)} \end{pmatrix} + \begin{pmatrix} \sum_{i=1}^{w} v_i \cdot k_i^{(1)} \\ \sum_{i=1}^{w} v_i \cdot k_i^{(2)} \\ \vdots \\ \sum_{i=1}^{w} v_i \cdot k_i^{(t)} \end{pmatrix}, \qquad (3)
$$

where all the operations are in the field $\mathbb{F}_q$. If Eq.(3) holds, return 1, otherwise return 0.

- $\{0,1\} \leftarrow$ **Audit.** The client $\mathcal{V}$ executes the Interaction protocol u times.

  $b = 0;$
  for $i = 1$ to u **do** Interaction$(\mathcal{P}(M^*, pp) \leftrightarrows \mathcal{V}(sk, pp))$
  $\quad ch \leftarrow$ Challenge$(1^\lambda);$
  $\quad re \leftarrow$ Response$(pp, M^*, ch);$
  $\quad$ If Verification$(pp, ch, re) = 1$ then $b \leftarrow b + 1;$
  end for
  If $(b/u > \frac{1}{q})$ return 1, otherwise return 0.

In the audit, $b/u > \frac{1}{q}$ means $b/u - \frac{1}{q}$ is non-negligible, since u is polynomial in λ.

The *Correctness* of the above PoR scheme is guaranteed by the following facts. For all (sk, pp, M^*) such that $(sk, pp) \leftarrow$ KeyGen(1^λ) and $M^* \leftarrow$ Encode (sk, pp, M),

- the original file M is always recovered from the correctly encoded file M^*, due to the correctness of the encoding/decoding algorithms of Gabidulin codes;
- the interaction protocol between honest $\mathcal{P}$ and $\mathcal{V}$ results in $1 \leftarrow$ Verification(pp, sk, ch, re), hence the interaction protocol outputs a challenge/response, i.e, $(ch, re) \leftarrow$ Interaction$(\mathcal{P}(M^*, pp) \leftrightarrows \mathcal{V}(sk, pp))$, due to the following facts:

$$
\sum_{i=1}^{w} v_i \circ \sigma_i = (v_1, v_2, \cdots, v_w) \circ \begin{pmatrix} \sigma_1 \\ \sigma_2 \\ \vdots \\ \sigma_w \end{pmatrix} = (v_1, v_2, \cdots, v_w) \circ \left(\begin{pmatrix} C_1 \\ C_2 \\ \vdots \\ C_w \end{pmatrix} \cdot k + \begin{pmatrix} k_1 \\ k_2 \\ \vdots \\ k_w \end{pmatrix} \right)
$$

$$
= \left(\sum_{i=1}^{w} v_i \circ c_{i1}, \sum_{i=1}^{w} v_i \circ c_{i2}, \cdots, \sum_{i=1}^{w} v_i \circ c_{in} \right) \cdot k + \sum_{i=1}^{w} v_i \circ k_i
$$

$$
= (\bar{c}_1, \bar{c}_2, \cdots, \bar{c}_n) \cdot k + \sum_{i=1}^{w} v_i \circ k_i,
$$

where $\bar{c}_j = \left(\bar{c}_j^{(1)}, \bar{c}_j^{(2)}, \cdots, \bar{c}_j^{(t)} \right)^T$, $k = \left(k^{(1)}, k^{(2)}, \cdots, k^{(n)} \right)^T$ and $k_i = \left(k_i^{(1)}, k_i^{(2)}, \cdots, k_i^{(t)} \right)^T$, which are vectors over $\mathbb{F}_q$.

5 Performance Analysis

To evaluate the efficiency of the proposed PoR scheme, we will analyze the local storage of the client, the expansion rate θ of the storage, which is defined as the ratio of the length of encoded file M^* to that of the original file M, the length of the challenge, denoted by $|ch|$, the length of the response, denoted by $|re|$, the computational complexity of the storage provider to compute the response, and the computational complexity of the client to verify the response.

Let $\mathsf{Mul}_{\mathbb{F}_q}$ denote a multiplication and $\mathsf{Add}_{\mathbb{F}_q}$ denote an addition over finite field $\mathbb{F}_q$.

We will use a pseudo-random function $\mathsf{PRF} : \{0,1\}^\lambda \times \{0,1\}^* \to \mathbb{F}_{q^t}$ as an instantiation.

Local Storage: The client will store the key $\mathsf{k} \in \mathbb{F}_{q^n}$, the seed $k' \in \{0,1\}^\lambda$ of PRF, and the parity check matrix $\mathsf{H}_{n \times (n-k)}$ of the $[q,k,n,t]$ Gabidulin code. The parity check matrix is determined by $h_i \in \mathbb{F}_{q^t}$, $i = 1, 2, \cdots, n$ according to Eq.(1). Hence the local storage is $(n \log q + \lambda + nt \log q)$ bits.

Storage Expansion Rate: $\theta = \frac{|M^*|}{|M|} = \frac{n+1}{k}$.

Length of Challenge: $ch \in (\mathbb{F}_q)^w$, hence $|ch| = w \log q$ bits.

Length of Response: re consists of a Gabidulin codeword and a tag, hence $|re| = (n+1)t \log q$ bits.

Computational Complexity of the Storage Server: To compute re, the storage server will do $(n+1)tw(q-1)/q$ multiplications and $(n+1)t(w-1)(q-1)/q$ additions over $\mathbb{F}_q$ on average. Hence there are totally $(n+1)tw(q-1)/q\mathsf{Mul}_{\mathbb{F}_q} + (n+1)t(w-1)(q-1)/q\mathsf{Add}_{\mathbb{F}_q}$ on average.

Computational Complexity of the Client: To test the consistency of (ch, re), the client needs $(n-k)n$ multiplications and $(n-k)(n-1)$ additions over $\mathbb{F}_{q^t}$ to test Gabidulin codeword, and another $tn + wt(q-1)/q$ multiplications and $t(n-1)+t(w-1)(q-1)/q$ additions over $\mathbb{F}_q$ on average. Hence there are totally $(n-k)n\mathsf{Mul}_{\mathbb{F}_{q^t}} + (n-k)(n-1)\mathsf{Add}_{\mathbb{F}_{q^t}} + (tn + wt(q-1)/q)\mathsf{Mul}_{\mathbb{F}_q} + (t(n-1) + t(w-1)(q-1)/q)\mathsf{Add}_{\mathbb{F}_q}$.

Now we instantiate the PoR scheme with security parameter $\lambda = 80$, and a $[q,k,n,t]$ Gabidulin Code with $q = 2, k = 128, n = t = 256$ and $d = 129$. $q = 2$ means that the addition over the binary field is reduced to XOR.

We consider a file M of size $1GB$. The number of blocks is $w = 2^{18}$.

During an interaction, the server will implement 2^{33} bit-XOR to prepare a response re. To verify the consistency of the response, the client's computation

Table 2. Instantiation of PoR Scheme with $[2, 128, 256, 256]$-Gabidulin Code

Local	Rate θ	$|ch|$	$|re|$	Server Comput.	Client Comput.
$|sk| = 336$ bits, $|pp| = 8$KB	≈ 2	32KB	≈ 8KB	$O(2^{33})$ bit-XOR	$O(2^{31})$ bit-XOR

is dominated by $2^{15}\mathsf{Mul}_{\mathbb{F}_{2^{256}}}$. One $\mathsf{Mul}_{\mathbb{F}_{2^{256}}}$ needs $O(256 \cdot 256) = O(2^{16})$ bit operations. Hence the client's computation complexity is $O(2^{31})$.

Consider a modular exponentiation in RSA with a 1024-bit modulus. It will take 1024 modular squares and about 512 modular multiplications. One modular multiplication needs $O(1024 \cdot 1024) = O(2^{20})$ bit operations. So a modular exponentiation in RSA with a 1024-bit modulus has computation complexity of $O(2^{30})$.

Therefore, to audit the storage of $1GB$ file, the computational complexity of both client and server in an interaction is comparable to 2 and 8 modular exponentiations with a 1024-bit modulus respectively.

6   The Security of the Proposed PoR Scheme

Recall that in the audit of the PoR scheme, the audit strategy is determined by a threshold $\frac{1}{q}$. Only if ϵ fraction, $\epsilon > \frac{1}{q}$, of the u executions of Interaction protocol is successful, does the audit claim success.

The ϵ-*soundness* of the PoR scheme will justifiy the sufficiency of the threshold $\frac{1}{q}$. We will prove that as long as a storage provider replies a response re that passes verification with probability $\epsilon > \frac{1}{q}$, there exists a PPT extractor recovering the original file M as long as the number of executions of Interaction protocol is big enough.

Definition 6. *A response re is called* **valid** *to a challenge ch if $re =$ Response(pp, M^*, ch) and the challenge/response (ch, re) is called a* **valid** *pair. A response re is called* **consistent** *to a challenge ch if* Verification(pp, sk, ch, re) $= 1$, *and the challenge/response (ch, re) is called a* **consistent** *pair.*

Given a challenge ch, there may exists many **consistent** responses, but there is only one **valid** response due to the deterministic algorithm Response. Hence, a consistent pair is not necessarily a valid pair.

Before the formal proof of *soundness* of the MRD-based PoR scheme, we will slightly change the PoR scheme. The key sequence $k_i = \mathsf{PRF}(k', i), i = 1, 2, \cdots, w$, which is used to compute tags for blocks and to verify the consistency of a challeng/response pair, is replaced with a truly random sequence over $\mathbb{F}_{q^t}$. Then we have the following lemma.

Lemma 1. *Suppose that $k_i, i = 1, 2, \cdots, w$ is randomly chosen from $\mathbb{F}_{q^t}$ instead of setting $k_i = \mathsf{PRF}(k', i)$. In an execution of Interaction Protocol of the PoR scheme, given a valid challenge/response pair (ch, re), any adversary $\mathcal{A}$ outputs a consistent but invalid response re' with respect to the same challenge ch, i.e., $re' \neq re$ but* Verification(pp, sk, ch, re') $= 1$, *with probability at most $1/q^d$, where d is the minimum rank distance of the MRD Code.*

The proof is omitted here due to the space limitation. See [13] for the full version of this paper.

6.1   ε-Soundness of the PoR Scheme

Now we consider how a PPT Extractor extracts the original file M through executions of the Interaction protocol with an ϵ-admissible storage provider. The idea is as follows: ϵ should be big enough to ensure that Extractor always gains information about M as the number of interactions with $\tilde{\mathcal{P}}_\epsilon$ increases. When the number of interactions in the audit is big enough, M can be recovered by solving equations.

Theorem 2. *The MRD-code-based PoR system is ϵ-sound for $\epsilon > \frac{1}{q}$, given secure PRF and $[q, k, n, t]$ Gabidulin code with $t \geq n$ and $n - k + 1 = \Omega(\lambda)$.*

The proof will be given in the full version [13] of the paper due to the space limitation.

7   Conclusion

In this paper, we propose a PoR scheme based on MRD codes. The MRD codes helps in two ways. Firstly, the MRD code can be applied over small field, and that help the storage provider efficiently computes responses in an audit. As to the binary field, the computation can be as simple as XOR. Secondly, the rank property of the MRD codewords helps the security proof of the PoR scheme. Even if the storage provider knows a correct response with respect to a challenge, it still cannot forge a different response to pass the client verification. This helps to prove the soundness of the PoR scheme.

References

1. Maximilien, G., Zhiyuan, Y.: Properties of codes with the rank metric. Arxiv preprint cs/0610099 (2006)
2. Roth, R.: Maximum-rank array codes and their application to crisscross error correction. IEEE Transactions on Information Theory 32(2), 328–336 (1991)
3. Gabidulin, E.: Theory of code with maximum rank distance. Problems of Information Transmission 21(1), 1–12 (1985)
4. Delsarte, P.: Bilinear forms over a finite field, with applications to coding theory. Journal of Combinatorial Theory, Series A 25(3), 226–241 (1978)
5. Ateniese, G., Burns, R., Curtmola, R., Herring, J., Kissner, L., Peterson, Z., Song, D.: Provable data possession at untrusted stores. In: De Capitani di Vimercati, S., Syverson, P. (eds.) Proceedings of the 14th ACM Conference on Computer and Communications Security (CCS 2007), pp. 598–609. ACM, New York (2007)
6. Dodis, Y., Vadhan, S., Wichs, D.: Proofs of retrievability via hardness amplification. In: Reingold, O. (ed.) TCC 2009. LNCS, vol. 5444, pp. 109–127. Springer, Heidelberg (2009)
7. Gabidulin, E., Pilipchuk, N.: Error and erasure correcting algorithms for rank codes. Designs, Codes and Cryptography 49(1-3), 105–122 (2008)
8. Juels, A., Kaliski, B.: PORs: proofs of retrievability for large files. In: De Capitani di Vimercati, S., Syverson, P. (eds.) Proceedings of the 14th ACM Conference on Computer and Communications Security (CCS 2007), pp. 584–597. ACM, New York (2007)

9. Shoup, V.: Sequences of games: a tool for taming complexity in security proofs. IACR Cryptology ePrint Archive, Report 2004/332 (2004)
10. Schwarz, T., Miller, E.: Store, forget, and check: using algebraic signatures to check remotely administered storage. In: Ahamad, M., Rodrigues, L. (eds.) Proceedings of ICDCS 2006, p. 12. IEEE Computer Society, Los Alamitos (2006)
11. Shacham, H., Waters, B.: Compact proofs of retrievability. In: Pieprzyk, J. (ed.) ASIACRYPT 2008. LNCS, vol. 5350, pp. 90–107. Springer, Heidelberg (2008)
12. Wachter, A., Sidorenko, A., Bossert, M.: A fast linearized Euclidean algorithm for decoding Gabidulin codes. In: Twelfth International Workshop on Algebraic and Combinatorial Coding Theory (ACCT 2010), pp. 298–303 (2010)
13. Han, S., Liu, S., Chen, K., Gu, D.: Proofs of data possession and retrievability based on MRD codes. IACR Cryptology ePrint Archive, Report 2013/789 (2013)
14. Oggier, F., Fathi, H.: An authentication code against pollution attacks in network coding. IEEE/ACM Transactions on Networking (TON) 19(6), 1587–1596 (2011)

TIMER: Secure and Reliable Cloud Storage against Data Re-outsourcing

Tao Jiang[1], Xiaofeng Chen[1], Jin Li[2], Duncan S. Wong[3],
Jianfeng Ma[1], and Joseph Liu[4]

[1] State Key Laboratory of Integrated Service Networks (ISN),
Xidian University, Xi'an, P.R. China
jiangt2009@gmail.com, {xfchen,jfma}@xidian.edu.cn
[2] School of Computer Science, Guangzhou University, China
lijin@gzhu.edu.cn
[3] Department of Computer Science, City University of Hong Kong, Hong Kong
duncan@cityu.edu.hk
[4] Institute for Infocomm Research, Singapore
ksliu@i2r.a-star.edu.sg

Abstract. The semi-trusted servers in cloud environment may outsource
the files of their clients to some low expensive servers to increase their
profit. To some extent, such behavior may violate the wishes of cloud
users and impair their legitimate rights and interests. In this paper, a
probabilistic challenge-response scheme is proposed to prove that the
clients' files are available and stored in a specified cloud server. In order to resist the collusion of cloud servers, common cloud infrastructure
with some reasonable limits, such as rational economic security model,
semi-collusion security model and response time bound, are exploited.
These limits guarantee that a malicious cloud server could not conduct a
t-round communication in a finite time. We analyze the security and performance of the proposed scheme and demonstrate that our scheme provides strong incentives for economically rational cloud providers against
re-outsourcing the clients' data to some other cloud providers.

Keywords: Cloud storage, Economical server collusion, Storage security, Probabilistic scheme.

1 Introduction

In the cloud computing environment, the Cloud Storage Providers (CSPs) offer
paid storage space on its infrastructure to store customers' data. Since the CSPs
are not necessarily trusted in cloud storage system, efficient and secure schemes
should be built to constrain their malicious activities.

For sensitive data, legitimate concerns are necessary when using cloud storage services. The failure of cloud storage server at Amazon results in the per-
manent loss of customer data [4]. Also, there are a variety of economical and
legal restrictions that may compel a customer to choose to store data in a specific cloud storage provider. For example, many companies are willing to store

X. Huang and J. Zhou (Eds.): ISPEC 2014, LNCS 8434, pp. 346–358, 2014.
© Springer International Publishing Switzerland 2014

their sensitive data in the same cloud storage server and many privacy laws in Nova Scotia, British Columbia, Australia and EU [8] require personal data stored within a political border or other nations with comparable protections. Further, the cross server deduplication will greatly reduce the storage overhead of cloud servers, which will reduce the costs of the service providers and enhance their competitiveness. However, the data deduplication may violate the intention of users and undermine the interests of them. Therefore, we see that it is necessary to constrain the activity of the CSPs and verify that their activity meet the storage obligations. Since the clients data is stored in remote server without a local copy, it is very difficult to provide transparency to the users that their sensitive data is correctly handled by the cloud provider. We need to use challenge-response scheme to provide an efficient method to prove the malicious storage re-outsourcing activity. However, the existing challenge-response scheme could not provide a proof that the data of clients stored in a semi-trusted remote cloud storage is not re-outsourced in the economical server collusion network model [6, 7].

In this paper, we demonstrate that it is possible to design a challenge-response protocol which imposes a strong incentive onto the cloud providers to store their clients' data at rest. In particular, we present a probabilistic challenge-response scheme where semi-collusion bound, communication and computation bound and response time bound are adopted. A malicious cloud server S who has re-outsourced its client data to some other cloud server S' should conduct a t-round communication with S' to generate a correct response. If t is large enough, the malicious server could not generate the response in time even if with unlimited computation power. It is demonstrated that our scheme is secure under cryptography assumption and our analysis shows that as long as the designed communication round t is large enough, TIMER scheme will provide a strong incentive for the rational economic cloud providers to store the data of their clients in their storage servers.

2   Related Works

Provable Data Possession: To protect the availability of the clients' files stored in remote data storage server, Ateniese et al. [1] proposed a formalized model called Provable Data Possession (PDP). Unlike the low efficiency deterministic schemes [10, 14, 23] and probability scheme [22], PDP could efficiently check whether the clients' files stored in remote server have been tampered or deleted with very high probability. Several variations of their proposed scheme, such as static PDP schemes [11, 18, 24] and limited dynamic or dynamic schemes [2, 13], are proposed to achieve efficient proof of remote data availability.

Secure Deduplication: Conducting deduplication will reduce the data storage burden and maintenance cost, which can promote price reductions of data storage service and enhance the competition of CSPs. Recent researches on storage deduplication [12, 25] show that deduplication achieves a higher level of scalability, availability, and durability. However, Harnik et al. [16] point out that client-side deduplication introduces security problems that an attacker is able to get the entire file from the server by learning just a small piece of the hash value about the file. Therefore, Halevi et al. [15] proposed a scheme called Proofs of Ownership (PoWs), where a client proves to the server that it actually holds a copy of the file and not just some short information about it based on Merkle trees [20] and specific encodings.

Location Sensitive Services: In data storage system, users' data is important for some location sensitive services. Some schemes [19, 26] proposed to use semi-trusted landmarks to provide geolocation solutions for data storage. Also, to provide the security against the colluding of adversaries, hidden landmarks are used in geolocation system [5] in wireless networks. Bowers et al. [4] proposed an hourglass scheme to verify a cloud storage service provider is duplicate data from multiple drives through the measurements of network delay. Gondree and Peterson proposed a provable data geolocation and they detect the network delay of different distance and they point that their system could be built on any exiting PDP scheme.

The PDP relevant solutions are proposed to realize efficient data availability check on remote data storage servers. The data storage deduplication relevant solution PoWs is proposed to protect against an attacker from gaining access to potentially huge files of other users based on a very small amount of side information. However, all these schemes focus on the authentication of data integrity and availability problems between clients and servers, which could not prevent a semi-trusted server from re-outsourcing clients' data to some other servers to save its storage space or increase its profit. Such behavior may reduce the security and availability guarantee of clients' data and the benefit of the clients may be violated in this situation.

3 Problem Statement and Design Goals

3.1 System and Threat Model

In cloud storage environment, the clients' data may be re-outsourced multiple times and stored in some unknown servers with low quality of service, which will cause some serious economical and security problems in cloud storage outsourcing service.

Conspiracy to Profit: A CSP may offload the clients' data to some other CSPs when the sum of their payment is lower than that from its clients. Thus, on one hand, the CSP will be able to enlarge its profit by the difference between the payment of itself and the sum payment of all the other CSPs. Also, data re-outsourcing may be used to save the storage space to store the data from other clients. On the other hand, the colluded CSPs will get payment from the CSP. As a result, the conspiracy to profit model will promote the collusion of CSPs driven by the interests.

Storage Location Security: In the multiple time storage re-outsourcing scenario, the data owner will not be able to control the data re-outsourcing behavior of the malicious CSP and the location of its data is uncontrollable.

Therefore, the clients' data may be stored in some servers controlled by its competitors or in some servers beyond the scope of legal protection. Then, some data security and privacy issues will arise.

Low Service Quality: If the cloud storage service is provided in a multi-hop mode in storage re-outsourcing scenario, the CSPs may not be able to respond the request from their clients in time. Worse still, the CSPs will not be able to respond the clients when any CSP in the storage re-outsourcing chain is out of service. Also, the client's data will be stored in a lower payment data store which usually provides lower data security and quality of service guarantee.

3.2 Design Goals

To design a secure and practical TIMER scheme, our system should achieve the following security and performance guarantees.

1. Correctness: Any cloud server that faithfully follows the mechanism must produce an output that can be decrypted and verified by the customer.
2. Soundness: No cloud server can generate an incorrect output that can be decrypted and verified by the customer with non-negligible probability.
3. Efficiency: The local computations done by customer should be substantially less than the whole data.

4 Proposed Scheme

In this section, we first present the bounds of our scheme. Then, we introduce the definition and designing detail of our scheme.

4.1 Construction Overview

As the first idea, we have to make a cryptography design where the challenges from the client C could not be responded correctly in time, when a cloud server S storing the client's files F colludes with some other cloud server S' and re-outsources F to it. Thus, we propose probabilistic TIMER scheme based on communication time delay to prove that the client data is available and stored in specified data store. The proposed scheme adopts cryptographical assumption and network delay to restrict the collusion re-outsourcing behavior of cloud servers. We properly parameterize some bounds on the protocol as follow:

Semi-Collusion Bound (SC-Bound): *In TIMER scheme, every cloud provider runs the public key generation algorithm and produces a pair of keys* (pk, sk). *The cloud provider then publicizes its public key pk and keeps its private key sk secret. It should be emphasized that a cloud provider will not conduct a full proxy signature delegation activity [28] with any other cloud server even in the collusion situation.*

Communication and Computation Bound (CC-Bound): *The cloud providers are rational. They would not like to sign for every possible combination* *of u tags, chosen from n tags, beforehand and outsourcing all the clients' files with these singed tags.(Actually, it is impossible for a cloud provider to conduct this kind of activity when u and n are relative large.)*

Time Bound (T-Bound): *The time for a cloud storage provider to compute the proof TC is much less than the time to conduct a 1-round challenge-response commutation TT. The maximum time delay for an honest server to response the client in the TIMER scheme is Δt. S and S' could not conduct t-round communication in Δt, even if they collude with each other.(Since multi-hop re-outsourcing needs much more response time than the 1-hop re-outsourcing, we only need to analyze the 1-hop re-outsourcing security in our scheme.)*

With the above bounds, we could provide an explanation of our TIMER scheme based on network delay. On one hand, Papagiannaki et al. [21] showed that the single-hop average communication delay of packet in the backbone experience is around 0.1ms. On the other hand, Jansma et al. [17] showed that 10ms is needed to compute an RSA signature on an Intel P4 2.0GHz machine with 512MB of RAM. As in $T - Bound$, we assume that the cloud storage providers have much powerful computation ability which makes the time to generate a proof TC much less than the time TT. Thus the maximum time for an honest server S to response the challenge in TIMER scheme is $Time_1 = TT + tTC + \Delta t$ where TC is the proof computation time of S. The minimum time for a dishonest server S, who has re-outsourced file F to another server S', to response the challenge is $Time_2 = (t+1)TT + tTC'$ where TC' is the joint computation time of server S and S'. According to the $T - Bound$, TC and TC' is much less than TT and Δt is smaller than tTC. We obtain that $\frac{Time_2}{Time_1} = \frac{(t+1)TT + t \times TC' \times TC + \Delta t}{TT + t}$ and the challenger C will be able to prove that its file F is not stored in the data storage server S.

In general, TIMER scheme is a challenge-response scheme based on PDP and it forces S to conduct a t-round communication with S' when the file F is offloaded from S and stored at S'. The colluded servers S and S' would not be able to generate a correct proof in a time delay Δt if t is chosen properly.

4.2   TIMER Scheme

In this section, we present the constructions of TIMER scheme. We start by introducing some additional notations used by the constructions. Let $p = 2p' + 1$ and $q = 2q' + 1$ be secure primes and let $N = pq$ be an RSA modulus. Let g be a generator of QR_N, the unique cyclic subgroup of Z_N^* of order $p'q'$. We can obtain g as $g = a^2$, where $a \xleftarrow{R} Z_N^*$ such that $\gcd(a \pm 1, N) = 1$. All exponentiations are performed modulo N, and we sometimes omit writing it explicitly for simplicity. Let $h : \{0,1\}^* \to QR_N$ be a secure deterministic hash function that maps strings uniformly to QR_N. Let k, l, λ be security parameters (λ is a positive integer) and let H be a cryptographic full domain hash function as used in the provably secure FDH signature scheme [3, 9]. We get $H : \{0,1\}^k \to \mathbb{Z}_N^*$. In addition, we make use of a pseudo-random function (PRF) f and a pseudo-random permutation (PRP) π that $f : \{0,1\}^k \times \{0,1\}^{log_2(n)} \to \{0,1\}^l$ and $\pi : \{0,1\}^k \times \{0,1\}^{log_2(n)} \to \{0,1\}^{log_2(n)}$.

We write $f_k(x)$ to denote f keyed with key k applied on input x. The algorithms of TIMER scheme are described in Algorithm 1. We are able to maintain 1-round communication cost between C and S with a combined value ρ, and verification materials T_l and $\rho_l (0 \leq l \leq t-1)$.

As previously defined, let f be a pseudo-random function, π be a pseudo-random permutation and H be a cryptographic hash function.

According to the TIMER algorithms in Algorithm 1, We construct the TIMER system in two phases, Setup and Challenge:

Setup: The client C runs $\mathsf{Gen}_C(1^k) \to (pk_C, sk_C)$, stores (sk_C, pk_C) and sets $(N_C, g) = pk_C, (e_C, d_C, v) = sk_C$. C then runs $\mathsf{Tag}(pk_C, sk_C, b_i, i) \to (T_{i,b_i}, W_i)$ for all $1 \leq i \leq n$ and sends pk_C, F and $TAG = (T_{1,b_1}, ..., T_{n,b_n})$ to S for storage. C may now delete F and TAG from its local storage.

Challenge: C requests proof of possession for $c = ut$ distinct blocks of the file F (with $1 \leq c \leq n$):

1. C generates the challenge $CHAL = (r, k_0, k', g^s, u, t)$, where $k_1 \overset{R}{\leftarrow} \{0,1\}^k$, $k' \overset{R}{\leftarrow} \{0,1\}^k$, $g_s = g^s \bmod N$, $s \overset{R}{\leftarrow} \mathbb{Z}_N^*$, CT_1 is the machine time when C sends the challenge, u and t are used to decide the number of blocks to verify and the round number that S has to sign the intermediate results and Δt is the upper bound of time for S to respond a challenge. C sends $CHAL$ to S and stores the current system time CT_1.

2. S runs $\mathsf{Gen}_S(1^k) \to (pk_S, sk_S)$ and then runs $\mathsf{Prof}(pk_C, sk_S, F, CHAL, TAG) \to \mathcal{V}$ and sends to C the proof of possession $\mathcal{V}$.

3. When C receives the response from S, it stores the current system time CT_2. Then C sets $CHAL = (k_1, k', u, t, s, CT_1, CT_2, \Delta t)$ and checks the validity of the proof $\mathcal{V}$ by running $\mathsf{Vrfy}(pk_S, pk_C, sk_C, CHAL, \mathcal{V})$.

It is obvious that, the additional tags do not change the storage requirements for the server, since the size of the file is $O(n)$. Considering the efficiency of the proposed scheme, we need to remark that $2t + 1$ values are needed among the communication between C and S. It means that the client needs to conduct t times signatures verification in each request. In the TIMER system, we consider a 1024-bit modulus N. In the Challenge phase, C sends to S 5 value with total 298 bytes (r and g_s are both 128 bytes, k_0 is 16 bytes, k' is 20 bytes, u is 4 byte and t is 1 byte). The values contained in the server's response are related with the communication round t and the total length is $(148t + 20)$ bytes ($T_l(0 \leq l \leq t-1)$ is 128 bytes, $\rho_l(0 \leq l \leq t-1)$ is 20 bytes and ρ is 20 bytes). The communication rounds t is decided according to Δt in full data re-outsourcing situation. However, in partial data re-outsourcing, it will grow when the allowed percent of the re-outsourced data becomes smaller, and we will provide a detailed analysis in the next section. According to out TIMER system above, we only need to send a small number of values and the server does not need to send back to the client the file blocks. The storage of a client is $O(1)$, and the communication overhead and computation overhead of a client are both $O(t)$.

Algorithm 1. The TIMER Algorithms

$\mathsf{Gen}_C(1^k)$:

1. Generate $pk_C = (N, g)$ and $sk_C = (e_C, d_C, v)$, such that $e_C d_C \equiv 1 (\bmod\ p'_C q'_C)$, $e_C > \lambda$ is a large secret prime and $d_C > \lambda$, g is a generator of QR_N and $v \xleftarrow{R} \{0,1\}^k$.
2. Output (pk_C, sk_C).

$\mathsf{Gen}_S(1^k)$:

1. Generate $pk_S = (N, e_S)$ and $sk_S = (N, d_S)$, such that $ed \equiv 1 (\bmod\ p'_S q'_S)$, $e_S > \lambda$ is a large secret prime and $d_S > \lambda$, g is a generator of QR_N.
2. Output (pk_S, sk_S).

$\mathsf{Tag}(pk_C = (N, g), sk_C = (d_C, v), b, i)$:

1. Generate $W_i = v || i$. Compute $T_{i,b} = (h(W_i) \cdot g^b)^{d_C} \bmod N$.
2. Output (T_i, b, W_i).

$\mathsf{Prof}(pk_C = (N, g), sk_S = d_S, F = (b_1, ..., b_n), CHAL = (r, k_0, k', g_s, u, t), TAG = (T_{1,b_1}, ..., T_{n,b_n}))$:

1. Let $c = ut$.
   for $0 \le l \le t - 1$ **do**
   > **for** $1 \le j \le u$ **do**
   >> Compute coefficients:$a_{l,j} = f_{k'}(ul + j)$; Compute the indices of the blocks for which the proof is generated: $i_{l,j} = \pi_{k_l}(ul + j)$;
   >
   > Compute $T_l = (h(W_{i_{l,1}})^{a_{l,1}} \cdot ... \cdot h(W_{i_{l,u}})^{a_{l,u}} \cdot g^{a_{l,1}b_{i_{l,1}} + ... + a_{l,u}b_{i_{l,u}}})^{d_C}$;
   > Compute $\rho_l = (H(T_l || r))^{d_S}$. let $k_{l+1} = \rho_l$;
2. Compute $\rho = H(\prod_{l=0}^{t-1} g_s^{a_{l,1}b_{i_{l,1}} + ... + a_{l,u}b_{i_{l,u}}} \bmod N)$;
3. Output $\mathcal{V} = (\rho, T_0, ..., T_{t-1}, \rho_0, ..., \rho_{t-1})$.

$\mathsf{Vrfy}(pk_S = e_S, pk_C = (N, g), sk_C = (e_C, v), CHAL = (r, k_0, k, u, t, s, CT_1, CT_2, \Delta t), \mathcal{V} = (\rho, T_0, ..., T_{t-1}, \rho_0, ..., \rho_{t-1}))$:

> **if** $CT_2 - CT_1 < \Delta t$ **then**
>> Compute $T = T_0 \cdot ... \cdot T_{t-1} = (\prod_{l=0}^{t-1} h(W_{i_{l,1}})^{a_{l,1}} \cdot ... \cdot h(W_{i_{l,u}})^{a_{l,u}} g^{a_{l,1}b_{i_{l,1}} + ... + a_{l,u}b_{i_{l,u}}})$; **for** $0 \le l \le t - 1$ **do**
>>> Compute $H(T_l \parallel r) = \theta_l$ Let $k_{l+1} = \rho_l$ and $\tau = T^{e_C}$. **for** $1 \le j \le u$ **do**
>>>> Compute $a_{l,j} = f_{k'}(ul + j)$;// Compute $i_{l,j} = \pi_{k_l}(ul + j), W_{i_{l,j}} = v || i_{l,j}$, and ;
>>
>> **if** $\theta_l = (\rho_l)^{e_S} (0 \le l \le t - 1)$ and $H(\tau^s \bmod N) = \rho$ **then**
>>> Output Accept.
>
> **else**
>> Output reject.

---

5   Security and Performance Analysis

In this section, we present the security and performance analysis of our TIMER scheme.

5.1   Security Proof of TIMER Scheme

We suppose that the maximum time delay that a client allows the server to respond the proof is Δt. According to the $T - Bound$, when the file F is re-outsourced to S' from S, the collusion servers would not conduct a t round communication between each other. However, S will be able to forge a proof of possession $\mathcal{V}$ for the blocks indicated by $CHAL$ without conducting a t-round interaction with S'. Thus, we have to prove that the colluded servers could forge a valid proof in each phase $Ph_i(0 \leq i \leq t - 1)$ with a negligible probability.

The initial key k_0, used to choose the blocks, is from the client while the phase key used to choose the blocks in each phase is generated from the result of the previous phase of the current phase. Thus, we have to prove that a Probability Polynomial Time (PPT) adversary will forge each phase key $k_l(1 \leq l \leq t - 1)$ with only a negligible probability. If the PDP scheme [1] adopted in our scheme is secure under the RSA and KEA-r assumption [27], we could start the security proof for TIMER system by the phrase key unforgeability. We construct the phase key generation scheme according to our TIMER scheme as follow:

The Phrase Key Generation Scheme

   Let f and π be the pseudo-random function and pseudo-random permutation respectively as defined before and some other parameters r, k_0 k', F and TAG are as defined in TIMER algorithms.

Key Generation: Compute$(N, e, d) \leftarrow$ GenRSA (1^k) and the public key is (N, e) and the secret is d. Let $H : \{0,1\}^k \rightarrow \mathbb{Z}_N^*$ be a hash function.

Phrase Key Generation: When $k_l(1 \leq l \leq t - 1)$ is needed to compute, the parameter T_{l-1} has been computed as defined in TIMER algorithms. Then compute $\rho_l = (H(T_l||r))^{d_S} \mod N$ and $k_{l+1} = \rho_l$. At last, output $(r, k_0, k', \{T_0, T_1, ..., T_{t-1}\}, \{k_1, k_2, ..., k_{t-1}\})$.

Phrase Key Verification: Input $(r, k_0, k', \{T_0', T_1', ..., T_{t-1}'\}, \{k_1', k_2', ..., k_{t-1}'\})$ and check whether all the $\rho_l'^{e_S} \overset{?}{=} H(T_l' \parallel r)$ and $k_{l+1}' = \rho_l'$ where $0 \leq l \leq t - 1$.

Theorem 1. *If the PDP scheme is provably secure under the RSA and KEA1-r assumption, and H and h are modeled as random oracles, the construction of the Phase Key Generation Scheme is unforgeable under adaptive chosen-message attack.*

Proof. On one hand, the PDP scheme is secure under RSA and KEA1-r assumption, which assures that an adversary can forge T_0 with only a negligible probability. On the other hand, the RSA-signature is a trapdoor permutation and H is assumed to be a full-domain hash function, which guarantees that the output of the signature scheme in the phrase key generation scheme has a unique signature. Then, we get that the probability for an adversary to forge a phase key $k_1' = \rho_0'$ and $\rho_0'^{es} = H(T_0' \parallel r)$ is negligible. As a result, if a PPT adversary could forge the key k_l' with only a negligible probability, the probability that k_{l+1}' can be correctly generated is negligible. Consequently, the phase key $\{k_1, k_2, ..., k_{t-1}\}$ is unforgeable when the phase key seed k_0 is determined.

Theorem 2. *For any phase* $Ph_l (0 \le l \le t-1)$, *on input* d_S, $\{k_0, k_1, ..., k_{l-1}\}$ *and* $\{T_0, T_1, ..., T_{l-1}\}$, *the probability that* S *could forge a signature* $T_l = (h(W_{i_{l,1}})^{a_{l,1}} \cdot ... \cdot h(W_{i_{l,u}})^{a_{l,u}} \cdot g^{a_{l,1}b_{i_{l,1}} + ... + a_{l,u}b_{i_{l,u}}})^{d_C}$ *is negligible without interacting with* S'; *On input* $F = b_1, ..., b_n$, W *and* $\{k_0, k_1, ..., k_{l-1}\}$, *the probability that* S' *could forge the phase key* k_{l+1} *is negligible without interacting with* S.

Proof. We model h as a random oracle. Then, the block identity $i_{l,j} = h_{k_{l-1}}(j)(1 \le j \le u)$ is uniform distribution. Since S has re-outsourced $F = b_1, ..., b_n$ to S', S could not compute a value $T_l = (h(W_{i_{l,1}})^{a_{l,1}} \cdot ... \cdot h(W_{i_{l,u}})^{a_{l,u}} \cdot g^{a_{l,1}b_{i_{l,1}} + ... + a_{l,u}b_{i_{l,u}}})^{d_C}$ from a random set of u blocks without communicating with S'. Then, we have to prove that S' could not forge $T_\alpha(l+1 \le \alpha \le t-1)$ without communicating with S.

According to the $SC - Bound$, S would not conduct a full proxy signature with S'. Thus, S' will not get the secret key d_S of S. Under the assumption $SC - Bound$, We consider a game in which a challenger generates an RSA key (N, e), chooses random $m \in \{0,1\}^k$ and $r \in Z_N^*$, and sends $(N, e, y = h(m\|r) \in Z_N)$ to adversary $\mathcal{A}$. The goal is for $\mathcal{A}$ to compute $y^{1/e}$ mod N. Assume that $\mathcal{A}$ can query the random oracle $H : Z_N^* \to Z_N^*$ at any sequence of points $x_1, ..., x_\ell \in Z_N^*$ receiving in return the output values $y_1 = H(x_1), ..., y_\ell = H(x_\ell)$ and, without loss of generality, these points are distinct. The challenger then gives to $\mathcal{A}$ the value $y^{1/e}$ mod N for all i, assuming that the challenger knows the factorization of N and can compute these values. We claim that $\mathcal{A}$ still can not compute a signature $\sigma = y^{1/e}$ mod N except with negligible probability. We construct the following adversary $\mathcal{A}'$ which computes $y^{1/e}$ mod N with the same probability at $\mathcal{A}$, but without any additional help from the challenger:

Algorithm 2. Algorithm $\mathcal{A}'$

Given (N, e, y) as input, and its goal is to compute $y^{1/e}$ mod N.

1. Run $\mathcal{A}$ on input (N, e, y).
2. Oracle Query:
   for *each random oracle query* $H(x_i)$ *of* $\mathcal{A}$ **do**
   $\quad \lfloor$ Choose $R_i \leftarrow Z_N^*$. Answer the query using $y_i := R_i^e$ mod N.
3. Give $R_1, ...R_\ell$ to $\mathcal{A}$, output whatever value is output by $\mathcal{A}$.

According to Theorem 1 and Theorem 2, if server S has re-outsourced F to S', it must conduct a t-round interaction with S' to generate a correct proof. Combining with $T - Bound$, they will not respond in time and the client will detect the malicious behavior of server S.

5.2 Probabilistic Analysis of Data Re-outsourcing

Our TIMER scheme is a probability scheme, where server S may re-outsource x blocks of the n-block file F to S' to break through the $T - Bound$. Let u be the number of different blocks for which client C asks proof in each phase of a challenge. Let X be a discrete random variable that is defined to be the number of blocks chosen by C that matches the blocks deleted by S. We could compute the probability P_X that at least one of the blocks picked by C matches one of the blocks re-outsourced to S' by S in each phases. We have:

$$
\begin{aligned}
P_X &= P\{X \geq 1\} = 1 - P\{X = 0\} \\
&= 1 - \frac{n-x}{n} \cdot \frac{n-x-1}{n-1} \cdot \ldots \cdot \frac{n-u+1-x}{n-u+1}.
\end{aligned}
\tag{1}
$$

Since $\frac{n-i-x}{n-i} \geq \frac{n-i-1-x}{n-i-1}$, we get:

$$
1 - \left(\frac{n-x}{n}\right)^u \leq P_X \leq 1 - \left(\frac{n-u+1-x}{n-u+1}\right)^u
\tag{2}
$$

If x blocks of F are offloaded to S' from S, P_X indicates the probability that a challenger C will detect the misbehavior of server S, when it asks proof for u out of n blocks. Since secure parameter t is the maximum communication rounds in a finite time delay Δt according to $T - Bound$, we have to guarantee that server S should conduct the communication rounds not less than t from the viewpoint of probability. Then, we get the relation between ideal communication rounds t and the actual communication rounds t' as $t' \times P_X = t$. That is:

$$
t' = \frac{t}{P_X} \geq \frac{t}{1 - \left(\frac{n-x}{n}\right)^u}.
\tag{3}
$$

Then, we assume that S re-outsources y out of n blocks of file F. Let Y be a discrete random variable that is defined to be the number of blocks chosen by C and matches the blocks destroyed by S. The probability P_Y that at least one of the blocks picked by C matches one of the blocks destroyed by S in each phase can be computed. We have:

$$
\begin{aligned}
P_Y &= P\{Y \geq 1\} = 1 - P\{Y = 0\} \\
&= 1 - \frac{n-y}{n} \cdot \frac{n-y-1}{n-1} \cdot \ldots \cdot \frac{n-u+1-y}{n-u+1}.
\end{aligned}
\tag{4}
$$

We define the probability P that, in all the t' phases, at least one of the blocks picked in each phase matches one of the blocks destroyed by S. we get:

$$
P = 1 - [1 - P_Y]^{t'}.
\tag{5}
$$

Then we have:

$$1 - (\frac{n-y}{y})^{ut'} \leq P \leq 1 - (\frac{n-u+1-y}{n-u+1})^{ut'}. \tag{6}$$

Let $c = ut'$ be the number of blocks chosen for the proof of data availability in PDP [1]. The lower bound of inequalities (5) is the same as detection probability expressed in PDP. If y equals to 1% of n, then C needs to ask for $ut = 460$ blocks and $ut = 300$ blocks in order to achieve P of at least 99% and 95%, respectively. Fig.1 shows the relation between t' and t when the total blocks asked by C are 460 and 300 respectively.

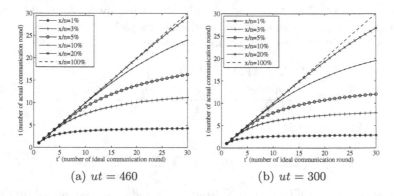

(a) $ut = 460$ (b) $ut = 300$

Fig. 1. Relationship between the ideal communication round t and the actual communication round t' when different percents of file are re-outsourced

According to Fig. 1, it is obvious that $t' = t$ when F is re-outsourced from S to S'. However, when only a part of F is re-outsourced from S to S', the TIMER scheme should also be able to tolerate a t-round communication delay. Thus, t' rounds communication needs to be adopted to prevent from partial data re-outsourcing and the relation between t and t' is shown in Fig. 1. We need to choose appropriate t' to prevent against different percent of data re-outsourcing, because the smaller t' is , the more efficient our scheme will be. If t' is relatively small, it means the allowed response delay Δt is not very large compared with a 1-round communication time delay in the network. From this point of view, the efficiency of our scheme, to some extent, depends on precise measurement of the maximum response delay Δt.

TIMER scheme is efficient when t' is relative small and the total challenge block number $c = ut'$ is fixed. However, to detect the malicious activity of S, when only a small percent data is re-outsourced, 1 percent or even smaller, t' may become too large compared to t. As a result, $u = c/t'$ may become a relative small number and the package composition number C_n^u may not be large enough as a secure parameter. In this situation, we need to fix u and compute the relative t'. Therefore, the total number of random blocks that C challenges will be linear correlation with the actual communication rounds t'.

6   Conclusion

Server side clients' data re-outsourcing may cause some security problems in cloud storage environment. In this paper, the proposed probabilistic TIMER scheme will provide an efficient way to detect this malicious behavior of cloud servers. It adopts cryptographic assumptions and network delay to prevent servers from collusion in cloud storage, which will provide a strong incentive for the economically rational cloud server to store clients' data in their stores. We provide a security and performance analysis of our scheme. The analysis shows that our scheme is secure and efficient. The storage overhead of clients in TIMER scheme is $O(1)$ and the computation and communication overhead are both $O(t)$ in full data re-outsourcing scenario and the client storage overhead, computation and communication overhead become $O(1)$, $O(t')$ and $O(t')$, respectively. However, t and t' will become relative large when only a small percent of clients' data is re-outsourced. In the future, we will explore some new methods to construct a scheme with constant computation and communication overhead.

Acknowledgement. This work is supported by the National Natural Science Foundation of China (Nos. 61272455 and 61100224), Doctoral Fund of Ministry of Education of China (No. 20130203110004), Program for New Century Excellent Talents in University (No. NCET-13-0946), China 111 Project (No. B08038), and the Fundamental Research Funds for the Central Universities (No. BDY151402).

References

1. Ateniese, G., et al.: Provable data possession at untrusted stores. In: Proc. of ACM CCS, Virginia, USA, pp. 598–609 (October 2007)
2. Ateniese, G., et al.: Scalable and efficient provable data possession. In: Proc. of SecureComm, VA, USA, pp. 1–10 (September 2008)
3. Bellare, M., Rogaway, P.: Random oracles are practical: A paradigm for designing effficient protocols. In: Proc. of ACM CCS, VA, USA, pp. 62–73 (November 1993)
4. Bowers, K.D., et al.: How to tell if your cloud files are vulnerable to drive crashes. In: Proceedings of the ACM Conference on Computer and Communications Security, IL, USA, pp. 501–514 (October 2011)
5. Capkun, S., Cagalj, M., Srivastava, M.: Secure localization with hidden and mobile base stations. In: Proceedings of the IEEE International Conference on Computer Communications, Catalunya, Spain, pp. 1–10 (April 2006)
6. Chen, X., Li, J., Susilo, W.: Efficient fair conditional payments for outsourcing computations. IEEE Transactions on Information Forensics and Security 7(6), 1687–1694 (2012)
7. Chen, X., Li, J., Ma, J., Tang, Q., Lou, W.: New algorithms for secure outsourcing of modular exponentiations. In: Foresti, S., Yung, M., Martinelli, F. (eds.) ESORICS 2012. LNCS, vol. 7459, pp. 541–556. Springer, Heidelberg (2012)
8. Commission, E.: Regulation of the european parliament and of the council on the protection of individuals with regard to the processing of personal data and on the free movement of such data. general data protection regulation, directive 95/46/EC (2012)

9. Coron, J.-S.: On the exact security of full domain hash. In: Bellare, M. (ed.) CRYPTO 2000. LNCS, vol. 1880, pp. 229–235. Springer, Heidelberg (2000)
10. Deswarte, Y., Quisquater, J.J., Saidane, A.: Remote integrity checking. In: Proc. of Conference on Integrity and Internal Control in Information Systems (IICIS 2003), Lausanne, Switzerland, pp. 1–11 (November 2003)
11. Dodis, Y., Vadhan, S., Wichs, D.: Proofs of retrievability via hardness amplification. In: Reingold, O. (ed.) TCC 2009. LNCS, vol. 5444, pp. 109–127. Springer, Heidelberg (2009)
12. Dubnicki, C., et al.: Hydrastor a scalable secondary storage. In: Proc. of the 7th USENIX Conference on File and Storage Technologies, CA, USA, pp. 197–210 (February 2009)
13. Erway, C., Kupcu, A., Papamanthou, C., Tamassia, R.: Dynamic provable data possession. In: Proc. of ACM CCS. pp. 213–222. Illinois, USA (November 2009)
14. Filho, D.L.G., Baretto, P.S.L.M.: Demonstrating data possession and uncheatable data transfer. IACR ePrint archive 2006 (2006),
    http://eprint.iacr.org/2006/150
15. Halevi, S., Harnik, D., Pinkas, B., Shulman-Peleg, A.: Proof of ownership in remote storage system. In: Proc. of ACM CCS, Illinois, USA, pp. 491–500 (October 2011)
16. Harnik, D., Pinkas, B., Shulman-Peleg, A.: Side channels in cloud services: Deduplication in cloud storage. In: Proc. of IEEE Security & Privicy, CA, USA, pp. 40–47 (November 2010)
17. Jansma, N., Arrendondo, B.: Performance comparison of elliptic curve and rsa digital signatures. Tech. Rep. MI, University of Michigan, Ann Arbor (May 2004)
18. Juels, A., Kaliski, B.S.: Pors: Proofs of retrievability for large files. In: Proc. of ACM CCS, Virginia, USA, pp. 584–597 (2007)
19. Laki, S., et al.: A detailed path-latency model for router geolocation. In: The International Conference on Testbeds and Research Infrastructures for the Development of Networks Communities and Workshops, DC, USA, pp. 1–6 (April 2009)
20. Merkle, R.C.: A certified digital signature. In: Brassard, G. (ed.) CRYPTO 1989. LNCS, vol. 435, pp. 218–238. Springer, Heidelberg (1990)
21. Papagiannaki, K., et al.: Provable data possession at untrusted stores. In: Proc. IEEE INFOCOM 2002, NY, USA, pp. 535–544 (June 2002)
22. Schwarz, T.S.J., Miller, E.L.: Store, forget, and check: Using algebraic signatures to check remotely administered storage. In: Proceedings of ICDCS 2006, Lisboa, Portugal, pp. 1–12 (July 2006)
23. Sebe, F., et al.: Time-bounded remote file integrity checking. Tech. Rep. 04429, Universitat Rovira i Virgili, Tarragona, Spain (July 2004)
24. Shacham, H., Waters, B.: Compact proofs of retrievability. In: Proc. of ASIACRYPT, Melbourne, Australia, pp. 90–107 (December 2008)
25. Ungureanu, C., et al.: Hydrafs A high-throughput file system for the hydrastor content-addressable storage system. In: Proc. of the 8th USENIX Conference on File and Storage Technologies, CA, USA, p. 17 (February 2010)
26. Wong, B., Stoyanov, I., Sirer, E.G.: Octant: A comprehensive framework for the geolocalization of internet hosts. In: Proceedings of the USENIX Networked Systems Design and Implementation, MA, USA, pp. 313–326 (April 2007)
27. Yamamoto, G., Fujisaki, E., Abe, M.: An efficiently-verifiable zero-knowledge argument for proofs of knowledge. IEICE Technical Report ISEC2005-48 105, 41–45 (July 2005)
28. Zhang, F., Kim, K.: Efficient id-based blind signature and proxy signature from bilinear pairings. In: Safavi-Naini, R., Seberry, J. (eds.) ACISP 2003. LNCS, vol. 2727, pp. 312–323. Springer, Heidelberg (2003)

Improvement of a Remote Data Possession Checking Protocol from Algebraic Signatures*

Yong Yu[1,2], Jianbing Ni[1], Jian Ren[3], Wei Wu[4], Lanxiang Chen[4], and Qi Xia[1]

[1] School of Computer Science and Engineering,
University of Electronic Science and Technology of China, Chengdu, 611731, China
{yyucd2012,nimengze,weiwu81,xiaqi0769}@gmail.com
[2] State Key Laboratory of Information Security, Institute of Information Engineering,
Chinese Academy of Sciences, Beijing 100093, China
[3] Department of Electrical and Computer Engineering,
Michigan State University, MI, 4882, USA
renjian@egr.msu.edu
[4] School of Mathematics and Computer Science,
Fujian Normal University, Fuzhou, 350007, China
lxiangchen@fjnu.edu.cn

Abstract. Cloud storage allows cloud users to enjoy the on-demand and high quality data storage services without the burden of local data storage and maintenance. However, the cloud servers are not necessarily fully trusted. As a consequence, whether the data stored on the cloud are intact becomes a major concern. To solve this challenging problem, recently, Chen proposed a remote data possession checking (RDPC) protocol using algebraic signatures. It achieves many desirable features such as high efficiency, small challenges and responses, non-block verification. In this paper, we find that the protocol is vulnerable to replay attack and deletion attack launched by a dishonest server. Specifically, the server can either fool the user to believe that the data is well maintained but actually only a proof of the challenge is stored, or can generate a valid response in the integrity checking process after deleting the entire file of the user. We then propose an improved scheme to fix the security flaws of the original protocol without losing the desirable features of the original protocol.

1 Introduction

Cloud storage provides a novel service model wherein data are maintained, managed and backed up remotely and accessed by the users over the network at

* This work is supported by the NSFC of China under Grants 61003232, 61370203, 61202450, the National Research Foundation for the Doctoral Program of Higher Education of China under Grants 20100185120012, 20123503120001, the NSFC of China for International Young Scientists under Grant 61250110543, Department of Education, Fujian Province, A-Class Project under Grant JA12076, and the Fundamental Research Funds for the Central Universities under Grant ZYGX2011J067.

X. Huang and J. Zhou (Eds.): ISPEC 2014, LNCS 8434, pp. 359–372, 2014.

anytime and from anywhere [1]. Although cloud storage is targeted to take up much of the workload from the client, it is fraught with security risks [2]. On the one hand, frequent data access increases the probability of disk corruption, as a result, loss of the data may occur constantly. Simultaneously, cloud service providers may try to hide data loss incidents in order to maintain their reputation. On the other hand, cloud providers are not fully trusted and thus, they might discard the data that have not been or are rarely accessed for monetary reasons. Therefore, whether the stored data keeps virgin is a major concern of the cloud users.

In order to check the data integrity at untrusted stores, in 2007, Ateniese et al. [3, 4] proposed the notion of provable data possession (PDP) for the first time and presented two efficient and provably-secure PDP schemes based on homomorphic verifiable tags. In their protocols, users are allowed to verify data integrity without accessing the entire file. At the same time, Juels et al. [5] formalized the model of proof of retrievability (PoR) which enables the server to produce a concise proof that a user can retrieve data, and then, presented a sentinel-based PoR scheme using error-correcting code. In 2008, Shacham and Waters [6, 7] described two efficient and compact PoR schemes. In 2009, Ateniese et al. [8] provided a framework for building public-key homomorphic linear authenticators from any identification protocol, and then described how to turn any public-key homomorphic linear authenticator into a publicly-verifiable PDP scheme with an unbounded number of verifications. Subsequently, a number of data auditing protocols [9–16] from some efficient PDP and PoR schemes [5–7, 17–19], were proposed to ensure the integrity of users' data. In 2013, Chen [20] proposed an algebraic signature based remote data possession checking (RDPC) protocol, which is a similar notion inherited from PDP, but the number of verifications in their basic protocol is limited. To overcome this drawback, an improved scheme supporting to refresh tags after t verifications was also proposed in [20]. Both protocols provide a number of desirable features of a remote data possession checking protocol such as high efficiency, small challenges and responses, no-block verification and were suggested to be adopted to the cloud storage scenario.

Our Contribution. In this paper, we identify several security flaws in the RDPC protocols in [20]. Firstly, neither the basic protocol nor the improved one is secure against the replay attack, in which the server is able to generate a valid proof from the previous proofs, without accessing the actual data. Consequently, the server needs only to store a previous proof and replay it as a valid response when required. Secondly, the improved protocol is vulnerable to a malicious server's deletion attack; namely, the server can generate a valid response in the integrity checking process after deleting the original data file. Then, we propose a new RDPC protocol to fix these security problems. Finally, we show the fixed protocol is secure based on the security model due to Ateniese et al. [3] and maintains the desirable features of the original protocol on performance.

Organization. Section 2 gives some preliminaries used in this paper. Section 3 reviews the RDPC protocols in [20] and discusses the security of the protocols. Section 4 describes our new RPDC protocol. Section 5 provides security proofs for the new RDPC protocol and Section 6 concludes the paper.

2 Preliminaries

In this section, we review basic knowledge of the RDPC protocols, including security model, components and security requirements of a RDPC protocol.

2.1 System Model

The remote data possession checking architecture for cloud storage involves two kinds of entities: a cloud server and its users. The cloud server, which has significant storage space and computation resources, stores users' data and provides data access service. The users have large amount of data to be stored on the cloud in order to eliminate the overhead of local storage. As users no longer possess the entire data locally and the cloud server is not fully-trusted, it is of critical importance for users to ensure their data are correctly stored and maintained in the cloud. Therefore, the users should be able to efficiently check the integrity and correctness of their outsourced data.

2.2 Components of a RDPC Protocol

A remote data possession checking protocol, which can be used to verify the integrity of the users' data, consists of five phases: **Setup**, **TagBlock**, **Challenge**, **ProofGen** and **ProofVerify** [3, 4].

- **Setup** is a probabilistic algorithm run by the user to setup the protocol. It takes a security parameter κ as input and returns k as the secret key of the user.
- **TagBlock** is a probabilistic algorithm that is run by the user to generate tags for a file. It takes the secret key k and a file F as input and returns the set of tags T for file F.
- **Challenge** is a probabilistic algorithm that is run by the user to generate a challenge. It takes the security parameter κ as input and returns the challenge $chal$.
- **ProofGen** is a deterministic algorithm that is run by the cloud server in order to generate a proof of possession. It takes the blocks of file F and the set of tags T as input and returns a proof of possession R for the challenged blocks in F.
- **ProofVerify** is a deterministic algorithm that is run by the user in order to evaluate a proof of possession. It takes his secret key k, the challenge $chal$ and the proof of possession R as input, and returns whether the proof is a correct proof of possession for the blocks challenged by $chal$.

2.3   Security Requirements

In cloud storage, the cloud server could be self-interested and might hide data corruption incidents to maintain its reputation. So a practical remote data possession checking protocol should be secure against the internal attacks a cloud server can launch, namely replace attack, forge attack, replay attack and deletion attack [14].

- Replace attack: The server may choose another valid pair of data block and tag (F_i, T_i) to replace a challenged pair of data block and tag (F_j, T_j), when it has already discarded F_j or T_j.
- Forge attack: The server may forge valid tags of data blocks to deceive the user.
- Replay attack: The server may generate a valid proof of possession R from previous proofs or other information, without accessing the outsourced data.
- Deletion attack: The server may generate a valid proof R making use of the tags T or other information, even the user's entire file has been deleted.

The security game due to Ateniese et al. [4] covers all the attacks mentioned above by capturing that an adversary cannot produce a valid proof without possessing all the blocks corresponding to a given challenge, unless it guesses all the missing blocks. The details of the game are as follows:

- Setup: The challenger runs **Setup** algorithm to generate a secret key k and keeps it secret.
- Query: The adversary chooses some data blocks $F_i(i = 1, \cdots, n)$ and makes tag queries adaptively. The challenger computes the corresponding tags $T_i(i = 1, \cdots, n)$ for the blocks and sends them back to the adversary.
- Challenge: The challenger generates a challenge *chal* and requests the adversary to respond a proof of possession R for the challenged blocks.
- Forge: The adversary computes a proof R for the challenged blocks and returns it to the challenger.

The adversary wins the game if **VerifyProof**$(k, chal, T_i(i = 1, \cdots, n), R)$ holds. A RDPC protocol is secure against a malicious server if for any (probabilistic polynomial-time) adversary the probability that it wins the security game on a set of file blocks is negligible.

3   On the Security of the RDPC Protocols

In this section, we review the basic RDPC protocol and the improved one in [20] and show that both protocols are insecure against the replay attack, and the improved scheme is also susceptible to the deletion attack.

3.1   A Brief Review of the RDPC Protocols

The following symbols are used in the RDPC protocols in [20].

- t: the number of verifications;
- c: the number of blocks challenged in each challenge;
- $E_{kt}(\cdot)$, $D_{kt}(\cdot)$: the encryption and decryption algorithms of a symmetric cryptosystem, where kt is the symmetric key;
- $F = F[1], \cdots, F[n]$: F denotes a file name, and $F[i]$ denotes the ith data block of the file F;
- $T = T_1, \cdots, T_t$: T denotes the set of block tags and T_i denotes the ith tag;
- $f(\cdot)$: $\{0,1\}^\kappa \times \{0,1\}^l \to \{0,1\}^l$, denotes a pseudo-random function (PRF);
- $\sigma(\cdot)$: $\{0,1\}^\kappa \times \{1, \cdots, n\} \to \{1, \cdots, n\}$, denotes a pseudo-random permutation (PRP);
- $AS_g(\cdot)$: denotes an algebraic signature algorithm. Here the algebraic signature on a block $s_0, s_1, \cdots, s_{n-1}$ is defined as:

$$AS_g(s_0, s_1, \cdots, s_{n-1}) = \sum_{i=0}^{n-1} s_i \cdot g^i,$$

where g is a primitive element of a Galois field [21].

The details of the basic RDPC protocol in [20] are described in Figure 1.

Setup: The user generates a master key $k \xleftarrow{R} \{0,1\}^\kappa$, an encryption key $kt \xleftarrow{R} \{0,1\}^\kappa$, and two random values $r_1, r_2 \xleftarrow{R} \{0,1\}^\kappa$.	**Challenge**: For the ith challenge, the user computes $k_i = f_k(r_1 + i)$, and sends $< r_2, k_i >$ to the server.
TagBlock:	**ProofGen**:
$0 < i \le t$ $\qquad k_i = f_k(r_1 + i)$ $\qquad s = 0$ $\qquad$ for $0 < j \le c$ $\qquad\qquad l_j = \sigma_{k_i}(r_2 + j)$ $\qquad\qquad s = s + F[l_j]$ $\qquad \delta_i = AS_g(s)$ $\qquad T_i = E_{kt}(\delta_i)$ The user sends $< F, T >$ to the server.	$F_i' = 0$ for $0 < j \le c$ $\qquad l_j = \sigma_{k_i}(r_2 + j)$ $\qquad F_i' = F_i' + F[l_j]$ return $< F_i', T_i' >$. **ProofVerify**:The user checks whether $AS_g(F_i') = D_{kt}(T_i')$ holds.

Fig. 1. The basic RDPC protocol in [20]

An improved scheme using challenge updating was proposed as well to overcome the drawback of limited number of data verifications in the basic protocol. The new tag generation and challenge updating are shown in Figure 2 and the other processes are the same as those of the basic protocol.

Setup: The user picks a master key $k \xleftarrow{R} \{0,1\}^\kappa$, the encryption key $kt \xleftarrow{R} \{0,1\}^\kappa$, and three random numbers $r_1, r_2, r_3 \xleftarrow{R} \{0,1\}^\kappa$.

TagBlock:	**Challenge-updating:**
for $0 < i \leq n$	For the mth updating
$\qquad \tau_i = AS_g(F[i])$	$k_m^u = f_k(r_3 + m)$
$\qquad$ for $0 < i \leq t$	for $0 < i \leq t$
$\qquad\qquad s = 0$	$\qquad s=0$
$\qquad\qquad k_i = f_k(r_1 + i)$	$\qquad k_i = f_{k_m^u}(r_1 + i)$
$\qquad\qquad$ for $0 < j \leq c$	$\qquad$ for $0 < j \leq c$
$\qquad\qquad\qquad l_j = \sigma_{k_i}(r_2 + j)$	$\qquad\qquad l_j = \sigma_{k_i}(r_2 + j)$
$\qquad\qquad\qquad s = s + \tau_{l_j}$	$\qquad\qquad s = s + \tau_{l_j}$
$\qquad\qquad T_i = E_{kt}(s)$	$\qquad T_i'' = E_{kt}(s)$
Forward $< F, T, \tau >$ to the server.	Send $< T'' >$ to the server.

Fig. 2. The improved RDPC protocol in [20]

3.2 Replay Attacks on the Protocols

The User	The Server
1.For the first challenge,	
$\quad$ compute $k_1 = f_k(r_1 + 1)$ $\xrightarrow{\ <r_2, k_1>\ }$	
	2.Compute $l_j = \sigma_{k_1}(r_2 + j)$ for
$\xleftarrow{\ <F_1', T_1'>\ }$	$\quad 1 \leq j \leq c$ and $F_1' = \sum_{j=1}^c F[l_j]$
3.Verify $AS_g(F_1') = D_{kt}(T_1')$	
	4.If the proof is available, discard
	$\quad < F, T >$, and keep $< F_1', T_1' >$
5.For the ith challenge,	
$\quad$ compute $k_i = f_k(r_1 + i)$ $\xrightarrow{\ <r_2, k_i>\ }$	
$\xleftarrow{\ <F_1', T_1'>\ }$ 6.Replay $< F_1', T_1' >$	
7.Verify $AS_g(F_1') = D_{kt}(T_1')$	

Fig. 3. Replay attack on the RDPC protocols

The replay attack, a serious security threat to RDPC protocols, says that the server can generate a valid proof from previous proofs or other information without accessing the actual data of the user. In the RDPC protocols in [20], since the replayed proof $< F_1', T_1' >$ can always make the equation $AS_g(F_1') = D_{kt}(T_1')$ hold and as a consequence, the server only needs to keep $< F_1', T_1' >$ instead of the entire file and verifiable tags $< F, T >$ of the user. Thus, the RPDC protocols in [20] are insecure against replay attack as shown in Figure 3.

3.3 Deletion Attack on the Improved Protocol

The deletion attack enables the server to generate a valid proof from the block tags or other information after deleting all the stored data of the user. In the improved protocol in [20], the server can launch deletion attack to fool the user to believe that the data in the cloud are well maintained, while actually only the block tags are stored. The details of the attack are shown below:

– Receiving the stored file $< F, T, \tau >$ from the user, the server keeps the values $< T, \tau >$ and discards the file F.
– When receiving the ith challenge $< r_2, k_i >$ from the user, the server computes $l_j = \sigma_{k_i}(r_2 + j)$ for each $j \in [1, c]$, and generates the l_j-th data block $F^*[l_j] = s^*_{l_j,0}, \cdots, s^*_{l_j,n-1}$ using τ_{l_j} as follows: pick $n - 1$ random values $s^*_{l_j,1}, \cdots, s^*_{l_j,n-1}$, and compute $s^*_{l_j,0}$ as:

$$s^*_{l_j,0} = \tau_{l_j} - \sum_{j=1}^{n-1} s^*_{l_j,j} \cdot g^j.$$

– After generating all the challenged data blocks $\{F^*_{l_1}, \cdots, F^*_{l_c}\}$, the server computes $F^*_i = \sum_{j=1}^c F^*_{l_j}$ and responds the proof $< F^*_i, T_i >$ to the user.

The verification equation $AS_g(F^*_i) = D_{kt}(T_1)$ holds since F^*_i is equal to F_i and thus, the user believes that the data in the cloud are well maintained. But in fact, the server stores only the block tags of the file $< T, \tau >$ instead of the whole data $< F, T, \tau >$. As a consequence, the server can delete the file F and rent the storage space to other cloud users without being detected by the user in data possession checking process.

4   Our RDPC Protocol

To enhance the security of original RDPC protocols in [20], we incorporate the basic RDPC scheme and the tricks due to Shacham and Waters [6, 7], namely, we involve the name of the file F_{id} and the block sequence numbers i in generating block tags. Besides, since algebraic signatures in [20] are non-cryptographic encoding methods rather than digital signatures, the server can generate a valid proof using the block tags τ after deleting all the data of the user. In our protocol, we enhance the algebraic signature algorithm by involving pseudo-random functions. Moreover, to improve the efficiency of the RDPC protocol, we make use of the random sampling technique to challenge the server. It's not necessary for the user to update the tags after t times verifications in the new protocol. Besides, the communication flows of our RDPC protocol should be transmitted via an authenticated and reliable channel in order to avoid the attack by Ni et al. [22]. The details of **Setup**, **TagBlock**, **Challenge**, **ProofGen** and **ProofVerify** are shown below.

- **Setup:** κ denotes the security parameter which determines the size of a prime q. Let G_1 be a cyclic group generated by g with order q. The user generates a secret key $k \xleftarrow{R} Z_q^*$, and defines two pseudo-random functions (PRF): δ: $\{0,1\}^* \times Z_q^* \to Z_q^*$ and ϕ: $Z_q^* \times Z_q^* \to Z_q^*$. π: $Z_q^* \times \{1, \cdots, n\} \to \{1, \cdots, n\}$ represents a pseudo-random permutation (PRP); H: $\{0,1\}^* \to Z_q^*$ stands for a hash function. Choose k_{enc} as the secret key of a symmetric encryption scheme $Enc(\cdot)$ and $Dec(\cdot)$.

- **TagBlock:** Given a file F, the user firstly splits F into m blocks $F = \{F[1], \cdots, F[m]\}$, further divides each block say $F[i]$ into n sectors $\{s_{i,1}, \cdots, s_{i,n}\}$. Next, the user picks n random values $\{\alpha_1, \cdots, \alpha_n\}$ in Z_q^* and generates $\tau = F_{id}||m||n||Enc_{k_{enc}}(\alpha_1||\cdots||\alpha_n)$ as the file tag of the file F where F_{id} is the name of the file F. Then, the user computes the verifiable tag of $F[i]$ as

$$T_i = \sum_{j=1}^{n} (\alpha_j \cdot s_{i,j} + H(F_{id}||g_{id}||i)) \cdot g_{id}^j,$$

where g_{id} is computed as $g_{id} = \delta_k(F_{id})$. Finally, the user sets $T = \{T_1, \cdots, T_m\}$ and sends (τ, F, T) to the server.

- **Challenge:** The user chooses a value c as the number of the blocks challenged, and generates two random numbers $k_1 \xleftarrow{R} Z_q^*$, $k_2 \xleftarrow{R} Z_q^*$, then sends the challenge $chal = (c, k_1, k_2)$ to the server.

- **ProofGen:** Upon receiving the challenge from the user, the server computes the $l_t = \pi_{k_1}(t)$ and $a_t = \phi_{k_2}(t)$ for $1 \le t \le c$. Then the server generates $\sigma = \sum_{t=1}^{c} a_t \cdot T_{l_t}$ and $\rho_j = \sum_{t=1}^{c} a_t s_{l_t,j}$ for $1 \le j \le n$. Finally, the server sets $\rho = \{\rho_1, \rho_2, \cdots, \rho_n\}$ and responds (τ, σ, ρ) to the user.

- **ProofVerify:** Upon receiving the proof from the server, the user computes $l_t = \pi_{k_1}(t)$, $a_t = \phi_{k_2}(t)$ for $1 \le t \le c$ and $g_{id} = \delta_k(F_{id})$, then decrypts $\alpha_1||\cdots||\alpha_n = Dec_{k_{enc}}(Enc_{k_{enc}}(\alpha_1||\cdots||\alpha_n))$ and checks whether the identity holds:

$$\sigma = \sum_{j=1}^{n} (\alpha_j \cdot \rho_j + \sum_{t=1}^{c} (a_t \cdot H(F_{id}||g_{id}||l_t))) \cdot g_{id}^j.$$

If the equation holds, it indicates the user's data are well maintained; Otherwise, the data have been corrupted. The protocol is illustrated in Figure 4.

The User	The Server
1.Compute τ and $T_i =$ $\sum_{j=1}^{n}(\alpha_j s_{i,j} + H(F_{id}\|g_{id}\|i))g_{id}^j$ for $F[i]$ where $g_{id} = \delta_k(F_{id})$.	

$\xrightarrow{\quad (\tau, F, T) \quad}$ 2.Store (τ, F, T).

3.Generate a random challenge:

$\quad chal = (c, k_1, k_2)$ $\xrightarrow{\quad (c, k_1, k_2) \quad}$ 4.Compute $l_t = \pi_{k_1}(t)$ and

$\qquad\qquad\qquad\qquad\qquad\qquad a_t = \phi_{k_2}(t)$ for $1 \leq t \leq c$.

$\qquad\qquad\qquad\qquad\qquad$ 5.Generate $\sigma = \sum_{t=1}^{c} a_t \cdot T_{l_t}$.

$\qquad\qquad\qquad\qquad\qquad$ 6.Generate $\rho_j = \sum_{t=1}^{c} a_t s_{l_t,j}$

$\xleftarrow{\quad (\tau, \sigma, \rho) \quad}$

7.Compute $l_t = \pi_{k_1}(t)$ and $\qquad\qquad\qquad$ for $1 \leq j \leq n$.

$a_t = \phi_{k_2}(t)$ for $1 \leq t \leq c$

and $g_{id} = \delta_k(F_{id})$.

8.Decrypt τ and check whether the equation

$\sigma = \sum_{j=1}^{n}(\alpha_j \cdot \rho_j + \sum_{t=1}^{c}(a_t \cdot H(F_{id}\|g_{id}\|l_t))) \cdot g_{id}^j$ holds.

Fig. 4. Our new RDPC protocol

The correctness of the protocol is elaborated as follows:

$$\sigma = \sum_{t=1}^{c} a_t \cdot T_{l_t} \tag{1}$$

$$= \sum_{t=1}^{c} a_t \cdot \sum_{j=1}^{n}(\alpha_j \cdot s_{l_t,j} + H(F_{id}\|g_{id}\|l_t)) \cdot g_{id}^j \tag{2}$$

$$= \sum_{j=1}^{n}\sum_{t=1}^{c} a_t(\alpha_j \cdot s_{l_t,j} + H(F_{id}\|g_{id}\|l_t)) \cdot g_{id}^j \tag{3}$$

$$= \sum_{j=1}^{n}(\sum_{t=1}^{c} a_t \cdot \alpha_j \cdot s_{l_t,j} + \sum_{t=1}^{c} a_t \cdot H(F_{id}\|g_{id}\|l_t)) \cdot g_{id}^j \tag{4}$$

$$= \sum_{j=1}^{n}(\alpha_j \cdot \rho_j + \sum_{t=1}^{c}(a_t \cdot H(F_{id}\|g_{id}\|l_t))) \cdot g_{id}^j \tag{5}$$

5   Security Proofs

In this section, we prove that our RDPC protocol is secure under the security model of Ateniese et al. [3] using the tricks due to Shacham and Waters [6, 7]. Intuitively, without maintaining the whole file, an adversary cannot generate a valid response to a challenge. That is, we will prove that the **ProofVerify** algorithm will reject except when the prover's ρ_j are computed correctly, i.e. are such that $\rho_j = \sum_{t=1}^{c} a_t s_{l_t,j}$.

Theorem 1. *If the pseudo-random function is secure and the symmetric encryption scheme is semantically secure, then there exists no adversary to break our RDPC protocol, that cause the user to accept a corrupted proof in the remote data possession checking process, within non-negligible probability, except the responding proof (σ, ρ) is computed correctly by* **ProofGen** *phase.*

In order to prove theorem 1, we construct a series of games and interleave the game description by limiting the difference in adversary's behavior between successive games.

Game 0. The first game, Game 0, is defined the same as the security game defined in Section 2.3.

Game 1. In Game 1, the challenger uses the a random bit-string of the same length as encryption of $\alpha_1 || \cdots || \alpha_n$ to replace the ciphertext. When given a challenged tag, the adversary can distinguish the encrypted value of the tag, rather than attempting to decrypt the ciphertext, the challenger declares failure and aborts.

Analysis. In Game 1, the challenger keeps a table of plaintexts $\alpha_1 || \cdots || \alpha_n$ and their tags to respond queries in decryption oracles. The challenger can break the semantic security of the symmetric encryption scheme employing the adversary if the probability of the adversary's success between Game 0 and Game 1 is non-negligible. In order to bridge the gap between Game 0 and Game 1, we must use a hybrid argument between "all valid encryption" and "no valid encryption", which will cause the reduction suffer a $1/q_s$ security loss, where q_s is the number of queries made by the adversary.

Specifically, the challenger interacts with the adversary $\mathcal{A}$ following the security game in section 2.3 and keeps track of the files stored by $\mathcal{A}$. Then, if $\mathcal{A}$ succeeds in some data integrity checking interaction with a proof that is different from that would be generated by the **ProofGen** algorithm, the challenger aborts and outputs 1; Otherwise, outputs 0. Assume the challenger outputs 1 with some non-negligible probability ϵ_0 if its behavior is as specified in Game 0, and the challenger outputs 1 with some non-negligible probability ϵ_1 if its behavior is as specified in Game 1, we will show that the gap between ϵ_0 and ϵ_1 is negligible as long as the symmetric encryption scheme is semantic secure.

In game 0, the challenger uses the ciphertext of $\alpha_1 || \cdots || \alpha_n$ to generate each tag. In Game 1, the challenger encrypts a random string of the same length in generating each tag. Suppose that $|\epsilon_1 - \epsilon_0|$ is non-negligible. Consider the hybrid argument in which the challenger generates the first i tags using random ciphertexts, and the remaining $q_s - i$ tags involving random values. Thus, there must be a value of i such that the difference between the challenger's outputs in hybrid i and hybrid $i+1$ is at least $|\epsilon_1 - \epsilon_0|/q_s$, which is non-negligible. According to this, we will construct an algorithm $\mathcal{B}$ to break the security of the symmetric encryption scheme.

The encryption oracle for k_{enc} is accessible to $\mathcal{B}$, as well as a left-or-right oracle which given strings m_0 and m_1 of the same length, outputs the encryption of m_b, where b is a random bit. $\mathcal{B}$ interacts with $\mathcal{A}$ acting as the challenger. In answering $\mathcal{A}$'s first i queries, $\mathcal{B}$ uses its encryption oracle to obtain the encryption of $\alpha_1 || \cdots || \alpha_n$, which includes in the tag. In answering $\mathcal{A}$'s the $(i + 1)$th query, $\mathcal{B}$ generates the correct plaintext $m_0 = \alpha_1 || \cdots || \alpha_n$ and a random plaintext m_1 of the same length and submits both to its left-or-right oracle. In answering $\mathcal{A}$'s remaining queries, $\mathcal{B}$ encrypts a random plaintext which has the same length as the correct plaintext using its encryption oracles and includes the result in the tags. $\mathcal{B}$ keeps track of the files stored by the adversary. If $\mathcal{A}$ succeeds in some data possession checking interaction but the proof is different from that would be generated by the **ProofGen** algorithm, the challenger aborts and outputs 1; Otherwise, outputs 0.

If the left-or-right oracle receives its left input, $\mathcal{B}$ is interacting with $\mathcal{A}$ according to hybrid i. If the left-or-right oracle receives its right input, $\mathcal{B}$ is interacting with $\mathcal{A}$ according to hybrid $i + 1$. There is a non-negligible difference in $\mathcal{A}$'s behavior and therefore in $\mathcal{B}$'s, which breaks the security of the symmetric encryption scheme. Note that, since the values $\alpha_1 || \cdots || \alpha_n$ are randomly chosen and independent with each file, the values given by $\mathcal{B}$ to its left-or-right oracle are consistent with a query it makes to its encryption oracle with negligible probability.

Game 2. In Game 2, the challenger uses truly random values in Z_p^* instead of the outputs of the pseudo-random function δ, remembering these values to use in verifying the validation of the adversary's responses in data possession checking instances. More specifically, the challenger evaluates g_{id} not by applying the PRF $g_{id} = \delta_k(F_{id})$, but by generating a random value $r \leftarrow Z_q^*$ and inserting an entry (k, F_{id}, r) in a table; it queries this table when evaluating the PRF δ to ensure consistency.

Analysis. In Game 2, the challenger uses random values to replace the outputs of the PRF δ and then keeps a table of (k, F_{id}, r) to ensure the verification of the adversary's proof. If there is a difference in the adversary's success probability between Games 1 and 2, we can use the adversary to break the security of the PRF δ. This means that if the adversary can distinguish random values from the outputs of PRF, the challenger can break the security of the PRF involving the adversary.

As in the analysis of Game 2, the difference in behavior we use to break the security of PRF is the event that the adversary succeeds in a data possession checking interaction but responded values (σ, ρ) are different from those that would be by the **ProofGen** algorithm. Similar to the analysis of Game 1, a hybrid argument is necessary to proof Game 2 with a security loss $1/(mq_s)$ in the reduction, where m is a bound on the number of blocks in any file the adversary requests to have stored.

Game 3. In Game 3, the challenger handles RDPC protocol executions initiated by the adversary differently than in Game 2. In each such RDPC protocol execution, the challenger issues a challenge as before. However, the challenger verifies the adversary's response differently from what it specified in **ProofVerify** phase.

The challenger keeps a table of the **TagBlock** queries made by the adversary and the corresponding responses to maintain consistency; the challenger knows the values ρ_j and σ that the sever would have produced in response to the query it issued. If the values the adversary sent were exactly these values, the challenger accepts the adversary's response. If in any of these interactions the adversary responds in such a way that (1) passes the verification algorithm but (2) is not what would have been computed by an honest server, the challenger declares failure and aborts.

Analysis. The adversary's view is different in Game 3 and Game 2 only when the response of adversary (1) can make the verification algorithm satisfied but (2) is not what would have been computed by the challenger, which acts as an honest server, in some RDPC protocol interaction. We show that the probability that this happens is negligible.

Before analyzing the difference in probabilities between Game 3 and Game 2, we firstly describe the notion and draw a few conclusions. Suppose the file F that causes the abort is divided into m data blocks $F = F[1], \cdots, F[m]$, further divides each block into n sectors $F[i] = s_{i,1}, \cdots, s_{i,n}$. F_{id} denotes the name of the file F and i represents the block number of $F[i]$. Assume $chal = (c, k_1, k_2)$ is the query that causes the challenger to abort and the adversary's response to that query is (σ^*, ρ^*). If the adversary's response satisfies the verification–i.e., if

$$\sigma^* = \sum_{j=1}^{n}(\alpha_j \cdot \rho_j^* + \sum_{t=1}^{c}(a_t \cdot H(F_{id}||r||l_t))) \cdot r^j,$$

where $l_t = \pi_{k_1}(t)$ and $a_t = \phi_{k_2}(t)$ for $1 \leq t \leq c$ and r is the random value substituted by Game 2 for g_{id}. Let the expected response, which would have been obtained from an honest prover, be (σ, ρ), where $\sigma = \sum_{t=1}^{c} a_t \cdot T_{l_t}$ and $\rho_j = \sum_{t=1}^{c} a_t s_{l_t,j}$. Because of the correctness of the protocol, the expected response can pass the verification equation, that is

$$\sigma = \sum_{j=1}^{n}(\alpha_j \cdot \rho_j + \sum_{t=1}^{c}(a_t \cdot H(F_{id}||r||l_t))) \cdot r^j.$$

Observe that if $\rho_j^* = \rho_j$ for each j, the value of σ^* should be equal to σ, which contradicts our assumption above. Therefore, let us define $\Delta\sigma = \sigma^* - \sigma$ and $\Delta\rho_j = \rho_j^* - \rho_j$ for $1 \leq j \leq n$ and subtracte the verification equation for σ from that for σ^*, we have

$$\Delta\sigma = \sum_{j=1}^{n} \alpha_j \cdot \Delta\rho_j \cdot r^j.$$

The bad event occurs exactly when some $\Delta\rho_j$ is not zero, which means that the adversary's submitting a convincing response is different from an honest server's response.

However, the values $\{\alpha_1, \cdots, \alpha_n\}$ for every file are randomly chosen and therefore independent of the adversary's view. There is no other needed to consider the encryption in generating the tags, and the appearance is in computing $T_i = \sum_{j=1}^{n}(\alpha_j \cdot s_{i,j} + H(F_{id}||r||i)) \cdot r^j$, where $H(F_{id}||r||i)$ is a secure hash function. Since the output of δ is replaced by a random value r, T_i is independent of $\{\alpha_1, \cdots, \alpha_n\}$. Therefore, the probability that the bad event happens if the challenger first picks the random values $\{\alpha_1, \cdots, \alpha_n\}$ for each stored file and then undertakes the data possession checking interactions is the same as the probability that the bad event happens if the challenger first undertakes the data possession checking interactions and then chooses the value $\{\alpha_1, \cdots, \alpha_n\}$ for each file.

Consider the values $\Delta\rho_j$ and $\Delta\sigma$ in responses from the adversary and the choice of $\{\alpha_1, \cdots, \alpha_n\}$. The probability makes the equation $\Delta\sigma = \sum_{j=1}^{n} \alpha_j \cdot \Delta\rho_j \cdot r^j$ hold for a specific entry in an interaction is $1/p$. Therefore, the probability that the equation holds for a nonzero number of entries is at most q_P/p, where q_P is the number of RDPC protocol interactions initiated by the adversary. Thus, except with negligible probability q_P/p, the adversary never generates a convincing response which is different from an honest server's response, so the probability of the challenger aborts is negligible.

Wrapping Up. Yet we have argued that, assuming the PRF is secure and the symmetric encryption is semantic security, there is only a negligible difference in the success probability of the adversary in Game 3 compared to Game 0, where the adversary is not constrained in this manner. This completes the proof of Theorem 1.

6   Conclusion

In this paper, we presented a security analysis on a remote data possession checking protocol using algebraic signature in [20], and showed that it suffers from the replay attack and deletion attack. We also proposed an improved protocol by using the techniques of Shacham and Waters [6,7] to fix these security flaws. Involving the security model due to Ateniese et al [3], we provided formal security proofs of our new RDPC protocol.

References

1. Buyyaa, R., Yeoa, C., Broberga, J., Brandicc, I.: Cloud computing and emerging IT platforms: Vision, hype, and reality for delivering computing as the 5th utility. Future Generation Computer Systems 25(6), 599–616 (2009)
2. Zissis, D., Lekkas, D.: Addressing cloud computing security issues. Future Generation Computer Systems 28(3), 583–592 (2012)
3. Ateniese, G., Burns, R.C., Curtmola, R., Herring, J., Kissner, L., Peterson, Z.N.J., Song, D.: Provable data possession at untrusted stores. In: Proceeding of ACM CCS 2007, Alexandria, Virginia, USA, pp. 598–609. ACM (2007)
4. Ateniese, G., Burns, R.C., Curtmola, R., Herring, J., Kissner, L., Peterson, Z.N.J., Song, D.: Remote data checking using provable data possession. ACM Trans. Inf. Syst. Security 14(1), 12 (2011)

5. Juels, A., Kaliski, B.S.: PORs: proofs of retrievability for large files. In: Proceeding of ACM CCS 2007, Alexandria, Virginia, USA, pp. 584–597. ACM (2007)
6. Shacham, H., Waters, B.: Compact proofs of retrievability. In: Pieprzyk, J. (ed.) ASIACRYPT 2008. LNCS, vol. 5350, pp. 90–107. Springer, Heidelberg (2008)
7. Shacham, H., Waters, B.: Compact proofs of retrievability. Journal of Cryptology 26(3), 442–483 (2013)
8. Ateniese, G., Kamara, S., Katz, J.: Proofs of storage from homomorphic identification protocols. In: Matsui, M. (ed.) ASIACRYPT 2009. LNCS, vol. 5912, pp. 319–333. Springer, Heidelberg (2009)
9. Wang, Q., Wang, C., Li, J., Ren, K., Lou, W.: Enabling public verifiability and data dynamics for storage security in cloud computing. In: Backes, M., Ning, P. (eds.) ESORICS 2009. LNCS, vol. 5789, pp. 355–370. Springer, Heidelberg (2009)
10. Wang, Q., Wang, C., Ren, K., Lou, W., Li, J.: Enabling public auditability and data dynamics for storage security in cloud computing. IEEE Trans. Parallel Distrib. Syst. 22(5), 847–859 (2012)
11. Wang, C., Ren, K., Lou, W., Li, J.: Toward public auditable secure cloud data storage services. IEEE Network 24(4), 19–24 (2010)
12. Zhu, Y., Hu, H., Ahn, G.J., Stephen, S.: Yau: efficient audit service outsourcing for data integrity in clouds. Journal of Systems and Software 85(5), 1083–1095 (2012)
13. Zhu, Y., Hu, H., Ahn, G.J., Yu, M.: Cooperative provable data possession for integrity verification in multicloud storage. IEEE Trans. Parallel Distrib. Syst. 23(12), 2231–2244 (2012)
14. Yang, K., Jia, X.: An efficient and secure dynamic auditing protocol for data storage in cloud computing. IEEE Trans. Parallel Distrib. Syst. 24(9), 1717–1726 (2013)
15. Zhu, Y., Wang, S.B., Hu, H., Ahn, G.J., Ma, D.: Secure collaborative integrity verification for hybrid cloud environments. Int. J. Cooperative Inf. Syst. 21(3), 165–198 (2012)
16. Wang, C., Chow, S.S.M., Wang, Q., Ren, K., Lou, W.: Privacy-preserving public auditing for secure cloud storage. IEEE Trans. Computers 62(2), 362–375 (2013)
17. Curtmola, R., Khan, O., Burns, R.: Robust remote data checking. In: Proceeding of Storage SS 2008, Fairfax, Virginia, USA, pp. 63–68. ACM (2008)
18. Bowers, K.D., Juels, A., Oprea, A.: Proofs of retrievability: theory and implementation. In: Proceeding of CCSW 2009, Chicago, Illinois, USA, pp. 43–54. ACM (2009)
19. Dodis, Y., Vadhan, S., Wichs, D.: Proofs of retrievability via hardness amplification. In: Reingold, O. (ed.) TCC 2009. LNCS, vol. 5444, pp. 109–127. Springer, Heidelberg (2009)
20. Chen, L.: Using algebraic signatures to check data possession in cloud storage. Future Generation Computer Systems 29(7), 1709–1715 (2013)
21. Schwarz, T., Miller, E.: Store, forget, and check: using algebraic signatures to check remotely administered storage. In: Proceeding of ICDCS 2006, Lisbon, Portugal, p. 12. IEEE Computer Society (2006)
22. Ni, J., Yu, Y., Mu, Y., Xia, Q.: On the security of an efficient dynamic auditing protocol in cloud storage. IEEE Transactions on Parallel and Distributed Systems (2013), doi:10.1109/TPDS.2013.199
23. Erway, C., Kupcu, A., Papamanthou, C., Tamassia, R.: Dynamic provable data possession. In: Proceeding of ACM CC 2009, Hyatt Regency Chicago, Chicago, IL, USA, pp. 213–222. ACM (2009)
24. Ateniese, G., Pietro, R.D., Mancini, L.V., Tsudik, G.: Scalable and efficient provable data possession. In: Proceeding of SecureComm 2008, Stanbul, Turkey, pp. 1–10. IEEE Computer Society (2008)

Distributed Pseudo-Random Number Generation and Its Application to Cloud Database

Jiageng Chen, Atsuko Miyaji, and Chunhua Su

School of Information Science,
Japan Advanced Institute of Science and Technology, Japan
{jg-chen,miyaji,su}@jaist.ac.jp

Abstract. Cloud database is now a rapidly growing trend in cloud computing market recently. It enables the clients run their computation on out-sourcing databases or access to some distributed database service on the cloud. At the same time, the security and privacy concerns is major challenge for cloud database to continue growing. To enhance the security and privacy of the cloud database technology, the pseudo-random number generation (PRNG) plays an important roles in data encryptions and privacy-preserving data processing as solutions. In this paper, we focus on the security and privacy risks in cloud database and provide a solution for the clients who want to generate the pseudo-random number collaboratively in a distributed way which can be reasonably secure, fast and low cost to meet requirement of cloud database. We provide two solutions in this paper, the first one is a construction of distributed PRNG which is faster than the traditional Linux PRNG. The second one is a protocol for users to execute the random data perturbation collaboratively before uploading the data to the cloud database.

Keywords: cloud database, pseudo-random number generators, distributed computation, data randomization.

1 Introduction

In the so-called "big data" era, huge volumes of data are being created from the organizations procedure, business activities, social network and scientific research. Databases are ubiquitous and of immense importance and the cloud database technology offers many benefits such as data storage and outsource computing to meet the new technological requirements. Many cloud database service and computation are in the distributed environment, as an important security primitive, pseudo-random number generator play an extremly important role in such cloud based data service. In this paper, we propose a framework for pseudo-random number generator (PRNG) which is used in distributed cloud database, our proposal is based on the collection of high entropy from operation system such as Linux.

X. Huang and J. Zhou (Eds.): ISPEC 2014, LNCS 8434, pp. 373–387, 2014.

In Linux PRNG, there are two devices dev/random and dev/urandom. dev/random is nearly a true random number generator consists of a physical non deterministic phenomenon produces a raw binary sequence and a deterministic function, compress this sequence in order to reduce statistical weakness. But these procedures to produce the nearly true random number sequences from dev/random are expensive and low-speed for practical cloud database application. So usually for practical usage, we use pseudo-random number generators which are deterministic random bit generators such as Linux dev/urandom, Linux dev/urandom use algorithms for generating a sequence of numbers that approximates the properties of true random number but with lower security bound. Our research purpose is to make the robust and secure dev/random which is more secure and robust to be faster to meet the need of cloud database service.

1.1 Related Works

Many random number generators exists (e.g., [15,18,23,1,20,21]. Shamir was first to provide SPRNG [23] while Blum-Blum-Shub [1] and many other PRNGs followed. A high-quality source of randomness must be used to design a high-quality true random data generator for cryptographic purposes. In a typical environment of general purpose computer systems, some good sources of randomness may exist in almost any user input - the exact timing of keystrokes and the exact movements of mouse are well known. Some other possible sources are for example microphone (if unplugged then A/D convertor yields electronic noise [9]), video camera (focused ideally on some kind of chaotic source as lava lamp [16]), or fluctuations in hard disk access time [6].

Following the unsuitability of the so called statistical PRNGs for cryptographical purposes, special PRNGs, intended for cryptography uses, were developed. The most related works to ours are Linux PRNG. The first security analysis of Linux PRNGs was given in 2006 by Gutterman *et. al* [10], based on kernel version 2.6.10 released in 2004. In 2012, Lacharme *et. al* [19] gave a detailed analyze the PRNG architecture in the Linux system and provide its first accurate mathematical description and a precise analysis of the building blocks, including entropy estimation and extraction.

1.2 Problem Definition and Our Contributions

There are two common deployment models of cloud database: users can run databases on the cloud independently, using a virtual machine image, or they can purchase access to a database service, maintained by a cloud database provider such as Distributed database as a service (DBaaS). However, cloud database adoption may be hampered by concerns about security, privacy, and proprietary issues, such distributed DBaaS are vulnerable to threats such as unauthorized access and malicious adversaries who want to compromise the privacy of the data storage. Our protocol is constructed based on Linux kernel, the internal state of the Linux PRNG is composed of three pools, namely the input pool, the blocking pool for dev/random output and the nonblocking pool for dev/urandom output, according to the source code. We assume that there are many severs who provide outsourcing distributed database services and need to generate pseudo-random number for encryption or data random perturbation. If the blocking pool cannot accumulate enough entropy, the PRNG output will be blocked. However, the Linux OS dev/random is extremely suitable for use when very high quality randomness is desired (for example, for key generation, one-time pads and sensitive data randomization), but it will only return a maximum of the number of bits of randomness contained in the entropy pool. The major problem we focus in this paper is to construct a fast dev/random in the distributed environment to achieve a higher speed.

- For the cryptographic purposes, the distributed clients and the cloud servers may need to generate encryption or decryption keys to secure their communication or create some fresh nonce or to execute the protocols for authentication. In this case, pseudo-random numbers are necessary for both key generations, encryption authentication.
- For data privacy purpose, the clients who purchase the services for the cloud database may store their database on the cloud servers. In order to aggregate information that contains personal data without involving a trusted aggregator, two important constraints must be fulfilled: 1) privacy of individuals or data subjects whose data are being collected, and 2) security of data contributors who need to protect their data from other contributors as well as the untrusted aggregation.

For an OS-based pseudo-random generator, Linux PRNG is a good candidate for the distributed environment. Because it is an open-source OS and it plays a huge role in virtualized cloud operations including the DBaaS. The theory of computational pseudo-randomness discussed in our paper emerged from cryptography, where researchers sought a definition that would ensure that using pseudo-random bits instead of truly random bits would retain security against all computationally feasible attacks.

Our Contributions. In this paper, we propose a framework for pseudo-random number generators under the distributed environment.

- We clarify the necessary conditions for implementing secure and fast PRNGs for the distributed cloud database.
- We propose a protocol based on Linux PRNG for the distributed pseudo-random number generation which is faster than stand-alone Linux PRNG. We let all parties execute the collection of entropy for distributed random source and then mix them securely to form a local random pool for the pseudo-random number generation. The second one is to apply Barak-Shaltiel-Tromer randomness extractor randomness exactor to generate the pseudo-random number with the same probability distribution for the data aggregation in cloud database.
- We also provide the security proof and show that the security of our proposals holds as long as the adversary has limited influence on the high-entropy source.

The rest of the paper is constructed as follows: We outline preliminaries for pseudo-random number generator in Section 2. The constructions of our schemes are in Section 3 and Section 4, respectively. In Section 5, we provide the security proofs for our proposed distributed PRNGs and our experimental analysis. We draw the conclusions in Section 6.

2   Preliminaries

In this section, we give a brief descriptions about the building blocks used in our schemes and the security definition.

2.1   Building Blocks

Linux PRNG. The Linux PRNG is part of the Linux kernel since 1994. The original version was written by Tsfo [24], and later modified by Mackall [22]. The PRNG is implemented in C with more than about 1700 lines code in a single source file, drivers/char/random.c. There are many build-in function which we can use to construct our distributed PRNG.

Barak-Halevi Model. Let us briefly recall construction of PRNG with input due to Barak and Halevi [3]. This model (which we call BH model) involves a randomness extraction function: $Extract : \{0,1\}^p \rightarrow \{0,1\}^n$ and a standard deterministic PNRG $G; \{0,1\}^n \rightarrow \{0,1\}^{n+l}$ In the Barak-Halevi's framework, two functions are defined in the pseudo-random number generator: function $\mathsf{next}(s)$ that generates the next output and then updates the state accordingly and a function $\mathsf{refresh}(s, x)$ that refreshes the current state s using some additional input x.

Twisted Generalized Feedback Shift Register (TGFSR)[20]. It is a improved version of Generalized Feedback Shift Register (GFSR) which can be used to run w Linear Feed Back Registers (LFSR) in parallel, where w is the size of the machine word and its cycle length $2^p - 1$ with a memory of p words. TGFSR achieves a period of $2^{wp} - 1$ and removes the dependence of a initialized sequence in GFSR, without the necessary of polynomial being a trinomial.

Verifiable Secret Sharing. The VSS protocol has a two-phase structure: In a primary phase, the dealer D distributes a secret s, while in a second, later phase, the players cooperate in order to retrieve it. More specifically, the structure is as follows:

- Sharing phase: The dealer initially holds secret $s \in K$ where K is a finite field of sufficient size; and each player P_i finally holds some private information v_i.
- Reconstruction phase: In this phase, each player P_i reveals (some of) his private information v_i. Then, on the revealed information v_i' (a dishonest player may reveal $v_i' \neq v_i$), a reconstruction function is applied in order to compute the secret, $s = Rec(v_1', ..., v_n')$

2.2   Security Definitions and Model

A deterministic function $G : \{0,1\}^d \rightarrow \{0,1\}^m$ is a (t,ϵ) pseudo-random generator (G) if $d < m$, $G(U_d)$ and U_m are (t,ϵ) indistinguishable. Information disclosure in G refers to the leaking of the internal state, or seed value, of a PRNG. Leaks of this kind can make predicting future output from the PRNG in use much easier. Here in this paper. we follow the formal security model for PRNGs with input was proposed in 2005 by Barak and Halevi (BH model) [3] and its extension by Dodis et al. [8].There is a proof that the security definition imply the following security notions in [8].

- Resilience: The internal state and future output of PRNG must not able to predict even if an adversary can influence or attain the entropy source used to initialize or refresh the internal state of the PRNG;
- Forward security and backward security: an adversary must not be able to predict past and future outputs even if he can compromise the internal state of the PRNG.

Our security model is based on Dodis et al. [8]'s modified BH model, the adversary $\mathcal{A}$ can access several oracle calls as follows:

- D-refresh. This is the key procedure where the distribution sampler D is run, and where its output I is used to refresh the current state ST. Additionally, one adds the amount of fresh entropy to the entropy counter c, and resets the corrupt flag to false when c crosses the threshold γ.
- get-state and set-state. These procedures provide $\mathcal{A}$ with the ability to either learn the current state ST, or set it to any value ST^*. In either case c is reset to 0 and corrupt is set to true. We denote by q_S the total number of calls to get-state and set-state.
- next-ror and get-next. These procedures provide $\mathcal{A}$ with either the real-or-random challenge (provided that corrupt = false) or the true PRNG output. As a small subtlety, a gprematureh call to get-next before corrupt = false resets the counter c to 0, since then $\mathcal{A}$ might learn something non-trivial about the (low-entropy) state ST in this case. We denote by q_R the total number of calls to next-ror and get-next.

This model involves an internal state that is refreshed with a (potentially biased) external random source, and a cryptographic function that outputs random numbers from the continually internal state. The game continues in this fashion until the attacker decides to halt with some output in $\{0,1\}$. For a particular construction $G = $ (setup, next, refresh), we let $Pr[A(m,H)^{\mathrm{I(G)}} = 1]$ denote the probability that adversary $\mathcal{A}$ outputs the bit 1 after interacting as above with the system. Here I(G) stands for the ideal random process and note that we only use G in this game to answer queries that are made while the compromised flag is set to true.

Definition 1. *We say that* $G = $ *(setup, next, refresh) is a robust pseudo-random generator (with respect to a family $\mathcal{H}$ of distributions) if for every probabilistic polynomial-time attacker algorithm $\mathcal{A}$, the difference*

$$Pr[A(m, H)^G = 1] - Pr[A(m, H)^{I(G)} = 1] < \epsilon$$

in some security parameter as follows:

- *G with input has $(t, qD, \gamma^*, \epsilon)$-recovering security if for any adversary $\mathcal{A}$ and legitimate sampler D, both running in time t, the advantage of recovering the internal state with parameters q_D is at most ϵ.*
- *G with input has (t, ϵ)-preserving security if the advantage of any adversary $\mathcal{A}$ running in time t of distinguishable G output and internal state from true random sample is at most $a\epsilon$.*

3   Our Proposal on Distributed PRNG

The PRNG used by the cloud server relies on external entropy sources. Entropy samples are collected from system events inside the kernel, asynchronously and independently from output generation. These inputs are then accumulated into the input pool. Beyond the difficulty of collecting truly random data from various randomness sources, the problem of insufficient amount of truly random data which can be effectively solved by using pseudo-random data is also important. Our protocol overcomes this problem by sharing the collecting the entropy in cloud computing environment.

1. We apply a hash function or symmetric key encryption scheme to protect the vulnerable PRNG outputs. If a PRNG is suspected to be vulnerable to direct cryptanalytic attack, then outputs from the PRNG should be preprocessed with a cryptographic hash function.
2. Occasionally generate a new starting PRNG state, a whole new PRNG state should occasionally be generated from the current PRNG. This will ensure that any PRNG can fully reseed itself, given enough time and input entropy. The best way to resist all the state-compromise extension attacks is simply never to have the PRNG's state compromised.

3.1   Distributed Pseudo-Random Number Generator

A nice PRNG should always have a component for harvesting entropy. Even if entropy is only used to seed a PRNG, the infrastructures using PRNG should still harvest their own entropy, because experience shows that pawning the responsibility for entropy harvesting onto clients leads to a large number of systems with inadequately seeded PRNGs. Entropy gathering should be a separate component from the PRNG. This component is responsible for producing outputs that are believed to be truly random. The following work reviewed is due to Gutterman, Pinkas and Reinman [10].

Our work focus on how to overcome the security problems in existing PRNG based on Linux. Furthermore, we apply the Lacharme's linear corrector [17] to implement the entropy addition and update to get more high entropy compared to existing Linx-based PRNG [10].

We assume that there are k distributed users or cloud servers online to generate the pseudo-random number. Let $G_i : \{0,1\}^m \to \{0,1\}^{n+l}$ be a distributed pseudo-random generator, where $1 \le i \le k$, and a ensemble of external input I. We then model our PRNG construction as follows:

- Initial phase: It uses a function setup() to generate the $seed = (s, s') \leftarrow \{0,1\}^{n+l}$ at first.
- State refresh phase: Given $seed = (s, s')$ as input, the refresh algorithm refresh(ST, I) outputs a next internal state ST'
- Random bits output phase: The generator G_i outputs a random string R and a new state ST'.

The Protocol for Distributed Pseudo-random Number Generation

1. Each party translates system events into bits which represent the underlying entropy and then share out their entropy to other parties.
2. Each party also collecting entropy for other other party. Because the system cannot consume more entropy than it has collected, and once the entropy counter for the input pool has reached its maximum value, the party starts ignoring any incoming events in order to save CPU resources. Thus, it collects no more entropy.
3. Each party run the setup() to get the initial seeds as input of PRNG G, after that each party adds these bits to the generator pools using add_input_randomness() function in Linux PRNG.
4. Each party use function refresh() to extract entropy and update the entropy pool. If the accumulated entropy from both internal events and external events of other parties can pass the test of entropy estimator, send the bits as input of function next().
5. When bits are read from the generator, each party uses function next() to generates the output of the generator and the feedback which is entered back into the pool.
6. Each party runs its internal G, let the random data generation be done in blocks of 10 output bytes. For each output block, 20 bytes, produced during the process, are injected and mixed back into the source pool to update it.

Fig. 1. The Distributed PRNG

3.2 The Details of Our Protocol

There are four asynchronous procedures: the initialization, the entropy accumulation, pool updating with entropy addition and the random number output. We provide some details of our construction in the following paragraphs.

Initialization. Operating system start-up includes a sequence of routine actions. This sequence, including initializing the PRNG with constant OS parameters and time-of-day, can easily be predicted by an adversary. If no special actions are taken, the PRNG state will include very low entropy. The time of day is given as seconds and micro-seconds, each is 32-bits. In reality this has very limited entropy as one can find computer uptime within an accuracy of a minute, which leads to a brute-force search of $60_{seconds} \times 106_{microseconds} < 2^{26}$ which is feasible according the [11]. Even if the adversary cannot get the system uptime, he can check the last modification time of files that are created or modified during the system start-up, and know the uptime in an accuracy of minutes.

To solve this problem, PRNG simulate continuity along shut-downs and start-ups. This is done by skipping system boots. A random-seed is saved at shut-down and is written to the pools at start-up. A script that is activated during system start-ups and shut-downs uses the read and write capabilities of /dev/urandom interface to perform this maintenance.

The script saves 512 bytes of randomness between boots in a file. During shut-down it reads 512 bytes from /dev/random and writes them to the file, and during start-up these bits are written back to /dev/random. Writing to /dev/random modifies the primary pool and not the random pool, as one could expect. The secondary and the random pool get their entropy from the primary pool, so the script operation actually affects all three pools.

The author of [24] instructs Linux distribution developers to add the access control of initial seed in order to ensure unpredictability at system start-ups. This implies that the security of the PRNG is not completely stand-alone but dependent on an external component which can be predictable in a certain Linux distribution.

2. Collecting and Sharing Entropy. Each party collects entropy from events originating from the keyboard, mouse, disk and interrupts on each client's local computer while collecting the event entropy from other parties. When such an event occurs, four 32-bit words are used as input to the entropy pools: For each entropy event fed into the Linux PRNG, three 32-bit values are considered: the num value, which is specific to the type of event 2, the current CPU cycle count and the jiffies count at the time the event is mixed into the pool. Here, we can use three functions for Linux PRNG: add_disk_randomness(), add_input_randomness() and add_interrupt_randomness().

The sequence from the three function represent the *jiffies* counts (the time between two ticks of the system timer interrupt) of the events, and is thus an increasing sequence. Since the estimation of the entropy should not depend on the time elapsed since the system was booted (beginning of the jiffies count), only the sequence of time differences are considered. A built-in estimator *Ent* is used to give an estimation of the entropy of the input data used to refresh the state *ST*. It is implemented in function add_timer_randomness which is used to refresh the input pool.

3. *Entropy Addition and Pool Updating.* LINUX PRNG uses an internal mixing function which is implemented in the built-in function mix_pool_bytes. It is used in two contexts, once to refresh the internal state with new input and secondly to transfer data between the input pool and the output pools., used to refresh the internal state with new input and to transfer data between the pools. The design of the mixing function relies on a Twisted Generalized Feedback Shift Register (TGFSR) as defined in Section 2. In the entropy pools, we add Lacharme's linear corrector with mixing function to update the pool, it is a deterministic function to compress random sequence in order to reduce statistical weakness [17]. Let C the $[255, 21, 111]$ BCH code, D the $[256, 234, 6]$ dual code of C, with generator polynomial

$$H(X) = X^{21} + X^{19} + X^{14} + X^{10} + X^7 + X^2 + 1 \qquad (1)$$

The input 255-tuple $(m^1, ..., m^{255})$ is coded by a binary polynomial $m(X) = \sum_{i=1}^2 55 m_i X^i$. Therefore the function f mapping F_2^{255} to F_2^{21}, defined by $m(X) \mapsto m(X) \bmod H(X)$ is a $(255, 21, 110)$-resilient function. This polynomial reduction is implemented by a shift register of length 21 with only seven xor gates.In this case, with an important input bias $e/2 = 0.25$, it give an output bias of: $\forall y \in F_2^{21} |P(f(X) = y) - 2^{-21}| \leq 2^{-111}$. Therefore, the minimal entropy of the output is very close to 21.

We can use a general constructions of good post-processing functions. We have shown that linear correcting codes and resilient functions provide many correctors achieving good bias reduction with variable input sizes. Linear feedback shift register are suitable for an hardware implementation where the chip area is limited.

If input pool does not contain enough entropy. Otherwise, estimated entropy of the input pool is increased with new input from external event. Entropy estimation of the output pool is decreased on generation. Data is transferred from the input pool to the output pools if they require entropy. When the pools do not contain enough entropy, no output can be generated with /dev/random.

4. *Random Bits Output.* Entropy estimations of the participating pools are updated according to the transferred entropy amount. Extracting entropy from a pool involves hashing the extracted bits, modifying the pool inner-state ST and decrementing the entropy amount estimation by the number of extracted bits. Such tasks are executed by next() function in G. It extracts 80 random bytes from the secondary pool one time.It uses SHA-1 and entropy-addition operations before actually outputting entropy in order to avoid backtracking attacks. In addition it uses folding to blur recognizable patterns from 160 bits SHA-1 output into 80 bits.

Once mixed with the pool content, the 5 words computed in the first step are used as an initial value or chaining value when hashing another 16 words from the pool. These 16 words overlap with the last word changed by the feedback data. In the case of an output pool (pool length = 32 words), they also overlap with the first 3 changed words. The 20 bytes of output from this second hash are folded in half to compute 11 the 10 bytes to be extracted: if $w\,[m...n]$ denotes the bits $m, ..., n$ of the word w, the folding operation of the five words w_0, w_1, w_2, w_3, w_4 is done by $w_0 \oplus w_3, w_1 \oplus w_4, w_2\,[0...15] \oplus w_2\,[16...31]$. Finally, the estimated entropy counter of the affected pool is decremented by the number of generated bytes.

4   Application to Distributed Data Random Perturbation

Data random perturbation is a technology when preserve the data privacy by adding the random noise to the original data, in recent years, it has been reviewed and the such as differential privacy is the state-of-the-art privacy notion [7] that gives a strong and provable privacy guarantee for aggregated data. The basic idea is partial random noise is generated by all participants, which draw random variables from Gamma or Gaussian distributions, such that the aggregated noise follows Laplace distribution to satisfy differential privacy.

Here in this section, we propose a application of our distributed PRNG. Combined with randomness extractor We assume that the adversary has some control over the environment in which the device operates (temperature, voltage, frequency, timing, etc.), and it is possible that that changes in this environment affect the distribution of X. In the Barak-Shaltiel-Tromer model, they assumed that the adversary can control at most t boolean properties of the environment, and can thus create at most 2^t different environments.

Definition 2. *(Barak-Shaltiel-Tromer randomness extractor [2]) A function $\mathcal{E}$: $\{0,1\}^n \times \{0,1\}^t \to \{0,1\}^m$ is a (k,ϵ)-extractor if for every random variable X of min-entropy at least k it holds that $\mathcal{E}(X, U_t)$ is ϵ-close to the uniform distribution over $\{0,1\}^m$.*

Definition 3. *(The security definition of Barak-Shaltiel-Tromer randomness extractor [2])*

- *An adversary chooses 2^t distributions $D_1, \ldots, D_{2^t}$ over $\{0,1\}^n$, such that $H_\infty(D_i) > k$ for all $i = 1 \cdots, 2^t$.*
- *A public parameter π is chosen at random and independently of the choices of D_i.*
- *The adversary is given π, and selects $i \in \{1, ..., 2^t\}$.*
- *The user computes $\mathcal{E}^\pi(X)$, where X is drawn from D_i.*

Given n, k, m, ϵ, δ and t, an extractor $\mathcal{E}$ is t-resilient if, in the above setting, with probability 1-ϵ over the choice of the public parameter the statistical distance between $\mathcal{E}^\pi(X)$ and U_m is at most δ.

We can apply this random extractor to a distributed environment with k participated database owners $P_i, i = 1, ..., k$ by using the Verifiable Secret Sharing scheme [5] which allows any party distributes his shares of a secret, which can be verified for consistency. The Gaussian noise can be generated and all the participants cooperatively verify that the shared values are legitimate. Finally, each party site $P_i, i = 1, ..., n$ can cooperatively reconstruct the original datadensity by using the reconstruction technique of the verifiable secret sharing scheme. In our proposal, we need that all parties must generate the noise from the same probability distribution. y_i and b_i can be generated interactively among all parties. The protocol is shown in Fig.2.

Protocol for distributed random noise generation for cloud database service

1. Before upload data to cloud database, the client i will generate random bits string using the G we proposed in last section and get $a_{1,i}, ..., a_{k,i}$.
2. Every client collaborative executing the coin tossing protocol some random bits $b_1, ..., b_n$ with a pre-determined distribution and share out those bits via verifiable secret sharing.
3. The client i can apply a randomness extractor $Ext()$ with the input $\pi_i(b_1, ..., b_n)$ where π_i is a random permutation and get the random bits $c_{1,i}, ..., c_{k,i}$
4. Then client i computes $a_{1,i} \oplus c_{k,i}, ..., a_{1,i} \oplus c_{k,i}$ and then converts these random bits $GF(2)$ to random noise on $GF(q)$. The sequences of random noise is serially uncorrelated and the output has good statistical characteristics due to the randomness extractor.

Fig. 2. The Distributed Random Noise Generation

Each party i shares a random bit by sharing out a value $b_i \in \{0,1\}_{GF(q)}$, using a non-malleable verifiable secret sharing scheme, where q is sufficiently large, and engages in a simple protocol to prove that the shared value is indeed in the specified set. And then suppose for a moment that we have a public source of unbiased bits, $c_1, c_2, ..., c_n$. By XORing together the corresponding b's and c's, we can transform the low quality bits b_i (in shares) into high-quality bits $b_i \oplus c_i$ in shares. Finally, each participant party sums her shares to get a share of the random noise.

The principal costs are the multiplications for verifying random noise in $\{0,1\}_{GF(q)}$ and the executions of verifiable secret sharing. Note that all the verifications of random noise parameters are performed simultaneously, so the messages from the different executions can be bundled together. The same is true for the verifications in the VSS. The total cost of the scheme is $\Theta(n)$ multiplications and additions in shares, which can be all done in a constant number of rounds.

5   Security Proofs and Experimental Analysis

In this section, we provide security proofs and the experimental analysis.

5.1   Security Proof of the Distributed PRNG

We show the security of our scheme in Theorem 1 and Theorem 2 as follows:

Theorem 1. *Our PRNG has t', q_D, ϵ-recovering security.*

Proof. The adversary $\mathcal{A}$ compromised a state and get the value ST_0 of the G, let's consider the game as follows:

- The challenger choose a seed $seed \leftarrow setup()$, after that he sample the D and get some assemble $\sigma_k, I_k, \gamma_k, z_k)$, where $k = 1, ..., q_D$. Here γ is some fresh entropy estimation of I, z is the leakage about I given to the $\mathcal{A}$.
- The adversay get $\gamma_1, ..., \gamma_{q_D}$ and $z_1, ..., z_{q_D}$, after that he launch an attack against $q_D + 1$ step computation of G, he can call D-fresh along with other oracle
- The challenger sequentially computes $ST_j = \mathsf{refresh}(ST_{j-1}, I_j, seed)$ for $j = 1, ..., d$. If $b = 0$, $\mathcal{A}$ is given $(ST^*, R) = \mathsf{next}(ST_d)$ and if $b = 1$, $\mathcal{A}$ is given $(ST^*, R) \leftarrow \{0, 1\}^{n+l}$.
- The adversary $\mathcal{A}$ output a bit b^*.

Adversary can query the oracles in security definition and try to distinguish the internal state from the random sample. Let Game 0 be the original recovering security game above: the game outputs a bit which is set to 1 iff the $\mathcal{A}$ guesses the challenge bit $b^* = b$. We define Game1 where, during the challengerfs computation of $(ST^*, R) \leftarrow \mathsf{next}(S_d)$ for the challenge bit $b = 0$, it chooses $U \leftarrow \{0, 1\}^m$ uniformly. We can know that $\Pr[(Game0) = 1] - \Pr[(Game1) = 1] \le \epsilon$ according the argument in [8].

Theorem 2. *Our PRNG has t, ϵ-preserving security.*

Proof. Intuitively, it says that if the state S_0 starts uniformly random and uncompromised, and then is refreshed with arbitrary (adversarial) samples. Here in this paper, we adapt the security notions which is simplified by Dodis [8] based on BH model we mentioned above. $I_1, ..., I_d$ resulting in some final state S_d, then the output $(S^*, R) \leftarrow \mathsf{next}(S_d)$ looks indistinguishable from uniform. Formally, we consider the following security game with an adversary $\mathcal{A}$ who try to compromise the PRNG. We consider the game as follows:

- The challenger chooses an initial state $S_0 \leftarrow \{0, 1\}^n$, a seed $seed \leftarrow \mathsf{setup}$, and a bit $b \leftarrow \{0, 1\}$ uniformly at random.
- $\mathcal{A}$ gets seed and specifies arbitrarily long sequence of values $I_1, ..., I_d$ with $I_j \in \{0, 1\}^n$ for all $j \in [d]$.
- The challenger sequentially computes $ST_j = \mathsf{refresh}(ST_{j-1}, I_j, seed)$ for $j = 1, ..., d$. If $b = 0$, $\mathcal{A}$ is given $(ST^*, R) = \mathsf{next}(ST_d)$ and if $b = 1$, $\mathcal{A}$ is given $(ST^*, R) \leftarrow \{0, 1\}^{n+l}$.
- $\mathcal{A}$ outputs a bit b^*.

Without loss of generality, we will assume that all compromised next queries that the $\mathcal{A}$ makes are to $get - next$. Let Game 0 be the original preserving security game: the game outputs a bit which is set to 1 iff the attacker guesses the challenge bit $b^* = b$. If the initial state is $ST_0 \leftarrow \{0, 1\}^n$, the seed is $seed =$

(X, X'), and the adversarial samples are $I_d, ..., I_0$ (indexed in reverse order where I_d is the earliest sample) then the refreshed state that incorporates these samples will be $S_d := S_0 \cdot X_d + P_j = I_j \cdot X_j$. As long as $X = 0$, the value ST_d is uniformly random (over the choice of S_0). We consider a modified Game 1, where the challenger simply chooses $ST_d \leftarrow \{0, 1\}^n$. We can use using the hybrid argument and get the advantage of $\mathcal{A}$ is $|\Pr[b] - \frac{1}{2}| < \epsilon$.

5.2 Security Analysis of Application of PRNG in Random Data Perturbation

In order to determine the effect of a perturbation method, it is necessary to consider the security provided by that method. If two data matrics X and X' differ in a single row, the statistical difference between X and X' is $1/n$. Let X be a random variable and $\Pr[X = x]$ be the probability that X assigns to an element x. Let $H_\infty(X) = \log(\frac{1}{max_{x \in X}\Pr[X=x]})$. By definition, it is easy to verify that the following claims:

- If $\max_{x \in X}\Pr[X = x] \leq 2^{-k}$ if and only if $H_\infty(X) \geq k$;
- If $\max_{x \in X}\Pr[X = x] \geq 2^{-k}$ if and only if $H_\infty(X) \leq k$.

To design randomness extractor $\mathcal{E}: \{0, 1\}^n \to \{0, 1\}^m$, we need to consider its input and mathematical structure. It is well-known result that one cannot extract m bits from a distribution X with $H_\infty(X) \leq m - 1$. $H_\infty(X) \leq m - 1$ implies $Pr[X = x] \geq 2^{-(m-1)}$. For any candidate extractor function $\mathcal{E}: \{0, 1\}^n \to \{0, 1\}^m$, we know that $Pr[y = \mathcal{E}(x)] \geq 2^{-(m-1)}$. It follows that $\mathcal{E}(x)$ is far from being uniformly distributed. Another well-known result is that there exists no single deterministic randomness extractor for all high-entropy sources X. Consider the goal of designing an extractor for all distributions X with $H_\infty(X) \leq n-1$. One can show that there exists a design for function $\mathcal{E}: \{0, 1\}^n \to \{0, 1\}$. For an arbitrary adversary $\mathcal{A}$, there are two statistically similar data matrix, only differ in on row, after the linear transformation, he can not indistinguish between the transcript $T(X)$ and $T(X')$. Because $T(X)/T(X')$ is at most $e^{-\frac{X-X'}{\sigma}}$, where σ is . Using the law of conditional probability, and writing t_i for the indices of t, $\frac{\Pr[T(X)=t]}{\Pr[X'+Y=t]} \in exp(\pm\frac{|X-X'|}{\sigma})$.

5.3 Experimental Analysis

Our experiment is executed on Note PCs with 2.6GHz, the OS is 32-bit Ubuntu 13.10. We collect the entropy from three other PC and generate the pseudo-random from 100 bytes to 1000 bytes. We did not use linux kernel APIs in linux/net.h and /linux/netpoll.h to send UDP packets, but to collect three PC's entropy and form them into a file which is used for the fourth experiment PC. So we only calculate the computation time as shown in Fig. 3.

From the Fig.3, we can see that our proposed is faster than the stand-alone Linux PRNG dev/random. We also can see that the time for generating pseudo-random number from dev/random does not always increases progressively with

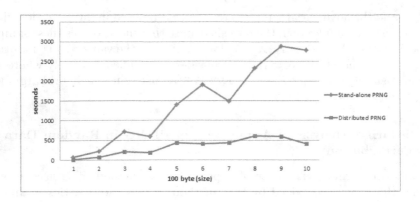

Fig. 3. A Comparison of Stand-alone Linux PRNG and our Distributed PRNG

the output size. That is due to the unpredictability of the event entropy which imply a stronger security and robustness than dev/urandom which repeatedly use the pool entropy without enough update input for random events.

6   Conclusion and Future Works

In this paper, we proposed a distributed pseudo-random number generator based on Linux kernel and its PRNG. After that, we provide a solution for using the proposed PRNG to do the distributed random data perturbation which can be used to preserve the data privacy before using the cloud database service. The future direction should be modifying the our PRNG to make it more efficient and secure, we may try to use of a newer hash function, for example SHA-3 or AES to do the extracting output. It would require a significant change of the design, and an investigation of Linux PRNG.

References

1. Blum, L., Blum, M., Shub, M.: Comparison of two pseudo-random number generators, pp. 61–78. Plenum Press, New York (1983)
2. Barak, B., Shaltiel, R., Tromer, E.: True Random Number Generators Secure in a Changing Environment. In: Walter, C.D., Koç, Ç.K., Paar, C. (eds.) CHES 2003. LNCS, vol. 2779, pp. 166–180. Springer, Heidelberg (2003)
3. Barak, B., Halevi, S.: A model and architecture for pseudo-random generation with applications to /dev/random. In: ACM Conference on Computer and Communications Security, pp. 203–212 (2005)
4. Bellare, M., Rompel, J.: Randomness-Efficient Oblivious Sampling FOCS, pp. 276–287 (1994)
5. Chor, B., Goldwasser, S., Micali, S., Awerbuch, B.: Verifiable Secret Sharing and Achieving Simultaneity in The Presence of Faults. In: Proceedings of the 26th Annual IEEE Symposium on Foundations of Computer Science, pp. 383–395 (1985)

6. Davis, D., Ihaka, R., Fenstermacher, P.: Cryptographic Randomness from Air Turbulence in Disk Drives. In: Desmedt, Y.G. (ed.) CRYPTO 1994. LNCS, vol. 839, pp. 114–120. Springer, Heidelberg (1994)
7. Dwork, C.: Differential privacy: A survey of results. In: Agrawal, M., Du, D.-Z., Duan, Z., Li, A. (eds.) TAMC 2008. LNCS, vol. 4978, pp. 1–19. Springer, Heidelberg (2008)
8. Dodis, Y., Pointcheval, D., Ruhault, S., Vergnaud, D., Wichs, D.: Security analysis of pseudo-random number generators with input: dev/random is not robust. In: Proceedings of the 2013 Conference on Computer & Communications Security, USA, pp. 647–658 (2013)
9. Ellison, C.: IEEE. P1363 Appendix E Cryptographic Random Numbers cme/P1363/ ranno.html (1995), http://theworld.com/~cme/P1363/ranno.html (online; accessed 2009)
10. Gutterman, Z., Pinkas, B., Reinman, T.: Analysis of the Linux Random Number Generator. In: Proc. of IEEE Security and Privacy, pp. 371 385 (2006)
11. Gutmann, P.: Cryptographic Security Architecture Design and Verification (2004) ISBN: 978-0-387-95387-8
12. Krawczyk, H.: How to predict congruential generators. In: Brassard, G. (ed.) CRYPTO 1989. LNCS, vol. 435, pp. 138–153. Springer, Heidelberg (1990)
13. Krhovjak, J., Kur, J., Lorenc, V., Matyas, V., Pecho, P., Riha, Z., Staudek, J., Svenda, P.: Zizkovsky. Smartcards, final report for the Czech National Security Authority (December 2008)
14. Knuth, D.E.: Seminumerical Algorithms, 3rd edn. The Art of Computer Programming, vol. 2. Addison-Wesley (2001)
15. Lehmer, D.H.: Mathematical methods in large-scale computing units. In: Proc. 2nd Sympos. on Large-Scale Digital Calculating Machinery, Cambridge, MA, pp. 141–146. Harvard University Press (1949, 1951)
16. The LavaRnd Random Number Generator (2000), http://www.lavarnd.org/ (online; accessed 2009)
17. Lacharme, P.: Post-Processing Functions for a Biased Physical Random Number Generator. In: Nyberg, K. (ed.) FSE 2008. LNCS, vol. 5086, pp. 334–342. Springer, Heidelberg (2008)
18. Lewis, T.G., Payne, W.H.: Generalized feedback shift register pseudorandom number algorithm. Journal of the ACM 20(3), 456–468 (1973)
19. Lacharme, P., Rock, A., Strubel, V., Videau, M.: The linux pseudorandom number generator revisited. Cryptology ePrint Archive, Report 2012/251 (2012)
20. Matsumoto, M., Kurita, Y.: Twisted GFSR generators. ACM Transactions on Modeling and Computer Simulation 2(3), 179–194 (1992)
21. Matsumoto, M., Nishimura, T.: Mersenne Twister: A 623-Dimensionally Equidistributed Uniform Pseudo-Random Number Generator. ACM Transactions on Modeling and Computer Simulation (TOMACS) 8(1), 3–30 (1998)
22. Mackall, M., Ts'o, T.: random.c A strong random number generator, /driver/char/random.c in Linux Kernel 2.6.30.7 (2009), http://www.kernel.org/
23. Shamir, A.: On the generation of cryptographically strong pseudo-random sequences. In: Even, S., Kariv, O. (eds.) ICALP 1981. LNCS, vol. 115, pp. 544–550. Springer, Heidelberg (1981)
24. Ts'o, T.: random.c Linux kernel random number generator, http://www.kernel.org

A Provably Secure Ring Signature Scheme with Bounded Leakage Resilience

Huaqun Wang[1,2], Qianhong Wu[3], Bo Qin[4],
Futai Zhang[5], and Josep Domingo-Ferrer[6]

[1]School of Information Engineering, Dalian Ocean University
[2]Shanghai Key Laboratory of Integrate Administration Technologies for Information Security
[3]School of Electronic and Information Engineering, Beihang University
[4]School of Information, Renmin University of China
[5]School of Computer Science and Technology, Nanjing Normal University
[6]Dept. of Computer Engineering and Maths, Universitat Rovira i Virgili, Catalonia
wanghuaqun@aliyun.com, qhwu@xidian.edu.cn, qinboo@xaut.edu.cn,
zhangfutai@njnu.edu.cn, josep.domingo@urv.cat

Abstract. Conventionally, the unforgeability of ring signature schemes is defined in an ideal environment where the attackers cannot access any information about the secret keys of the signers. This assumption is too strong to be satisfied in the real world since the cryptographic operations involves the secret key information leakage in various ways due to power/time consumption difference in operations on the 0/1 bits of the secret key. An attacker can obtain this information both passively by collecting power consumption information or actively by injecting faults during the signing operations. Thus, provably secure ring signature in the conventional security definition may be insecure in the real world due to the key information leakage. To address this problem, we formalize the first bounded leakage resilience definition for ring signature. A leakage resilient ring signature scheme remains secure even if arbitrary, but bounded, information about the secret key is leaked to an adversary. A bound on the leaked information is necessary because a ring signature cannot be secure if some signer's secret key is fully leaked. Then we propose the first ring signature scheme with bounded leakage resilience. Following the enhanced security definition with leakage resilience, the proposed scheme is provably secure based on the difficulty of the second l-representation problem in finite field.

Keywords: Ring signature, Secret key leakage, Leakage resilience.

1 Introduction

A useful model when proving the security of a cryptographic primitive is to think of it as a black box, that is, to assume that the adversary can only use and observe the primitive in a pre-specified and limited way. This simplified

X. Huang and J. Zhou (Eds.): ISPEC 2014, LNCS 8434, pp. 388–402, 2014.

model commonly assumes that no information on the secret key is accessible to the adversary. However, when cryptographic primitives are implemented in the real world, they actually become "translucent" boxes to a clever adversary. Indeed, the adversary may succeed in recovering significant information on the secret key through side-channel cryptanalysis [1,2], fault attacks [3,4], timing attacks [5], et al. As a result, some bits of the secret key are at risk of being leaked. The conventional security definitions of cryptosystem do not capture this kind of attacks. A secure cryptographic scheme should remain secure even if some bits of the secret key have been leaked to the adversary. It can make cryptographic schemes secure after they are implemented in the real world, not just theoretically secure in an ideal security model.

We formalize an appropriate model of what information the adversary can learn during a leakage attack. We also need to bound how much information the adversary can learn since a cryptographic scheme cannot be secure if all the bits of the secret key are leaked. Therefore, in this work we assume that the attacker can repeatedly and adaptively learn arbitrary function values of the secret key sk, as long as the total number of bits leaked during the lifetime of the system is bounded by some parameter l. A cryptographic scheme is said to be secure with bounded leakage resilience if it remains secure under this attack. Specially, we study secure ring signature scheme in the model of bounded leakage resilience. We allow the leakage function to be arbitrary as long as the total leakage is bounded as some function of the secret key length $|sk|$. If the secret key is unchanging, such a restriction on the leakage is essential.

1.1 Related Work

In recent years, there has been impressive progress in leakage-resilient cryptography. The early efforts were made to obtain leakage resilience encryption schemes [6,7]. In 2009, Akavia et al. proposed memory attacks and proved that two lattice-based public-key encryption schemes are secure in the face of these attacks [8]. Subsequently, Naor et al. proposed a leakage-resilient public-key encryption scheme based on a universal hash proof system [9].

There has also been works on leakage-resilient signatures. Katz et al. gave a signature scheme tolerating the secret key leakage [10]. Faust et al. gave a tree-based, stateful leakage-resilient signature scheme from any 3-time signature scheme [11]. Boyle et al. constructed fully leakage-resilient signature schemes without random oracles [12]. Malkin et al. [13] presented the first signature scheme that is resilient to fully continual leakage: memory leakage as well as leakage from processing during signing, key generation and updates (both of the secret key and the randomness). Faust et al. [14] proposed the first constructions of digital signature schemes that are secure in the auxiliary input model. They designed a digital signature scheme that is secure against chosen-message attacks when given an exponentially hard-to-invert function of the secret key. Phong et al. [15] considered the continual key leakage scenario of strong key-insulated signature design. Guo et al. proposed efficient online/offline signatures with computational leakage resilience in the online phase [16]. Alwen *et al.* studied the design of cryptographic primitives resilient to key leakage attacks [17].

Most efforts have been devoted to leakage-resilient signatures in the single-signer setting. Motivated by group-oriented applications, ring signature were introduced in 2001 by Rivest *et al.* [18]. In a ring signature scheme, one user can form an on-the-fly group in an *ad hoc* way by simply adding other users' public keys to the group key list, without getting other users' agreements. Then he can sign any message on behalf of that temporal group. The resulting signature is verifiable by anyone who knows the public keys of the group members in the temporal group. For a secure ring signature, it is required that only users in the group member list can generate a valid signature and the signatures generated by different members are theoretically indistinguishable. The former property is referred to as unforgeability and the latter as unconditional anonymity. It has been shown that ring signature is a very useful cryptographic primitive in many applications [19,20,21,22]. However, to the best of our knowledge, no leakage-resilient ring signature was proposed in the public literature. This motivates us to investigate security-enhanced ring signature that can withstand bounded leakage of the secret key.

1.2 Our Contribution

This paper focuses on leakage-resilient ring signature. More specifically, our contributions are twofold:

- First, we formalize the model of ring signature with bounded leakage resilience. We focus on existential unforgeability under adaptively chosen-message and bounded leakage attacks. In these attacks, an attacker is allowed not only to adaptively query for ring signature on any message of his choice, but also to access a leakage oracle through a leakage function f to gain information about the secret keys of the signers. The constraint is that the output of the leakage function after all the leakage queries should be bounded. Unforgeability states that no polynomial-time attacker can forge a valid ring signature with non-negligible probability in probabilistic polynomial time.
- Second, we propose the first ring signature scheme with bounded leakage resilience. Specifically, we follow the above model and prove that our scheme is unforgeable under the adaptively chosen message and bounded leakage attacks. The proof relies on the hardness of the second l-representation problem which is related to the well-known discrete logarithm problem. We also show that our ring signature scheme preserves unconditional anonymity even if the attacker is provided with the secret keys in the group. Thus, the anonymity of our ring signature scheme is perfectly leakage-resilient without any bound on the information leakage on the secret keys.

1.3   Plan of This Paper

The rest of this paper is organized as follows. Section 2 contains some technical preliminaries. Section 3 formalizes the security model of ring signature with bounded leakage resilience. Section 4 presents our concrete ring signature scheme with bounded leakage resilience. Section 5 evaluates the security of our scheme. Finally, Section 6 contains some conclusions and sketches future work directions.

2   Preliminaries

We review some information theory results and computational assumptions.

2.1   Information Theory Lemmas

The following two definitions come from the reference [23].

Definition 1 (Min-entropy). *The min-entropy of a random variable X, denoted by $H_\infty(X)$, is $H_\infty(X) \overset{def}{=} \min_{x \in \{0,1\}^n} \{-\log_2 Pr[X = x]\}$.*

Definition 2 (Average-conditional min-entropy). *The average-conditional min-entropy of a random variable X given Z, denoted as $\tilde{H}_\infty(X|Z)$, is*

$$\tilde{H}_\infty(X|Z) \overset{def}{=} -\log_2(E_{z \leftarrow Z}[\max_x Pr[X = x|Z = z]]) = -\log_2(E_{z \leftarrow Z}[2^{H_\infty[X|Z=z]}])$$

where $E_{z \leftarrow Z}(\cdot)$ means taking average of the argument over all values z of Z.

The following lemma is proven in [23].

Lemma 1. *Let X, Y, Z be random variables where Y takes values in a set of size at most 2^l. Then, $\tilde{H}_\infty(X|(Y,Z)) \geq \tilde{H}_\infty((X,Y)|Z) - l \geq \tilde{H}_\infty(X|Z) - l$, and in particular, $\tilde{H}_\infty(X|Y)) \geq \tilde{H}_\infty(X) - l$.*

The following lemma is proven in [10].

Lemma 2. *Let X be a random variable with $H \overset{def}{=} H_\infty(X)$, and fix $\Delta \in [0, H]$. Let f be an arbitrary function with range $\{0,1\}^\lambda$, and set*

$$Y \overset{def}{=} \{y \in \{0,1\}^\lambda | H_\infty(X|y = f(X)) \leq H - \Delta\}$$

Then, $Pr[f(X) \in Y] \leq 2^{\lambda - \Delta}$.

In other words, the probability that knowledge of $f(X)$ decreases the min-entropy of X by Δ or more is at most $2^{\lambda - \Delta}$. Put differently, the min-entropy of X after observing the value of $f(X)$ is greater than H' except with probability at most $2^{\lambda - H + H'}$.

2.2 Computational Assumptions

We recall the computationally difficult problems underlying our constructions. In this paper, let q and p denote two secure prime numbers that satisfy $q|(p-1)$. On the other hand, $\hat{k}$ is the security parameter.

Assumption 1 (Discrete logarithm problem). *Let $\mathscr{G}$ be a probabilistic algorithm which takes a security parameter $\hat{k}$ as input and outputs (G, q, p), where G is a finite cyclic subgroup of order q which belongs to a group of order p. We say the discrete logarithm problem is hard for the group G if, for any probabilistic polynomial-time (PPT) algorithm $\mathcal{A}$, the advantage of $\mathcal{A}$ is negligible. The advantage of $\mathcal{A}$ can be defined below*

$$\mathsf{Adv}_{\mathcal{A}}^{\mathrm{DLP}} = \Pr\left[\begin{array}{c}(G, q, p) \leftarrow \mathscr{G}(1^{\hat{k}}) \\ g, h \leftarrow G\end{array}\middle| x \leftarrow \mathcal{A}(G, q, g, h,) \wedge g^x = h\right]$$

where $x \in \mathbb{Z}_q^*, g^x = h \bmod p$, g is a generator of G.

Assumption 2 (First l-representation problem). *[10] We say that the first l-representation problem is hard for the group G if, for any PPT algorithm $\mathcal{A}$, the advantage of $\mathcal{A}$ is negligible. The advantage of $\mathcal{A}$ can be defined below*

$$\mathsf{Adv}_{\mathcal{A}}^{l\text{-}\mathrm{FRP}} = \Pr\left[\begin{array}{c}(G, q, p) \leftarrow \mathscr{G}(1^{\hat{k}}) \\ g_1, g_2, \cdots, g_l \leftarrow G\end{array}\middle| \begin{array}{c}\begin{pmatrix}x_1, x_2, \cdots, x_l \\ x_1', x_2', \cdots, x_l'\end{pmatrix} \leftarrow \mathcal{A}(G, q, g_1, g_2, \cdots, g_l) \\ \wedge \prod_i g_i^{x_i} = \prod_i g_i^{x_i'} \wedge \overrightarrow{x} \neq \overrightarrow{x}'\end{array}\right]$$

where q is the order of the group G, p is the size of G, $(x_1, x_2, \cdots, x_l) \in (\mathbb{Z}_q^*)^l$, $(x_1', x_2', \cdots, x_l') \in (\mathbb{Z}_q^*)^l$, $\prod_i g_i^{x_i} = \prod_i g_i^{x_i'} \bmod p$, g is a generator of G.

Notes: The discrete logarithm problem and the first l-representation problem are equivalent.

1. If the first l-representation problem is easy, then when $l = 2$, we can solve the discrete logarithm problem. Given g, h, then $\mathcal{A}$ can get two different tuples $(x, y), (x', y')$ that satisfy $g^x h^y = g^{x'} h^{y'} \bmod p$. Denote $h = g^\omega$, then we can get $\omega = \frac{x'-x}{y-y'} \bmod q$. Thus, the discrete logarithm problem is solved.
2. On the other hand, if the discrete logarithm problem is easy, then $\mathcal{A}$ can get r_i that satisfy $g_i = g^{r_i}$ for $1 \leq i \leq l$. $\mathcal{A}$ can pick a random tuple $\overrightarrow{x} = (x_1, x_2, \cdots, x_l)$ and compute $\hat{x} = \sum_{i=1}^{l} r_i x_i \bmod q$. Then, $\mathcal{A}$ solves the equation $\sum_{i=1}^{l} r_i x_i' = \hat{x} \bmod q$. It is easy to calculate another tuple $\overrightarrow{x'} = (x_1', x_2', \cdots, x_l')$ that satisfies $\sum_{i=1}^{l} r_i x_i = \sum_{i=1}^{l} r_i x_i' \bmod q$, i.e., $\prod_i g_i^{x_i} = \prod_i g_i^{x_i'}$. Thus, the first l-representation problem is solved.

According to the above analysis, we know that the discrete logarithm problem and the first l-representation problem are equivalent.

Assumption 3 (Second l-representation problem). *We say that the second l-representation problem is hard for the group G if, for any PPT algorithm $\mathcal{A}$, the advantage of $\mathcal{A}$ is negligible. The advantage of $\mathcal{A}$ is defined below*

$$\mathsf{Adv}_{\mathcal{A}}^{l\text{-SRP}} = \Pr\left[\begin{array}{l} (G, q, p) \leftarrow \mathcal{G}(1^k) \\ g_1, g_2, \cdots, g_l \leftarrow G \end{array} \middle| \begin{array}{l} (x'_1, x'_2, \cdots, x'_l) \leftarrow \mathcal{A}(G, q, g_1, g_2, \cdots, g_l, (x_1, \\ x_2, \cdots, x_l)) \wedge \prod_i g_i^{x_i} = \prod_i g_i^{x'_i} \wedge \vec{x} \neq \vec{x}' \end{array} \right]$$

where q is the order of the group G, p is the size of G, $(x_1, x_2, \cdots, x_l) \in (\mathbb{Z}_q^*)^l$ is randomly chosen beforehand, $(x'_1, x'_2, \cdots, x'_l) \in (\mathbb{Z}_q^*)^l$, $\prod_i g_i^{x_i} = \prod_i g_i^{x'_i} \bmod p$, g is a generator of G.

In this paper, our proposed leakage-resilient ring signature scheme is built on some subgroup of $\mathbb{Z}_p^*$ with the order q. The discrete logarithm problem, the first l-representation problem and the second l-representation problem are difficult on the subgroup of $\mathbb{Z}_p^*$.

Notes: The first l-representation problem assumption is stronger than the second l-representation problem assumption. If the assumption 3 does not hold, the adversary $\mathcal{A}$ can pick a random tuple $(x_1, x_2, \cdots, x_l)$ as the input, it can output another tuple $(x'_1, x'_2, \cdots, x'_l)$ by taking use of *the second l-representation* oracle. Thus, the adversary $\mathcal{A}$ gets the two tuples $\vec{x} = (x_1, x_2, \cdots, x_l)$ and $\vec{x}' = (x'_1, x'_2, \cdots, x'_l)$ that satisfy $\prod_i g_i^{x_i} = \prod_i g_i^{x'_i} \wedge \vec{x} \neq \vec{x}'$. Thus, the second l-representation problem assumption is weaker than the first l-representation problem assumption.

3 Modeling Ring Signature with Bounded Leakage Resilience

We provide a formal definition of bounded leakage-resilient ring signature, and we state some technical lemmas that will be used in our security analysis. The security definitions are the variants of the reference [10].

Definition 3 (Ring signature). *A ring signature scheme is a tuple of PPT algorithms (Setup, Ring-Sign, Ring-Vrfy) defined as follows.*

Setup. *Each potential user U_i generates his secret/public key pair (sk_i, pk_i) by using a key generation protocol that takes as input a security parameter $\hat{k}$.*

Ring-Sign. *If a user U_k wants to compute a ring signature on behalf of a ring $L = \{U_1, \cdots, U_n\}$ that contains himself, i.e., $U_k \in L$, U_k executes this probabilistic polynomial time algorithm with input a message m, the public keys $pk_1, \cdots, pk_n$ of the ring and his secret key sk_k. The output of this algorithm is a ring signature σ for the message m and the ring L.*

Ring-Vrfy. *This is a deterministic polynomial time algorithm that takes as input a message m and a ring signature σ, that includes the public keys of all the members of the corresponding ring L, and outputs "True" if the ring signature is valid, or "False" otherwise.*

The resulting ring signature scheme must satisfy the following properties:

1. *Correctness*: A ring signature generated in a correct way must be accepted by any verifier with overwhelming probability.
2. *Anonymity*: If a signer computes a ring signature on behalf of a ring of n members, any verifier not belonging to the ring should not have probability greater than $\frac{1}{n}$ to guess the signer's identity. If the verifier is a member of the signer's ring, but is not the signer himself, then his probability of guessing the signer's identity should not be greater than $\frac{1}{n-1}$.
3. *Unforgeability*: Any attacker has only negligible probability in forging a valid ring signature for some message m on behalf of a ring that does not contain him, even if he knows valid ring signature for messages, different from m, that he can adaptively choose.

The definition of ring signature with bounded leakage resilience is the same as the standard definition of ring signature. The security model definition of ring signature with bounded leakage resilience is similar to the standard security model definition of ring signature, except that we additionally allow the adversary to specify arbitrary leakage functions $\{f_i\}$ and obtain the value of these functions applied to the secret key. The formal security properties of ring signature with bounded leakage resilience are stated next.

Definition 4 (Unforgeability of ring signature with bounded leakage resilience). *Let* $\prod =\{Setup, Ring\text{-}Sign, Ring\text{-}Vrfy\}$ *be a ring signature scheme, and let* λ *be a function. Given an adversary* $\mathcal{A}$, *the experiment is defined as follows:*

1. *The user* U_i *can obtain the corresponding secret/public key pair* (sk_i, pk_i) *by running* $(sk_i, pk_i) \leftarrow Gen(1^{\hat{k}}, r_i)$, $1 \leq i \leq n$, *where* Gen *denotes an algorithm that can generate the secret/public key pair.*
2. *Run* $\mathcal{A}(1^{\hat{k}}, pk_1, \cdots, pk_n)$. *The adversary may adaptively access a ring signing oracle* $Ring\text{-}Sign(\cdot)$ *and a leakage oracle* $Leak(\cdot)$ *that have the following functionalities:*
   - *Let the* i*-th ring signature query be* $Ring\text{-}Sign_{sk_k}(m_i, pk_{j_1}, \cdots, pk_{j_i})$, *where* $L_i = \{pk_{j_1}, \cdots, pk_{j_i}\} \subseteq \{pk_1, \cdots, pk_n\}$ *and* $pk_k \in L_i$. *The ring signature oracle computes* $\sigma_i = Ring\text{-}Sign_{sk_k}(m_i, pk_{j_1}, \cdots, pk_{j_i})$, *and returns* σ_i *to* $\mathcal{A}$.
   - *In order to respond to the* i*-th leakage query* $Leak(f_i, sk_k)$ *(where* f_i *is specified as a circuit), the leakage oracle returns* $f_i(sk_k)$ *to* $\mathcal{A}$, *where* sk_k *is the secret key to be used for computing the ring signature.* sk_k *may be other secret key whose corresponding public key belongs to the signing set* L_i *and* $\mathcal{A}$ *queries* U_k *to sign the message. (To make the definition meaningful in the random oracle model, the* $\{f_i\}$ *are allowed to be oracle circuits that depend on the random oracle.) The* $\{f_i\}$ *can be arbitrary,*

> *subject to the restriction that the total output length of all the $f_i(sk_k)$ is at most $\lambda(|sk_k|)$.*

3. *At some point, $\mathcal{A}$ outputs (m, L, σ) where $L \subseteq \{pk_1, pk_2, \cdots, pk_n\}$.*

We say $\mathcal{A}$ succeeds if (1) $Ring\text{-}Vrfy_{pk_{j_1}, \cdots, pk_{j_l}}(m, \sigma) = 1$, and (2) m was not previously queried to the $Ring\text{-}Sign_{sk_j}(\cdot)$ oracle. We denote the probability of this event by $Pr_{\mathcal{A},\Pi}^{\lambda-leakage}(\hat{k})$. If $Pr_{\mathcal{A},\Pi}^{\lambda-leakage}(\hat{k})$ is negligible for any PPT adversary $\mathcal{A}$, we say Π is λ-leakage resilient.

Definition 4 gives the unforgeability of ring signature with bounded leakage resilience. Unconditional anonymity is another important security property of ring signature that can be defined as follows.

Definition 5 (Anonymity of ring signature with bounded leakage resilience). *If a signer computes a ring signature on behalf of a ring of n members, any verifier not belonging to the ring should not have probability greater than $\frac{1}{n}$ to guess the signer's identity even some bits of the secret key are leaked . If the verifier is a member of the signer's ring, but is not the signer himself, then his probability of guessing the signer's identity should not be greater than $\frac{1}{n-1}$ even if some bits of the secret key are leaked .*

Note that unconditional anonymity means that the scheme remains anonymous even all the secret keys are exposed to the adversary. Thus, if we can prove that a ring signature scheme satisfies unconditional anonymity, then this scheme remains anonymous with bounded leakage.

The anonymity property is closely related to the witness indistinguishability notion [24]. In general, an $\mathcal{NP}$ statement may have multiple witnesses. For example, a Hamiltonian graph may have multiple Hamiltonian cycles; a 3-colorable graph may have multiple (non-isomorphic) 3-colorings; etc. In leakage-resilient public-key cryptography, we are interested in proof systems (for languages in $\mathcal{NP}$) that do not leak information about which witness the prover is using, even to a malicious verifier. In the sequel, we let $\langle \mathcal{A}(y), \mathcal{B}(z) \rangle(x)$ denote the view (*i.e.*, inputs, internal coin tosses, incoming messages) of $\mathcal{B}$ when interacting with $\mathcal{A}$ on common input x, $\mathcal{A}$ has auxiliary input y and $\mathcal{B}$ has auxiliary input z. The definition of witness indistinguishability can be used to decide whether our proposed scheme satisfies the property. It is also important to prove our scheme's unforgeability based on witness indistinguishability.

Definition 6 (Witness indistinguishability). *Let $L \in \mathcal{NP}$ and let $(\mathcal{P}, \mathcal{V})$ be an interactive proof system for L with perfect completeness. We say that $(\mathcal{P}, \mathcal{V})$ is witness-indistinguishable (WI) if for every PPT algorithm $\mathcal{V}^*$ and every two sequences $\{\omega_x^1\}_{x \in L}$ and $\{\omega_x^2\}_{x \in L}$ such that ω_x^1 and ω_x^2 are both witnesses for x, the following ensembles are computationally indistinguishable:*

1. $\{\langle \mathcal{P}(\omega_x^1), \mathcal{V}^*(z) \rangle(x)\}_{x \in L, z \in \{0,1\}^*}$
2. $\{\langle \mathcal{P}(\omega_x^2), \mathcal{V}^*(z) \rangle(x)\}_{x \in L, z \in \{0,1\}^*}$

(When the security parameter is not written explicitly, we simply take $|x| = \hat{k}$ without confusion.) In particular, we may have $z = (\omega_x^1, \omega_x^2)$.

4 Our Ring Signature Scheme with Bounded Leakage Resilience

In this section, we describe our ring signature scheme with bounded leakage resilience. Our concrete scheme is based on Schnorr signature [25] and Rivest et al.'s ring signature construction skeleton [18]. Here, by $a \in_R \mathbb{Z}_q^*$ we denote drawing a random number a from $\mathbb{Z}_q^*$ according to the uniform distribution. Also, by $H : \{0,1\}^* \to \mathbb{Z}_q^*$ we denote a collision-resistant hash function. Our scheme consists of three phases: **Setup, Ring-Sign, Ring-Vrfy**.

Setup. Suppose that there exist n users in the system. Assume that $g_1, \cdots, g_l$ are generators of some subgroup S_G of $\mathbb{Z}_p^*$, where the order of the subgroup S_G is q. Let $(n, p, q, g_1, \cdots, g_l)$ be the publicly accessible global system parameters. For $i = 1, 2, \cdots, n$ and $j = 1, 2, \cdots, l$, select $x_{ij} \in \mathbb{Z}_q^*$. Then, the i-th user's secret/public key pair is (sk_i, pk_i), where

$$sk_i = (x_{i1}, x_{i2}, \cdots, x_{il}), \quad pk_i = \prod_{j=1}^{l} g_j^{x_{ij}} \bmod p.$$

Ring-Sign. Suppose that the actual signer is U_k. He selects a signer set L containing U_k. Without loss of generality, we assume that $L = \{U_1, U_2, \cdots, U_{k-1}, U_k, U_{k+1}, \cdots, U_s\}$. The actual signer U_k performs the procedures as follows.

1. Pick $\alpha_1, \cdots, \alpha_l \in_R \mathbb{Z}_q^*$ and calculate

$$c_{k+1} = H(L, m, g_1^{\alpha_1} g_2^{\alpha_2} \cdots g_l^{\alpha_l} \bmod p)$$

2. For $i = k+1, \cdots, s, 1, \cdots, k-1$, pick $s_{i1}, s_{i2}, \cdots, s_{il} \in_R \mathbb{Z}_q^*$ and calculate

$$c_{i+1} = H(L, m, g_1^{s_{i1}} g_2^{s_{i2}} \cdots g_l^{s_{il}} pk_i^{c_i} \bmod p)$$

where $1 = s + 1 \bmod s$, i.e., they are cycle.

3. Calculate $s_{k1} = \alpha_1 - x_{k1} c_k \bmod q$, $\cdots$, $s_{kl} = \alpha_l - x_{kl} c_k \bmod q$. Finally, U_k outputs $\{c_1, s_{ij}, 1 \le i \le s, 1 \le j \le l\}$ as the ring signature for m, L.

Ring-Vrfy. Upon receiving the ring signature $\{c_1, s_{ij}, 1 \le i \le s, 1 \le j \le l\}$ for m and L, the verifier does:

1. For $i = 1, \cdots, s$, calculate $e_i = g_1^{s_{i1}} \cdots g_l^{s_{il}} pk_i^{c_i} \bmod p$, $c_{i+1} = H(L, m, e_i)$.

2. Check whether $c_1 \stackrel{?}{=} H(L, m, e_s)$ holds or not. If it holds, accept this signature. Otherwise, reject it.

Theorem 1 (Correctness). *If the signer and the verifier are honest, our ring signature with bounded leakage resilience can pass the verification.*

Proof. Without loss of generality, suppose the actual signer is U_k. The received ring signature is $\{c_1, s_{ij}, 1 \le i \le s, 1 \le j \le l\}$ for m and L. According to the signature process, we know that if $e_k = g_1^{\alpha_1} g_2^{\alpha_2} \cdots g_l^{\alpha_l} \bmod p$ holds, it is straightforward that our ring signature scheme can pass the verification.

According to the signature process, we know that

$$
\begin{aligned}
g_1^{\alpha_1} g_2^{\alpha_2} \cdots g_l^{\alpha_l} \bmod p &= g_1^{s_{k1}+x_{k1}c_k} g_2^{s_{k2}+x_{k2}c_k} \cdots g_l^{s_{kl}+x_{kl}c_k} \bmod p \\
&= g_1^{s_{k1}} g_2^{s_{k2}} \cdots g_l^{s_{kl}} g_1^{x_{k1}c_k} g_2^{x_{k2}c_k} \cdots g_l^{x_{kl}c_k} \bmod p \\
&= g_1^{s_{k1}} g_2^{s_{k2}} \cdots g_l^{s_{kl}} pk_k^{c_k} \bmod p \\
&= e_k
\end{aligned}
$$

Thus, our scheme satisfies the correctness.   □

5   Security Analysis

A secure ring signature scheme with bounded leakage resilience must satisfy the following requirements: unconditional anonymity and unforgeability.

Theorem 2. *Our proposed ring signature scheme with bounded leakage resilience is unconditionally anonymous.*

Proof. From the above ring signature process, we know that $(s_{i1}, s_{i2}, \cdots, s_{il}) \in_R \mathbb{Z}_q^{*l}$, where $i \in \{1, 2, \cdots, k-1, k+1, \cdots, s\}$. For the signer's subscript k, we have that $s_{k1}, s_{k2}, \cdots, s_{kl}$ are also uniformly distributed over $\mathbb{Z}_q^*$ because $(\alpha_{k1}, \cdots, \alpha_{kl}) \in_R \mathbb{Z}_q^{*l}$. Therefore, for fixed (L, m), $(s_{i1}, s_{i2}, \cdots, s_{il})$, $1 \leq i \leq s$ has q^{sl} variations that are equally likely regardless of the signer's subscript k. The remaining element c_1 is a hash value which is determined uniquely by (L, m), $s_{sj}, 1 \leq j \leq l$ and pk_s. In random oracle model, c_1 is a random value which does not expose the true signer's identity. Thus, our proposed ring signature scheme is unconditionally anonymous.   □

Lemma 3. *Our proposed ring signature scheme with bounded leakage resilience satisfies the property of witness indistinguishability.*

Proof. To prove this, for two different witnesses, $(x_{k1}, x_{k2}, \cdots, x_{kl})$ and $(x'_{k1}, x'_{k2}, \cdots, x'_{kl})$ satisfying $pk_k = \prod_{j=1}^{l} g_j^{x_{kj}} = \prod_{j=1}^{l} g_j^{x'_{kj}} \bmod p$ (1), we show that even an infinitely powerful adversary $\mathcal{B}$ cannot determine which witness was used from the ring signature.

Let $\delta_{kj} = x'_{kj} - x_{kj} \bmod q$ where $1 \leq j \leq l$. Suppose the actual signer is U_k and the ring signature is $\{c_1, s_{ij}, 1 \leq i \leq s, 1 \leq j \leq l\}$ for m and L. Due to the ring signature procedures, we know that all the s_{ij} are random for $i \neq k, 1 \leq j \leq l$. When $i = k$ and $1 \leq j \leq l$, from the ring signature procedure, the following equation holds for the chosen random numbers α_{kj} that were picked in the phase of Ring-Sign.

$$
s_{kj} = \alpha_j - x_{kj}c_k = \alpha_j + \delta_{kj}c_k - (\delta_{kj} + x_{kj})c_k = \alpha_j + \delta_{kj}c_{k-1} - x'_{kj}c_{k-1} \bmod q
$$

From Equation (1), it follows that

$$
\prod_{j=1}^{l} g_j^{x_{kj}} = \prod_{j=1}^{l} g_j^{x_{kj}+\delta_{kj}} \bmod p, \qquad \prod_{j=1}^{l} g_j^{\delta_{kj}} = 1 \bmod p
$$

Let $\alpha_j' = \alpha_j + \delta_{kj}c_k$. We obtain

$$A_k = \prod_{j=1}^{l} g_j^{\alpha_j} = \prod_{j=1}^{l} g_j^{\alpha_j' - \delta_{kj}c_k} = \prod_{j=1}^{l} g_j^{\alpha_j'} \prod_{j=1}^{l} g_j^{-\delta_{kj}c_k}$$
$$= \prod_{j=1}^{l} g_j^{\alpha_j'} (\prod_{j=1}^{l} g_j^{\delta_{kj}})^{-c_k} = \prod_{j=1}^{l} g_j^{\alpha_j'} \bmod p$$

Thus, the distributions of $\overrightarrow{\alpha} = (\alpha_1, \cdots, \alpha_l)$ and $\overrightarrow{\alpha}' = (\alpha_1', \cdots, \alpha_l')$ are exactly equivalent. To the two different tuples $\overrightarrow{\alpha}$ and $\overrightarrow{\alpha}'$, the signer U_k can get the same ring signature $\{c_1, s_{ij}, 1 \le i \le s, 1 \le j \le l\}$ when it picks the same random numbers s_{ij} for $i \ne k, 1 \le j \le l$. Hence, even an infinitely powerful adversary $\mathcal{B}$ cannot determine which witness was used from the ring signature. Our proposed ring signature scheme with bounded leakage resilience satisfies the property of witness indistinguishability. □

Theorem 3. *Suppose $\mathcal{A}$ is a $(T, \epsilon, q_H, q_S, \lambda)$-forger against our ring signature scheme, i.e., $\mathcal{A}$ can forge a valid ring signature with probability ϵ within time T after q_H hash queries, q_S signature queries and leakage of at most $\lambda = (\frac{1}{2} - \frac{1}{2l} - \epsilon) \cdot l \cdot \log_2 q$ bits of the secret key, where the length of the secret key is $l \cdot \log_2 q$ bits. Then, the second l-representation problem can be solved with probability $\frac{1}{2n}(1 - \frac{q_H}{q^{2\epsilon l}})$ within time $T' \le \frac{144823 V_{q_h,n}(T + q_s T_s)}{\epsilon}$, where $V_{Q,n}$ denotes the number of n-permutations of Q elements, that is, $V_{Q,n} = Q(Q-1)\cdots(Q-n+1)$. Based on the difficulty of the second l-representation problem, our scheme is λ-leakage resilient.*

Proof. Let $\prod$ denote the scheme given above, and let $\mathcal{A}$ be a PPT adversary with success probability $\epsilon \stackrel{def}{=} Pr[Succ_{\mathcal{A},\prod}^{\lambda-leakage}(\hat{k})]$, where $\hat{k}$ is the security parameter. Input the second l-representation problem $(S_G, q, g_1, g_2, \cdots, g_l, (x_1, x_2, \cdots, x_l))$, we construct a challenger $\mathcal{B}$ solving the second l-representation problem with probability $\frac{1}{2}(1 - \frac{q_H}{q^{2\epsilon l}})$ within time $T' \le \frac{144823 V_{q_h,n}(T + q_s T_s)}{\epsilon}$.

$\mathcal{B}$ is given some secret keys $sk_i, 1 \le i \le n$, where sk_i is a secret key that corresponds to the user U_i. Algorithm $\mathcal{B}$ then answers the signing and leaking queries of $\mathcal{A}$ using the secret keys $sk_i, 1 \le i \le n$ that it knows. Since the secret keys are distributed identically to the secret key of an honest signer, the simulation for $\mathcal{A}$ is perfect.

Without loss of generality, we make a number of assumptions about $\mathcal{A}$. First, we assume that if $\mathcal{A}$ outputs $\{c_1, s_{ij}, 1 \le i \le s, 1 \le j \le l\}$ on m and L and computes the value $A_i = g_1^{s_{i1}} \cdots g_l^{s_{il}} pk_i^{c_i} \bmod p$, then (1) $\mathcal{A}$ at some point queried $H(m, L, A_k), 1 \le k \le s$ and (2) $\mathcal{A}$ never requested a signature on m. Second, for any leakage query $Leak(f_i)$ we assume $f_i(state)$ makes the same number of H-oracle calls regardless of the value of $state$ (this can always be ensured by adding dummy queries, as needed).

We construct a probabilistic polynomial-time algorithm $\mathcal{B}$ solving the second l-representation problem. Algorithm $\mathcal{B}$ proceeds as follows: Input $(S_G, q, g_1, g_2, \cdots, g_l, (x_1, x_2, \cdots, x_l))$, for $1 \le z \le n$, $\mathcal{B}$ designs $x_{z1} = x_1, x_{z2} = x_2, \cdots, x_{zl} = x_l$ and calculate $pk_z = \prod_{j=1}^{l} g_j^{x_{zj}} \bmod p$, then it chooses random $\{x_{ij}, 1 \le i \le n, 1 \le j \le l, i \ne z\}$ and computes $pk_i = \prod_{j=1}^{l} g_j^{x_{ij}} \bmod p, 1 \le i \le n$. It gives the system parameters $(p, q, g_1, \cdots, g_l)$ and public keys $pk_i, 1 \leq i \leq n$ to $\mathcal{A}$. Thus, the challenger $\mathcal{B}$ can easily respond to the ring signature queries and leakage queries because he knows one of the secret keys.

When $\mathcal{A}$ terminates, $\mathcal{B}$ examines $\mathcal{A}$'s output $\{c_{1,1}, s_{ij,1}, 1 \leq i \leq s, 1 \leq j \leq l\}$ on the message m and the set L of ring members. If $\mathcal{A}$'s output can pass the signature verification, this forged signature is successful. According to the forking lemma of ring signature [26], the attacker $\mathcal{A}$ can also forge another ring signature $\{c'_{1,1}, s_{ij,1}, 1 \leq i \leq s, 1 \leq j \leq l\}$ on the same message m, the same set L of ring members and the same randomness. With non-negligible probability, the two forged ring signatures satisfy the following properties:

1. $c_{j,1} \neq c'_{j,1}$ for one $j \in \{1, 2, \cdots, s\}$;
2. $c_{i,1} = c'_{i,1}$ for all $i = 1, \cdots, s$ such that $i \neq j$;

Thus, due to the same randomness, we can get

$$g_1^{s_{j1,1}} \cdots g_l^{s_{jl,1}} pk_i^{c_{j,1}} = g_1^{s'_{j1,1}} \cdots g_l^{s'_{jl,1}} pk_i^{c'_{j,1}} \bmod p$$
$$\prod_{i=1}^{l} g_i^{s_{ji,1}+c_{j,1}x'_{ji}} = \prod_{i=1}^{l} g_i^{s'_{ji,1}+c'_{j,1}x'_{ji}} \bmod p$$
$$\prod_{i=1}^{l} g_i^{(s_{ji,1}+c_{j,1}x'_{ji})-(s'_{ji,1}+c'_{j,1}x'_{ji})} = 1 \bmod p$$

We denote $g_1 = g^{\alpha_1}, g_2 = g^{\alpha_2}, \cdots, g_l = g^{\alpha_l}$. Then, we can get

$$\sum_{i=1}^{l} \alpha_i [(s_{ji,1} + c_{j,1}x'_{ji}) - (s'_{ji,1} + c'_{j,1}x'_{ji})] = 0 \bmod q$$

After sl times to perform the above procedures, we can get sl equations

$$\sum_{i=1}^{l} \alpha_i [(s_{ji,w} + c_{j,w}x'_{ji}) - (s'_{ji,w} + c'_{j,w}x'_{ji})] = 0 \bmod q$$

where $1 \leq j \leq s, 1 \leq w \leq sl + 1$. Thus, there must exist at least one user, denoted as $j = u$, has the following l equations which correspond to l different w:

$$\sum_{i=1}^{l} \alpha_i [(s_{ui,w} + c_{u,w}x'_{ui}) - (s'_{ui,w} + c'_{u,w}x'_{ui})] = 0 \bmod q$$

We can compute all the corresponding discrete logarithms α_i if $(s_{ui,w}+c_{u,w}x'_{ui})-(s'_{ui,w}+c'_{u,w}x'_{ui}) \neq 0 \bmod q$ by calculating the above equation group. Based on the difficulty of discrete logarithm problem, we know that all the $l + 1$ equations satisfy the following $(s_{ui,w} + c_{u,w}x'_{ui}) - (s'_{ui,w} + c'_{u,w}x'_{ui}) = 0 \bmod q$. The probability of $u = z$ is $\frac{s}{n} \times \frac{1}{s} = \frac{1}{n}$. When $u = z$, it must hold that $s'_{zi,1} + c'_{z,1}x'_{zi} = s_{zi,1} + c_{z,1}x'_{zi} \bmod q$, i.e., $x'_{zi} = \frac{s_{zi,1}-s'_{zi,1}}{c'_{z,1}-c_{z,1}} \bmod q$ for $1 \leq i \leq l$. At last, the challenger $\mathcal{B}$ gets another l-representation $(x_{z1}, x_{z2}, \cdots, x_{zl})$ of the value pk_z.

Next, we consider the success probability of $\mathcal{B}$ as follows.

Suppose that the adversary $\mathcal{A}$ can forge a valid ring signature with probability ϵ within time T. According to the forking lemma of ring signature [26], the adversary $\mathcal{A}$ can produce two valid ring signature such that $c_j \neq c'_j$, for some $j \in \{1, 2, \cdots, n\}$ and $c_i = c'_i$ for all $i = 1, \cdots, n$ such that $i \neq j$, in the expected time $T' \leq \frac{144823 V_{q_h, n}(T + q_s T_s)}{\epsilon}$. Then, we consider the probability that $\mathcal{B}$ can solve the second l-representation problem.

When $\mathcal{B}$ succeeds in obtaining two different forged ring signature, we need to evaluate the probability that the extracted l-representation $\vec{x}' = (x'_1, \cdots, x'_l)$ is equal to the original l-representation $\vec{x} = (x_1, \cdots, x_l)$.

Let $\lambda = (\frac{1}{2} - \frac{1}{2l} - \epsilon) \cdot l \cdot \log_2 q$, an upper bound on the number of leaked bits in each run of $\mathcal{A}$. The public key pk_j constrains $\vec{x}$ to lie in an $(l-1)$-dimensional vector space, and signature queries do not further constrain $\vec{x}$ [27]. Thus, the min-entropy of $\vec{x}$ conditioned on the public key and the observed signatures is $(l-1)\log_2 q$ bits. The views of $\mathcal{A}$ in its two runs contain only the following additional information about $\vec{x}$: at most $2 \cdot \lambda$ bits from the leakage functions (i.e., λ bits in each view), and $\log_2 q_H$ bits indicating the relevant state associated with the first forgery. According to Lemmas 2 and 3, we can see that the conditional min-entropy of $\vec{x}$ is greater than 0 except with probability at most

$$2^{2\lambda + \log_2 q_H - (l-1)\log_2 q} \leq q_H q^{-2\epsilon l}.$$

From the above analysis, if the adversary $\mathcal{A}$ can forge a valid ring signature with probability ϵ within time T, then the second l-representation problem can be solved with probability $\frac{1}{2}(1 - \frac{q_H}{q^{2\epsilon l}}) \times \frac{1}{n} = \frac{1}{2n}(1 - \frac{q_H}{q^{2\epsilon l}})$ within time

$$T' \leq \frac{144823 V_{q_h, n}(T + q_s T_s)}{\epsilon}$$

under the condition that $\lambda = (\frac{1}{2} - \frac{1}{2l} - \epsilon) \cdot l \cdot \log_2 q$ bits of the secret key are leaked. Based on the difficulty of the second l-representation problem, our scheme is secure. $\square$

Thus, based on Theorem 2 and Theorem 3, we know that our proposed ring signature scheme with bounded leakage resilience is provably secure.

6   Conclusions and Future Work

In this paper, we have proposed the first definition of ring signature resilient to bounded leakage and we have given a concrete instantiation of such ring signature. Based on the difficulty of the second l-representation problem, our proposed ring signature scheme with bounded leakage resilience is provably secure in the random oracle model. Our model does not cover attacks in which the attacker may obtain some information about the system's internal randomness state during the signing process. It seems interesting to explore as future work ring signature that can resist bounded leakage of the system's internal state. We plan to develop a more general leakage resiliency model for ring signature that takes internal state leaks into account.

Acknowledgement. This work was partly supported by the NSF of China through projects (No. 61272522, No. 61173154, No. 61370190, No. 61003214, No. 61170298), the Opening Project of Shanghai Key Laboratory of Integrate Administration Technologies for Information Security(No. AGK2013005), and by the Spanish Government through projects TIN2011-27076-C03-01 "CO-PRIVACY" and CONSOLIDER INGENIO 2010 CSD2007-00004 "ARES", by the Government of Catalonia under grant 2009 SGR 1135, by the European Commission under FP7 projects "DwB" and "Inter-Trust". The last author is partially supported as an ICREA-Acadèmia researcher by the Catalan Government; he leads the UNESCO Chair in Data Privacy, but this paper does not necessarily reflect the position of UNESCO nor does it commit that organization.

References

1. Kocher, P.C.: Timing attacks on implementations of Diffie-Hellman, RSA, DSS, and other systems. In: Koblitz, N. (ed.) CRYPTO 1996. LNCS, vol. 1109, pp. 104–113. Springer, Heidelberg (1996)
2. Kocher, P.C., Jaffe, J., Jun, B.: Differential power analysis. In: Wiener, M. (ed.) CRYPTO 1999. LNCS, vol. 1666, pp. 388–397. Springer, Heidelberg (1999)
3. Biham, E., Carmeli, Y., Shamir, A.: Bug attacks. In: Wagner, D. (ed.) CRYPTO 2008. LNCS, vol. 5157, pp. 221–240. Springer, Heidelberg (2008)
4. Boneh, D., DeMillo, R.A., Lipton, R.J.: On the importance of checking cryptographic protocols for faults. In: Fumy, W. (ed.) EUROCRYPT 1997. LNCS, vol. 1233, pp. 37–51. Springer, Heidelberg (1997)
5. Boneh, D., Brumley, D.: Remote timing attacks are practical. Computer Networks 48(5), 701–716 (2005)
6. Micali, S., Reyzin, L.: Physically observable cryptography. In: Naor, M. (ed.) TCC 2004. LNCS, vol. 2951, pp. 278–296. Springer, Heidelberg (2004)
7. Standaert, F.-X., Malkin, T.G., Yung, M.: A unified framework for the analysis of side-channel key recovery attacks. In: Joux, A. (ed.) EUROCRYPT 2009. LNCS, vol. 5479, pp. 443–461. Springer, Heidelberg (2009)
8. Akavia, A., Goldwasser, S., Vaikuntanathan, V.: Simultaneous hardcore bits and cryptography against memory attacks. In: Reingold, O. (ed.) TCC 2009. LNCS, vol. 5444, pp. 474–495. Springer, Heidelberg (2009)
9. Naor, M., Segev, G.: Public-key cryptosystems resilient to key leakage. In: Halevi, S. (ed.) CRYPTO 2009. LNCS, vol. 5677, pp. 18–35. Springer, Heidelberg (2009)
10. Katz, J., Vaikuntanathan, V.: Signature schemes with bounded leakage resilience. In: Matsui, M. (ed.) ASIACRYPT 2009. LNCS, vol. 5912, pp. 703–720. Springer, Heidelberg (2009)
11. Faust, S., Kiltz, E., Pietrzak, K., Rothblum, G.N.: Leakage-resilient signatures. In: Micciancio, D. (ed.) TCC 2010. LNCS, vol. 5978, pp. 343–360. Springer, Heidelberg (2010)
12. Boyle, E., Segev, G., Wichs, D.: Fully leakage-resilient signatures. In: Paterson, K.G. (ed.) EUROCRYPT 2011. LNCS, vol. 6632, pp. 89–108. Springer, Heidelberg (2011)
13. Malkin, T., Teranishi, I., Vahlis, Y., Yung, M.: Signatures resilient to continual leakage on memory and computation. In: Ishai, Y. (ed.) TCC 2011. LNCS, vol. 6597, pp. 89–106. Springer, Heidelberg (2011)

14. Faust, S., Hazay, C., Nielsen, J.-B., Nordholt, P.S., Zottarel, A.: Signature schemes secure against hard-to-invert leakage, http://eprint.iacr.org/2012/045.pdf
15. Phong, L.T., Matsuo, S., Yung, M.: Leakage resilient strong key-insulated signatures in public channel. In: Chen, L., Yung, M. (eds.) INTRUST 2010. LNCS, vol. 6802, pp. 160–172. Springer, Heidelberg (2011)
16. Guo, F., Mu, Y., Susilo, W.: Efficient online/offline signatures with computational leakage resilience in online phase. In: Lai, X., Yung, M., Lin, D. (eds.) Inscrypt 2010. LNCS, vol. 6584, pp. 455–470. Springer, Heidelberg (2011)
17. Alwen, J., Dodis, Y., Wichs, D.: Leakage-resilient public-key cryptography in the bounded-retrieval model. In: Halevi, S. (ed.) CRYPTO 2009. LNCS, vol. 5677, pp. 36–54. Springer, Heidelberg (2009)
18. Rivest, R.L., Shamir, A., Tauman, Y.: How to leak a secret. In: Boyd, C. (ed.) ASIACRYPT 2001. LNCS, vol. 2248, pp. 552–565. Springer, Heidelberg (2001)
19. Wang, J., Sun, B.: Ring signature schemes from lattice basis delegation. In: Qing, S., Susilo, W., Wang, G., Liu, D. (eds.) ICICS 2011. LNCS, vol. 7043, pp. 15–28. Springer, Heidelberg (2011)
20. Liu, J.K., Yuen, T.H., Zhou, J.: Forward secure ring signature without random oracles. In: Qing, S., Susilo, W., Wang, G., Liu, D. (eds.) ICICS 2011. LNCS, vol. 7043, pp. 1–14. Springer, Heidelberg (2011)
21. Zeng, S., Jiang, S., Qin, Z.: A new conditionally anonymous ring signature. In: Fu, B., Du, D.-Z. (eds.) COCOON 2011. LNCS, vol. 6842, pp. 479–491. Springer, Heidelberg (2011)
22. Fujisaki, E.: Sub-linear size traceable ring signatures without random oracles. In: Kiayias, A. (ed.) CT-RSA 2011. LNCS, vol. 6558, pp. 393–415. Springer, Heidelberg (2011)
23. Dodis, Y., Ostrovsky, R., Reyzin, L., Smith, A.: Fuzzy extractors: how to generate strong keys from biometrics and other noisy data. SIAM Journal on Computing 38(1), 97–139 (2008)
24. Feige, U., Shamir, A.: Witness indistinguishable and witness hiding protocols. In: 22nd ACM Symposium on Theory of Computing, pp. 416–426 (1990)
25. Schnorr, C.P.: Efficient identification and signatures for smart cards. In: Brassard, G. (ed.) CRYPTO 1989. LNCS, vol. 435, pp. 239–252. Springer, Heidelberg (1990)
26. Herranz, J., Sáez, G.: Forking lemmas for ring signature schemes. In: Johansson, T., Maitra, S. (eds.) INDOCRYPT 2003. LNCS, vol. 2904, pp. 266–279. Springer, Heidelberg (2003)
27. Okamoto, T.: Provably secure and practical identification schemes and corresponding signature schemes. In: Brickell, E.F. (ed.) CRYPTO 1992. LNCS, vol. 740, pp. 31–53. Springer, Heidelberg (1993)

Two-Party (Blind) Ring Signatures
and Their Applications

Man Ho Au and Willy Susilo*

Centre for Computer and Information Security Research (CCISR)
School of Computer Science and Software Engineering
University of Wollongong, Australia
{aau,wsusilo}@uow.edu.au

Abstract. Ring signatures, introduced by Rivest, Shamir and Tauman, attest the fact that one member from a ring of signers has endorsed the message but no one can identify who from the ring is actually responsible for its generation. It was designed canonically for secret leaking. Since then, various applications have been discovered. For instance, it is a building block of optimistic fair exchange, destinated verifier signatures and ad-hoc key exchange. Interestingly, many of these applications require the signer to create a ring signature on behalf of two possible signers (a two-party ring signature) only. An efficient two-party ring signature scheme due to Bender, Katz, and Morselli, is known. Unfortunately, it cannot be used in many of the aforementioned applications since it is secure only in a weaker model. In this paper, we revisit their construction and proposed a scheme that is secure in the strongest sense. In addition, we extend the construction to a two-party blind ring signature. Our proposals are secure in the standard model under well-known number-theoretic assumptions. Finally, we discuss the applications of our construction, which include designated verifier signatures, optimistic fair exchange and fair outsourcing of computational task.

1 Introduction

The notion of ring signatures, introduced by Rivest, Shamir and Tauman [14], is a group-oriented signature which takes into account privacy concerns. A user can autonomously sign on behalf of a group, while group members can be totally unaware of being included in the group. Any verifier can be assured that a message has been endorsed by one of the members in this group, but the actual identity of the signer remains hidden. Unlike group signatures [6], there is no group manager and no revocation. Following the terminology, the group is usually called a ring since the original proposal arrange the group members in a ring during the process of signature generation. The formation of the ring is spontaneous and the original motivation is for Whistle Blowing.

If the ring consists of two members only, the resulting signature is called a two-party ring signature, which is the focus of this paper. The reason is that most of the applications of ring signatures only require a ring size of 2. Nonetheless, even with this

---

* This work is supported by ARC Future Fellowship FT0991397.

X. Huang and J. Zhou (Eds.): ISPEC 2014, LNCS 8434, pp. 403–417, 2014.

relaxation, construction in the standard model under well-established assumption still remains daunting.

Chow et al. [8] gave a construction with a formal security analysis in the standard model under a new assumption. The general version of Bender et al. [2] uses generic ZAPs for NP as a building block and is inefficient. They also proposed an efficient two-party ring signature scheme under standard assumptions in a weaker security model. Shacham and Waters [17] proposed an efficient ring signature scheme without using random oracles but anonymity is computational and required a trusted setup assumption. Chandran et al. [4] presented a scheme in the untrusted common reference string model while providing "heuristically statistical" anonymity. Schäge and Schwenk [16] provided another ring signature scheme in the standard model using basic assumptions, again, in a weaker security model. Recently, Ghadafi [9] offered both ring signatures and blind ring signatures in the standard model. Again, the anonymity is computational and required a trusted setup assumption.

As mentioned, the focus of our paper is on two-party ring signatures. We start from the specific construction due to Bender et al. due to its simplicity and efficiency. All other existing schemes employ non-interactive proof of some sort in the signature and it is hard to improve their efficiency. In addition, due to the use of non-interactive proof, the anonymity is often computational due to the use of the Groth-Sahai proof system [11] which requires a trusted setup for the common reference string. The major issue with Bender et al.'s two-party ring signature scheme is its insecurity under the chosen key model where an attacker is allowed to generate its own public key. An attack of this kind in this model is presented in [17]. This limits the use of this scheme as a building block in a larger system involving multiple users who could be malicious and are allowed to generate their own keys.

We observe that the problem can be solved if all the keys introduced by the attackers are "certified" to be properly generated. In other words, if we require all users to make a zero-knowledge proof-of-knowledge of the secret keys, the system could be proven secure. For if this is the case, the simulator in the security proof could "extract" the secret key for each public key presented by the adversary and uses this key to answer the query. The only remaining issue is that the prove has to be non-interactive so that it could be viewed as part of this public key. In this regard, we make use of the proof system from Groth-Sahai and present two useful non-interactive protocols as building blocks. The advantage of our approach is that these complex non-interactive proof are only added as part of the public key which only needs to be verified once in practice. Thus, our proposal retains most of the computational advantage of the two-party ring signature scheme from Bender et al. Finally, we equip our scheme with a blind signature generation protocol. We believe our construction can be used as a building block for many larger systems.

1.1 Our Contribution

1. We present efficient non-interactive zero-knowledge proof-of-knowledge protocols for discrete logarithm and commitment.

2. We present an efficient two-party ring signature construction in the standard model and equip it with a blind signing procedure.
3. We discuss various applications of two-party (blind) ring signatures.

Organization. The rest of the paper is organized as follows. In Sec. 2, we review the syntax of a two-party (blind) ring signature scheme its security definitions. We present two non-interactive zero-knowledge proof-of-knowledge protocols in Sec. 3. Based on our protocols, we present an efficient construction of two-party ring signatures and its blind version in Sec. 4. We discuss various applications of our proposal in Sec. 5 before concluding our paper in Sec. 6.

2 Preliminary

If n is a positive integer, we use $[n]$ to denote the set $\{1, \ldots, n\}$. We review the following well-known computational assumptions.

Definition 1 (DL Assumption). *Let $\mathbb{G} = \langle g \rangle$ be a cyclic group of prime order p. The discrete logarithm assumption states that given a tuple $(g, Z) \in (\mathbb{G}, \mathbb{G})$, it is computationally infeasible to compute the value $z \in \mathbb{Z}_p$ such that $Z = g^z$.*

Definition 2 (CDH Assumption). *Let $\mathbb{G} = \langle g \rangle$ be a cyclic group of prime order p. The computational Diffie-Hellman assumption states that given a tuple $(g, g^a, g^b) \in (\mathbb{G}, \mathbb{G}, \mathbb{G})$, it is computationally infeasible to compute the value g^{ab}.*

Definition 3 (DLIN Assumption). *Let $\mathbb{G} = \langle g \rangle$ be a cyclic group of prime order p. The decision linear (DLIN) assumption states that given a tuple $(u, v, w, u^a, v^b, T) \in (\mathbb{G}, \mathbb{G}, \mathbb{G}, \mathbb{G}, \mathbb{G}, \mathbb{G})$, it is computationally infeasible to decide if $T = w^{a+b}$.*

2.1 Bilinear Pairing

Let $\mathbb{G}, \mathbb{G}_T$ be two cyclic groups of the same prime order p. Let g be a generator of $\mathbb{G}$. A mapping $\hat{e} : \mathbb{G} \times \mathbb{G} \to \mathbb{G}_T$ is a bilinear pairing if the following are true:

- (*Unique Representation*) Each element of $\mathbb{G}$ and $\mathbb{G}_T$ has a unique binary representation.
- (*Bilinear*) For all $a, b \in \mathbb{Z}_p$, $\hat{e}(g^a, g^b) = \hat{e}(g, g)^{ab}$.
- (*Non-degenerate*) $\hat{e}(g, g) \neq 1_{\mathbb{G}_T}$, where $1_{\mathbb{G}_T}$ is the identity element of the group $\mathbb{G}_T$.

The setting we present here is often referred to as a symmetric pairing. We abuse the notation and use 1 to represent the identity element regardless of the group. For example, we will use 1 to represent $1_{\mathbb{G}_T}$ in the subsequent text.

2.2   Groth-Sahai Non-interactive Witness-Indistinguishable Proof System

We briefly review the non-interactive witness-indistinguishable proof system developed by Groth and Sahai [11] (referred to as GS proof hereafter). They gave three instantiations and we employ the version that depends on the decision linear assumption since it is often regarded as the weakest assumption amongst the three and works in the symmetric pairing setting.

Consider a set of variables $\{X_i\}_{i=1}^n \in \mathbb{G}^n$ and public constants $\{A_i\}_{i=1}^n \in \mathbb{G}^n$, $\{b_{i,j} \in \mathbb{Z}_p\}_{i,j \in [n]}$, $t_T \in \mathbb{G}_T$. A pairing product equation is of the form:

$$\prod_{i=1}^n \hat{e}(X_i, A_i) \prod_{i=1}^n \prod_{j=1}^n \hat{e}(X_i, X_j)^{x_{i,j}} = t_T.$$

The GS proof system requires a common reference string which allows a prover to make commitments of a set of variables $\{X_i\}$. It also allows the prover to produce an non-interactive proof that these committed variables satisfy a set of pairing product equations. The proof is witness-indistinguishable in the sense the the proof generated by one set of variables is indistinguishable to another. There are two kinds of common reference string in a GS proof system, namely, soundness string and simulation string. The former allows the string creator to open the "commitments" and thus guarantees the soundness of the system. The latter provides perfectly hiding commitments and guarantees witness-indistinguishably. These two strings are computationally indistinguishable.

As an example, consider a variable X and a constants A and the following pairing product equation:

$$\hat{e}(X, X)\hat{e}(X, A) = 1.$$

A GS proof of a variable X satisfying the above equation could be produced using $X = 1$ or $X = A^{-1}$ and the proofs produced by these two values (often called witnesses) are indistinguishable. Indeed, proof of satisfaction of the above equation would assure the verifier that either $X = 1$ or $X = A^{-1}$.

Throughout this paper, we will use the following notation to represent a GS proof of knowledge of variables satisfying a set of pairing product equations. All symbols that appear on the left hand side inside the brackets are variables while all other symbols on the right hand side after the colon are the public constants of the pairing product equations. For example,

$$NIWI \left\{ (X_1, X_2, X_3) : \begin{array}{l} \hat{e}(X_1, X_1)\hat{e}(X_1, A) = 1 \wedge \\ \hat{e}(X_1, X_2)\hat{e}(X_2, X_3) = T \end{array} \right\}$$

means a proof of the variables X_1, X_2, X_3 that satisfies the two equations, with A and T being public constants.

2.3   Syntax of Two-Party Ring Signatures

We adapt the definitions and security models of ring signatures from various literatures. A ring signature scheme in the common reference string model consists of four algorithms, namely, Setup, Gen, Sign, Verify, whose functions are enumerated below.

param $\leftarrow$ Setup(1^λ): On input a security parameter λ, this algorithm outputs the public parameter param for the system. We assume param is an implicit input to all algorithms listed below.

(pk, sk) $\leftarrow$ Gen(): This algorithm outputs a key pair (pk, sk) for a signer. If (pk, sk) is an output of the algorithm Gen(), we say pk is the corresponding public key of sk (and vice versa).

$(\sigma, \mathcal{R}) \leftarrow$ Sign($sk_S, \mathcal{R}, m$) : On input a message m, a secret key of a signer sk_S (whose public key is pk_S) and a set public keys $\mathcal{R}$ with $pk_S \in \mathcal{R}$, this algorithm outputs a signature σ, which is a ring signature of m with respect to the ring $\mathcal{R}$.

valid/invalid $\leftarrow$ Verify($\sigma, \mathcal{R}, m$) : On input a public key a message m, a signature σ with a set of public keys $\mathcal{R}$, this algorithm verifies the signature and outputs valid/invalid.

A ring signature scheme must possess *Correctness*, *Unforgeability* and *Anonmity*, to be reviewed below.

Correctness. For any security parameter λ and param $\leftarrow$ Setup(1^λ), (pk_S, sk_S) $\leftarrow$ Gen() and $\mathcal{R} = \{pk_1, \ldots, pk_n\}$ such that (pk_i, sk_i) $\leftarrow$ Gen() for $i \in [n]$ with $pk_S \in \mathcal{R}$. For any message m, if $(\sigma, \mathcal{R}) \leftarrow$ Sign($sk_S, \mathcal{R}, m$), then valid $\leftarrow$ Verify($\sigma, \mathcal{R}, m$).

In this paper, our focus is on two-party ring signature. That is, $|\mathcal{R}| = 2$ for all signatures.

Unforgeability. The following game between a challenger $\mathcal{C}$ and an adversary $\mathcal{A}$ formally captures the requirement of *Unforgeability*.

Setup $\mathcal{C}$ invokes Setup(1^λ) and subsequently Gen() to obtain (param, $\{(pk_i, sk_i)\}_{i\in[n]}$). Denote the set $\{pk_i\}_{i\in[n]}$ by $\mathcal{R}$. (param, $pk_S, \mathcal{R}$) is given to $\mathcal{A}$.

Query $\mathcal{A}$ is allowed to make the following queries:
- Corruption Query. $\mathcal{A}$ submits a public key $pk_i \in \mathcal{R}$ and receives sk_i.
- Signature Query. $\mathcal{A}$ submits a message m, an arbitrary ring $\mathcal{R}' = \{pk_0', pk_1'\}$ and a bit b, and receives $(\sigma, \mathcal{R}') \leftarrow$ Sign($sk_b', \mathcal{R}', m$) where sk_b' is the corresponding private key of pk_b'.

Output $\mathcal{A}$ submits $(\sigma^*, \mathcal{R}^*, m^*)$ and wins if and only if
1. valid $\leftarrow$ Verify($\sigma^*, \mathcal{R}^*, m^*$) and $\mathcal{R}^* \subset \mathcal{R}$.
2. $\mathcal{A}$ has not submitted a Signature Query with input $m^*, \mathcal{R}^*$.
3. $\mathcal{A}$ has not submitted a Corruption Query on input pk such that pk $\in \mathcal{R}^*$.

Definition 4 (Unforgeability). *A two-party ring signature scheme is unforgeable if no PPT adversary wins the above game with non-negligible probability.*

Our definition of unforgeability is slightly stronger than the strongest notion, existential unforgeability with respect to insider corruption [2], in which we allow the adversary to issue signature query on behalf of arbitrary ring without supplying the corresponding secret key.

Anonymity. It means that given a message m and a signature $(\sigma, \mathcal{R})$, it is infeasible to determine who created the signature, even if all the secret keys are known. The formal definition is adapted from [2] for general ring signatures against full key exposure. Note that we allow the common reference string to be maliciously generated in this model.

The following game between a challenger C and an adversary A formally captures the requirement of *Anonymity*.

Setup A gives param to C. C invokes Gen() to obtain $\{(\mathsf{pk}_i, \mathsf{sk}_i)\}_{i \in [n]}$). Denote the set $\{\mathsf{pk}_i\}_{i \in [n]}$ by R. (pk_i, sk_i) for $i \in [n]$) is given to A.

Challenge A gives two indexes i_0, i_1 and a message m to C. C flips a fair coin b and computes $(\sigma, \{\mathsf{pk}_{i_0}, \mathsf{pk}_{i_1}\}) \leftarrow \mathsf{Sign}(\mathsf{sk}_b, m\{\mathsf{pk}_{i_0}, \mathsf{pk}_{i_1}\})$. σ is returned to A.

Output A submits a guess bit b' and wins if and only if $b' = b$.

Definition 5 (Anonymity). *A two-party ring signature is unconditionally anonymous if no computationally unbounded adversray A wins the above game with probability that is non-negligibly higher than $1/2$.*

2.4 Syntax of Two-Party Blind Ring Signatures

A signature is blind if there exists a protocol between the signer and a user in which the user obtains a signature from the signer on message m in such a way that the signer learns nothing about the m nor the signature issued. More formally, a blind signature scheme is a scheme with the following additional protocol BSign.

Setup, Gen, Verify are the same as above.

BSign : This is a protocol between the signer and a user. The common input is param and a ring of two public keys $R = (\mathsf{pk}_0, \mathsf{pk}_1)$. The signer has additionally a private input a private key (sk_b) such that the corresponding public key (pk_b) is in the ring R. The user has a private input m. Upon successful completion of the protocol, the user obtains a ring signature σ on message m with respect to ring R.

Unforgeability. The following game between a challenger C and an adversary A formally captures the requirement of *Unforgeability* for any two-party blind ring signatures.

Setup C invokes Setup(1^λ) and subsequently Gen() to obtain (param, $\{(\mathsf{pk}_i, \mathsf{sk}_i)\}_{i \in [n]}$). Denote the set $\{\mathsf{pk}_i\}_{i \in [n]}$ by R. (param, pk_S, R) is given to A.

Query A is allowed to make the following queries:
- Corruption Query. A submits a public key $\mathsf{pk}_i \in R$ and receives sk_i.
- Blind Sign Query. A submits an arbitrary ring $R' = \{\mathsf{pk}_0', \mathsf{pk}_1'\}$ and a bit b, and interacts with C who plays the role of a signer (with public key pk_b' and secret key sk_b').

Output A submits a ring R^* and $(k+1)$ distinct messages (m_i^*) and their corresponding signatures (σ_i^*) for $i = 1$ to $k+1$ and wins if and only if
  1. $R^* \subset R$ and A has not submitted a Corruption Query on input pk such that $\mathsf{pk} \in R^*$.
  2. `valid` $\leftarrow$ Verify(σ_i^*, R^*, m_i^*) for $i = 1$ to $k+1$.
  3. A has submitted at most k blind sign queries with input R^*.

Definition 6 (Unforgeability). *A two-party blind ring signature scheme is unforgeable if no PPT adversary wins the above game with non-negligible probability.*

Anonymity Anonymity for the blind version is shown as follows.

The following game between a challenger C and an adversary A formally captures the requirement of *Anonymity*.

Setup A gives param to C. C invokes Gen() to obtain $\{(\mathsf{pk}_i, \mathsf{sk}_i)\}_{i \in [n]}$. Denote the set $\{\mathsf{pk}_i\}_{i \in [n]}$ by $\mathcal{R}$. C gives (pk_i, sk_i) for $i \in [n]$ to A.

Challenge A gives two indexes i_0, i_1 to C. C filps a fair coin b and interacts with A as a signer in protocol BSign with private input sk_{i_b}.

Output A submits a guess bit b' and wins if and only if $b' = b$.

Definition 7 (Anonymity). *A two-party blind ring signature is unconditionally anonymous if no computationally unbounded adversray A wins the above game with probability that is non-negligibly higher than $1/2$.*

Blindness Blindness refers to the fact that the signer learns nothing about the message being signed nor the signature created during a blind sign protocol. The following game between a challenger C and an adversary A formally captures the requirement of *Blindness*.

Setup C invokes Setup() and subsequently Gen() to obtain param, $\{(\mathsf{pk}_i, \mathsf{sk}_i)\}_{i \in [n]}$. Denote the set $\{\mathsf{pk}_i\}_{i \in [n]}$ by $\mathcal{R}$. C gives param and (pk_i, sk_i) for $i \in [n]$ to A.

Challenge A gives a ring $\mathcal{R}^* \subset \mathcal{R}$ and two messages m_0, m_1 to C. C filps a fair coin b and obtains two signatures from A in protocol BSign in the following order: the first interaction is to obtain signature on message m_b and the second interaction is for signature on message m_{1-b}. C gives σ_0, σ_1 to A which are the resulting signatures from these interactions. Note that the index i is arbitrary, meaning that σ_i could be the result from the first run or the second interaction. Further, $\sigma_i = \perp$ if the interaction does not terminate successfully.

Output A submits a guess bit b' and wins if and only if $b' = b$.

Definition 8 (Blindness). *A two-party blind ring signature is blind if no PPT adversray A wins the above game with probability that is non-negligibly higher than $1/2$.*

3 Non-interactive Zero-Knowledge Proof-of-Knowledge

Our construction relies on an non-interactive zero-knowledge proof-of-knowledge of discrete logarithm satisfying the requirement of what is commonly referred to as signature proof-of-knowledge. More formally, it has to be simulatable and extractable under the same common reference string. Being simulatable means that given a trapdoor of the common reference string, there exists an efficient algorithm, called simulator, which is capable of simulating a proof-of-knowledge of discrete logarithm of an element without actually knowing the discrete logarithm. Being extractable means that given the trapdoor of the common reference string, there exists another efficient algorithm, called extractor, which is capable of outputting the discrete logarithm of an element given a proof-of-knowledge of discrete logarithm of that element.

Many secure constructions requires a proof system that allows simulations and extraction under the same string and this is not readily achievable in the GS proof system.

Nonetheless, Bernhard et al. [3], following the technique employed in [10], showed how a GS proof for pairing product equations can be turned into signature of knowledges offering simulatability and extractability simultaneously. Our protocol follows their concept and the difference is discussed after the presentation of the protocol.

3.1 Proof $\mathfrak{P}_{DL}$

We use the notation $\mathfrak{P}_{DL}\{(x) : Y = g^x\}$ to represent an non-interactive zero-knowledge proof-of-knowledge of the discrete logarithm of Y to base g. The protocol makes use of the GS witness-indistinguishable proof system on a set of pairing-product equations. Our protocol is inspired by various constructions in the literature and we introduce several optimizations for efficiency considerations.

Setup Let n be the security parameter. The common reference string of $\mathfrak{P}_{DL}$ consists of crs_{GS}, the soundness string of the GS proof system, and the following elements $v', v_1, \ldots, v_n, h_1, h_2 \in \mathbb{G}$ and a collision-resistant hash function $H : \{0,1\}^* \to \mathbb{Z}_p$.

Proof Generation Intuition We first present the intuition of the non-interactive proof of knowledge of x such that $Y = g^x$. The prover first express x as $\sum_{i=0}^{n-1} 2^i x[i]$ where $x[n-1]\ldots x[0]$ is the binary representation of x. The prover generates a witness-indistinguishable proof of the following fact:

$$NIWI \left\{ (X_0,\ldots,X_{n-1},S_1) : \begin{array}{c} \left(\begin{array}{c} \bigwedge_{i=0}^{n-1}(X_i = g^{2^i} \vee X_i = 1) \wedge \\ Y = \prod_{i=0}^{n-1} X_i \quad \wedge \\ \vee \end{array} \right) \\ \left(\hat{e}(S_1, h) = \hat{e}(h_1, h_2)\hat{e}(\mathcal{V}(statement), S_2) \right) \end{array} \right\}$$

where $\mathcal{V}(statement)$ is the waters hash of the statement being proved. Specifically, let C be the commitments of the witnesses of $\{X_i\}$'s in the GS proof system. Further, let $s = H(C\|Y\|S_2)$ and $\mathcal{V}(statement)$ is defined as $v' \prod v_i^{s[i]}$ where $s[i]$ is the i-th bit of s. The idea of the proof is that $X_i = g^{2^i}$ if $x[i]$ is 1 and $X_i = 1$ (the identity element of $\mathbb{G}$) if $x[i] = 0$. Due to the soundness of the GS proof system, knowing the set of X_i's implies knowing a set of values $x[i] \in \{0,1\}$. Since the later part assures the verifier that $Y = \prod_{i=0}^{n-1} X_i$, knowing a set of values $x[i] \in \{0,1\}$ is equivalent to knowing the value $x = \sum_{i=0}^{n-1} x[i]$ such that $Y = g^x$. One could view the final equation as knowing a Waters' signature on the statement. In fact, (S_1, S_2) is a Waters' signature on the value $s = H(C\|Y\|S_2)$. This is purely for the simulatablility of the proof as the simulator who generates the common reference string knows the "secret key" (α) such that $h_1 = h^\alpha$ would be capable of generating (S_1, S_2) and use it for the proof simulation. Due to witness-indistinguishability of the GS proof system, the simulated proof is indistinguishable to the proof generating using witness $\{X_i\}$. The remaining challenge is to transform the above idea into a set of pairing-product equations where the GS proof system can be used.

Proof Generation The prover randomly picks $r \in_R \mathbb{Z}_p$, computes $S_2 = h_1^r \in \mathbb{G}$ and computes the following GS proof.

$$
NIWI \left\{ (X_0, \ldots, X_{n-1}, S_1, S) : \begin{array}{cc} \hat{e}(S/h, S/h_1) = 1 & \wedge \\ \bigwedge_{i=0}^{n-1} (\hat{e}(X_i, X_i/g^{2^i}) = 1) & \wedge \\ \hat{e}(Y, S/h) = \hat{e}(\prod_{i=0}^{n-1} X_i, S/h) & \wedge \\ \hat{e}(S_1, S) = \hat{e}(h_2, h_1) \hat{e}(\mathcal{V}(statement), S_2) \end{array} \right\}
$$

using the set of witnesses $\{X_i = g^{x[i]2^i}\}$, $S = h_1, S_1 = \mathcal{V}(statement) h_2^r$. Again, let C be the commitments of $\{X_i\}$'s and S in the GS proof system. Let $s = H(C \| Y \| S_2)$ and $\mathcal{V}(statement)$ is defined as $v' \prod v_i^{s[i]}$ where $s[i]$ is the i-th bit of s.

Proof Verification The verifier validates the NIWI proof and that $S_2 \neq 1$.

Discussions Various optimization techniques have been employed for the realization of $\mathfrak{P}_{DL}$. Firstly, one could note that the variable S acts as a selector. The first equation guarantees that $S = h$ or $S = h_1$. When $S = h_1$, the prover can simulate the last equation without knowing the Waters signature on the statement as shown above. Specifically, the prover can set $S_2 = h_1^r$ and use the witness $S_1 = \mathcal{V}(statement) h_2^r$. In this setting, the prover is forced to set X_i to be $g^{x[i]2^i}$ so that the equation $\hat{e}(Y, h_1/h) = \hat{e}(\prod_{i=0}^n X_i, h_1/h)$ holds. Finally, one could note that the equation $\hat{e}(X_i, X_i/g^{2^i}) = 1$ guarantees that $X_i = 1$ or g^{2^i}.

To produce a simulated proof, the simulator would have to generate the common reference string so that it knows α such that $h_1 = h^\alpha$. With this trapdoor (α), the simulator could set $X_i = 1$, $S = h$ so that all but the last equation holds. For the last equation, the simulator creates a Waters signature on the statement. Specifically, it randomly picks $r \in_R \mathbb{Z}_p$, computes $S_2 = h^r$ and $S_1 = h_2^\alpha \mathcal{V}(statement)^r$.

While the general idea is similar to that of [3] in the construction of signature proof of knowledge, our realization contains several optimizations. Firstly, only part of the Waters' signature (S_1) is a variable. The reason is that S_2 can be computed without knowing the signing key and can be "simulated" by the real prover. Secondly, we make use of the symmetric pairing to save the number of variables for the "OR" proofs. For instance, proving the knowledge of variable X satisfying the relation $e(X/A, X/B) = 1$ is equivalent to proving $X = A$ or $X = B$ with one pairing-product equation in one variable.

3.2   Proof $\mathfrak{P}_{WH}$

Let $g, u_1, \ldots, u_n \in \mathbb{G}$ be generators of group $\mathbb{G}$. Consider a message $m \in \mathbb{Z}_p$, we consider the commitment of m as $\prod_{i=1}^n u_i^{m[i]} g^r$ for a random value $r \in_R \mathbb{Z}_p$ where $m[i]$ is the i-th bit of m. We use the notation $\mathfrak{P}_{WH}\{(m, r) : M = \prod_{i=1}^n u_i^{m[i]} g^r\}$ to represent the non-interactive zero-knowledge proof-of-knowledge of how the commitment M can be openned.

Common Reference String is the same as the proof $\mathfrak{P}_{DL}$.

Proof Generation The prover randomly picks $t \in_R \mathbb{Z}_p$, computes $S_2 = h_1^t \in \mathbb{G}$ and computes the following GS proof.

$$
NIWI \left\{ \begin{pmatrix} R_0, \ldots, R_{n-1}, \\ U_1, \ldots, U_n, \\ S_1, S \end{pmatrix} : \begin{array}{ll} \hat{e}(S/h, S/h_1) = 1 & \wedge \\ \bigwedge_{i=1}^{n}(\hat{e}(U_i, U_i/u_i) = 1) & \wedge \\ \bigwedge_{i=0}^{n-1}(\hat{e}(R_i, R_i/g^{2^i}) = 1) & \wedge \\ \hat{e}(M, S/h) = \hat{e}(\prod_{i=1}^{n} U_i \prod_{i=0}^{n-1} R_i, S/h) & \wedge \\ \hat{e}(S_1, S) = \hat{e}(h_2, h_1)\hat{e}(\mathcal{V}(statement), S_2) \end{array} \right\}
$$

using the set of witnesses $\{R_i = g^{r[i]2^i}\}$, $\{U_i = u_i^{m[i]}\}$, $S = h_1$, $S_1 = \mathcal{V}(statement)h_2^t$. Here $r[n-1] \ldots r[0]$ is the binary representation of r. Again, let C be the commitments of $\{R_i\}$'s, $\{U_i\}$'s and S in the GS proof system. Let $s = H(C||M||S_2)$ and $\mathcal{V}(statement)$ is defined as $v' \prod v_i^{s[i]}$ where $s[i]$ is the i-th bit of s.

Proof Verification The verifier validates the NIWI proof and that $S_2 \neq 1$.

Regarding the security of these two non-interactive proofs, we have the following theorem whose proof can be found in Appendix A.

Theorem 1. $\mathfrak{P}_{DL}$ *and* $\mathfrak{P}_{WH}$ *are simulatable under the DLIN assumption and extractable under the CDH assumption in the standard model.*

4 Constructions

We first describe our construction of a two-party ring signature, which is essentially the scheme from [2] with a proof-of-correctness added to the public key.

4.1 A Two-Party Ring Signature Scheme

param $\leftarrow$ Setup(1^λ): On input a security parameter λ, this algorithm chooses two cyclic groups $\mathbb{G}$, $\mathbb{G}_T$ of prime order p such that $|p| = \lambda$ and that there exists a bilinear map $\hat{e} : \mathbb{G} \times \mathbb{G} \to \mathbb{G}_T$. It also generates the common reference string of the non-interactive proof system discussed in section 3. Finally, it chooses several generator $g, u', u_1, \ldots, u_n \in \mathbb{G}$, where n is the bit-length of the message.

(pk, sk) $\leftarrow$ Gen(): This algorithm randomly picks $x \in_R \mathbb{Z}_p$ and computes $Y = g^x$. It also computes the non-interactive proof $\pi_Y = \mathfrak{P}_{DL}\{(x) : Y = g^x\}$. The public key is (Y, π_Y) and the secret key is x.

$(\sigma, \mathcal{R}) \leftarrow$ Sign(sk$_S$, $\mathcal{R}$, m) : On input a message m, a secret key of a signer x and two public keys (Y, π_Y) and $(Y', \pi_{Y'})$ where $Y = g^x$, this algorithm first validates $\pi_{Y'}$. Next, it computes $M = u' \prod_{i=1}^{n} u_i^{m[i]}$. It then chooses $r \in_R \mathbb{Z}_p$, computes $S_2 = g^r$ and $S_1 = Y'^x M^r$. Output σ as (S_1, S_2) and the ring as $\{(Y, \pi_Y), (Y', \pi_{Y'})\}$.

valid/invalid $\leftarrow$ Verify(σ, $\mathcal{R}$, m) : On input a a message m, a signature σ and a rinf $\{(Y, \pi_Y), (Y', \pi_{Y'})\}$, this algorithm first validates π_Y and $\pi_{Y'}$. Next, it outputs valid if and only if

$$
\hat{e}(S_1, g) = \hat{e}(Y, Y')\hat{e}(u' \prod_{i=1}^{n} u_i^{m[i]}, S_2).
$$

Note that the signature size is only 2 elements. While the validations of π_Y and $\pi_{Y'}$ is quite expensive, it is required to be conducted once per each public key. Thus, in a long run, our scheme is nearly as efficient as the original scheme from [2] if the public key of the users are relatively stable.

4.2 A Blind Signature Generation Protocol for Our Two-Party Ring Signature Scheme

The blind signature generation protocol is a two-round protocol described below. The public keys of the ring, (Y, π_Y) and $(Y', \pi_{Y'})$ are known to both the signer and the user. Without loss of generality, the signer has an additional input x such that $Y = g^x$. The user has an additional input m.

The user validates (Y, π_Y) and $(Y', \pi_{Y'})$. Then it computes a commitment of m as $M' = \prod_{i=1}^{n} u_i^{m[i]} g^r$ for some random $r \in_R \mathbb{Z}_p$ and the non-interactive proof $\pi_{M'} = \mathfrak{P}_{\mathsf{WH}}\{(m, r) : M' = \prod_{i=1}^{n} u_i^{m[i]} g^r\}$. It sends $M', \pi_{M'}$ to the signer.

Upon receive $M', \pi_{M'}$, the signer validates $\pi_{M'}$ and $\pi_{Y'}$. Next, it computes $S_2 = g^t$ for some randomly generated $t \in_R \mathbb{Z}_p$, $S_1 = Y'^x (u'M')^t$ and returns (S_1', S_2') to the user.

The user picks $a \in_R \mathbb{Z}_p$, computes $S_1 = (S_1'/(S_2')^r)(u'M')^a$ and $S_2 = S_2' g^a$. It outputs the signature on m as (S_1, S_2).

It is straightforward to see that the signature created using the blind signature generation protocol has the same distribution as those outputted from the sign algorithm.

Regarding the security of our two-party ring signatures, we have the following theorem whose proof can be found in Appendix B.

Theorem 2. *Our construction of two-party ring signatures is unforgeable under the DLIN and CDH assumption. It is unconditionally anonymous. The blind signature version possesses blindness under the DLIN and CDH assumption.*

5 Applications

Designated Verifier Signatures A direct application of our two-party ring signature scheme is on designated verifier signatures, Jakobsson, Sako and Impagliazzo [13], and independently by Chaum [5] in 1996. A DVS scheme allows a signer Alice to convince a designated verifier Bob that Alice has endorsed the message while Bob cannot transfer this conviction to anyone else. As discussed in [15], if Alice create a ring signature on behalf of the ring with Alice and Bob and sends the ring signature to Bob, Bob will be convinced that the message has been endorsed by Alice. On the other hand, the signature will not be able to convince any outsider since Bob could have been the creator of the signature. Hence, a two-party ring signature is sufficient for the construction of designated verifier signature. Our construction secure in the strong model is necessary for it allows the resulting designated verifier signatures to be secure against the vogue key attack [13,18]. On the other hand, some existing schemes make use of some ad-hoc techniques [20] to defend against this attack.

Optimistic Fair Exchange. Optimistic fair exchange, introduced by Asokan, Schunter and Waidner [1] allows two parties, Alice and Bob, to exchange digital signatures with the help of a passive trusted third party. Haung et al. [12] presents an elegant realization based on a secure two-party ring signatures. Their construction is generic in which any secure two-party ring signature scheme can be used. Having said that, since optimistic fair exchange is supposed to work in the multi-user setting, the security requirement of the underlying ring signature is stronger than the model guaranteed by the two-party ring signatures in [2]. On the other hand, our scheme satisfies their security requirements and can be used. We also make the following observation. If the blind version of our ring signature scheme is employed, the resulting optimistic fair exchange protocol enjoys an additional property in which the trusted third party cannot learn anything about the messages and signatures being exchanged even if it is called upon for protocol completion. This will improve the applicability of this protocol since they exchanging parties might be reluctant to reveal the information of the exchange.

Fair Outsourcing. Following the fair exchange paradigm, Chen et al. [7] consider the problem of the exchange of payment and outsourcing computation. In their proposal, the job owner outsourced some computationally expensive task to a set of workers and upon completion of its assigned computation, the worker shall receive the payment from the job owner. A fair exchange protocol is used to ensure fairness. Specifically, the computation result is used in exchange of the job owner's payment. As a two-party ring signature can be used as a building block for a fair exchange protocol, our construction is also useful in the fair outsourcing system.

6   Conclusion

In this paper, we present two useful non-interactive zero-knowledge proof-of-knowledge protocols. With these protocols, we proposed an efficient two-party ring signatures and its extension to support blind signature generation. Finally, we discussed several applications of our constructions.

References

1. Asokan, N., Schunter, M., Waidner, M.: Optimistic protocols for fair exchange. In: Graveman, R., Janson, P.A., Neumann, C., Gong, L. (eds.) ACM Conference on Computer and Communications Security, pp. 7–17. ACM (1997)
2. Bender, A., Katz, J., Morselli, R.: Ring signatures: Stronger definitions, and constructions without random oracles. In: Halevi, S., Rabin, T. (eds.) TCC 2006. LNCS, vol. 3876, pp. 60–79. Springer, Heidelberg (2006)
3. Bernhard, D., Fuchsbauer, G., Ghadafi, E.: Efficient signatures of knowledge and DAA in the standard model. In: Jacobson, M., Locasto, M., Mohassel, P., Safavi-Naini, R. (eds.) ACNS 2013. LNCS, vol. 7954, pp. 518–533. Springer, Heidelberg (2013)
4. Chandran, N., Groth, J., Sahai, A.: Ring signatures of sub-linear size without random oracles. In: Arge, L., Cachin, C., Jurdziński, T., Tarlecki, A. (eds.) ICALP 2007. LNCS, vol. 4596, pp. 423–434. Springer, Heidelberg (2007)
5. Chaum, D.: Private Signature and Proof Systems, US Patent 5,493,614 (1996)

6. Chaum, D., van Heyst, E.: Group signatures. In: Davies, D.W. (ed.) EUROCRYPT 1991. LNCS, vol. 547, pp. 257–265. Springer, Heidelberg (1991)
7. Chen, X., Li, J., Susilo, W.: Efficient fair conditional payments for outsourcing computations. IEEE Transactions on Information Forensics and Security 7(6), 1687–1694 (2012)
8. Chow, S.S.M., Liu, J.K., Wei, V.K., Yuen, T.H.: Ring Signatures Without Random Oracles. In: ASIACCS 2006, pp. 297–302. ACM Press (2006)
9. Ghadafi, E.: Sub-linear blind ring signatures without random oracles. Cryptology ePrint Archive, Report 2013/612 (2013), http://eprint.iacr.org/
10. Groth, J.: Simulation-sound NIZK proofs for a practical language and constant size group signatures. In: Lai, X., Chen, K. (eds.) ASIACRYPT 2006. LNCS, vol. 4284, pp. 444–459. Springer, Heidelberg (2006)
11. Groth, J., Sahai, A.: Efficient non-interactive proof systems for bilinear groups. In: Smart, N. (ed.) EUROCRYPT 2008. LNCS, vol. 4965, pp. 415–432. Springer, Heidelberg (2008)
12. Huang, Q., Yang, G., Wong, D.S., Susilo, W.: Efficient optimistic fair exchange secure in the multi-user setting and chosen-key model without random oracles. In: Malkin, T. (ed.) CT-RSA 2008. LNCS, vol. 4964, pp. 106–120. Springer, Heidelberg (2008)
13. Jakobsson, M., Sako, K., Impagliazzo, R.: Designated Verifier Proofs and Their Applications. In: Maurer, U.M. (ed.) EUROCRYPT 1996. LNCS, vol. 1070, pp. 143–154. Springer, Heidelberg (1996)
14. Rivest, R.L., Shamir, A., Tauman, Y.: How to Leak a Secret. In: Boyd, C. (ed.) ASIACRYPT 2001. LNCS, vol. 2248, pp. 552–565. Springer, Heidelberg (2001)
15. Saeednia, S., Kremer, S., Markowitch, O.: An Efficient Strong Designated Verifier Signature Scheme. In: Lim, J.-I., Lee, D.-H. (eds.) ICISC 2003. LNCS, vol. 2971, pp. 40–54. Springer, Heidelberg (2004)
16. Schäge, S., Schwenk, J.: A CDH-based ring signature scheme with short signatures and public keys. In: Sion, R. (ed.) FC 2010. LNCS, vol. 6052, pp. 129–142. Springer, Heidelberg (2010)
17. Shacham, H., Waters, B.: Efficient ring signatures without random oracles. In: Okamoto, T., Wang, X. (eds.) PKC 2007. LNCS, vol. 4450, pp. 166–180. Springer, Heidelberg (2007)
18. Shim, K.-A.: Rogue-key Attacks on the Multi-designated Verifiers Signature Scheme. Inf. Process. Lett. 107(2), 83–86 (2008)
19. Shoup, V.: Sequences of games: A tool for taming complexity in security proofs. IACR Cryptology ePrint Archive 2004, 332 (2004)
20. Zhang, Y., Au, M.H., Yang, G., Susilo, W.: (Strong) multi-designated verifiers signatures secure against rogue key attack. In: Xu, L., Bertino, E., Mu, Y. (eds.) NSS 2012. LNCS, vol. 7645, pp. 334–347. Springer, Heidelberg (2012)

A   Proof of Theorem 1

We sketch the proof idea for $\mathfrak{P}_{DL}$. The proof for $\mathfrak{P}_{WH}$ is similar and is thus omitted.

Simulatability. In the intuition of $\mathfrak{P}_{DL}$, we already discussed how a simulator, with the knowledge of α such that $h_1 = h^\alpha$ can produce a simulated proof $\mathfrak{P}_{DL}$. It remains to argue this simulated proof is indistinguishable from the real proof. The argument makes use of the game-hoping technique [19] which involves a sequence of games defined below.

1. $Game_0$: This is the real game.

2. Game$_1$: Same is Game$_0$ except the common reference string of the GS proof system crs$_{GS}$ is chosen in the simulation setting instead of the soundness setting.
3. Game$_2$: Same as Game$_1$ except the non-interactive proofs $\mathfrak{P}_{DL}$ given to the adversary is generated by the simulator.
4. Game$_3$: Same as Game$_2$ except the common reference string of the GS proof system crs$_{GS}$ is chosen to be in the soundness setting instead of the simulation setting.

The setting in Game$_3$ is where the adversary is given simulated proofs instead of real proofs. It remains to show the advantage of an adversary trying to distinguish whether it is playing Game$_0$ and Game$_3$ is negligible. The argument goes as follows. The difference between Game$_0$ and Game$_1$ is negligible under the DLIN assumption due to the computational indistinguishably of the common reference string of the GS proof system. For Game$_1$ and Game$_2$, observe that the distribution of S_2 is the same (uniformly at random from $\mathbb{G}$) and that the distribution of the GS proof is also the same (since the commitments are perfectly hiding in the simulation string), the difference between Game$_1$ and Game$_2$ is negligible. Finally, the difference between Game$_2$ and Game$_3$ is negligible under the DLIN assumption. Thus, $\mathfrak{P}_{DL}$ is simulatable under the DLIN assumption.

Extractability. Due to the soundness of the GS proof system, the extractor can always extracts from $\mathfrak{P}_{DL}$ a set of witnesses $(X_0, \ldots, X_{n-1}, S_1, S)$ satisfying the set of pairing product equations. From the equation

$$\hat{e}(S/h, S/h_1) = 1,$$

S can only be h or h_1. If $S = h$, the last equation

$$\hat{e}(S_1, S) = \hat{e}(h_2, h_1)\hat{e}(\mathcal{V}(statement), S_2)$$

means that the witness S_1 together with the value S_2 is a Waters signature on the message "statement". Since the adversary must be producing a new statement. It is easy to setup the simulator which breaks the existential unforgeability of Waters signature, which is equivalent to solve the CDH problem. (The simulator is given a signing oracle of the Waters signature and use it to produce all the simulated proof. Finally, we then adversary produces a new proof, the simulator extracts a new Waters signature.)
When $S = h_1$, we have

$$\hat{e}(Y, S/h) = \hat{e}(\prod_{i=0}^{n-1} X_i, S/h),$$

which implies $Y = \prod_{i=0}^{n-1} X_i$. Recall that for all i,

$$\hat{e}(X_i, X_i/g^{2^i}) = 1,$$

it means $X_i = 1$ or $X_i = g^{2^i}$. From this, the simulator can calculate $x = \sum_{i=0}^{n-1} x[i]2^i$ where $x[i] = 0$ if $X_i = 1$ and $x[i] = 2^i$ otherwise.
Thus, $\mathfrak{P}_{DL}$ is extractable under the CDH assumption.

B   Proof of Theorem 2

We sketch the proof idea for our construction of two-party (blind) ring signatures.

Unforgeability. The signature generation and verification is the same as the construction of [2], which is unforgeable against chosen sub-ring attack. The only difference is the addition of the non-interactive proof of knowledge of the secret key attached in the public key. For all public keys presented by the adversary, the simulator can extract the corresponding signing keys and use it to answer all queries related to these keys chosen by the adversary. This in turns allow our scheme to be proven secure in the stronger model where the adversary can introduce keys into the system. For the blind signature generation protocol, the simulator can always extract from $\mathfrak{P}_{\mathsf{WH}}$ the message to be signed in the protocol and the rest is the same as the origin version. Due to the need to produce a simulated proof for the challenge public key and the need of extractions, our construction is secure under the CDH and the DLIN assumption in the standard model.

Anonymity. The original two-party ring signature of [2] is unconditionally anonymous and it is straightforward to see our construction retains this desirable property. Consider a given signature $(S_1, S_2), \{PK, PK'\}$ on message m. For any public key $PK = (Y, \pi_Y)$, there exists a random value r such that $S_1 = g^{yy'}(u' \prod_{i=1}^{m} u_i^{m[i]})^r$ and $S_2 = g^r$. In other words, it can be generated by user with public key PK or PK' and thus the signature is unconditionally anonymous.

Blindness. Consider two transcripts of the blind signature generation protocol $(M', \pi_{M'}, S_1', S_2')$ and $(\bar{M}', \pi_{\bar{M}'}, \bar{S}_1', \bar{S}_2')$ and a given message-signature pair (m, S_1, S_2).

There exists a set of randomness (r, a) such that $M' = \prod_{i=1}^{n} u_i^{m[i]} g^r$, $S_2 = S_2' g^a$ and $S_1 = (u'M')^a S_1'/(S_2')^r$ (this only holds when S_1', S_2' are correctly computed by the signer for M' yet if the signer does not, the user can detect this misbehavior and abort).

At the same time, there exists another set of randomness $(\bar{r}, \bar{a})$ such that $M' = \prod_{i=1}^{n} u_i^{m[i]} g^{\bar{r}}$, $S_2 = \bar{S}_2' g^{\bar{a}}$ and $S_1 = (u'M')^{\bar{a}} \bar{S}_1'/(\bar{S}_2')^{\bar{r}}$ (again, assume S_1' and S_2' are correctly computed).

This means that a message-signature pair can be the result of interaction M', S_1', S_2' or $\bar{M}', \bar{S}_1', \bar{S}_2'$. Finally, due to the simulatablility of $\mathfrak{P}_{\mathsf{WH}}$, $\pi_{M'}$ nor $\pi_{\bar{M}'}$ leaks no information about m and r under the DLIN and CDH assumption. Thus, our construction possesses blindness under the DLIN and CDH assumption.

Efficient Leakage-Resilient Signature Schemes in the Generic Bilinear Group Model[*]

Fei Tang[1,2], Hongda Li[1,2], Qihua Niu[1,2], and Bei Liang[1,2]

[1] The Data Assurance and Communication Security Research Center
of Chinese Academy of Sciences, Beijing, China
[2] State Key Laboratory of Information Security, Institute of Information Engineering
of Chinese Academy of Sciences, Beijing, China
tangfei127@163.com, hdli@ucas.ac.cn, {niuqihua,liangbei}@iie.ac.cn

Abstract. We extend the techniques of Kiltz et al. (in ASIACRYPT 2010) and Galindo et al. (in SAC 2012) to construct two efficient leakage-resilient signature schemes. Our schemes based on Boneh-Lynn-Shacham (BLS) short signature and Waters signature schemes, respectively. Both of them are more efficient than Galindo et al.'s scheme, and can tolerate leakage of $(1 - o(1))/2$ of the secret key at every signature invocation. The security of the proposed schemes are proved in the generic bilinear group model (in our first scheme which is based on the BLS signature, a random oracle is needed for the proof).

Keywords: Digital signature, leakage-resilient cryptography, generic bilinear group model.

1 Introduction

In the traditional security proof of the cryptographic schemes, there has a basic assumption that the secret state is completely hidden to the adversary. However, it is almost impossible to realize this assumption in the real world. Many cryptographic engineers have designed some side-channel attacks can detect some leakage information about the secret state. For example, power consumption [23], fault attacks [5,8], and timing attacks [7], etc.

Leakage-resilient cryptography is a countermeasure to resist such side-channel attacks with some algorithmic techniques, which means that designing algorithms such that their description already provides security against those attacks. Leakage-resilient cryptography is an increasingly active area in recent years and many leakage models have been proposed, such as only computation leaks information (OCLI) [18,20,24,22], memory leakage [1,17], bounded retrieval [2,3,14], and auxiliary input models [15,20,19], etc. In this work, we design leakage-resilient signature schemes based on the following two leakage models:

---

[*] This research is supported by the National Natural Science Foundation of China (Grant No. 60970139), the Strategic Priority Program of Chinese Academy of Sciences (Grant No. XDA06010702), and the IIEs Cryptography Research Project.

X. Huang and J. Zhou (Eds.): ISPEC 2014, LNCS 8434, pp. 418–432, 2014.

- *OCLI model:* leakage is assumed to only occur on values that currently accessed during the computation.
- *Continual leakage model:* the amount of leakage is assumed to be bounded only in between any two successive key refreshes but the overall amount can be unbounded.

Bounded leakage model [21,6] is a weaker notion, corresponding to the continual leakage model, means that the amount of the leakage information is bounded with a fixed value throughout the lifetime of the system. Obviously, the continual leakage model is more closer to the real-world scenarios. Note that in the continual leakage setting, the secret state should be stateful, i.e., the secret state should be updated after (or before) every round of the invocation of the secret state. Otherwise, the entire secret state will be completely leaked after multiple invocations.

Kiltz and Pietrzak [22] designed a leakage-resilient PKE scheme which is a bilinear version of the ElGamal key encapsulation mechanism and it is secure in the presence of continual leakage in the *generic bilinear group* (GBG) model [10]. It is more important that their scheme is very efficient, just less than a little time slower than the standard ElGamal scheme. Galindo and Vivek [20] then adapted their techniques (i.e., blinding the secret key) to construct a practical signature scheme based on the Boneh-Boyen IBE scheme [9]. Its efficiency is close to the non leakage-resilient one and it tolerates leakage of almost half of the bits of the secret key at every signature invocation.

In this paper, we follow the techniques by Kiltz et al. [22] and Galindo et al. [20], construct two leakage-resilient signature schemes based on the OCLI and continual leakage models. Our first scheme is based on the BLS signature scheme [12], its signing algorithm is deterministic, we adapt it to a probabilistic one and the resulting scheme can tolerate leakage of $(1-o(1))/2$ of the secret key at every signature invocation. Our second scheme is based on the Waters signature scheme [28], the resulting scheme also can tolerate leakage of $(1 - o(1))/2$ of the secret key at every signature invocation. Both of them are provable leakage-resilience in the GBG model (the BLS-based one needs an additional random oracle for the proof), and more efficient than Galindo and Vivek's signature scheme, more precisely, one exponentiation is decreased in the signing and verification algorithm, respectively.

2   Preliminaries

In this section, we review some basic notions and preliminaries for this paper: bilinear groups and two intractability assumptions CDH and DBDH, generic bilinear groups model, entropy, and Schwartz-Zippel lemma.

The following notations will be used in this paper. Let $\mathbb{Z}$ be the set of integers and $\mathbb{Z}_p$ be the ring modulo p. 1^k denotes the string of k ones for $k \in \mathbb{N}$. $|x|$ denotes the length of the bit string x. $s \xleftarrow{\$} S$ means randomly choosing an element s form the set S. $[n]$ is a shorthand for the set $\{1, 2, \ldots, n\}$. We write $y \leftarrow \mathsf{A}(x)$ to indicate that running the algorithm A with input x and then outputs y, $y \xleftarrow{\$} A(x)$ has the same indication except that A is a probabilistic algorithm, and if we want to explicitly denote the randomness r used during the computation we write it $y \xleftarrow{r} A(x)$. Lastly we write PPT for the probabilistic polynomial time.

2.1 Bilinear Groups

Let G_1 and G_2 be two multiplicative cyclic groups with a same prime order p, and g be an arbitrary generator of G_1. We say that $\hat{e} : G_1 \times G_1 \to G_2$ be an admissible bilinear mapping if it satisfies the the following properties:

- *Bilinearity:* $\hat{e}(g^a, g^b) = \hat{e}(g, g)^{ab}$ for all $a, b \in \mathbb{Z}_p$.
- *Non-degeneracy:* $\hat{e}(g, g) \neq 1$.
- *Computability:* there exists efficient algorithm to calculate $\hat{e}(g^a, g^b)$ for all $a, b \in \mathbb{Z}_p$.

We assume that $\mathsf{BGen}(1^k)$ be a PPT algorithm can generate parameters $\mathbb{P} = (G_1, G_2, p, g, \hat{e})$ to satisfy the above properties on input a security parameter k. The group G_1 is said to be a bilinear group, and it is also called the base group and G_2 be the target group.

Definition 1. (CDH Assumption). For any PPT adversary $\mathcal{A}$, any polynomial $p(\cdot)$, and all sufficiently large $k \in \mathbb{N}$,

$$\Pr \left[\begin{array}{l} (G_1, G_2, p, g, \hat{e}) \leftarrow \mathsf{BGen}(1^k); \\ a, b \xleftarrow{\$} \mathbb{Z}_p; \\ v \leftarrow \mathcal{A}(G_1, p, g, g^a, g^b) \end{array} : v = g^{ab} \right] < \frac{1}{p(k)}.$$

Definition 2. (DBDH Assumption). For any PPT adversary $\mathcal{A}$, any polynomial $p(\cdot)$, and all sufficiently large $k \in \mathbb{N}$,

$$\left| \Pr \left[\begin{array}{l} (G_1, G_2, p, g, \hat{e}) \leftarrow \mathsf{BGen}(1^k); \\ a, b, c \xleftarrow{\$} \mathbb{Z}_p; \\ d \leftarrow \mathcal{A}(\mathbb{P}, g^a, g^b, g^c, \hat{e}(g, g)^{abc}) \end{array} : d = 1 \right] - \right.$$

$$\left. \Pr \left[\begin{array}{l} (G_1, G_2, p, g, \hat{e}) \leftarrow \mathsf{BGen}(1^k); \\ a, b, c, r \xleftarrow{\$} \mathbb{Z}_p; \\ d \leftarrow \mathcal{A}(\mathbb{P}, g^a, g^b, g^c, \hat{e}(g, g)^r) \end{array} : d = 1 \right] \right| < \frac{1}{p(k)}.$$

2.2 Generic Bilinear Group Model

In the generic group model [25], the elements of the group encoded by unique but randomly chosen strings, and thus the only property that can be tested by adversary is equality. Boneh et al. [10] extended it to a generic bilinear group (GBG) model. In the GBG model, the encoding is given by randomly chosen injective functions $\xi_1 : \mathbb{Z}_p \to \Xi_1$ and $\xi_2 : \mathbb{Z}_p \to \Xi_2$ which are the representations of the elements of the base group G_1 and target group G_2, respectively (w.l.o.g., we assume that $\Xi_1 \cap \Xi_2 = \emptyset$). The operations of the groups and the bilinear map are performed by three public oracles $\mathcal{O}_1, \mathcal{O}_2$, and $\mathcal{O}_{\hat{e}}$, respectively. For any $a, b \in \mathbb{Z}_p$,

- $\mathcal{O}_1(\xi_1(a), \xi_1(b)) \to \xi_1(a + b) \pmod{p}$
- $\mathcal{O}_2(\xi_2(a), \xi_2(b)) \to \xi_2(a + b) \pmod{p}$
- $\mathcal{O}_{\hat{e}}(\xi_1(a), \xi_1(b)) \to \xi_2(ab) \pmod{p}$

For a fixed generator g of G_1 we have $g = \xi_1(1)$ and $g_T = \hat{e}(g, g) = \xi_2(1)$.

2.3 Entropy

Let X be a finite random variable, then the *min-entropy* of X defined by $H_\infty(X) \stackrel{def}{=} -\log_2(\max_x \Pr[X = x])$, and the *average conditional min-entropy* of X given a random variable Y defined by $\widetilde{H}_\infty(X|Y) \stackrel{def}{=} -\log_2(\mathbb{E}_{y \leftarrow Y}[\max_x \Pr[X = x|Y = y]])$.

We have the following lemma which is from [16].

Lemma 1. *Let $f : X \to \{0,1\}^\Delta$ be a function on X. Then $\widetilde{H}_\infty(X|f(X)) \geq H_\infty(X) - \Delta$.*

2.4 Schwartz-Zippel Lemma

We follow the result of [20,25], it is a simple variant of the Schwartz-Zippel lemma [26,29].

Lemma 2. *Let $F \in \mathbb{Z}_p[X_1, \ldots, X_n]$ be a non-zero polynomial of total degree at most d. Let $P_i(i = 1, \ldots, n)$ be probability distributions on $\mathbb{Z}_p$ such that $H_\infty(P_i) \geq \log p - \Delta$, where $0 \leq \Delta \leq \log p$. If $x_i \stackrel{P_i}{\leftarrow} \mathbb{Z}_p (i = 1, \ldots, n)$ are chosen independently, then $\Pr[F(x_1, \ldots, x_n) = 0] \leq \frac{d}{p} 2^\Delta$.*

This lemma can be proved by mathematical induction (please refer to [20,25] for detailed proof). Based on this lemma, we can get the following result directly.

Corollary 1. *If $\Delta = (1 - o(1)) \log p$ in Lemma 2, then $\Pr[F(x_1, \ldots, x_n) = 0]$ is negligible (in $\log p$).*

3 Definitions

3.1 Signature Scheme

A signature scheme Σ generally consists of three algorithms, key generation, signing, and verification, denoted by KGen, Sign, and Vrfy, respectively.

Definition 3. *Σ=(KGen, Sign, Vrfy) is a signature scheme if it satisfies:*

- KGen is a PPT algorithm takes as input a security parameter k, then outputs the signer's public key pk and secret key sk. We write it $(pk, sk) \overset{\$}{\leftarrow} \mathsf{KGen}(1^k)$.
- Sign is a PPT algorithm run by the signer who takes as input its secret key sk and a message m_i, then outputs a signature σ_i. We write it $\sigma_i \overset{\$}{\leftarrow} \mathsf{Sign}(sk, m_i)$.
- Vrfy is a deterministic algorithm run by the verifier who takes as input the signer's public key pk, the signed message m_i, and the corresponding signature σ_i, then outputs 1 if it is valid, else outputs 0. We write it $1/0 \leftarrow \mathsf{Vrfy}(pk, m_i, \sigma_i)$.

For any index i, we require that $1 \leftarrow \mathsf{Vrfy}(pk, m_i, \mathsf{Sign}(sk, m_i))$.

We say that a signature scheme is stateful if its signing algorithm is stateful, it means that the secret key will be updated before (or after) each signing algorithm invocation while the public key remains fixed.

3.2 Security

The notion of existential unforgeability against adaptive chosen message attack (EUF-CMA) for the signature scheme is defined by the following game $\mathcal{G}_{\Sigma,\mathcal{A}}^{euf-cma}$.

Game $\mathcal{G}_{\Sigma,\mathcal{A}}^{euf-cma}(1^k)$	Oracle $\mathcal{O}_{\mathsf{Sign}}(m_i)$
$(pk, sk) \overset{\$}{\leftarrow} \mathsf{KGen}(1^k)$	$\sigma_i \overset{\$}{\leftarrow} \mathsf{Sign}(sk, m_i)$
$(m^*, \sigma^*) \overset{\$}{\leftarrow} \mathcal{A}^{\mathcal{O}_{\mathsf{Sign}}}(pk)$	return σ_i and set $i \leftarrow i+1$
if $1 \leftarrow \mathsf{Vrfy}(pk, m^*, \sigma^*)$ and $m^* \notin \{m_1, \ldots, m_i\}$	
then output 1 else output 0	

Adversary $\mathcal{A}$ wants to give a forgery (m^*, σ^*) by means of adaptively query to the signing oracle $\mathcal{O}_{\mathsf{Sign}}$. We denote the advantage of $\mathcal{A}$ wins the above game by $\mathbf{Adv}_{\Sigma,\mathcal{A}}^{euf-cma}$.

Definition 4. The signature scheme Σ is EUF-CMA secure if have no PPT adversary can win the above game with a non-negligible advantage.

3.3 Security in the Presence of Leakage

Following the techniques of [20,22], we split the signing key into two parts, and store them in two different parts of the memory. Then the signing process be divided into two corresponding phases. However, the input/output behavior will exactly the same as in the original one.

Formally, $\Sigma^* = (\mathsf{KGen}^*, \mathsf{Sign}^*, \mathsf{Vrfy}^*)$ be a stateful signature scheme, in the KGen^* algorithm, the secret key sk is split into two initial states S_0 and S_0', correspondingly, the signing algorithm is processed with a sequence of two phases $\mathsf{Sign}^* = (\mathsf{Sign}_{Phase1}^*, \mathsf{Sign}_{Phase2}^*)$. The ith invocation of signing (with secret state (S_{i-1}, S_{i-1}')) is computed as

$$(S_i, w_i) \overset{r_i}{\leftarrow} \mathsf{Sign}_{Phase1}^*(S_{i-1}, m_i); (S_i', \sigma_i) \overset{r_i'}{\leftarrow} \mathsf{Sign}_{Phase2}^*(S_{i-1}', w_i), \quad (1)$$

where the parameter w_i is some state information passed from Sign^*_{Phase1} to Sign^*_{Phase2}. After this round of signing, the secret state will be updated to (S_i, S'_i).

In the presence of leakage, an adversary $\mathcal{A}^*$ can obtain some leakage information in addition to the signatures for some messages of its choice. In order to model such behavior, we define a Sign&Leak oracle $\mathcal{O}^{\text{Leak}}_{\text{Sign}}$. In this oracle, besides the messages chosen by $\mathcal{A}^*$ to the signing oracle, it also allowed to specify two leakage functions f_i and h_i with bounded range $\{0,1\}^\lambda$ (where λ be the leakage parameter). The leakage functions defined as

$$\Lambda_i = f_i(S_{i-1}, r_i); \Lambda'_i = h_i(S'_{i-1}, r'_i, w_i). \tag{2}$$

We define the security notion of existential unforgeability under adaptive chosen message and leakage attacks (EUF-CMLA) through the following game $\mathcal{G}^{euf-cmla}_{\Sigma^*, \mathcal{A}^*}$, where $|f_i|$ denotes the length of the output of f_i.

Game $\mathcal{G}^{euf-cmla}_{\Sigma^*, \mathcal{A}^*}(1^k)$	Oracle $\mathcal{O}^{\text{Leak}}_{\text{Sign}}(m_i, f_i, h_i)$
$(pk, (S_0, S'_0)) \xleftarrow{\$} \text{KGen}^*(1^k), i \leftarrow 1$	if $|f_i| \neq \lambda$ or $|h_i| \neq \lambda$, return $\perp$
$(m^*, \sigma^*) \xleftarrow{\$} \mathcal{A}^{*\mathcal{O}^{\text{Leak}}_{\text{Sign}}}(pk)$	$(S_i, w_i) \xleftarrow{r_i} \text{Sign}^*_{Phase1}(S_{i-1}, m_i)$
if $1 \leftarrow \text{Vrfy}^*(pk, m^*, \sigma^*)$ and	$(S'_i, \sigma_i) \xleftarrow{r'_i} \text{Sign}^*_{Phase2}(S'_{i-1}, w_i)$
$m^* \notin \{m_1, \ldots, m_i\}$	$\Lambda_i = f_i(S_{i-1}, r_i)$
then output 1 else output 0	$\Lambda'_i = h_i(S'_{i-1}, r'_i, w_i)$
	return $(\sigma_i, \Lambda_i, \Lambda'_i)$ and set $i \leftarrow i+1$

Adversary $\mathcal{A}^*$ wants to give a forgery (m^*, σ^*) by means of adaptively query to the Sign&Leakage oracle $\mathcal{O}^{\text{Leak}}_{\text{Sign}}$. We denote the advantage of $\mathcal{A}^*$ wins the above game by $\text{Adv}^{euf-cmla}_{\Sigma^*, \mathcal{A}^*}$.

Definition 5. We say that the signature scheme Σ^* is EUF-CMLA secure if have no polynomial-bounded adversary can win the above game with a non-negligible advantage.

4   Boneh-Lynn-Shacham Signature Scheme

In ASIACRYPT 2001, Boneh, Lynn, and Shacham [12] proposed a very efficient short signature scheme. (See [12] for the BLS signature scheme construction.) It has been received great attention and adopted to construct many more complicated cryptographic schemes (e.g. [11,13]).

4.1   Probabilistic BLS Signature Scheme

We adapt the deterministic BLS signature to a probabilistic scheme. We denote it by $\Sigma_{\text{pBLS}} = (\text{KGen}_{\text{pBLS}}, \text{Sign}_{\text{pBLS}}, \text{Vrfy}_{\text{pBLS}})$, it constructed as follows:

- $\mathsf{KGen}_{\mathsf{pBLS}}(1^k)$:
  - Run $(G_1, G_2, p, g, \hat{e}) \overset{\$}{\leftarrow} \mathsf{BGen}(1^k)$ and choose a cryptographic hash function $H : \{0,1\}^* \to G_1$, then set the system public parameter as $\mathbb{P} = (G_1, G_2, p, g, \hat{e}, H)$.
  - Choose random $x \overset{\$}{\leftarrow} \mathbb{Z}_p$, then compute $X = g^x \in G_1$ and $X_T = \hat{e}(X, g) = \hat{e}(g, g)^x \in G_2$.
  - Output $pk = X_T$ and $sk = X$.
- $\mathsf{Sign}_{\mathsf{pBLS}}(\mathbb{P}, sk, m)$:
  - Choose random $r \overset{\$}{\leftarrow} \mathbb{Z}_p$.
  - Compute and output $\sigma = (\sigma_1, \sigma_2) = (X \cdot H(m)^r, g^r)$.
- $\mathsf{Vrfy}_{\mathsf{pBLS}}(\mathbb{P}, pk, m, \sigma)$: Check whether $\frac{\hat{e}(\sigma_1, g)}{\hat{e}(\sigma_2, H(m))} \overset{?}{=} X_T$.

In fact, the above probabilistic BLS signature scheme is similar to Galindo et al.'s basic signature scheme (cf. Section 3 of [20]). In their scheme, $\sigma_1 = X \cdot (X_0 \cdot X_1^m)^r$, it can be regarded as a design without random oracles. However, the probabilistic BLS signature has advantages of efficiency and the length of the public key.

Similarly to the Galindo et al.'s basic scheme (cannot proved in the standard model), we cannot prove the security of the probabilistic BLS scheme in the random oracle model as the original BLS scheme does. In the following theorem, we prove it in the combinational model of the random oracle and generic bilinear group, this means that in the generic bilinear groups model, the hash function H is treated as a random oracle.

Theorem 1. *The probabilistic BLS signature scheme Σ_{pBLS} is EUF-CMA secure w.r.t. the Definition 4 in the combinational models of random oracle and generic bilinear group. The advantage of a q-query adversary is $O(\frac{q^2}{p})$.*

Proof. Let $\mathcal{A}$ be an adversary can break the security of the scheme Σ_{pBLS}. Without loss of generality, we assume that $\mathcal{A}$ is allowed to make totally at most q queries, which contains q_g group oracles $(\mathcal{O}_1, \mathcal{O}_2, \mathcal{O}_{\hat{e}})$ queries, q_h random oracle $(\mathcal{O}_H)$ queries, and q_s signing oracle $(\mathcal{O}_{\mathsf{Sign}})$ queries, i.e., $q_g + q_h + q_s \leq q$. We bound the advantage of $\mathcal{A}$ against Σ_{pBLS} in the following game $\mathcal{G}$. $\mathcal{A}$ plays the game $\mathcal{G}$ with a simulator $\mathcal{S}$ as follows.

Game $\mathcal{G}$: Let $X, \{H_i : i \in [q_h]\}, \{R_i : i \in [q_s]\}, \{Y_i : i \in [q_{g_1}], q_{g_1} \in [0, 2q_g + 2]\}$, and $\{Z_i : i \in [q_{g_2}], q_{g_2} \in [0, 2q_g]\}$ be indeterminates. They correspond to randomly chosen group elements in the scheme Σ_{pBLS}, or more precisely their discrete logarithms, that is to say, X corresponds to x. R_i corresponds to the randomness r_i that used in the signature invocation. Besides that, $\mathcal{A}$ can query the group oracles with some bit strings that not previously obtained from the group oracles. In order to record thus values we introduce indeterminates Y_i and Z_i which correspond to the discrete logarithm of the elements of G_1 and G_2, respectively. H_i corresponds to the discrete logarithms of the random and independent elements chosen from G_1, it means the hash values of the messages.

Without loss of generality, we assume that the first q_s queries of the $\mathcal{O}_H$, i.e., $\{H_i : i \in [q_s]\}$, correspond to the hash values of messages $\{m_i : i \in [q_s]\}$ that chosen by $\mathcal{A}$ used to query to the signing oracle, and the $(q_s + 1)^{th}$ query, i.e., H_{q_s+1}, corresponds to message m^* that also chosen by $\mathcal{A}$ as the message of its forgery. For simplicity sake, we denote them by $\{R\}, \{Y\}, \{Z\}$, and $\{H\}$, respectively.

$\mathcal{S}$ maintains the following two lists of polynomial-string pair to answer and record $\mathcal{A}$'s queries

$$\mathcal{L}_1 = \{(F_{1,i}, \xi_{1,i}) : i \in [\tau_1]\}, \tag{3}$$

$$\mathcal{L}_2 = \{(F_{2,i}, \xi_{2,i}) : i \in [\tau_2]\}, \tag{4}$$

where $F_{1,i} \in \mathbb{Z}_p[X, \{H\}, \{R\}, \{Y\}], F_{2,i} \in \mathbb{Z}_p[X, \{H\}, \{R\}, \{Y\}, \{Z\}]$ and $\xi_{1,i}, \xi_{2,i}$ are bit strings from the encoding sets Ξ_1 (of group G_1) and Ξ_2 (of group G_2), respectively.

Initially, i.e., at step $\tau = 0$ and $\tau_1 = 2q_s + q_h + q_{g_1} + 1, \tau_2 = q_{g_2} + 1$, $\mathcal{S}$ creates the following lists

$$\mathcal{L}_1 = \Big\{ (1, \xi_{1,1}), \{(H_i, \xi_{1,i+1}) : i \in [q_h]\}, \{(Y_i, \xi_{1,i+q_h+1}) : i \in [q_{g_1}]\},$$
$$\{(X + R_i H_i, \xi_{1,2i+q_h+q_{g_1}}), (R_i, \xi_{1,2i+q_h+q_{g_1}+1}) : i \in [q_s]\} \Big\},$$
$$\mathcal{L}_2 = \Big\{ (X, \xi_{2,1}), \{(Z_i, \xi_{2,i+1}) : i \in [q_{g_2}]\} \Big\},$$

where $\xi_{1,i}, \xi_{2,i}$ are chosen randomly and distinctly from Ξ_1 and Ξ_2, respectively. We assume that the entries in the sets Ξ_1 and Ξ_2 are recorded in order, and thus given a string $\xi_{1,i}$ or $\xi_{2,i}$, it is able to determine its index in the lists if it exists. Similarly, the entries $\{(H_i, \xi_{1,i+1}) : i \in [q_h]\}$ has an ordering and thus given a message m, then it is able to determine its index in these entries if it exists. At step $\tau \in [0, q_g + q_h]$ of the game,

$$\tau_1 + \tau_2 = \tau + 2q_s + q_h + q_{g_1} + q_{g_2} + 2. \tag{5}$$

For the initial entries of the two lists, they correspond to the group elements of the public parameters and the signatures on the corresponding messages chosen by $\mathcal{A}$. $\{Y\}$ and $\{Z\}$ correspond to the group elements that $\mathcal{A}$ will guess in the actual interaction. In the game, $\mathcal{A}$ can query the group oracles with at most two new (guessed) elements and it also will output two new elements from G_1 as the forgery, hence $q_{g_1} + q_{g_2} \leq 2q_g + 2$. Therefore, from the equation (5) we have (w.l.o.g., assuming $q_h + q_s \geq 4$)

$$\tau_1 + \tau_2 \leq q_g + q_h + 2q_s + q_h + 2q_g + 2 + 2 \leq 3(q_g + q_h + q_s) \leq 3q. \tag{6}$$

Random Oracle $\mathcal{O}_H$: $\mathcal{A}$ queries the random oracle $\mathcal{O}_H$ with input m, $\mathcal{S}$ searches the entries $\{(H_i, \xi_{1,i}) : i \in [q_h]\}$ in $\mathcal{L}_1$, if there exists entry $\{(H_k, \xi_{1,k})\}$ for $k \leq q_h$ corresponds to m, then $\mathcal{S}$ returns $\xi_{1,k}$ to $\mathcal{A}$. Otherwise, it first increments the counter $\tau_1 := \tau_1 + 1$ and $\tau := \tau + 1$, then returns a random string $\xi_{1,i}$ distinct from those already contained in $\mathcal{L}_1$ to $\mathcal{A}$. Finally, adding $(H_i, \xi_{1,i})$ to $\mathcal{L}_1$.

Group Oracles $\mathcal{O}_1, \mathcal{O}_2$: For the group operations in group G_1, $\mathcal{A}$ takes as input two elements $\xi_{1,i}, \xi_{1,j} (i, j \in [\tau_1])$ in $\mathcal{L}_1$ and specifies whether to multiply or divide them. $\mathcal{S}$ first increments the counters $\tau_1 := \tau_1 + 1$ and $\tau := \tau + 1$, then computes $F_{1,\tau_1} = F_{1,i} + F_{1,j}$ if $\mathcal{A}$ calls for multiplication, or else $F_{1,\tau_1} = F_{1,i} - F_{1,j}$. If there exists $k < \tau_1$ such that $F_{1,\tau_1} = F_{1,k}$, then sets $\xi_{1,\tau_1} := \xi_{1,k}$. Otherwise, $\mathcal{S}$ chooses a random string ξ_{1,τ_1} that distinct from those already contained in $\mathcal{L}_1$. Finally, $\mathcal{S}$ adds the entry $(F_{1,\tau_1}, \xi_{1,\tau_1})$ to $\mathcal{L}_1$. Note that the degree of the polynomials $F_{1,i}$ in $\mathcal{L}$ is at most *two*. Similarly, $\mathcal{S}$ answers $\mathcal{A}$'s queries to the oracle $\mathcal{O}_2$, updates the list $\mathcal{L}_2$ and the counters τ_2 and τ.

Pairing Oracle $\mathcal{O}_{\hat{e}}$: $\mathcal{A}$ takes as input two elements $\xi_{1,i}, \xi_{1,j} (i, j \in [\tau_1])$ from the list $\mathcal{L}_1$ to this oracle. $\mathcal{S}$ first increments the counters $\tau_2 := \tau_2 + 1$ and $\tau := \tau + 1$, and then computes $F_{2,\tau_2} = F_{1,i} \cdot F_{1,j}$. If there exists $k < \tau_2$ such that $F_{2,\tau_1} - F_{2,k}$, then sets $\xi_{2,\tau_1} := \xi_{2,k}$. Otherwise, $\mathcal{S}$ chooses random string ξ_{2,τ_2} that distinct from those already contained in $\mathcal{L}_2$. Finally, $\mathcal{S}$ adds the entry $(F_{2,\tau_2}, \xi_{2,\tau_2})$ to the list $\mathcal{L}_2$. The degree of the polynomials $F_{2,i} \in \mathcal{L}_2$ is at most *four*.

Output: After finishing the queries, $\mathcal{A}$ outputs $(m^*, (\xi_{1,\sigma_1}, \xi_{1,\sigma_2})) \in \mathbb{Z}_p \times \mathcal{L}_1 \times \mathcal{L}_1 (\sigma_1, \sigma_2 \in [\tau_1])$. It corresponds to the forgery outputted by $\mathcal{A}$ in the actual interaction and m^* was not taken as input to the signing oracle. Let F_{1,σ_1} and F_{1,σ_2} be the polynomials that correspond to ξ_{1,σ_1} and ξ_{1,σ_2} in $\mathcal{L}_1$, respectively. $\mathcal{S}$ computes the polynomial

$$F_{1,\sigma} = X + F_{1,\sigma_2} H_{q_s+1} - F_{1,\sigma_1}. \tag{7}$$

The degree of $F_{1,\sigma}$ is at most *three*. Then $\mathcal{S}$ chooses random and independent values $x, \{h\}, \{r\}, \{y\}$ and $\{z\}$ from $\mathbb{Z}_p$ and evaluates the polynomials in the lists $\mathcal{L}_1$ and $\mathcal{L}_2$. We say that $\mathcal{A}$ wins the game $\mathcal{G}$ if one of the following cases occurs:

- *Case 1*: $F_{1,i}(x, \{h\}, \{r\}, \{y\}) = F_{1,j}(x, \{h\}, \{r\}, \{y\})$ in $\mathbb{Z}_p$, for some two polynomials $F_{1,i} \neq F_{1,j}$ in list $\mathcal{L}_1$.
- *Case 2*: $F_{2,i}(x, \{h\}, \{r\}, \{y\}, \{z\}) = F_{2,j}(x, \{h\}, \{r\}, \{y\}, \{z\})$ in $\mathbb{Z}_p$, for some two polynomials $F_{2,i} \neq F_{2,j}$ in list $\mathcal{L}_2$.
- *Case 3*: $F_{1,\sigma}(x, \{h\}, \{r\}, \{y\}) = 0$ in $\mathbb{Z}_p$.

Game $\mathcal{G}$ **vs. actual EUF-CMA game**: The success probability of $\mathcal{A}$ in the actual EUF-CMA game is bounded by its success probability in the above game $\mathcal{G}$ with a negligible probability gap. The reasons are as follows:

- Case 1 means that $\mathcal{A}$ can provoke collisions among group elements of G_1, i.e., $F_{1,i} \neq F_{1,j}$ but $g^{F_{1,i}(x,\{h\},\{r\},\{y\})} = g^{F_{1,j}(x,\{h\},\{r\},\{y\})}$ in the actual EUF-CMA game with a fixed generator g of the group G_1, this can be used to solve the discrete logarithm problem of the group G_1 (cf. Lemma 1 of the full version of the paper [22]). Similarly, case 2 means that $\mathcal{A}$ can provoke collisions among group elements of G_2. As long as these two cases do not occur, then the view of $\mathcal{A}$ is identical that in the game $\mathcal{G}$ and in the actual interaction. Therefore, if $\mathcal{A}$ cannot provoke collisions, then its adaptive strategies are no more powerful than non-adaptive ones (for more details, please refer to [25]).

- Case 3 means that $(\xi_{1,\sigma_1}, \xi_{1,\sigma_2})$ is a valid forgery on a new message m^*.

Advantage: We now analyze the advantage of $\mathcal{A}$ in the game $\mathcal{G}$. Since $F_{1,i} \neq F_{1,j} \Leftrightarrow F' = F_{1,i} - F_{1,j} \neq 0$, and the degree of the polynomials in the list $\mathcal{L}_1$ at most two. According to the Schwartz-Zippel lemma (with $\Delta = 0$), $\Pr[F'(x, \{h\}, \{r\}, \{y\}) = 0] \leq \frac{2}{p}$. The list $\mathcal{L}_1$ has τ_1 entries, so there exists at most $C_{\tau_1}^2$ distinct pairs $(F_{1,i}, F_{1,j})$, the probability of the case 1 occurs is at most $C_{\tau_1}^2 \cdot \frac{2}{p}$. Similarly, the probability of the case 2 occurs is at most $C_{\tau_2}^2 \cdot \frac{4}{p}$. The degree of the polynomial $F_{1,\sigma}$ is at most three, so if it is non-zero (proved in Lemma 3 below), then we can use the Schwartz-Zippel Lemma to compute the probability of the case 3 occurs is at most $\frac{3}{p}$. In conclusion, the advantage of $\mathcal{A}$ wins the game $\mathcal{G}$ is

$$\mathbf{Adv}_{\Sigma_{\mathsf{pBLS}},\mathcal{A}}^{euf-cma} \leq C_{\tau_1}^2 \cdot \frac{2}{p} + C_{\tau_2}^2 \cdot \frac{4}{p} + \frac{3}{p} \leq \frac{2}{p}(\tau_1 + \tau_2)^2 \leq \frac{18q^2}{p} = O(\frac{q^2}{p}). \quad (8)$$

Therefore, let $q = poly(\log p)$, then $\mathbf{Adv}_{\Sigma_{\mathsf{pBLS}},\mathcal{A}}^{euf-cma}$ is negligible.

Lemma 3. $F_{1,\sigma}$ is a non-zero polynomial in $\mathbb{Z}_p[X, \{H\}, \{R\}, \{Y\}]$.

Proof. From the design of the group oracles and the initial elements of the list $\mathcal{L}_1$, we can see that any polynomial in $\mathcal{L}_1$ is computed by either adding or subtracting two polynomials previously existing in the list. Therefore, w.l.o.g., we can write the forgery $(F_{1,\sigma_1}, F_{1,\sigma_2})$ as follows

$$F_{1,\sigma_1} = c_1 + \sum_{i=1}^{q_h} c_{2,i} H_i + \sum_{i=1}^{q_s} c_{3,i} R_i + \sum_{i=1}^{q_{g_1}} c_{4,i} Y_i + \sum_{i=1}^{q_s} c_{5,i}(X + R_i H_i), \quad (9)$$

$$F_{1,\sigma_2} = d_1 + \sum_{i=1}^{q_h} d_{2,i} H_i + \sum_{i=1}^{q_s} d_{3,i} R_i + \sum_{i=1}^{q_{g_1}} d_{4,i} Y_i + \sum_{i=1}^{q_s} d_{5,i}(X + R_i H_i), \quad (10)$$

where $c_1, d_1, c_{j,i}, d_{j,i}(j = 2, 3, 4, 5) \in \mathbb{Z}_p$ are chosen by $\mathcal{A}$. We divide them into two cases:

- *Case 1:* $c_{5,i} = d_{5,i} = 0$, for $\forall i \in [q_s]$.
  In this case, both F_{1,σ_1} and F_{1,σ_2} do not contain the indeterminate X. Hence the polynomial $F_{1,\sigma_2} H_{q_s+1} - F_{1,\sigma_1}$ in (7) also does not contain the determinate X. Therefore, in the polynomial $F_{1,\sigma}$, the coefficient of the term X is non-zero, and thus $F_{1,\sigma}$ is non-zero.
- *Case 2:* $c_{5,k} \neq 0$ or $d_{5,k} \neq 0$, for $\exists k \in [q_s]$.
  • If $d_{5,k} \neq 0$, then the coefficient of the term $R_k H_k H_{q_s+1}$ is non-zero, and thus $F_{1,\sigma}$ is non-zero.
  • If $c_{5,k} \neq 0$, then the coefficient of the term $R_k H_k$ is non-zero, and thus $F_{1,\sigma}$ is non-zero.

Therefore, the polynomial $F_{1,\sigma}$ is non-zero. This completes the proof of Theorem 2. $\qquad \square$

4.2   Leakage-Resilient Probabilistic BLS Signature Scheme

We now adapt the probabilistic BLS signature scheme to the leakage-resilient setting, i.e., leakage-resilient probabilistic BLS signature scheme. It denoted by $\Sigma^*_{\mathsf{pBLS}} = (\mathsf{KGen}^*_{\mathsf{pBLS}}, \mathsf{Sign}^*_{\mathsf{pBLS}}, \mathsf{Vrfy}^*_{\mathsf{pBLS}})$ and constructed as follows:

- $\mathsf{KGen}^*_{\mathsf{pBLS}}(1^k)$:
  - Run $(G_1, G_2, p, g, \hat{e}) \xleftarrow{\$} \mathsf{BGen}(1^k)$ and choose a cryptographic hash function $H : \{0,1\}^* \to G_1$, then set the system public parameter as $\mathbb{P} = (G_1, G_2, p, g, \hat{e}, H)$.
  - Choose random $x \xleftarrow{\$} \mathbb{Z}_p$, then compute $X = g^x \in G_1$ and $X_T = \hat{e}(X, g) = \hat{e}(g, g)^x \in G_2$.
  - Choose random $l_0 \xleftarrow{\$} \mathbb{Z}_p$ and set $(S_0, S'_0) = (g^{l_0}, g^{x-l_0})$.
  - Output $pk = X_T$ and $sk_0 = (S_0, S'_0)$.
- $\mathsf{Sign}^*_{\mathsf{pBLS}}(\mathbb{P}, sk_{i-1}, m)$:
  - *Phase 1* $(\mathbb{P}, S_{i-1}, m)$:
    * Choose random $l_i \xleftarrow{\$} \mathbb{Z}_p$ and compute $S_i = S_{i-1} \cdot g^{l_i}$.
    * Choose random $r \xleftarrow{\$} \mathbb{Z}_p$ and compute $(\sigma'_1, \sigma'_2) = (S_i \cdot H(m)^r, g^r)$.
    * Output $w_i = (l_i, \sigma'_1, \sigma'_2)$.
  - *Phase 2* $(\mathbb{P}, S'_{i-1}, w_i)$:
    * Compute $S'_i = S'_{i-1} \cdot g^{-l_i}$.
    * Compute and output $\sigma = (\sigma_1, \sigma_2) = (S'_i \cdot \sigma'_1, \sigma'_2)$.
- $\mathsf{Vrfy}^*_{\mathsf{pBLS}}(\mathbb{P}, pk, m, \sigma)$: Check whether $\frac{\hat{e}(\sigma_1, g)}{\hat{e}(\sigma_2, H(m))} \overset{?}{=} X_T$.

At the beginning of the each signing phase, the partial secret key will be re-randomized, however, for any i, let $L_i := \sum_{j=0}^{i} l_j$, then $S_i \cdot S'_i = g^{L_i} \cdot g^{\alpha - L_i} = X$. Hence the signatures of the scheme Σ^*_{pBLS} identical to that from scheme Σ_{pBLS}, however, precisely because of the re-randomized process, adversary cannot collect enough leakage information from the "fresh" secret state to recover the real secret key X.

In the first phase of the the signing algorithm, it requires three exponentiations, and no exponentiation in the second phase if we see g^{-l} as the inverse element of g^l which has been calculated in the first phase. Hence it requires three exponentiations in every signature calculation. In addition, it requires two pairing operations in the verification algorithm.

Because of the values of the input and output of the schemes Σ^*_{pBLS} and Σ_{pBLS} are identical, the security of Σ^*_{pBLS} in the non-leakage setting is obvious.

Lemma 4. *The probabilistic BLS signature scheme Σ^*_{pBLS} is EUF-CMA secure w.r.t. the Definition 4 in the combinational models of random oracle and generic bilinear group. The advantage of a q-query adversary is $O(\frac{q^2}{p})$.*

The security of the above scheme in the leakage-resilient setting is as follows. For the sake of space, we give the following theorem, please see the full version [27] for the detailed proof.

Theorem 2. *The probabilistic BLS signature scheme Σ^*_{pBLS} is EUF-CMLA secure w.r.t. the Definition 5 in the combinational models of random oracle and generic bilinear group. The advantage of a q-query adversary who gets at most λ bits of leakage per each invocation of Sign^*_{Phase1} or Sign^*_{Phase2} is $O(\frac{q^2}{p}2^{2\lambda})$.*

5   Waters Signature Scheme

In this section we construct a leakage-resilient signature scheme based on the Waters signature [28].

5.1   Leakage-Resilient Waters Signature Scheme

We now adapt the Waters signature scheme to the leakage-resilient setting, i.e., leakage-resilient Waters signature scheme $\Sigma^*_{\mathsf{W}} = (\mathsf{KGen}^*_{\mathsf{W}}, \mathsf{Sign}^*_{\mathsf{W}}, \mathsf{Vrfy}^*_{\mathsf{W}})$, it constructed as follows:

- $\mathsf{KGen}^*_{\mathsf{W}}(\mathbb{P})$:

  - Run $\mathbb{P} = (G_1, G_2, p, g, \hat{e}) \xleftarrow{\$} \mathsf{BGen}(1^k)$.
  - Choose random $x_1, x_2 \xleftarrow{\$} \mathbb{Z}_p$ and compute $(X_1, X_2) = (g^{x_1}, g^{x_2})$, then set $X_T = \hat{e}(X_1, X_2)$.
  - Choose random $u_i \xleftarrow{\$} \mathbb{Z}_p, i \in [0, n]$ and compute $U_i = g^{u_i} \in G_1$, then set $\mathcal{U} = \{U_i\}_{i \in [0,n]}$.
  - Choose random $l_0 \xleftarrow{\$} \mathbb{Z}_p$ and set $(S_0, S'_0) = (X_2^{l_0}, X_2^{x_1-l_0})$.
  - Output $pk = (X_T, \mathcal{U})$ and $sk_0 = (S_0, S'_0)$.
- $\mathsf{Sign}^*_{\mathsf{W}}(\mathbb{P}, sk_{i-1}, m)$:
  - *Phase 1* $(\mathbb{P}, S_{i-1}, m)$:

    * Let $m = m_1 m_2 \cdots m_n$, where m_i denotes the ith bit of the m.
    * Choose random $l_i \xleftarrow{\$} \mathbb{Z}_p$ and compute $S_i = S_{i-1} \cdot X_2^{l_i}$.
    * Choose random $r \xleftarrow{\$} \mathbb{Z}_p$ and compute $(\sigma'_1, \sigma'_2) = (S_i \cdot (U_0 \prod_{i \in \mathcal{M}} U_i)^r, g^r)$.
    * Output $w_i = (l_i, \sigma'_1, \sigma'_2)$.

  - *Phase 2* $(\mathbb{P}, S'_{i-1}, w_i)$:

    * Compute $S'_i = S'_{i-1} \cdot X_2^{-l_i}$.
    * Compute and output $\sigma = (\sigma_1, \sigma_2) = (S'_i \cdot \sigma'_1, \sigma'_2)$.
- $\mathsf{Vrfy}^*_{\mathsf{W}}(\mathbb{P}, pk, m, \sigma)$: Check whether $\frac{\hat{e}(\sigma_1, g)}{\hat{e}(\sigma_2, U_0 \prod_{i \in \mathcal{M}} U_i)} \stackrel{?}{=} X_T$.

At the beginning of the each signing phase, the partial secret key will be re-randomized, however, for any i, let $L_i := \sum_{j=0}^{i} l_j$, then $S_i \cdot S'_i = X_2^{L_i} \cdot X_2^{x_1-L_i} = X$. Hence the signature of this scheme Σ^*_{W} identical to that from scheme Σ_{W}.

In the first phase of the the signing algorithm, it requires three exponentiations, and no exponentiation in the second phase if we see X_2^{-l} as the inverse element of X_2^l which has been calculated in the first phase. Hence it requires three exponentiations in every signature calculation. In addition, it requires two pairing operations in the verification algorithm.

Because of the input-output behavior of the schemes Σ_W^* and Σ_W are identical, the security of Σ_W^* in the non-leakage setting is obvious.

Lemma 5. *The signature scheme Σ_W^* is EUF-CMA secure in standard model based on the DBDH assumption.*

The security of the scheme Σ_W^* in the leakage-resilient setting is as follows. For the sake of space, the detailed proof of the following theorem is given in the full version [27].

Theorem 3. *The signature scheme Σ_W^* is EUF-CMLA secure w.r.t. the Definition 5 in the generic bilinear group model. The advantage of a q-query adversary who gets at most λ bits of leakage per each invocation of* Sign^*_{Phase1} *or* Sign^*_{Phase2} *is $O(\frac{q^2}{p} 2^{2\lambda})$.*

6   Comparison

We compare our schemes Σ_{pBLS}^* and Σ_W^* to Galindo et al.'s scheme Σ_{BB}^* [20]. All of them have similar security results: if allowing λ bits of leakage at every signing process then the security of the schemes decreased by at most a factor $2^{2\lambda}$, and thus they can tolerate $\frac{1-o(1)}{2} \log p$ bits per each signing invocation. We now compare them from the aspects of their length of public key, signing cost, and verification cost, respectively. The results of the comparison in the table below, where $|G_1|, |G_2|$ denote the length of the element in group G_1 and G_2, respectively, e denotes an exponentiation computation and p denotes a pairing computation.

Table 1. Comparing the three schemes

Scheme	Length of public key	Signing cost	Verification cost
Σ_{BB}^*	$2|G_1| + |G_2|$	$4e$	$e + 2p$
Σ_{pBLS}^*	$|G_2|$	$3e$	$2p$
Σ_W^*	$(n+1)|G_1| + |G_2|$	$3e$	$2p$

From the above table we can see that both of our two schemes are more efficient than the scheme Σ_{BB}^*, especially the scheme Σ_{pBLS}^* not only has a low computation cost, but also has a short public key. The public key of the scheme Σ_W^* is long, however, its security can be guaranteed in the standard model in the black-box model, that is to say, there is no information leakage (both Σ_{BB}^* and Σ_{pBLS}^* do not have this property), and from this point of view, we can see that proving cryptographic scheme's security in the leakage-resilient setting is more intractable than in the traditional black-box model.

Acknowledgement. The authors would like to thank anonymous reviewers for their helpful comments and suggestions.

References

1. Akavia, A., Goldwasser, S., Vaikuntanathan, V.: Simultaneous hardcore bits and cryptography against memory attacks. In: Reingold, O. (ed.) TCC 2009. LNCS, vol. 5444, pp. 474–495. Springer, Heidelberg (2009)
2. Alwen, J., Dodis, Y., Wichs, D.: Leakage-resilient public-key cryptography in the bounded-retrieval model. In: Halevi, S. (ed.) CRYPTO 2009. LNCS, vol. 5677, pp. 36–54. Springer, Heidelberg (2009)
3. Alwen, J., Dodis, Y., Naor, M., Segev, G., Walfish, S., Wichs, D.: Public-key encryption in the bounded-retrieval model. In: Gilbert, H. (ed.) EUROCRYPT 2010. LNCS, vol. 6110, pp. 113–134. Springer, Heidelberg (2010)
4. Aggarwal, D., Maurer, U.: The leakage-resilience limit of a computational problem is equal to its unpredictability entropy. In: Lee, D.H., Wang, X. (eds.) ASIACRYPT 2011. LNCS, vol. 7073, pp. 686–701. Springer, Heidelberg (2011)
5. Biham, E., Carmeli, Y., Shamir, A.: Bug attacks. In: Wagner, D. (ed.) CRYPTO 2008. LNCS, vol. 5157, pp. 221–240. Springer, Heidelberg (2008)
6. Boyle, E., Segev, G., Wichs, D.: Fully leakage-resilient signatures. In: Paterson, K.G. (ed.) EUROCRYPT 2011. LNCS, vol. 6632, pp. 89–108. Springer, Heidelberg (2011)
7. Boneh, D., Brumley, D.: Remote timing attacks are practical. Computer Networks 48(5), 701–716 (2005)
8. Boneh, D., DeMillo, R.A., Lipton, R.J.: On the importance of checking cryptographic protocols for faults. In: Fumy, W. (ed.) EUROCRYPT 1997. LNCS, vol. 1233, pp. 37–51. Springer, Heidelberg (1997)
9. Boneh, D., Boyen, X.: Efficient selective-ID secure identity-based encryption without random oracles. In: Cachin, C., Camenisch, J.L. (eds.) EUROCRYPT 2004. LNCS, vol. 3027, pp. 223–238. Springer, Heidelberg (2004)
10. Boneh, D., Boyen, X., Goh, E.-J.: Hierarchical identity based encryption with constant size ciphertext. In: Cramer, R. (ed.) EUROCRYPT 2005. LNCS, vol. 3494, pp. 440–456. Springer, Heidelberg (2005)
11. Boneh, D., Gentry, C., Lynn, B., Shacham, H.: Aggregate and verifiably encrypted signatures from bilinear maps. In: Biham, E. (ed.) EUROCRYPT 2003. LNCS, vol. 2656, pp. 416–432. Springer, Heidelberg (2003)
12. Boneh, D., Lynn, B., Shacham, H.: Short signatures from the weil pairing. In: Boyd, C. (ed.) ASIACRYPT 2001. LNCS, vol. 2248, pp. 514–532. Springer, Heidelberg (2001)
13. Boldyreva, A.: Threshold signatures, multisignatures and blind signatures based on the gap-diffie-hellman-group signature scheme. In: Desmedt, Y.G. (ed.) PKC 2003. LNCS, vol. 2567, pp. 31–46. Springer, Heidelberg (2002)
14. Chow, S.S.M., Dodis, Y., Rouselakis, Y., Waters, B.: Practical leakage-resilient identity-based encryption from simple assumptions. In: CCS 2010, pp. 152–161. ACM (2010)
15. Dodis, Y., Kalai, Y., Lovett, S.: On cryptography with auxiliary input. In: STOC 2009, pp. 621–630. ACM (2009)
16. Dodis, Y., Ostrovsky, R., Reyzin, L., Smith, A.: Fuzzy extractors: how tow generate strong keys from biometrics and other noisy data. SIAM J. Comput. 38(1), 97–139 (2008)

17. Dodis, Y., Haralambiev, K., Lopez-Alt, A., Wichs, D.: Cryptography against continuous memory attacks. In: Proceedings of the 51st Annual IEEE Symposium on Foundations of Computer Science, pp. 511–520 (2010)

18. Faust, S., Kiltz, E., Pietrzak, K., Rothblum, G.N.: Leakage-resilient signatures. In: Micciancio, D. (ed.) TCC 2010. LNCS, vol. 5978, pp. 343–360. Springer, Heidelberg (2010)

19. Faust, S., Hazay, C., Nielsen, J.B., Nordholt, P.S., Zottarel, A.: Signature schemes secure against hard-to-invert leakage. In: Wang, X., Sako, K. (eds.) ASIACRYPT 2012. LNCS, vol. 7658, pp. 98–115. Springer, Heidelberg (2012)

20. Galindo, D., Vivek, S.: A practical leakage-resilient signature scheme in the generic group model. In: Knudsen, L.R., Wu, H. (eds.) SAC 2012. LNCS, vol. 7707, pp. 50–65. Springer, Heidelberg (2013)

21. Katz, J., Vaikuntanathan, V.: Signature schemes with bounded leakage resilience. In: Matsui, M. (ed.) ASIACRYPT 2009. LNCS, vol. 5912, pp. 703–720. Springer, Heidelberg (2009)

22. Kiltz, E., Pietrzak, K.: Leakage resilient elGamal encryption. In: Abe, M. (ed.) ASIACRYPT 2010. LNCS, vol. 6477, pp. 595–612. Springer, Heidelberg (2010)

23. Kocher, P.C., Jaffe, J., Jun, B.: Differential power analysis. In: Wiener, M. (ed.) CRYPTO 1999. LNCS, vol. 1666, pp. 388–397. Springer, Heidelberg (1999)

24. Micali, S., Reyzin, L.: Physically observable cryptography. In: Naor, M. (ed.) TCC 2004. LNCS, vol. 2951, pp. 278–296. Springer, Heidelberg (2004)

25. Shoup, V.: Lower bounds for discrete logarithms and related problems. In: Fumy, W. (ed.) EUROCRYPT 1997. LNCS, vol. 1233, pp. 256–266. Springer, Heidelberg (1997)

26. Schwartz, J.T.: Fast probabilistic algorithms for verfication of polynomial identities. J. ACM 27(4), 701–717 (1980)

27. Tang, F., Li, H., Niu, Q., Liang, B.: Efficient leakage-resilient signature schemes in the generic bilinear group model. In: Cryptology ePrint Archive, Report 2013/785 (2013) http://eprint.iacr.org/

28. Waters, B.: Efficient identity-based encryption without random oracles. In: Cramer, R. (ed.) EUROCRYPT 2005. LNCS, vol. 3494, pp. 114–127. Springer, Heidelberg (2005)

29. Zippel, R.: Probabilistic algorithms for sparse polynomials. In: Ng, K.W. (ed.) EUROSAM 1979 and ISSAC 1979. LNCS, vol. 72, pp. 216–226. Springer, Heidelberg (1979)

Attribute-Based Signature
with Message Recovery

Kefeng Wang, Yi Mu, Willy Susilo, and Fuchun Guo

Centre for Computer and Information Security Research
School of Computer Science and Software Engineering
University of Wollongong, Wollongong NSW 2522, Australia
{kw909,ymu,wsusilo,fuchun}@uow.edu.au

Abstract. We present a new notion called the *attribute-based signature with message recovery*. Compared with the existing attribute-based signature schemes, an attribute-based signature with message recovery scheme does not require transmission of the original message to verify the validity of the signature, since the original message can be recovered from the signature. Therefore, this scheme shortens the total length of the original message and the appended attribute-based signature. The contributions of this paper are threefold. First, we introduce the notion of attribute-based signature with message recovery. Second, we present a concrete construction of an attribute-based signature with message recovery scheme based on bilinear pairing. Finally, we extend our scheme to deal with large messages. The proposed schemes support flexible threshold predicates and are proven to be existentially unforgeable against adaptively chosen message attacks in the random oracle model under the assumption that the Computational Diffie-Hellman problem is hard. We demonstrate that the proposed schemes are also equipped with the attribute privacy property.

Keywords: Signature, Attribute-Based Signature, Message Recovery.

1 Introduction

Essentially, there are two general classes of digital signature schemes. Signature schemes with appendix require the original message as input to the verification algorithm. Signature schemes with message recovery do not require the original message as input to the verification algorithm. In networks with limited bandwidth and lightweight mobile devices, long digital signatures will obviously be a drawback. Apart from shortening the signature itself, the other effective approach for saving bandwidth is to eliminate the requirement of transmitting the signed original message for the sake of verifying the attached digital signature. In this work, we consider the latter approach. In signature schemes with message recovery, all or part of the original message is embedded within the signature and can be recovered from the signature itself. It is somewhat related to the problem of signing short messages using a scheme that minimizes the total length of the

X. Huang and J. Zhou (Eds.): ISPEC 2014, LNCS 8434, pp. 433–447, 2014.

original message and the appended signature, and hence it is useful in an organization where bandwidth is one of the main concerns and useful for applications in which short messages should be signed.

An attribute-based signature is an elaborated cryptographic notion that supports fine-grain access control in anonymous authentication systems. A related approach, but much simpler, to an attribute-based signature is identity-based signature. Compared with an identity-based signature in which a single string representing the signer's identity, in an attribute-based signature, a signer who obtains a certificate for a set of attributes from the attribute authority is defined by a set of attributes. An attribute-based signature attests not to the identity of the individual who signed a message, but assures the verifier that a signer whose set of attributes satisfies a predicate has endorsed the message. In an attribute-based signature, the signature reveals no more than the fact that a single user with some set of attributes satisfying the predicate has attested to the message. In particular, the signature hides the attributes used to satisfy the predicate and any identifying information about the signer. Furthermore, users cannot collude to pool their attributes together.

Our Contributions. In this paper, we introduce the notion of attribute-based signature with message recovery. This notion allows fine-grain access control as well as enjoys the shortness of message-signature length. We propose two efficient schemes supporting flexible threshold predicate. The first one embeds short original message in the signature and it will be recovered in the process of verification, while keeping the signature size the same as existing scheme which requires transmission of the original message to verify the signature. For large messages, the second scheme separates the original message to two parts. The signature is appended to a truncated message and the discarded bytes can be recovered by the verification algorithm. The security of our schemes are proven to be existentially unforgeable against adaptively chosen message attacks in the random oracle model under the assumption that the CDH problem is hard. These schemes are also equipped with attribute-privacy property.

Paper Organization. The rest of this paper is organized as follows: In Section 2, we introduce some related work that has been studied in the literature. In Section 3, we introduce some preliminaries used throughout this paper. In Section 4, we propose a notion of attribute-based signature with message recovery scheme and present a concrete scheme based on bilinear pairing. We also present a security model and security proofs about existential unforgeability against adaptively chosen message attacks and attribute-privacy property. Section 5 extends the first scheme in order to deal with large messages. Section 6 concludes the paper.

2   Related Work

Attribute-based signatures extend the identity-based signature of Shamir [11] by allowing the identity of a signer to be a set of descriptive attributes rather than a single string. As a related notion to attribute-based signature, fuzzy identity-based signature was proposed and formalized in [13], which enables users to generate signatures with part of their attributes. An attribute-based signature was also proposed in [12], to achieve almost the same goal. However, these kinds of signatures do not consider the anonymity for signers. Khader [3,2] proposed a notion called attribute-based group signatures. This primitive hides the identity of the signer, but reveals which attributes the signer used to satisfy the predicate. It also allows a group manager to identify the signer of any signature. In Khader [4] and Maji et al. [7,8], they treated attribute-privacy as a fundamental requirement of attribute-based signatures.

Maji et al. [7] constructed an attribute-based signature scheme that supports a powerful set of predicates, namely, any predicate consists of AND, OR and Threshold gates. However, their construction is only proved in the generic group model. Li and Kim [6] first proposed an attribute-based signature scheme that is secure under the standard CDH assumption. Their scheme only considered (n, n)-threshold, where n is the number of attributes purported in the signature. Shahandashti and Safavi-Naini [10] extended Li and Kim's scheme [6] and presented an attribute-based signature scheme supporting (k, n)-threshold. Li et al. [5] explored a new signing technique integrating all the secret attributes components into one. Their constructions provide better efficiency in terms of both the computational cost and signature size.

In order to minimize the total length of the original message and the appended signature, message recovery schemes were introduced (e.g. [9]). Zhang et al. [14] presented the seminal construction of an identity-based message recovery signature scheme. Inspired by the schemes due to Zhang et al. [14] and Li et al. [5], we propose our attribute-based signature with message recovery scheme.

Comparison. As we have mentioned above, the scheme of Li et al. [5] have improved schemes of [6,10] to provide better efficiency in terms of both the computational cost and signature size. Compared with the scheme of Li et al. [5] which requires transmission of the original message, our scheme embeds the original message in the signature while keeping the signature size same as that of [5]. We also note that Gagné et al. [1] proposed a new threshold attribute-based signature scheme which they claimed the signature size is independent of the number of attributes. However, this result is restricted only to a very special (t, t) threshold scenario. For general attribute policies such as (t, n) threshold scenario, the signature size still grows linearly with the number of attributes used to generate the signature. Furthermore, the scheme of Gagné et al. [1] only deals with fixed threshold. While our scheme can deal with flexible threshold from 1 to d which is predefined in the setup step.

3 Preliminaries

3.1 Lagrange Interpolation

Given d points $q(1), \cdots, q(d)$ on a $d - 1$ degree polynomial, let S be this d-element set. The Lagrange coefficient $\Delta_{j,S}(i)$ of $q(j)$ in the computation of $q(i)$ is:

$$\Delta_{j,S}(i) = \prod_{\eta \in S, \eta \neq j} \frac{i - \eta}{j - \eta}$$

We can use Lagrange interpolation to compute $q(i)$ for any $i \in \mathbb{Z}_p$.

3.2 Bilinear Pairing

Let $\mathbb{G}_1$ be a cyclic additive group whose order is a prime p. Let $\mathbb{G}_2$ be a cyclic multiplicative group with the same order p. Let $\hat{e} : \mathbb{G}_1 \times \mathbb{G}_1 \rightarrow \mathbb{G}_2$ be a bilinear mapping with the following properties:

- Bilinearity: $\hat{e}(aP, bQ) = \hat{e}(P, Q)^{ab}$ for all $\{P, Q\} \in \mathbb{G}_1, \{a, b\} \in \mathbb{Z}_q$.
- Non-degeneracy: There exists $P \in \mathbb{G}_1$ such that $\hat{e}(P, P) \neq 1$.
- Computability: There exists an efficient algorithm to compute $\hat{e}(P, Q)$ for all $\{P, Q\} \in \mathbb{G}_1$.

3.3 CDH Problem

Let $\mathbb{G}_1$ be a group of prime order p. Let g be a generator of $\mathbb{G}_1$. Let $\mathcal{A}$ be an attacker. $\mathcal{A}$ tries to solve the following problem: Given (g, g^a, g^b) for some unknown $a, b \in \mathbb{Z}_p^*$, compute g^{ab}.

The CDH problem is said to be intractable, if for every probabilistic polynomial time algorithm $\mathcal{A}$, the success probability is negligible.

4   Attribute-Based Signature with Message Recovery

4.1 Definitions

We assume there is a universal set of attributes U. Each signer is associated with a subset $\omega \subset U$ of attributes that is verified by an attribute authority. Our scheme consists of the following four algorithms.

Setup: On input of a security parameter, this algorithm selects the master secret key and generates the corresponding public key.

Extract: When a party requires its attribute private key $\{D_i\}_{i \in \omega}$ corresponding to an attribute set ω, this algorithm generates the attribute private key using the master key and attributes in ω if he is eligible to be issued with these attributes.

Sign: This scheme supports all predicates $\Upsilon_{t,\bar{\omega}}(\cdot) \rightarrow 0/1$ consisting of t out of n threshold gates, in which $\bar{\omega}$ is an n-element attribute set with threshold value t flexible from 1 to d where $\Upsilon_{t,\bar{\omega}}(\omega) = 1$ when $|\omega \cap \bar{\omega}| \geq t$. On input a message m, a predicate $\Upsilon_{t,\bar{\omega}}(\cdot) \rightarrow 0/1$, and a sender's private key $\{D_i\}_{i \in \omega}$, this algorithm generates a signature σ when $|\omega \cap \bar{\omega}| \geq t$.

Verify: When receiving a signature σ and a predicate $\Upsilon_{t,\bar{\omega}}(\cdot) \rightarrow 0/1$, this algorithm checks whether the signature is valid corresponding to the predicate $\Upsilon_{t,\bar{\omega}}(\cdot) \rightarrow 0/1$. If the signature σ is valid, this algorithm recovers the original message m.

4.2 Our Scheme

Setup: First, define the attributes in universe U as elements in $\mathbb{Z}_p^*$ where p is a sufficient large prime. A $(d-1)$ default attribute set from $\mathbb{Z}_p^*$ is given as $\Omega = \{\Omega_1, \Omega_2, \cdots, \Omega_{d-1}\}$. Select a random generator $g \in \mathbb{G}_1$, a random $x \in \mathbb{Z}_p^*$, and set $g_1 = g^x$. Next, pick a random element $g_2 \in \mathbb{G}_1$. Five hash functions are also chosen such that $H_1 : \mathbb{Z}_p^* \to \mathbb{G}_1$, $H_2 : \{0,1\}^* \to \mathbb{Z}_p^*$, $H_3 : \{0,1\}^* \to \mathbb{G}_1$, $F_1 : \{0,1\}^{k_2} \to \{0,1\}^{k_1}$, $F_2 : \{0,1\}^{k_1} \to \{0,1\}^{k_2}$. The public parameters are $params = (g, g_1, g_2, d, H_1, H_2, H_3, F_1, F_2)$, the master secret key is x.

Extract: To generate private key for an attribute set ω,

- First, randomly choose a $(d-1)$ degree polynomial $q(z)$ such that $q(0) = x$;
- Generate a new attribute set $\hat{\omega} = \omega \cup \Omega$. For each $i \in \hat{\omega}$, choose $r_i \in_R \mathbb{Z}_p$ and compute $d_{i0} = g_2^{q(i)} \cdot H_1(i)^{r_i}$ and $d_{i1} = g^{r_i}$;
- Finally, output $D_i = (d_{i0}, d_{i1})$ as the private key for each $i \in \hat{\omega}$.

Sign: Suppose one has private key for the attribute set ω. To sign a message m which length is equal to k_2 with predicate $\Upsilon_{t,\bar{\omega}}(\cdot)$, namely, to prove owning at least t attributes among an n-element attribute set $\bar{\omega}$, he selects a t-element subset $\omega' \subseteq \omega \cap \bar{\omega}$ and selects randomly an element j from subset $\bar{\omega}/\omega'$, and proceeds as follows:

- First, select a default attribute subset $\Omega' \subseteq \Omega$ with $|\Omega'| = d - t$ and choose $(n + d - t - 1)$ random values $r_i' \in \mathbb{Z}_p^*$ for $i \in (\bar{\omega}/j) \cup \Omega'$, choose a random value $s \in \mathbb{Z}_p^*$;
- Compute $v = e(g_1, g_2)$;
- Compute $f = F_1(m) \| (F_2(F_1(m)) \oplus m)$;
- Compute $r = H_2(v) + f$;
- Compute $\sigma_i = d_{i1}^{\Delta_{i,s}(0)} \cdot g^{r_i'}$ for $i \in \omega' \cup \Omega'$;
- Compute $\sigma_i = g^{r_i'}$ for $i \in \bar{\omega}/(\omega' \cup j)$;
- Compute $\sigma_j = g^s$;
- Compute $\sigma_0 = \left[\prod_{i \in \omega' \cup \Omega'} d_{i0}^{\Delta_{i,s}(0)} \right] \cdot \left[\prod_{i \in (\bar{\omega} \cup \Omega')/j} H_1(i)^{r_i'} \right]$
  $\cdot \left(H_1(j) \cdot H_3(r, \{\sigma_i\}_{i \in (\bar{\omega} \cup \Omega')/j}, \sigma_j) \right)^s$;
- Finally, output the signature $\sigma = (r, \sigma_0, \{\sigma_i\}_{i \in (\bar{\omega} \cup \Omega')/j}, \sigma_j)$.

To sign a message m which length is shorter than k_2, one can just pad spaces after the message until k_2.

Verify: To verify the validity of a signature $\sigma = (r, \sigma_0, \{\sigma_i\}_{i \in (\bar{\omega} \cup \Omega')/j}, \sigma_j)$ with threshold t for attributes $\bar{\omega}$, the verifier performs the following verification procedure to recover the message m:

$$\frac{e(g, \sigma_0)}{\prod_{i \in \bar{\omega} \cup \Omega'} e(H_1(i), \sigma_i) \cdot e\left(\sigma_j, H_3\left(r, \{\sigma_i\}_{i \in (\bar{\omega} \cup \Omega')/j}, \sigma_j\right)\right)} = v$$

$$r - H_2(v) = f.$$

Then, $m = [f]_{k_2} \oplus F_2([f]^{k_1})$ is recovered from f. The verifier checks whether the equation $[f]^{k_1} = F_1(m)$ holds. If it holds, output accept and the message m is recovered. Otherwise, output reject to denote the signature is not valid.

In the above computation, the subscript k_2 of f denotes the least significant k_2 bits of f, and the superscript k_1 of f denotes the most significant k_1 bits of f.

4.3   Security Model

Existential Unforgeability against Chosen Message Attacks
It can be defined using a game between an adversary $\mathcal{A}$ and a challenger $\mathcal{C}$.

The adversary $\mathcal{A}$ knows the public key of the signer. Its goal is to forge a valid signature of a message m^* with a predicate $\Upsilon_{t,\bar{\omega}}(\cdot) \to 0/1$ that his attributes do not satisfy.

Firstly, challenger $\mathcal{C}$ runs the Setup algorithm to get the master secret key with respect to a security parameter and the system's public parameters $params$. Then, $\mathcal{C}$ sends $params$ to adversary $\mathcal{A}$. $\mathcal{A}$ can access polynomially bounded number of the following oracles.

H_1 Oracle: For each H_1 hash query with respect to an attribute $i \in \mathbb{Z}_p^*$, $\mathcal{C}$ returns a hash value $H_1(i) \in_R \mathbb{G}_1$ corresponding to the attribute i.
H_3 Oracle: For each H_3 hash query with respect to a tuple $(r, \{\sigma_i\}_{i \in (\bar{\omega} \cup \Omega')/j}, \sigma_j)$ in which the first $r \in \mathbb{Z}_p^*$ and the rest elements all come from group $\mathbb{G}_1$, $\mathcal{C}$ returns a hash value $H_3(r, \{\sigma_i\}_{i \in (\bar{\omega} \cup \Omega')/j}, \sigma_j) \in_R \mathbb{G}_1$ corresponding to the tuple $(r, \{\sigma_i\}_{i \in (\bar{\omega} \cup \Omega')/j}, \sigma_j)$.
Extract Oracle: For each Extract query with respect to an attribute set ω such that $|\bar{\omega} \cap \omega| < t$, $\mathcal{C}$ returns $D_i = (d_{i0}, d_{i1})$ for each $i \in \omega$ as the private key of attribute set ω.
Sign Oracle: For each Sign query on arbitrary designated attribute set ω and arbitrary message m, $\mathcal{C}$ returns a valid signature σ with respect to m on behalf of the designated signer who possesses the attribute set ω.
Output: $\mathcal{A}$ outputs an alleged signature σ^* on message m^* on behalf of a user who possesses an attribute set ω^* such that $|\bar{\omega} \cap \omega^*| \geq t$. If no Sign queries of message m^* with an attribute set ω such that $|\bar{\omega} \cap \omega| \geq t$ and no Extract queries with respect to an attribute set ω such that $|\bar{\omega} \cap \omega| \geq t$ have been queried, $\mathcal{A}$ wins the game if the signature σ^* is valid.

If there is no such polynomial-time adversary $\mathcal{A}$ that can forge a valid signature in the game described above, we say this scheme is secure against existential forgery under chosen message attacks.

It is worth noting that this model also guarantees *collusion resistance*. This is because if a group of signers can cooperate to construct a signature that none of them could individually produce, then they can build another adversary which can forge a valid signature to win the above game.

Attribute Privacy
In an attribute-based signature scheme, a legitimate signer is indistinguishable among all the users whose attributes satisfying the predicate specified in the signature. The signature reveals nothing about the identity or attributes of the signer beyond what is explicitly revealed by the claim being made.

It can be defined using a game between an adversary $\mathcal{A}$ and a challenger $\mathcal{C}$.

The adversary $\mathcal{A}$ even knows the master secret key. So he could generate all signer's private keys as well as public keys. Its goal is to distinguish between two signers which one generates the valid signature of a message with a predicate such that both of their attributes satisfy the predicate.

Firstly, challenger $\mathcal{C}$ runs the Setup algorithm to get the master secret key and the public parameters $params$. Then, $\mathcal{C}$ sends $params$ as well as the master secret key to adversary $\mathcal{A}$. $\mathcal{A}$ can access polynomially bounded number of $\mathbf{H}_1$ and $\mathbf{H}_3$ oracles which are the same as described in the previous game. $\mathcal{A}$ can generate private keys and signatures itself, because he has got the master secret key.

Challenge: $\mathcal{A}$ outputs a message m^*, two attribute sets ω_0^*, ω_1^*, and challenged attribute set ω^* for signature query, where $\omega^* \subseteq \omega_0^* \cap \omega_1^*$. $\mathcal{C}$ chooses $b \in \{0,1\}$, computes the challenge signature σ^* on behalf of the signer who possesses attribute set ω^* selected from ω_b^* and provides σ^* to $\mathcal{A}$.

Guess: $\mathcal{A}$ tries to guess which attribute set between ω_0^* and ω_1^* is used to generate the challenge signature σ^*. Finally, $\mathcal{A}$ outputs a guess $b' \in \{0,1\}$ and wins the game if $b' = b$.

If there is no such polynomial-time adversary $\mathcal{A}$ that can win the game described above, we say this scheme holds attribute privacy property.

It is worth noting that this property holds even for the attribute authority, because the master secret key is also given to the adversary.

4.4 Security Analysis

Theorem 1. *This attribute-based signature with message recovery scheme is correct.*

Proof. The correctness of this scheme can be justified as follows:

$$
\frac{e\left(g, \sigma_0\right)}{\prod_{i \in \bar{\omega} \cup \Omega'} e\left(H_1(i), \sigma_i\right) \cdot e\left(\sigma_j, H_3\left(r, \{\sigma_i\}_{i \in (\bar{\omega} \cup \Omega')/j}, \sigma_j\right)\right)}
$$

$$
= \frac{e\left(g, \left[\prod_{i \in \omega' \cup \Omega'} d_{i0}^{\Delta_{i,s}(0)}\right] \cdot \left[\prod_{i \in (\bar{\omega} \cup \Omega')/j} H_1(i)^{r_i}\right] \cdot H_1(j)^s\right)}{\prod_{i \in \bar{\omega} \cup \Omega'} e\left(H_1(i), \sigma_i\right)}
$$

$$
= \frac{e\left(g, \left[\prod_{i \in \omega' \cup \Omega'} d_{i0}^{\Delta_{i,s}(0)}\right] \cdot \left[\prod_{i \in (\bar{\omega} \cup \Omega')/j} H_1(i)^{r_i}\right] \cdot H_1(j)^s\right)}{\prod_{i \in \omega' \cup \Omega'} e\left(H_1(i), d_{i1}^{\Delta_{i,s}(0)} \cdot g^{r_i}\right) \cdot \prod_{i \in \bar{\omega}/(\omega' \cup j)} e\left(H_1(i), g^{r_i}\right) \cdot e\left(H_1(j), g^s\right)}
$$

$$
= \frac{e\left(g, \prod_{i \in \omega' \cup \Omega'} d_{i0}^{\Delta_{i,s}(0)}\right) \cdot e\left(g, \prod_{i \in (\bar{\omega} \cup \Omega')/j} H_1(i)^{r_i}\right)}{\prod_{i \in \omega' \cup \Omega'} e\left(H_1(i), d_{i1}^{\Delta_{i,s}(0)} \cdot g^{r_i'}\right) \cdot \prod_{i \in \bar{\omega}/(\omega' \cup j)} e\left(H_1(i), g^{r_i'}\right)}
$$

$$
= \frac{e\left(g, \prod_{i \in \omega' \cup \Omega'} d_{i0}^{\Delta_{i,s}(0)}\right) \cdot e\left(g, \prod_{i \in \omega' \cup \Omega'} H_1(i)^{r_i'}\right) \cdot e\left(g, \prod_{i \in \bar{\omega}/(\omega' \cup j)} H_1(i)^{r_i'}\right)}{\prod_{i \in \omega' \cup \Omega'} e\left(H_1(i), d_{i1}^{\Delta_{i,s}(0)} \cdot g^{r_i'}\right) \cdot \prod_{i \in \bar{\omega}/(\omega' \cup j)} e\left(H_1(i), g^{r_i'}\right)}
$$

$$
= \frac{e\left(g, \prod_{i \in \omega' \cup \Omega'} d_{i0}^{\Delta_{i,s}(0)}\right) \cdot e\left(g, \prod_{i \in \omega' \cup \Omega'} H_1(i)^{r'_i}\right)}{\prod_{i \in \omega' \cup \Omega'} e\left(H_1(i), d_{i1}^{\Delta_{i,s}(0)} \cdot g^{r_i}\right)}
$$

$$
= \frac{e\left(g, \prod_{i \in \omega' \cup \Omega'} d_{i0}^{\Delta_{i,s}(0)}\right)}{\prod_{i \in \omega' \cup \Omega'} e\left(H_1(i), d_{i1}^{\Delta_{i,s}(0)}\right)}
$$

$$
= \frac{e\left(g, \prod_{i \in \omega' \cup \Omega'} \left(g_2^{q(i)} \cdot H_1(i)^{r_i}\right)^{\Delta_{i,s}(0)}\right)}{\prod_{i \in \omega' \cup \Omega'} e\left(H_1(i), (g^{r_i})^{\Delta_{i,s}(0)}\right)}
$$

$$
= e\left(g, g_2^{\sum_{i \in \omega' \cup \Omega'} q(i) \Delta_{i,s}(0)}\right)
$$

$$
= v
$$

Then, using this v and r, we can recover f from the following computation.

$$
r - H(v) = f
$$

Since f is computed from $f = F_1(m) \| (F_2(F_1(m)) \oplus m)$, the original message m will be recovered from f like this:

$$
[f]_{k_2} \oplus F_2([f]^{k_1})
$$
$$
= [F_1(m) \| (F_2(F_1(m)) \oplus m)]_{k_2} \oplus F_2([F_1(m) \| (F_2(F_1(m)) \oplus m)]^{k_1})
$$
$$
= F_2(F_1(m)) \oplus m \oplus F_2(F_1(m))
$$
$$
= m \qquad \qquad \square
$$

Theorem 2. *This attribute-based signature with message recovery scheme is existentially unforgeable under chosen message attacks in the random oracle model, under the assumption that the CDH problem is hard.*

Proof. Assume there is an algorithm $\mathcal{A}$ that can forge a valid signature under chosen message attacks. There will be another algorithm $\mathcal{B}$ that can run the algorithm $\mathcal{A}$ as a subroutine to solve the CDH problem.

We assume that the instance of the CDH problem consists of group elements $(g, g^x, g^y) \in \mathbb{G}_1^3$, and our goal is to compute an element $g^{xy} \in \mathbb{G}_1$.

Setup: Let the default attribute set be $\Omega = \{\Omega_1, \Omega_2, \cdots, \Omega_{d-1}\}$. Since the threshold in our scheme is flexible from 1 to d, without loss of generality, we fix the threshold to $t \le d$ in this proof. Firstly, $\mathcal{B}$ selects randomly a subset $\Omega' \subseteq \Omega$ with $|\Omega'| = d - t$. $\mathcal{B}$ selects g as the generator of $\mathbb{G}_1$, and sets $g_1 = g^x$ and $g_2 = g^y$. $\mathcal{B}$ sends public system parameters *params* to adversary $\mathcal{A}$.

H_1 Queries: $\mathcal{B}$ creates and keeps one list H_1-List to simulate H_1 Oracle. This list is used to store tuples like $(i, \alpha_i, H_1(i))$. In this type of tuples, the first element $i \in \mathbb{Z}_p^*$ indicates an attribute. The second element α_i is a random number in $\mathbb{Z}_p^*$. The last element $H_1(i)$ is a random element selected from $\mathbb{G}_1$.

Upon receiving an H_1 hash query with respect to an attribute i, if this i is not included in this H_1-List and $i \in \bar{\omega} \cup \Omega'$, $\mathcal{B}$ randomly selects a number $\alpha_i \in \mathbb{Z}_q^*$ and returns $H_1(i) = g^{\alpha_i}$ as the H_1 hash value of this i. Then, $\mathcal{B}$ records the tuple $(i, \alpha_i, g^{\alpha_i})$ in this H_1-List. If this i is not included in this H_1-List and $i \notin (\bar{\omega} \cup \Omega')$, $\mathcal{B}$ randomly selects a number $\alpha_i \in \mathbb{Z}_q^*$ and returns $H_1(i) = g_1^{-\alpha_i}$ as the H_1 hash value of this i. Then, $\mathcal{B}$ records the tuple $(i, \alpha_i, g_1^{-\alpha_i})$ in this H_1-List. If the i is already in a record in this H_1-List, $\mathcal{B}$ only returns the corresponding $H_1(i)$ in the record as the H_1 hash value.

H_3 Queries: $\mathcal{B}$ creates and keeps one list H_3-List to simulate H_3 Oracle. This list is used to store tuples like

$$\left((r, \{\sigma_i\}_{i \in (\bar{\omega} \cup \Omega')/j}, \sigma_j), \quad \beta, \quad H_3(r, \{\sigma_i\}_{i \in (\bar{\omega} \cup \Omega')/j}, \sigma_j) \right).$$

In this type of tuples, the first tuple $(r, \{\sigma_i\}_{i \in (\bar{\omega} \cup \Omega')/j}, \sigma_j)$ includes an element in $\mathbb{Z}_p$ and some other elements in $\mathbb{G}_1$. The second element β is a random number in $\mathbb{Z}_q^*$. The last element $H_3(r, \{\sigma_i\}_{i \in (\bar{\omega} \cup \Omega')/j}, \sigma_j)$ is a random element selected from $\mathbb{G}_1$.

Part of the records in this H_3-List corresponding to the queries which are queried by the adversary $\mathcal{A}$. We will discuss this situation soon. The other part of the records in this H_3-List corresponding to the queries which are conducted by the simulator $\mathcal{B}$ when $\mathcal{B}$ responds to the Sign queries. We will postpone to discuss this situation in the Sign Queries.

Upon receiving the k-th H_3 hash query which is conducted by the adversary $\mathcal{A}$ with respect to a tuple $(r, \{\sigma_i\}_{i \in (\bar{\omega} \cup \Omega')/j}, \sigma_j)_k$, if this tuple is not included in this H_3-List, $\mathcal{B}$ randomly selects a number $\beta_k \in \mathbb{Z}_q^*$ and returns $H_3((r, \{\sigma_i\}_{i \in (\bar{\omega} \cup \Omega')/j}, \sigma_j)_k) = g^{\beta_k}$ as the H_3 hash value of this tuple. $\mathcal{B}$ records $((r, \{\sigma_i\}_{i \in (\bar{\omega} \cup \Omega')/j}, \sigma_j)_k, \beta_k, g^{\beta_k})$ in this H_3-List. If the tuple is already in a record in this H_3-List, $\mathcal{B}$ only returns the corresponding $H_3((r, \{\sigma_i\}_{i \in (\bar{\omega} \cup \Omega')/j}, \sigma_j)_k)$ in the record as the H_3 hash value.

Extract Queries: $\mathcal{A}$ can make requests for private keys of attribute set ω such that $|\bar{\omega} \cap \omega| < t$. First define three sets Γ, Γ', S in the following manner: $\Gamma = (\omega \cap \bar{\omega}) \cup \Omega'$, Γ' such that $\Gamma \subseteq \Gamma' \subseteq S$ and $|\Gamma'| = d - 1$, and $S = \Gamma' \cup \{0\}$.

Similar to the case in the normal scheme, $\mathcal{B}$ should randomly choose a $(d - 1)$ degree polynomial $q(z)$ such that $q(0) = x$. We will show how $\mathcal{B}$ simulate private keys for attribute sets although $\mathcal{B}$ does not know exactly the value of x.

For $i \in \Gamma'$, $\mathcal{B}$ randomly selects two numbers $\tau_i, r_i \in \mathbb{Z}_p^*$. In this case, $\mathcal{B}$ assumes the value $q(i)$ corresponding to this i of the randomly chosen $(d - 1)$ degree polynomial $q(z)$ is $q(i) = \tau_i$. Then, $\mathcal{B}$ can compute D_i for $i \in \Gamma'$ as follows:

$$D_i = (g_2^{q(i)} \cdot H_1(i)^{r_i}, g^{r_i}) = (g_2^{\tau_i} \cdot H_1(i)^{r_i}, g^{r_i})$$

For $i \notin \Gamma'$, $\mathcal{B}$ looks up the H_1-List which is created by H_1 Oracle to find the record about attribute i and get the corresponding α_i. $\mathcal{B}$ randomly selects a number $r_i' \in \mathbb{Z}_p^*$, and let

$$r_i = \frac{\Delta_{0,S}(i)}{\alpha_i} y + r_i'$$

We will show how $\mathcal{B}$ simulate private keys for attribute $i \notin \Gamma'$ although $\mathcal{B}$ does not know exactly the value of y. In case of the values $q(i)$ for $i \in \Gamma'$ are determined in the previous stage, $\mathcal{B}$ can compute the value $q(i)$ corresponding to $i \notin \Gamma'$ of the randomly chosen $(d-1)$ degree polynomial $q(z)$ by using Lagrange interpolation as

$$q(i) = \sum_{j \in \Gamma'} \Delta_{j,S}(i) \cdot q(j) + \Delta_{0,S}(i) \cdot q(0)$$

in which $q(0) = x$. Then, $\mathcal{B}$ can compute D_i for $i \notin \Gamma'$ as follows:

$$D_i = (g_2^{q(i)} \cdot H_1(i)^{r_i}, g^{r_i})$$
$$= (g_2^{\sum_{j \in \Gamma'} \Delta_{j,S}(i) \cdot q(j)} \cdot (g_1^{-\alpha_i})^{r_i'}, g_2^{\frac{\Delta_{0,S}(i)}{\alpha_i}} \cdot g^{r_i'})$$

although $\mathcal{B}$ does not know exactly the value of x and y.

$\mathcal{B}$ returns D_i for each $i \in (\omega \cup \Omega)$ as the private key of ω.

Sign Queries: For a Sign query on message m with respect to an attribute set ω. If $|\bar{\omega} \cap \omega| < t$, $\mathcal{B}$ can get a simulated private key with respect to ω by querying the Extract Oracle, and compute a signature on message m with respect to ω normally.

If $|\bar{\omega} \cap \omega| \geq t$, $\mathcal{B}$ selects a t-element subset $\omega' \subseteq \bar{\omega} \cap \omega$ and selects randomly an element j from subset $\bar{\omega}/\omega'$, and simulates the signature as follows:

Firstly, $\mathcal{B}$ selects a random $(d-t)$-element subset Ω' from Ω. Then, $\mathcal{B}$ chooses two random numbers r_i and r_i'' for each $i \in \omega' \cup \Omega'$, and let $r_i' = r_i \cdot \Delta_{i,S}(0) + r_i''$. It is obviously that r_i' is still a random number for each $i \in \omega' \cup \Omega'$. $\mathcal{B}$ also chooses random number r_i' for each $i \in \bar{\omega}/(\omega' \cup j)$. $\mathcal{B}$ also chooses two random values $\beta_h, s' \in \mathbb{Z}_p^*$ and let $s = \frac{1}{\beta_h}y + s'$ which is also a random number because β_h and s' are randomly chosen. We will show how $\mathcal{B}$ simulate a correct signature although $\mathcal{B}$ does not know exactly the value of y.

Firstly, $\mathcal{B}$ computes the following parts by using previous parameters as in the normal scheme:

- Compute $v = e(g_1, g_2)$;
- Compute $f = F_1(m) \| (F_2(F_1(m)) \oplus m)$;
- Compute $r = H_2(v) + f$;
- Compute $\sigma_i = (g^{r_i})^{\Delta_{i,S}(0)} \cdot g^{r_i''} = g^{r_i \cdot \Delta_{i,S}(0) + r_i''} = g^{r_i'}$ for $i \in \omega' \cup \Omega'$;
- Compute $\sigma_i = g^{r_i'}$ for $i \in \bar{\omega}/(\omega' \cup j)$;
- Compute $\sigma_j = g^s = g^{\frac{1}{\beta_h}y + s'} = g_2^{\frac{1}{\beta_h}} \cdot g^{s'}$;

After this computation, $\mathcal{B}$ inserts a record $((r, \{\sigma_i\}_{i \in (\bar{\omega} \cup \Omega')/j}, \sigma_j), \beta_h, g_1^{-\beta_h})$ in the H_3-List. Then, $\mathcal{B}$ computes σ_0 as follows:

$$\sigma_0 = g_2^x \cdot \left[\prod_{i \in (\bar{\omega} \cup \Omega')/j} H_1(i)^{r_i'} \right] \cdot H_1(j)^s \cdot H_3(r, \{\sigma_i\}_{i \in (\bar{\omega} \cup \Omega')/j}, \sigma_j)^s$$

$$= g_2^x \cdot H_3(r, \{\sigma_i\}_{i \in (\bar{\omega} \cup \Omega')/j}, \sigma_j)^s \cdot \left[\prod_{i \in (\bar{\omega} \cup \Omega')/j} H_1(i)^{r_i'} \right] \cdot H_1(j)^s$$

$$= g_2^x \cdot (g_1^{-\beta_h})^{\frac{1}{\beta_h} y + s'} \cdot \left[\prod_{i \in (\bar{\omega} \cup \Omega')/j} H_1(i)^{r_i'} \right] \cdot (g^{\alpha_j})^{\frac{1}{\beta_h} y + s'}$$

$$= g_2^x \cdot g_1^{-y} \cdot g_1^{-\beta_h s'} \cdot \left[\prod_{i \in (\bar{\omega} \cup \Omega')/j} H_1(i)^{r_i'} \right] \cdot (g_2^{\frac{\alpha_j}{\beta_h}} \cdot g^{\alpha_j s'})$$

$$= g_1^{-\beta_h s'} \cdot (g_2^{\frac{\alpha_j}{\beta_h}} \cdot g^{\alpha_j s'}) \cdot \left[\prod_{i \in (\bar{\omega} \cup \Omega')/j} H_1(i)^{r_i'} \right]$$

We will show this simulated σ_0 have the same form as in the normal scheme as follows:

$$\sigma_0 = g_2^x \cdot \left[\prod_{i \in (\bar{\omega} \cup \Omega')/j} H_1(i)^{r_i'} \right] \cdot (H_1(j) \cdot H_3(r, \{\sigma_i\}_{i \in (\bar{\omega} \cup \Omega')/j}, \sigma_j))^s$$

$$= g_2^{\sum_{i \in \omega' \cup \Omega'} q(i) \cdot \Delta_{i,s}(0)} \cdot \prod_{i \in \omega' \cup \Omega'} H_1(i)^{r_i'} \cdot \prod_{i \in \bar{\omega}/(\omega' \cup j)} H_1(i)^{r_i'}$$

$$\cdot (H_1(j) \cdot H_3(r, \{\sigma_i\}_{i \in (\bar{\omega} \cup \Omega')/j}, \sigma_j))^s$$

$$= \prod_{i \in \omega' \cup \Omega'} g_2^{q(i) \cdot \Delta_{i,s}(0)} \cdot \prod_{i \in \omega' \cup \Omega'} H_1(i)^{r_i \cdot \Delta_{i,s}(0)} \cdot \prod_{i \in \omega' \cup \Omega'} H_1(i)^{r_i''}$$

$$\cdot \prod_{i \in \bar{\omega}/(\omega' \cup j)} H_1(i)^{r_i'} \cdot (H_1(j) \cdot H_3(r, \{\sigma_i\}_{i \in (\bar{\omega} \cup \Omega')/j}, \sigma_j))^s$$

$$= \prod_{i \in \omega' \cup \Omega'} (g_2^{q(i)} \cdot H_1(i)^{r_i})^{\Delta_{i,s}(0)} \cdot \prod_{i \in \omega' \cup \Omega'} H_1(i)^{r_i''} \cdot \prod_{i \in \bar{\omega}/(\omega' \cup j)} H_1(i)^{r_i'}$$

$$\cdot (H_1(j) \cdot H_3(r, \{\sigma_i\}_{i \in (\bar{\omega} \cup \Omega')/j}, \sigma_j))^s$$

Compared with a signature generated from the normal scheme, we will find out that this simulated signature can be regarded as a normal signature which is generated by a signer who possesses private keys $D_i = (g_2^{q(i)} \cdot H_1(i)^{r_i}, g^{r_i})$ for attribute $i \in \omega' \cup \Omega'$ in which $q(z)$ is a random $(d-1)$ degree polynomial such that $q(0) = x$. It is worth noting that although r_i'' and r_i' are not the same form at the first glance, they are indeed the same form because both of r_i'' and r_i' are random numbers. So the two parts $\prod_{i \in \omega' \cup \Omega'} H_1(i)^{r_i''}$ and $\prod_{i \in \bar{\omega}/(\omega' \cup j)} H_1(i)^{r_i'}$ can be merged into one part as $\prod_{i \in (\bar{\omega} \cup \Omega')/j} H_1(i)^{r_i'}$ in the normal scheme.

Verify: While $|\bar{\omega} \cap \omega| < t$, the simulated signature on message m with respect to ω is computed by querying the Extract Oracle to get a simulated private key with respect to ω normally. It will certainly pass the normal verification process. While $|\bar{\omega} \cap \omega| \geq t$, we can check that the simulated signature can also pass the normal verification process by straight-forward substitutions.

Finally, The adversary outputs a forged signature σ^* on message m^* for attribute set ω^* such that $|\bar{\omega} \cap \omega^*| \geq t$. It satisfies the verification equation, which means that

$$\sigma^* = \{r^*, g_2^x \cdot \left[\prod_{i \in (\bar{\omega} \cup \Omega')/j} H_1(i)^{r_i} \right] \cdot H_1(j)^s \cdot H_3(r^*, \{\sigma_i^*\}_{i \in (\bar{\omega} \cup \Omega')/j}, \sigma_j^*)^s,$$

$$\{g^{r_i'}\}_{i \in (\bar{\omega} \cup \Omega')/j}, g^s\}.$$

Then, $\mathcal{B}$ can compute

$$\frac{\sigma_0^*}{\prod_{i \in (\bar{\omega} \cup \Omega')/j} (\sigma_i^*)^{\alpha_i} \cdot (\sigma_j^*)^{\alpha_j} \cdot (\sigma_j^*)^{\beta_k}} = g^{xy}.$$

So, $\mathcal{B}$ can solve an CDH problem if $\mathcal{A}$ is able to forge valid signatures.

If there is no such polynomial-time adversary that can forge a valid attribute-based signature with a predicate that his attributes do not satisfy, we say that this attribute-based signature with message recovery scheme is secure against existential forgery under chosen message attacks.   □

Theorem 3. *This attribute-based signature with message recovery scheme is equipped with the attribute privacy property in the random oracle model.*

Proof. **Setup:** First, a $(d-1)$ default attribute set from $\mathbb{Z}_p^*$ is given as $\Omega = \{\Omega_1, \Omega_2, \cdots, \Omega_{d-1}\}$ for some predefined integer d. $\mathcal{C}$ selects a random generator $g \in \mathbb{G}_1$, a random $x \in \mathbb{Z}_p^*$ as the master secret key, and set $g_1 = g^x$. Next, $\mathcal{C}$ picks a random element $g_2 \in \mathbb{G}_1$. $\mathcal{C}$ sends these public parameters *params* as well as the master secret key x to adversary $\mathcal{A}$.

Both of the $\mathbf{H}_1$ oracle and $\mathbf{H}_3$ oracle are the same as described in Theorem 2.

Challenge: The adversary outputs two attribute sets ω_0^* and ω_1^*. Both the adversary $\mathcal{A}$ and the challenger $\mathcal{C}$ can generate secret keys corresponding to these two attribute sets as D_i^0 for $i \in \omega_0^* \cup \Omega$ and D_i^1 for $i \in \omega_1^* \cup \Omega$ respectively. Then, the adversary outputs a message m^* and a t-element challenge attribute subset $\omega^* \subseteq \omega_0^* \cap \omega_1^*$. The adversary $\mathcal{A}$ asks the challenger to generate a signature on message m^* with respect to ω^* from either ω_0^* or ω_1^*. The challenger $\mathcal{C}$ chooses a random bit $b \in \{0, 1\}$, a $(d-t)$-element subset $\Omega' \subseteq \Omega$, and outputs a signature $\sigma^* = \{r^*, \sigma_0^*, \{\sigma_i^*\}_{i \in (\bar{\omega} \cup \Omega')/j}, \sigma_j^*\}$ by running algorithm which is described as the Sign oracle in Theorem 2 using the secret key D_i^b for $i \in \omega_b^* \cup \Omega$.

As we have mentioned in Theorem 2, part of the signature σ_0^* can be written as $\prod_{i \in \omega^* \cup \Omega'} (g_2^{q(i)} \cdot H_1(i)^{r_i})^{\Delta_{i,s}(0)} \cdot \prod_{i \in \omega^* \cup \Omega'} H_1(i)^{r_i''} \cdot \prod_{i \in \bar{\omega}/(\omega^* \cup j)} H_1(i)^{r_i'} \cdot (H_1(j) \cdot H_3(r, \{\sigma_i\}_{i \in (\bar{\omega} \cup \Omega')/j}, \sigma_j))^s$, σ_i for $i \in \omega^* \cup \Omega'$ can be written as $\sigma_i = (g^{r_i})^{\Delta_{i,s}(0)} \cdot g^{r_i''} = g^{r_i \cdot \Delta_{i,s}(0) + r_i''} = g^{r_i'}$.

So, the challenge signature can be regarded as generated by a signer who possesses private keys $D_i = (g_2^{q(i)} \cdot H_1(i)^{r_i}, g^{r_i})$ for attributes $i \in \omega^* \cup \Omega'$ in which $q(z)$ is a random $(d-1)$ degree polynomial such that $q(0) = x$. Thus, if this challenge signature is generated by using the secret key D_i^0 for $i \in \omega_0^* \cup \Omega$, it can also be generated by using the secret key D_i^1 for $i \in \omega_1^* \cup \Omega$ since the secret key D_i^1 for $i \in \omega_1^* \cup \Omega$ also satisfy the situation mentioned above. Similarly, if this challenge signature is generated by using the secret key D_i^1 for $i \in \omega_1^* \cup \Omega$, it can also be generated by using the secret key D_i^0 for $i \in \omega_0^* \cup \Omega$.

Therefore, even the adversary has access to the master secret key and has unbounded computation ability, he cannot distinguish between two signers which one generates a valid signature of a message with a predicate such that both of their attributes satisfy the predicate. $\square$

5   Extended Scheme

In order to deal with messages which are larger than k_2, we can extend the previous scheme as follows.

Setup: The Setup algorithm is same as in the previous scheme.

Extract: The Extract algorithm is also same as in the previous scheme.

Sign: Suppose one has private key for the attribute set ω. To sign a message m which length is larger than k_2 with predicate $\Upsilon_{t,\bar{\omega}}(\cdot)$, namely, to prove owning at least t attributes among an n-element attribute set $\bar{\omega}$, he selects a t-element subset $\omega' \subseteq \omega \cap \bar{\omega}$ and selects randomly an element j from subset $\bar{\omega}/\omega'$, and proceeds as follows:

- First, separate the message m into two parts $m = m_1 \| m_2$, and let the length of m_1 be k_2.
- Select a default attribute subset $\Omega' \subseteq \Omega$ with $|\Omega'| = d - t$ and choose $(n + d - t - 1)$ random values $r_i' \in \mathbb{Z}_p^*$ for $i \in (\bar{\omega}/j) \cup \Omega'$, choose a random value $s \in \mathbb{Z}_p^*$;
- Compute $v = e(g_1, g_2)$;
- Compute $f = F_1(m_1) \| (F_2(F_1(m_1)) \oplus m_1)$;
- Compute $r = H_2(v) + f$;
- Compute $c = H_2(r, m_2)$;
- Compute $\sigma_i = d_{i1}^{\Delta_{i,s}(0)} \cdot g^{r_i'}$ for $i \in \omega' \cup \Omega'$;
- Compute $\sigma_i = g^{r_i}$ for $i \in \bar{\omega}/(\omega' \cup j)$;
- Compute $\sigma_j = g^s$;
- Compute $\sigma_0 = \left[\prod_{i \in \omega' \cup \Omega'} d_{i0}^{\Delta_{i,s}(0)} \right] \cdot \left[\prod_{i \in (\bar{\omega} \cup \Omega')/j} H_1(i)^{r_i'} \right]$
  $\cdot (H_1(j) \cdot H_3(c, \{\sigma_i\}_{i \in (\bar{\omega} \cup \Omega')/j}, \sigma_j))^s$;
- Finally, output the signature $\sigma = (m_2, r, \sigma_0, \{\sigma_i\}_{i \in (\bar{\omega} \cup \Omega')/j}, \sigma_j)$.

Verify: To verify the validity of a signature $\sigma = (m_2, r, \sigma_0, \{\sigma_i\}_{i \in (\bar{\omega} \cup \Omega')/j}, \sigma_j)$ with threshold t for attributes $\bar{\omega}$, the verifier performs the following verification procedure to recover the message m_1:

$$\frac{e(g, \sigma_0)}{\prod_{i \in \bar{\omega} \cup \Omega'} e(H_1(i), \sigma_i) \cdot e(\sigma_j, H_3(H_2(r, m_2), \{\sigma_i\}_{i \in (\bar{\omega} \cup \Omega')/j}, \sigma_j))} = v$$

$$r - H_2(v) = f.$$

Then, $m_1 = [f]_{k_2} \oplus F_2([f]^{k_1})$ is recovered from f. The verifier checks whether the equation $[f]^{k_1} = F_1(m_1)$ holds. If it holds, output accept. Then the verifier combines $m = m_1 \| m_2$ and the message m is recovered. Otherwise, output reject to denote the signature is not valid.

In the above computation, the subscript k_2 of f denotes the least significant k_2 bits of f, and the superscript k_1 of f denotes the most significant k_1 bits of f.

Theorem 4. *This extended attribute-based signature with message recovery scheme is correct.*

Proof. Correctness can be verified similarly with the above attribute-based signature with message recovery scheme in Theorem 1.   □

Theorem 5. *This extended attribute-based signature with message recovery scheme is existentially unforgeable under chosen message attacks in the random oracle model, under the assumption that the CDH problem is hard.*

Proof. This proof is similar to the proof of Theorem 2 and therefore it is omitted.
                                                                                □

Theorem 6. *This extended attribute-based signature with message recovery scheme is equipped with the attribute privacy property in the random oracle model.*

Proof. This proof is similar to the proof of Theorem 3 and therefore it is omitted.
                                                                                □

6   Conclusion

We proposed a new notion of attribute-based signature with message recovery, and presented two concrete attribute-based signature with message recovery schemes based on bilinear pairing that support flexible threshold predicates. The first scheme allows the signer to embed the original message in the signature without the need of sending the original message to the verifier, while keeping the same signature size. The original message can be recovered from the signature. Therefore, our first scheme minimizes the total length of the original message and the appended signature. The second scheme is extended from the first scheme in order to deal with large messages. These schemes have been proven to be existentially unforgeable against adaptively chosen message attacks in the random oracle model under the assumption that the CDH problem is hard. These schemes have also been proven to have the attribute privacy property.

References

1. Gagné, M., Narayan, S., Safavi-Naini, R.: Short pairing-efficient threshold-attribute-based signature. In: Abdalla, M., Lange, T. (eds.) Pairing 2012. LNCS, vol. 7708, pp. 295–313. Springer, Heidelberg (2013)

2. Khader, D.: Attribute based group signature with revocation. IACR Cryptology ePrint Archive 2007, 241 (2007)
3. Khader, D.: Attribute based group signatures. IACR Cryptology ePrint Archive 2007, 159 (2007)
4. Khader, D.: Authenticating with attributes. IACR Cryptology ePrint Archive 2008, 31 (2008)
5. Li, J., Au, M.H., Susilo, W., Xie, D., Ren, K.: Attribute-based signature and its applications. In: Proceedings of the 5th ACM Symposium on Information, Computer and Communications Security, pp. 60–69. ACM (2010)
6. Li, J., Kim, K.: Attribute-based ring signatures. IACR Cryptology ePrint Archive 2008, 394 (2008)
7. Maji, H.K., Prabhakaran, M., Rosulek, M.: Attribute-based signatures: Achieving attribute-privacy and collusion-resistance. IACR Cryptology ePrint Archive 2008, 328 (2008)
8. Maji, H.K., Prabhakaran, M., Rosulek, M.: Attribute-based signatures. In: Topics in Cryptology–CT-RSA 2011, pp. 376–392. Springer (2011)
9. Nyberg, K., Rueppel, R.: A new signature scheme based on the dsa giving message recovery. In: Proceedings of the 1st ACM Conference on Computer and Communications Security, pp. 58–61. ACM (1993)
10. Shahandashti, S.F., Safavi-Naini, R.: Threshold attribute-based signatures and their application to anonymous credential systems. In: Preneel, B. (ed.) AFRICACRYPT 2009. LNCS, vol. 5580, pp. 198–216. Springer, Heidelberg (2009)
11. Shamir, A.: Identity-based cryptosystems and signature schemes. In: Blakely, G.R., Chaum, D. (eds.) CRYPTO 1984. LNCS, vol. 196, pp. 47–53. Springer, Heidelberg (1985)
12. Shaniqng, G., Yingpei, Z.: Attribute-based signature scheme. In: International Conference on Information Security and Assurance, ISA 2008, pp. 509–511. IEEE (2008)
13. Yang, P., Cao, Z., Dong, X.: Fuzzy identity based signature. In: IACR Cryptology ePrint Archive, p. 2 (2008)
14. Zhang, F., Susilo, W., Mu, Y.: Identity-based partial message recovery signatures (or how to shorten id-based signatures). In: Patrick, A.S., Yung, M. (eds.) FC 2005. LNCS, vol. 3570, pp. 45–56. Springer, Heidelberg (2005)

An Adaptively CCA-Secure Ciphertext-Policy Attribute-Based Proxy Re-Encryption for Cloud Data Sharing

Kaitai Liang[1], Man Ho Au[2], Willy Susilo[2,*], Duncan S. Wong[1,**],
Guomin Yang[2], and Yong Yu[2,***]

[1] Department of Computer Science, City University of Hong Kong, China
kliang4-c@my.cityu.edu.hk, duncan@cityu.edu.hk
[2] Centre for Computer and Information Security Research, School of Computer
Science and Software Engineering, University of Wollongong, Wollongong, NSW 2522,
Australia
{aau,wsusilo,gyang,yyong}@uow.edu.au

Abstract. A Ciphertext-Policy Attribute-Based Proxy Re-Encryption (CP-ABPRE) employs the PRE technology in the attribute-based encryption cryptographic setting, in which the proxy is allowed to convert an encryption under an access policy to another encryption under a new access policy. CP-ABPRE is applicable to many real world applications, such as network data sharing. The existing CP-ABPRE systems, however, leave how to achieve adaptive CCA security as an interesting open problem. This paper, for the first time, proposes a new CP-ABPRE to tackle the problem by integrating the dual system encryption technology with selective proof technique. The new scheme supports any monotonic access structures. Although our scheme is built in the composite order bilinear group, it is proven adaptively CCA secure in the standard model without jeopardizing the expressiveness of access policy.

Keywords: Ciphertext-Policy Attribute-Based Encryption, Ciphertext-Policy Attribute-Based Proxy Re-Encryption, Adaptive Chosen-Cipher text Security.

1 Introduction

Attribute-Based Encryption (ABE) [10,21], which is a generalization of Public Key Encryption (PKE), provides flexibility of data sharing for system users such that a data encryptor is allowed to specify some descriptive values x for an encryption and thus, the encryption can be decrypted successfully by a secret

* W. Susilo is partially supported by the Australian Research Council Linkage Project LP120200052.
** D. S. Wong is supported by a grant from the RGC of the HKSAR, China (Project No. CityU 121512).
*** Y. Yu is supported by the Vice Chancellor's research fellowship of University of Wollongong and the NSFC of China under Grant 61003232.

X. Huang and J. Zhou (Eds.): ISPEC 2014, LNCS 8434, pp. 448–461, 2014.

key associated with some descriptive values y matching x. ABE has many applications, such as audit log applications [10]. It usually has two classifications: Key-Policy ABE (KP-ABE) and Ciphertext-Policy ABE (CP-ABE). In a KP-ABE system, ciphertexts are associated with attribute sets and secret keys are associated with access policies. However, CP-ABE is complementary. This paper deals with the case of CP-ABE.

In a cloud storage system, a user, say Alice, may encrypt a data under a specified access policy such that other system users satisfying this policy can access the data. She might encrypt her profile under a policy $AP_1 = $ ("*Department* : *Human Resource*" and "*Position* : *Team manager or above*") before uploading to the cloud. The system users satisfying AP_1 then can download the ciphertext from the cloud, and next access the data by using the corresponding secret keys. This data sharing pattern, nonetheless, does not scale well when the policy needs to be updated frequently. Suppose the policy above is updated as $AP_2 = $ ("*Department* : *Human Resource or Materials Storage*" and "*Position* : *Team manager only*"), Alice then should generate a new encryption accordingly. If Alice does not back up the data locally, she needs to download the ciphertext so as to recovers the data first. If the access policy is updated N times, Alice needs to construct N new encryptions. This might not be desirable as Alice's workload is linearly in N. Besides, if she is off-line or using some resource-limited devices which cannot afford such heavy computational cost, the data sharing might not be handled effectively.

To efficiently share data, we may leverage Proxy Re-Encryption (PRE). PRE is introduced by Mambo and Okamoto [19], and further studied by Blaze, Bleumer and Strauss [5]. It is an interesting extension of PKE providing the delegation of decryption rights. Specifically, it allows a *semi-trusted* proxy to transform a ciphertext intended for Alice into another ciphertext of the same plaintext intended for another system user, say Bob, without revealing knowledge of the secret keys and the underlying plaintext. It is applicable to many network applications, such as secure distributed files systems [1] and email forwarding [5].

To integrate PRE in the ABE cryptographic setting, Liang et al. [16] defined Ciphertext-Policy Attribute-Based PRE (CP-ABPRE), and proposed a concrete CP-ABPRE system enabling proxy to transform an encryption under a specified access policy into another encryption under a new access policy. We refer to this special functionality as *attribute-based re-encryption*. By using the technology of CP-ABPRE, Alice can share the data more efficiently. She first generates a re-encryption key from her own attribute set to a new access policy AP_2, and next uploads the key to the cloud such that the cloud server then can convert the original encryption under AP_1 to a new encryption under AP_2. The server, nevertheless, cannot learn the data during the conversion of cipehrtexts.

Although CP-ABPRE explores the applications of PRE, they leave us interesting open problems. All the existing CP-ABPRE schemes in the literature are secure against *selective chosen-plaintext attacks* (selective CPA) only except [15] which is *selective chosen-ciphertext attacks* (selective CCA) secure. We state that CPA security might not be sufficient enough in an open network as it only guarantees the secrecy of data which only allows an encryption to be secure against "static" adversaries. Nevertheless, in a real network scenario, there might exist "active" adversaries trying to tamper an encryption in transit and next observing its decryption so as to obtain useful information related to the underlying data. Accordingly, a CP-ABPRE system being secure against CCA is needed as CCA security not only helps the system preclude the above subtle attacks but also enables the system to be further developed and next securely "embedded" to a large protocol/system implementing in arbitrary network environments. In addition, a CP-ABPRE system with selective security, which limits an adversary to choose an attack target before playing security game, might not scale in practice as well. This is so because a realistic adversary can adaptively choose his attack target upon attacking a cryptosystem. Therefore, an *adaptively CCA secure* CP-ABPRE scheme is needed in most of practical network applications.

The expressiveness of access policy is another crucial factor for a practical CP-ABPRE system. An access policy should be embedded with AND, OR gates, and even more meaningful expression. For instance, Alice might choose to share her profile with some officials of the same company under the access policy $AP_3 = ("Department: allexcept Human$
$Resource"$ and $"Position: Project head or team manager")$. Nevertheless, most of the existing CP-ABPRE schemes only support access policy with AND gates operating over attributes. This limits their practical use. Thus it is desirable to propose a CP-ABPRE system supporting more expressive access policy.

1.1 Our Contributions

This work first formalizes the notion of adaptive CCA security for CP-ABPRE systems. Compared to the selective CPA security notion, our new notion enables an adversary to commit to a target access policy in the challenge phase, and to gain access to re-encryption and decryption oracles additionally. To tackle the open problems mentioned previously, this paper proposes a novel single-hop unidirectional CP-ABPRE system. In addition, the new system supports any monotonic access policy such that system users are allowed to fulfill more flexible delegation of decryption rights. Despite our scheme is built in the composite order bilinear group, it is proven adaptively CCA secure in the standard model by integrating the dual system encryption technology with the selective proof technique.

1.2 Related Work

Below we review some ABE systems related to this work. Following the introduction of ABE due to Sahai and Waters [21], Goyal et al. [10] proposed the first KP-ABE system. Later, Bethencourt, Sahai and Waters [4] defined a complementary notion, i.e. CP-ABE. After that there are some CP-ABE schemes (e.g. [7,9,22,2]) that have been proposed. Recently, Waters [23] proposed a deterministic finite automata-based functional encryption where policy is expressed by arbitrary-size regular language.

The aforementioned schemes, nonetheless, are only selective secure (except for [4] being proven in the generic group model). To convert one of the CP-ABE systems [22] to achieve fully security, Lewko et al. [13] leveraged the dual system encryption technology. But their conversion yields some loss of expressiveness. Later, Lewko and Waters [14] introduced a new method to guarantee the expressiveness by employing the selective proof technique into the dual system encryption technology. Inspired by [14,22], this paper focuses on constructing the first CP-ABPRE with adaptive CCA security in the standard model.

Decryption rights delegation is introduced in [19]. Later, Blaze, Bleumer and Strauss [5] defined PRE. PRE can be classified as: unidirectional and bidirectional PRE, and single-hop and multi-hop PRE [1]. This present work deals with the single-hop unidirectional case. Since its introduction many PRE systems have been proposed, e.g., [1,6,12,17,11,24,25,26].

To employ PRE in the context of ABE, Liang et al. [16] defined CP-ABPRE, and further extended [7] to support proxy re-encryption. Their work provides AND gates over positive and negative attributes. Luo et al. [18] proposed an extension of [16] supporting policy with AND gates on multi-valued and negative attributes. To combine ABE with IBE by using PRE technique, Mizuno and Doi [20] proposed a special type of CP-ABPRE scheme where encryptions in the form of ABE can be converted to the ones being decrypted in the context of IBE. The previously introduced systems, however, are selectively CPA secure, and their policies are lack of expressiveness due to supporting AND gates over attributes only. Thus an adaptively CCA-secure CP-ABPRE scheme with more expressive access policy remains open. This paper deals with this problem.

Below we compare this work with some CP-ABPRE schemes. We let p be the number of attributes used in an access policy, a be the number of attributes embedded in a user's secret key and u be the total number of attributes used in the system. In the worst case, an access policy and a user's secret key might be embedded with all system attributes, that is $p = a = u$. Thus we have $p, a \leq u$. We use c_e and c_p to denote the computational cost of an exponentiation and a bilinear pairing. To the best of our knowledge, our scheme is the first to achieve adaptive CCA security, and to support any monotonic access formula.

Table 1. Comparison with [16,18,20]

Schemes	Public/Secret Key Size	Ciphertext Size	Re-Encryption Cost	Adaptive Security	CCA Security
[16]	$\mathcal{O}(u)/\mathcal{O}(u)$	$\mathcal{O}(u)$	$\mathcal{O}(u) \cdot c_p$	✗	✗
[18]	$\mathcal{O}(u^2)/\mathcal{O}(u)$	$\mathcal{O}(u)$	$\mathcal{O}(u) \cdot c_p$	✗	✗
[20]	$\mathcal{O}(u)/\mathcal{O}(u)$	$\mathcal{O}(u)$	$\mathcal{O}(1) \cdot c_e + \mathcal{O}(u) \cdot c_p$	✗	✗
Ours	$\mathcal{O}(u)/\mathcal{O}(a)$	$\mathcal{O}(p)$	$\mathcal{O}(a) \cdot c_e + \mathcal{O}(a) \cdot c_p$	✓	✓

2 Definitions and Security Models

We review the definition of CP-ABPRE systems, and next define the adaptive CCA security notion. Due to limited space we refer the reader to [22] for the details of access structure and Linear Secret Sharing Schemes.

2.1 Definition of CP-ABPRE

We review the definition of single-hop unidirectional CP-ABPRE [16,18].

Definition 1. *A Single-Hop Unidirectional Ciphertext-Policy Attribute-Based Proxy Re-Encryption (CP-ABPRE) scheme consists of the following algorithms:*

1. $(param, msk) \leftarrow Setup(1^k, \mathcal{U})$: *on input a security parameter $k \in \mathbb{N}$ and an attribute universe $\mathcal{U}$, output the public parameters param and a master secret key msk.*
2. $sk_S \leftarrow KeyGen(param, msk, S)$: *on input param, msk and an attribute set S describing the key, output a secret key sk_S for S.*
3. $rk_{S \rightarrow (A', \rho')} \leftarrow ReKeyGen(param, sk_S, (A', \rho'))$: *on input param, sk_S, and an access structure (A', ρ') for attributes over $\mathcal{U}$, output a re-encryption key $rk_{S \rightarrow (A', \rho')}$ which can be used to transform a ciphertext under (A, ρ) to another ciphertext under (A', ρ'), where $S \models (A, \rho)$, $S \nvDash (A', \rho')$, (A, ρ) and (A', ρ') are two disjoint access structures. Note by two disjoint access structures we mean for any attribute x satisfies (A, ρ), x does not satisfy (A', ρ').*
4. $C \leftarrow Encrypt(param, (A, \rho), m)$: *on input param, (A, ρ), and a message $m \in \{0, 1\}^k$, output an original ciphertext C which can be further re-encrypted. Note (A, ρ) is implicitly included in the ciphertext.*
5. $C_R \leftarrow ReEnc(param, rk_{S \rightarrow (A', \rho')}, C)$: *on input param, $rk_{S \rightarrow (A', \rho')}$, and a C under (A, ρ), output a re-encrypted ciphertext C_R under (A', ρ') if $S \models (A, \rho)$ or a symbol $\perp$ indicating either C is invalid or $S \nvDash (A, \rho)$. Note C_R cannot be further re-encrypted.*
6. $m \leftarrow Dec(param, sk_S, C)$: *on input param, sk_S, and a C under (A, ρ), output a message m if $S \models (A, \rho)$ or a symbol $\perp$ indicating either C is invalid or $S \nvDash (A, \rho)$.*
7. $m \leftarrow Dec_R(param, sk_S, C_R)$: *on input param, sk_S, and a C_R under (A, ρ), output a message m if $S \models (A, \rho)$ or a symbol $\perp$ indicating either C_R is invalid or $S \nvDash (M, \rho)$.*

2.2 Security Models

Definition 2. *A single-hop unidirectional CP-ABPRE scheme is IND-CCA secure at original ciphertext if no Probabilistic Polynomial Time (PPT) adversary $\mathcal{A}$ can win the game below with non-negligible advantage. Below $\mathcal{C}$ is the game challenger.*

1. **Setup.** *$\mathcal{C}$ runs $Setup(1^k, \mathcal{U})$ and sends param to $\mathcal{A}$.*

2. **Phase 1.**
   (a) Secret key extraction oracle $\mathcal{O}_{sk}(S)$: on input an attribute set S, $\mathcal{C}$ runs $sk_S \leftarrow KeyGen(param, msk, S)$ and returns sk_S to $\mathcal{A}$.
   (b) Re-encryption key extraction oracle $\mathcal{O}_{rk}(S, (A', \rho'))$: on input S, and an access structure (A', ρ'), $\mathcal{C}$ outputs $rk_{S \to (A', \rho')} \leftarrow ReKeyGen$ $(param, sk_S, (A', \rho'))$, where $sk_S \leftarrow KeyGen(param, msk, S)$.
   (c) Re-encryption oracle $\mathcal{O}_{re}(S, (A', \rho'), C)$: on input S, (A', ρ'), an original ciphertext C under (A, ρ), $\mathcal{C}$ outputs $C_R \leftarrow ReEnc(param, rk_{S \to (A', \rho')}, C)$, where $rk_{S \to (A', \rho')} \leftarrow ReKeyGen(param, sk_S, (A', \rho'))$, $sk_S \leftarrow KeyGen(param, msk, S)$ and $S \models (A, \rho)$.
   (d) Original ciphertext decryption oracle $\mathcal{O}_{dec}(S, C)$: on input S and a C under (A, ρ), $\mathcal{C}$ returns $m \leftarrow Dec(param, sk_S, C)$ to $\mathcal{A}$, where $sk_S \leftarrow KeyGen(param, msk, S)$ and $S \models (A, \rho)$.
   (e) Re-encrypted ciphertext decryption oracle $\mathcal{O}_{dec_R}(S, C_R)$: on input S and a C_R under (A, ρ), $\mathcal{C}$ returns $m \leftarrow Dec_R(param, sk_S, C_R)$, where $sk_S \leftarrow KeyGen(param, msk, S)$ and $S \models (A, \rho)$.

   If ciphertexts issued to $\mathcal{O}_{re}$, $\mathcal{O}_{dec}$ and $\mathcal{O}_{dec_R}$ are invalid, outputs $\bot$.
3. **Challenge.** $\mathcal{A}$ outputs two equal length messages m_0 and m_1, and a challenge access structure (A^*, ρ^*) to $\mathcal{C}$. If the following queries

$$\mathcal{O}_{sk}(S) \text{ for any } S \models (A^*, \rho^*); \text{ and}$$
$$\mathcal{O}_{rk}(S, (A', \rho')) \text{ for any } S \models (A^*, \rho^*), \mathcal{O}_{sk}(S') \text{ for any } S' \models (A', \rho')$$

are never made, $\mathcal{C}$ returns $C^* = Encrypt(param, (A^*, \rho^*), m_b)$ to $\mathcal{A}$, where $b \in_R \{0, 1\}$.
4. **Phase 2.** $\mathcal{A}$ continues making queries except the followings:
   (a) $\mathcal{O}_{sk}(S)$ for any $S \models (A^*, \rho^*)$;
   (b) $\mathcal{O}_{rk}(S, (A', \rho'))$ for any $S \models (A^*, \rho^*)$, and $\mathcal{O}_{sk}(S')$ for any $S' \models (A', \rho')$;
   (c) $\mathcal{O}_{re}(S, (A', \rho'), C^*)$ for any $S \models (A^*, \rho^*)$, and $\mathcal{O}_{sk}(S')$ for any $S' \models (A', \rho')$;
   (d) $\mathcal{O}_{dec}(S, C^*)$ for any $S \models (A^*, \rho^*)$; and
   (e) $\mathcal{O}_{dec_R}(S, C_R)$ for any C_R under (A, ρ), $S \models (A, \rho)$, where C_R is a derivative of C^*. As of [6], the derivative of C^* is defined as:
      i. C^* is a derivative of itself.
      ii. If $\mathcal{A}$ has issued a re-encryption key query on $(S^*, (A', \rho'))$ to get $rk_{S^* \to (A', \rho')}$, obtained $C_R \leftarrow ReEnc(param, rk_{S^* \to (A', \rho')}, C^*)$ such that $Dec_R(param, sk_{S'}, C_R) \in \{m_0, m_1\}$, then C_R is a derivative of C^*, where $S^* \models (A^*, \rho^*)$ and $S' \models (A', \rho')$.
      iii. If $\mathcal{A}$ has issued a re-encryption query on $(S, (A', \rho'), C^*)$ and obtained the re-encrypted ciphertext C_R, then C_R is a derivative of C^*, where $S \models (A^*, \rho^*)$.
5. **Guess.** $\mathcal{A}$ outputs a guess bit $b' \in \{0, 1\}$. If $b' = b$, $\mathcal{A}$ wins.

$\mathcal{A}$'s advantage is defined as $Adv_{CP\text{-}ABPRE, \mathcal{A}}^{IND\text{-}CCA\text{-}Or}(1^k, \mathcal{U}) = |Pr[b' = b] - \frac{1}{2}|$.

Definition 3. *A single-hop unidirectional CP-ABPRE scheme is IND-CCA se-cure at re-encrypted ciphertext if the advantage $Adv_{CP\text{-}ABPRE,\mathcal{A}}^{IND\text{-}CCA\text{-}Re}(1^k, \mathcal{U})$ is neg-ligible for any PPT adversary $\mathcal{A}$ in the following experiment. Set $\mathcal{O} = \{\mathcal{O}_{sk}, \mathcal{O}_{rk}, \mathcal{O}_{dec}, \mathcal{O}_{dec_R}\}$.*

$$Adv_{CP\text{-}ABPRE,\mathcal{A}}^{IND\text{-}CCA\text{-}Re}(1^k, \mathcal{U}) = |Pr[b' = b : (param, msk) \leftarrow Setup(1^k, \mathcal{U});$$

$$(m_0, m_1, (A^*, \rho^*), (A, \rho)) \leftarrow \mathcal{A}^{\mathcal{O}}(param); b \in_R \{0, 1\};$$

$$C_R^* \leftarrow ReEnc(param, rk_{S \rightarrow (A^*, \rho^*)}, C); b' \leftarrow A^{\mathcal{O}}(C_R^*)] - \frac{1}{2}|,$$

where (A, ρ) and (A^*, ρ^*) are disjoint, (A^*, ρ^*) is the challenge access structure, $S \models (A, \rho)$, $rk_{S \rightarrow (A^*, \rho^*)} \leftarrow ReKeyGen(param, sk_S, (A^*, \rho^*))$, $C \leftarrow Encrypt(param, (A, \rho), m_b)$, $\mathcal{O}_{sk}, \mathcal{O}_{rk}, \mathcal{O}_{dec}, \mathcal{O}_{dec_R}$ are the oracles defined in Definition 2. However, these oracles are restricted by the following constraints. For $\mathcal{O}_{sk}$, any query $S \models (A^*, \rho^*)$ is rejected. There is no restriction to $\mathcal{O}_{rk}$ and $\mathcal{O}_{dec}$ (note invalid ciphertexts issued to $\mathcal{O}_{dec}$ are rejected). If $\mathcal{A}$ queries to $\mathcal{O}_{dec_R}$ on either (S, C_R^*) in which $S \models (A^*, \rho^*)$ or any invalid re-encrypted ciphertext, the oracle outputs $\perp$.

Remarks. Definition 3 implies collusion resistance. If $\mathcal{A}$ can compromise sk_{S^*} from either $rk_{S^* \rightarrow (A, \rho)}$ or $rk_{S \rightarrow (A^*, \rho^*)}$, $\mathcal{A}$ wins the game with non-negligible probability, where $S \models (A, \rho)$, $S^* \models (A^*, \rho^*)$ and sk_S is given.

3   An Adaptively CCA-Secure CP-ABPRE

3.1   Construction

Due to limited space we review composite order bilinear groups, complexity assumptions, and one-time symmetric encryption in Appendix A.

1. **Setup**$(1^k, \mathcal{U})$. Run $(N, \mathbb{G}, \mathbb{G}_T, e) \leftarrow \mathcal{G}(1^k)$, where $N = p_1 p_2 p_3$ is the or-der of group $\mathbb{G}$ and p_1, p_2, p_3 are distinct primes. Let $\mathbb{G}_{p_i}$ denote the sub-group of order p_i in group $\mathbb{G}$. Choose $a, \alpha, \kappa, \beta, \epsilon \in_R \mathbb{Z}_N$, $g, \hat{g}_1 \in_R \mathbb{G}_{p_1}$, two Target Collision Resistance hash functions [8] $TCR_1 : \mathbb{G}_T \rightarrow \mathbb{Z}_N$, $TCR_2 : \mathbb{G}_T \rightarrow \{0, 1\}^{poly(1^k)}$, a CCA-secure one-time symmetric encryp-tion system SYM and a strongly existential unforgeable one-time signature system [3] OTS. For each attribute $i \in \mathcal{U}$, choose $h_i \in_R \mathbb{Z}_N$. The $param$ is $(N, g, \hat{g}_1, g^a, g^\kappa, g^\beta, g^\epsilon, e(g, g)^\alpha, \forall i \in \mathcal{U} \ H_i = g^{h_i}, TCR_1, TCR_2, SYM, OTS)$, and the msk is (g^α, g_3), where g_3 is a generator of $\mathbb{G}_{p_3}$.
2. **KeyGen**$(param, msk, S)$. Choose $t, u \in_R \mathbb{Z}_N, R, R', R'', \{R_i\}_{i \in S} \in_R \mathbb{G}_{p_3}$, and set the secret key sk_S as

$$(S, K = g^\alpha g^{at} g^{\kappa u} R, K' = g^u R', K'' = g^t R'', \forall i \in S \ K_i = H_i^t R_i).$$

3. **Encrypt**$(param, (A, \rho), m)$. Given an LSSS access structure (A, ρ) and a message $m \in \mathbb{G}_T$ in which A is an $l \times n$ matrix and ρ is a map from each row A_j to an attribute $\rho(j)$,

(a) Choose a random vector $v = (s, v_2, ..., v_n) \in_R \mathbb{Z}_N^n$.

(b) For each A_j, choose $r_j \in_R \mathbb{Z}_N$, run $(ssk, svk) \leftarrow OTS.KeyGen(1^k)$ and set

$$B_0 = m \cdot e(g,g)^{\alpha s}, B_1 = g^s, B_2 = (g^\kappa)^s, B_3 = (\hat{g}_1^{svk} g^\beta)^s, B_4 = (g^\epsilon)^s,$$
$$\forall j \in [1,l](C_j = (g^a)^{A_j v} H_{\rho(j)}^{-r_j}, D_j = g^{r_j}),$$
$$E = OTS.Sign(ssk, (B_0, B_1, B_3, \forall j \in [1,l] \ (C_j, D_j))).$$

(c) Output $C = (svk, B_0, B_1, B_2, B_3, B_4, \forall j \in [1,l] \ (C_j, D_j), E)$. Note $\{\rho(j) | 1 \le j \le l\}$ are the attributes used in (A, ρ).

4. **ReKeyGen**$(param, sk_S, (A', \rho'))$. Given $sk_S = (S, K, K', K'', \forall i \in S \ K_i)$ and an LSSS access structure (A', ρ'),

(a) Choose $\theta_1, \theta_2, \theta_3 \in_R \mathbb{Z}_N, \delta \in_R \mathbb{G}_T$, set $rk_1 = (Kg^{\kappa\theta_1} g^{a\theta_2})^{TCR_1(\delta)} g^{\epsilon\theta_3}$, $rk_2 = (K'g^{\theta_1})^{TCR_1(\delta)}$, $rk_3 = (K''g^{\theta_2})^{TCR_1(\delta)}$, $rk_4 = g^{\theta_3}$, $\forall i \in S \ rk_{5,i} = (K_i H_i^{\theta_2})^{TCR_1(\delta)}$.

(b) Choose a random vector $v^{(rk)} = (s^{(rk)}, v_2^{(rk)}, ..., v_n^{(rk)}) \in_R \mathbb{Z}_N^n$. For each row A'_j of A', choose $r_j^{(rk)} \in_R \mathbb{Z}_N$, run $(ssk^{(rk)}, svk^{(rk)}) \leftarrow OTS.KeyGen(1^k)$ and set rk_6 as

$$svk^{(rk)}, B_0^{(rk)} = \delta \cdot e(g,g)^{\alpha s^{(rk)}}, B_1^{(rk)} = g^{s^{(rk)}}, B_2^{(rk)} = (g^\kappa)^{s^{(rk)}},$$
$$B_3^{(rk)} = (\hat{g}_1^{svk^{(rk)}} g^\beta)^{s^{(rk)}}, \forall j \in [1,l] \ (C_j^{(rk)} = (g^a)^{A'_j v^{(rk)}} H_{\rho'(j)}^{-r_j^{(rk)}},$$
$$D_j^{(rk)} = g^{r_j^{(rk)}}), E^{(rk)} = OTS.Sign(ssk^{(rk)}, (B_0^{(rk)}, B_1^{(rk)}, B_3^{(rk)},$$
$$\forall j \in [1,l] \ (C_j^{(rk)}, D_j^{(rk)}))).$$

(c) Output $rk_{S\to(A',\rho')} = (rk_1, rk_2, rk_3, rk_4, \forall i \in S \ rk_{5,i}, rk_6)$.

5. **ReEnc**$(param, rk_{S\to(A',\rho')}, C)$. Parse the original ciphertext C under (A, ρ) as $(svk, B_0, B_1, B_2, B_3, B_4, \forall j \in [1,l] \ (C_j, D_j), E)$, and the re-encryption key $rk_{S\to(A',\rho')}$ as $(rk_1, rk_2, rk_3, rk_4, \forall i \in S \ rk_{5,i}, rk_6)$.

(a) Check the validity of the original ciphertext C as

$$e(B_1, g^\kappa) \overset{?}{=} e(B_2, g), e(B_1, \hat{g}_1^{svk} g^\beta) \overset{?}{=} e(B_3, g), e(B_1, g^\epsilon) \overset{?}{=} e(B_4, g),$$
$$e(\prod_{\rho(j)\in S} C_j^{w_j}, g) \overset{?}{=} e(B_1, g^a) \cdot \prod_{\rho(j)\in S} (e(D_j^{-1}, H_{\rho(j)}^{w_j})), S \overset{?}{\models} (A, \rho),$$
$$OTS.Verify(svk, (E, (B_0, B_1, B_3, \forall j \in [1,l] \ (C_j, D_j)))) \overset{?}{=} 1, \qquad (1)$$

where w_j are chosen by the proxy so that $\sum_{\rho(j)\in S} w_j A_j = (1, 0, ..., 0)$. If Eq. (1) does not hold, output $\bot$. Otherwise, proceed.

(b) Compute $F = \frac{e(B_1, rk_1)e(B_2, rk_2)^{-1}e(B_4, rk_4)^{-1}}{(\prod_{\rho(j)\in S}(e(C_j, rk_3)e(D_j, rk_{5,i})))^{w_j}}$, run $\sigma_1 = SYM.Enc(TCR_2(key), G)$, where $G = (C||rk_6||F)$ and $key \in_R \mathbb{G}_T$.

(c) Choose a random vector $v^{(re)} = (s^{(re)}, v_2^{(re)}, ..., v_n^{(re)}) \in_R \mathbb{Z}_N^n$. For each row A'_j of A', choose $r_j^{(re)} \in_R \mathbb{Z}_N$, run $(ssk^{(re)}, svk^{(re)}) \leftarrow$

$OTS.KeyGen(1^k)$ and set σ_2 as

$$svk^{(re)}, B_0^{(re)} = key \cdot e(g,g)^{\alpha s^{(re)}}, B_1^{(re)} = g^{s^{(re)}}, B_2^{(re)} = (g^\kappa)^{s^{(re)}},$$

$$B_3^{(re)} = (\hat{g}_1^{svk^{(re)}} g^\beta)^{s^{(re)}}, \forall j \in [1,l] \ (C_j^{(re)} = (g^a)^{A'_j v^{(re)}} H_{\rho'(j)}^{-r_j^{(re)}},$$

$$D_j^{(re)} = g^{r_j^{(re)}}), E^{(re)} = OTS.Sign(ssk^{(re)}, (B_0^{(re)}, B_1^{(re)}, B_3^{(re)},$$

$$\forall j \in [1,l] \ (C_j^{(re)}, D_j^{(re)}))).$$

(d) Output $C_R = (\sigma_1, \sigma_2)$ under (A', ρ').

6. **Dec**$(param, sk_S, C)$. Parse the original ciphertext C under (A, ρ) as $(svk, B_0, B_1, B_2, B_3, B_4, \forall j \in [1,l] \ (C_j, D_j), E)$, and the secret key sk_S as $(S, K, K', K'', \forall i \in S \ K_i)$. The decryption algorithm chooses a set of constants $w_j \in_R \mathbb{Z}_N$ such that $\sum_{\rho(j) \in S} w_j A_j = (1, 0, ..., 0)$, and next recovers the message as follows.

(a) If Eq. (1) does not hold, output $\bot$. Otherwise, proceed.

(b) Compute $e(B_1, K)e(B_2, K')^{-1}/(\prod_{\rho(j) \in S}(e(C_j, K'')e(D_j, K_{\rho(j)}))^{w_j})$
$= e(g,g)^{\alpha s}$, and output the message $m = B_0/e(g,g)^{\alpha s}$.

7. **Dec**$_R(param, sk_S, C_R)$. Parse the re-encrypted ciphertext C_R under (A', ρ') as (σ_1, σ_2), and the secret key sk_S as $(S, K, K', K'', \forall i \in S \ K_i)$.

(a) Check the validity of σ_2 as

$$e(B_1^{(re)}, g^\kappa) \stackrel{?}{=} e(B_2^{(re)}, g), e(B_1^{(re)}, \hat{g}_1^{svk^{(re)}} g^\beta) \stackrel{?}{=} e(B_3^{(re)}, g),$$

$$e(\prod_{\rho'(j) \in S} (C_j^{(re)})^{w_j^{(re)}}, g) \stackrel{?}{=} e(B_1^{(re)}, g^a) \cdot \prod_{\rho'(j) \in S} (e((D_j^{(re)})^{-1}, H_{\rho'(j)}^{w_j^{(re)}})),$$

$$OTS.Verify(svk^{(re)}, (E^{(re)}, (B_0^{(re)}, B_1^{(re)}, B_3^{(re)},$$

$$\forall j \in [1,l] \ (C_j^{(re)}, D_j^{(re)})))) \stackrel{?}{=} 1, S \stackrel{?}{\models} (A', \rho'), \tag{2}$$

where $w_j^{(re)}$ are chosen by the decryptor so that $\sum_{\rho'(j) \in S} w_j^{(re)} A'_j = (1, 0, ..., 0)$. If Eq. (2) does not hold, output $\bot$. Otherwise, proceed.

(b) Compute $e(B_1^{(re)}, K)e(B_2^{(re)}, K')^{-1}/(\prod_{\rho'(j) \in S}(e(C_j^{(re)}, K'')e(D_j^{(re)}, K_{\rho'(j)}))^{w_j^{(re)}}) = e(g,g)^{\alpha s^{(re)}}$, and output $key = B_0^{(re)}/e(g,g)^{\alpha s^{(re)}}$.

(c) Run $G = SYM.Dec(TCR_2(key), \sigma_1)$.

(d) Parse G as (C, rk_6, F). If either Eq. (1) or the following verification for rk_6 does not hold, output $\bot$. Otherwise, proceed.

$$e(B_1^{(rk)}, g^\kappa) \stackrel{?}{=} e(B_2^{(rk)}, g), e(B_1^{(rk)}, \hat{g}_1^{svk^{(rk)}} g^\beta) \stackrel{?}{=} e(B_3^{(rk)}, g),$$

$$e(\prod_{\rho'(j) \in S} (C_j^{(rk)})^{w_j^{(rk)}}, g) \stackrel{?}{=} e(B_1^{(rk)}, g^a) \cdot \prod_{\rho'(j) \in S} (e((D_j^{(rk)})^{-1}, H_{\rho'(j)}^{w_j^{(rk)}})),$$

$$OTS.Verify(svk^{(rk)}, (E^{(rk)}, (B_0^{(rk)}, B_1^{(rk)}, B_3^{(rk)},$$

$$\forall j \in [1,l] \ (C_j^{(rk)}, D_j^{(rk)})))) \stackrel{?}{=} 1, S \stackrel{?}{\models} (A', \rho'), \tag{3}$$

where $w_j^{(rk)}$ are chosen by the decryptor so that $\sum_{\rho'(j) \in S} w_j^{(rk)} A'_j = (1, 0, ..., 0)$.

(e) Compute $e(B_1^{(rk)}, K)e(B_2^{(rk)}, K')^{-1}/(\prod_{\rho'(j) \in S}(e(C_j^{(rk)}, K'')e(D_j^{(rk)}, K_{\rho'(j)}))^{w_j^{(rk)}}) = e(g, g)^{\alpha s^{(rk)}}$, and then $B_0^{(rk)}/e(g, g)^{\alpha s^{(rk)}} = \delta$. Compute $F^{TCR_1(\delta)^{-1}} = e(g, g)^{\alpha s}$, and finally output $m = B_0/e(g, g)^{\alpha s}$.

3.2 Security Analysis

Theorem 1. *Suppose Assumption 1, the general subgroup decision assumption, the three party Diffie-Hellman assumption in a subgroup, and the source q-parallel BDHE assumption in a subgroup hold, SYM is a CCA-secure one-time symmetric encryption, OTS is a strongly existential unforgeable one-time signature, and TCR_1, TCR_2 are the TCR hash functions, our system is IND-CCA secure in the standard model.*

We prove our scheme by following [14]. Due to limited space, we present our construction for semi-functional ciphertexts and semi-functional keys in the full version.

We will prove Theorem 1 in a hybrid argument over a sequence of games. We let the total number of queries be $q = q_{sk} + q_{rk} + q_{re} + q_{dec}$, where $q_{sk}, q_{rk}, q_{re}, q_{dec}$ denote the number of the secret key, re-encryption key, re-encryption and decryption queries, respectively. $Game_{real}$ is the first game that is the IND-CCA security game for CP-ABPRE systems in which the challenge ciphertext (original ciphertext/re-encrypted ciphertext) is normal. Here, $\mathcal{C}$ will use normal secret keys to respond secret key extraction queries. Besides, $\mathcal{C}$ will first generate normal secret keys, and next leverage these keys to respond the re-encryption key, re-encryption and decryption queries, namely, the re-encryption keys, re-encryption results and decryption results are indirectly computed from the normal secret keys. $Game_0$ is the second game which is identical to $Game_{real}$ except that the challenge ciphertext is semi-functional.

Hereafter by "keys" (resp. "key") we mean the secret key(s) (constructed by $\mathcal{C}$) used to respond the secret key extraction, re-encryption key extraction, re-encryption and decryption queries. In the following, we will convert the "keys" to be semi-functional one by one. But for clarity we first turn the "keys" for the secret key extraction queries, and then convert the "keys" for the re-encryption key queries, the re-encryption queries and the decryption queries in sequence. Besides, $\mathcal{A}$ issues one query in each of the following games. We define $Game_i$ as follows, where $i \in [1, q]$. We let $j_\tau \in [1, q_\tau]$, where $\tau \in \{sk, rk, re, dec\}$. In $Game_{j_\tau}$ we define two sub-games $Game_{j_\tau}^N$ and $Game_{j_\tau}^T$ in which the challenge ciphertext is semi-functional. In $Game_{j_\tau}^N$ the first $(j - 1)_\tau$ "keys" are semi-functional, the j_τ-th "key" is nominal semi-functional, and the rest of "keys" are normal. In $Game_{j_\tau}^T$ the first $(j - 1)_\tau$ "keys" are semi-functional, the j_τ-th "key" is temporary semi-functional, and the remaining "keys" are normal.

To transform $Game_{(j-1)_\tau}$ (where j_τ-th "key" is normal) to $Game_{j_\tau}$ (where j_τ-th "key" is semi-functional) , we first convert $Game_{(j-1)_\tau}$ to $Game_{j_\tau}^N$, then to $Game_{j_\tau}^T$, and finally to $Game_{j_\tau}$. To get from $Game_{j_\tau}^N$ to $Game_{j_\tau}^T$, we treat the simulations for the queries of Phase 1 and that of Phase 2 differently: the former is based on the three party Diffie-Hellman assumption, and the latter is based on the source group q-parallel BDHE assumption. In $Game_q = Game_{q_{dec}}$ all "keys" are semi-functional, and the challenge ciphertext is semi-functional for one of the given messages. $Game_{final}$ is the final game where all "keys" are semi-functional and the challenge ciphertext is semi-functional for a random message, independent of the two message given by $\mathcal{A}$. We will prove the above games to be indistinguishable by the following lemmas. Note we implicitly assume SYM is a CCA-secure one-time symmetric encryption, OTS is a strongly existential unforgeable one-time signature, TCR_1, TCR_2 are TCR hash functions and it is hard to find a non-trivial factor of N (for Lemma 3 and Lemma 4).

Lemma 1. *If there is an algorithm $\mathcal{A}$ such that $Game_{real}Adv_{\mathcal{A}}^{CP\text{-}ABPRE} - Game_0 Adv_{\mathcal{A}}^{CP\text{-}ABPRE} = \varphi$, we build an algorithm $\mathcal{C}$ that breaks the general subgroup decision assumption with advantage φ.*

Lemma 2. *If there is an algorithm $\mathcal{A}$ such that $Game_{(j-1)_\tau}Adv_{\mathcal{A}}^{CP\text{-}ABPRE} - Game_{j_\tau}^N Adv_{\mathcal{A}}^{CP\text{-}ABPRE} = \varphi$ (for any $j_\tau \in [1, q_\tau]$), we build an algorithm $\mathcal{C}$ that breaks the general subgroup decision assumption with advantage φ.*

Lemma 3. *If there is an algorithm $\mathcal{A}$ such that $Game_{j_\tau}^N Adv_{\mathcal{A}}^{CP\text{-}ABPRE} - Game_{j_\tau}^T Adv_{\mathcal{A}}^{CP\text{-}ABPRE} = \varphi$ for a j_τ belonging to the Phase 1 queries, we build an algorithm $\mathcal{C}$ that breaks the three party Diffie-Hellman assumption in a subgroup with advantage φ.*

Lemma 4. *If there is an algorithm $\mathcal{A}$ such that $Game_{j_\tau}^N Adv_{\mathcal{A}}^{CP\text{-}ABPRE} - Game_{j_\tau}^T Adv_{\mathcal{A}}^{CP\text{-}ABPRE} = \varphi$ for a j_τ belonging to the Phase 2 queries, we build an algorithm $\mathcal{C}$ that breaks the source group q-parallel BDHE assumption in a subgroup with advantage φ.*

Lemma 5. *If there is an algorithm $\mathcal{A}$ such that $Game_{j_\tau}^T Adv_{\mathcal{A}}^{CP\text{-}ABPRE} - Game_{j_\tau}Adv_{\mathcal{A}}^{CP\text{-}ABPRE} = \varphi$ (for any $j_\tau \in [1, q_\tau]$), we build an algorithm $\mathcal{C}$ that breaks the general subgroup decision assumption with advantage φ.*

Lemma 6. *If there is an algorithm $\mathcal{A}$ such that $Game_q Adv_{\mathcal{A}}^{CP\text{-}ABPRE} - Game_{final}Adv_{\mathcal{A}}^{CP\text{-}ABPRE} = \varphi$, we can build a reduction algorithm $\mathcal{C}$ that breaks Assumption 1 with advantage φ.*

Due to limited space, we will provide the proofs of the lemmas in the full version of this paper.

4   Conclusions

This paper defined the IND-CCA security notion for CP-ABPRE systems, and proposed the first adaptively CCA-secure CP-ABPRE scheme without loss of expressiveness on access policy by integrating the dual system encryption technology with selective proof technique. Following the proof framework introduced by Lewko and Waters, our scheme was proved in the standard model. This paper also motivates interesting open problems, such as, converting our system in the prime order bilinear group.

References

1. Ateniese, G., Fu, K., Green, M., Hohenberger, S.: Improved proxy re-encryption schemes with applications to secure distributed storage. ACM Trans. Inf. Syst. Secur. 9(1), 1–30 (2006)
2. Attrapadung, N., Herranz, J., Laguillaumie, F., Libert, B., de Panafieu, E., Rafols, C.: Attribute-based encryption schemes with constant-size ciphertexts. Theoretical Computer Science 422, 15–38 (2012)
3. Bellare, M., Shoup, S.: Two-tier signatures, strongly unforgeable signatures, and fiat-shamir without random oracles. In: Okamoto, T., Wang, X. (eds.) PKC 2007. LNCS, vol. 4450, pp. 201–216. Springer, Heidelberg (2007)
4. Bethencourt, J., Sahai, A., Waters, B.: Ciphertext-policy attribute-based encryption. In: IEEE Symposium on Security and Privacy, pp. 321–334. IEEE Computer Society (2007)
5. Blaze, M., Bleumer, G., Strauss, M.: Divertible protocols and atomic proxy cryptography. In: Nyberg, K. (ed.) EUROCRYPT 1998. LNCS, vol. 1403, pp. 127–144. Springer, Heidelberg (1998)
6. Canetti, R., Hohenberger, S.: Chosen-ciphertext secure proxy re-encryption. In: Ning, P., di Vimercati, S.D.C., Syverson, P.F. (eds.) ACM Conference on Computer and Communications Security, pp. 185–194. ACM (2007)
7. Cheung, L., Newport, C.C.: Provably secure ciphertext policy ABE. In: Ning, P., di Vimercati, S.D.C., Syverson, P.F. (eds.) ACM Conference on Computer and Communications Security, pp. 456–465. ACM (2007)
8. Cramer, R., Shoup, V.: Design and analysis of practical public-key encryption schemes secure against adaptive chosen ciphertext attack. SIAM J. Comput. 33(1), 167–226 (2004)
9. Goyal, V., Jain, A., Pandey, O., Sahai, A.: Bounded ciphertext policy attribute based encryption. In: Aceto, L., Damgård, I., Goldberg, L.A., Halldórsson, M.M., Ingólfsdóttir, A., Walukiewicz, I. (eds.) ICALP 2008, Part II. LNCS, vol. 5126, pp. 579–591. Springer, Heidelberg (2008)
10. Goyal, V., Pandey, O., Sahai, A., Waters, B.: Attribute-based encryption for fine-grained access control of encrypted data. In: Juels, A., Wright, R.N., di Vimercati, S.D.C. (eds.) ACM Conference on Computer and Communications Security, pp. 89–98. ACM (2006)
11. Hanaoka, G., Kawai, Y., Kunihiro, N., Matsuda, T., Weng, J., Zhang, R., Zhao, Y.: Generic construction of chosen ciphertext secure proxy re-encryption. In: Dunkelman, O. (ed.) CT-RSA 2012. LNCS, vol. 7178, pp. 349–364. Springer, Heidelberg (2012)
12. Isshiki, T., Nguyen, M.H., Tanaka, K.: Proxy re-encryption in a stronger security model extended from CT-RSA2012. In: Dawson, E. (ed.) CT-RSA 2013. LNCS, vol. 7779, pp. 277–292. Springer, Heidelberg (2013)
13. Lewko, A., Okamoto, T., Sahai, A., Takashima, K., Waters, B.: Fully secure functional encryption: Attribute-based encryption and (hierarchical) inner product encryption. In: Gilbert, H. (ed.) EUROCRYPT 2010. LNCS, vol. 6110, pp. 62–91. Springer, Heidelberg (2010)

14. Lewko, A., Waters, B.: New proof methods for attribute-based encryption: Achieving full security through selective techniques. In: Safavi-Naini, R., Canetti, R. (eds.) CRYPTO 2012. LNCS, vol. 7417, pp. 180–198. Springer, Heidelberg (2012)

15. Liang, K., Fang, L., Susilo, W., Wong, D.S.: A ciphertext-policy attribute-based proxy re-encryption with chosen-ciphertext security. In: INCoS, pp. 552–559. IEEE (2013)

16. Liang, X., Cao, Z., Lin, H., Shao, J.: Attribute based proxy re-encryption with delegating capabilities. In: Li, W., Susilo, W., Tupakula, U.K., Safavi-Naini, R., Varadharajan, V. (eds.) ASIACCS, pp. 276–286. ACM (2009)

17. Libert, B., Vergnaud, D.: Unidirectional chosen-ciphertext secure proxy re-encryption. In: Cramer, R. (ed.) PKC 2008. LNCS, vol. 4939, pp. 360–379. Springer, Heidelberg (2008)

18. Luo, S., Hu, J., Chen, Z.: Ciphertext policy attribute-based proxy re-encryption. In: Soriano, M., Qing, S., López, J. (eds.) ICICS 2010. LNCS, vol. 6476, pp. 401–415. Springer, Heidelberg (2010)

19. Mambo, M., Okamoto, E.: Proxy cryptosystems: Delegation of the power to decrypt ciphertexts. IEICE Transactions E80-A(1), 54–63 (1997)

20. Mizuno, T., Doi, H.: Hybrid proxy re-encryption scheme for attribute-based encryption. In: Bao, F., Yung, M., Lin, D., Jing, J. (eds.) Inscrypt 2009. LNCS, vol. 6151, pp. 288–302. Springer, Heidelberg (2010)

21. Sahai, A., Waters, B.: Fuzzy identity-based encryption. In: Cramer, R. (ed.) EUROCRYPT 2005. LNCS, vol. 3494, pp. 457–473. Springer, Heidelberg (2005)

22. Waters, B.: Ciphertext-policy attribute-based encryption: An expressive, efficient, and provably secure realization. In: Catalano, D., Fazio, N., Gennaro, R., Nicolosi, A. (eds.) PKC 2011. LNCS, vol. 6571, pp. 53–70. Springer, Heidelberg (2011)

23. Waters, B.: Functional encryption for regular languages. In: Safavi-Naini, R., Canetti, R. (eds.) CRYPTO 2012. LNCS, vol. 7417, pp. 218–235. Springer, Heidelberg (2012)

24. Weng, J., Chen, M., Yang, Y., Deng, R.H., Chen, K., Bao, F.: CCA-secure unidirectional proxy re-encryption in the adaptive corruption model without random oracles. Science China Information Sciences 53(3), 593–606 (2010)

25. Weng, J., Yang, Y., Tang, Q., Deng, R.H., Bao, F.: Efficient conditional proxy re-encryption with chosen-ciphertext security. In: Samarati, P., Yung, M., Martinelli, F., Ardagna, C.A. (eds.) ISC 2009. LNCS, vol. 5735, pp. 151–166. Springer, Heidelberg (2009)

26. Weng, J., Zhao, Y., Hanaoka, G.: On the security of a bidirectional proxy re-encryption scheme from PKC 2010. In: Catalano, D., Fazio, N., Gennaro, R., Nicolosi, A. (eds.) PKC 2011. LNCS, vol. 6571, pp. 284–295. Springer, Heidelberg (2011)

A   Preliminaries

Due to limited space, we refer the reader to [14] for the definition of composite order bilinear groups, assumption 1, the general subgroup decision assumption, the three party Diffie-Hellman assumption in a subgroup, the source group q-parallel BDHE assumption in a subgroup. We here review the one-time symmetric encryption system.

One-time Symmetric Encryption. A one-time symmetric encryption [8] consists of the following algorithms. Note let $\mathcal{K}_D$ be the key space $\{0,1\}^{poly(1^k)}$, and SYM be a symmetric encryption scheme, where $poly(1^k)$ is the fixed polynomial size (bound) with respect to the security parameter k. The encryption algorithm $SYM.Enc$ intakes a key $K \in \mathcal{K}_D$ and a message M, outputs a ciphertext C. The decryption algorithm $SYM.Dec$ intakes K and C, outputs M or a symbol $\perp$. The CCA security model for SYM systems is given in [12], we hence omit the details.

Multi-recipient Encryption
in Heterogeneous Setting

Puwen Wei[1,*], Yuliang Zheng[2,*], and Wei Wang[1,*]

[1] Key Laboratory of Cryptologic Technology and Information Security,
Ministry of Education, Shandong University, Jinan 250100, China
{pwei,weiwangsdu}@sdu.edu.cn
[2] Department of Software and Information Systems,
University of North Carolina at Charlotte, Charlotte, NC 28223, USA
yzheng@uncc.edu

Abstract. This paper presents an efficient method for securely broadcasting a message to multiple recipients in a heterogeneous environment where each recipient is allowed to choose his or her preferred secure encryption scheme independently of other recipients' choices. Previous work pertinent to this direction of research, namely multi-recipient encryption scheme (MRES), generally requires all recipients adhere to the same public key encapsulation mechanism (KEM) for the sake of delivering promised savings in computation and bandwidth via randomness reuse. Our work eliminates the requirement of using the same KEM by all recipients, whereby removing a practical barrier to the adoption of MRES in real world applications. A second advantage is the method's capability to cope with a dynamically changing group of recipients where old recipients may be deleted and new recipients may be added, while ensuring the security of messages shared in future. Additional features of our method include decryption by a sender, anonymity of recipients and stateful key encapsulation which significantly reduces computational costs for securely transmitting or sharing new messages. All these attributes would be useful in building applications for secure data sharing in a cloud computing environment.

Keywords: multi-recipient, public key encryption, sender recovery, KEM, DEM.

1 Introduction

The primary goal of multi-recipient encryption is for a sender to transmit encrypted messages to multiple recipients in an efficient manner in terms of computation and bandwidth. Although in its broadest form multi-recipient encryption could be defined to allow multiple messages intended for different recipients to be included in a single ciphertext, we focus our attention on the case of most relevance to practical applications, namely single message multi-recipient encryption whereby the same message is transmitted to all intended recipients.

---

* Corresponding Authors.

X. Huang and J. Zhou (Eds.): ISPEC 2014, LNCS 8434, pp. 462–480, 2014.
© Springer International Publishing Switzerland 2014

A simple construction for a multi-recipient encryption scheme (MRES) could follow an approach specified in S/MIME [1]: generate a symmetric key k for a data encapsulation mechanism (DEM), encrypt k for intended recipients followed by encrypting the message using the DEM under k. It is however unclear whether the ad hoc construction admits provable security under reasonable assumptions. A further issue is with efficiency in terms of computational and bandwidth requirements when a full-fledged public key encryption scheme is employed as a key encapsulation mechanism (KEM) for each recipient.

In pursuit of a more efficient MRES that admits a rigorous security analysis, Kurosawa [2] proposed the first MRES with a shortened ciphertext. Smart [3] introduced the notion of mKEM, which can be viewed as an efficient key encapsulation technique for multiple recipients. Bellare et al. [4][5] systematically studied the technique of randomness reuse and provided several generic and efficient constructions for MRES. Specifically, they introduced a so-called reproducibility theorem [5] to determine whether a standard encryption scheme permits secure randomness reuse. This was followed by Barbosa and Farshim [6] who proposed the notion of weak reproducibility which enabled them to construct a wider class of efficient (single message) MRESs. Hiwatari et al. [7] considered yet another approach by way of examining the behavior of a simulator in a security proof. We also note an earlier effort to design a multi-recipient signcryption scheme in which a sender and all recipients share the same group parameters [8]. While (public key) broadcast encryption [9] and multi-recipient encryption share a similar goal, researchers differentiate between these two types of security techniques by noting how public/secret key pairs for recipients are generated. Generally speaking, with broadcast encryption all recipients' public/secret key pairs are generated centrally by a sender or by a trusted key generation center, whereas with multi-recipient encryption each recipient is allowed to generate his or her own public/seciret key pair. In theory, multi-recipient encryption offers more flexibility for recipients than does broadcast encryption. In practice though, the flexibility is curtailed by previously proposed MRESs which generally require that all recipients use the same KEM or at the least share some easy-to-handle mathematical structures such as the same cyclic group. The main reason for the necessity of imposing limitations on recipients' choices of public/secret key pairs is due to the fact that these early MRESs employ randomness reuse as a tool to achieve savings in computation and bandwidth. We believe that the limitation as explained above would be a barrier to the adoption of MRES in some real world applications where each recipient may prefer to choose his or her own public/secret key pairs due to either organizational policy requirements or purely personal preferences. As a concrete example, one can imagine that in a cloud computing environment, recipient 1 might have to use RSA in order to comply with his company's security policy, recipient 2 might prefer to use elliptic curve cryptography (ECC), recipient 3 might be quite happy to use the latest standard technique for lattice based cryptography, and recipient 4 might want to stick to her choice of group parameters for ECC that are different from those for recipient 2.

1.1   Our Contributions

The goal of this paper is to address the above problem by designing an efficient MRES with provable security for a heterogeneous environment where a recipient is free to choose a secure KEM of his or her liking. Further, our scheme can be optimized in a stateful manner. That is, state information that includes randomness and other data used to generate a ciphertext can be reused to improve the efficiency of the multi-recipient encryption scheme. More interestingly, the scheme can be securely extended to a more general, heterogeneous setting where some of the recipients may not possess public/secret key pairs but instead share with the sender some symmetric keys which may be established in an out-of-band manner or as an outcome of a previous secure communication session. An added feature of our scheme is decryption of a ciphertext by the sender which was first advocated in [10,11]. Such a property would be useful in practice when the sender wishes to recover a message he or she sent earlier from the ciphertext only without access to the original plaintext or any of the recipients' secret decryption keys.

In some applications it may be important to protect the identity of a recipient. We show how to adapt our scheme in such a way that other than the sender and an intended recipient herself, no-one else can determine whether the recipient is an intended one or not. For the security model of anonymity, we mostly follow the idea of [12] on the definition of anonymity for broadcast encryption. However, modifications must be made to reflect a major difference: unlike broadcast encryption, the public/secret key pairs of our MRES are generated by different recipients instead of a key generation center. So it provides a potential opportunity for an adversary to choose public keys of his liking and compromise anonymity. We define a security model for anonymity in a heterogeneous environment and prove that our adapted scheme satisfies the stringent requirement of anonymity. All these attributes make our scheme a useful tool for secure data sharing in a heterogeneous environment, e.g., encrypted file system in a cloud computing environment.

1.2   Overview of Main Techniques

Map t Strings to One String. As mentioned above, researchers constructed efficient MRES by employing a key encapsulation mechanism (KEM) in lieu of full-fledged public key encryption. However, previous efficient schemes, e.g., [2,3,4,5,6,7] are not applicable in a heterogeneous public key setting. The main difficulty of employing KEMs is how to map ephemeral keys that are independently generated with different recipients' KEMs, to the same string that is used as a key in a symmetric data encapsulation mechanism (DEM). We overcome this difficulty with the help of a universal hash function family with collision accessibility. Cryptographic applications of a universal hash function family with collision accessibility, denoted by UH_{CA}, were discussed extensively in early work including [13] and explored more recently in [11]. Simply speaking, a

t-universal hash function family with collision accessibility is one that, given t initial strings, the hash values of them can be made to collide with one another. By using UH_{CA}, [11] provides an efficient method for public key encryption with sender recovery. Extending the work of [11], we find that ephemeral keys for different recipients' KEMs can be mapped into the same symmetric key for a DEM thanks to the collision accessibility of UH_{CA}. However, it turns out that this straightforward extension has its drawback in that it is not quite scalable when the number of recipients increases. To address this drawback we consider alternative structures to a "flat" t-universal hash function family. An example of such alternatives is derived from the Merkle-Damgard hash chain. Another example takes the form of a hash tree. These alternative structures enable us to use a 2-universal hash function family only to realize in an efficient and scalable manner the "collision" of t ephemeral keys and more importantly, to work out a security proof using an idea similar to length-extension attack.

Secure State Reuse. Stateful public key cryptosystem introduced in [14] permits the reuse of state information across different encryptions, resulting in a more efficient technique. The authors of [14] demonstrated stateful versions of the DHIES and Kurosawa-Desmedt schemes which requires one exponentiation only to encrypt. A potential problem with the randomness reuse, when applied to a stateful (single message) MRES as advocated in [14,5], lies in the fact that the symmetric key for a subsequent DEM is fixed. This issue of fixed DEM keys can be seen clearly when one applies the above randomness reuse technique to the construction of stateful MRESs from concrete MRESs in [3,6,7]. With a fixed DEM key, the resultant stateful MRESs are exposed to potential attacks when a recipient is removed from the group of intended recipients, as the removed recipient would still be able to decrypt future ciphertexts as long as the sender does not reset the state. While resetting the state could prevent such attacks, it would severely decrease the efficiency of a stateful MRES. To better understand it we note that all previous MRESs work more or less like this: a symmetric key (or the seed of the symmetric key) k is chosen at random and then "mapped"[1] to t ciphertexts for KEMs, which correspond exactly to t recipients. Since the state depends on k, it has to be changed once k is changed.

The MRES we propose in this paper can be viewed as the exact opposite of the above: t random ephemeral keys and their corresponding KEM ciphertexts, say $(k_1, c_1), (k_2, c_2), ..., (k_t, c_t)$, are generated for all t recipients independently; they are then "mapped" to the same DEM key k by UH_{CA}. One can see that if $(k_1, c_1), (k_2, c_2), ..., (k_t, c_t)$ are cached the first time when they are computed, they can be reused in subsequent encryptions for the same recipients. When a recipient, say U_1, is removed from the group of recipients, the sender can still reuse the remaining $(k_2, c_2), ..., (k_t, c_t)$ to generate a new DEM key k which will be no longer accessible to the removed recipient. An example is given in Table 1, which shows that when recipient U_1 is removed, the subsequent computational costs for the current recipients $U_2, U_3, ..., U_t$ in our MRES are less than that of

---

[1] Indeed, k is encrypted as a symmetric key for all recipients or reused as randomness in a ciphertext for a KEM.

the traditional method, e.g, the method specified in S/MIME. If on the other hand a new recipient U_{t+1} is added to the group, the sender needs to generate a new pair (k_{t+1}, c_{t+1}) for the new recipient only while keeping existing pairs $(k_1, c_1), (k_2, c_2), ..., (k_t, c_t)$ unchanged. These $t + 1$ pairs can then be used to generate a new DEM key k. By recycling (k_i, c_i)s, computational costs for each recipient can be reduced to merely two multiplications and one multiplicative inversion in $GF(2^{256})$.

Table 1. Efficiency comparison of encryption of our MRES with traditional method. RSA 2048, ElGamal 1024, ElGamal 2048,..., ECIES 256 are the public key encryption schemes used by recipient $U_2, U_3, ..., U_t$, respectively. Inv-$GF(2^{256})$ denotes the multiplicative inversion in $GF(2^{256})$. Exp-xxx and ECMul-xxx denotes the exponentiation and the elliptic curve point multiplication on the corresponding groups, respectively.

	U_2 RSA 2048	U_3 ElGamal 1024	U_4 ElGamal 2048	...	U_t ECIES 256
Our MRES	1 Inv-$GF(2^{256})$	1 Inv-$GF(2^{256})$	1 Inv-$GF(2^{256})$	...	1 Inv-$GF(2^{256})$
Traditional method	1 Exp-2048	2 Exp-1024	2 Exp-2048	...	2 ECMul-256

2   Basic Definitions

Notation. If x is a string, then $|x|$ is the length of x. $x||y$ denotes the concatenation of x and y. If X is a set, then $x \xleftarrow{R} X$ denotes the operation of picking an element x of X uniformly at random. If A is an algorithm, then $z \leftarrow A(x, y, ...)$ denotes the operation of running A on input $(x, y, ...)$ with its output being saved in z.

Key Encapsulation Mechanism. A key encapsulation mechanism (KEM) consists of three algorithms $KEM.Gen$, $KEM.Enc$ and $KEM.Dec$. $KEM.Gen$ takes as input a security parameter 1^λ and outputs a public/secret key pair (pk, sk). $KEM.Enc$ takes as input a public key pk and outputs a ciphertext c and an ephemeral key k. Let $\{0, 1\}^{\lambda_k}$ denote the KEM's key space, where λ_k is a polynomial in security parameter λ. $KEM.Dec$ takes as input a secret key sk and a ciphertext c, and outputs the ephemeral key k or a special failure symbol "$\perp$".

A standard notion of security for a KEM is indistinguishability security against adaptive chosen ciphertext attack, or IND-CCA2 security. This notion is defined by a two-party game played between a challenger and an adversary A. Throughout the game, the adversary can query a KEM oracle $\mathcal{O}_{KEM}$, which upon a decapsulation query c returns $KEM.Dec(sk, c)$.

Game$_{KEM}^{IND-CCA2}$:

$(pk, sk) \leftarrow KEM.Gen(1^\lambda)$

$(c^*, k_0^*) \leftarrow KEM.Enc(pk),\ k_1^* \xleftarrow{R} \{0,1\}^{\lambda_k},\ b \xleftarrow{R} \{0,1\}$

$b' \leftarrow A^{\mathcal{O}_{KEM}}(pk, c^*, k_b^*)$

Note that after receiving (c^*, k_b^*), the adversary can query $\mathcal{O}_{KEM}$ with any ciphertext c with the restriction that $c \neq c^*$. We say that A wins the game if $b = b'$. A KEM is said to be ϵ_{KEM}-IND-CCA2 secure if $|Pr[b = b'] - 1/2| \leq \epsilon_{KEM}$ for any probabilistic polynomial time (PPT) adversary, where ϵ_{KEM} is a negligible function in security parameter λ.

Data Encapsulation Mechanism. A data encapsulation mechanism (DEM) is composed of two algorithms, these being an encryption algorithm $DEM.Enc$ and a decryption algorithm $DEM.Dec$. $DEM.Enc$ takes as input a symmetric key k and a plaintext m and outputs a ciphertext c. The key space for the algorithm is denoted by $\{0,1\}^{\lambda_{Enc}}$, where λ_{Enc} is a polynomial in the security parameter λ. $DEM.Dec$ takes as input a symmetric key k and a ciphertext c and outputs m.

For the security of DEM, we adopt the notion of one-time symmetric-key encryption against passive attack (IND-OPA) [15] defined by the following game involving an adversary A:

Game$_{DEM}^{IND-OPA}$:

A chooses a pair of plaintexts (m_0, m_1), where $|m_0| = |m_1|$

$k \xleftarrow{R} \{0,1\}^{\lambda_{Enc}},\ c^* \leftarrow DEM.Enc(k, m_b),\ b \xleftarrow{R} \{0,1\}$

$b' \leftarrow A(c^*)$

We say that the adversary A wins the game if $b = b'$. An one-time symmetric-key encryption is said to be ϵ_{DEM}-IND-OPA secure if $|Pr[b = b'] - 1/2| \leq \epsilon_{DEM}$ for any PPT adversary, where ϵ_{DEM} is a negligible function in λ.

One-Time Signature. An one-time signature $Sig = (Gen_{Sig}, Sign, Vrfy)$ requires a signer generate new verification/signing keys each time when he signs a message. It consists of three algorithms specified below. Gen_{Sig} takes as input a security parameter 1^λ and outputs a verification/signing key pair (vk, sk_{Sig}). $Sign$ takes as input sk_{Sig} and a message m and outputs a signature σ. $Vrfy$ takes as input vk, m and σ and outputs "1" if σ is valid; otherwise, "0".

The security of Sig required in this paper is the strong unforgeability under chosen message attack (SU-CMA), which is defined by the following game.

Game$_{Sig}^{SU-CMA}$:

$(vk, sk_{Sig}) \leftarrow Gen_{Sig}(1^\lambda)$

$(m^*, \sigma^*) \leftarrow A^{\mathcal{O}_{Sign}}(vk)$

Notice that A can make at most one query m to the signing oracle $\mathcal{O}_{Sign}$, which returns the corresponding signature $\sigma = Sign(sk_{Sig}, m)$. We say the adversary wins the game if $Vrfy(vk, m^*, \sigma^*) = 1$ and $(m^*, \sigma^*) \neq (m, \sigma)$. Sig is said to be

ϵ_{Sig}-SU-CMA secure if $\Pr[A \text{ wins}] \leq \epsilon_{Sig}$ for any PPT adversary, where ϵ_{Sig} is a negligible function in λ.

A Useful Lemma

Lemma 1. *[16] Let A_1, A_2, B be events defined over a probability space such that $\Pr[A_1 \cap \overline{B}] = \Pr[A_2 \cap \overline{B}]$. Then we have $|\Pr[A_1] - \Pr[A_2]| \leq \Pr[B]$.*

3   Security Model

In this section, we define a multi-recipient encryption scheme with sender recovery (MRES-SR) together with a security model for MRES-SR.

Let U_i denote the i-th recipient, for $1 \leq i \leq t$. A MRES-SR is a tuple of algorithms $(Gen_{MR}, Enc_{MR}, Dec_{MR}, Rec_{MR})$ defined as follows:

- A probabilistic key generation algorithm Gen_{MR}, which in turn consists of sub-algorithms $Gen_{MR}.S$ and $Gen_{MR}.U_i$, for all $1 \leq i \leq t$.
  - $Gen_{MR}.S$ takes as input the security parameter 1^λ and outputs a sender's secret recovery key sk_{rcv}.
  - $Gen_{MR}.U_i$ takes as input the security parameter $1^{\lambda^{(i)}}$ and outputs a recipient U_i's public/secret key pair (pk_i, sk_i).
- An encryption algorithm Enc_{MR}, which takes as input the sender's secret recovery key sk_{rcv}, the recipients' public keys $\mathbf{pk} = (pk_1, pk_2, ..., pk_t)$ and a plaintext m, outputs a ciphertext c_{MR}.
- A decryption algorithm Dec_{MR} (of U_i), which takes as input the recipient's secret key sk_i and a ciphertext c_{MR}, outputs the corresponding plaintext m or the error symbol "$\perp$".
- A recovery algorithm Rec_{MR}, which takes as input sk_{rcv} and c_{MR}, outputs the corresponding plaintext m or the error symbol "$\perp$".

Remark. Since recipients may use different types of public key encryption algorithms, descriptions of Enc_{MR} (or Dec_{MR}) are dependent on specific recipients' algorithms. For simplicity, we use the same notation Enc_{MR} (Dec_{MR}) for all recipients.

IND-CCA2 Security of MRES-SR. The security of MRES-SR is defined by an IND-CCA2 game $\mathbf{Game}_{MR}^{IND-CCA2}$ played between an adversary A and a challenger. During the game, the adversary A has access to three oracles: (1) an encryption oracle $\mathcal{O}_{Enc}$, which upon an encryption query $q_{Enc} = (\mathbf{pk}', m)$ returns a ciphertext $c_{MR} = Enc_{MR}(sk_{rcv}, \mathbf{pk}', m)$. (2) a decryption oracle $\mathcal{O}_{Dec\ i}$ for recipient U_i, which upon a decryption query $q_{Dec} = c_{MR}$ returns $Dec_{MR}(sk_i, c_{MR})$. (3) a recovery oracle $\mathcal{O}_{Rec}$, which upon a recovery query $q_{Rec} = c_{MR}$ returns $Rec_{MR}(sk_{rcv}, c_{MR})$. $\mathbf{Game}_{MR}^{IND-CCA2}$ proceeds as follows.

- The challenger runs Gen_{MR} to generate a target sender's secret recovery key sk_{rcv} and target recipient U_i's public/secret key pair (pk_i, sk_i), for $1 \leq i \leq t$. Let $\mathbf{pk} = (pk_1, pk_2, ..., pk_t)$.

- The adversary A generates a pair of plaintexts (m_0, m_1) such that $|m_0| = |m_1|$, and sends (m_0, m_1) to the challenger. The challenger returns a target ciphertext $c_{MR}^* \leftarrow Enc_{MR}(sk_{rcv}, \mathbf{pk}, m_b)$, where $b \xleftarrow{R} \{0, 1\}$.
- Finally, A terminates by returning a guess b'.

Notice that after the challenge phase, the adversary A can still query all the three oracles $\mathcal{O}_{Enc}$, $\mathcal{O}_{Dec\ i}$ and $\mathcal{O}_{Rec}$ with any input, provided that $q_{Dec} \neq c_{MR}^*$ and $q_{Rec} \neq c_{MR}^*$.

The above game models a sender transmitting a message to recipients $U_1,...,U_t$, who have public keys $pk_1,...,pk_t$, respectively. The adversary A can make query $q_{Enc} = (\mathbf{pk}', m)$ with any public keys $\mathbf{pk}'$, which captures the security of MRES-SR under maliciously chosen recipients' public keys. Unlike a traditional security model for MRES, queries q_{Enc} and q_{Rec} should be considered in our security model since the sender's secret key sk_{rcv} is taken as part of the inputs to Enc_{MR} and Rec_{MR}.

We say that the adversary A wins the above game if $b' = b$. MRES-SR is said to be ϵ-IND-CCA2 secure if, for any PPT adversary A, $|\Pr[A \text{ wins}] - 1/2| \leq \epsilon$.

4   Constructions

The main idea of constructing a MRES-SR is that the sender runs t different recipients' KEMs to generate t different ephemeral keys and then maps those keys to the same random string, which is used to generate a symmetric key for a DEM. During the decryption phase, a ciphertext for the DEM can be decrypted using any of t ephemeral keys. Hence, the function which maps t strings to one string plays a central role in our MRES-SR. Let us first show how to realize this function efficiently.

4.1   Map t Strings to One String

We follow ideas presented in [13] to employ universal hash function families UH_{CA} with t-collision accessibility property. Such functions can map t different strings, say $k_0, k_1, ..., k_{t-1} \in GF(2^{2\lambda})$, to the same string, say $k_{CA} \in GF(2^\lambda)$. To construct UH_{CA} such that $UH_{CA}(k_0) = UH_{CA}(k_1) = ... = UH_{CA}(k_{t-1}) = k_{CA}$, we choose $w_0,...,w_{t-1}$ and k_{CA} at random from $GF(2^\lambda)$ and solve the following set of linear equations for $a_0, a_1, ..., a_{t-1} \in GF(2^{2\lambda})$:

$$
\begin{cases}
w_0 || k_{CA} = a_0 + a_1 k_0 + a_2 k_0^2 + ... + a_{t-1} k_0^{t-1} \\
w_1 || k_{CA} = a_0 + a_1 k_1 + a_2 k_1^2 + ... + a_{t-1} k_1^{t-1} \\
\quad\vdots \\
w_{t-1} || k_{CA} = a_0 + a_1 k_{t-1} + a_2 k_{t-1}^2 + ... + a_{t-1} k_{t-1}^{t-1}
\end{cases}
$$

The description of UH_{CA} can be completely specified by $(a_0, a_1, ..., a_{t-1})$ and the output of $UH_{CA}(k_i)$ is k_{CA}, which is part of $a_0 + a_1 k_i + a_2 k_i^2 + ... + a_{t-1} k_i^{t-1}$.

Notice that the computational cost for solving the above equations grows as a cubic function of t, the number of recipients. This does not really scale well for a large t, say when $t > 10,000$. To overcome this problem, we considered an iterated version of UH_{CA}, which adopts a MD like structure and uses UH_{CA} with 2-collision accessibility as a building block. (Other types of structures such as tree structure can also realize the "collision" of different strings using UH_{CA} with 2-collision accessibility.) The resulting construction is illustrated in Fig. 1, where $k_{CA,0}$, k_1,...,k_{t-1} are mapped to $k_{CA,t-1}$. In an iteration, $k_{CA,i-1}$ and k_i are mapped to the same string $k_{CA,i}$ by UH_{CA} with 2-collision accessibility. For a large t, the generation of $t-1$ UH_{CA} with 2-collision accessibility is significantly more efficient than that of UH_{CA} with t-collision accessibility.

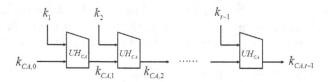

Fig. 1. UH_{CA} with MD like structure

We note that $k_{CA,i}$ the output of one UH_{CA} cannot be taken as input directly to generate the UH_{CA} of the next iteration, since the output length of UH_{CA} is shorter than its input length. Hence, additional randomness should be added to generate the next UH_{CA}. To that end, we resort to the verification key of one-time signature and hash functions, which is shown in the construction of MRES-SR.

A Useful Claim. Suppose the description $(a_0, a_1) \in \{0,1\}^{\lambda_1} \times \{0,1\}^{\lambda_1}$ of a UH_{CA} with 2-collision accessibility is generated by (1),

$$
\begin{cases}
w_0 \| k_{CA} = a_0 + a_1 s_0 \\
w_1 \| k_{CA} = a_0 + a_1 s_1
\end{cases}
\tag{1}
$$

and $(w_0, w_1, k_{CA}, s_0, s_1) \in \{0,1\}^{\lambda_3} \times \{0,1\}^{\lambda_3} \times \{0,1\}^{\lambda_4} \times \{0,1\}^{\lambda_1} \times \{0,1\}^{\lambda_1}$ is said to be a valid tuple if $s_0 \neq s_1$, where $\lambda_1 = \lambda_3 + \lambda_4$. The following claim, which is proved in [11], is a very useful property of UH_{CA} with 2-collision accessibility.

Claim 1. *[11] Consider the following ensemble,*

$$
W_\beta = \{(a_0^{(1)}, a_1^{(1)}, s_1^{(1)}), (a_0^{(2)}, a_1^{(2)}, s_1^{(2)}), ..., (a_0^{(N-1)}, a_1^{(N-1)}, s_1^{(N-1)}), (a_0^*, a_1^*, s_1^*)\},
$$

where $(a_0^{(i)}, a_1^{(i)}, s_1^{(i)})$, $1 \le i \le N-1$, are generated by (1) using random and valid tuples and $\beta \overset{R}{\leftarrow} \{0,1\}$. If $\beta = 0$, then (a_0^*, a_1^*, s^*) is generated by UH_{CA} using a random and valid tuple $(w_0^*, w_1^*, k_{CA}^*, s_0^*, s_1^*) \in \{0,1\}^{\lambda_3} \times \{0,1\}^{\lambda_3} \times \{0,1\}^{\lambda_4} \times \{0,1\}^{\lambda_1} \times \{0,1\}^{\lambda_1}$. Otherwise, (a_0^*, a_1^*, s_1^*) is chosen uniformly at random from $\{0,1\}^{\lambda_1} \times \{0,1\}^{\lambda_1} \times \{0,1\}^{\lambda_1}$. Then the statistical difference between W_0 and W_1 is at most $\frac{1}{2^{\lambda_3 - 1}}$.

4.2   Basic Multi-recipient Encryption with Sender Recovery

In this section we describe the construction of a basic MRES-SR, which will be further optimized in the next section. Since ephemeral keys generated by different KEMs may be of different lengths or on different groups, we cannot use those keys to generate the description of UH_{CA} directly. To solve the problem, we prepare two hash functions $H_0 : \{0,1\}^* \to \{0,1\}^{2\lambda_1}$, $H_1 : \{0,1\}^* \to \{0,1\}^{\lambda_1+\lambda_3}$, and a key derivation function $H_{KDF} : \{0,1\}^* \to \{0,1\}^{\lambda_k}$ to generate UH_{CA}. To realize the sender recovery property, the sender's recovery key together with other ephemeral keys are mapped to the same string, which is the symmetric key of a DEM. An one-time signature $Sig = (Gen_{Sig}, Sign, Vrfy)$ is applied to thwart adaptively chosen ciphertext attacks.

The generation of UH_{CA} must take into account a verification key vk for an one-time signature in addition to $(k_i, k_{CA,i-1})$. The advantage of adding vk is two fold. First, vk is used to generate the description of UH_{CA} and the sender can recover the ephemeral key $k_{CA,t}$ by vk. Second, the ephemeral keys and the ciphertexts of KEM can be reused thanks to a fresh vk, which will be explained later. More details of the basic MRES-SR are described below and Fig 2 illustrates the structure of the basic MRES-SR.

- Key generation Gen_{MR}
    - $Gen_{MR}.U_i$: Each recipient U_i, where $1 \leq i \leq t$, runs his key generation algorithm $KEM.Gen$ to generate a public/secret key pair (pk_i, sk_i). Let $\{0,1\}^{\lambda_{KEM}^{(i)}}$ denote U_i's KEM keyspace. Let $\mathbf{pk} = (pk_1, pk_2, ..., pk_t)$.
    - $Gen_{MR}.S$: The sender chooses at random $sk_{rcv} \in \{0,1\}^{\lambda_1}$ as her secret key for the recovery of a message from a ciphertext.
- Encryption $Enc_{MR}(sk_{rcv}, \mathbf{pk}, m)$ by the sender
    1. $(vk, sk_{Sig}) \leftarrow Gen_{Sig}(1^\lambda)$. Set $k_{CA,0} = sk_{rcv}$.
       For $i = 1, ..., t$, do
       (a) $(k_i, c_i) \leftarrow KEM.Enc(pk_i)$, $w_{0,i-1}||s_{0,i-1}||k_{CA,i} \leftarrow H_0(k_{CA,i-1}||vk)$ and $w_{1,i}||s_{1,i} \leftarrow H_1(k_i||vk)$. If $s_{1,i} = s_{0,i-1}$, compute $(k_i, c_i) \leftarrow KEM.Enc(pk_i)$ and $w_{1,i}||s_{1,i} \leftarrow H_1(k_i||vk)$ until $s_{1,i} \neq s_{0,i-1}$. Note that the lengths of $w_{j,i}$, $s_{j,i}$ and $k_{CA,i}$ are λ_3, λ_1 and λ_4, respectively.
       (b) Solve the system of linear equations below for $(a_{0,i}, a_{1,i})$.

$$\begin{cases} w_{0,i-1}||k_{CA,i} = a_{0,i} + a_{1,i}s_{0,i-1} \\ w_{1,i}||k_{CA,i} = a_{0,i} + a_{1,i}s_{1,i} \end{cases}$$

      Let $\mathbf{a} = \{(a_{0,i}, a_{1,i})\}$ and $\mathbf{c}_{KEM} = (c_1, c_2, ..., c_t)$, where $\{(a_{0,i}, a_{1,i})\}$ denotes an ordered list of $(a_{0,1}, a_{1,1}), ..., (a_{0,t}, a_{1,t})$.
    2. $k_{Enc} \leftarrow H_{KDF}(k_{CA,t}||\mathbf{a})$ and $c_{DEM} \leftarrow DEM.Enc(k_{Enc}, m)$. $tag \leftarrow Sign(sk_{Sig}, \mathbf{a}||\mathbf{c})$, where $\mathbf{c} = (\mathbf{c}_{KEM}, c_{DEM})$.
    3. Output $\mathbf{c}_{MR} = (vk, \mathbf{a}, \mathbf{c}, tag)$.
- Decryption $Dec_{MR}(sk_i, \mathbf{c}_{MR})$ by a recipient U_i
    1. If $Vrfy(vk, \mathbf{a}||\mathbf{c}, tag) \neq 1$, output $\bot$ and halt.
    2. Let $k_i \leftarrow KEM.Dec(sk_i, c_i)$. If $k_i = \bot$, output $\bot$ and halt.

3. Let $w_{1,i}||s_{1,i} \leftarrow H_1(k_i||vk)$ and $w'_{1,i}||k_{CA,i} \leftarrow a_{0,i}+a_{1,i}s_{1,i}$. If $w'_{1,i} \neq w_{1,i}$, output $\perp$ and halt.
4. If $i = t$, go to step 5. Otherwise, for $j = i+1, ..., t$, do
   - $w_{0,j-1}||s_{0,j-1}||k_{CA,j} \leftarrow H_0(k_{CA,j-1}||vk)$.
5. $k_{Enc} \leftarrow H_{KDF}(k_{CA,t}||a)$, $m' \leftarrow DEM.Dec(k_{Enc}, c_{DEM})$.
6. Output m'.

- Recovery $Rec_{MR}(sk_{rcv}, c_{MR})$ by the sender
  1. If $Vrfy(vk, a||c, tag) \neq 1$, output $\perp$ and halt.
  2. Let $w_{0,0}||s_{0,0}||k_{CA,1} \leftarrow H_0(sk_{rcv}||vk)$ and $w'_{0,0}||k'_{CA,1} \leftarrow a_{0,1} + a_{1,1}s_{0,0}$. If $w'_{0,0}||k'_{CA,1} \neq w_{0,0}||k_{CA,1}$, output $\perp$ and halt.
  3. For $j = 2, ..., t$, do
     - $w_{0,j-1}||s_{0,j-1}||k_{CA,j} \leftarrow H_0(k_{CA,j-1}||vk)$.
  4. $k_{Enc} \leftarrow H_{KDF}(k_{CA,t}||a)$, $m' \leftarrow DEM.Dec(k_{Enc}, c_{DEM})$.
  5. Output m'.

Note that $KEM.Gen$, $KEM.Enc$ and $KEM.Dec$ could be different for each

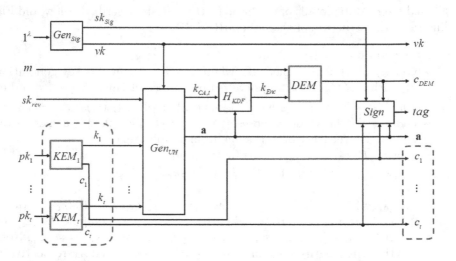

Fig. 2. Encrypting with MRES-SR, where Gen_{UH} denotes the generation of a and $k_{CA,t}$

recipient, being determined by the specific public key cryptosystem used by the recipient. For simplicity, we use the same notations. On the other hand, $DEM.Dec$ and the verification algorithm $Vrfy$ for the one-time signature are the same across all recipients. In order to decrypt correctly, each recipient U_i needs to know the "position" of his ciphertext $(c_i, a_{0,i}, a_{1,i})$ in c_{MR}, which is usually an implicit requirement for multi-recipient encryption.

MRES-SR with Tree Structure. Computational costs for recipients are not the same in that U_{i-j} has to compute j more hashing operations than does U_i, for $0 \leq j < i \leq t$. Although the differences may be immaterial in most applications, we do need to keep in mind that the depth of the hash chain increases linearly with the number of recipients. This problem can be alleviated by a logarithmic factor by the use of the tree structured construction. More precisely, a tree can be defined recursively starting at leaf nodes: sk_{rcv}, $k_1,...,k_t$ are set to leaf nodes $k_{CA,0}^{[0]},...,k_{CA,0}^{[t]}$, respectively, and each pair of nodes, say $k_{CA,0}^{[i]}$ and $k_{CA,0}^{[i+1]}$, for $i = 0, 2, 4, ...$, are mapped to their parent node, say $k_{CA,1}^{[i]}$, using UH_{CA}. If the number of nodes on a level is odd, the rightmost node on that level is set to his parent node directly. Finally, sk_{rcv}, $k_1,...,k_t$ are mapped to the same root node, which can be generated using any one of the leaf nodes and the corresponding leaf to root path. Security of the tree structured MRES-SR can be proven by following a similar analysis to that for the basic MRES-SR shown in section 4.3. Details of the proof will be provided in the full version of the paper.

4.3 Security Analysis

Theorem 1. *The basic MRES-SR is ϵ-IND-CCA2 secure in the random oracle model if recipient U_i's KEM is $\epsilon_{KEM}^{(i)}$-IND-CCA2 secure, for $1 \leq i \leq t$, DEM is ϵ_{DEM}-IND-OPA secure and Sig is ϵ_{Sig}-SU-CMA secure where $\epsilon \leq 2t\epsilon_{KEM} + \epsilon_{DEM} + \epsilon_{Sig} + (\frac{1}{2^{\lambda_1 - 1}} + \frac{1}{2^{\lambda_k - 1}})N_{RO} + (\frac{1}{2^{\lambda_1 - 2}} + \frac{1}{2^{\lambda_3 - 1}})N_{Rec} + \frac{1}{2^{\lambda_1}} + \frac{1}{2^{\lambda_3 - 1}}$, $\epsilon_{KEM} = max\{\epsilon_{KEM}^{(1)}, ..., \epsilon_{KEM}^{(t)}\}$, N_{Rec} denotes an upper bound on the number of recovery queries, $N_{RO} = max\{N_0, N_1\}$, and N_0 and N_1 denote upper bounds on the numbers of queries on H_0 and H_1, respectively.*

Proof. In order to show that any PPT adversary can win the IND-CCA2 game of MRES-SR with a negligible advantage only, we introduce three new games described below.

- Game 0 is the same as the original IND-CCA2 game of MRES-SR. During the challenge phase, the target ciphertext $\mathbf{c}_{MR}^* = (vk^*, \mathbf{a}^*, \mathbf{c}^*, tag^*)$ is computed as follows.
  - $(vk^*, sk_{Sig}^*) \leftarrow Gen_{Sig}(1^\lambda)$, $k_{CA,0}^* \leftarrow sk_{rcv}$.
    For $i = 1, ..., t$, do
    1. $(k_i^*, c_i^*) \leftarrow KEM.Enc(pk_i)$, $w_{0,i-1}^* \| s_{0,i-1}^* \| k_{CA,i}^* \leftarrow H_0(k_{CA,i-1}^* \| vk^*)$ and $w_{1,i}^* \| s_{1,i}^* \leftarrow H_1(k_i^* \| vk^*)$ such that $s_{1,i}^* \neq s_{0,i-1}^*$.
    2. Solve the system of linear equations below for $(a_{0,i}^*, a_{1,i}^*)$.

$$\begin{cases} w_{0,i-1}^* \| k_{CA,i}^* = a_{0,i}^* + a_{1,i}^* s_{0,i-1}^* \\ w_{1,i}^* \| k_{CA,i}^* = a_{0,i}^* + a_{1,i}^* s_{1,i}^* \end{cases}$$

Let $\mathbf{a}^* = \{(a_{0,i}^*, a_{1,i}^*)\}$ and $\mathbf{c}_{KEM}^* = (c_1^*, c_2^*, ..., c_t^*)$.
  - $k_{Enc}^* \leftarrow H_{KDF}(k_{CA,t}^* \| \mathbf{a}^*)$, $c_{DEM}^* \leftarrow DEM.Enc(k_{Enc}^*, m_b)$ and $tag^* \leftarrow Sign(sk_{Sig}^*, \mathbf{a}^* \| \mathbf{c}^*)$, where $\mathbf{c}^* = (\mathbf{c}_{KEM}^*, c_{DEM}^*)$.
- Game 1 is similar to Game 0, but with the following differences:

- At the beginning of the game, the challenger computes part of the target ciphertext as follows: $(vk^*, sk^*_{Sig}) \leftarrow Gen_{Sig}(1^\lambda)$, $k^*_{CA,0} \leftarrow sk_{rcv}$, $(k^*_i, c^*_i) \leftarrow KEM.Enc(pk_i)$ and $k^{**}_i \overset{R}{\leftarrow} \{0,1\}^{\lambda^{(i)}_{KEM}}$, for $1 \leq i \leq t$. Then let $\mathbf{c}^*_{KEM} = (c^*_1, c^*_2, ..., c^*_t)$.
  For $i = 1, ..., t$, do
  1. $w^*_{0,i-1}||s^*_{0,i-1}||k^*_{CA,i} \leftarrow H_0(k^*_{CA,i-1}||vk^*)$ and $w^{**}_{1,i}||s^{**}_{1,i} \leftarrow H_1(k^{**}_i||vk^*)$ such that $s^{**}_{1,i} \neq s^*_{0,i-1}$.
  2. Solve the system of linear equations below for $(a^{**}_{0,i}, a^{**}_{1,i})$.

$$\begin{cases} w^*_{0,i-1}||k^*_{CA,i} = a^{**}_{0,i} + a^{**}_{1,i}s^*_{0,i-1} \\ w^{**}_{1,i}||k^*_{CA,i} = a^{**}_{0,i} + a^{**}_{1,i}s^{**}_{1,i} \end{cases}$$

  Let $k^{**}_{Enc} \leftarrow H_{KDF}(k^*_{CA,t}||\mathbf{a}^{**})$, where $\mathbf{a}^{**} = \{(a^{**}_{0,i}, a^{**}_{1,i})\}$.
- In the challenge phase, $c^{**}_{DEM} \leftarrow DEM.Enc(k^{**}_{Enc}, m_b)$ and $tag^{**} \leftarrow Sign(sk^*_{Sig}, \mathbf{a}^{**}||\mathbf{c}^{**})$, where $\mathbf{c}^{**} = (\mathbf{c}^*_{KEM}, c^{**}_{DEM})$. The target ciphertext of Game 1 is $\mathbf{c}^{**}_{MR} = (vk^*, \mathbf{a}^{**}, \mathbf{c}^{**}, tag^{**})$.
- After the challenge phase, $\mathcal{O}_{Dec\ j}$ returns $\perp$ for decryption queries $c_{MR} = (vk, \mathbf{a}, (c_1, ..., c_t, c_{DEM}), tag)$ satisfying $c_j = c^*_j$, for $j \in \{1, ..., t\}$.
- Game 2 is similar to Game 1 except that the challenger randomly chooses $(a^+_{0,1}, a^+_{1,1})$ and k^+_{Enc} in place of $(a^{**}_{0,1}, a^{**}_{1,1})$ and k^{**}_{Enc}, respectively. Let $\mathbf{a}^+ = \{(a^+_{0,1}, a^+_{1,1}), (a^{**}_{0,2}, a^{**}_{1,2}), ..., (a^{**}_{0,t}, a^{**}_{1,t})\}$. In the challenge phase, $c^+_{DEM} \leftarrow DEM.Enc(k^+_{Enc}, m_b)$, and $tag^+ \leftarrow Sign(sk^*_{Sig}, \mathbf{a}^+||\mathbf{c}^+)$, where $\mathbf{c}^+ = (\mathbf{c}^*_{KEM}, c^+_{DEM})$. The target ciphertext is $c^+_{MR} = (vk^*, \mathbf{a}^+, \mathbf{c}^+, tag^+)$.

Claim 2. *If recipient U_i's KEM is $\epsilon^{(i)}_{KEM}$-IND-CCA2 secure, for $1 \leq i \leq t$, and Sig is ϵ_{Sig}-SU-CMA secure, then $|\Pr[Game\ 0 = 1] - \Pr[Game\ 1 = 1]| \leq \frac{1}{2^{\lambda_1}} + (t+1)\epsilon_{KEM} + \epsilon_{Sig}$, where $\epsilon_{KEM} = max\{\epsilon^{(1)}_{KEM}, \epsilon^{(2)}_{KEM}, ..., \epsilon^{(t)}_{KEM}\}$ and $\Pr[Game\ j = 1]$ denotes the probability that the adversary wins in Game j.*

Proof. We proceed with a sequence of t games to show the indistinguishability between Game 0 and Game 1.

- Game $0^{(0)}$ is similar to Game 0, except that, after the challenge phase, $\mathcal{O}_{Dec\ j}$ returns $\perp$ for decryption queries $c_{MR} = (vk, \mathbf{a}, (c_1, ..., c_t, c_{DEM}), tag)$ satisfying $c_j = c^*_j$, for $j \in \{1, ..., t\}$.
- Game $0^{(1)}$ is similar to Game $0^{(0)}$, except for the following modifications. At the beginning of the game, the challenger computes part of the target ciphertext: Compute vk^* and $\mathbf{c}^*_{KEM}$ as in the challenge phase. Then, let $k^{**}_1 \overset{R}{\leftarrow} \{0,1\}^{\lambda^{(1)}_{KEM}}$. k^{**}_1 instead of k^*_1 will be used to compute the target ciphertext.

$\vdots$

- Game $0^{(i)}$ is similar to Game $0^{(i-1)}$, but at the beginning of the game, $k^{**}_i \overset{R}{\leftarrow} \{0,1\}^{\lambda^{(i)}_{KEM}}$ and k^{**}_i instead of k^*_i will be used to compute the target ciphertext.

$\vdots$

- Game $0^{(t)}$ is similar to Game $0^{(t-1)}$, but at the beginning of the game, $k_t^{**} \xleftarrow{R} \{0,1\}^{\lambda_{KEM}^{(t)}}$ and k_t^{**} instead of k_t^* will be used to compute the target ciphertext. Indeed, $\Pr[Game\ 0^{(t)} = 1] = \Pr[Game\ 1 = 1]$.

We call c_{MR} is valid if c_{MR} can pass the validity check in step 1, 2 and 3 of decryption. Notice that A may query $\mathcal{O}_{Dec\ j}$ with a valid $c_{MR} = (vk, \mathbf{a}, (c_1, ..., c_t, c_{DEM}), tag)$ such that $c_{MR} \neq c_{MR}^*$ and $c_j = c_j^*$. Let $VALID$ denote such an event. If $VALID$ does not happen, Game 0 and Game $0^{(0)}$ are the same. That is, $\Pr[Game\ 0 = 1|\overline{VALID}] = \Pr[Game\ 0^{(0)} = 1|\overline{VALID}]$. Therefore,

$$\Pr[Game\ 0 = 1] - \Pr[Game\ 0^{(0)} = 1] \leq \Pr[VALID].$$

Next, we show $\Pr[VALID]$ is negligible by considering two cases below.

- $vk = vk^*$. If this case happens with a non-negligible probability, we can construct an algorithm to break the security of the underlying one-time signature and we have $\Pr[VALID] \leq \epsilon_{Sig}$.
- $vk \neq vk^*$.
  - A presents queries $k_j^{*real}\|vk$ to H_1 where k_j^{*real} is the real ephemeral key corresponding to c_j^*. If this case happens with a non-negligible probability, we can construct an algorithm to break the IND-CCA security of one of t underlying KEMs. Hence, $\Pr[VALID] \leq t\epsilon_{KEM}$, where $\epsilon_{KEM} = max\{\epsilon_{KEM}^{(1)}, \epsilon_{KEM}^{(2)}, ..., \epsilon_{KEM}^{(t)}\}$.
  - A did not make queries $k_j^{*real}\|vk$ to oracle H_1. Since the output of $H_1(k_j^{*real}\|vk)$ is distributed uniformly over the range of H_1, the probability that the ciphertext can pass the validity check in step 3 of decryption is at most $\frac{1}{2^{\lambda_1}}$.

Therefore we have $\Pr[VALID] \leq \frac{1}{2^{\lambda_1}} + t\epsilon_{KEM} + \epsilon_{Sig}$.

Indistinguishability between Game $0^{(i-1)}$ and Game $0^{(i)}$ relies on the IND-CCA2 security of U_i's KEM, for $i = 1, ..., t$. It is not difficult to prove that $|\Pr[Game\ 0^{(i-1)}] - \Pr[Game\ 0^{(i)}]| \leq \epsilon_{KEM}^{(i)}$ and $|\Pr[Game\ 0^{(0)}] - \Pr[Game\ 0^{(t)}]| \leq t\epsilon_{KEM}$. Therefore, $|\Pr[Game\ 0 = 1] - \Pr[Game\ 1 = 1]| \leq |\Pr[Game\ 0 = 1] - \Pr[Game\ 0^{(0)} = 1]| + |\Pr[Game\ 0^{(0)} = 1] - \Pr[Game\ 0^{(t)} = 1]| \leq \frac{1}{2^{\lambda_1}} + 2t\epsilon_{KEM} + \epsilon_{Sig}$.

Claim 3. $|\Pr[Game\ 1 = 1] - \Pr[Game\ 2 = 1]| \leq (\frac{1}{2^{\lambda_1-1}} + \frac{1}{2^{\lambda_k-1}})N_{RO} + (\frac{1}{2^{\lambda_1-2}} + \frac{1}{2^{\lambda_3-1}})N_{Rec} + \frac{1}{2^{\lambda_3-1}}$, where $N_{RO} = max\{N_0, N_1\}$ and N_0 and N_1 denote upper bounds on the numbers of queries on H_0 and H_1, respectively.

Sketch of Proof. Indistinguishability between Game 1 and Game 2 is closely related to Claim 1. Assume that there exists a PPT adversary A_{12} such that $|\Pr[Game\ 1 = 1] - \Pr[Game\ 2 = 1]|$ is non-negligible, we show how to construct a PPT algorithm M_{UH}, which takes as input

$$W_\beta = \{(a_0^{(1)}, a_1^{(1)}, s_1^{(1)}), (a_0^{(2)}, a_1^{(2)}, s_1^{(2)}), ..., (a_0^{(N-1)}, a_1^{(N-1)}, s_1^{(N-1)}), (a_0^*, a_1^*, s_1^*)\}$$

and outputs β with a non-negligible advantage.

The main idea of the proof is similar to that of [11], where there is only one UH_{CA}. Notice that if the inputs to a random oracle $H(\cdot)$ are different, the corresponding outputs are uniformly and independently distributed. Due to the unforgeability of the one-time signature, vk which is part of the inputs to H_0 and H_1 are usually different in each encryption and the corresponding outputs $w_{0,i-1}||s_{0,i-1}||k_{CA,i}$ and $w_{1,i}||s_{1,i}$ are uniformly and independently distributed. Therefore, (a_0, a_1)s in W_β can be considered as parts of the ciphertexts in the simulated game. However, our scheme uses t UH_{CA}s with the MD like iterated structure. To compute a simulated target ciphertext, the first iteration of UH_{CA} is generated using (a_0^*, a_1^*, s_1^*) and the remaining $t-1$ iterations can be generated following the idea of a length-extension attack. More details of the proof are omitted due to lack of space.

Claim 4. $|\Pr[Game\ 2 = 1] - 1/2| \leq \epsilon_{Sig} + \epsilon_{DEM}$ *if the underlying DEM is* ϵ_{DEM}-*IND-OPA secure and Sig is* ϵ_{Sig}-*SU-CMA secure.*

Proof. If there exists a PPT adversary, say A_2, which can win Game 2 with a non-negligible advantage, we show how to construct an algorithm M_{DEM} to break the IND-OPA security of the underlying DEM.

M_{DEM} sets parameters and answers queries $q_{Enc}, q_{Dec}, q_{Rec}$ from A_2 as in Game 2, except that when A_2 submits $q_{Dec} = (vk^*, \mathbf{a}', \mathbf{c}', tag')$ or $q_{Rec} = (vk^*, \mathbf{a}', \mathbf{c}', tag')$, M_{DEM} responds with "$\perp$". However, M_{DEM}'s answers may be wrong when such queries are valid. Denote such an event by Bad_2. When receiving (m_0, m_1) from A_2, M_{DEM} sends (m_0, m_1) to the challenger of IND-OPA game and gets the answer c_{DEM}^+. M_{DEM} sets the target ciphertext to $(vk^*, \mathbf{a}^+, (\mathbf{c}_{KEM}^*, c_{DEM}^+), tag^+)$. Finally, A_2 will terminates with output a bit, which is also the output of M_{DEM}. Notice that M_{DEM} perfectly simulates Game 2 for A_2 if Bad_2 does not happen. That is, $\Pr[Game\ 2 = 1 \cap \overline{Bad_2}] = \Pr[M_{DEM}\ wins \cap \overline{Bad_2}]$. Hence, we have $|\Pr[Game\ 2 = 1] - \frac{1}{2}| \leq |\Pr[Game\ 2 = 1] - \Pr[M_{DEM}\ wins]| + |\Pr[M_{DEM}\ wins] - \frac{1}{2}| \leq \Pr[Bad_2] + \epsilon_{DEM}$, where the last inequality follows from Lemma 1.

In fact, $\Pr[Bad_2]$ is negligible, which relies on the unforgeability of one-time signature. That is, $\Pr[Bad_2] \leq \epsilon_{Sig}$. Therefore, $|\Pr[Game\ 2 = 1] - \frac{1}{2}| \leq \epsilon_{Sig} + \epsilon_{DEM}$, which completes the proof of Claim 4.

From Claims 2, 3 and 4, it follows that $|\Pr[Game\ 0 = 1] - \frac{1}{2}| \leq |\Pr[Game\ 0 = 1] - \Pr[Game\ 1 = 1]| + |\Pr[Game\ 1 = 1] - \Pr[Game\ 2 = 1]| + |\Pr[Game\ 2 = 1] - \frac{1}{2}| \leq 2t\epsilon_{KEM} + \epsilon_{DEM} + \epsilon_{Sig} + (\frac{1}{2^{\lambda_1 - 1}} + \frac{1}{2^{\lambda_k - 1}})N_{RO} + (\frac{1}{2^{\lambda_1 - 2}} + \frac{1}{2^{\lambda_3 - 1}})N_{Rec} + \frac{1}{2^{\lambda_1}} + \frac{1}{2^{\lambda_3 - 1}}$, which completes the proof of Theorem 1.

4.4   Stateful MRES-SR

We find that $(k_1, c_1), ..., (k_t, c_t)$ can be cached as part of the state information for the scheme and reused later for improved efficiency. Specifically, the sender can use the same (k_i, c_i) for each recipient U_i when running Enc_{MR}. As a result, the main cost of computing $\mathbf{c}_{KEM}$, e.g. exponentiations in large cyclic groups, is minimized for subsequent applications of the encryption algorithm. As a specific example, if we set $\lambda_1 = 256$ and $\lambda_3 = \lambda_4 = 128$, the main cost of a subsequent encryption for the same recipients is dominated by $2t$ multiplications, t inversions in $GF(2^{256})$ and a symmetric encryption operation.

Notice that the verification key vk is usually different in each encryption if the underlying one-time signature is unforgeable. Thanks to the randomness of vk, $\mathbf{a}$ and k_{Enc} are fresh each time when a new message is encrypted, even with the fixed state. Additionally, even if the group of recipients is changed, most part of the state could be still reused. As an example, if U_1 leaves the group of recipients, $(k_2, c_2), ..., (k_t, c_t)$ can still be reused and U_1 is denied the ability of decrypting a new ciphertext due to the use of a fresh symmetric key. On the other hand, if a new recipient U_{t+1} joins the group, the sender can generate a new pair (k_{t+1}, c_{t+1}) for the new recipient and then update the state to $(k_1, c_1), ..., (k_t, c_t), (k_{t+1}, c_{t+1})$.

Security Analysis. The security model for MRES-SR is carried over to the stateful version of our MRES-SR, where the encryption oracle computes the ciphertexts using a fixed state. The method of security proof of the basic MRES-SR, which is shown in section 4.3, still holds for the stateful MRES-SR.

The main difference between proofs of the stateful MRES-SR and the basic MRES-SR is that the sender uses the fixed state $(k_1^*, c_1^*), ..., (k_t^*, c_t^*)$ to answer the encryption queries from the beginning of Game 0, Game 1 and Game 2. (Note that $k_1^*, ..., k_t^*$ in Game 1 and Game 2 are strings chosen at random.) Only minor modifications need to be made in the proof of Claim 2. In Game $0^{(0)}$ of the proof of Claim 2, $\mathcal{O}_{Dec\ j}$ returns $\bot$ for decryption queries $c_{MR} = (vk, \mathbf{a}, (c_1, ..., c_t, c_{DEM}), tag)$ satisfying that $c_j = c_j^*$. However, in the game of stateful MRES-SR, it is possible for the adversary to make valid decryption queries c_{MR} such that $c_{MR} \neq c_{MR}^*$ and $c_j = c_j^*$. For instance, such c_{MR} could be returned by $\mathcal{O}_{Enc}$ since the state c_j^* is fixed. To reduce the possibility of returning $\bot$ for a valid ciphertext, a list $\mathcal{L}_{Enc}$ is used to record the encryption queries and the corresponding answers from $\mathcal{O}_{Enc}$. The modified description of Game $0^{(0)}$ are as follows. During the game, $\mathcal{O}_{Dec\ j}$ returns $\bot$ for decryption queries $c_{MR} = (vk, \mathbf{a}, (c_1, ..., c_t, c_{DEM}), tag)$ satisfying that c_{MR} is not in $\mathcal{L}_{Enc}$ and $c_j = c_j^*$. In addition, Game $0^{(i)}$ is similar to Game $0^{(i-1)}$, for $i = 1, ..., t$, except that a random k_i^{**} instead of k_i^* is used to answer the encryption queries and compute the target ciphertext. For the proof of $|\Pr[Game\ 0^{(i-1)}] - \Pr[Game\ 0^{(i)}]| \leq \epsilon_{KEM}^{(i)}$, the simulator can use $\mathcal{L}_{Enc}$ to answer the decryption queries c_{MR}s which are returned by $\mathcal{O}_{Enc}$.

5   Anonymous Multi-recipient Encryption

In this section, we show how our MRES-SR can be easily converted to an anonymous MRES-SR, denoted by ANOMRES-SR. Let $\mathcal{U} = \{U_1, U_2, ..., U_t\}$ be the universe of all legitimate recipients and $\mathbf{pk} = (pk_1, pk_2, ..., pk_t)$ be an ordered list of recipients' public keys. Let S, a subset of $\mathcal{U}$, be a group of recipients to whom a sender intends to send a message. Anonymity of recipients can be accomplished by sending the message in an encrypted form to all legitimate recipients in such a way that only intended recipients can decrypt the ciphertext correctly. Specifically, the sender takes as input to the encryption algorithm sk_{rcv}, **pk** and m together with S the set of all intended recipients. During the encryption phase, if U_i is a legitimate recipient but not an intended one for this particular message m, that is $U_i \in \mathcal{U}$ and $U_i \notin S$, a randomly chosen k_i in place of the "real" k_i generated by $KEM.Enc(pk_i)$ is used to generate a ciphertext. As a result, the unintended recipient $U_i \notin S$ is denied the ability to decrypt the ciphertext. Decryption and recovery are the same as that of MRES-SR. More details of the modified encryption algorithm follow.

- Encryption $Enc_{MR}(sk_{rcv}, \mathbf{pk}, S, m)$ by the sender
    1. $(vk, sk_{Sig}) \leftarrow Gen_{Sig}(1^\lambda)$. Set $k_{CA,0} = sk_{rcv}$.
       For $i = 1, ..., t$, do
       (a) $(k_i, c_i) \leftarrow KEM.Enc(pk_i)$. If $U_i \notin S$, replace k_i with a random element in the keyspace of KEM. Compute $w_{0,i-1} || s_{0,i-1} || k_{CA,i} \leftarrow H_0(k_{CA,i-1} || vk)$ and $w_{1,i} || s_{1,i} \leftarrow H_1(k_i || vk)$. If $s_{1,i} = s_{0,i-1}$, compute $(k_i, c_i) \leftarrow KEM.Enc(pk_i)$ and $w_{1,i} || s_{1,i} \leftarrow H_1(k_i || vk)$ until $s_{1,i} \neq s_{0,i-1}$.

The remaining steps of encryption are the same as that of MRES-SR.

The IND-CCA2 security of ANOMRES-SR can be proven in a similar way to that of MRES-SR and we only discuss the anonymity of ANOMRES-SR.

5.1   Analysis of Anonymity

Since the public/secret key pairs of MRES-SR are generated by recipients rather than a key generation center as in broadcast encryption, the adversary may choose public keys of his liking to compromise anonymity. In order to capture such attacks, in our security model we allow recipients' public keys to be generated by the adversary. What follows is our new model for anonymity described in its entirety.

- The challenger generates the sender's recovery key sk_{rcv} and a target recipient U_i's public/secret key pair (pk_i, sk_i), for $1 \leq i \leq t$. Let $S_t = \{U_1, U_2, ..., U_t\}$ and $S_c = \{\phi\}$ denote the set of the target recipients and the set of corrupted recipients, respectively. Let $\mathbf{pk} = (pk_1, pk_2, ..., pk_t)$. **pk** is sent to an adversary A who has access to four oracles described below.
    • A private key extraction oracle $\mathcal{O}_{Key}$, which upon a key extraction query $q_{Key} = pk_i$ returns sk_i, where $pk_i \in \mathbf{pk}$. If pk_i is queried, add U_i to S_c.
    • An encryption oracle $\mathcal{O}_{Enc}$, which upon an encryption query $q_{Enc} = (\mathbf{pk}', S, m)$ returns a ciphertext $c_{MR} = Enc_{MR}(sk_{rcv}, \mathbf{pk}', S, m)$. Public keys in $\mathbf{pk}'$ could be generated by the adversary.

- A decryption oracle $\mathcal{O}_{Dec\ i}$ for recipient $U_i \in S_t$, which upon a decryption query $q_{Dec} = c_{MR}$ returns $Dec_{MR}(sk_i, c_{MR})$.
- A recovery oracle $\mathcal{O}_{Rec}$, which upon a recovery query $q_{Rec} = c_{MR}$ returns $Rec_{MR}(sk_{rcv}, c_{MR})$.

- A chooses a message m, $\mathbf{pk}^*$ and two distinct sets $S_0 \subseteq \mathcal{U}^*$ and $S_1 \subseteq \mathcal{U}^*$ such that $(S_0 \backslash S_1) \bigcup (S_1 \backslash S_0) \subseteq S_t \backslash S_c$, where $\mathcal{U}^* = \{U_1^*, U_2^*, ..., U_t^*\}$ is the set of recipients corresponding to $\mathbf{pk}^*$. The challenger returns a target ciphertext $c_{MR}^* \leftarrow Enc_{MR}(sk_{rcv}, \mathbf{pk}^*, S_b, m)$, where $b \stackrel{R}{\leftarrow} \{0,1\}$.
- A can make queries as described above, except that, for $U_i \in (S_0 \backslash S_1) \bigcup (S_1 \backslash S_0)$, A cannot query $\mathcal{O}_{Dec\ i}$ on $q_{Dec} = c_{MR}^*$ or query $\mathcal{O}_{Key}$ on $q_{Key} = pk_i$. Finally, the adversary terminates by returning a guess b'.

MRES-SR is said to be ϵ_{ANO}-anonymous if $|\Pr[Game_{ANO}^{b=0} = 1] - \Pr[Game_{ANO}^{b=1} = 1]| \leq \epsilon_{ANO}$, where $Game_{ANO}^{b=0} = 1$ $(Game_{ANO}^{b=1} = 1)$ denotes the event that $b = b'$ when $b = 0$ $(b = 1)$.

Theorem 2. *ANOMRES-SR is ϵ_{ANO}-anonymous if recipient U_i's KEM is $\epsilon_{KEM}^{(i)}$-IND-CCA2 secure, for $1 \leq i \leq t$, and Sig is ϵ_{Sig}-SU-CMA secure, where $\epsilon_{ANO} \leq \frac{2}{2^{\lambda_1}} + 3t\epsilon_{KEM} + 2\epsilon_{sig}$.*

Theorem 2 can be proven using similar methods in [12] and Claim 2. Descriptions of the proof are omitted due to space limitations.

6   Concluding Remarks

We have proposed an efficient method of constructing a (single message) multi-recipient encryption scheme in a heterogeneous setting, which offers an efficient solution to secure data sharing in a cloud computing environment. The resulting scheme can be used in a stateful manner, achieving significant savings in computation when multiple messages are sent to the same group of recipients. In addition, our scheme enjoys the sender recovery property and can be adapted to offer anonymity of recipients. One of the main techniques we use is the function which maps t strings to one string. A direction for future research is to identify more efficient ways to map t strings to one string without random oracles.

Acknowledgements. This work has been supported by 973 program (No. 2013CB834205), National Natural Science Foundation of China (No. 61103237, No. 61272035), Research Fund for the Doctoral Program of Higher Education of China (No. 20100131120015), Outstanding Young Scientists Foundation Grant of Shandong Province (No. BS2012DX018), Program for New Century Excellent Talents in University of China (No. NCET-13-0350) and Interdisciplinary Research Foundation of Shandong University (No.2012JC018).

References

1. RFC 3851: Secure/multipurpose internet mail extensions (s/mime) version 3.1 message specification, https://tools.ietf.org/html/rfc3851
2. Kurosawa, K.: Multi-recipient public-key encryption with shortened ciphertext. In: Naccache, D., Paillier, P. (eds.) PKC 2002. LNCS, vol. 2274, pp. 48–63. Springer, Heidelberg (2002)
3. Smart, N.P.: Efficient key encapsulation to multiple parties. In: Blundo, C., Cimato, S. (eds.) SCN 2004. LNCS, vol. 3352, pp. 208–219. Springer, Heidelberg (2005)
4. Bellare, M., Boldyreva, A., Staddon, J.: Multi-recipient encryption schemes: Security notions and randomness re-use. In: Desmedt, Y.G. (ed.) PKC 2003. LNCS, vol. 2567, pp. 85–99. Springer, Heidelberg (2002)
5. Bellare, M., Boldyreva, A., Kurosawa, K., Staddon, J.: Multirecipient encryption schemes: How to save on bandwidth and computation without sacrificing security. IEEE Transactions on Information Theory 53(11), 3927–3943 (2007)
6. Barbosa, M., Farshim, P.: Randomness reuse: Extensions and improvements. In: Galbraith, S.D. (ed.) Cryptography and Coding 2007. LNCS, vol. 4887, pp. 257–276. Springer, Heidelberg (2007)
7. Hiwatari, H., Tanaka, K., Asano, T., Sakumoto, K.: Multi-recipient public-key encryption from simulators in security proofs. In: Boyd, C., González Nieto, J. (eds.) ACISP 2009. LNCS, vol. 5594, pp. 293–308. Springer, Heidelberg (2009)
8. Zheng, Y.: Digital signcryption or how to achieve cost (Signature & encryption) << cost(Signature) + cost(Encryption). In: Kaliski Jr., B.S. (ed.) CRYPTO 1997. LNCS, vol. 1294, pp. 165–179. Springer, Heidelberg (1997)
9. Fiat, A., Naor, M.: Broadcast encryption. In: Stinson, D.R. (ed.) CRYPTO 1993. LNCS, vol. 773, pp. 480–491. Springer, Heidelberg (1994)
10. Wei, P., Zheng, Y., Wang, X.: Public key encryption for the forgetful. In: Naccache, D. (ed.) Cryphtography and Security: From Theory to Applications. LNCS, vol. 6805, pp. 185–206. Springer, Heidelberg (2012)
11. Wei, P., Zheng, Y.: Efficient public key encryption admitting decryption by sender. In: De Capitani di Vimercati, S., Mitchell, C. (eds.) EuroPKI 2012. LNCS, vol. 7868, pp. 37–52. Springer, Heidelberg (2013)
12. Libert, B., Paterson, K.G., Quaglia, E.A.: Anonymous broadcast encryption: Adaptive security and efficient constructions in the standard model. In: Fischlin, M., Buchmann, J., Manulis, M. (eds.) PKC 2012. LNCS, vol. 7293, pp. 206–224. Springer, Heidelberg (2012)
13. Zheng, Y., Hardjono, T., Pieprzyk, J.: The sibling intractable function family (SIFF): Notion, construction and applications. IEICE Transactions on Fundamentals of Electronics, Communications and Computer Science E76-A(1), 4–13 (1993)
14. Bellare, M., Kohno, T., Shoup, V.: Stateful public-key cryptosystems: how to encrypt with one 160-bit exponentiation. In: Proceedings of the 13th ACM Conference on Computer and Communications Security, CCS 2006, pp. 380–389. ACM, New York (2006)
15. Cramer, R., Shoup, V.: Design and analysis of practical public-key encryption schemes secure against adaptive chosen ciphertext attack. SIAM Journal on Computing 33(1), 167–226 (2003)
16. Shoup, V.: OAEP reconsidered. In: Kilian, J. (ed.) CRYPTO 2001. LNCS, vol. 2139, pp. 239–259. Springer, Heidelberg (2001)

ACP-lrFEM: Functional Encryption Mechanism with Automatic Control Policy in the Presence of Key Leakage

Mingwu Zhang[1,2,*]

[1] School of Computer Sciences, Hubei University of Technology
[2] State Key Laboratory of Information Security,
Institute of Information Engineering, Chinese Academy of Sciences
csmwzhang@gmail.com

Abstract. We present a leakage-resilient functional encryption from finite automata control policy, in which the ciphertext is associated with an input string w and the private key is connected to a finite automata $\mathcal{M}$. The decryption will succeed iff the automata accepts the string, i.e., $Accept(\mathcal{M}, w) = 1$. In our scheme, we allow the leakage of sensitive key by allowing the attacker to provide an efficiently computable function (leakage function) adaptively, and to receive the output of the function taking the private key as input. Our security model considers two sides: *key-leakage resilience* and *plaintext confidentiality*. Not only can the attacker request the reveal of all *non-match keys* of finite automata, but can query the leakage for the *match key*. We also deploy an update algorithm to support the continual leakage resilience. We give the construction in bilinear groups of composite order and prove the security in dual system framework. The analysis shows that the maximum leakage of the key can be 33%.

Keywords: Deterministic Finite Automata, Leakage resilience, Match key.

1 Introduction

BACKGROUND Traditional provable security is implemented in an idealized environment, in which the sensitive information such as private keys and internal states are perfectly hidden from the attacker. That is, the attacker must not see any bit of the sensitive information in the cryptosystem, but is able to access to the input/output of the cryptographic algorithms. Otherwise, the provable security reduction will fail. However, in practice, the key may be leaked to the possible attacker. For example, the attacker can obtain the partial sensitive key by measuring the timing, power-consumption, temperature, radiation, acoustics and so on [4,18,2,5,8,20]. A large body of work has investigated techniques to improve the security of cryptographic implementations. Motivated by the challenge

* Supported by the National Natural Science Foundation of China (#61370224), the Key Program of Natural Science Foundation of Hubei Province (#2013CFA046), and the Open Fund Program for State Key Laboratory of Information Security.

X. Huang and J. Zhou (Eds.): ISPEC 2014, LNCS 8434, pp. 481–495, 2014.

in the key leakage setting, several works have also considered the possibility to evaluate the effectiveness of countermeasures against side-channel attacks in a more formal manner, and to design new primitives against such attacks. There have two methods to countermeasure these attacks. One is to reduce or avoid the leakage by reinforcing the hardware. The other method is to provide a leakage-resilient scheme to survive the leakage. In this paper, we consider the latter model, in which the attacker is allowed to observe leakage from the private key. Leakage-resilient cryptosystems[7,9,12,19,25] are designed to keep secure even though partial information about the key is leaked.

Functional encryption is a type of public-key encryption in which possessing a private key allows one to learn a function of what the ciphertext is encrypting, which was proposed by Sahai and Waters in 2005[22] and later formalized by Boneh, Sahai and Waters[3]. Ideally, it is possible to derive secret keys DK_F for any function F. However, most instantiations of this type of encryption supported only limited function classes such as boolean formulae[22,14].

In order to provide a more general functional encryption system, Waters[23] proposed a scheme for regular language policy. Recently, in [21], Ramanna constructed a deterministic finite automata encryption with adaptive security, however, the restriction of the scheme is that the keys associated with the automata is only one unique final state and a single transition corresponding to each symbol. Also, in their scheme the key leakage is not allowed. Goldwasser et al.[11] considered how to perform the Turing machines on the encryption data, which is considered as a generalized data protect and access control over the ciphertext space. However, as the complex functionality of the Turing machine (evaluating an algorithm over encrypted data is as slow as the worst-case running time of the algorithm), the authors constructed several schemes in different control policies.

In this work, we focus on the leakage-resilient security model of functional encryption from the finite automata policy, in which the ciphertext is associated with an input string w and the key is associated with a deterministic finite automata $\mathcal{M}$. The decryption succeeds if and only if the automata accepts the string, i.e., $Accept(\mathcal{M}, w) = 1$. We take a methodical approach, by studying resilience to key leakage within the framework of functional encryption, in which the attacker allows to obtain any polynomial-time computable function of the key in every time-period, as long as the information thus obtained is *bounded*.

OUR TECHNIQUE We give the leakage-resilient semantic security model of functional encryption for finite automatic policy. In this model, the attacker can gain the sensitive key by providing an efficiently computable function (leakage function) and gaining the output of the function taking the private key as input. The attacker can select different leakage functions at different point of time based on its view and prior leakage information.

One of the main challenge in leakage-resilient cryptography is to obtain proofs of security, under realistic assumptions and for efficient constructions. We divide the queried key (including extracted keys and leaked keys) into two parts: *non-match key* and *match key*. We call the key $DK_{\mathcal{M}}$ of finite automata $\mathcal{M}$ to be matched if the key can decrypt the challenge ciphertext CT_w, i.e.,

$Accept(\mathcal{M}, \boldsymbol{w}) = 1$. Otherwise the key is non-matched if $Accept(\mathcal{M}, \boldsymbol{w}) = 0$. In the traditional partition proof technique, the attacker cannot query the match key. However, in our model, we allow the attacker to perform the leakage query for the match key. We give the concrete construction in the dual system framework, and implement the proofs by virtue of a series of dual system transformations. We organize two types of semi-functional key: *type-1 semi-functional* and *type-2 semi-functional*. In type-1 semi-functional key, all components have virtual $\mathcal{G}_2$ part and in type-2 semi-functional key only the components associated with the master key have $\mathcal{G}_2$ part.

In order to show that, even the attacker obtains at most L bits key leakage and has negligible advantage to decrypt the challenge ciphertext $\mathtt{CT}_{\boldsymbol{w}}$. We extend the type-2 semi-functional key into two types: *truly type-2* semi-functional and *nominally type-2* semi-functional. A truly semi-functional key can not gain non-negligible in decrypting the challenge semi-functional ciphertext, and a nominally semi-functional key can decrypt the challenge ciphertext with some probability. By the algebra lemma 1, we prove that an attacker has no advantage in transforming a truly semi-functional key into a nominally semi-functional form even the attacker can gain some leakage on the key.

We employ a key update algorithm to achieve the continual leakage resilience. More interesting, unlike in updating the private key using additional secret information that never leaks (named *floppy model*) by Agrawal et al.[1], we consider that any user can update his secret key only taking his key and automata as inputs.

2   Encryption with Automatic Control Policy in the Presence of Key Leakage

We give the formal model and security definition of leakage-resilient functional encryption from finite automatic policy (`ACP-lrFEM`), where the key is associated with a deterministic finite automata and the ciphertext is associated with an input string. Let $\mathcal{P}$ and $\mathcal{C}$ be the plaintext space and the ciphertext space, respectively, and let $\mathcal{F}$ be the computable leakage function family.

Definition 1. *(Deterministic finite automata (DFA))[13] A finite automata is a finite state machine that accepts/rejects finite strings of symbols and only produces a unique run of the automation for each input string. A DFA $\mathcal{M}$ is formally defined as a 5-tuple $(X, \Sigma, \delta, q_0, Y)$:*

1. *A finite set of states X;*
2. *A finite set of input symbols called the alphabet Σ;*
3. *A transition function $\delta: X \times \Sigma \to X$;*
4. *A start state $q_0 \in X$;*
5. *A set of accept states $Y \subseteq X$.*

Let $\boldsymbol{w} = w_1 w_2 \cdots w_n$ be a string over the alphabet Σ. The automation $\mathcal{M}$ accepts the string $\boldsymbol{w}$ if a sequence of states, $r_0, r_1, \cdots, r_n$, exists in X with the following conditions:

1. $r_0 = q_0$, which denotes that the machine $\mathcal{M}$ starts from the start state q_0;
2. $r_{i+1} = \delta(r_i, w_{i+1})$, for $i = 1, 2, \cdots, n-1$, which means that given each character of string w, the machine $\mathcal{M}$ will transition from a state r_i to another state r_{i+1} according to the transition function δ on the input w_{i+1};
3. $r_n \in Y$, which means that the machine $\mathcal{M}$ accepts w if the last input of string w causes the machine to halt in one of the accepting states in Y. We write the machine $\mathcal{M}$ accepts(rejects) the string w by $Accept(\mathcal{M}, w) = 1(0)$.

The structure of the DFA is determined by its transition function δ, which maps each state r_i and a given input symbol w_{i+1} to a new state r_{i+1}. the output function of a DFA $\mathcal{M}$ for all input $w_1 w_2 \cdots w_n$ is defined as

$$Accept(\mathcal{M}, w) = \begin{cases} 1, & \text{if } \delta(r_{n-1}, w_n) \in Y \\ 0, & \text{if } \delta(r_{n-1}, w_n) \notin Y \end{cases} \tag{1}$$

Definition 2. *(ACP-lrFEM) A leakage-resilient functional encryption from finite automatic policy (ACP-lrFEM) is comprised of the following five probabilistic polynomial-time algorithms.*

1. $(PP, MK) \leftarrow SysGen(1^\kappa, \Sigma, L)$ *The system setup algorithm takes a security parameter κ, a universe of alphabet Σ and an allowable private-key leakage bound L as inputs, and outputs system public key PP and master key MK. Note that the system public key can be seen by all participants in the system and will be the input in all other algorithms. In the rest of this paper, all algorithms will take implicitly the public key PP as their inputs.*
2. $DK_\mathcal{M} \leftarrow KeyExt(MK, \mathcal{M})$ *The key generation algorithm takes the master key MK, and a deterministic finite automata $\mathcal{M}$ as inputs, and outputs a private key $DK_\mathcal{M}$.*
3. $DK'_\mathcal{M} \leftarrow KeyUpd(DK_\mathcal{M}, \mathcal{M})$ *The key update algorithm takes a private key $DK_\mathcal{M}$ and its automata as inputs and outputs a re-randomized key $DK'_\mathcal{M}$.*
4. $CT_w \leftarrow Enc(M, w)$ *The encryption algorithm takes a plaintext M and a string $w = w_1 w_2 \cdots w_n$ as inputs, and outputs a ciphertext CT_w.*
5. $M/\bot \leftarrow Dec(CT_w, DK_\mathcal{M})$ *The decryption algorithm takes a ciphertext CT_w and a key $DK_\mathcal{M}$ as inputs, and outputs M if and only if the string w is accepted by the automata $\mathcal{M}$, i.e., $Accept(\mathcal{M}, w) = 1$.*

Definition 3. *(Consistency) Assume κ to be a security parameter. For all correctly generated PP and MK, and $DK_\mathcal{M}$ is created from any deterministic finite automata in ACP-lrFEM scheme. The amount leakage of $DK_\mathcal{M}$ is prescribed a limit L, i.e., $\sum_i f_i(DK_\mathcal{M}) \le L$. For the leakage function family $\mathcal{F}$, the consistency of ACP-lrFEM is guaranteed by the following probability in parameter κ:*

$$\Pr \begin{bmatrix} (PP, MK) \leftarrow SysGen(1^\kappa, \Sigma, L); \ \forall \mathcal{M}, w, s.t.\ Accept(\mathcal{M}, w) = 1; \\ DK_\mathcal{M} \leftarrow KeyExt(MK, \mathcal{M}); \ \forall i, f_i \in \mathcal{F}, \ \sum_i f_i(DK_\mathcal{M}) \le L; \\ DK'_\mathcal{M} \leftarrow KeyUpd(DK_\mathcal{M}, \mathcal{M}); \ \forall i, g_i \in \mathcal{F}, \ \sum_i g_i(DK'_\mathcal{M}) \le L; \\ CT_w \leftarrow Enc(M, w); \ Dec(CT_w, DK'_\mathcal{M}) \ne M. \end{bmatrix} = \varepsilon(\kappa) \tag{2}$$

where the probability is taken over the coins of algorithms SysGen, KeyExt, KeyUpd and Enc.

Our security model considers twofold: key-leakage resilience and message confidentiality. We follow the natural key-leakage resilient security definition from [2], which roughly states that an encryption is L-leakage-resilient if it remains secure despite the fact that an attacker can learn up to L bits of arbitrary information on the private key of being attacked.

We also achieve the plaintext confidentiality for the encryption scheme. Indistinguishability requires that no efficient attacker is able to distinguish a real distribution from an idealized one (e.g. uniform randomness) with non-negligible advantage. A functional encryption scheme is leakage-resilient semantically secure (indistinguishability against adaptive chosen-plaintext attacks in the presence of leakage) when the attacker obtain partial information on the decryption key. We model the key leakage by allowing the attacker to query the leakage oracle that taking the private key as input and obtaining the (leakage) output of the key. In order to record the queried and leaked keys, we set two initially empty lists: $\mathcal{L}_1 = \langle \chi, w \rangle$, $\mathcal{L}_2 = \langle \chi, w, \mathrm{DK}_{\mathcal{M}}, l \rangle$ to store the records, where all records are associated with a handle χ.

Definition 4. *(Key leakage fraction) The leakage fraction γ is defined as the relative leakage of a key DK, i.e., $\gamma = \frac{L}{|DK|}$, where L is an allowable leakage bound and $|DK|$ is the size of a key DK.*

Definition 5. *(Leakage-resilient experiment) The leakage-resilient experiment $\Lambda_0(1^\kappa, \Sigma, L)$ works between a challenger $\mathcal{C}$ and an attacker $\mathcal{A}$ as follows.*

Step 1: **Setup phase.** *In this stage, the challenger $\mathcal{C}$ runs the setup algorithm to generate public key PP and master key MK, and starts the interaction with $\mathcal{A}$. In this stage, $\mathcal{C}$ also creates two empty lists $\mathcal{L}_1$ and $\mathcal{L}_2$ defined as aforementioned.*

Step 2: **Lunch query phase.** *In this stage, attacker $\mathcal{A}$ can request the following oracles for some information about the key knowledge adaptively:*

   i. **Key extraction oracle (Ω_E):**
   ii. **Key leakage oracle (Ω_L):**
   iii. **Key update oracle (Ω_U):**

Step 3: **Challenge phase.** *$\mathcal{A}$ outputs two challenged plaintexts $(M^{(0)}, M^{(1)})$ and a string w s.t. $\forall w \in \mathcal{L}_2$ $Accept(\mathcal{M}, w) = 0$, i.e., $\mathcal{M}$ rejects the string w. $\mathcal{C}$ at random toss a coins η and then responds the challenge ciphertext as $CT^{(\eta)} = Enc(M^{(\eta)}, w)$.*

Step 4: **Supper query.** *$\mathcal{A}$ continues to issues the queries like in Lunch query with the restriction that $\mathcal{A}$ can not request for the leakage oracle Ω_L in this stage.*

Step 5: **Output.** *Finally, in this stage, $\mathcal{A}$ outputs a bit $\eta' \in \{0, 1\}$ as the guess for the random coin η in the challenge phase. Adversary $\mathcal{A}$'s advantage in experiment $\Lambda_0(1^\kappa, \Sigma, L)$ is defined as $Adv_{\mathcal{A}}(1^\kappa, \Sigma, L) = |2Pr[(\eta = \eta')] - 1|$.*

Definition 6. *(Adaptively key-leakage resilient semantic security) Suppose that the system security parameter is κ, the leakage bound is L and a polynomial-time attacker has at most Q queries for keys. A leakage-resilient functional encryption scheme is adaptively (Q, L, γ)-semantically secure if the advantage of the attacker in winning $\Lambda_0(\kappa, \Sigma, L)$ is less than $\varepsilon(\kappa)$ in security parameter κ and leakage bound L, where γ is defined as $\gamma = \frac{L}{|DK|}$. More concretely, for any attacker in the experiment $\Lambda_0(\kappa, \Sigma, L)$, the attacker gains at most γ fraction for each key, and the advantage $Adv_A(1^\kappa, \Sigma, L)$ is computationally negligible parameterized by κ.*

Definition 7. *(Selectively key-leakage resilient semantic security) A leakage-resilient functional encryption scheme is selectively (Q, L, γ)-semantically secure, if in the experiment $\lambda_\rangle(\kappa, \Sigma, L)$ the challenge finite automata $\mathcal{M}$ had to provide ahead of Step 1 (in Step 0, the attacker provides the challenge $\mathcal{M}$ before the public key and master key build), and the advantage $Adv_A(1^\kappa, \Sigma, L)$ is computationally negligible parameterized by κ.*

3   Construction of ACP-lrFEM

In this section, we give the concrete construction for our scheme.

ACP-lrFEM.SysGen($1^\kappa, \Sigma, L$) Taking as input a security parameter $\kappa \in \mathcal{Z}^+$, an alphabet set Σ for the finite automata, and a leakage bound L, this algorithm creates system public key PP and master key MK as follows:

S1. Run the bilinear group generator algorithm GCP(κ) to produce (p_1, p_2, p_3, $\mathcal{G}, \mathcal{H}, e$), where p_1, p_2 and p_3 are distinct primes, i.e., $e : \mathcal{G} \times \mathcal{G} \to \mathcal{H}$, and $gcd(p_1, p_2, p_3) = 1$.[1] Set subgroups $\mathcal{G}_1 = \langle P_1 \rangle$, $\mathcal{G}_2 = \langle P_2 \rangle$ and $\mathcal{G}_3 = \langle P_3 \rangle$ of orders p_1, p_2 and p_3 respectively, and P_1, P_2 and P_3 are the generators of subgroups $\mathcal{G}_1, \mathcal{G}_2$ and $\mathcal{G}_3$ respectively; Define $\mathcal{G} = \mathcal{G}_1 \times \mathcal{G}_2 \times \mathcal{G}_3$ and set $N = p_1 p_2 p_3$.

S2. Select $\tau \in \mathbb{R}^+$ such that $\varepsilon = p_2^{-\tau}$ is small enough, and compute $\omega = \lceil 1 + 2\tau + L/|p_2| \rceil$.

S3. Select random elements $Z, H_{st}, H_{end} \in \mathcal{G}_1$.

S4. At random choose $y \in \mathcal{Z}_N$; For each $\sigma \in \Sigma$, pick $H_\sigma \in \mathcal{G}_1$.

S5. Set the master key

$$MK = \langle (\boldsymbol{\beta}_i P_1)_{i \in [\omega]}, (y + \langle \boldsymbol{\alpha}, \boldsymbol{\beta} \rangle) P_1 \rangle$$

S6. Publish the system public key

$$PP = \langle \Theta, Z, P_1, P_3, H_{st}, H_{end}, \forall \sigma \in \Sigma \ H_\sigma, (\boldsymbol{\alpha}_i P_1)_{i \in [\omega]}, (T_i)_{i \in \Sigma}, e(P_1, P_1)^y \rangle$$

Here $\Theta = (N, \mathcal{G}, \mathcal{H}, e)$. In the setting, the parameter ω, mainly decided by L, can be varied to achieve desired key leakage and size of keys/ciphertexts. Obviously, the larger L, the larger of keys and ciphertexts.

---

[1] $gcd(p_1, p_2) = gcd(p_2, p_3) = gcd(p_1, p_3) = 1$.

ACP-lrFEM.Enc$(M, \boldsymbol{w} = w_1 w_2 \cdots w_n)$ Taking as input a plaintext M and a string $\boldsymbol{w} = w_1 w_2 \cdots w_n$, this algorithm at random picks $s_0, s_1, \cdots, s_n \in \mathcal{Z}_N$, and calculates the ciphertext $\mathtt{CT}_{\boldsymbol{w}}$ as:

$$
\mathtt{CT}_{\boldsymbol{w}} = \begin{pmatrix} \boldsymbol{w}, & C_m \\ C_{st,1}, & C_{st,2} \\ C_{1,1}, & C_{1,2} \\ \vdots & \vdots \\ C_{n,1}, & C_{n,2} \\ C_{end,1}, & C_{end,2} \\ C_{fin} \end{pmatrix} = \begin{pmatrix} \boldsymbol{w}, & M \cdot e(P_1, P_1)^{y s_n} \\ s_0 P_1, & s_0 H_{st} \\ s_1 P_1, & s_1 H_{w_1} + s_0 Z \\ \vdots & \vdots \\ s_n P_1, & s_n H_{w_n} + s_{n-1} Z \\ s_n P_1, & s_n H_{end} \\ (\boldsymbol{\alpha}_i^{s_n} P_1)_{i \in [\omega]} \end{pmatrix} \tag{3}
$$

ACP-lrFEM.KeyExt$(\mathtt{MK}, \mathcal{M} = (X, \Sigma, q_0, \delta, Y))$ Assume the automata $\mathcal{M}$ including a set X of states $q_0, q_1, \cdots, q_{|X|-1}$, in which q_0 is the start state. Taking as input the master key $\mathtt{MK}$ and a finite automata $\mathcal{M}$, this algorithm creates the key $\mathtt{DK}_{\mathcal{M}}$ as follows:

K1. At random pick $D_0, D_1, \cdots, D_{|X|-1} \in \mathcal{G}_1$, and associate each q_i with D_i.

K2. Choose $r_{st}, r_{end} \in \mathcal{Z}_N$ and $R_{st,1}, R_{st,2}, R_{end,1}, R_{end,2} \in \mathcal{G}_3$ randomly, and for each transition $t \in \mathcal{T}$ (t is defined by a triple $(q_x, q_y, \delta) \in X \times X \times \Sigma$) select $r_t \in \mathcal{Z}_N$.

K3. For $t \in \mathcal{T}$, select $R_{t,1}, R_{t,2}, R_{t,3} \in \mathcal{G}_3$ randomly.

K4. Calculate $K_{st,1} = D_0 + r_{st} H_{st} + R_{st,1}$, $K_{st,2} = r_{st} P_1 + R_{st,2}$.

K5. For all $t \in \mathcal{T}$ with $t = (q_x, q_y, \delta)$, calculate $K_{t,1} = -D_x + r_t Z + R_{t,1}$, $K_{t,2} = r_t P_1 + R_{t,2}$ and $K_{t,3} = D_y + r_t H_\sigma + R_{t,3}$.

K6. For each $q_y \in Y$, at random select $r_{end_y} \in \mathcal{Z}_N$, $R_{end_y,1}, R_{end_y,2} \in \mathcal{G}_3$, and calculate $K_{end_y,1} = (y + \langle \boldsymbol{\alpha}, \boldsymbol{\beta} \rangle) P_1 + D_y + r_{end_y} H_{end} + R_{end_y,1}$, and $K_{end_y,2} = r_{end_y} P_1 + R_{end_y,2}$.

K7. For $i \in [\omega]$ at random pick $R_{fin,i} \in \mathcal{G}_3$, and calculate $K_{fin,i} = \boldsymbol{\beta}_i P_1 + R_{fin,i}$.

K8. Finally, output

$$
\mathtt{DK}_{\mathcal{M}} = \langle (K_{st,1}, K_{st,2}), (K_{t,1}, K_{t,2}, K_{t,3})_{t \in \mathcal{T}}, (K_{end_y,1}, K_{end_y,2})_{q_y \in Y}, (K_{fin,i})_{i \in [\omega]} \rangle \tag{4}
$$

ACP-lrFEM.KeyUpd$(\mathtt{DK}_{\mathcal{M}}, \mathcal{M} = (X, \Sigma, q_0, \delta, Y))$ Let a secret key $\mathtt{DK}_{\mathcal{M}} = \langle K_{st,1}, K_{st,2}, (K_{t,1}, K_{t,2}, K_{t,3})_{t \in \mathcal{T}}, (K_{end_y,1}, K_{end_y,2})_{q_y \in Y}, (K_{fin,i})_{i \in [\omega]} \rangle$. The algorithm proceeds the following steps to refresh a key:

U1. At random pick $r'_{st} \in \mathcal{Z}_N$ and $R'_{st,1}, R'_{st,2} \in \mathcal{G}_3$, and update the start part key: $K'_{st,1} = K_{st,1} + r'_{st} H_{st} + R'_{st,1}$, $K'_{st,2} = K_{st,2} + r'_{st} P_1 + R'_{st,2}$.

U2. For all $t \in \mathcal{T}$ with $t = (q_x, q_y, \delta)$, at random select $r'_t \in \mathcal{Z}_N$, $R'_{t,1}, R'_{t,2}, R'_{t,3} \in \mathcal{G}_3$, and update the transition key: $\forall t \in \mathcal{T}$ with $t = (q_x, q_y, \delta)$, set $K'_{t,1} = K_{t,1} + r'_t Z + R'_{t,1}$, $K'_{t,2} = K_{t,2} + r'_t P_1 + R'_{t,2}$ and $K'_{t,3} = K_{t,3} + r'_t H_\sigma + R'_{t,3}$.

U3. For each $q_y \in Y$, at random select $r'_{end_y} \in \mathcal{Z}_N$, $R'_{end_y,1}, R'_{end_y,2} \in \mathcal{G}_3$, and update the end part key: $K'_{end_y,1} = K_{end_y,1} + r'_{end_y} H_{end} + R'_{end_y,1}$, and $K'_{end_y,2} = K_{end,2} + r'_{end_y} P_1 + R'_{end,2}$.

U4. At random select $R_{fin,i} \in \mathcal{G}_3$ for $i \in [\omega]$, and update key final part key: $K'_{fin,i} = K_{fin,i} + R'_{fin,i}$.

U5. Delete $\mathrm{DK}_\mathcal{M}$ and output the new key

$$\mathrm{DK}'_\mathcal{M} = \langle (K'_{st,1}, K'_{st,2}), (K'_{t,1}, K'_{t,2}, K'_{t,3})_{t \in \mathcal{T}}, (K'_{end_y,1}, K'_{end_y,2})_{q_y \in Y}, (K'_{fin,i})_{i \in [\omega]} \rangle$$

$\mathrm{ACP\text{-}1rFEM.Dec}(\mathrm{CT}_w, \mathrm{DK}_\mathcal{M})$ If $Accept(\mathcal{M}, w) = 1$, that is, the finite automata $\mathcal{M}$ accepts string w, then there exist a sequence of $n+1$ states $u_0, u_1, \cdots, u_n$ and n transitions $t_1, t_2, \cdots, t_n$ such that $u_0 = q_0$ and $u_n \in Y$. For $i = 1, \cdots, n$, we have $t_i = (u_{i-1}, u_i, w_i) \in \mathcal{T}$. The decryption procedure is performed as follows:

D1. At first calculate the initialization state:

$$B_0 = \frac{e(C_{st,1}, K_{st,1})}{e(C_{st,2}, K_{st,2})} = e(D_0, C_{st,1}) = e(D_0, P_1)^{s_0}$$

D2. For $i = 1$ to n, calculate iteratively:

$$B_i = B_{i-1} \cdot \frac{e(C_{i-1,1}, K_{t_i,1}) e(C_{i,1}, K_{t_i,3})}{e(C_{i,2}, K_{t_i,2})} = e(D_{u_i}, C_{i,1}) = e(D_{u_i}, P_1)^{s_i}$$

D3. As the automata $\mathcal{M}$ accepts the string w, then the last state u_n must halt in Y. That is, $u_n = q_y$ for some $q_y \in Y$ and $B_n = e(D_y, P_1)^{s_n}$. Calculate:

$$B_{end} = B_n \cdot \frac{e(C_{end,2}, K_{end_y,2})}{e(C_{end,1}, K_{end_y,1})} = e(P_1, P_1)^{-s_n(y + \langle \alpha, \beta \rangle)}$$

D4. Calculate $B_{fin} = B_{end} \cdot e_n(C_{fin}, K_{fin}) = e(P_1, P_1)^{-y s_n}$

D5. Extract the plaintext from C_m by $M \leftarrow C_m \cdot B_{fin}$.

4   Analysis

4.1   Consistency

First, we show that any key component in $\mathcal{G}_3$ will cancel since subgroups $\mathcal{G}_1$ and $\mathcal{G}_3$ are orthogonal but the ciphertext in $\mathcal{G}_1$ and the key in $\mathcal{G}_1 \times \mathcal{G}_3$. We give the correctness and consistency as below:

$$
\begin{aligned}
B_0 &= \frac{e(C_{st,1}, K_{st,1})}{e(C_{st,2}, K_{st,2})} = \frac{e(s_0 P_1, D_0 + r_{st} H_{st} + R_{st,1})}{e(s_0 H_{st}, r_{st} P_1 + R_{st,2})} \\
&= \frac{e(s_0 P_1, D_0) e(s_0 P_1, r_{st} H_{st})}{e(s_0 H_{st}, r_{st} P_1)} = e(D_0, P_1)^{s_0}
\end{aligned}
\tag{5}
$$

$$B_i = B_{i-1} \cdot \frac{e(C_{i-1,1}, K_{t_i,1}) e(C_{i,1}, K_{t_i,3})}{e(C_{i,2}, K_{t_i,2})}$$

$$= \frac{e(D_{i-1}, P_1)^{s_{i-1}} e(s_{i-1}P_1, -D_{x_i} + r_{t_i}Z) e(s_i P_1, D_{y_i} + r_{t_i}H_{w_i})}{e(s_i H_{w_i} + s_{i-1}Z, r_{t_i}P_1)}$$

$$= \frac{e(s_{i-1}P_1, r_{t_i}Z) e(s_i P_1, D_{y_i}) e(s_i P_1, r_{t_i}H_{w_i})}{e(s_i H_{w_i}, r_{t_i}P_1) e(s_{i-1}Z, r_{t_i}P_1)}$$

$$= e(s_i P_1, D_{y_i}) = e(D_{y_i}, P_1)^{s_i} \tag{6}$$

$$B_{end} = B_n \cdot \frac{e(C_{end,2}, K_{end_y,2})}{e(C_{end,1}, K_{end_y,1})}$$

$$= \frac{e(D_{y_i}, P_1)^{s_n} e(s_n H_{end}, r_{end_y}P_1 + R_{end,2})}{e(s_n P_1, (y + \langle \alpha, \beta \rangle)P_1 + D_{y_i} + r_{end_y}H_{end})}$$

$$= \frac{e(D_{y_i}, P_1)^{s_n} e(s_n H_{end}, r_{end_y}P_1)}{e(s_n P_1, (y + \langle \alpha, \beta \rangle)P_1 + D_{y_i} + r_{end_y}H_{end})}$$

$$= \frac{e(D_{y_i}, P_1)^{s_n} e(s_n H_{end}, r_{end_y}P_1)}{e(s_n P_1, yP_1) e(s_n P_1, P_1)^{\langle \alpha, \beta \rangle} e(s_n P_1, D_{y_i}) e(s_n P_1, r_{end_y}H_{end})}$$

$$= \frac{1}{e(P_1, P_1)^{s_n y} e(P_1, P_1)^{s_n \langle \alpha, \beta \rangle}} = \frac{1}{e(P_1, P_1)^{s_n (y + \langle \alpha, \beta \rangle)}} \tag{7}$$

$$B_{fin} = B_{end} \cdot e_n(C_{fin}, K_{fin}) = \frac{\prod_{i \in [\omega]} e(s_n \alpha_i P_1, \beta_i P_1)}{e(P_1, P_1)^{s_n (y + \langle \alpha, \beta \rangle)}}$$

$$= \frac{e(P_1, P_1)^{\Sigma_{i \in [\omega]} s_n \alpha_i \beta_i}}{e(P_1, P_1)^{s_n (y + \langle \alpha, \beta \rangle)}} = e(P_1, P_1)^{-y s_n} \tag{8}$$

4.2   Subspaces for Leakage Resilience over Transformation

We provide the algebraic tool to apply in our scheme. More specifically, we give an algebraic theorem and its claim that essentially say that the subspaces are resilient to continual leakage.

Lemma 1. *(Subspace for Leakage Map)[6]* Let $m, l, d \in \mathcal{Z}^+$, $2d \le l \le m$ and p be a prime. Let $A_1 \xleftarrow{R} \mathcal{Z}_p^{m \times l}$ and $A_2 \xleftarrow{R} \mathcal{Z}_p^{m \times d}$, and $T \xleftarrow{R} Rank_d(\mathcal{Z}_p^{l \times d})$ *(i.e., the rank of matrix T is d). For any transformation $f : \mathcal{Z}_p^{m \times d} \to \{0, 1\}^L$, there exists $\Delta((A_1, f(A_1 T)), (A_1, f(A_2))) \le \varepsilon(\cdot)$, as long as $L \le 4(1 - 1/p) \cdot p^{l-2d+1} \cdot \varepsilon(\cdot)^2$.*

We note that, if the leakage $f(A_1 T)$ reveals bounded information A_1, then $(A_1, f(A_1 T))$ and $(A_1, f(A_2))$ are statistically close. A_2 is a random vector and the leakage function $f(A_2)$ reveals nothing about the space A_1. By setting $d = 1$ and $l = m - 1$, we have the following claim.

Claim. Let $W, \boldsymbol{S} \xleftarrow{R} \mathcal{Z}_p^\omega$ and $\boldsymbol{S}'$ be selected uniformly randomly from the set of vector in $\mathcal{Z}_p^\omega$ which are orthogonal to W under the inner product modulo p_2. For any transformation $f : \mathcal{Z}_{p_2}^\omega \to \{0,1\}^L$, where the function output is bounded by the length L, then $\Delta((W, f(\boldsymbol{S})), (W, f(\boldsymbol{S}'))) \leq \varepsilon(\cdot)$, as long as $L \leq 4p_2^{\omega-3}(p_2 - 1) \cdot \varepsilon(\cdot)^2$.

4.3 Leakage-resilient Semantic Security

The key-leakage resilience and plaintext-adaptive confidentiality will be proven under the framework of dual system encryption[17,24] and Theorem 1. By means of dual system encryption mechanism, we first give the semi-functional ciphertext/key generation algorithms and convert the challenge ciphertext and queried keys into semi-functional form. We also define two types of semi-functional key: type-1 form and type-2 form. Let P_2 be a random generator of subgroup $\mathcal{G}_2$. The semi-functional key and ciphertext are constructed as follows:

KeyExtSF algorithm. Let $\mathrm{DK}_{\mathcal{M}} = \langle K_{st,1}, K_{st,2}, (K_{t,1}, K_{t,2}, K_{t,3})_{t \in \mathcal{T}}, (K_{end_y,1}, K_{end_y,2})_{q_y \in Y}, (K_{fin,i})_{i \in [\omega]} \rangle$ be a normal key that is produced by **KeyExt** algorithm, a semi-functional key is constructed as:

Type 1: In type-1 semi-functional key, all components are attached with $\mathcal{G}_2$ parts.

$$
\hat{\mathrm{DK}}_{\mathcal{M}} = \underbrace{\begin{pmatrix} K_{st,1}, & K_{st,2} \\ (K_{t_i,1}, & K_{t_i,2}, & K_{t_i,3})_{t_i \in \mathcal{T}} \\ (K_{end_{y_i},1}, & K_{end_{y_i},2})_{y_i \in Y} \\ (K_{fin,i})_{i \in [\omega]} \end{pmatrix}}_{\text{Normal key}}
$$

$$
+ \underbrace{\begin{pmatrix} z_0 + \mu_{st}\pi_{st}, & \mu_{st} \\ (z_x + \mu_{t_i}, & \mu_{t_i}, & z_y + \mu_{t_i})_{t_i \in \mathcal{T}} \\ (z_{f_{y_i}} + \tau_{end_{y_i}}, & \mu_{end_{y_i}})_{y_i \in Y} \\ (\vartheta_{fin,i})_{i \in [\omega]} \end{pmatrix}}_{\text{Mixed } \mathcal{G}_2 \text{ part}} P_2 \qquad (9)
$$

where $z_0, z_x, z_y, \mu_{st}, \mu_{st_i}, \mu_{end_{y_i}}, \vartheta_{fin,i}$ are randomly chosen from $\mathcal{Z}_N$.

Type 2: In this type of semi-functional key, only the components $K_{end_{y_i},1}$, $K_{end_{y_i},2}$ and K_{fin} contain $\mathcal{G}_2$ part, which means that only the components involved the master key y have $\mathcal{G}_2$ part. Also, in this form, the term $z_{f_{y_i}}$ is removed from the components, that is, $\hat{K}_{end_{y_i},1} = K_{end_{y_i},1} + \tau_{end_{y_i}}P_2$, $\hat{K}_{end_{y_i},2} = K_{end_{y_i},2} + \mu_{end_{y_i}}P_2$, $\hat{K}_{fin,i} = K_{fin,i} + P_2$ and the other components are unchanged.

EncSF algorithm. Let $\mathrm{CT}_{\boldsymbol{w}} = \langle \boldsymbol{w}, C_m, C_{st,1}, C_{st,2}, (C_{i,1}, C_{i,2})_{i \in [n]}, C_{end,1}, C_{end,2}, \boldsymbol{C}_{fin} \rangle$ be a normal ciphertext generated by **Enc** algorithm, a semi-functional ciphertext is converted as:

$$
\hat{\mathrm{CT}}_{w} =
\underbrace{
\begin{pmatrix}
w, & C_m \\
C_{st,1}, & C_{st,2} \\
C_{1,1}, & C_{1,2} \\
\vdots & \vdots \\
C_{n,1}, & C_{n,2} \\
C_{end,1}, & C_{end,2} \\
C_{fin} &
\end{pmatrix}
}_{\text{Normal ciphertext}}
+
\underbrace{
\begin{pmatrix}
0, & 0 \\
\gamma_0, & \gamma_0 \pi_{st} \\
\gamma_1, & \gamma_1 \pi_{w_i} + \gamma_{i-1} \\
\vdots & \vdots \\
\gamma_n, & \gamma_n \pi_{w_n} + \gamma_{n-1} \\
\gamma_n, & \pi_{end} \\
\boldsymbol{\theta}_{fin} &
\end{pmatrix} P_2
}_{\text{Mixed } \mathcal{G}_2 \text{ part}}
\tag{10}
$$

where $\gamma_0, \gamma_1, \cdots, \gamma_n, \pi_{st}, \pi_{w_1}, \cdots, \pi_{w_n}, \pi_{end}$ and $\theta_{fin,1}, \cdots, \theta_{fin,\omega}$ are randomly selected from $\mathcal{Z}_N$. Actually, all components except w and C_m are attached with $\mathcal{G}_2$ part (w is the input string and C_m is in $\mathcal{H}$).

In the intermediate games, we need at most one key to be type-1 form and the rest keys to be type-2 form. Actually, for an acceptable automata for a string w, i.e., $Accept(\mathcal{M}, w) = 1$, if we use a type-2 semi-functional key to decrypt a semi-functional ciphertext, we will obtain extra term $e(P_2, P_2)^{\langle \boldsymbol{\theta}, \boldsymbol{\vartheta} \rangle - \mu_{end}\pi_{end} - \gamma_n \tau_{end}}$. If the exponent is zero, that is, $\langle \boldsymbol{\theta}, \boldsymbol{\vartheta} \rangle - \mu_{end}\pi_{end} - \gamma_n\tau_{end} = 0$, then during the decryption the $\mathcal{G}_2$ part will cancel out and we call the key *nominally semi-functional*, otherwise we call the key *truly semi-functional*.

The leakage-resilient semantic security proof has two steps: At first we use a series of indistinguishable games to prove that the scheme is adaptively secure in unacceptable string between the queried key and challenge ciphertext, which is derived from the idea of dual system machanism[16,25]. We do so by proving that, in the view of the attacker, the valid private keys are indistinguishable from keys that are random in the subgroup in which the plaintext is embedded. Secondly, we prove that, even the attacker has at most L bits leakage on each key (especially for a match key), one has negligible advantage to decrypt the ciphertext. We give the following theorem:

Theorem 1. *If a dual system* $\prod_{\mathsf{DDFA\text{-}lrFE}} = (SysGen, KeyExt, KeyUpd, Enc, Dec, KeyExtSF, EncSF)$ *has semi-functional ciphertext invariance, semi-functional key invariance, and semi-functional security under the leakage bound* L, *then the* $ACP\text{-}lrFEM$ *scheme* $\prod = (SysGen, KeyExt, KeyUpd, Enc, Dec)$ *is* (Q, L, γ)-*semantically secure in the presence of key leakage, where* Q *is the number of key that attacker queries,* L *is the allowable bound and* $\gamma = \frac{L}{|DK|}$ *is the leakage fraction.*

Proof. Let Q be the number of key queries that the attacker makes in the leakage-resilient experiment in definition 5, then our proof considers a sequence of $2Q+4$ games between an attacker $\mathcal{A}$ and a challenger $\mathcal{C}$ as follow:

$$
\Lambda_0, \Lambda_1, \Lambda_2, (\Lambda_{3,1}, \Lambda_{4,1}, \cdots, \Lambda_{3,k}, \Lambda_{4,k}, \cdots, \Lambda_{3,Q}, \Lambda_{4,Q}), \Lambda_5
$$

In game Λ_0, the key and the challenge ciphertext in this game described in Section 3 are all normal (no $\mathcal{G}_2$ part). We use a series of computationally indistinguishable conversions to implement our proofs. In game Λ_0, we replace the key

Table 1. Games

Games	Functionalities	Remarks
Λ_0	Real experiment defined in definition 5	The keys and challenge ciphertext are all normal
Λ_1	update oracle replace by extraction oracle	
Λ_2	Challenge ciphertext is converted to semi-functional	
$\Lambda_{3,k}$	First $k-1$ keys are type-2's, k^{th} is type-1's, and the rest keys are normal	Ω_E for non-match key, $1 \le k \le Q$
$\Lambda_{4,k}$	The kth is converted to nominal form	Ω_L: Under the leakage of match key, the semi-functional key cannot convert into a nominal one
Λ_5	C_0 is replaced by a random element from $\mathcal{H}$	All components in keys and ciphertexts are semi-functional except C_m (C_m is randomized)

update oracle with key extraction oracle since the update can be considered as a particular key extraction. Thus in the next games, we do not consider the update oracle. In Game Λ_2, we transform the challenge ciphertext to be semi-functional, and show that in the view of attacker this transformation is oblivious.

In the next games we transform the queried keys into semi-functional forms one by one. In particular, for $k = 1, 2, \cdots, Q$, we first transform the first $k - 1$ keys to be type-2 formed, the k-th key to be type-1 formed and the rest to be normal. Then, we convert the k-th key into type-2 form. Obviously, all keys are semi-functional when $k = Q$.

Next, we consider whether these keys are truly nominal or not when the keys may partially leak. In $\Lambda_{5,k}$, we indicate that any key cannot convert into a nominal semi-functional form even though at most L-bit leakage occurs.

All components in $\texttt{CT}_w$ and $\texttt{DK}_{\mathcal{M}}$ are paired by bilinear map except C_m. From the transformations as above, these components are attached with $\mathcal{G}_2$ parts and the decryption will fail by the dual system mechanism. In the last game, we replace the plaintext component C_m in challenge ciphertext with a random element of $\mathcal{H}$, which means that the plaintext is information-theoretically hidden in the ciphertext. We give the Claims to show that these games are computationally indistinguishable and then conclude the proof, in which the Claims appear in the full version. □

5   Performance and Discussion

5.1   Performance of Leakage Resilience

In the system, we set $\omega = \lceil 1 + 2\tau + \frac{L}{|p_2|} \rceil \approx 1 + \frac{L}{|p_2|}$, and thus $L = (\omega - 1)|p_2|$. Obviously, if $\omega = 1$, then $L = 0$ and $\tau = 0$, which means that the scheme is non-leakage resilient. The larger ω, the better leakage-resilience. We also require that p_1, p_2 and p_3 are distinct primes with same length, i.e., $|p_1| = |p_2| = |p_3|$ and $|N| = 3|p_2|$. Let $\mathcal{G}, \mathcal{H}$ be the bilienar groups of elliptic curve and e be the η pairing. The ciphertext size is $|\mathcal{H}| + (2n + 4 + \omega)|\mathcal{G}| = (6n + 18 + 3\omega)|p_2|$ and the key size is $3(2 + |\mathcal{T}| + Q + \omega)|p_2|$. The leakage fraction

$$\gamma = \frac{L}{|\mathsf{DK}|} = \frac{\omega - 1}{3(2 + |\mathcal{T}| + Q + \omega)} \approx \frac{1}{3(1 + \frac{|\mathcal{T}|+Q}{\omega})}$$

where $|\mathcal{T}|$ is the number of transitions in finite automata $\mathcal{M}$, and Q is the number of end states in set Y. We can set ω large enough to tolerate the maximum leakage to be $\frac{1}{3}|\mathsf{DK}| - o(1)$.

Table 2. Comparison of encryption with automata control policy

scheme	[23]	[21]	ours
order	prime	composite	composite
# accept states	≥ 1	1	≥ 1
# group elements of CT	$6 + 2n$	$6 + 2n$	$6 + 2n + \omega$
# group elements of DK	$2 + 3|\mathcal{T}| + 2|Y|$	$4 + 3|\mathcal{T}|$	$2 + \omega + 3|\mathcal{T}| + 2|Y|$
leakage fraction	$\emptyset$	$\emptyset$	33%

The size of an element of $\mathcal{H}$ is twice of $\mathcal{G}$. $\omega = \lceil 1 + 2\tau + L/|p_2|\rceil$ is the leakage parameter and L is the leakage bound. n is the length of input string of automata. $|\mathcal{T}|$ is the size of transition function of automata. $|Y|$ is the number of accept states.

5.2 Discussion

The implementation of dual system can derived from the finite groups of prime order[23] or composite order[17,25]. Freeman[10] and Lewko[15] respectively proposed the methods in converting the construction of composite-order group into prime-order model. Also, they gave the negative result that some schemes and models cannot be converted. In our scheme, the subgroup $\mathcal{G}_2$ has two functionalities: the hidden intractable order p_2 from group $\mathcal{G}$ for adaptive security proof and the subspace orthogonality for leakage tolerance in Lemma 1. We leave it as open problem whether we can use the technique and tool in [10,15] to transform our composite-order construction to prime-order one.

Waters[23] and Ramanna[21] also provided the encryption schemes that employs the deterministic finite automata as the encryption policy. However, [23] is only selective secure without the leakage resilience. [21] is adaptively secure but the automata is only one unique final state and a single transition corresponding to each symbol. Also, the key leakage is forbidden in [23] and [21]. The comparison is listed in Table 2.

5.3 Application Scenario

A finite automata can model the execution of software that decides whether online user-input such as email addresses are valid or not, and then network firewalls perform the filtering rules. In practice, deterministic finite automates are one of the most practical models of computation, since there is a trivial linear time, constant-space, online algorithm to simulate the model on a stream of input. Furthermore, compared Turing machine, there are efficient algorithms to find a deterministic finite automata recognizing. For example, in email firewall, an efficient way of filtering and matching is building and execution of a deterministic finite automaton. Traditionally, the rule is stored in the firewall server and the server performs the filter check by running the automata that taking the email as the input. However, in practice, there have some flaws in twofold: (1)the server will fail if the email is encrypted; (2)the attacker can attack the server and gains the clear filter rule so as to bypass the rule. We can deploy our encryption module to perform the filter: transform the finite automata into the key form and store it in the server; the email is encrypted as a string; instead of the filter match in cleartext, the server check the match in ciphertext/key space. Even the key is partially leaked to the other attacker, the attacker cannot gain any useful information from the encrypted email.

6   Conclusions

We have provided the model and presented a concrete construction of functional encryption from finite automata control policy in the presence of key leakage. In the scheme, the automata control policy has much attention for general function description that the length of input is arbitrary. The automata can run in ciphertext/key spaces such that a ciphertext is associated with a string and a secret key is associated with a finite automata, whereas the possible 33% leakage on the key is allowed. We leave it is an interesting open problem of the scheme against full leakage construction (e.g., key leakage, randomness leakage and internal state leakage, simultaneously).

References

1. Agrawal, S., Dodis, Y., Vaikuntanathan, V., Wichs, D.: On continual leakage of discrete log representations. In: Sako, K., Sarkar, P. (eds.) ASIACRYPT 2013, Part II. LNCS, vol. 8270, pp. 401–420. Springer, Heidelberg (2013)
2. Akavia, A., Goldwasser, S., Vaikuntanathan, V.: Simultaneous hardcore bits and cryptography against memory attacks. In: Reingold, O. (ed.) TCC 2009. LNCS, vol. 5444, pp. 474–495. Springer, Heidelberg (2009)
3. Boneh, D., Sahai, A., Waters, B.: Functional encryption: Definitions and challenges. In: Ishai, Y. (ed.) TCC 2011. LNCS, vol. 6597, pp. 253–273. Springer, Heidelberg (2011)
4. Boyle, E., Garg, S., Jain, A., Kalai, Y.T., Sahai, A.: Secure computation against adaptive auxiliary information. In: Canetti, R., Garay, J.A. (eds.) CRYPTO 2013, Part I. LNCS, vol. 8042, pp. 316–334. Springer, Heidelberg (2013)
5. Brakerski, Z., Goldwasser, S.: Circular and leakage resilient public-key encryption under subgroup indistinguishability. In: Rabin, T. (ed.) CRYPTO 2010. LNCS, vol. 6223, pp. 1–20. Springer, Heidelberg (2010)
6. Brakerski, Z., Kalai, Y.T., Katz, J., Vaikuntanathan, V.: Overcoming the hole in the bucket: Publickey cryptography resilient to continual memory leakage. In: FOCS 2010, pp. 501–510 (2010)

7. Chow, S., Dodis, Y., Rouselakis, Y., Waters, B.: Practical leakage-resilient identity-based encryption from simple assumptions. In: ACM-CCS 2010, pp. 152–161 (2010)
8. Dodis, Y., Haralambiev, K., López-Alt, A., Wichs, D.: Efficient public-key cryptography in the presence of key leakage. In: Abe, M. (ed.) ASIACRYPT 2010. LNCS, vol. 6477, pp. 613–631. Springer, Heidelberg (2010)
9. Dodis, Y., Lewko, A., Waters, B., Wichs, D.: Storing secrets on continually leaky devices. In: FOCS 2011, pp. 688–697 (2011)
10. Freeman, D.M.: Converting pairing-based cryptosystems from composite-order groups to prime-order groups. In: Gilbert, H. (ed.) EUROCRYPT 2010. LNCS, vol. 6110, pp. 44–61. Springer, Heidelberg (2010)
11. Goldwasser, S., Kalai, Y.T., Popa, R.A., Vaikuntanathan, V., Zeldovich, N.: How to run turing machines on encrypted data. In: Canetti, R., Garay, J.A. (eds.) CRYPTO 2013, Part II. LNCS, vol. 8043, pp. 536–553. Springer, Heidelberg (2013)
12. Hazay, C., López-Alt, A., Wee, H., Wichs, D.: Leakage-resilient cryptography from minimal assumptions. In: Johansson, T., Nguyen, P.Q. (eds.) EUROCRYPT 2013. LNCS, vol. 7881, pp. 160–176. Springer, Heidelberg (2013)
13. Hopcroft, J.E., Motwani, R., Ullman, J.: Introduction to automata theory, languages and computation, 2nd edn. Addison Wesley (2000)
14. Katz, J., Sahai, A., Waters, B.: Predicate encryption supporting disjunctions, polynomial equations, and inner products. In: Smart, N.P. (ed.) EUROCRYPT 2008. LNCS, vol. 4965, pp. 146–162. Springer, Heidelberg (2008)
15. Lewko, A.: Tools for simulating features of composite order bilinear groups in the prime order setting. In: Pointcheval, D., Johansson, T. (eds.) EUROCRYPT 2012. LNCS, vol. 7237, pp. 318–335. Springer, Heidelberg (2012)
16. Lewko, A., Waters, B.: New proof methods for attribute-based encryption: Achieving full security through selective techniques. In: Safavi-Naini, R., Canetti, R. (eds.) CRYPTO 2012. LNCS, vol. 7417, pp. 180–198. Springer, Heidelberg (2012)
17. Lewko, A., Rouselakis, Y., Waters, B.: Achieving leakage resilience through dual system encryption. In: Ishai, Y. (ed.) TCC 2011. LNCS, vol. 6597, pp. 70–88. Springer, Heidelberg (2011)
18. Mather, L., Oswald, E., Bandenburg, J., Wójcik, M.: Does my device leak information? An a priori statistical power analysis of leakage detection tests. In: Sako, K., Sarkar, P. (eds.) ASIACRYPT 2013, Part I. LNCS, vol. 8269, pp. 486–505. Springer, Heidelberg (2013)
19. Naor, M., Segev, G.: Public-key cryptosystems resilient to key leakage. In: Halevi, S. (ed.) CRYPTO 2009. LNCS, vol. 5677, pp. 18–35. Springer, Heidelberg (2009)
20. Qin, B., Liu, S.: Leakage-resilient chosen-ciphertext secure public-key encryption from hash proof system and one-time lossy filter. In: Sako, K., Sarkar, P. (eds.) ASIACRYPT 2013, Part II. LNCS, vol. 8270, pp. 381–400. Springer, Heidelberg (2013)
21. Ramanna, S.C.: DFA-based functional encryption: adaptive security from dual system encryption. IACR Cryptology ePrint Archive 2013, 638 (2013)
22. Sahai, A., Waters, B.: Fuzzy identity-based encryption. In: Cramer, R. (ed.) EUROCRYPT 2005. LNCS, vol. 3494, pp. 457–473. Springer, Heidelberg (2005)
23. Waters, B.: Functional encryption for regular languages. In: Safavi-Naini, R., Canetti, R. (eds.) CRYPTO 2012. LNCS, vol. 7417, pp. 218–235. Springer, Heidelberg (2012)
24. Zhang, M., Shi, W., Wang, C., Chen, Z., Mu, Y.: Leakage-resilient attribute-based encryption with fast decryption: Models, analysis and constructions. In: Deng, R.H., Feng, T. (eds.) ISPEC 2013. LNCS, vol. 7863, pp. 75–90. Springer, Heidelberg (2013)
25. Zhang, M., Yang, B., Takagi, T.: Bounded leakage-resilient funtional encryption with hidden vector predicate. The Computer Journal, Oxford 56(4), 464–477 (2013)

Provably Secure Certificateless Authenticated Asymmetric Group Key Agreement

Lei Zhang[1], Qianhong Wu[2], Bo Qin[3], Hua Deng[4],
Jianwei Liu[2], and WenChang Shi[3]

[1] Shanghai Key Laboratory of Trustworthy Computing,
Software Engineering Institute, East China Normal University, Shanghai, China
leizhang@sei.ecnu.edu.cn
[2] School of Electronic and Information Engineering, Beihang University, China
{qianhong.wu,liujianwei}@buaa.edu.cn
[3] School of Information, Renmin University of China, Beijing, China
{bo.qin,wenchang}@ruc.edu.cn
[4] School of Computer, Wuhan University, Wuhan, China
denghuar0804@163.com

Abstract. Asymmetric group key agreement allows a group of members to establish a public group encryption key while each member has a different secret decryption key. Knowing the group encryption key, a sender can encrypt to the group members so that only the members can decrypt. This paper studies authenticated asymmetric group key agreement in certificateless public key cryptography. We formalize the security model of certificateless authenticated asymmetric group key agreement and capture typical attacks in the real world. We next present a strongly unforgeable stateful certificateless batch multi-signature scheme as building block and realize a one-round certificatless authenticated asymmetric group key agreement protocol to resist active attacks. Both the new multi-signature scheme and the resulting group key agreement protocol are shown to be secure under the well-established computational Diffie-Hellman and the k-Bilinear Diffie-Hellman exponent assumptions in the random oracle model, respectively.

Keywords: Certificateless public key cryptography, group key agreement, asymmetric group key agreement.

1 Introduction

The proliferation of applications, e.g., IP telephony, video conference, collaborative workspace, interactive chats and multi-user games that rely on group communicationa prompt the need for secure broadcast channels. A widely used mechanism for secure broadcast channels is the use of Group Key Agreement (GKA) protocols which allow a group of users to share keys over a distributed network. However, conventional GKA protocols have several limitations. Firstly, in a conventional GKA protocol, the key established is a common secret key. Only the group users who learn the common secret key can securely broadcast

X. Huang and J. Zhou (Eds.): ISPEC 2014, LNCS 8434, pp. 496–510, 2014.

to others. Secondly, to establish a secret key, existing conventional GKA protocols [4,6,7,8,9,11] require two or more rounds without using multilinear maps [3,13]. Further, an additional round is required for each member to confirm the established secret key. Though plausible multilinear maps [13] are constructed recently and can be used to realize one round GKA, an additional round is still required for key confirmation.

Recently, a notion called Asymmetric Group Key Agreement (AGKA) is introduced [19]. In an AGKA protocol, instead of a common secret key, the keys established are a common encryption key and respective secret decryption key of each group user. To confirm the established keys, a group user just needs to encrypt a message m using the encryption key then decrypt the corresponding ciphertext using her secret decryption key. If the decrypted message is equal to m, then the user may confirm that she obtains the correct keys. Therefore, the key confirmation step can be done locally and the round for key confirmation is eliminated. Once the encryption and decryption keys are established, the encryption key can be published and anyone who knows the encryption key can securely send messages to the users in group. In [19], a concrete AGKA protocol is proposed. To establish the encryption and decryption keys, it only requires one round which implies that the protocol participants needs not to be online at the same time. This property makes that the one round protocols have more advantages than two or more rounds protocols. For instance, a group of friends wishing to share their private files via the insecure internet; doing so with a two or more rounds key agreement protocol would require all of them to be online at the same time. However, if they live in different time zones, it is difficult for them to be online concurrently.

The basic AGKA protocol in [19] and its plain extensions [20,21] does not authenticate the protocol participants. Therefore, it cannot be used in open networks where active adversaries may control the message flows during the execution of the protocol. Authenticated AGKA (AAGKA) aims to assurance that no party other than the group users can possibly compute the established group decryption key(s). Recently, AAGKA protocols are studied in traditional PKI based public key cryptosystem [23] and identity-based public key cryptosystem [17,22] in which a third party called private key generator (PKG) is employed to issue private keys for the system members. However, the former system has the certificate management problem while the latter one suffers from the key escrow problem. Certificateless public key cryptosystem (CL-PKC) [1] may successfully solve those drawbacks in traditional and identity-based public key cryptosystems. In CL-PKC, no certificate is required to bind a user with her public key. Further, though a third party called KGC is used to help a user to generate her private key, it only has access to the partial private key of the user. A user's full private key is composed of the partial private key comes from the KGC and a secret information chosen by herself. Since the KGC does not hold the full private key of the user in the system, it cannot represent any user to do cryptographical operations without being detected. The key escrow problem is accordingly eliminated.

The first provably secure AAGKA is proposed in [22]. It is built on a new notion referred to as identity-based batch multi-signature (IB-B-MS), which allows multiple signers to sign t messages in an efficient way and captures the typical security requirements of GKA protocols, *i.e.*, *secrecy, known-key security* and *partial forward secrecy* [5,22] (See Section 3). We note that partial forward secrecy cannot guarantee the secrecy of the messages if an attacker learns all the private keys of the group users. In ID-PKC, since the PKG has the knowledge of all the private keys of the users in the system, it can always decrypt the messages encrypted under the negotiated public key, which is not desirable in most application environments. Further, even an AAGKA in identity-based public key cryptosystem achieves perfect forward secrecy and session key escrow freeness (i.e., the secrecy of previous messages is not violated even if the PKG is corrupted), the PKG may still impersonate a user or launch a man-in-the-middle attack to obtain the secret session key without being caught due to the key escrow problem. Recently, AAGKA protocols are studied in CL-PKC [16,18]. However, the formal security analysis of the protocol in [18] is not provided. Although, the protocol in [16] is presented with a formal security analysis, an attacker cannot get any decryption key related to the target user.

1.1 Our Contribution

In this paper, we study AAGKA in CL-PKC. Firstly, we define a security model for CertificateLess AAGKA (CL-AAGKA) protocols which captures the typical security requirements of GKA protocols (*i.e.*, *secrecy, known-key security* and *partial forward secrecy*) as well as the abilities of two types of adversaries (See Section 3.2). Different from the model in [16], in our model, an attacker can obtain any decryption key of any user, except the decryption keys generated in the target session. Secondly, we propose a one-round CL-AAGKA protocol. Our proposal enjoys a modular design by exploiting a new batch multi-signature scheme as building block. In our batch multi-signature scheme, even an attacker obtains a batch multi-signature on t messages under a state information, he cannot generate a new batch multi-signature on the same messages under the same state information. The security of our protocol is reduced to the hardness of the k-Bilinear Diffie-Hellman Exponent problem and the strong unforgeability of our batch multi-signature. Since the KGC does not have the knowledge of the private keys of the group users, it does not suffer from the key escrow problem. In fact, without the full private key of even one group user, an attacker cannot know any useful information about the confidential communications protected by the proposed protocol. Hence, our protocol is suitable for most applications.

1.2 Outline

The rest of the paper is organized as follows. Section 2 reviews bilinear maps and complexity assumptions. We define the security model for CL-AAGKA protocols in Section 3. Section 4 proposes a strongly unforgeable stateful CL-B-MS signature scheme. The CL-AAGKA protocol is proposed in Section 5. We conclude our paper in Section 6.

2   Bilinear Maps and Complexity Assumption

Our scheme is realized in groups which allowing efficient bilinear maps. Let G_1 be an additive group of prime order q and G_2 be a multiplicative group of the same order. A map $\hat{e} : G_1 \times G_1 \longrightarrow G_2$ is called a bilinear map if it satisfies the following properties:

1. Bilinearity: $\hat{e}(aP, bQ) = \hat{e}(P, Q)^{ab}$ for all $P, Q \in G_1, a, b \in Z_q^*$.
2. Non-degeneracy: There exists $P, Q \in G_1$ such that $\hat{e}(P, Q) \neq 1$.
3. Computability: There exists an efficient algorithm to compute $\hat{e}(P, Q)$ for any $P, Q \in G_1$.

The security of our protocol is based on the hardness of the Computational Diffie-Hellman (CDH) problem and the k-Bilinear Diffie-Hellman Exponent (BDHE) problem [2,19], which are briefly reviewed next.

CDH Problem: Given P, aP, bP for unknown $a, b \in Z_q$, compute abP.

CDH Assumption: Let $\mathcal{B}$ be an algorithm which has advantage

$$\mathsf{Adv}(\mathcal{B}) = \Pr\left[\mathcal{B}(P, aP, bP) = abP\right]$$

in solving the CDH problem. The CDH assumption states that $\mathsf{Adv}(\mathcal{B})$ is negligible for any polynomial-time algorithm $\mathcal{B}$.

k-**BDHE Problem:** Given P, H, and $Y_i = \alpha^i P$ in G_1 for $i = 1, 2, ..., k, k + 2, ..., 2k$ as input, compute $\hat{e}(P, H)^{\alpha^{k+1}}$. Since the input vector lacks the term $\alpha^{k+1} P$, the bilinear map does not seem helpful to compute $\hat{e}(P, H)^{\alpha^{k+1}}$.

k-**BDHE Assumption:** Let $\mathcal{B}$ be an algorithm which has advantage

$$\mathsf{Adv}(\mathcal{B}) = \Pr\left[\mathcal{B}(P, H, Y_1, ..., Y_k, Y_{k+2}, ..., Y_{2k}) = \hat{e}(P, H)^{\alpha^{k+1}}\right]$$

in solving k-BDHE problem. The k-BDHE assumption states that $\mathsf{Adv}(\mathcal{B})$ is negligible for any polynomial-time algorithm $\mathcal{B}$.

3   Security Model

The security model for AGKA protocols was first studied in [19], in which passive attackers are considered. In [22], security model for AAGKA protocols was defined for the first time. This model is for AAGKA protocols in identity-based public key cryptosystem and captures the identity-based variation of the typical security requirements: secrecy, known-key security and partial forward secrecy. Secrecy guarantees that, except the group members, no entity can learn the messages encrypted under the negotiated public key. Known-key security means that, if an adversary learns the group encryption/decryption keys of other sessions, he cannot compute subsequent group decryption keys. Partial forward secrecy ensures that the disclosure of one or more long-term private keys of group members must not compromise the secrecy of the messages in the earlier runs of the protocol. A stronger notion is perfect forward secrecy which requires that the secrecy of previous messages is not violated even if all the long-term private keys of the group members are disclosed. In the following, we propose the security model for CL-AAGKA protocols which aims to capture the certificateless variation of the typical security requirements: secrecy, known-key security and partial forward secrecy.

3.1 Participants and Notations

Suppose a set of users $\{\mathcal{U}_1, ..., \mathcal{U}_n\}$ decide to launch a CL-AAGKA protocol run. We define following variables for a participant $\mathcal{U}_i$.

- $\Pi_{\mathcal{U}_i}^{\pi}$ denotes instance π of participant $\mathcal{U}_i$ involved with other partner participants $\{\mathcal{U}_1, ..., \mathcal{U}_{i-1}, \mathcal{U}_{i+1}, ..., \mathcal{U}_n\}$ in a session.
- $\mathrm{pid}_{\mathcal{U}_i}^{\pi}$ denotes the *partner ID* of instance $\Pi_{\mathcal{U}_i}^{\pi}$. It contains the identity of $\mathcal{U}_i$ and the identities of all the partner participants of $\mathcal{U}_i$. The identities in $\mathrm{pid}_{\mathcal{U}_i}^{\pi}$ are assumed to be ordered lexicographically.
- $\mathrm{sid}_{\mathcal{U}_i}^{\pi}$ denotes the *session ID* of instance $\Pi_{\mathcal{U}_i}^{\pi}$. Similar to [15], we assume that when the protocol is initiated, a unique session ID is provided by some higher-level protocol. Therefore, all members taking part in a given execution of a protocol will have the same session ID.
- $\mathrm{ms}_{\mathcal{U}_i}^{\pi}$ is the messages sent and received by $\Pi_{\mathcal{U}_i}^{\pi}$ during its execution. The messages in $\mathrm{ms}_{\mathcal{U}_i}^{\pi}$ are ordered by round, and within each round lexicographically by the identities of the purported senders.
- $\mathrm{ek}_{\mathcal{U}_i}^{\pi}$ is the encryption key held by $\Pi_{\mathcal{U}_i}^{\pi}$.
- $\mathrm{dk}_{\mathcal{U}_i}^{\pi}$ is the decryption key held by $\Pi_{\mathcal{U}_i}^{\pi}$.
- $\mathrm{state}_{\mathcal{U}_i}^{\pi}$ represents the current (internal) state of instance $\Pi_{\mathcal{U}_i}^{\pi}$. We say $\Pi_{\mathcal{U}_i}^{\pi}$ has *terminated*, if it finishes sending and receiving messages. If a CL-AAGKA protocol has been *accepted* in the instance $\Pi_{\mathcal{U}_i}^{\pi}$, then it possesses $\mathrm{ek}_{\mathcal{U}_i}^{\pi}(\neq null)$, $\mathrm{dk}_{\mathcal{U}_i}^{\pi}(\neq null)$, $\mathrm{pid}_{\mathcal{U}_i}^{\pi}$ and $\mathrm{sid}_{\mathcal{U}_i}^{\pi}$.

Definition 1 (Partnering). *We say instances $\Pi_{\mathcal{U}_i}^{\pi}$ and $\Pi_{\mathcal{U}_j}^{\pi'}$ (with $i \neq j$) are partnered iff (1) they are accepted; (2) $\mathrm{pid}_{\mathcal{U}_i}^{\pi} = \mathrm{pid}_{\mathcal{U}_j}^{\pi'}$; and (3) $\mathrm{sid}_{\mathcal{U}_i}^{\pi} = \mathrm{sid}_{\mathcal{U}_j}^{\pi'}$.*

3.2 The Model

As defined in [1], a protocol in CL-PKC has to resist the attacks from type I and type II adversaries. The former may replace the public key of any user, while the latter has the knowledge of the master-key but cannot perform public key replacement. The ability of type II adversary is later enhanced by allowing he to replace the public key of any user except the target one(s) [10,14,24]. In our security model, we treat the type II adversary as the enhanced one.

The security model of CL-AAGKA protocols is defined by the following game which is played between a challenger $\mathcal{C}$ and an adversary $\mathcal{A}$. $\mathcal{A}$ is either a type I or II adversary and controls all the message flows. The game has following three stages.

Initial: At this stage, $\mathcal{C}$ generates the system parameters params and the master-key of the KGC. If $\mathcal{A}$ is of type I, params is passed to $\mathcal{A}$; otherwise, master-key is given to $\mathcal{A}$ as well.

Attacking: At this stage, $\mathcal{A}$ may access the following oracles which are controlled by $\mathcal{C}$.

- Send$(\Pi_{\mathcal{U}_i}^{\pi}, \Lambda)$: Send a message Λ to instance $\Pi_{\mathcal{U}_i}^{\pi}$, and output the reply generated by this instance. If Λ is incorrect, the query returns $null$. When $\Lambda = (\mathsf{sid}, \mathsf{pid})$, it prompts $\mathcal{U}_i$ to initiate the protocol using session ID sid and partner ID pid. The identity of $\mathcal{U}_i$ should be in pid.
- Corrupt.PPK$(\mathcal{U}_i)$: Output the partial private key of participant $\mathcal{U}_i$.
- Corrupt.SK$(\mathcal{U}_i)$: Output the secret key of participant $\mathcal{U}_i$.
- Corrupt$(\mathcal{U}_i)$: Output the full private key of participant $\mathcal{U}_i$. The oracle can be simulated via calls both Corrupt.PPK$(\mathcal{U}_i)$ and Corrupt.SK$(\mathcal{U}_i)$. Hence, this oracle is not considered in this paper.
- PK$(\mathcal{U}_i)$: Output the public key of participant $\mathcal{U}_i$.
- Replace$(\mathcal{U}_i, P_i')$: Replace the public key of participant $\mathcal{U}_i$ to be P_i'.
- Ek.Reveal$(\Pi_{\mathcal{U}_i}^{\pi})$: Output the encryption key $\mathsf{ek}_{\mathcal{U}_i}^{\pi}$.
- Dk.Reveal$(\Pi_{\mathcal{U}_i}^{\pi})$: Output the decryption key $\mathsf{dk}_{\mathcal{U}_i}^{\pi}$. We will use it to model *known-key security*.
- Test$(\Pi_{\mathcal{U}_i}^{\pi})$: At some point, $\mathcal{A}$ returns two messages (m_0, m_1) ($|m_0| = |m_1|$) and a fresh instance $\Pi_{\mathcal{U}_i}^{\pi}$ (see Definition 2). The challenger $\mathcal{C}$ chooses $b \in \{0, 1\}$ at random, generates a ciphertext c by encrypting m_b under $\mathsf{ek}_{\mathcal{U}_i}^{\pi}$, and returns c to $\mathcal{A}$. This query is used to model *secrecy* and can be submitted only once.

Response: $\mathcal{A}$ returns a bit b'. We say that $\mathcal{A}$ wins if $b' = b$. $\mathcal{A}$'s advantage is defined to be $\mathsf{Adv}(\mathcal{A}) = |2\Pr[b = b'] - 1|$.

Definition 2 (Freshness). *An instance $\Pi_{\mathcal{U}_i}^{\pi}$ is fresh if none of the following happens:*

1. *At some point, $\mathcal{A}$ queried* Dk.Reveal$(\Pi_{\mathcal{U}_i}^{\pi})$ *or* Dk.Reveal$(\Pi_{\mathcal{U}_j}^{\pi'})$, *where $\Pi_{\mathcal{U}_j}^{\pi'}$ is partnered with $\Pi_{\mathcal{U}_i}^{\pi}$.*
2. *$\mathcal{A}$ corrupted the partial private key of a participant in $\mathsf{pid}_{\mathcal{U}_i}^{\pi}$ before $\Pi_{\mathcal{U}_i}^{\pi}$ terminated if $\mathcal{A}$ is of type I, or, $\mathcal{A}$ corrupted the secret key or replaced the public key of a participant in $\mathsf{pid}_{\mathcal{U}_i}^{\pi}$ before $\Pi_{\mathcal{U}_i}^{\pi}$ terminated if $\mathcal{A}$ is of type II.*
3. *All the partial private keys of the participants associated with $\mathsf{sid}_{\mathcal{U}_i}^{\pi}$ are corrupted if $\mathcal{A}$ is of type I, or, all the secret keys of the participants with $\mathsf{sid}_{\mathcal{U}_i}^{\pi}$ are corrupted if $\mathcal{A}$ is of type II.*

In the above definition of *freshness*, since we do not allow $\mathcal{A}$ to corrupt the partial private keys or secret keys of all the participants in the same session, our game captures partial forward secrecy.

Definition 3. *A CL-AAGKA protocol is said to be secure against semantically indistinguishable under chosen plaintext attacks (Ind-CPA), if the advantage*

$$\mathsf{Adv}(\mathcal{A}) = |2\Pr[b = b'] - 1|$$

for polynomial-time bounded adversary $\mathcal{A}$ to win in the above game is negligible.

In the above model, if $\mathcal{A}$ may additionally submit ciphertexts to $\mathcal{C}$ to obtain the corresponding plaintexts during the **Attacking** stage and the challenging ciphertext has never been queried for the plaintext in the Test query, then the model captures a stronger attack against CL-AAGKA protocols called indistinguishable chosen ciphertext attack (Ind-CCA). Generic constructions of AAGKA protocols secure against Ind-CCA can be found in [12,19,22]. Therefore, we will focus on CL-AAGKA protocol secure against Ind-CPA.

4 Strongly Unforgeable Stateful CL-B-MS Scheme

Our CL-AAGKA protocol is built on a strongly unforgeable stateful CL-B-MS scheme. A stateful CL-B-MS scheme allows a signer to generate a certificateless batch signature on t messages under a state information using the same random input. Later, the certificateless batch signatures on the same messages under the same state information may be aggregated into a CL-B-MS which can be separated into t individual certificateless multi-signatures. Informally, a stateful CL-B-MS is strongly unforgeable, if an attacker cannot forge a new CL-B-MS on t messages under a state information even the attacker has already obtained a CL-B-MS on the same t messages under the same state information. Precise definition will be given in Section 4.2. In the precise definition, we will show that if a stateful CL-B-MS is strongly unforgeable, an attacker cannot even forge a new certificateless multi-signature.

4.1 Definition

A CL-B-MS scheme consists of the following seven algorithms.

- Setup: On input a security parameter, it generates a master key master-key of the KGC and a list of system parameters params.
- Extract.PPK: On input params, master-key and a user's identity, it outputs the user's partial private key.
- SK.Gen: On input params and a user's identity, it outputs the user's secret key.
- PK.Gen: On input params and a user's identity and secret key, it outputs the user's public key.
- Sign: On input params, a one-time-use state information ψ, t messages, a signer's identity, public key, partial private key and secret key, this algorithm outputs a certificateless batch signature.
- Aggregate: On input params, the identities and public keys of x signers, a collection of x certificateless batch signatures on t messages under the same state information ψ from the x signers, this algorithm outputs a CL-B-MS.
- Verify: This algorithm is used to check the validity of a CL-B-MS. It outputs 1 if the CL-B-MS is valid; otherwise, it outputs 0.

4.2   The Model

Similarly, we also need to consider two types of adversaries as that in the security model of CL-AAGKA protocols. The model is defined via the following game between a challenger C and an adversary A of type I or II.

Initial: C first runs Setup to obtain a master-key and the system parameter list params, then sends params to A if A is a type I adversary; otherwise master-key is also passed to A.

Attacking: A can perform a polynomially bounded number of the following types of queries in an adaptive manner.

- Corrupt.PPK(ID_i): Output the partial private key of the user with identity ID_i.
- Corrupt.SK(ID_i): Output the secret key of the user with identity ID_i.
- PK(ID_i): Output the public key of the user with identity ID_i.
- Replace(ID_i, P'_i): Replace the public key of the user with identity ID_i to be P'_i.
- Sign($ID_i, P_i, \psi, m_1, ..., m_t$): Output a certificateless batch signature on state information ψ and messages $(m_1, ..., m_t)$. It requires that the batch signature is valid under (ID_i, P_i) and ψ.

Forgery: A outputs x identities $\{ID_1^*, ..., ID_x^*\}$ and corresponding public keys $\{P_1^*, ..., P_x^*\}$, a message m^*, a state information ψ^* and a certificateless multi-signature σ^*. We say that A wins the above game if the following conditions are satisfied:

1. σ^* is a valid multi-signature on message m^* under $\{ID_1^*, ..., ID_x^*\}$, $\{P_1^*, ..., P_x^*\}$ and ψ^*.
2. If A is a type I adversary, it requires that none of the identities in $\{ID_1^*, ..., ID_x^*\}$ has been submitted during the Corrupt.PPK queries; else, it requires that none of the identities in $\{ID_1^*, ..., ID_x^*\}$ has been submitted during the Corrupt.SK and Replace queries.
3. The certificateless multi-signature is not generated by using the certificateless batch signatures output by calling the Sign queries with $(ID_i^*, P_i^*, \psi^*, m_{1_i}, ..., m^*, ..., m_{t_i})$ as input, for $i \in \{1, ..., x\}$.

Similarly to the security model in [22], A is only required to output a single multi-signature in the above model. This is due to fact that a CL-B-MS can be separated into t individual certificateless multi-signatures.

Definition 4. *A CL-B-MS scheme is strongly existentially unforgeable under adaptive chosen-message attacks if and only if the success probability of any polynomial-time bounded adversary in the above game is negligible.*

4.3   Our CL-B-MS Scheme

The specification of the scheme is as follows:

- Setup: Given a security parameter ℓ, the KGC chooses a cyclic additive group G_1 which is generated by P with prime order q, chooses a cyclic multiplicative group G_2 of the same order and a bilinear map $\hat{e} : G_1 \times G_1 \longrightarrow G_2$. The KGC also chooses a random $\lambda \in Z_q^*$ as the master-key and sets $P_T = \lambda P$, chooses cryptographic hash functions $H_1 \sim H_3 : \{0,1\}^* \longrightarrow G_1$, $H_4 : \{0,1\}^* \longrightarrow Z_q^*$. The system parameter list is

$$\mathsf{params} = (q, G_1, G_2, \hat{e}, P, P_T, H_1 \sim H_4).$$

- Extract.PPK: This algorithm accepts params, master-key λ and a user's identity $ID_i \in \{0,1\}^*$, and generates the partial private key for the user as follows:
  1. Compute $Q_{i,0} = H_1(ID_i, 0)$, $Q_{i,1} = H_1(ID_i, 1)$.
  2. Output the partial private key

$$(D_{i,0}, D_{i,1}) = (\lambda Q_{i,0}, \lambda Q_{i,1}).$$

- SK.Gen: This algorithm takes as input params, a user's identity ID_i, selects $x_i, y_i \in Z_q^*$ and sets (x_i, y_i) as her secret key.
- PK.Gen: This algorithm takes as input params, a user's identity ID_i, secret key (x_i, y_i) and sets her public key as

$$P_i = (P_{i,0}, P_{i,1}) = (x_i P, y_i P).$$

- Sign: To sign t messages $(m_1, ..., m_t)$ using the signing key $(x_i, y_i, D_{i,0}, D_{i,1})$, the signer, whose identity is ID_i and public key is

$$P_i = (P_{i,0}, P_{i,1}) = (x_i P, y_i P),$$

first chooses a state information ψ then performs the following steps:
  1. Choose a random $r_i \in Z_q^*$, compute $R_i = r_i P$.
  2. Compute
$$h_i = H_4(R_i, \psi, ID_i, P_{i,0}, P_{i,1}), V = H_3(\psi).$$

  3. For $1 \le j \le t$, compute

$$T_j = H_2(\psi, m_j), S_{i,j} = D_{i,0} + h_i D_{i,1} + (x_i + h_i y_i)V + r_i T_j.$$

  4. Output

$$\sigma_i = (R_i, S_{i,1}, ..., S_{i,t})$$

as the batch signature.

- **Aggregation:** For an aggregating set (which has the same state information ψ) of x users with identities $\{ID_1, \cdots, ID_x\}$ and the corresponding public keys $\{P_1, \cdots, P_x\}$, and t signatures

$$(\sigma_1 = (R_1, S_{1,1}, ..., S_{1,t}), \cdots, \sigma_t = (R_x, S_{x,1}, ..., S_{x,t}))$$

on $(m_1, ..., m_t)$ from the x users respectively, anyone can compute

$$S_j = \sum_{i=1}^{n} S_{i,j}$$

and output the batch multi-signature

$$\sigma = (R_1, ..., R_x, S_1, ..., S_t).$$

- **Verify:** To verify the above batch multi-signature, a verifier performs the following steps:
  1. Compute $V = H_3(\psi), R = \sum_{i=1}^{x} R_i$.
  2. For $1 \leq i \leq x$, compute

$$h_i = H_4(R_i, \psi, ID_i, P_{i,0}, P_{i,1}), Q_{i,0} = H_1(ID_i, 0), Q_{i,1} = H_1(ID_i, 1).$$

  3. For $1 \leq j \leq t$, compute $T_j = H_2(\psi, m_j)$, verify

$$\hat{e}(S_j, P) \overset{?}{=} \hat{e}(P_T, \sum_{i=1}^{x} Q_{i,0} + \sum_{i=1}^{x} h_i Q_{i,1}) \hat{e}(V, \sum_{i=1}^{x} P_{i,0} + \sum_{i=1}^{x} h_i P_{i,1}) \hat{e}(T_j, R).$$

If all equation hold, output *true*. Otherwise, output $\perp$.

4.4 Security Analysis

The following theorems shows that our stateful CL-B-MS scheme is strongly unforgeable.

Theorem 1. *Suppose a type I adversary $\mathcal{A}$ who asks at most q_{H_i} queries to H_i for $1 \leq i \leq 4$, q_{cp} queries to Corrupt.PPK, q_p queries to PK, q_{cs} queries to Corrupt.SK, q_s queries to Sign, and wins the game with advantage ε in time τ. Then there exists an algorithm to solve the CDH problem with advantage*

$$\frac{q_{H_2}}{e^{x+2}} \left(\frac{x+2}{q_{H_2} + q_{cp} + x + 1} \right)^{x+2} \varepsilon$$

in time $\tau + \mathcal{O}(2q_{H_1} + q_{H_2} + q_{H_3} + 4q_p + 2q_{cs} + 6Nq_s)\tau_{G_1}$, where τ_{G_1} is the time to compute a scalar multiplication in G_1, x is the scale of the identity set related to the forged signature, N is the largest message scale in the Sign queries.

Due to page limitation, the proof will be presented in the full version of this paper.

Theorem 2. *Suppose a type II adversary $\mathcal{A}$ who asks at most q_{H_i} queries to H_i for $2 \leq i \leq 4$, q_p queries to PK, q_{cs} queries to Corrupt.SK, q_s queries to Sign, and wins the game with advantage ε in time τ. Then there exists an algorithm to solve the CDH problem with advantage*

$$\frac{q_{H_2}}{e^{x+2}}\left(\frac{x+2}{q_{H_2}+q_{cs}+x+1}\right)^{x+2}\varepsilon$$

in time $\tau + \mathcal{O}(q_{H_2} + q_{H_3} + 4q_p + 4q_{cs} + 7Nq_s)\tau_{G_1}$.

Due to page limitation, the proof will be presented in the full version of this paper.

5   The CL-AAGKA Protocol

5.1   The Proposal

Our CL-AAGKA protocol is based on the above CL-B-MS scheme. The concrete protocol comes as follows:

- Setup: The same as that of our CL-B-MS scheme, except an additional hash function $H_5 : \{0,1\}^* \longrightarrow \{0,1\}^\varsigma$ is chosen, where ς defines the bit-length of plaintexts. The system parameter list is

$$\mathsf{params} = (q, G_1, G_2, \hat{e}, P, P_T, H_1 \sim H_5, \varsigma).$$

- Extract.PPK: The same as that of our CL-B-MS scheme.
- SK.Gen: The same as that of our CL-B-MS scheme.
- PK.Gen: The same as that of our CL-B-MS scheme.
- Agreement: Assume the group scale is n and the session ID is sid_λ. A protocol participant, whose identity is ID_i, public key is $(P_{i,0}, P_{i,1})$, secret key is (x_i, y_i) and partial private key is $(D_{i,0}, D_{i,1})$, performs the following steps:

  1. Choose $r_i \in \mathbb{Z}_q^*$ and compute $R_i = r_i P$.
  2. For $1 \leq j \leq n$, compute $T_j = H_2(\mathsf{sid}_\lambda, j)$.
  3. Compute

$$V = H_3(\mathsf{sid}_\lambda), h_i = H_4(R_i, \mathsf{sid}_\lambda, ID_i, P_{i,0}, P_{i,1}).$$

  4. For $1 \leq j \leq n$, compute

$$Z_{i,j} = D_{i,0} + h_i D_{i,1} + (x_i + h_i y_i)V + r_i T_j.$$

  5. Publish

$$\sigma_i = (ID_i, P_{i,0}, P_{i,1}, R_i, \{Z_{i,j}\}_{j\in\{1,...,n\},j\neq i}).$$

- Enc.Key.Gen: To get the group encryption key, a user computes $V = H_3(\text{sid}_\lambda)$; and for $1 \le i \le n$ computes

$$Q_{i,0} = H_1(ID_i, 0), Q_{i,1} = H_1(ID_i, 1), h_i = H_4(R_i, \text{sid}_\lambda, ID_i, P_{i,0}, P_{i,1}).$$

Define $\Delta = 1$, if Equations (1) and (2) hold, and $\Delta = 0$ in other cases.

$$\hat{e}(Z_{1,2}, P) \overset{?}{=} \hat{e}(P_T, Q_{1,0} + h_1 Q_{1,1})\hat{e}(V, P_{1,0} + h_1 P_{1,1})\hat{e}(T_2, R_1) \qquad (1)$$

$$\hat{e}(\prod_{i=2}^{n} Z_{i,1}, P)$$

$$\overset{?}{=} \hat{e}(P_T, \sum_{i=2}^{n} Q_{i,0} + \sum_{i=2}^{n} h_i Q_{i,1})\hat{e}(V, \sum_{i=2}^{n} P_{i,0} + \sum_{i=2}^{n} h_i P_{i,1})\hat{e}(T_1, \sum_{i=2}^{n} R_i) \qquad (2)$$

The Δ is used to check whether R_i is well formatted, where $T_j = H_2(\text{sid}_\lambda, j)$, $j \in \{1, 2\}$. If $\Delta = 1$, the user outputs (R, Ω) as the group encryption key, where

$$R = \sum_{i=1}^{n} R_i, \quad \Omega = \hat{e}(P_T, \sum_{i=1}^{n} Q_{i,0} + \sum_{i=1}^{n} h_i Q_{i,1})\hat{e}(V, \sum_{i=1}^{n} P_{i,0} + \sum_{i=1}^{n} h_i P_{i,1});$$

otherwise it aborts. We note that a protocol participant does not need to test the value of Δ, since it will do a similar check in the following Dec.Key.Gen stage.

- Dec.Key.Gen: Each participant $\mathcal{U}_i$ computes

$$T_i = H_2(\text{sid}_\lambda, i), V = H_3(\text{sid}_\lambda),$$

$$Q_{i,0} = H_1(ID_i, 0), Q_{i,1} = H_1(ID_i, 1), h_i = H_4(R_i, \text{sid}_\lambda, ID_i, P_{i,0}, P_{i,1}),$$

computes

$$R = \sum_{l=1}^{n} R_l, \Gamma_i = \hat{e}(T_i, R), S_i = \sum_{l=1}^{n} Z_{l,i},$$

$$\Omega = \hat{e}(P_T, \sum_{l=1}^{n} Q_{l,0} + \sum_{l=1}^{n} h_l Q_{l,1})\hat{e}(V, \sum_{l=1}^{n} P_{l,0} + \sum_{l=1}^{n} h_l P_{l,1})$$

and tests

$$\hat{e}(S_i, P) \overset{?}{=} \Omega \cdot \Gamma_i.$$

If the equation holds, $\mathcal{U}_i$ accepts S_i as the group decryption key; otherwise, it aborts. The above test is also used by $\mathcal{U}_i$ to determine whether the group encryption key is valid.

- Enc: To encrypt a plaintext m, a user does the following steps:
  1. Select $s \in Z_q^*$ and compute

$$C_1 = sP, C_2 = sR, C_3 = m \oplus H_5(\Omega^s).$$

2. Output the ciphertext $C = (C_1, C_2, C_3)$.
- Dec: To decrypt the ciphertext $C = (C_1, C_2, C_3)$, $\mathcal{U}_i$, whose group decryption key is S_i, computes

$$m = C_3 \oplus H_5(\hat{e}(S_i, C_1)\hat{e}(T_i^{-1}, C_2)).$$

5.2   Security Analysis

In this section, we show that the security of our CL-AAGKA protocol can be reduced to the difficulty of solving the k-BDHE problem and the strong unforgeability of our CL-B-MS scheme.

Theorem 3. *Suppose a type I adversary $\mathcal{A}$ who asks at most q_{H_i} queries to H_i for $1 \le i \le 5$, q_{cp} queries to Corrupt.PPK, q_s queries to Send, q_{er} queries to Ek.Reveal and q_{dr} queries to Dk.Reveal, and wins the game with advantage ϵ in time τ. Then there exists an algorithm to solve the k-BDHE problem with advantage*

$$\frac{4n(1 - 2\varepsilon)}{q_{H_5}(q_{cp} + q_{dr} + n + 1)^2 e^2}\epsilon$$

in time $\tau + \mathcal{O}(10q_{er})\tau_{\hat{e}} + \mathcal{O}(2q_{H_1} + q_{H_2} + q_{H_3} + 4q_p + 2q_{cs} + 7q_s + 6q_{er})\tau_{G_1}$, where ε is the advantage for $\mathcal{A}$ to forge a valid CL-B-MS in time τ, $\tau_{\hat{e}}$ is the time to compute a pairing and τ_{G_1} is the time to compute a scalar multiplication in G_1.

Due to page limitation, the proof will be presented in the full version of this paper.

Theorem 4. *Suppose a type II adversary $\mathcal{A}$ who asks at most q_{H_i} queries to H_i for $2 \le i \le 5$, q_{cs} queries to Corrupt.SK, q_s queries to Send, q_{er} queries to Ek.Reveal and q_{dr} queries to Dk.Reveal, and wins the game with advantage ϵ in time τ. Then there exists an algorithm to solve the k-BDHE problem with advantage*

$$\frac{4n(1 - 2\varepsilon)}{q_{H_5}(q_{cs} + q_{dr} + n + 1)^2 e^2}\epsilon$$

in time $\tau + \mathcal{O}(10q_{er})\tau_{\hat{e}} + \mathcal{O}(q_{H_2} + q_{H_3} + 2q_p + 2q_{cs} + 7q_s + 6q_{er})\tau_{G_1}$, where ε is the advantage for $\mathcal{A}$ to forge a valid CL-B-MS in time τ, $\tau_{\hat{e}}$ is the time to compute a pairing and τ_{G_1} is the time to compute a scalar multiplication in G_1.

Due to page limitation, the proof will be presented in the full version of this paper.

6   Conclusion

We have defined the security model for CL-AAGKA protocols, which captures the typical security requirements of GKA protocols. A one-round CL-AAGKA protocol is proposed and proven secure in our model. Unlike the existing AAGKA protocol in identity-based cryptosystem, our CL-AAGKA protocol does not suffer from the key escrow problem.

Acknowledgments. This paper is supported by the Natural Science Foundation of China through projects 61202465, 61021004, 61103222, 61370190, 61173154, 61003214, 61272501 and 61070192, the Shanghai NSF under grant 12ZR1443500, 11ZR1411200, the Shanghai Chen Guang Program (12CG24), the Science and Technology Commission of Shanghai Municipality under grant 13JC1403500, the National Key Basic Research Program (973 program) through project 2012CB315905, the Beijing Natural Science Foundation through project 4132056 and 4122041, the Research Fund for the Doctoral Program of Higher Education of China under Grant No. 20110076120016, the Fundamental Research Funds for the Central Universities through the Research Funds of East China Normal University, the project 2012211020212 of Wuhan University and the Research Funds of Renmin University of China through project 14XNLF02, the Open Research Fund of The Academy of Satellite Application and the Open Research Fund of Beijing Key Laboratory of Trusted Computing, and by the European Commission under FP7 projects DwB and Inter-Trust, the Spanish Government 777 through projects IPT-2012-0603-430000, TIN2012-32757 and TIN2011-27076-C03-01.

References

1. Al-Riyami, S.S., Paterson, K.G.: Certificateless public key cryptography. In: Laih, C.-S. (ed.) ASIACRYPT 2003. LNCS, vol. 2894, pp. 452–473. Springer, Heidelberg (2003)
2. Boneh, D., Boyen, X., Goh, E.-J.: Hierarchical identity based encryption with constant size ciphertext. In: Cramer, R. (ed.) EUROCRYPT 2005. LNCS, vol. 3494, pp. 440–456. Springer, Heidelberg (2005)
3. Boneh, D., Silverberg, A.: Applications of multilinear forms to cryptography. Contemporary Mathematics 324, 71–90 (2003)
4. Boyd, C., González-Nieto, J.: Round-optimal contributory conference key agreement. In: Desmedt, Y.G. (ed.) PKC 2003. LNCS, vol. 2567, pp. 161–174. Springer, Heidelberg (2002)
5. Boyd, C., Mathuria, A.: Protocols for authentication and key establishment, pp. 9–10. Springer (2003) ISBN:3-540-43107-1
6. Bresson, E., Catalano, D.: Constant round authenticated group key agreement via distributed computation. In: Bao, F., Deng, R., Zhou, J. (eds.) PKC 2004. LNCS, vol. 2947, pp. 115–129. Springer, Heidelberg (2004)
7. Bresson, E., Chevassut, O., Pointcheval, D., Quisquater, J.: Provably authenticated group Diffie-Hellman key exchange. In: ACM CCS 2001, pp. 255–264 (2001)
8. Burmester, M., Desmedt, Y.G.: A secure and efficient conference key distribution system. In: De Santis, A. (ed.) EUROCRYPT 1994. LNCS, vol. 950, pp. 275–286. Springer, Heidelberg (1995)
9. Choi, K.Y., Hwang, J.Y., Lee, D.H.: Efficient ID-based group key agreement with bilinear maps. In: Bao, F., Deng, R., Zhou, J. (eds.) PKC 2004. LNCS, vol. 2947, pp. 130–144. Springer, Heidelberg (2004)
10. Dent, A.W., Libert, B., Paterson, K.G.: Certificateless encryption schemes strongly secure in the standard model. In: Cramer, R. (ed.) PKC 2008. LNCS, vol. 4939, pp. 344–359. Springer, Heidelberg (2008)
11. Dutta, R., Barua, R.: Provably secure constant round contributory group key agreement in dynamic setting. IEEE Trans. Inf. Theory 54(5), 2007–2025 (2008)

12. Fujisaki, E., Okamoto, T.: Secure integration of asymmetric and symmetric encryption schemes. In: Wiener, M. (ed.) CRYPTO 1999. LNCS, vol. 1666, pp. 537–554. Springer, Heidelberg (1999)
13. Garg, S., Gentry, C., Halevi, S.: Candidate multilinear maps from ideal lattices. In: Johansson, T., Nguyen, P.Q. (eds.) EUROCRYPT 2013. LNCS, vol. 7881, pp. 1–17. Springer, Heidelberg (2013)
14. Huang, X., Mu, Y., Susilo, W., Wong, D.S., Wu, W.: Certificateless signature revisited. In: Pieprzyk, J., Ghodosi, H., Dawson, E. (eds.) ACISP 2007. LNCS, vol. 4586, pp. 308–322. Springer, Heidelberg (2007)
15. Katz, J., Shin, J.: Modeling insider attacks on group key-exchange protocols. In: ACM CCS 2005, pp. 180–189 (2005)
16. Lv, X., Li, H., Wang, B.: Authenticated asymmetric group key agreement based on certificateless cryptosystem. International Journal of Computer Mathematics (2013), http://dx.doi.org/10.1080/00207160.2013.806653
17. Shamir, A.: Identity-based cryptosystems and signature schemes. In: Blakely, G.R., Chaum, D. (eds.) CRYPTO 1984. LNCS, vol. 196, pp. 47–53. Springer, Heidelberg (1985)
18. Wei, G., Yang, X., Shao, J.: Efficient certificateless authenticated asymmetric group key agreement protocol. KSII Transactions on Internet and Information Systems 6(12) (2012)
19. Wu, Q., Mu, Y., Susilo, W., Qin, B., Domingo-Ferrer, J.: Asymmetric group key agreement. In: Joux, A. (ed.) EUROCRYPT 2009. LNCS, vol. 5479, pp. 153–170. Springer, Heidelberg (2009)
20. Wu, Q., Qin, B., Zhang, L., Domingo-Ferrer, J., Farràs, O.: Bridging Broadcast Encryption and Group Key Agreement. In: Lee, D.H., Wang, X. (eds.) ASIACRYPT 2011. LNCS, vol. 7073, pp. 143–160. Springer, Heidelberg (2011)
21. Wu, Q., Qin, B., Zhang, L., Domingo-Ferrer, J., Manjón, J.A.: Fast Transmission to Remote Cooperative Groups: A New Key Management Paradigm. IEEE/ACM Trans. Netw. 21(2), 621–633 (2013)
22. Zhang, L., Wu, Q., Qin, B., Domingo-Ferrer, J.: Identity-based authenticated asymmetric group key agreement protocol. In: Thai, M.T., Sahni, S. (eds.) COCOON 2010. LNCS, vol. 6196, pp. 510–519. Springer, Heidelberg (2010)
23. Zhang, L., Wu, Q., Qin, B., Domingo-Ferrer, J.: Asymmetric group key agreement protocol for open networks and its application to broadcast encryption. Computer Networks 55(15), 3246–3255 (2011)
24. Zhang, L., Zhang, F., Wu, Q., Domingo-Ferrer, J.: Simulatable certificateless two-party authenticated key agreement protocol. Information Sciences 180(6), 1020–1030 (2010)

New Variants of Lattice Problems and Their NP-Hardness

Wulu Li

School of Mathematical Science
Peking University
Beijing, China
liwulu@pku.edu.cn

Abstract. We introduce some new variants of lattice problems: Quadrant-SVP, Quadrant-CVP and Quadrant-GapCVP'. All of them are NP-hard under deterministic reductions from subset sum problem. These new type of lattice problems have potential in construction of cryptosystems. Moreover, these new variant problems have reductions with standard SVP (shortest vector problem) and CVP (closest vector problem), this feature gives new way to study the complexity of SVP and CVP, especially for the proof of NP-hardness of SVP under deterministic reductions, which is an open problem up to now.

Keywords: lattice, complexity, NP-hard, deterministic reduction.

1 Introduction

Lattice has been widely studied in cryptography in these years, for its problems enjoy very strong security proofs based on worst-case hardness, and they have potential against quantum attack.

A lattice $\mathcal{L}$ is a discrete subgroup of the Euclidean space $\mathbb{R}^m$, and it is generated by linearly independent vectors $\mathbf{b}_1, \mathbf{b}_2, \cdots, \mathbf{b}_n$, namely:

$$\mathcal{L} = \{\sum_{i=1}^{n} x_i \mathbf{b}_i | x_i \in \mathbb{Z}, \mathbf{b}_i \in \mathbb{R}^m\}.$$

Denoted by $\mathcal{L} = \mathcal{L}(\mathbf{b}_1, \mathbf{b}_2, \cdots, \mathbf{b}_n)$, m, n are called the dimension and the rank of it. Usually, we consider lattices with rational generating vectors, and it is called the rational lattices.

Lattice was first studied as a part of geometry of numbers, and was developed Gauss, Hermite, Zolotarev, Dirichlet, Minkowski [18] and Voronoi [22]. There are mainly two classical problems over lattices: SVP and CVP.

SVP (shortest vector problem): given lattice and norm (such as ℓ_2 norm, etc), find the shortest nonzero vector in it;

CVP (closest vector problem): given lattice, norm and a target vector $\mathbf{t} \in \mathbb{R}^m$, find the closest lattice vector from $\mathbf{t}$.

X. Huang and J. Zhou (Eds.): ISPEC 2014, LNCS 8434, pp. 511–523, 2014.

Since the historic work introduced by Lenstra *et.al* [13]: the LLL algorithm, which is the first algorithm for approximate SVP with factor $\phi = O((2/\sqrt{3})^n)$. In 1986, algorithm for approximate CVP was introduced by Babai [4], using the LLL method; Schnorr [20] improved the LLL algorithm and decreased the approximate factor to $(1+\epsilon)^n$; in 2001, Ajtai, Kumar and Sivakumar [3] proposed a new sieve method for solving SVP; Blömer [5] improved the AKS algorithm for solving GSVP and CVP; recently a new algorithm for SVP based on voronoi cell was introduced by Micciancio [17], with single exponential running time.

There are a variety of cryptosystems building on lattice assumptions. In 1996, the Ajtai-Dwork [2] public-key cryptosystem was proposed, the security is based on the worst-case hardness of unique-SVP, it was the first lattice based public-key cryptosystem with provable security; GGH [10] was proposed by Goldreich, Goldwasser and Halevi in 1996; in 1997, Hoffstein, Pipher and Silverman introduced NTRU [11], it is the most efficient lattice based cryptosystem; Oded Regev [19] proposed LWE and cryptosystem built from it, its security was based on the hardness of worst-case hardness of CVP; in 2009, Gentry [8] proposed the first fully-homomorphic encryption scheme based on lattice.

1.1   NP-Hardness Result of SVP and CVP

The complexity of lattice problems has been studied since 1980s. In 1981, van Emde Boas [21] proved the NP-hardness of CVP in ℓ_p norm and NP-hardness of SVP in ℓ_∞ norm, also he conjectured the NP-hardness of SVP in ℓ_p norm; in 1996, Ajtai [1] proved that SVP in ℓ_2 norm is NP-hard, under randomized reduction; Cai [6] improved Ajtai's work, showed approximating SVP in ℓ_p norm within factor $O(1+1/n^\epsilon)$ is NP-hard, his result also based on randomized reduction; Micciancio [14]proved approximating SVP in ℓ_p norm within factor $\sqrt[p]{2}$ is NP-hard under randomized reduction; Knot [12] proved that under assumption "NP$\neq$RTIME", approximate SVP within factor $\gamma(n) = 2^{\log^{1/2-\epsilon}(n)}$ is NP-hard; a recent work by Micciancio [15] improved Knot's result, showed NP-harness of approximating SVP within constant factor under RUR-reduction. But there are no deterministic reductions to prove the NP-hardness of SVP up to now.

On the other side, Goldreich and Goldwasser [9] showed that under approximate factor $\gamma = \sqrt{n/O(\log n)}$, if approximating SVP is NP-hard, then coNP$\subseteq$AM, which is thought to be impossible in complexity theory, so proving the hardness of SVP from constant factor c to $\sqrt{n/O(\log n)}$ is still an open problem.

Actually, the NP-hardness under randomized reductions is not a standard complexity result, how to find a deterministic reduction to prove the NP-hardness of lattice problem is also an open problem. In this paper, we focus on variants of lattice problems and prove their NP-hardness under deterministic reductions.

1.2   Our Results and Open Problems

We introduce 3 new variants of lattice problem: Quadrant-SVP, Quadrant-CVP and Quadrant-CVP', all these problems have NP-hardness under deterministic reductions. The Quadrant-SVP, defined similar to SVP, is to find the shortest nonzero lattice vector in given subset of $\mathbb{R}^n$, usually we call the subset "quadrant" of Euclid space, in this paper, we use quadrant $Q_1 = \{\mathbf{x} = (x_1, \cdots, x_m) | \forall i \in [m], x_i \geq 0\}$.

(Quadrant-SVP) Given lattice $\mathcal{L}$ in $\mathbb{R}^m$, ℓ_p norm and Q_1, find the shortest nonzero vector in $\mathcal{L} \cap Q_1$.

(Quadrant-CVP) Given lattice $\mathcal{L}$ in $\mathbb{R}^m$, ℓ_p norm and a target vector $\mathbf{t} \in \mathbb{R}^m$, find a lattice vector $\mathbf{v}$ such that $||\mathbf{v} - \mathbf{t}|| = min\{||\mathbf{x} - \mathbf{t}|| \,|\, \mathbf{x} \in \mathcal{L}, \mathbf{x} - \mathbf{t} \in Q_1\}$.

The main result of this paper is contained in the following theorem:

Theorem 1. *For any given lattice $\mathcal{L}$ and ℓ_p norm, there exist no polynomial time algorithms to solve Quadrant-SVP, Quadrant-CVP and Quadrant-CVP', unless P=NP.*

We give the first construction of Quadrant lattice problems and prove their NP-hardness, which is the main contribution of this paper. Besides, we give a deterministic reduction from Quadrant-CVP' to CVP, the result can be seen as a new proof of NP-hardness of CVP, this Quadrant method can be used in studying the complexity of SVP and CVP.

By proving the NP-hardness of Quadrant-SVP, we get closer to prove the NP-hardness of SVP under deterministic reduction, which is still an open problem; on the other hand, how to prove the NP-hardness of Quadrant lattice problems with larger approximate factor is also an open problem.

1.3   Organization

In section 2 we give readers some preliminaries; in section 3 we give the definition of Quadrant lattice problems and prove their NP-hardness; in section 4 we discuss the approximate variants of Quadrant lattice problems and prove their NP-hardness; in section 5 we give the conclusion.

2   Preliminaries

2.1   Lattice

Lattice is a subgroup of Euclidian space $\mathbb{R}^m$, it is generated by n independent vectors, namely:

$$\mathcal{L}(\mathbf{b}_1, \ldots, \mathbf{b}_n) = \{\sum_{i=1}^{n} x_i \mathbf{b}_i | \mathbf{x} = (x_1, \cdots, x_m) \in \mathbb{Z}^m\}$$

Where m is the dimension of $\mathcal{L}$, n is its rank, the vectors $\mathbf{b}_1, \cdots, \mathbf{b}_n$ is the basis of $\mathcal{L}$.

The Gram-Schmidt orthogonalization of a basis $\mathbf{B}$ is the sequence of orthogonal vectors $\widetilde{\mathbf{b}}_1, \ldots, \widetilde{\mathbf{b}}_n$, where $\widetilde{\mathbf{b}}_i$ is the component of $\mathbf{b}_i$ orthogonal to

$span(\mathbf{b}_1, \cdots, \mathbf{b}_{i-1})$, clearly, $||\widetilde{\mathbf{b}_i}|| \leq ||\mathbf{b}_i||$, where $|| \cdot ||$ denotes the Euclidian norm in $\mathbb{R}^m$, namely, the ℓ_p norm.

The ith successive minimum λ_i is defined as the smallest r that $\mathbf{b}_r$ contains at least i independent vectors in $\mathbb{R}^m$ (λ_i can be defined in different norms, such as ℓ_p), λ_1 is the length of the shortest vector in $\mathcal{L}$. For a linearly independent vector set $\mathbf{S} \subset \mathcal{L}$, where $\mathbf{S} = \{\mathbf{s}_1 \ldots \mathbf{s}_r\}$, we denote r as the rank of $\mathbf{S}$ and denote $||\mathbf{S}||$ as the longest norm of $\mathbf{s}_1 \ldots \mathbf{s}_r$, namely:

$$||\mathbf{S}|| = \max_i\{||\mathbf{s}_1|| \ldots ||\mathbf{s}_r||\}.$$

If the $\mathbf{S}$ has rank n, we call $\mathbf{S}$ a full rank independent vector set. So λ_n is the norm of shortest full rank independent vector set.

2.2 SVP and CVP

Lattice is attractive in cryptography for its problems including SVP (*Gap*SVP), CVP (*Gap*CVP), all of these problems achieve NP-hardness under deterministic or randomized reductions, we define these problems in the following:

Definition 2. *(SVP) For any given lattice $\mathcal{L}$ and the ℓ_p norm, the goal is to find the shortest nonzero vector $\mathbf{v} \in \mathcal{L}$. In other words, the goal of SVP is to find $\mathbf{v} \in \mathcal{L}$ such that $||\mathbf{v}|| = \lambda_1$.*

Definition 3. *(CVP) For any given lattice $\mathcal{L}$, ℓ_p norm and a target vector $\mathbf{t} \in \mathbb{R}^m$, the goal is to find $\mathbf{v} \in \mathcal{L}$ such that $||\mathbf{v} - \mathbf{t}|| = min_{\mathbf{x} \in \mathcal{L}}||\mathbf{x} - \mathbf{t}||$.*

There are decision versions of SVP and CVP, we omit the definition for simplicity. There are also promise version of SVP and CVP, which is often used in building of cryptosystems.

Definition 4. *(GapSVP_γ) For input a lattice basis $\mathbf{B}$ and a real d, it is a **Yes** instance if $\lambda_1 \leq d$, and is a **No** instance if $\lambda_1 > \gamma d$, if $d < \lambda_1 \leq \gamma d$, then both **Yes** and **No** would be correct.*

Definition 5. *(GapCVP_γ) For input a lattice basis $\mathbf{B}$, a vector $\mathbf{t} \in \mathbb{R}^m$ and a real d, it is a **Yes** instance if $dist(\mathcal{L}, \mathbf{t}) \leq d$, and is a **No** instance if $dist(\mathcal{L}, \mathbf{t}) > \gamma d$, where "dist" is defined by arbitrary norm (ℓ_p norm in this paper) in $\mathbb{R}^m$, $d < dist(\mathcal{L}, \mathbf{t}) \leq \gamma d$, then both **Yes** and **No** would be correct.*

It is obvious that when $\gamma = 1$, $GapSVP_\gamma$ and $GapCVP_\gamma$ is the decision version of SVP and CVP.

2.3 NP-Hardness of Lattice Problems

In this subsection we review the NP-hardness results of several lattice problems, both SVP (GapSVP), CVP (GapCVP) are proved to be NP-hard, we introduce some of them in the following lemmas:

Lemma 6. *([21]) CVP is NP-hard in ℓ_p norm under deterministic reduction; SVP is NP-hard in ℓ_∞ under deterministic reduction.*

Lemma 7. *([1]) SVP in ℓ_2 norm is NP-hard under randomized reduction.*

Lemma 8. *([16]) GapCVP$_\gamma$ is NP-hard in ℓ_p norm under deterministic reduction, where $\gamma = 2^{\log^{1-\epsilon}(n)}$.*

Lemma 9. *([12]) GapSVP$_\gamma$ is NP-hard in ℓ_p norm under randomized reduction, where $\gamma = 2^{\log^{1/2-\epsilon}(n)}$.*

Since there are no NP-hardness results for SVP (GapSVP) under deterministic reductions except for ℓ_p norm, the NP-hardness of Quadrant-SVP is the first deterministic NP-hardness result for SVP type problems.

2.4 Subset Sum Problem

In this paper, we use subset sum (SS) in the construction of reduction, the SS problem is widely studied in cryptography and complexity theory.

Definition 10. *(SS) The input is an integer s and a set of integer $\mathbf{A} = \{a_1, \cdots, a_n\}$, the goal is to determine whether there exists $\mathbf{x} \in \{0,1\}^n$, such that $\sum_{i=1}^{n} x_i a_i = s$.*

SS is a classic NP-complete problem [7], we will use SS in all reduction of this paper.

Theorem 11. *([7]) Subset sum problem is NP-complete.*

Proof. Omitted for brevity. □

3 NP-Hardness of Quadrant-SVP (CVP)

3.1 Definition

In this subsection we give the definition of Quadrant-SVP, Quadrant-CVP, first of all, we define the "Quadrant" we use throughout the paper:

Definition 12. *(Quadrant) A quadrant Q is a subset of $\mathbb{R}^m$, with property that $\forall \mathbf{x} = (x_1, \cdots, x_m) \in Q$, $x_i \geq 0 (or \leq 0)$ for $i = 1, \cdots, m$.*

Obviously there are 2^m Quadrants in $\mathbb{R}^m$, Q_1 denotes $\{\mathbf{x} = (x_1, \cdots, x_m) | x_i \geq 0\}$, and Q_{2^m} denotes $\{\mathbf{x} = (x_1, \cdots, x_m) | x_i \leq 0\}$.

The Quadrant-SVP, defined as solving SVP in Q_i other than $\mathbb{R}^m$.

Definition 13. *(Quadrant-SVP) For any given lattice $\mathcal{L}$ of rank n and the ℓ_p norm, the goal is to find the shortest nonzero vector $\mathbf{v} \in \mathcal{L} \cap Q_i$, if there exist no nonzero vectors in Q_i, output $\emptyset$.*

In the rest of this paper, we will use Q_1 without loss of generosity, if fact, the hardness results of Quadrant lattice problems for any Quadrant Q_i is equivalent to problems for Q_1.

The Quadrant-CVP is defined as the same way:

Definition 14. *(Quadrant-CVP) Given lattice $\mathcal{L}$ in $\mathbb{R}^m$ of rank n, ℓ_p norm and a target vector $\mathbf{t} \in \mathbb{R}^m$, find a lattice vector $\mathbf{v}$ such that $||\mathbf{v} - \mathbf{t}|| = min\{||| \mathbf{x} - \mathbf{t}||| \mathbf{x} \in \mathcal{L}, \mathbf{x} - \mathbf{t} \in Q_1\}$, if there exists no vectors satisfy $\mathbf{x} - \mathbf{t} \in Q_1\}$, output $\emptyset$.*

3.2   Proof of NP-Hardness

In this subsection we prove the NP-hardness of Quadrant-SVP and Quadrant-CVP, using reductions from subset sum problem, our reduction is deterministic.

Theorem 15. *Subset sum problem can be reduced to Quadrant-SVP in polynomial time, under ℓ_p norm $(1 \le p \le \infty)$.*

Proof. For SS problem instance $(a_1, \cdots, a_n; s)$, choose an integer $M > 2n$, we have the following lattice basis matrix:

$$\mathbf{H} = \begin{bmatrix} Ma_1, \cdots, Ma_n & -Ms \\ -\mathbf{I}_n & \mathbf{1}_n \\ \mathbf{I}_{n+1} & \end{bmatrix}.$$

Notice that $\mathbf{I}_n$ stands for the unit matrix of dimension n, and $\mathcal{L}(\mathbf{H})$ is an integer lattice with dimension $2n + 2$. Any vector in $\mathcal{L}(\mathbf{H})$ can be written as:

$$\mathbf{Hx} = \begin{pmatrix} M(\sum_{i=1}^{n} x_i a_i - x_{n+1}s) \\ x_{n+1} - x_1 \\ \vdots \\ x_{n+1} - x_n \\ x_1 \\ \vdots \\ x_{n+1} \end{pmatrix}$$

Where $\mathbf{x} = (x_1, \cdots, x_{n+1})$. We will prove that, if we can solve Quadrant-SVP in the above lattice, we will get the solution of the SS problem. Actually, if the SS problem has a solution, then the Quadrant-SVP has a solution $\mathbf{v}$ such that $||\mathbf{v}||_{\ell_p} \le \sqrt[p]{2n+1}$; if the SS problem has no solutions at all, then the Quadrant-SVP also has no solutions or has solution $\mathbf{v}$ such that $||\mathbf{v}||_{\ell_p} > \sqrt[p]{2n+1}$.

We will divide the proof into two parts, one for $1 \le p < \infty$ and the other for $p = \infty$.

$(1 \le p < \infty)$:

1. If SS problem has a solution $(x_1, \cdots, x_n) \in \{0, 1\}^n$ such that $\sum_{i=1}^{n} x_i a_i = s$, then there exists lattice vector

$$\mathbf{v} = \mathbf{H}(x_1, \cdots, x_n, 1)^T = (0, 1 - x_1, \cdots, 1 - x_n, x_1, \cdots, x_n, 1)^T.$$

Since $x_i = 0, 1$, we get $\mathbf{v} \in Q_1$ and $||\mathbf{v}||_{\ell_p} \leq \sqrt[p]{n+1}$, so there exists solution of Quadrant-SVP in $\mathcal{L}(\mathbf{H})$ with norm less than $\sqrt[p]{n+1}$.

2. If SS problem has no solutions, we prove that the Quadrant-SVP has no solutions or has solution $\mathbf{v}$ with $||\mathbf{v}||_{\ell_p} > \sqrt[p]{2n+1}$. We assume that there exists a solution of Quadrant-SVP, $\mathbf{v} \in Q_1$, that $||\mathbf{v}|| \leq \sqrt[p]{2n+1}$.

   · If $x_{n+1} \geq 2$, since $x_i \geq 0$ and $x_{n+1} - x_i \geq 0$. Among $x_1, \cdots, x_n$, we assume there are k_0 elements equal 0, k_1 elements equal 1, k_2 elements equal or bigger than 2, then $n = k_1 + k_2 + k_3$, and

$$||\mathbf{v}||_{\ell_p}^p \geq 2k_1 + 2^p + k_0 2^p + k_2 2^p$$

$$= 2(n + 2^{p-1}) + (2^p - 2)(n - k_1) \geq 2n + 2.$$

   · If $x_{n+1} = 1$, we know that for all $1 \leq i \leq n$, $x_i = 0, 1$, since the SS problem has no solutions, we get $\sum_{i=1}^{n} x_i a_i \neq s$, then $||\mathbf{v}||_{\ell_p}^p \geq M^p \geq 2^p n^p > 2n + 1$.

   · If $x_{n+1} = 0$, then for all $1 \leq i \leq n$, $x_i = 0$, we get $\mathbf{v} = \mathbf{0}$, it can not be a solution for the Quadrant-SVP problem.

   In all of the 3 situations, we get contradiction against the fact we are assuming, then we know that the Quadrant-SVP has no solutions or has solution $\mathbf{v}$ such that $||\mathbf{v}||_{\ell_p} > \sqrt[p]{2n+1}$.

The correctness of the theorem easily followed by the above argument, when $1 \leq p < \infty$.
$(p = \infty)$:

1. If SS problem has a solution, use similar method, we easily get there exists solution of Quadrant-SVP in $\mathcal{L}(\mathbf{H})$ with ℓ_∞ norm less than 1.

2. If SS problem has no solutions, we get that the Quadrant-SVP has no solutions or has solution $\mathbf{v}$ with $||\mathbf{v}||_{\ell_\infty} \geq 2$.

By above argument, we can solve the SS problem by determine whether the Quadrant-SVP has a solution with norm equal or less than $\sqrt[p]{n+1}$ (or 1) when $1 \leq p < \infty$ (or $p = \infty$). □

We can easily get the NP-hardness of Quadrant-SVP under deterministic reduction:

Corollary 16. *Quadrant-SVP is NP-hard under deterministic reductions, in other words, there exist no polynomial time algorithms to solve Quadrant-SVP, unless P=NP.*

As for Quadrant-CVP, we use similar method to construct the reduction from SS problem.

Theorem 17. *Subset sum problem can be reduced to Quadrant-CVP in polynomial time, under $\ell_p (1 \leq p \leq \infty)$.*

Proof. For SS problem instance $(a_1, \cdots, a_n; s)$, choose an integer $M > 2n$, we have the following lattice basis matrix and target vector:

$$\mathbf{T} = \begin{bmatrix} Ma_1, \cdots, Ma_n \\ -\mathbf{I}_n \\ \mathbf{I}_n \end{bmatrix}, \quad \mathbf{t} = (Ms, -\mathbf{1}_n, \mathbf{0}_n)^T.$$

Notice that $\mathbf{I}_n$ stands for the unit matrix of dimension n, and $\mathcal{L}(\mathbf{T})$ is an integer lattice with dimension $n + 1$. For any $\mathbf{x} = (x_1, \cdots, x_n)^T$,

$$\mathbf{Tx} - \mathbf{t} = (M(\sum_{i=1}^{n} x_i a_i - s), 1 - x_1, \cdots, 1 - x_n, x_1, \cdots, x_n)^T.$$

We will also divide the proof into two parts, one for $1 \leq p < \infty$ and the other for $p = \infty$.
$(1 \leq p < \infty)$:

1. If the SS problem has a solution, say $\mathbf{x} = (x_1, \cdots, x_n)^T$, such that $\sum_{i=1}^{n} x_i a_i = s$, then there exists a lattice vector $\mathbf{v} = \mathbf{Tx}$ such that $\mathbf{v} - \mathbf{t} = (0, 1 - x_1, \cdots, 1 - x_n, x_1, \cdots, x_n)^T \in Q_1$, thus $x_i = 0, 1$, we have $||\mathbf{v} - \mathbf{t}||_{\ell_p} = \sqrt[p]{n}$, then the solution of Quadrant-CVP is within distance $\sqrt[p]{n}$ from $\mathbf{t}$.
2. If the SS problem has no solutions, we assume that there exists a solution of Quadrant-CVP, say $\mathbf{v} = \mathbf{Tx}$ such that $\mathbf{v} - \mathbf{t} \in Q_1$ and $||\mathbf{v} - \mathbf{t}||_{\ell_p} \leq \sqrt[p]{n}$, then we have $x_i = 0, 1$, and $s \neq \sum_{i=1}^{n} x_i a_i$, we have $||\mathbf{v} - \mathbf{t}||_{\ell_p}^p \geq M^p \geq (n+1)^p \geq n + 1$, which contradicts to the fact that $||\mathbf{v} - \mathbf{t}||_{\ell_p} \leq \sqrt[p]{n}$.

The correctness of the theorem followed by the above argument, when $1 \leq p < \infty$.
$(p = \infty)$:

1. If SS problem has a solution, use similar method, we easily get there exists solution $\mathbf{v}$ of Quadrant-CVP in $\mathcal{L}(\mathbf{T})$ with $||\mathbf{v} - \mathbf{t}||_{\ell_\infty} \leq 1$.
2. If SS problem has no solutions, we get that the Quadrant-CVP has no solutions or has solution $\mathbf{v}$ with $||\mathbf{v} - \mathbf{t}||_{\ell_\infty} \geq M$.

From the above discussion, we can solve the SS problem by determine whether there exists lattice vector $\mathbf{v}$ within ℓ_p (or ℓ_∞) distance $\sqrt[p]{n}$ (or 1) from $\mathbf{t}$, satisfying $\mathbf{v} - \mathbf{t} \in Q_1$. $\qquad \square$

Notice the above reduction is deterministic, we get similar corollary:

Corollary 18. *Quadrant-CVP is NP-hard under deterministic reductions, in other words, there exist no polynomial time algorithms to solve Quadrant-CVP, unless P=NP.*

4 NP-Hardness of Promise Variants of Quadrant Lattice Problems

4.1 Definitions

There are also promise version of Quadrant lattice problem, defined similar to GapSVP and GapCVP in section 2.2, we define another 3 promise versions of Quadrant lattice problems, they are Quadrant-GapSVP, Quadrant-GapCVP, Quadrant-GapCVP'. In the rest of this paper, we use symbol $\lambda_1^{(1)}$ denotes $min_{0 \neq \mathbf{x} \in \mathcal{L}(\mathbf{B}) \cap Q_1} \{ \|\mathbf{x}\|_{\ell_p} \}$.

Definition 19. *(Quadrant-GapSVP$_\gamma$) For input a lattice basis $\mathbf{B}$ and a real d, it is a **Yes** instance if $\lambda_1^{(1)} \leq d$, and is a **No** instance if $\lambda_1^{(1)} > \gamma d$ or there are no nonzero lattice vectors in Q_1, if $d < \lambda_1^{(1)} \leq \gamma d$, then both **Yes** and **No** would be correct.*

We also use symbol $dist^{(1)}(\mathbf{t}, \mathcal{L})$ denotes $min_{\mathbf{v} \in \mathcal{L}, \mathbf{v} - \mathbf{t} \in Q_1} \{ \|\mathbf{v} - \mathbf{t}\|_{\ell_p}$ in the rest of this paper.

Definition 20. *(Quadrant-GapCVP$_\gamma$) For input a lattice basis $\mathbf{B}$, a target vector $\mathbf{t}$ and a real d, it is a **Yes** instance if $dist^{(1)}(\mathbf{t}, \mathcal{L}) \leq d\}$, and a **No** instance if $dist^{(1)}(\mathbf{t}, \mathcal{L}) > \gamma d\}$, or there are no vectors satisfying $\mathbf{v} - \mathbf{t} \in Q_1$, if $d < dist^{(1)}(\mathbf{t}, \mathcal{L}) \leq \gamma d$, then both **Yes** and **No** would be correct.*

4.2 NP-Hardness Proofs

Theorem 21. *The SS problem $(a_1, \cdots, a_n; s)$ can be reduced to Quadrant-GapSVP$_\gamma$ where $\gamma = \sqrt[p]{2} - \epsilon$ for $p < \infty$ and $\gamma = 2 - \epsilon$ for $p = \infty$, where $\epsilon > 0$ is a negligible constant.*

Proof. As proved in Theorem 15, we divide the proof into two parts, one for $1 \leq p < \infty$ and the other for $p = \infty$.
$(1 \leq p < \infty)$: We set $\mathcal{L}(\mathbf{H})$, $d = \sqrt[p]{n+1}$, $\gamma = \sqrt[p]{2} - \epsilon$ as the input of Quadrant-GapSVP$_\gamma$, where ϵ is positive small enough.

1. If the SS problem has a solution, we know from Theorem 15 that $\lambda_1^{(1)} \leq \sqrt[p]{n+1} = d$, which is not a **No** instance of Quadrant-GapSVP$_\gamma$;
2. If the SS problem has no solutions, we know that $\lambda_1^{(1)} \geq \sqrt[p]{2n+2} = \sqrt[p]{2}d > \gamma d$ or $\mathcal{L} \cap Q_1 = \{\mathbf{0}\}$, which is not a **Yes** instance of Quadrant-GapSVP$_\gamma$.

By the answer of Quadrant-GapSVP$_\gamma$, we can determine whether the SS problem has a solution, namely, if the output of Quadrant-GapSVP$_\gamma$ is **Yes**, then SS has a solution; if the output of Quadrant-GapSVP$_\gamma$ is **No**, then SS has no solutions.
$(p = \infty)$: We set $\mathcal{L}(\mathbf{H})$, $d = 1$, $\gamma = \sqrt[p]{2} - \epsilon$ as the input of Quadrant-GapSVP$_\gamma$ as above.

1. If the SS problem has a solution, we know from Theorem 15 that $\lambda_1^{(1)} \leq 1 = d$, which is not a **No** instance of Quadrant-GapSVP$_\gamma$;

2. If the SS problem has no solutions, we know that $\lambda_1^{(1)} \geq 2 = 2d > \gamma d$ or $\mathcal{L} \cap Q_1 = \{\mathbf{0}\}$, which is not a **Yes** instance of Quadrant-$GapSVP_\gamma$.

Similarly, if the output of Quadrant-$GapSVP_\gamma$ is **Yes**, then SS has a solution; if the output of Quadrant-$GapSVP_\gamma$ is **No**, then SS has no solutions. $\qquad\square$

Notice the above reduction is deterministic in polynomial time, then we easily get the NP-hardness of Quadrant-$GapSVP_\gamma$:

Corollary 22. *Quadrant-$GapSVP_\gamma$ is NP-hard under deterministic reductions, where $\gamma = \sqrt[p]{2} - \epsilon$ in $\ell_{p<\infty}$ norm and $\gamma = 2 - \epsilon$ in ℓ_∞ norm.*

The result for Quadrant-$GapCVP_\gamma$ is similar, according to Theorem 17 and Theorem 21.

Theorem 23. *The SS problem $(a_1, \cdots, a_n; s)$ can be reduced to Quadrant-$GapCVP_\gamma$ where $\gamma = poly(n)$, where $poly(n)$ denotes for any polynomial with input n.*

Proof. $(1 \leq p < \infty)$: For SS instance $(a_1, \cdots, a_n; s)$, choose $M = \gamma \sqrt[p]{n} + 1$, which is still polynomial of n, build a lattice $\mathcal{L}(\mathbf{T})$ as in Theorem 17, we set $\mathcal{L}(\mathbf{T})$, γ, $\mathbf{t}$, $d = \sqrt[p]{n}$ as the input for Quadrant-$GapCVP_\gamma$:

1. If the SS problem has a solution, we know that $dist^{(1)}(\mathbf{t}, \mathcal{L}) \leq \sqrt[p]{n}$, which is not a **No** instance of Quadrant-$GapCVP_\gamma$;
2. If the SS problem has no solutions, we know that $dist^{(1)}(\mathbf{t}, \mathcal{L}) \geq M = \gamma \sqrt[p]{n} + 1 > \gamma d$ or $\mathcal{L} \cap Q_1 = \{\mathbf{0}\}$, which is not a **Yes** instance of Quadrant-$GapCVP_\gamma$.

We can solve the SS by solving the Quadrant-$GapCVP_\gamma$, if the output of Quadrant-$GapCVP_\gamma$ is **Yes**, then SS has a solution; if the output of Quadrant-$GapCVP_\gamma$ is **No**, then SS has no solutions.
$(1 \leq p < \infty)$: Omitted for brevity. $\qquad\square$

Corollary 24. *Quadrant-$GapCVP_{\gamma=poly(n)}$ is NP-hard under deterministic reductions.*

4.3   Mixed Problem and Relationship with GapCVP

In this subsection we mix the original GapCVP with the Quadrant-GapCVP, propose a new type of promise problem and prove its NP-hardness under deterministic reduction, we also give reduction between the new type problem and standard GapCVP.

Definition 25. *(Quadrant-GapCVP') For input a lattice basis $\mathbf{B}$, a target vector $\mathbf{t}$ and a real d, it is a **Yes** instance if $dist^{(1)}(\mathbf{t}, \mathcal{L}) \leq d$, and a **No** instance if $dist(\mathbf{t}, \mathcal{L}) > d$, or there are no vectors satisfying $\mathbf{v} - \mathbf{t} \in Q_1$, if $d < dist^{(1)}(\mathbf{t}, \mathcal{L})$ and $dist(\mathbf{t}, \mathcal{L}) \leq d$, then both **Yes** and **No** would be correct.*

Theorem 26. *The SS problem $(a_1, \cdots, a_n; s)$ can be reduced to Quadrant-GapCVP'.*

Proof. $(1 \leq p < \infty)$: For SS instance $(a_1, \cdots, a_n; s)$, choose $M = \sqrt[p]{n} + 1$, which is still polynomial of n, build a lattice $\mathcal{L}(\mathbf{T})$ as in Theorem 17, we set $\mathcal{L}(\mathbf{T})$, γ, $\mathbf{t}$, $d = \sqrt[p]{n}$ as the input for Quadrant-GapCVP':

1. If the SS problem has a solution, we know that $dist^{(1)}(\mathbf{t}, \mathcal{L}) \leq \sqrt[p]{n}$, which is not a **No** instance of Quadrant-GapCVP';
2. If the SS problem has no solutions, we assume that $dist(\mathbf{t}, \mathcal{L}) \leq \sqrt[p]{n}$, then there exists lattice vector $\mathbf{v} = \mathbf{Tx}$ such that $\mathbf{v} - \mathbf{t} = (M(\sum_{i=1}^{n} x_i a_i - s), 1 - x_1, \cdots, 1 - x_n, x_1, \cdots, x_n)^T$ and $||\mathbf{v} - \mathbf{t}|| \leq \sqrt[p]{n}$. Since $M = \sqrt[p]{n} + 1$, we know that $\sum_{i=1}^{n} x_i a_i - s = 0$, then $\exists i$ such that $x_i \neq 0, 1$, we have $max\{|1 - x_i|, |x_i|\} \geq 2$, then $||\mathbf{v} - \mathbf{t}|| \geq \sqrt[p]{n + 2^p} > \sqrt[p]{n}$, which contradicts to the fact we are assuming, so it is not a **Yes** instance of Quadrant-GapCVP'.

So we can solve the SS by solving the Quadrant-GapCVP', if the output of Quadrant-GapCVP' is **Yes**, then SS has a solution; if the output of Quadrant-GapCVP' is **No**, then SS has no solutions.
$(1 \leq p < \infty)$: Omitted for brevity. $\square$

Corollary 27. *Quadrant-GapCVP' is NP-hard under deterministic reductions.*

We get the NP-hardness of Quadrant-GapCVP' by reduction from SS problem, since we know the fact that GapCVP is also NP-hard under deterministic reduction, a natural question may be asked, what is the relationship between GapCVP and Quadrant-GapCVP'? Is one question harder than another? Actually, we have the following result:

Theorem 28. *There exists deterministic reduction from Quadrant-GapCVP' to $GapCVP_{\gamma=1}$.*

Proof. Given Quadrant-GapCVP' instance $(\mathcal{L}, d, \mathbf{t})$, we solve GapCVP with the same input.

1. If the $(\mathcal{L}, d, \mathbf{t})$ is not a **Yes** instance for Quadrant-GapCVP', which means $dist(\mathbf{t}, \mathcal{L}) > d$. For GapCVP, it is also not a **Yes** instance for Quadrant-GapCVP';
2. If the $(\mathcal{L}, d, \mathbf{t})$ is not a **No** instance for Quadrant-GapCVP', which means $dist^{(1)}(\mathbf{t}, \mathcal{L}) \leq d$, since $dist(\mathbf{t}, \mathcal{L}) \leq dist^{(1)}(\mathbf{t}, \mathcal{L})$, we get $dist(\mathbf{t}, \mathcal{L}) \leq d$, which is not a **No** instance for GapCVP.

The reduction easily followed by the above argument, and the reduction is deterministic. $\square$

Form Theorem 28 we know that Quadrant-GapCVP' is easier than GapCVP, but still achieves NP-hardness. It has potential in construction of cryptosystem as GapCVP.

5   Conclusion

In this paper we study a variety of new lattice problems, they are Quadrant-SVP(CVP), Quadrant-GapSVP(CVP), Quadrant-GapCVP'. All the five problems are NP-hard under deterministic reduction, and they have reduction with the standard lattice problem. These new lattice problems are attractive for their hardness and potential in cryptography.

Although, from our point of view, there are still many open questions about the Quadrant lattice problems, such as the worst-case to average-case reduction; hardness under larger approximate factor; specific relationship with standard lattice problems.

References

1. Ajtai, M.: The shortest vector problem in l 2 is np-hard for randomized reductions. In: Proceedings of the Thirtieth Annual ACM Symposium on Theory of Computing, pp. 10–19. ACM (1998)
2. Ajtai, M., Dwork, C.: A public-key cryptosystem with worst-case/average-case equivalence. In: Proceedings of the Twenty-ninth Annual ACM Symposium on Theory of Computing, pp. 284–293. ACM (1997)
3. Ajtai, M., Kumar, R., Sivakumar, D.: A sieve algorithm for the shortest lattice vector problem. In: Proceedings of the Thirty-third Annual ACM Symposium on Theory of Computing, pp. 601–610. ACM (2001)
4. Babai On, L.: lovászlattice reduction and the nearest lattice point problem. Combinatorica 6(1), 1–13 (1986)
5. Blömer, J., Naewe, S.: Sampling methods for shortest vectors, closest vectors and successive minima. In: Arge, L., Cachin, C., Jurdziński, T., Tarlecki, A. (eds.) ICALP 2007. LNCS, vol. 4596, pp. 65–77. Springer, Heidelberg (2007)
6. Cai, J.-Y., Nerurkar, A.: Approximating the svp to within a factor $(1+ 1/\dim e)$ is np-hard under randomized reductions. Journal of Computer and System Sciences 59(2), 221–239 (1999)
7. Gary, M.R., Johnson, D.S.: Computers and intractability: A guide to the theory of np-completeness (1979)
8. Gentry, C.: Fully homomorphic encryption using ideal lattices (2009)
9. Goldreich, O., Goldwasser, S.: On the limits of non-approximability of lattice problems. In: Proceedings of the Thirtieth Annual ACM Symposium on Theory of Computing, pp. 1–9. ACM (1998)
10. Goldreich, O., Goldwasser, S., Halevi, S.: Public-key cryptosystems from lattice reduction problems. In: Kaliski Jr., B.S. (ed.) CRYPTO 1997. LNCS, vol. 1294, pp. 112–131. Springer, Heidelberg (1997)
11. Hoffstein, J., Pipher, J., Silverman, J.H.: NTRU: A ring-based public key cryptosystem. In: Buhler, J.P. (ed.) ANTS 1998. LNCS, vol. 1423, pp. 267–288. Springer, Heidelberg (1998)
12. Khot, S.: Hardness of approximating the shortest vector problem in lattices. Journal of the ACM (JACM) 52(5), 789–808 (2005)
13. Lenstra, A.K., Lenstra, H.W., Lovász, L.: Factoring polynomials with rational coefficients. Mathematische Annalen 261(4), 515–534 (1982)
14. Micciancio, D.: The shortest vector in a lattice is hard to approximate to within some constant. SIAM Journal on Computing 30(6), 2008–2035 (2001)

15. Micciancio, D.: Inapproximability of the shortest vector problem: Toward a deterministic reduction. Theory of Computing 8(1), 487–512 (2012)
16. Micciancio, D., Goldwasser, S.: Complexity of lattice problems: a cryptographic perspective, vol. 671. Springer (2002)
17. Micciancio, D., Voulgaris, P.: A deterministic single exponential time algorithm for most lattice problems based on voronoi cell computations. In: Proceedings of the 42nd ACM Symposium on Theory of Computing, pp. 351–358. ACM (2010)
18. Minkowski, H.: Geometrie der zahlen. BG Teubner (1910)
19. Regev, O.: On lattices, learning with errors, random linear codes, and cryptography. J. ACM 56(6), 34:1–34:40 (2009)
20. Schnorr, C.-P.: A hierarchy of polynomial time lattice basis reduction algorithms. Theoretical Computer Science 53(2), 201–224 (1987)
21. van Emde-Boas, P.: Another NP-complete partition problem and the complexity of computing short vectors in a lattice, Department, Univ. (1981)
22. Voronoï, G.: Nouvelles applications des paramètres continus à la théorie des formes quadratiques. deuxième mémoire. recherches sur les parallélloèdres primitifs. Journal für die reine und angewandte Mathematik 134, 198–287 (1908)

Improved Preimage Attacks against Reduced HAS-160*

Ronglin Hao[1,2], Bao Li[2], Bingke Ma[2], and Xiaoqian Li[2]

[1] Department of Electronic Engineering and Information Science,
University of Science and Technology of China, Hefei, 230027, China
haorl@mail.ustc.edu.cn
[2] State Key Laboratory of Information Security, Institute of Information
Engineering, Chinese Academy of Sciences, Beijing, 100093, China
{lb,bkma,xqli}@is.ac.cn

Abstract. HAS-160 is a Korean industry standard for hash functions. It has a similar structure to SHA-1 and produces a 160-bit hash value. In this paper, we propose improved preimage attacks against step-reduced HAS-160 using the differential meet-in-the-middle technique and initial structure. Our work finds a pseudo-preimage of 70 steps of HAS-160 with a complexity of $2^{155.71}$ and this pseudo-preimage attack can be converted to a preimage attack with a complexity of $2^{158.86}$. Moreover, we reduce the complexity of previous pseudo-preimage attack on 65-step HAS-160 from $2^{143.4}$ to $2^{139.09}$. To the best of our knowledge, our result on 70 steps is the best preimage attack on HAS-160 in terms of attacked steps.

Keywords: HAS-160, hash function, preimage attack, differential meet-in-the-middle.

1 Introduction

Cryptographic hash function is one of the most crucial parts of modern cryptography. A hash function takes a message of arbitrary length and produces a bit string of fixed length. Secure hash functions need to fulfill three main properties: preimage resistance, second-preimage resistance, and collision resistance. Suppose that the length of the hash value is n bits. A generic attack needs at least 2^n computations of the hash function to find a preimage or a second-preimage.

HAS-160 is a Korean industry standard (TTAS.KO-12.0011/R1) [2] for hash functions which is widely used in Korea. The structure of HAS-160 is similar to SHA-1 [4]. However, there are two key differences between them. Firstly, as Norbert *et al.* pointed out in [1] that HAS-160 uses multiple sets of rotation

---

* This work was supported by the National Basic Research Program of China (973 Project, No.2013CB338002), the National High Technology Research and Development Program of China (863 Program, No.2013AA014002), the National Natural Science Foundation of China (No.61379137), the IIE's Cryptography Research Project (No.Y3Z0027103), and the Strategic Priority Research Program of Chinese Academy of Sciences under Grant XDA06010702.

X. Huang and J. Zhou (Eds.): ISPEC 2014, LNCS 8434, pp. 524–536, 2014.

constants within the compression function, while SHA-1 uses the single set of rotation constants. Secondly, the message schedule of HAS-160 is non-recursive and can be regarded as a mixture of designs of MD5 [5] and SHA-0 [6].

Many cryptanalysis results on HAS-160 have been proposed. Collision attacks on step-reduced HAS-160 are analyzed in [17–20]. The best result with practical complexity in terms of attacked steps is the semi-free-start collision for 65 steps [20] exhibited at ICISC 2011. The second-order collisions for the full HAS-160 compression function are discussed in [21, 22]. In particular, a practical distinguisher has been generated in [22] recently. At ICISC 2008, preimage attacks on 48 and 52 steps of HAS-160 were presented in [13], which used the splice-and-cut, partial-matching and partial-fixing techniques [3]. After that, several new techniques for (pseudo) preimage attacks against MD4-like hash functions were developed, such as the initial structure and improved partial-fixing technique for unknown carry behavior [14], and the kernel computing approach for chunk separation [11]. Combining these techniques, Deukjo *et al.* showed an improved preimage attack against 68-step HAS-160 [12] at ICISC 2009. As far as we know, no progress on preimage attack has been made since 2009.

Our Contributions. In this paper, we investigate the preimage resistance of HAS-160. Using the differential meet-in-the-middle technique [7] and initial structure, we are able to attack the middle 70 steps (Steps 6-75)[1] out of 80 steps of HAS-160. According to the experiment result, a pseudo-preimage can be found with an expected time complexity of $2^{155.71}$ and a memory of 2^7 words. Then, the pseudo-preimages are converted to a preimage with a complexity of $2^{158.86}$. Based on the same chunk separation, the complexity of the original pseudo-preimage attack on 65 steps [12] is reduced from $2^{143.4}$ to $2^{139.09}$. Slight improvements are also obtained for attacks on 67 and 68 steps of HAS-160. Finally, we provide a security margin for preimage attack on full HAS-160 applying the brute-force attack. The previous results and our results are listed in Table 1.

Organization. Section 2 gives a brief description of HAS-160. Section 3 introduces the techniques used in the meet-in-the-middle preimage attack. Section 4 presents pseudo-preimage and preimage attacks on step-reduced HAS-160. Section 5 briefly provides a security benchmark for actual attacks on full HAS-160. Section 6 concludes the paper.

2   Specification of HAS-160

HAS-160 [2] is a hash function based on the Merkle-Damgård structure that produces 160-bit hash values. The original message M is padded to be a multiple of 512 bits. A single bit 1, a variable number of 0s, and the 64-bit binary

---

[1] We attack the middle 70 steps rather than the first 70 steps in this paper. Since the best previous preimage attacks on HAS-160 work on the middle steps as well, we think our attack is meaningful.

Table 1. Preimage attacks against HAS-160

Steps	Step Number	Pseudo-preimage	Preimage	Memory (words)	Reference
48	1-48	2^{128}	2^{145}	$2^{32} \times 6$	[13]
52	12-63	2^{144}	2^{153}	$2^{48} \times 9$	[13]
52	12-63	2^{144}	2^{153}	$2^{16} \times 9$	[12]
65	0-64	$2^{143.4}$	$2^{152.7}$	$2^{16} \times 6$	[12]
67	0-66	2^{154}	2^{158}	$2^{10} \times 7$	[12]
68	12-79	$2^{150.7}$	$2^{156.3}$	$2^{12} \times 7$	[12]
65	0-64	$2^{139.09}$	$2^{150.55}$	$2^{24} \times 5$	Sec. 4.3
67	0-66	$2^{152.2}$	$2^{157.1}$	$2^{10} \times 3$	App. A
68	12-79	$2^{149.32}$	$2^{155.66}$	$2^{13} \times 2$	App. A
70	6-75	$2^{155.71}$	$2^{158.86}$	2^7	Sec. 4.2
80	0-79	-	$2^{159.04}$	$2^{31} \times 5$	Sec. 5

representation of the length of M are appended at the end. Then the padded message is split into L 512-bit message blocks $M^0, M^1, \ldots, M^{L-1}$. The hash value is computed as follows:

$$H^0 = IV, \ H^{j+1} = E(M^j, H^j) + H^j, \ 0 \le j < L,$$

where E is the internal block cipher of HAS-160, H^j is a 160-bit chaining value which consists of five 32-bit words, and IV represents the initial value specified by the designers. The last chaining value H^L is the output of the hash function.

The internal cipher E is divided into 4 rounds, 20 steps per round. The operation of $E(M^j, H^j)$ consists of two parts: the message expansion and the state update transformation.

Message Expansion. The message schedule of HAS-160 splits M^j into sixteen 32-bit message words $m_0, \ldots, m_{15}$ at first. Then based on the original 16 message words, HAS-160 produces 4 additional message words $m_{16}, \ldots, m_{19}$ for each round. The expanded message word w_i used in each step i ($i = 0, 1, \ldots, 79$) is shown in Table 2.

State Update Transformation. The chaining value p_i right before step i is denoted by $(a_i, b_i, c_i, d_i, e_i)$, i.e., $p_0 = H^j$. Fig. 1 shows the transformation of step i ($i = 0, \ldots, 79$). Note that f_i, k_i, and $\lll s$ denote bitwise Boolean function, constant number and s-bit left rotation depending on each step, respectively. The corresponding definitions are shown in Table 3.

3 Related Works: Techniques for Meet-in-the-Middle Preimage Attacks

3.1 Converting Pseudo-preimages to a Preimage

Given a hash value H^n, a pseudo-preimage is a pair (H^{n-1}, M) such that $CF(H^{n-1}, M) = H^n$, where $H^{n-1} \ne IV$ and CF is the compression function.

Table 2. Message expansion of HAS-160

Round 1	$w_0, w_1, \ldots, w_9$	m_{18}	m_0	m_1	m_2	m_3	m_{19}	m_4	m_5	m_6	m_7
	$w_{10}, w_{11}, \ldots, w_{19}$	m_{16}	m_8	m_9	m_{10}	m_{11}	m_{17}	m_{12}	m_{13}	m_{14}	m_{15}
Round 2	$w_{20}, w_{21}, \ldots, w_{29}$	m_{18}	m_3	m_6	m_9	m_{12}	m_{19}	m_{15}	m_2	m_5	m_8
	$w_{30}, w_{31}, \ldots, w_{39}$	m_{16}	m_{11}	m_{14}	m_1	m_4	m_{17}	m_7	m_{10}	m_{13}	m_0
Round 3	$w_{40}, w_{41}, \ldots, w_{49}$	m_{18}	m_{12}	m_5	m_{14}	m_7	m_{19}	m_0	m_9	m_2	m_{11}
	$w_{50}, w_{51}, \ldots, w_{59}$	m_{16}	m_4	m_{13}	m_6	m_{15}	m_{17}	m_8	m_1	m_{10}	m_3
Round 4	$w_{60}, w_{61}, \ldots, w_{69}$	m_{18}	m_7	m_2	m_{13}	m_8	m_{19}	m_3	m_{14}	m_9	m_4
	$w_{70}, w_{71}, \ldots, w_{79}$	m_{16}	m_{15}	m_{10}	m_5	m_0	m_{17}	m_{11}	m_6	m_1	m_{12}

	Round 1	Round 2	Round 3	Round 4
m_{18}	$m_8 \oplus m_9$ $\oplus m_{10} \oplus m_{11}$	$m_{11} \oplus m_{14}$ $\oplus m_1 \oplus m_4$	$m_4 \oplus m_{13}$ $\oplus m_6 \oplus m_{15}$	$m_{15} \oplus m_{10}$ $\oplus m_5 \oplus m_0$
m_{19}	$m_{12} \oplus m_{13}$ $\oplus m_{14} \oplus m_{15}$	$m_7 \oplus m_{10}$ $\oplus m_{13} \oplus m_0$	$m_8 \oplus m_1$ $\oplus m_{10} \oplus m_3$	$m_{11} \oplus m_6$ $\oplus m_1 \oplus m_{12}$
m_{16}	$m_0 \oplus m_1$ $\oplus m_2 \oplus m_3$	$m_3 \oplus m_6$ $\oplus m_9 \oplus m_{12}$	$m_{12} \oplus m_5$ $\oplus m_{14} \oplus m_7$	$m_7 \oplus m_2$ $\oplus m_{13} \oplus m_8$
m_{17}	$m_4 \oplus m_5$ $\oplus m_6 \oplus m_7$	$m_{15} \oplus m_2$ $\oplus m_5 \oplus m_8$	$m_0 \oplus m_9$ $\oplus m_2 \oplus m_{11}$	$m_3 \oplus m_{14}$ $\oplus m_9 \oplus m_4$

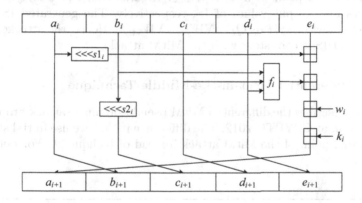

Fig. 1. Step transformation of HAS-160

Table 3. Boolean function f, constant k, and rotations $s1$ and $s2$ of HAS-160

Round	Step i	$f_i(X, Y, Z)$	k_i	$s2_i$
1	$0-19$	$(X \wedge Y) \vee (\neg X \wedge Z)$	0x00000000	10
2	$20-39$	$X \oplus Y \oplus Z$	0x5a827999	17
3	$40-59$	$Y \oplus (X \vee \neg Z)$	0x6ed9eba1	25
4	$60-79$	$X \oplus Y \oplus Z$	0x8f1bbcdc	30

$i \bmod 20$	0	1	2	3	4	5	6	7	8	9	10	11	12	13	14	15	16	17	18	19
$s1_i$	5	11	7	15	6	13	8	14	7	12	9	11	8	15	6	12	9	14	5	13

For the narrow-pipe Merkle-Damgård based hash functions with an n-bit output, there is a generic algorithm from [15, Fact 9.99] which can convert pseudo-preimages to a preimage with a total complexity of $2^{(n+c)/2+1}$, where the complexity of a pseudo-preimage attack is 2^c ($c < n-2$).

3.2   Splice-and-Cut and Initial Structure

In the splice-and-cut framework developed by Aoki and Sasaki [3], the first and last steps of the compression function can be considered as consecutive steps via the feed-forward. Thus, we can start the meet-in-the-middle (MitM) attack from any step and find more appropriate chunk separations with independent neutral message words. Since the initial chaining value is determined by the effective matching and may not be equal to IV, only a pseudo-preimage rather than a preimage can be obtained.

Instead of starting the computations from a single state, the initial structure (IS) technique [14] can be applied to set several consecutive steps as the splitting point, which can increase the total number of attacked steps. Given the neutral words NW_{for} and NW_{back} involved by IS, IS needs to be constructed properly so that the backward computation is independent from NW_{for} and the forward computation is independent from NW_{back}. Assume that P_{IS} and Q_{IS} are the input values and output values of IS, respectively. The generated IS can be regarded as a function $IS(P_{IS}, Q_{IS}, NW_{for}, NW_{back})$. Hence, the attacker should make sure that IS is consistent with the MitM attack.

3.3   The Differential Meet-in-the-Middle Technique

This section describes the differential MitM pseudo-preimage attack proposed by Knellwolf et al. at CRYPTO 2012. The difference is that we use initial structure as the starting point of the MitM attack instead of biclique [9]. For details, we refer to [7].

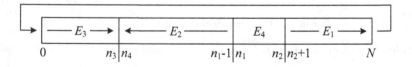

Fig. 2. Separation of E for pseudo-preimage attacks

Suppose the internal block cipher E used in HAS-160 has an n-bit block size and a k-bit key size ($k > n$). The equation $A =_T B$ means $A \wedge T = B \wedge T$, where $T \in \{0,1\}^n$ denotes a truncation mask. First, E is separated into four subparts, $E = E_1 \circ E_4 \circ E_2 \circ E_3$ as shown in Fig. 2. The initial structure is constructed for E_4. E_1 and E_3 via the feed-forward denote the forward chunk, and E_2 is the backward chunk. Assume that h is the target hash value and S denotes the randomly fixed chaining values in the initial structure. Then, the attacker tries to find two linear spaces $D_1, D_2 \subset \{0,1\}^k$, which consist of the same number of message differences as follows:

- $D_1 \cap D_2 = \{0\}$.
- For each $\delta_1 \in D_1$ and uniformly chosen M and S, $E_1 \circ E_4(M,S) = E_1 \circ E_4(M \oplus \delta_1, S)$, and also there exists a difference $\Delta_1 \in \{0,1\}^n$ such that $\Delta_1 =_T E_3(M,S) \oplus E_3(M \oplus \delta_1, S)$ holds with probability p_1 ($0 < p_1 \le 1$).
- For each $\delta_2 \in D_2$ and uniformly chosen M and S, there exists a difference $\Delta_2 \in \{0,1\}^n$ such that $\Delta_2 =_T E_2^{-1} \circ E_4^{-1}(M,S) \oplus E_2^{-1} \circ E_4^{-1}(M \oplus \delta_2, S)$ holds with probability p_2 ($0 < p_2 \le 1$).

Algorithm 1. Testing $M \oplus D_1 \oplus D_2$ for a candidate pseudo-preimage

---

Input: $D_1, D_2 \subset \{0,1\}^k$, $\{\Delta_1\}, \{\Delta_2\} \subset \{0,1\}^n$, $T, S \in \{0,1\}^n$, $M \in \{0,1\}^k$
Output: A candidate pseudo-preimage if one is contained in $M \oplus D_1 \oplus D_2$.
  for all $\delta_2 \in D_2$ **do**
    $L_1[\delta_2] = E_3(M \oplus \delta_2, h - E_1 \circ E_4(M \oplus \delta_2, S)) \oplus \Delta_2$.
  end for
  for all $\delta_1 \in D_1$ **do**
    $L_2[\delta_1] = E_2^{-1} \circ E_4^{-1}(M \oplus \delta_1, S) \oplus \Delta_1$.
  end for
  for all $(\delta_1, \delta_2) \in D_1 \times D_2$ **do**
    if $L_1[\delta_2] =_T L_2[\delta_1]$ **then**
      return $M \oplus \delta_1 \oplus \delta_2$
    end if
  end for
  return No candidate pseudo-preimage in $M \oplus D_1 \oplus D_2$

The active bits corresponding to D_1 (resp. D_2) can be regarded as neutral words for the backward (resp. forward) chunk. If the dimension of the two linear spaces D_1 and D_2 is d, $2^{2d} = 2^d \times 2^d$ different messages are included in the set $M \oplus D_1 \oplus D_2$ for a random message M. According to the hypothesis test, a candidate pseudo-preimage $M \oplus \delta_1 \oplus \delta_2$ is falsely rejected by Algorithm 1 with probability $\alpha = 1 - p_1 \cdot p_2$ (type I error probability defined in [7]). For all $(\delta_1, \delta_2) \in D_1 \times D_2$, the average type I error probability $\overline{\alpha}$ can be estimated by experiment. Thus, in order to obtain a pseudo-preimage, we have to test $2^n/(1-\overline{\alpha})$ messages with an expected complexity of $(2^{n-d}\Gamma + 2^{n-r}\Gamma_{re})/(1-\overline{\alpha})$, where Γ denotes the cost of one computation of E, Γ_{re} is the cost of rechecking a candidate pseudo-preimage and r is the Hamming weight of T. Note that the probabilities p_1 and p_2 should be high enough to make the attack valid.

4   Preimage Attack on 70-Step HAS-160

In [12], Deukjo *et al.* proposed a preimage attack on the last 68 steps of HAS-160, but the variant with 70 steps was not attacked due to the limitation of attack

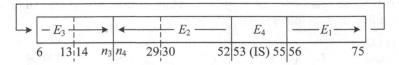

Fig. 3. Selected chunks for the 70 steps

techniques used. In this section, we show how to generate a preimage for 70-step HAS-160 faster than exhaustive search.

The attack target is from Step 6 to Step 75 and the corresponding chunks are shown in Fig. 3. The initial structures are constructed from Step 53 to Step 55. For the backward chunk from Step 52 to Step 30, m_{11} and m_{12} are neutral words satisfying $\Delta m_{11} = \Delta m_{12}$. That is, $m_{11} \oplus m_{12} = const$ and $const$ is not necessarily $zero$. Similarly, for the forward chunk from Step 56 to Step 75 and Step 6 to Step 13, the neutral words m_3, m_6, m_8 and m_{15} need to fulfill $\Delta m_3 = \Delta m_6 = \Delta m_8 = \Delta m_{15}$. The partial-matching part involving neutral words for two chunks starts from Step 14 to Step 29.

4.1   Initial Structure

The 3-step initial structure is shown in Fig. 4, which is similar to the one in [12]. Note that the expanded word used in Step 55 is $m_{11} \oplus const_b$, where $const_b = m_0 \oplus m_9 \oplus m_2$. To generate the initial structure, we first fix a_{53}, b_{53}, t_{53}, t_{54} and t_{55} to randomly chosen values. Then, in the forward direction, a_{54}, a_{55}, a_{56} are computed independently from the backward chunk and in the backward direction, e_{55}, e_{54}, e_{53} are computed independently from the forward chunk.

4.2   Finding Appropriate Attack Parameters

In order to apply Algorithm 1 with the above chunk separation, we need to find the remaining attack parameters: the linear spaces $D_1, D_2 \subset \{0,1\}^k$ of the same dimension d, the corresponding output difference Δ_1 (resp. Δ_2) for each message difference $\delta_1 \in D_1$ (resp. $\delta_2 \in D_2$), and a truncation mask $T \in \{0,1\}^n$. From a differential view, m_{11} and m_{12} are active in D_1 and the other message words have zero difference. Similarly, m_3, m_6, m_8 and m_{15} are the only active message words in D_2.

Given the chunk separation, D_1 and D_2, we can calculate the output differences by linearization: $\Delta_1 = \overline{E}_3 \circ \overline{E}_1 \circ \overline{E}_4(\delta_1, 0)$ and $\Delta_2 = \overline{E}_2^{-1} \circ \overline{E}_4^{-1}(\delta_2, 0)$. The linearization of HAS-160 is similar to SHA-1 [7], except that the non-linear boolean functions $f_i(B, C, D)$ in round 1 and 3 are replaced with 0 and C respectively. The same substitution has been used to find a semi-free-start collision for 65 steps of HAS-160 [20]. And this better choice has been partially verified by counting the sum of hamming weights of the forward and backward linear characteristics when all combinations of the 4-bit message difference for D_1 and D_2 are enumerated in the partial-matching part. Due to the choice of neutral

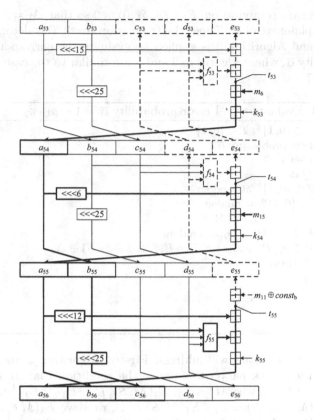

Fig. 4. Initial structure skipping 3 steps

Algorithm 2. Find a truncation mask T for matching

Input: $D_1, D_2 \subset \{0,1\}^k$, r $(0 < r \leq n)$
Output: A truncation mask $T \in \{0,1\}^n$ of Hamming weight r.

$c =$ an array of n counters set to 0
for $q = 1$ to Q **do**
   Choose $M \in \{0,1\}^k$ at random
   Choose $S \in \{0,1\}^n$ at random
   $P = E_3^{-1} \circ E_2^{-1} \circ E_4^{-1}(M, S)$
   Choose $(\delta_1, \delta_2) \in D_1 \times D_2$ at random
   $\Delta = E_3(M \oplus \delta_1, P) \oplus \Delta_1 \oplus E_2^{-1} \circ E_4^{-1}(M \oplus \delta_2, S) \oplus \Delta_2$
   for $i = 0$ to $n-1$ **do**
     if the i-th bit of Δ is 1 **then**
       $c[i] \leftarrow c[i] + 1$
     end if
   end for
end for
Set those r bits of T to 1 which have the lowest counters.

---

words for backward computation, $E_1 \circ E_4(\delta_1, 0) = 0$ so that $\Delta_1 = \overline{E}_3(\delta_1, 0)$. Let P denote the plaintext of E. Then, the truncation mask T is determined using Algorithm 2, and Algorithm 3 is applied to evaluate the corresponding type I error probability $\overline{\alpha}$, where Algorithm 2 and 3 are similar to the case of one-block preimages in [7].

Algorithm 3. Evaluate type I error probability $\overline{\alpha} = 1 - p_1 \cdot p_2$

Input: $D_1, D_2 \subset \{0,1\}^k$, $T \in \{0,1\}^n$
Output: Average probability $\overline{\alpha}$.
  c = a counter set to 0
  for $q = 1$ to Q **do**
    Choose $M \in \{0,1\}^k$ at random
    Choose $S \in \{0,1\}^n$ at random
    $P = E_3{}^{-1} \circ E_2{}^{-1} \circ E_4{}^{-1}(M, S)$
    Choose $(\delta_1, \delta_2) \in D_1 \times D_2$ at random
    $\Delta = E_3(M \oplus \delta_1, P) \oplus \Delta_1 \oplus E_2{}^{-1} \circ E_4{}^{-1}(M \oplus \delta_2, S) \oplus \Delta_2$
    if $\Delta \neq_T 0^n$ **then**
      $c \leftarrow c + 1$
    end if
  end for
  return c/Q

There are two issues we will address. Firstly, Algorithm 2 and 3 are used to determine the attack parameters under the condition that M is a pseudo-preimage for $h = P+C$, where $C = E_1 \circ E_4(M, S)$, $P = E_3{}^{-1} \circ E_2{}^{-1} \circ E_4{}^{-1}(M, S)$. Since $E_1 \circ E_4(M \oplus \delta_1, S) = E_1 \circ E_4(M, S) = C$, we have $E_3(M \oplus \delta_1, h - (E_1 \circ E_4(M \oplus \delta_1, S))) = E_3(M \oplus \delta_1, P)$. That is, type I probability is a conditional probability where the condition is that M is already a pseudo-preimage, so M just needs to be consistent with $h = P+C$ instead of a fixed hash value. Secondly, we have tried several values for Q, such as 2^l, $l \in \{16, 17, \ldots, 24\}$. The results obtained are almost identical for these choices. In order to reduce the time for determining the attack parameters, we set $Q = 2^{16}$ in both algorithms without loss of correctness of results.

Attack Parameters for N=70. The best result obtained by extensive experiments is as follows: $d = 7$, $r = 5$, $n_3 = 22$, $n_4 = 23$. Given a single element $x_0 \| \cdots \| x_{15}$ of the basis of D_1 (resp. D_2), the basis of D_1 (resp. D_2) can be generated by word-wise rotation as $(x_0 \lll i) \| \cdots \| (x_{15} \lll i)$ for $i = 0, \ldots, d-1$.

  D_1 : 0x00000000 0x00000000 0x00000000 0x00000000 0x00000000 0x00000000
       0x00000000 0x00000000 0x00000000 0x00000000 0x00000000 0x08000000
       0x08000000 0x00000000 0x00000000 0x00000000

  D_2 : 0x00000000 0x00000000 0x00000000 0x80000000 0x00000000 0x00000000
       0x80000000 0x00000000 0x80000000 0x00000000 0x00000000 0x00000000
       0x00000000 0x00000000 0x00000000 0x80000000

   T : 0x00000000 0x00000000 0x00000000 0x00000000 0x00007c00

The estimated type I error probability $\overline{\alpha} = 0.752$. Since all non-zero bits lie in the rightmost word of T, 4 steps can be skipped in the partial-matching part. Hence, we make a slight change in Algorithm 1 by setting $n_3 = 18$, $n_4 = 23$, because $L_1[\delta_2]$ corresponds to p_{19} and $L_2[\delta_1]$ corresponds to p_{23}, we only need to check if $(a_{19} \lll s2_{20}) =_{T_e} e_{23}$ in the last loop, where T_e denotes the rightmost word of T. This results in a pseudo-preimage attack with an expected complexity of $2^{n-d}((N-4)/N + 2^{d-r}(16-4)/N)/(1-\overline{\alpha}) = 2^{155.71}$ and a memory of 2^7 words.

According to the padding and length encoding rules, message words m_{14} and m_{15} are used to encode the length. Because m_{15} is chosen as a neutral word for forward computation, the value of m_{15} will be determined by the attack procedure. We need to convert the pseudo-preimages to a preimage, but the exact value of m_{15} may lead to a message with a random length. Luckily by using the expandable messages [16] to satisfy the message length restraint, pseudo-preimages can still be converted to a preimage with $2^{158.86}$ computations of the compression function.

4.3 Improved Preimage Attack on 65-Step HAS-160

The original preimage attack on the first 65 steps of HAS-160 [12] didn't use the initial structure and only 7 steps were skipped in the partial-matching part. Instead of using the partial-fixing technique for unknown carry behavior to match in the middle, we exploit Algorithm 2 and 3 to determine the proper attack parameters for partial-matching. The same chunk separation and neutral words for 65 steps will be used in the attack.

Attack Parameters for N=65. The best result obtained is as follows: $d = 24$, $r = 21$, $n_3 = 39$, $n_4 = 40$.

D_1 : 0x00004000 0x00000000 0x00000000 0x00000000 0x00000000 0x00000000
      0x00000000 0x00000000 0x00000000 0x00000000 0x00004000 0x00000000
      0x00000000 0x00000000 0x00000000 0x00000000

D_2 : 0x00000000 0x00000000 0x00000000 0x00000000 0x00000000 0x00000000
      0x00000000 0x00000000 0x00000000 0x00000000 0x00000000 0x00000000
      0x80000000 0x00000000 0x80000000 0x00000000

T : 0x00000001 0x00000000 0xff000000 0xff000001 0xc0000001

The average type I error probability $\overline{\alpha} = 0.782$, and a pseudo-preimage can be found with an expected complexity of $2^{139.09}$ and a memory of $2^{24} \times 5$ words. Hence, a preimage is generated from pseudo-preimages with $2^{150.55}$ computations of the compression function. We also slightly improve the preimage attacks on 67 and 68 steps of HAS-160 [12]. Due to the space limitation, these results are given in Appendix A.

Remark. We have also studied the preimage resistance of HAS-160 reduced to 71 steps (Steps 2-72) with 5-step initial structure and 17-step partial-matching. After the initial structure is constructed from Step 5 to Step 9, we run experiments according to the methods described in this paper. The experiments result to a pseudo-preimage attack with a very large complexity, and the pseudo-preimage attack can no longer be converted to a preimage attack faster than brute-force attack. Comparing to the results of SHA-1 in [7] where more than 25 steps can be skipped in the probabilistic matching part, no more than 17 steps can be skipped in the probabilistic matching part of HAS-160, since the multiple sets of rotation constants and the message schedule of HAS-160 makes the difference propagation faster than SHA-1.

5   Accelerated Brute-Force Search for Full HAS-160

The main idea of the accelerated brute-force search [7, 8] is to not recompute parts of E which share the same expanded message words. It can be applied to any number of rounds. For the variant with N steps, the speed-up factor is about $N/(N - n')$, where n' denotes the number of steps which are not recomputed during the brute-force attack.

Message words m_{12} and m_{13} are set as neutral words for the backward chunk, and m_2 and m_7 are set as neutral words for the forward chunk. Note that these message words should satisfy $\Delta m_{12} = \Delta m_{13}$ and $\Delta m_2 = \Delta m_7$. In order to fulfill the padding rule, the certain bit of m_{13} must be 1. Hence, only 31 bits of m_{13} are active in D_1. If the truncation mask $T = (\texttt{0xffffffff}, \texttt{0x00000000}, \texttt{0x00000000}, \texttt{0x00000000}, \texttt{0x00000000})$, additional 4 steps will be skipped. Further, we can move the addition of m_{12} downwards to Step 17 and move m_2 upwards to Step 61 with no constraint by using the technique in the initial structure [10]. That is, n' can be increased to $16 + 17 + 4 + 1 + 1 = 39$. When $N = 80$, a one-block preimage with correct padding for full HAS-160 can be found with a complexity of $2^{160} \cdot (80 - 39)/80 = 2^{159.04}$ and a memory of $2^{31} \times 5$ words.

6   Conclusion

In this paper, we propose a preimage attack on 70-step HAS-160 and further reduce the complexities of previous preimage attacks. The improvements essentially come from the use of a more effective probabilistic matching in the differential meet-in-the-middle framework, as compared to the partial-fixing technique for unknown carry behavior in previous attacks. For 70 steps of HAS-160, we find a pseudo-preimage with a complexity of $2^{155.71}$ and a preimage with a complexity of $2^{158.86}$. We also improve the complexities of previous attacks on 65, 67 and 68 steps. Finally, we accelerate the brute-force preimage search to $2^{159.04}$ compression function calls. As far as we know, our result on 70-step HAS-160 is the best preimage attack in terms of attacked steps.

Acknowledgements. We would like to thank the anonymous reviewers for their valuable comments and suggestions.

References

1. Pramstaller, N., Rechberger, C., Rijmen, V.: Impact of Rotations in SHA-1 and Related Hash Functions. In: Preneel, B., Tavares, S. (eds.) SAC 2005. LNCS, vol. 3897, pp. 261–275. Springer, Heidelberg (2006)
2. Telecommunications Technology Association. Hash Function Standard Part 2: Hash Function Algorithm Standard (HAS-160), TTAS.KO-12.0011/R1 (2000)
3. Aoki, K., Sasaki, Y.: Preimage attacks on one-block MD4, 63-step MD5 and more. In: Avanzi, R.M., Keliher, L., Sica, F. (eds.) SAC 2008. LNCS, vol. 5381, pp. 103–119. Springer, Heidelberg (2009)
4. U.S. Department of Commerce, National Institute of Standards and Technology. Announcing the SECURE HASH STANDARD (Federal Information Processing Standards Publication 180-3) (2008),
   http://csrc.nist.gov/publications/fips/fips180-3/fips180-3_final.pdf
5. Rivest, R.L.: Request for Comments 1321: The MD5 Message Digest Algorithm. The Internet Engineering Task Force (1992),
   http://www.ietf.org/rfc/rfc1321.txt
6. U.S. Department of Commerce, National Institute of Standards and Technology. Secure Hash Standard. Federal Information Processing Standard Publication # 180-1 (1995)
7. Knellwolf, S., Khovratovich, D.: New Preimage Attacks against Reduced SHA-1. In: Safavi-Naini, R., Canetti, R. (eds.) CRYPTO 2012. LNCS, vol. 7417, pp. 367–383. Springer, Heidelberg (2012)
8. Bogdanov, A., Khovratovich, D., Rechberger, C.: Biclique cryptanalysis of the full AES. In: Lee, D.H., Wang, X. (eds.) ASIACRYPT 2011. LNCS, vol. 7073, pp. 344–371. Springer, Heidelberg (2011)
9. Khovratovich, D., Rechberger, C., Savelieva, A.: Bicliques for Preimages: Attacks on Skein-512 and the SHA-2 Family. In: Canteaut, A. (ed.) FSE 2012. LNCS, vol. 7549, pp. 244–263. Springer, Heidelberg (2012)
10. Aoki, K., Guo, J., Matusiewicz, K., Sasaki, Y., Wang, L.: Preimages for step-reduced SHA-2. In: Matsui, M. (ed.) ASIACRYPT 2009. LNCS, vol. 5912, pp. 578–597. Springer, Heidelberg (2009)
11. Aoki, K., Sasaki, Y.: Meet-in-the-middle preimage attacks against reduced SHA-0 and SHA-1. In: Halevi, S. (ed.) CRYPTO 2009. LNCS, vol. 5677, pp. 70–89. Springer, Heidelberg (2009)
12. Hong, D., Koo, B., Sasaki, Y.: Improved Preimage Attack for 68-Step HAS-160. In: Lee, D., Hong, S. (eds.) ICISC 2009. LNCS, vol. 5984, pp. 332–348. Springer, Heidelberg (2010)
13. Sasaki, Y., Aoki, K.: A preimage attack for 52-step HAS-160. In: Lee, P.J., Cheon, J.H. (eds.) ICISC 2008. LNCS, vol. 5461, pp. 302–317. Springer, Heidelberg (2009)
14. Sasaki, Y., Aoki, K.: Finding preimages in full MD5 faster than exhaustive search. In: Joux, A. (ed.) EUROCRYPT 2009. LNCS, vol. 5479, pp. 134–152. Springer, Heidelberg (2009)
15. Menezes, A.J., van Oorschot, P.C., Vanstone, S.A.: Handbook of Applied Cryptography. CRC Press, Boca Raton (1997)

16. Kelsey, J., Schneier, B.: Second preimages on n-bit hash functions for much less than 2^n work. In: Cramer, R. (ed.) EUROCRYPT 2005. LNCS, vol. 3494, pp. 474–490. Springer, Heidelberg (2005)
17. Yun, A., Sung, S.H., Park, S., Chang, D., Hong, S.H., Cho, H.-S.: Finding collision on 45-step HAS-160. In: Won, D.H., Kim, S. (eds.) ICISC 2005. LNCS, vol. 3935, pp. 146–155. Springer, Heidelberg (2006)
18. Cho, H.-S., Park, S., Sung, S.H., Yun, A.: Collision search attack for 53-step HAS-160. In: Rhee, M.S., Lee, B. (eds.) ICISC 2006. LNCS, vol. 4296, pp. 286–295. Springer, Heidelberg (2006)
19. Mendel, F., Rijmen, V.: Colliding message pair for 53-step HAS-160. In: Nam, K.-H., Rhee, G. (eds.) ICISC 2007. LNCS, vol. 4817, pp. 324–334. Springer, Heidelberg (2007)
20. Mendel, F., Nad, T., Schläffer, M.: Cryptanalysis of Round-Reduced HAS-160. In: Kim, H. (ed.) ICISC 2011. LNCS, vol. 7259, pp. 33–47. Springer, Heidelberg (2012)
21. Sasaki, Y., Wang, L., Takasaki, Y., Sakiyama, K., Ohta, K.: Boomerang distinguishers for full HAS-160 compression function. In: Hanaoka, G., Yamauchi, T. (eds.) IWSEC 2012. LNCS, vol. 7631, pp. 156–169. Springer, Heidelberg (2012)
22. Kircanski, A., AlTawy, R., Youssef, A.M.: A heuristic for finding compatible differential paths with application to HAS-160. In: Sako, K., Sarkar, P. (eds.) ASIACRYPT 2013, Part II. LNCS, vol. 8270, pp. 464–483. Springer, Heidelberg (2013)

A   Improved Attacks on 67 and 68 Steps

Attack Parameters for N=67. The best result obtained is as follows: $d = 10$, $r = 9$, $n_3 = 41$, $n_4 = 44$.

D_1 : 0x00400000 0x00000000 0x00000000 0x00000000 0x00000000 0x00000000
0x00000000 0x00000000 0x00000000 0x00000000 0x00400000 0x00000000
0x00000000 0x00000000 0x00000000 0x00000000

D_2 : 0x00000000 0x00000000 0x00000000 0x00000000 0x00000000 0x00000000
0x00000000 0x00000000 0x00000000 0x80000000 0x00000000 0x80000000
0x80000000 0x00000000 0x80000000 0x00000000

T : 0x00000038 0x06000000 0xe0000001 0x00000000 0x00000000

The average type I error probability $\overline{\alpha} = 0.717$, and a pseudo-preimage can be found with an expected complexity of $2^{152.20}$ and a memory of $2^{10} \times 3$ words.

Attack Parameters for N=68. The best result obtained is as follows: $d = 13$, $r = 11$, $n_3 = 54$, $n_4 = 58$.

D_1 : 0x00000000 0x00000000 0x00000000 0x00000001 0x00000000 0x00000000
0x00000001 0x00000000 0x00000001 0x00000000 0x00000000 0x00000000
0x00000000 0x00000000 0x00000000 0x00000001

D_2 : 0x00000000 0x00000000 0x00080000 0x00000000 0x00000000 0x00000000
0x00000000 0x00000000 0x00080000 0x00000000 0x00000000 0x00000000
0x00000000 0x00000000 0x00000000 0x00000000

T : 0x07c00000 0x0fc00000 0x00000000 0x00000000 0x00000000

The average type I error probability $\overline{\alpha} = 0.702$, and a pseudo-preimage can be found with an expected complexity of $2^{149.32}$ and a memory of $2^{13} \times 2$ words.

Modular Inversion Hidden Number Problem Revisited

Jun Xu[1,2,3], Lei Hu[1], Zhangjie Huang[1], and Liqiang Peng[1]

[1] State Key Laboratory of Information Security, Institute of Information
Engineering, Chinese Academy of Sciences, Beijing 100093, China
[2] Data Assurance and Communications Security Research Center, Chinese Academy
of Sciences, Beijing 100093, China
[3] School of Mathematical Science, Anhui University, Hefei 230601, Anhui, China
{jxu,hu,zhjhuang,lqpeng}@is.ac.cn

Abstract. In this paper we revisit the modular inversion hidden number problem, which is to find a hidden number given several integers and partial bits of the corresponding modular inverse integers (in the sense of modulo a prime number) of the sums of the known integers and that unknown integer. Along with another direction different to the previous study, we present a better polynomial time algorithm to solve the problem by utilizing a technique of priority queue computation and by constructing related lattices from algebraically dependent polynomials. Let n be the number of known integers, our algorithm assumes to know about $\left(\frac{1}{2} + \frac{1}{(n+1)!} \right)$ of the bits of the modular inverses, which means about $\frac{2}{3}$ of bits are required to be known in our algorithm when $n = 2$, while in the case that only $\frac{2}{3}$ of bits of the modular inverses are required to be known, the result of Boneh et al. and the latest algorithm of Ling et al. in Journal of Symbolic Computation need more samples (i.e., known integers and the corresponding partial bits). Our algorithm is also better for other n.

Keywords: Hidden number problem, modular inversion hidden number problem, lattice, LLL algorithm, Coppersmith's algorithm.

1 Introduction

The hidden number problem (HNP) was introduced by Boneh and Venkatesan [3, 4] as an object with wide applications in cryptography. The modular inversion hidden number problem (ModInv-HNP) is a class of HNP, which, roughly speaking, is a problem of finding a hidden number $\alpha \in \mathbb{Z}_p$, given a prime number p, several, say n, independent and uniformly distributed elements $t_i \in \mathbb{Z}_p \setminus \{-\alpha\}$ and the l most significant bits of the corresponding integers $(\alpha + t_i)^{-1} \pmod{p}$, where an element of $\mathbb{Z}_p$ is regarded as an integer from $\{0, 1, \ldots, p-1\}$. The elements t_i and the partial bits are called the samples. The modular inversion hidden number problem was proposed by Boneh et al. in 2001 [2] and has been used for constructing cryptography algorithms such as pseudorandom number

X. Huang and J. Zhou (Eds.): ISPEC 2014, LNCS 8434, pp. 537–551, 2014.

generator and message authentication code. More results and applications on HNP are presented in the survey [18].

The ways of finding small roots to modular univariate polynomial equations and bivariate integer polynomial equations were first proposed by Coppersmith in 1996 and 1997 [6–8], and a heuristic strategy for the multivariate polynomial equation case was presented by May et al. in 2006 [13]. Variants of these methods have been widely used in the field of cryptanalysis such as attacking the RSA variants [17] and pseudorandom number generators [11].

Boneh et al. first analyzed ModInv-HNP [2] and described two heuristic algorithms for this problem respectively for the two cases that the number l of known partial bits satisfies $l \approx \frac{2}{3} \log_2 p$ and $l \approx \frac{1}{3} \log_2 p$ in an asymptotic sense that n is sufficiently large, however these two algorithms need many samples or a large n and they did not give an estimate on how large concretely the n should be. Moreover, for their second algorithm that requires about $\frac{1}{3} \log_2 p$ bits to be known, they did not explicitly give a concrete construction of the corresponding lattice and the algorithm needs to assume a very large number of samples.

Recently, to consider more precisely the ModInv-HNP problem for concrete number of samples n and achieve an explicit relation between n and the number of partial bits l, Ling et al. presented an algorithm for ModInv-HNP, which requires l is at least $(\frac{2}{3} + \varepsilon)$ of the bit-length of p, where ε is a small number depending on n and satisfies $n = \lceil \frac{2}{9\varepsilon} \rceil + 1$, and they analysed the probability of success for their algorithm [16]. For small numbers of samples, and the number of presumptively known partial bits in Ling et al.'s algorithm is $l > \frac{8}{9} \log_2 p$ when $n = 2$ and $l > \frac{7}{9} \log_2 p$ when $n = 3$, and hence, this algorithm is not ideal in terms of the number of partial bits when n is a small integer. If n is very large, the ratio $l/\log_2 p$ tends to $2/3$, which goes to a similar result on the ratio $l/\log_2 p$ in the first algorithm of Boneh et al.

In this paper, to obtain a better ratio $l/\log_2 p$ for small n, we propose an algorithm which requires l is about $(\frac{1}{2} + \frac{1}{(n+1)!}) \log_2 p$. Such an l is $l \approx \frac{2}{3} \log_2 p$ if $n = 2$ and $l \approx \frac{13}{24} \log_2 p$ if $n = 3$. We first give an algorithm by a technique of priority queue to construct some polynomials, and then construct a lattice using these polynomials. Although these polynomials are algebraically dependent, they are useful for decreasing the bound on $l/\log_2 p$. To the best of our knowledge, it is the first time that algebraically dependent polynomials are used in the construction of lattices. Finally, we get small roots of modular multivariate polynomials by the Coppersmith method and recover the hidden number α.

The rest of this paper is organized as follows. In Section 2, we recall some terminology and preliminary knowledge. In Section 3, we present our algorithm for solving ModInv-HNP, and give a proof of the algorithm in Section 4. In Section 5, we list our experimental results to confirm the correctness of our algorithm. Section 6 is the conclusion.

2   Preliminaries

2.1   Lattice

A lattice L is a set of all integer linear combination of $\{b_1,\ldots,b_m\}$, where $\{b_1,\ldots,b_m\}$ are linearly independent row vectors in $\mathbb{R}^n$ and $m \leq n$. The vector set $\{b_1,\ldots,b_m\}$ is known as a basis of the lattice, and the determinant of L is $\det(L) = \sqrt{\det(BB^T)}$, where $B = [b_1^T,\ldots,b_m^T]^T$ is the matrix represented by this basis. The dimension of L is $\dim(L) = m$. Finding the shortest vector is a very hard problem in the lattice with a large dimension [1], however, by applying the LLL basis reduction algorithm, we can obtain an approximately shortest vector in polynomial time.

Lemma 1 (LLL, [15]). *Let L be a lattice. In polynomial time, the LLL algorithm outputs reduced basis vectors $v_1,\ldots,v_m$ that satisfy*

$$\|v_1\| \leq \|v_2\| \leq \cdots \leq \|v_i\| \leq 2^{\frac{m(m-1)}{4(m+1-i)}} \det(L)^{\frac{1}{m+1-i}}, 1 \leq i \leq m.$$

In order to find small integer roots of a modular equation, we need to combine the following lemma due to Howgrave-Graham with the LLL reduction. In Lemma 2, the norm of a polynomial $f(x_1,\ldots,x_n) = \sum a_{i_1,\ldots,i_n} x_1^{i_1} \ldots x_n^{i_n}$ is the Euclidean norm of its coefficient vector, i.e., $\|f(x_1,\ldots,x_n)\| = \sqrt{\sum |a_{i_1,\ldots,i_n}|^2}$.

Lemma 2 (Howgrave-Graham, [12]). *Let $g(x_1,\ldots,x_n) \in \mathbb{Z}[x_1,\ldots,x_n]$ be an integer polynomial that consists of at most ω monomials. Suppose that*

1. $g(x_1^{(0)},\ldots,x_n^{(0)}) = 0 \pmod{N}$ *for* $|x_1^{(0)}| \leq X_1,\ldots,|x_n^{(0)}| \leq X_n$; *and*
2. $\|g(X_1 x_1,\ldots,X_n x_n)\| < \frac{N}{\sqrt{\omega}}$,

then $g(x_1^{(0)},\ldots,x_n^{(0)}) = 0$ holds over integers.

To apply Lemma 1 and Lemma 2 to find n polynomials $g_i(x_1,\ldots,x_n)$ with $g_i(x_1^{(0)},\ldots,x_n^{(0)}) = 0$ for $1 \leq i \leq n$, we need

$$2^{\frac{m(m-1)}{4(m+1-n)}} \det(L)^{\frac{1}{m+1-n}} < \frac{N}{\sqrt{m}}. \tag{1}$$

We expect that these polynomials are algebraically independent, then we can compute their common roots using the resultant [10] or Gröbner basis [9] methods. In theory, these polynomials corresponding to the lattice vectors are linearly independent. In practice, we find that they are also algebraically independent in most cases. Hence we give the following heuristic assumption.

Assumption 1. *The polynomials corresponding to the first n LLL-reduced vectors are algebraically independent.*

By neglecting the terms that do not depend on N in (1) and letting them contribute to an error term ε, we simply use the condition

$$\det(L) < N^m. \tag{2}$$

2.2 Priority Queue

A priority queue is a data structure for maintaining a set of elements, each with an associated priority. A priority queue supports at least the following two operations:

1. EXTRACT-MAX: extracts the highest priority element, i.e., removes and returns the element with the highest priority.
2. INSERT: inserts with priority, i.e., adds an element to the queue with an associated priority.

For more details on priority queue, please refer to the book [14].

3 ModInv-HNP and Main Result

In this section, we give a description about modular inverse hidden number problem (ModInv-HNP), and then present our main result.

3.1 ModInv-HNP

Problem. Let p be a k-bit prime and α be a random element of $\mathbb{Z}_p$. Given n independent and uniformly distributed elements t_i in $\mathbb{Z}_p \setminus \{-\alpha\}$ and integers u_i such that

$$|(\alpha + t_i)^{-1} \bmod p - u_i| \le p/2^l, \quad 1 \le i \le n,$$

where the u_i are denoted by $\mathrm{MSB}_{l,p}((\alpha+t_i)^{-1} \bmod p)$ in general, n is the number of samples and l is the number of known bits of the modular inverses, our goal is to recover this hidden element α.

Let $\tilde{x}_i = (\alpha + t_i)^{-1} \bmod p - u_i$ with $|\tilde{x}_i| \le p/2^l$. Clearly,

$$(u_i + \tilde{x}_i)(\alpha + t_i) = 1 \pmod{p}, \quad 1 \le i \le n. \tag{3}$$

For any two equations in (3), we eliminate α and get

$$\frac{1}{u_i + \tilde{x}_i} - t_i = \frac{1}{u_j + \tilde{x}_j} - t_j \pmod{p}, \tag{4}$$

where $i < j$. Rearranging (4), we have

$$\tilde{x}_i \tilde{x}_j + a_{i,j} \tilde{x}_i + b_{i,j} \tilde{x}_j + c_{i,j} = 0 \pmod{p},$$

where

$$a_{i,j} = u_j + (t_i - t_j)^{-1} \bmod p,$$

$$b_{i,j} = u_i - (t_i - t_j)^{-1} \bmod p,$$

$$c_{i,j} = u_i u_j + (u_i - u_j)(t_i - t_j)^{-1} \bmod p.$$

Then $(\tilde{x}_i, \tilde{x}_j)$ is a root of $f_{i,j}(x_i, x_j) = 0 \bmod p$, where $f_{i,j}(x_i, x_j) = x_i x_j + a_{i,j} x_i + b_{i,j} x_j + c_{i,j}$. For convenience, we let $f_{j,i} = f_{i,j}$ for $1 \le i < j \le n$.

Remark 1. For any $1 \leq i < j < k \leq n$, $f_{i,j}$, $f_{i,k}$, $f_{j,k}$ are algebraically dependent, i.e., we can derive any one of them from the remaining two polynomials.

Clearly, recovering the hidden number α is equivalent to finding a root $(\tilde{x}_i, \tilde{x}_j)$ of the bivariate modular polynomial equation $f_{i,j} = 0 \bmod p$. When $n=2$, the root $(\tilde{x}_i, \tilde{x}_j)$ is heuristic solved if $l > \frac{2}{3}k$ by using a variant of Coppersmith's algorithm [13]. This bound on l is the same as our bound when $n = 2$. In this paper, for $n \geq 3$, we use algebraically dependent polynomials $f_{i,j}$ for the first time to construct lattices, and get a better bound when $n \geq 3$ in the following Theorem 1.

3.2 Main Result

Theorem 1. *Assume the k-bit prime number p is public, given n samples*

$$\left(t_i, \mathrm{MSB}_{l,p}\left((\alpha + t_i)^{-1} \bmod p\right)\right), \quad 1 \leq i \leq n,$$

with $t_i \in \mathbb{Z}_p \setminus \{-\alpha\}$ chosen randomly and uniformly. Then, under Assumption 1, we can recover α in polynomial time when

$$l \geq \left(\frac{1}{2} + \frac{1}{(n+1)!} + \varepsilon\right) k,$$

where ε is a small number depending on n which can be arbitrarily small theoretically.

Remark 2. For example, when $n = 2$, the hidden number α is recovered if $l \geq (\frac{2}{3} + \varepsilon)k$ using our heuristic algorithm. However, the deterministic algorithm in [16] needs that $l \geq \frac{8}{9}k$. And when $n = 3$, we can recover α when $l \geq (\frac{13}{24} + \varepsilon)k$, but they need $l \geq \frac{7}{9}k$ in [16].

4 The Strategy and Proof of Main Result

In this section we give a strategy to find the roots $\tilde{x}_1, \tilde{x}_2, \ldots, \tilde{x}_n$ of polynomials $f_{i,j}, 1 \leq i < j \leq n$. Then we prove our main result.

4.1 The Strategy

Step 1. Fix a positive integer d, for any integers i_j satisfying $0 \leq i_j \leq d$, $1 \leq j \leq n$, construct a polynomial

$$r_{i_1,i_2,\ldots,i_n} = \left(\prod_k x_k^{t_k}\right) \cdot \left(\prod_{i,j} f_{i,j}^{t_{i,j}}\right),$$

where $t_j, t_{i,j} \in \mathbb{N}$, such that the leading monomial in $r_{i_1,i_2,\ldots,i_n}$ is $x_1^{i_1} x_2^{i_2} \ldots x_n^{i_n}$ according to the graded lexicographic order on n-variable monomials. Denote by $R(i_1, i_2, \ldots, i_n)$ the total sum of the multiplicities of $f_{i,j}$ appearing in the expression of $r_{i_1,i_2,\ldots,i_n}$, i.e., $R(i_1, i_2, \ldots, i_n) = \sum_{i,j} t_{i,j}$. We have

$$r_{i_1,i_2,\ldots,i_n}(\tilde{x}_1, \tilde{x}_2, \ldots, \tilde{x}_n) = 0 \quad (\mathrm{mod}\ p^{R(i_1,i_2,\ldots,i_n)}).$$

We take a positive integer $W = \max_{0 \le i_1,i_2,\ldots,i_n \le d} R(i_1, i_2, \ldots, i_n)$. Then

$$p^{W-R(i_1,i_2,\ldots,i_n)} r_{i_1,i_2,\ldots,i_n}(\tilde{x}_1, \tilde{x}_2, \ldots, \tilde{x}_n) = 0 \quad (\mathrm{mod}\ p^W).$$

Step 2. Let $|\tilde{x}_i| < X_i$, $1 \le i \le n$, construct a lattice L generated by the coefficient vectors of polynomials in

$$\left\{ p^{W-R(i_1,i_2,\ldots,i_n)} r_{i_1,i_2,\ldots,i_n}(X_1 x_1, X_2 x_2, \ldots, X_n x_n) \right\},$$

where $(i_1, i_2, \ldots, i_n)$ is ordered by the graded lexicographic order. The matrix of the coefficient vectors is lower triangular and its diagonal elements are

$$p^{W-R(i_1,i_2,\ldots,i_n)} X_1^{i_1} X_2^{i_2} \ldots X_n^{i_n}.$$

Step 3. Apply the LLL algorithm to the lattice L and obtain n polynomials $r_i(x_1, x_2, \ldots, x_n)$ satisfying Lemma 2.

Step 4. Under Assumption 1, we obtain a univariate polynomial $r(x_i)$ by using the resultant or Gröbner basis method for $r_i(x_1, x_2, \ldots, x_n)$. Finally, we solve the equation $r(x_i) = 0$ over integers to find the x_i.

4.2 Proof of Main Result

We know that the dimension of the lattice L is equal to the number of polynomials $r_{i_1,i_2,\ldots,i_n}$, where $0 \le i_1, i_2, \ldots, i_n \le d$, thus,

$$\dim(L) = (d+1)^n.$$

Note that the basis matrix of L is lower triangular and its diagonal entries are $p^{W-R(i_1,i_2,\ldots,i_n)} X_1^{i_1} X_2^{i_2} \ldots X_n^{i_n}$, then the determinant of the lattice L is given by

$$\det(L) = X^{\frac{nd(d+1)^n}{2}} \cdot p^{(d+1)^n W - \sum_{0 \le i_1,i_2,\ldots,i_n \le d} R(i_1,i_2,\ldots,i_n)},$$

where $X_i = p/2^l =: X$. Substituting the expressions of $\det(L)$ and $\dim(L)$ into (2), we have

$$X^{\frac{nd(d+1)^n}{2}} \cdot p^{(d+1)^n W - \sum_{0 \le i_1,i_2,\ldots,i_n \le d} R(i_1,i_2,\ldots,i_n)} < p^{(d+1)^n W}.$$

Rearranging the above relation, we get

$$X^{\frac{nd(d+1)^n}{2}} < p^{\sum_{0 \le i_1,i_2,\ldots,i_n \le d} R(i_1,i_2,\ldots,i_n)}. \tag{5}$$

Algorithm 1. Construct polynomial $g_{i_1,i_2,\ldots,i_n}(x_1, x_2, \ldots, x_n)$

Input: Monomial $x_1^{i_1} x_2^{i_2} \ldots x_n^{i_n}$
Output: A polynomial $g_{i_1,i_2,\ldots,i_n}(x_1, x_2, \ldots, x_n) \in \mathbb{Z}[x_1, x_2, \ldots, x_n]$ corresponding to monomial $x_1^{i_1} x_2^{i_2} \ldots x_n^{i_n}$ in constructing the lattice
1: Make a list of tuples in form $\langle i_k, x_k \rangle$ from monomial $x_1^{i_1} x_2^{i_2} \ldots x_n^{i_n}$, where x_k is a variable appears in $x_1^{i_1} x_2^{i_2} \ldots x_n^{i_n}$ and i_k its degree
2: Maintenance a priority queue Q whose elements are tuples $\langle i_k, x_k \rangle$ and associate each queue element with priority defined as: an element is with higher priority if and only if its first component is larger
3: $g_{i_1,i_2,\ldots,i_n}(x_1, x_2, \ldots, x_n) \leftarrow 1$
4: **while** $length(Q) \geq 2$ **do**
5:   $\langle i_{j_1}, x_{j_1} \rangle \leftarrow$ EXTRACT-MAX(Q)
6:   $\langle i_{j_2}, x_{j_2} \rangle \leftarrow$ EXTRACT-MAX(Q)
7:   $g_{i_1,i_2,\ldots,i_n}(x_1, x_2, \ldots, x_n) \leftarrow g_{i_1,i_2,\ldots,i_n}(x_1, x_2, \ldots, x_n) \cdot f_{j_1,j_2}$
8:   INSERT$(Q, \langle i_{j_1} - 1, x_{j_1} \rangle)$ if $i_{j_1} - 1 > 0$
9:   INSERT$(Q, \langle i_{j_2} - 1, x_{j_2} \rangle)$ if $i_{j_2} - 1 > 0$
10: **end while**
11: **if** $length(Q) = 1$ **then**
12:   $\langle i_{j_3}, x_{j_3} \rangle \leftarrow$ EXTRACT-MAX(Q)
13:   $g_{i_1,i_2,\ldots,i_n}(x_1, x_2, \ldots, x_n) \leftarrow g_{i_1,i_2,\ldots,i_n}(x_1, x_2, \ldots, x_n) \cdot x_{j_3}^{i_{j_3}}$
14: **end if**
15: **return** $g_{i_1,i_2,\ldots,i_n}(x_1, x_2, \ldots, x_n)$

Denote

$$P_{i_1,i_2,\ldots,i_n} = \left\{ \left(\prod_k x_k^{t_k} \right) \cdot \left(\prod_{i,j} f_{i,j}^{t_{i,j}} \right) \; \middle| \; t_k + \sum_{j \neq k} t_{k,j} = i_k, \; 1 \leq k \leq n \right\},$$

then $r_{i_1,i_2,\ldots,i_n} \in P_{i_1,i_2,\ldots,i_n}$. Clearly, any polynomial in the set $P_{i_1,i_2,\ldots,i_n}$ can be chosen as $r_{i_1,i_2,\ldots,i_n}$ in Step 1. Our aim is to make the bound X as large as possible, according to (5), for any tuple $(i_1, i_2, \ldots, i_n)$, we expect to use those polynomials $r_{i_1,i_2,\ldots,i_n}$ that maximizes $R(i_1, i_2, \ldots, i_n)$.

Our approach is for any tuple $(i_1, i_2, \ldots, i_n)$, to use the priority queue technique in Section 2.2 to generate a polynomial $r_{i_1,i_2,\ldots,i_n}$ which we denote as $g_{i_1,i_2,\ldots,i_n}(x_1, x_2, \ldots, x_n)$, see Algorithm 1. Let $G(i_1, i_2, \ldots, i_n)$ denote the sum of multiplicities of the $f_{i,j}$ which appear in the expression of $g_{i_1,i_2,\ldots,i_n}(x_1, x_2, \ldots, x_n)$. The following Lemma 3 computes the value of $G(i_1, i_2, \ldots, i_n)$, then in Theorem 2 we will prove that Algorithm 1 indeed outputs a polynomial $r_{i_1,i_2,\ldots,i_n}$ which maximizes $R(i_1, i_2, \ldots, i_n)$, namely,

$$G(i_1, i_2, \ldots, i_n) = \max \left\{ R(i_1, i_2, \ldots, i_n) : \; r_{i_1,i_2,\ldots,i_n} \in P_{i_1,i_2,\ldots,i_n} \right\}.$$

Lemma 3. *Denote* $M = \max\{i_1, i_2, \ldots, i_n\}$. *Then*

$$G(i_1, i_2, \ldots, i_n) = \begin{cases} \sum\limits_{k=1}^{n} i_k - M, & \text{if } M > (\sum_{k=1}^{n} i_k)/2, \\ \left\lfloor \left(\sum\limits_{k=1}^{n} i_k\right) \middle/ 2 \right\rfloor, & \text{otherwise.} \end{cases}$$

Proof. For the case of $M > (\sum_{k=1}^{n} i_k)/2$, i.e., $M > \sum_{k=1}^{n} i_k - M$, according to Algorithm 1 we have

$$G(i_1, i_2, \ldots, i_n) = \sum_{k=1}^{n} i_k - M.$$

Otherwise, $M \le (\sum_{k=1}^{n} i_k)/2$. Suppose there exist m elements which are equal to M, without loss of generality, let $i_1 = \cdots = i_m = M$, where $1 \le m \le n$. If $M = 0$, then $g_{i_1, i_2, \ldots, i_n} = 1$, and $G(i_1, i_2, \ldots, i_n) = 0$. If $M = 1$, we have $G(i_1, i_2, \ldots, i_n) = \lfloor m/2 \rfloor = \lfloor (\sum_{k=1}^{n} i_k)/2 \rfloor$. If $M \ge 2$, when m is even, we know

$$G(i_1, \ldots, i_m, i_{m+1}, \ldots, i_n) = G(i_1 - 1, \ldots, i_m - 1, i_{m+1}, \ldots, i_n) + \frac{m}{2}.$$

We now consider the maximum of $\{i_1 - 1, \ldots, i_m - 1, i_{m+1}, \ldots, i_n\}$. Obviously,

$$i_1 - 1 = \max\{i_1 - 1, \ldots, i_m - 1, i_{m+1}, \ldots, i_n\}.$$

Note that $i_1 - 1 = \cdots = i_m - 1$, we have

$$i_1 - 1 \le \frac{(i_1 - 1) + \cdots + (i_m - 1) + i_{m+1} + \cdots + i_n}{2},$$

According to the mathematical induction, we know

$$G(i_1 - 1, \ldots, i_m - 1, i_{m+1}, \ldots, i_n) = \left\lfloor \frac{(i_1 - 1) + \cdots + (i_m - 1) + i_{m+1} + \cdots + i_n}{2} \right\rfloor,$$

thus,

$$G(i_1, \ldots, i_n) = \left\lfloor \frac{i_1 + \cdots + i_n}{2} \right\rfloor.$$

Similarly, $G(i_1, \ldots, i_n)$ can be computed as $\lfloor \frac{i_1 + \cdots + i_n}{2} \rfloor$ when m is odd.   □

Remark 3. For any integer i_j satisfying $0 \le i_j \le d$, $1 \le j \le n$, we have $G(i_1, \ldots, i_n) \le \lfloor \frac{nd}{2} \rfloor$, and $G(d, \ldots, d) = \lfloor \frac{nd}{2} \rfloor$.

Now we show that the polynomial $g_{i_1, i_2, \ldots, i_n}$ output from Algorithm 1 is optimal in the sense that the corresponding $G(i_1, i_2, \ldots, i_n)$ maximizes $R(i_1, i_2, \ldots, i_n)$ for a fixed tuple $(i_1, i_2, \ldots, i_n)$.

Theorem 2. *Let the set* $P_{i_1, i_2, \ldots, i_n}$ *be defined as above, then the polynomial* $g_{i_1, i_2, \ldots, i_n}$ *Algorithm 1 outputs satisfies*

$$G(i_1, i_2, \ldots, i_n) = \max\left\{R(i_1, i_2, \ldots, i_n) : r_{i_1, i_2, \ldots, i_n} \in P_{i_1, i_2, \ldots, i_n}\right\}.$$

Proof. There exists some variable x_k such that the polynomial

$$g_{i_1,i_2,\ldots,i_n} = x_k^{t_k} \prod_{1 \le i < j \le n} f_{i,j}^{t_{i,j}},$$

where t_k is a non-negative integer, and its leading monomial under the graded lexicographic order is $x_1^{i_1} x_2^{i_2} \ldots x_n^{i_n}$, hence, $g_{i_1,i_2,\ldots,i_n} \in P_{i_1,i_2,\ldots,i_n}$. Note that the leading monomial of any polynomial $r_{i_1,i_2,\ldots,i_n} \in P_{i_1,i_2,\ldots,i_n}$ is always $x_1^{i_1} x_2^{i_2} \ldots x_n^{i_n}$, therefore the total sum of the multiplicities of $f_{i,j}$ appearing in the expression of $r_{i_1,i_2,\ldots,i_n}$ is no more than $\lfloor \frac{i_1+\cdots+i_n}{2} \rfloor$ since $f_{i,j}$ is quadratic. However, from Lemma 3, we know when $M \le (\sum_{k=1}^{\tilde{n}} i_k)/2$,

$$G(i_1, i_2, \ldots, i_n) = \left\lfloor \frac{i_1 + \cdots + i_n}{2} \right\rfloor,$$

which means that $g_{i_1,i_2,\ldots,i_n}$ is optimal.

For the case of $M > (\sum_{k=1}^{n} i_k)/2$, without loss of generality, assume $M = i_1 > i_2 + \cdots + i_n$. Then $i_1 > 0$ and any polynomial $r_{i_1,i_2,\ldots,i_n}$ in $P_{i_1,i_2,\ldots,i_n}$ must be of the form

$$\left(\prod_k x_k^{t_k}\right)\left(\prod_{1 \le i < j \le n} f_{i,j}^{t_{i,j}}\right), \ t_k, \ t_{i,j} \in \mathbb{N},$$

where $t_1 > 0$. Otherwise, if $t_1 = 0$, note that $t_1 + \sum_{j=2}^{n} t_{1,j} = i_1$, it leads to $i_1 = \sum_{j=2}^{n} t_{1,j}$. This is contradictory with that $i_1 > \sum_{j=2}^{n} i_j \ge \sum_{j=2}^{n} t_{1,j}$.

Furthermore, we expect that $R(i_1, i_2, \ldots, i_n)$ is as large as possible, therefore, the corresponding polynomial $r_{i_1,i_2,\ldots,i_n}$ in $P_{i_1,i_2,\ldots,i_n}$ must be of the form

$$x_1^{t_1} \prod_{1 \le i < j \le n} f_{i,j}^{t_{i,j}}, \ t_{i,j} \in \mathbb{N}, \ t_1 > 0. \tag{6}$$

Otherwise, there exists positive integers $l > \cdots > k \ge 2$ with positive $t_l, \ldots, t_k$, such that

$$r_{i_1,i_2,\ldots,i_n} = \left(x_1^{t_1} x_k^{t_k} \ldots x_l^{t_l}\right)\left(\prod_{1 \le i < j \le n} f_{i,j}^{t_{i,j}}\right), \ t_{i,j} \in \mathbb{N}, t_1 > 0.$$

We can construct another polynomial

$$\tilde{r}_{i_1,i_2,\ldots,i_n} = \left(f_{1,k} x_1^{t_1-1} x_k^{t_k-1} \ldots x_l^{t_l}\right)\left(\prod_{1 \le i < j \le n} f_{i,j}^{t_{i,j}}\right), \ t_{i,j} \in \mathbb{N}, t_1 > 0,$$

and obviously, $\tilde{r}_{i_1,i_2,\ldots,i_n} \in P_{i_1,i_2,\ldots,i_n}$, and the total sum of the multiplicities of $f_{i,j}$ appearing in the expression of $\tilde{r}_{i_1,i_2,\ldots,i_n}$ is more than $r_{i_1,i_2,\ldots,i_n}$.

Finally, due to (6) and the $f_{i,j}$ are quadratic, we have the following relations

$$\begin{cases} R(i_1, i_2, \ldots, i_n) = \sum_{j=2}^{n} t_{1,j} + \sum_{2 \le i < j \le n} t_{ij}, \\ \sum_{j=2}^{n} i_j = \sum_{j=2}^{n} t_{1,j} + 2 \sum_{2 \le i < j \le n} t_{ij}, \end{cases}$$

and then,

$$R(i_1, i_2, \ldots, i_n) = \sum_{j=2}^{n} i_j - \sum_{2 \le i < j \le n} t_{ij}.$$

For fixed integers $i_1, i_2, \ldots, i_n$, we know that

$$R(i_1, i_2, \ldots, i_n) = \sum_{j=2}^{n} i_j$$

is maximal when $t_{i,j} = 0$ for $2 \le i < j \le n$. Clearly, this corresponding polynomial is

$$x_1^{t_1} \prod_{1 < j \le n} f_{1,j}^{t_{1,j}}, \ t_{1,j} \in \mathbb{N}, \ t_1 > 0. \tag{7}$$

In fact, this polynomial is exactly the polynomial $g_{i_1, i_2, \ldots, i_n}$ that Algorithm 1 outputs. $\square$

To obtain the largest upper bound X, according to Theorem 2, we use the polynomials $g_{i_1, i_2, \ldots, i_n}$ instead of the polynomials $r_{i_1, i_2, \ldots, i_n}$ in the lattice L and take $W = \lfloor \frac{nd}{2} \rfloor$ in Step 1 of the strategy.

From (5), we have

$$X < p^{\frac{2F(n,d)}{nd(d+1)^n}}.$$

where

$$F(n, d) = \sum_{0 \le i_1, i_2, \ldots, i_n \le d} G(i_1, i_2, \ldots, i_n).$$

We give an explicit formula for $F(n, d)$ in the following lemma and leave its proof in Appendix A.

Lemma 4. *Given positive integers n and d, we have*

$$F(n, d)$$
$$= \begin{cases} \frac{1}{4} \left((d+1)^n (nd-1) - \frac{d(d+1)(n+2d-1)}{n^2-1} \binom{n+d-1}{n-2} + n \sum_{i=0}^{(d-1)/2} \binom{n+2i-2}{n-2} \right), & \text{if } d \text{ is odd,} \\ \frac{1}{4} \left((d+1)^n (nd-1) + 1 - \frac{d(d+1)(n+2d-1)}{n^2-1} \binom{n+d-1}{n-2} + n \sum_{i=1}^{d/2} \binom{n+2i-3}{n-2} \right), & \text{if } d \text{ is even.} \end{cases}$$

Note that $X = p/2^l$, we have

$$l > \left(1 - \frac{2F(n, d)}{nd(d+1)^n} \right) k.$$

For fixed n, we know that

$$\lim_{d \to \infty} \left(\binom{n+d-1}{n-2} \Big/ \frac{d^{n-2}}{(n-2)!} \right) = 1,$$

and when $d \to \infty$,

$$\sum_{i=1}^{d/2} \binom{n+2i-3}{n-2} = o\left(\binom{n+d-1}{n-2}\right),$$

$$\sum_{i=1}^{(d-1)/2} \binom{n+2i-2}{n-2} = o\left(\binom{n+d-1}{n-2}\right).$$

Then when $d \to \infty$,

$$F(n,d) \approx \frac{1}{4}\left(nd^{n+1} - \frac{2d^3}{n^2-1}\frac{d^{n-2}}{(n-2)!}\right) = \frac{1}{4}\left(1 - \frac{2}{(n+1)!}\right)nd^{n+1}.$$

Furthermore,

$$\lim_{d\to\infty} \frac{2F(n,d)}{nd(d+1)^n} = \frac{1}{2} - \frac{1}{(n+1)!}.$$

Thus,

$$l > \left(\frac{1}{2} + \frac{1}{(n+1)!} + \varepsilon\right)k,$$

where ε is a real number with very small absolute value depending on n and d.

5   Experiment Results

We implemented our algorithm on a desktop with a 2.83GHz quad-core Intel Core2 CPU and 4GB RAM. We show a selection of our experimental results for various parameter settings in Table 1. In order to find the roots from the system of equations corresponding to the first n LLL-reduced basis vectors, we can use the resultant or Gröbner basis technique. In our experiments, we found that for $n \le 3$, both methods worked well. But for $n \ge 4$, the first n equations will vanish to 0 after resultants computation. We also found that the LLL algorithm outputs more than n integer equations by choosing proper parameters namely when larger p or smaller l is needed. Actually, all vectors in the LLL-reduced basis correspond to an integer equation except the last vector in our experiments. This can benefit us in computing Gröbner basis.

Instead of using (1) to estimate the appropriate bounds for l in our experiments, we used (2) to calculate the theoretical values of l for specifically chosen n and d. In our experiments, we found that the length of the n-th vector in the LLL-reduced basis was approximately

$$\|\boldsymbol{v}_n\| \approx 1.02^{\dim(L)}(\det(L))^{1/\dim(L)},$$

when n was not too large. As in [5] we used 1.02 as the value for the so-called "LLL factor". The justification of the factor was confirmed by a number of experiments in our implementation. In our experiments, the factor never exceed 1.02. As we can see in Table 1, the fifth column (experimental results) and the sixth column (theoretical bounds) are perfectly matched, which means that we can solve ModInv-HNP with about half of the most significant bits of the inversions modulo p.

Table 1. Experimental results with different parameter settings. For comparison we include the parameter settings which cannot be checked by experiments due to much more computation or out of memory.

k $(\log_2 p)$	n	d	$\dim(L)$	l/k (experiment)	l/k (theory)	LLL (seconds)	Gröbner (seconds)
1000	2	2	9	0.723	0.722	0.203	0.296
1000	2	3	16	0.709	0.708	1.217	0.172
1000	2	4	25	0.701	0.700	9.516	1.248
1000	2	8	81	0.686	0.685	5272.974	428.925
1000	2	10	121	0.683	0.682	47043.443	3912.723
1000	3	1	8	0.668	0.667	0.031	0.000
1000	3	2	27	0.618	0.617	9.688	0.624
1000	3	3	64	0.598	0.597	859.378	33.150
1000	3	4	125	0.586	0.585	27049.622	1214.936
1000	4	1	16	0.626	0.625	0.359	0.031
1000	4	2	81	0.575	0.574	1301.532	55.677
-	4	4	625	-	0.544	-	-
-	4	8	6561	-	0.527	-	-
1000	5	1	32	0.601	0.600	6.131	2.246
-	5	2	243	-	0.554	-	-
-	5	3	1024	-	0.537	-	-
-	5	5	7776	-	0.529	-	-
1000	6	1	64	0.584	0.583	191.491	2.262
-	6	2	729	-	0.543	-	-
-	6	3	4096	-	0.529	-	-
1000	7	1	128	0.573	0.571	3536.917	24.414
-	7	2	2187	-	0.536	-	-

6 Conclusion

The modular inversion hidden number problem is revisited and a new polynomial time algorithm for solving the problem is presented. In our algorithm, to recover the hidden number when n samples are given, we need to know about $\left(\frac{1}{2} + \frac{1}{(n+1)!}\right)$ of the bits of the inversions modulo p. Compared with previous algorithms, assume the same number of partial bits of the modular inversions are known, our algorithm requires fewer samples.

Acknowledgements. The authors would like to thank anonymous reviewers for their helpful comments and suggestions. The work of this paper was supported by the National Key Basic Research Program of China (2013CB834203), the National Natural Science Foundation of China (Grant 61070172), and the Strategic Priority Research Program of Chinese Academy of Sciences under Grant XDA06010702.

References

1. Ajtai, M.: The shortest vector problem in l_2 is NP-hard for randomized reductions. In: Proceedings of the Thirtieth Annual ACM Symposium on Theory of Computing, pp. 10–19. ACM (1998)
2. Boneh, D., Halevi, S., Howgrave-Graham, N.: The modular inversion hidden number problem. In: Boyd, C. (ed.) ASIACRYPT 2001. LNCS, vol. 2248, pp. 36–51. Springer, Heidelberg (2001)
3. Boneh, D., Venkatesan, R.: Hardness of computing the most significant bits of secret keys in Diffie-Hellman and related schemes. In: Koblitz, N. (ed.) CRYPTO 1996. LNCS, vol. 1109, pp. 129–142. Springer, Heidelberg (1996)
4. Boneh, D., Venkatesan, R.: Rounding in lattices and its cryptographic applications. In: Proceedings of the Eighth Annual ACM-SIAM Symposium on Discrete Algorithms, Society for Industrial and Applied Mathematics, pp. 675–682 (1997)
5. Cohn, H., Heninger, N.: Approximate common divisors via lattices. Cryptology ePrint Archive, Report 2011/437 (2011), http://eprint.iacr.org/
6. Coppersmith, D.: Finding a small root of a bivariate integer equation; factoring with high bits known. In: Maurer, U.M. (ed.) EUROCRYPT 1996. LNCS, vol. 1070, pp. 178–189. Springer, Heidelberg (1996)
7. Coppersmith, D.: Finding a small root of a univariate modular equation. In: Maurer, U.M. (ed.) EUROCRYPT 1996. LNCS, vol. 1070, pp. 155–165. Springer, Heidelberg (1996)
8. Coppersmith, D.: Small solutions to polynomial equations, and low exponent RSA vulnerabilities. Journal of Cryptology 10(4), 233–260 (1997)
9. Cox, D.A.: Ideals, varieties, and algorithms: an introduction to computational algebraic geometry and commutative algebra. Springer (2007)
10. Gelfand, I., Gelfand, I., Kapranov, M., Zelevinsky, A.: Discriminants, Resultants, and Multidimensional Determinants. Mathematics (Birkhäuser). Birkhäuser Boston (2008)
11. Herrmann, M., May, A.: Attacking power generators using unravelled linearization: When do we output too much? In: Matsui, M. (ed.) ASIACRYPT 2009. LNCS, vol. 5912, pp. 487–504. Springer, Heidelberg (2009)
12. Howgrave-Graham, N.: Finding small roots of univariate modular equations revisited. In: Darnell, M.J. (ed.) Cryptography and Coding 1997. LNCS, vol. 1355, pp. 131–142. Springer, Heidelberg (1997)
13. Jochemsz, E., May, A.: A strategy for finding roots of multivariate polynomials with new applications in attacking RSA variants. In: Lai, X., Chen, K. (eds.) ASIACRYPT 2006. LNCS, vol. 4284, pp. 267–282. Springer, Heidelberg (2006)
14. Leiserson, C.E., Rivest, R.L., Stein, C., Cormen, T.H.: Introduction to algorithms. The MIT press (2001)
15. Lenstra, A.K., Lenstra, H.W., Lovász, L.: Factoring polynomials with rational coefficients. Mathematische Annalen 261(4), 515–534 (1982)
16. Ling, S., Shparlinski, I.E., Steinfeld, R., Wang, H.: On the modular inversion hidden number problem. Journal of Symbolic Computation 47(4), 358–367 (2012)
17. May, A.: Using LLL-reduction for solving rsa and factorization problems. In: The LLL algorithm, pp. 315–348. Springer (2010)
18. Shparlinski, I.E.: Playing hide-and-seek with numbers: the hidden number problem, lattices, and exponential sums. In: Proceeding of Symposia in Applied Mathematics, vol. 62, pp. 153–177 (2005)

A   Proof of Lemma 4

Before computing $F(n,d)$, we define $S_0(n,d)$ and $S_1(n,d)$:

$$S_0(n,d) = \sum_{0 \le i_1,i_2,\dots,i_n \le d} \left\lfloor \frac{i_1 + i_2 + \cdots + i_n}{2} \right\rfloor ,$$

$$S_1(n,d) = \sum_{0 \le i_1,i_2,\dots,i_n \le d} \left\lfloor \frac{1 + i_1 + i_2 + \cdots + i_n}{2} \right\rfloor ,$$

for positive integers n and d. We have the following lemma:

Lemma 5. *Given the above definition of $S_0(n,d)$ and $S_1(n,d)$, we have*

$$S_0(n,d) = \begin{cases} \frac{1}{4}(nd-1)(d+1)^n, & \text{if } d \text{ is odd,} \\ \frac{1}{4}(nd-1)(d+1)^n + \frac{1}{4}, & \text{if } d \text{ is even.} \end{cases}$$

$$S_1(n,d) = \begin{cases} \frac{1}{4}(nd+1)(d+1)^n, & \text{if } d \text{ is odd,} \\ \frac{1}{4}(nd+1)(d+1)^n - \frac{1}{4}, & \text{if } d \text{ is even.} \end{cases}$$

Proof. We first consider the case when d is even. In this case, we rewrite $S_0(n,d)$ as

$$S_0(n,d) = \sum_{0 \le i_1 \le d} \sum_{0 \le i_2,\dots,i_n \le d} \left\lfloor \frac{i_1 + i_2 + \cdots + i_n}{2} \right\rfloor$$

$$= S_0(n-1,d)\left(\frac{d}{2}+1\right) + S_1(n-1,d)\frac{d}{2} + \frac{1}{4}d^2(d+1)^{n-1}. \tag{8}$$

Analogously, we rewrite $S_1(n,d)$ as

$$S_1(n,d) = S_0(n-1,d)\frac{d}{2} + S_1(n-1,d)\left(\frac{d}{2}+1\right) + \frac{1}{4}d(d+2)(d+1)^{n-1}. \tag{9}$$

It is easy to know that when $n = 1$, $S_0(1,d) = d^2/4$ and $S_1(1,d) = d(d+2)/4$. Solve the recurrence equations (8) and (9) with initial values $S_0(1,d)$ and $S_1(1,d)$, we get

$$S_0(n,d) = \frac{1}{4}(nd-1)(d+1)^n + \frac{1}{4},$$

$$S_1(n,d) = \frac{1}{4}(nd+1)(d+1)^n - \frac{1}{4}.$$

The proof to the case of d being odd is similar, we omit the details here. □

Proof of Lemma 4.

1. When d is even, we have

$$S_0(n, d)$$

$$=F(n, d) + \sum_{M>(i_1+i_2+\cdots+i_n)/2} \left(\left\lfloor \frac{i_1 + i_2 + \cdots + i_n}{2} \right\rfloor - (i_1 + i_2 + \cdots + i_n - M) \right)$$

$$=F(n, d) + n \sum_{i_1=1}^{d} \sum_{i_2+\cdots+i_n<i_1} \left(\left\lfloor \frac{i_1 + i_2 + \cdots + i_n}{2} \right\rfloor - (i_2 + \cdots + i_n) \right)$$

$$=F(n, d) + n \sum_{i_1=1}^{d} \sum_{j=0}^{i_1-1} \left(\left\lfloor \frac{i_1 + j}{2} \right\rfloor - j \right) \binom{n+j-2}{n-2}$$

$$=F(n, d) + n \sum_{i_1=1}^{d} \sum_{j=0}^{i_1-1} \left(\frac{2i_1 - 2j - 1}{4} \right) \binom{n+j-2}{n-2} - \frac{n}{4} \sum_{i=1}^{d/2} \binom{n+2i-3}{n-2}$$

$$=F(n, d) + \frac{1}{4} \frac{d(d+1)(n+2d-1)}{n^2-1} \binom{n+d-1}{n-2} - \frac{n}{4} \sum_{i=1}^{d/2} \binom{n+2i-3}{n-2}.$$

Thus,

$$F(n, d)$$

$$=\frac{1}{4} \left((d+1)^n(nd-1) + 1 - \frac{d(d+1)(n+2d-1)}{n^2-1} \binom{n+d-1}{n-2} + n \sum_{i=1}^{d/2} \binom{n+2i-3}{n-2} \right).$$

2. When d is odd, we have

$$S_0(n, d)$$

$$=F(n, d) + n \sum_{i_1=1}^{d} \sum_{j=0}^{i_1-1} \left(\frac{2s_1 + 2j - 1}{4} \right) \binom{n+j-2}{n-2} - \frac{n}{4} \sum_{i=0}^{(d-1)/2} \binom{n+2i-2}{n-2},$$

then,

$$F(n, d)$$

$$=\frac{1}{4} \left((d+1)^n(nd-1) - \frac{d(d+1)(n+2d-1)}{n^2-1} \binom{n+d-1}{n-2} + n \sum_{i=0}^{(d-1)/2} \binom{n+2i-2}{n-2} \right).$$

$\square$

On the Recursive Construction of MDS Matrices for Lightweight Cryptography*

Hong Xu[1,2], Lin Tan[2], and Xuejia Lai[1]

[1] Shanghai Jiao Tong University, Shanghai, China
[2] Zhengzhou Information Science and Technology Institute, Zhengzhou, China

Abstract. Maximum distance separable (MDS) matrices are widely used in the diffusion layers of block ciphers and hash functions. Recently, Guo, Sajadieh and Wu *et al.* proposed to use recursive methods to construct MDS matrices from linear feedback shift registers, and Wu *et al.* presented some very compact MDS matrices constructed from cascade of several linear feedback shift registers. However, some of the MDS matrices constructed by them do not have simple inverses. In this paper, we further present some compact MDS matrices which have simple inverses. The cost is almost the same as Wu *et al.*'s, and the inverses are also MDS matrices and can be efficiently implemented as themselves.

Keywords: Diffusion Layers, Branch number, MDS matrices, Linear Feedback Shift Register (LFSR).

1 Introduction

Confusion and diffusion are two important standards considered in the design of block ciphers and hash functions [1]. Modern block ciphers and hash functions are usually cascades of several rounds and each round consists of confusion and diffusion layers [2]. The confusion component is usually a non-linear substitution boxes (S-boxes) on a small subblock and the diffusion component is a linear mixing of the subblocks in order to diffuse the statistics of the system. The diffusion layer plays an important role in providing resistance against the most well-known attacks such as differential cryptanalysis (DC) [3] and linear cryptanalysis (LC) [4].

In 1994, Vaudenay [5] [6] suggested using MDS matrices in cryptographic primitives to achieve perfect diffusion (multipermutations). He showed how to exploit imperfect diffusion to cryptanalyze functions that are not multipermutations. This notion was later used by Daemen [7] named as the branch number, and the most attractive diffusion layers are those with maximum branch numbers, which are also called perfect or MDS diffusion layers. Many block ciphers such as AES [8], use MDS matrices in the diffusion layers. How to construct MDS matrices efficiently is still a challenge for the designers.

* This work was supported by the NSF of China under Grant Numbers 61100200, 61272042, 61309017, and China Postdoctoral Science Foundation under Grant Number 2013M531174.

X. Huang and J. Zhou (Eds.): ISPEC 2014, LNCS 8434, pp. 552–563, 2014.
© Springer International Publishing Switzerland 2014

In the design of lightweight algorithms PHOTON [9] and LED [10], to further improve the efficiency, Guo *et al.* presented a strategy to construct $s \times s$ MDS matrices from an s-stage linear feedback shift register (LFSR) over F_{2^n} (See Figure 1). Later, Sajadieh *et al.* [2] and Wu *et al.* [11] further generalized their construction by replacing the finite field multiplication operations presented in PHOTON with simpler F_2-linear operations, and provided some perfect MDS matrices for $2 \leq s \leq 8$. In their constructions, Sajadieh *et al.* focused on constructing MDS matrices with fewer basic linear functions, whereas Wu *et al.* focused on constructing MDS matrices with fewer XOR operations. To further reduce the hardware costs, Wu *et al.* also considered to construct MDS matrices from cascade of several LFSRs and provided some examples for $s = 4, 6, 8$. The MDS matrices constructed by Sajadieh *et al.* have simple inverses. However, some of the 4×4 and 6×6 MDS matrices proposed by Wu *et al.* do not have simple inverses.

As is known, Feistel and SPN (substitution permutation network) structures are two fundamental structures of block ciphers. The Feistel structure possesses similarity of encryption and decryption, whereas the decryption process of SPN structures need to use inverse transformations. If the inverse transformations are not perfect, then the security of the decryption algorithm may be lower than that of the encryption algorithm. Thus in the design of diffusion layers, MDS matrices with simple inverses whose inverses are also MDS are preferred to ensure the security and efficiency of the algorithm.

In this paper, inspired by Wu *et al.*'s construction, we further present some examples of MDS matrices with simple inverses, and the inverses are also MDS matrices. Such MDS matrices can provide much flexibility in the design of perfect diffusion layers. The hardware cost of the MDS matrices constructed by us is almost the same as that of Wu *et al.*'s.

The rest of this paper is organized as follows. First, some definitions, properties and known results on the recursive constructions of MDS matrices are reviewed in Section 2. Then a systematic analysis on 4×4 and 6×6 MDS matrices constructed from cascade of several LFSRs are presented in Sections 3. All the MDS matrices constructed by us have simple inverses, and their inverses are usually also MDS matrices and can be efficiently implemented with the same computational complexity. Finally, a short conclusion is given in Section 4.

2 Preliminaries

In this section, we will review some basic definitions and properties of MDS matrices, and provide some known results on the recursive constructions of MDS matrices from LFSRs.

Definition 1. *[12] [13] Let F be a finite field, and p and q be two integers. Let $x \to M \times x$ be a mapping from F^p to F^q defined by the $q \times p$ matrix M.*

We say that it is an MDS matrix if the set of all pairs $(x, M \times x)$ is an MDS code, i.e. a linear code of dimension p, length $p + q$ and minimal distance $q + 1$.

In coding theory, MDS codes are usually constructed from RS codes [12], Cauchy matrices [14] and Vandermonde matrices [15]. The diffusion layer constructed by MDS matrices can reach maximal linear and differential branch number. The most widely used property for constructing MDS matrices is

Proposition 1. *[12] An $[m, s, d]$ code C with generator matrix $G = [I|A]$, where A is an $s \times (m - s)$ matrix, is MDS if and only if every square submatrix (formed from any i rows and any i columns, for any $i = 1, 2, ..., \min\{s, m - s\}$) of A is nonsingular.*

When considering a linear diffusion layer, A is always a square matrix, that is, $m = 2s$. A square matrix A over a field is nonsingular if and only if its determinant is nonzero. Since the entries of A^{-1} contains determinants of all the $(s-1) \times (s-1)$ submatrices of A, then from Proposition 1 we know that if A is an $s \times s$ MDS matrix over F_{2^n}, then all entries of A and A^{-1} are nonzero. Furthermore, Gupta *et al.* also presented the following useful result for the judgement of 4×4 MDS matrices.

Proposition 2. *[16] Any 4×4 matrix over F_{2^n} with all entries non zero is an MDS matrix if and only if it is a full rank matrix with the inverse matrix having all entries non zero and all of its 2×2 submatrices are full rank.*

MDS matrices are widely used in the diffusion layers of block ciphers and hash functions. In the design of lightweight primitives PHOTON [9] and LED [10], to further improve the efficiency and provide more compact serial implementation in lightweight cryptographic primitives, Guo *et al.* presented a strategy to construct $s \times s$ MDS matrices from an s-stage linear feedback shift register (LFSR) over F_{2^n} (See Figure 1). In each step, only the last register is updated by a linear

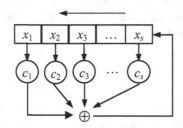

Fig. 1. An s-stage linear feedback shift register over F_{2^n}

combination of all of the registers while other registers are obtained by shifting the state vector by one position to the left. That is, the state transition matrix of the LFSR can be given as

$$
A = \begin{pmatrix}
0 & 1 & 0 & \cdots & 0 \\
0 & 0 & 1 & \cdots & 0 \\
\vdots & \vdots & \vdots & \ddots & \vdots \\
0 & 0 & 0 & \cdots & 1 \\
c_1 & c_2 & c_3 & \cdots & c_s
\end{pmatrix},
$$

where $c_i \in F_{2^n}$. For simplicity, we only extract the final row of A, that is, $A = [c_1, c_2, ..., c_s]_{lfsr}$. Guo $et\ al.$ tested all the possible values $c_1, c_2, ..., c_s \in F_{2^n}$, and picked the most compact candidate such that A^s is an MDS matrix. One example of the 4×4 MDS matrix presented by Guo $et\ al.$ was $\left([1, \alpha, 1, \alpha^2]_{lfsr}\right)^4$, which can be implemented by iterating the LFSR four times. Here α is the root of the defining polynomial of F_{2^n}.

Since the mapping $x \rightarrow c_i \cdot x$ can also be seen as a linear transformation over F_{2^n} (or F_2^n equivalently), Sajadieh $et\ al.$ [2] and Wu $et\ al.$[11] further generalized Guo $et\ al.$'s construction by replacing the finite field multiplication operations with simpler F_2-linear operations L over F_2^n, and provided some perfect MDS matrices for $2 \leq s \leq 8$. In their constructions, Sajadieh $et\ al.$ focused on constructing MDS matrices with fewer basic linear functions, whereas Wu $et\ al.$ focused on constructing MDS matrices with fewer XOR operations.

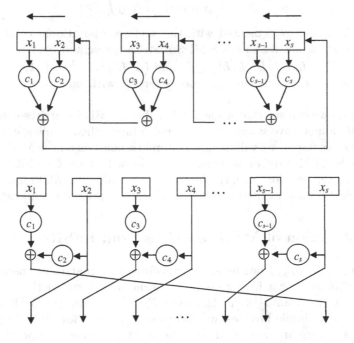

Fig. 2. Cascade of several 2-stage LFSRs

To further reduce the hardware costs, Wu *et al.* also considered to construct MDS matrices from cascade of several 2-stage LFSRs (see Figure 2), which can also be seen as a Generalized Feistel Structure in block ciphers. The corresponding state transition matrix can be given as

$$
A = \begin{pmatrix}
0 & 1 & 0 & 0 & \cdots & 0 & 0 & 0 & 0 \\
0 & 0 & c_3 & c_4 & \cdots & 0 & 0 & 0 & 0 \\
0 & 0 & 0 & 1 & \cdots & 0 & 0 & 0 & 0 \\
0 & 0 & 0 & 0 & \cdots & 0 & 0 & 0 & 0 \\
\vdots & \vdots & \vdots & \vdots & \ddots & \vdots & \vdots & \vdots & \vdots \\
0 & 0 & 0 & 0 & \cdots & 0 & 1 & 0 & 0 \\
0 & 0 & 0 & 0 & \cdots & 0 & 0 & c_{s-1} & c_s \\
0 & 0 & 0 & 0 & \cdots & 0 & 0 & 0 & 1 \\
c_1 & c_2 & 0 & 0 & \cdots & 0 & 0 & 0 & 0
\end{pmatrix},
$$

For simplicity, we denote by $A = [c_1, c_2, ..., c_s]_{gfs}$. It is clear that if $c_{2i-1} = 1$ for all $1 \leq i \leq s/2$, then

$$
A^{-1} = \begin{pmatrix}
c_2 & 0 & 0 & 0 & \cdots & 0 & 1 \\
1 & 0 & 0 & 0 & \cdots & 0 & 0 \\
0 & 1 & c_4 & 0 & \cdots & 0 & 0 \\
0 & 0 & 1 & 0 & \cdots & 0 & 0 \\
\vdots & \vdots & \vdots & \vdots & \ddots & \vdots & \vdots \\
0 & 0 & 0 & 0 & \cdots & c_s & 0 \\
0 & 0 & 0 & 0 & \cdots & 1 & 0
\end{pmatrix},
$$

which can be easily implemented with the same computational complexity as A. The best 4×4, 6×6 and 8×8 MDS matrices presented by Wu *et al.* were $([L, 1, 1, L]_{gfs})^4$, $([L, 1, 1, L^2, L, L^2]_{gfs})^6$, and $([1, L^4, 1, L^{-1}, 1, L, 1, L^2]_{gfs})^8$, respectively, where L is a linear operation over F_2^n with only one or two XOR gates.

From above we can see that some 4×4 and 6×6 MDS matrices constructed by Wu et al. do not have simple inverses, which limits their applications in SPN networks. In this paper, we will make a systematic analysis on the MDS matrices constructed by LFSRs and present some examples of 4×4 and 6×6 MDS matrices with simple inverses. Moreover, the inverses are usually also MDS matrices and can be efficiently implemented with the same computational complexity.

3   Construction of MDS Matrices from LFSRs

Let $A = [c_1, c_2, ..., c_s]_{gfs}$ be the state transformation matrix of cascades of $\frac{s}{2}$ 2-stage LFSRs as shown in Figure 2. We want to determine the parameters c_i's such that A^s is an MDS matrix over F_{2^n}. To ensure the MDS matrices constructed have simple inverses, we always set $c_{2i-1} = 1$ for all $1 \leq i \leq \frac{s}{2}$.

For any $s \times s$ square matrix M, denote by $M_{i,j}$ the entry appearing in the i-th row and j-th column of M, where $1 \leq i, j \leq s$.

From propositions 1 and 2 we know that if A^s is MDS over F_{2^n}, then all entries of A^s and A^{-s} are nonzero. Thus we can first obtain the following necessary conditions respect to c_i's.

Proposition 3. *Let* $A = [1, c_2, 1, c_4]_{gfs}$ *be the state transformation matrix of cascades of two 2-stage LFSRs. If* A^4 *is an MDS matrix over* F_{2^n}*, then* $c_2 \neq c_4$*,* $c_2 \neq 1$ *and* $c_4 \neq 1$*.*

Proof. The result follows from $(A^4)_{1,2} = c_2 + c_4 \neq 0$, $(A^{-4})_{1,1} = 1 + c_2^4 \neq 0$, and $(A^{-4})_{3,4} = 1 + c_4^4 \neq 0$.

Proposition 4. *Let* $A = [1, c_2, 1, c_4, 1, c_6]_{gfs}$ *be the state transformation matrix of cascades of three 2-stage LFSRs. If* A^6 *is an MDS matrix over* F_{2^n}*, then* $c_2 \neq 1$*,* $c_4 \neq 1$*,* $c_6 \neq 1$*,* $c_2 \neq c_4$*,* $c_2 \neq c_6$*,* $c_4 \neq c_6$ *and* $c_2 + c_4 + c_6 \neq 0$*.*

Proof. The result follows from $(A^{-6})_{1,1} = 1 + c_2^6 \neq 0$, $(A^{-6})_{3,6} = 1 + c_4^6 \neq 0$, $(A^{-6})_{5,6} = 1 + c_6^6 \neq 0$, $(A^{-6})_{3,4} = (c_2 + c_4)^3 \neq 0$, $(A^{-6})_{1,4} = (c_2 + c_6)^3 \neq 0$, $(A^{-6})_{6,3} = (c_4 + c_6)^3 \neq 0$, and $(A^6)_{1,2} = c_2 + c_4 + c_6 \neq 0$.

3.1 Construction of 4×4 MDS Matrices

Let $A = [1, c_2, 1, c_4]_{gfs}$ be the state transformation matrix of cascades of two 2-stage LFSRs as shown in Figure 2. We need to determine the parameters c_2's and c_4's, such that A^4 is an MDS matrix over F_{2^n}. From Proposition 3 we know that if A^4 is an MDS matrix, then $c_2 \neq c_4$, $c_2 \neq 1$ and $c_4 \neq 1$. To ensure efficiency, we restrict the values of c_2 and c_4 in the set $\{\alpha, \alpha^2, \alpha + 1\}$, where α is a root of the defining polynomial $f(x)$ of F_{2^n}. Thus the only candidates remained for (c_2, c_4) are belonging to the set $\{(\alpha, \alpha^2), (\alpha^2, \alpha), (\alpha, \alpha + 1), (\alpha + 1, \alpha)\}$.

For the above two cases we can show the following two results hold.

Theorem 1. *Let* $A = [1, c_2, 1, c_4]_{gfs}$ *with* $(c_2, c_4) \in \{(\alpha, \alpha^2), (\alpha^2, \alpha)\}$*. Then* A^4 *is an MDS matrix over* F_{2^n} *if and only if* $\deg f(x) \geq 4$ *and* $f(x) \neq x^4 + x^3 + 1$*,* $x^4 + x^3 + x^2 + x + 1$*,* $x^5 + x^4 + x^2 + x + 1$*,* $x^6 + x + 1$*,* $x^6 + x^3 + 1$*,* $x^7 + x + 1$*. Moreover, if such conditions are satisfied, then* A^4 *and* A^{-4} *will be MDS matrices simultaneously.*

Proof. We first show the result holds for $A = [1, \alpha, 1, \alpha^2]_{gfs}$. From Proposition 2 we know that A^4 is an MDS matrix if and only if all entries of A^4, A^{-4}, and all the determinants of 2×2 submatrices of A^4 are nonzero. We can calculate such values and obtain the corresponding canonical factorization of them over F_2 as follows:

$$
A^4 = \begin{pmatrix}
1 & \alpha(\alpha+1) & \alpha^3 & \alpha^5 \\
\alpha^5 & (\alpha+1)^2(\alpha^2+\alpha+1)^2 & \alpha(\alpha+1) & \alpha^4 \\
\alpha^3 & \alpha^4 & 1 & \alpha(\alpha+1) \\
\alpha(\alpha+1) & \alpha^2 & \alpha^4 & (\alpha+1)^2(\alpha^2+\alpha+1)^2
\end{pmatrix},
$$

$$A^{-4} = \begin{pmatrix} (\alpha+1)^4 & \alpha(\alpha+1) & \alpha^2(\alpha^2+\alpha+1) & \alpha^3 \\ \alpha^3 & 1 & \alpha(\alpha+1) & \alpha^2 \\ \alpha^2(\alpha^2+\alpha+1) & \alpha^6 & (\alpha+1)^8 & \alpha(\alpha+1) \\ \alpha(\alpha+1) & \alpha^4 & \alpha^6 & 1 \end{pmatrix},$$

and all the 36 determinants of 2×2 submatrices of A^4 are $(\alpha+1)(\alpha^3+\alpha+1)(\alpha^3+\alpha^2+1)$, $\alpha(\alpha^7+\alpha+1)$, $\alpha^4(\alpha+1)^2(\alpha^2+\alpha+1)^2$, $\alpha^2(\alpha+1)^3(\alpha^4+\alpha^3+1)$, $\alpha^6(\alpha+1)(\alpha^4+\alpha^3+\alpha^2+\alpha+1)$, α^6, α^5, $(\alpha+1)^2(\alpha^2+\alpha+1)^2$, $\alpha(\alpha^7+\alpha+1)$, $\alpha(\alpha^6+\alpha+1)$, $\alpha^2(\alpha^2+\alpha+1)(\alpha^5+\alpha^4+\alpha^2+\alpha+1)$, α^4, α^4, α^5, $(\alpha+1)(\alpha^3+\alpha+1)(\alpha^3+\alpha^2+1)$, α^6, $\alpha(\alpha^7+\alpha+1)$, α^3, α^3, α^4, α^6, $(\alpha+1)(\alpha^4+\alpha^3+\alpha^2+\alpha+1)$, $\alpha(\alpha^6+\alpha+1)$, α^2, $\alpha(\alpha^7+\alpha+1)$, $\alpha^2(\alpha^2+\alpha+1)(\alpha^5+\alpha^4+\alpha^2+\alpha+1)$, $\alpha^6(\alpha+1)(\alpha^4+\alpha^3+\alpha^2+\alpha+1)$, $\alpha^3(\alpha+1)(\alpha^3+\alpha+1)(\alpha^3+\alpha^2+1)$, $(\alpha^6+\alpha^3+1)^2$, $\alpha(\alpha^6+\alpha+1)$, α^6, $\alpha(\alpha^6+\alpha+1)$, $\alpha^2(\alpha+1)^3(\alpha^4+\alpha^3+1)$, $\alpha^2(\alpha+1)(\alpha^2+\alpha+1)^2$, $\alpha^3(\alpha+1)(\alpha^3+\alpha+1)(\alpha^3+\alpha^2+1)$, $(\alpha+1)(\alpha^4+\alpha^3+\alpha^2+\alpha+1)$, respectively.

From above we can see that exactly all irreducible polynomials of degree less than 3 appear in some entries of A^4 and A^{-4}, and the following eight new irreducible polynomials $\alpha^3+\alpha+1$, $\alpha^3+\alpha^2+1$, $\alpha^4+\alpha^3+1$, $\alpha^4+\alpha^3+\alpha^2+\alpha+1$, $\alpha^5+\alpha^4+\alpha^2+\alpha+1$, $\alpha^6+\alpha+1$, $\alpha^6+\alpha^3+1$, $\alpha^7+\alpha+1$ appear in the determinants of 2×2 submatrices of A^4. Thus A^4 is an MDS matrix if and only if all these irreducible polynomials respect to α are nonzero, that is,

$$\alpha \neq 0,$$
$$\alpha + 1 \neq 0,$$
$$\alpha^2 + \alpha + 1 \neq 0,$$
$$\alpha^3 + \alpha + 1 \neq 0,$$
$$\alpha^3 + \alpha^2 + 1 \neq 0,$$
$$\alpha^4 + \alpha^3 + 1 \neq 0,$$
$$\alpha^4 + \alpha^3 + \alpha^2 + \alpha + 1 \neq 0,$$
$$\alpha^5 + \alpha^4 + \alpha^2 + \alpha + 1 \neq 0,$$
$$\alpha^6 + \alpha + 1 \neq 0,$$
$$\alpha^6 + \alpha^3 + 1 \neq 0,$$
$$\alpha^7 + \alpha + 1 \neq 0. \tag{1}$$

Therefore α can not be the root of any irreducible polynomials of degree less than 4, and α can not be the root of the following six irreducible polynomials x^4+x^3+1, $x^4+x^3+x^2+x+1$, $x^5+x^4+x^2+x+1$, x^6+x+1, x^6+x^3+1, x^7+x+1. Hence we can deduce that A^4 is an MDS matrix if and only if $\deg f(x) \geq 4$ and $f(x) \neq x^4 + x^3 + 1, x^4 + x^3 + x^2 + x + 1, x^5 + x^4 + x^2 + x + 1, x^6 + x + 1, x^6 + x^3 + 1, x^7 + x + 1$.

To judge whether A^{-4} is an MDS matrix, we need to further calculate all the determinants of 2×2 submatrices of A^{-4}. By careful calculation, we find that the same eight new irreducible polynomials also appear in the determinants of 2×2 submatrices of A^{-4}. Thus from Proposition 2 we can deduce that A^4 and A^{-4} will be MDS matrices or non MDS matrices simultaneously, and they will be MDS matrices if and only if $\deg f(x) \geq 4$ and $f(x) \neq x^4 + x^3 + 1$, $x^4 + x^3 + x^2 + x + 1$, $x^5 + x^4 + x^2 + x + 1$, $x^6 + x + 1$, $x^6 + x^3 + 1$, $x^7 + x + 1$. So the result holds for $A = [1, \alpha, 1, \alpha^2]_{gfs}$.

Similarly we can show the result also holds for $A = [1, \alpha^2, 1, \alpha]_{gfs}$.

Similar as above, we can also show the following result holds. The proof is given in appendix for completeness.

Theorem 2. *Let $A = [1, c_2, 1, c_4]_{gfs}$ with $(c_2, c_4) \in \{(\alpha, \alpha+1), (\alpha+1, \alpha)\}$. Then A^4 is an MDS matrix over F_{2^n} if and only if $\deg f(x) \geq 5$ and $f(x) \neq x^5 + x^3 + 1$, $x^5 + x^4 + x^3 + x^2 + 1$. Moreover, if such conditions are satisfied, then A^4 and A^{-4} will be MDS matrices simultaneously.*

Remark 1. The parameter α in Theorem 1 and Theorem 2 can also be replaced by any other linear transformation L over F_{2^n} (or F_2^n equivalently). The matrix A^4 will be an MDS matrix if and only if the linear transformation L satisfies similar nonzero conditions as (1) and (2) given on α in the proofs of the theorems. In fact, there exist many linear transformations L with only one or two XOR gates that satisfy the conditions. Some of them are listed in the following table.

Table 1. Lightweight linear transformation L for $A = [1, c_2, 1, c_4]_{gfs}$

Length of the input	Example of L
$n = 5$	$[[2, 4], 3, 4, 5, 1]$
$n = 6$	$[[1, 2], 3, 4, 5, 6, 1]$
$n = 7$	$[[2, 5], 3, 4, 5, 6, 7, 1]$
$n = 8$	$[[2, 3], 3, [4, 7], 5, 6, 7, 8, 1]$
$n = 12$	$[[2, 5], 3, 4, ..., 12, 1]$
$n = 16$	$[[2, 3], 3, 4, ..., 16, 1]$
$n = 32$	$[[2, 4], 3, 4, ..., 32, 1]$
$n = 64$	$[[2, 6], 3, 4, ..., 64, 1]$

Here only the nonzero positions in each row of the matrix L is listed for simplicity, that is, $[[2, 4], 3, 4, 5, 1]$ is the representation of the matrix

$$\begin{pmatrix} 0 & 1 & 0 & 1 & 0 \\ 0 & 0 & 1 & 0 & 0 \\ 0 & 0 & 0 & 1 & 0 \\ 0 & 0 & 0 & 0 & 1 \\ 1 & 0 & 0 & 0 & 0 \end{pmatrix}.$$

The matrices L in Table 1 are selected such that their minimal polynomials do not contain the irreducible factors listed in conditions (1) and (2).

Note that the last two rows of the table is the same as Table 1 of [11]. Particularly if $A = [1, L, 1, L^2]_{gfs}$, or $[1, L^2, 1, L]_{gfs}$ as shown in Theorem 1, then L can be chosen as any linear transformation listed in Table 1 of [11]. For example, L can also be chosen as $[[2, 3], 3, 4, 1]$ for $n = 4$, and $[[5, 6], 7, 5, 8, 4, 3, 1, 2]$ for $n = 8$, which costs only one XOR gate as presented in [11].

On the other hand, if the defining polynomial of the finite field F_{2^n} is a trinomial, then the linear transformation $x \rightarrow \alpha \cdot x$ over F_{2^n} also contains only one XOR gate. For example, the matrices A^4 with $A = [1, \alpha, 1, \alpha^2]_{gfs}, [1, \alpha^2, 1, \alpha]_{gfs},$ $[1, \alpha, 1, \alpha+1]_{gfs},$ and $[1, \alpha+1, 1, \alpha]_{gfs}$ are all MDS matrices over F_{2^5} with defining polynomial $f(x) = x^5 + x^3 + 1$. Simultaneously, A^{-4} is also an MDS matrix over F_{2^5} with defining polynomial $f(x) = x^5 + x^3 + 1$. Except for the case when $8|n$, there exists many such trinomials.

3.2   Construction of 6×6 MDS Matrices

Let $A = [1, c_2, 1, c_4, 1, c_6]_{gfs}$ be the state transformation matrix of cascades of three 2-stage LFSRs as shown in Figure 2. From Proposition 4 we know that if A^6 is an MDS matrix over F_{2^n}, then $c_2 \neq 1$, $c_4 \neq 1$, $c_6 \neq 1$, $c_2 \neq c_4$, $c_2 \neq c_6$, $c_4 \neq c_6$ and $c_2 + c_4 + c_6 \neq 0$. Since c_2, c_4 and c_6 are pairwise distinct, by searching the parameters c_i's over the set $\{1, \alpha, \alpha^2, \alpha^3, \alpha^{-1}, \alpha+1, \alpha^2+1, \alpha^{-1}+1, \alpha^3+1\}$, we also find some 6×6 MDS matrices over F_{2^n} ($n \geq 8$) which have simple inverses.

By Proposition 1, to judge whether A^6 is an MDS matrix we should calculate the canonical factorization of all the entries of A^6, A^{-6}, and determinants of all the 850 submatrices of A^6. Since there are so many irreducible factors, we only list some examples of the defining polynomial $f(x)$ of F_{2^n} such that A^6 is an MDS matrix. We have verified that A^{-6} is also an MDS matrix in these cases.

Table 2. Example of defining polynomials for $A = [1, c_2, 1, c_4, 1, c_6]_{gfs}$

A_{gfs}	$n = 8$	$8 < n < 16$	$n = 16$	$n > 16$
$[1, \alpha, 1, \alpha^2, 1, \alpha^{-1}]$	84310	12, 5, 0	16,5,3,2,0	all
$[1, \alpha, 1, \alpha^2, 1, \alpha^2 + 1]$	84310	12, 5, 0	16,5,3,2,0	all
$[1, \alpha, 1, \alpha + 1, 1, \alpha^3]$	86540	12, 5, 0	16,5,3,2,0	all for $n > 28$

Here "84310" refers to the polynomial $x^8 + x^4 + x^3 + x + 1$ over F_2. For the first two cases, any irreducible polynomials with degree $n > 16$ can be chosen as the defining polynomial, and for the third case, any irreducible polynomials with degree $n > 28$ can be chosen as the defining polynomial. When $8 < n < 16$, there exist lots of irreducible trinomials $f(x)$ such that A^6 and A^{-6} are MDS matrices.

Remark 2. The parameter α in Table 2 can also be replaced by some linear transformations L over F_{2^n} (or F_2^n equivalently). For example, when

Table 3. Lightweight linear transformation L for $A = [1, L, 1, L^2, 1, L^{-1}]_{gfs}$

Length of the input	Example of L
$n = 8$	$[[2, 3], 3, [4, 7], 5, 6, 7, 8, 1]$
$n = 16$	$[[2, 4], 3, 4, [5, 11], 6, ..., 16, 1]]$
$n = 32$	$[[2, 3], 3, [1, 4], 5, ..., 32, 1]]$
$n = 64$	$[[2, 8], 3, 4, 5, 6, 7, [6, 8], 9, ..., 64, 1]]$

$A = [1, L, 1, L^2, 1, L^{-1}]_{gfs}$ and $n = 8, 16, 32, 64$, there exists many lightweight linear transformations L with only two XOR gates such that A^6 and A^{-6} are MDS matrices. Some of them are listed in the following table.

3.3 Comparison with Known Results

The following table presents a comparison of MDS matrices A_{gfs}^s constructed from LFSRs by us and Wu *et al.* The hardware cost to implement one iteration of LFSRs (A_{gfs}) is listed in the third column. The parameter L refer to the linear transformation $x \to \alpha \cdot x$ or other kind of linear transformations as listed in Table 1 and Table 3. All the MDS matrices constructed by us have simple inverses, and the inverses are usually also MDS matrices, whereas the MDS matrices constructed by Wu *et al.* do not have simple inverses.

Table 4. Comparison of MDS matrices constructed from LFSRs

s	A_{gfs}	Cost (XOR gates)	with simple inverse	Note
	$[L, 1, 1, L]$	$2n + 2\#L$	N	[11]
4	$[1, L, 1, L^2]$	$2n + \#L + \#L^2$	Y	Ours
	$[1, L, 1, L + 1]$	$3n + 2\#L$	Y	Ours
	$[L, 1, 1, L^2, L, L^2]$	$3n + 2\#L + 2\#L^2$	N	[11]
6	$[1, L, 1, L^2, 1, L^{-1}]$	$3n + \#L + \#L^{-1} + \#L^2$	Y	Ours
	$[1, L, 1, L^2, 1, L^2 + 1]$	$4n + \#L + 2\#L^2$	Y	Ours
	$[1, L, 1, L + 1, 1, L^3]$	$4n + 2\#L + \#L^3$	Y	Ours

From the table we can see that if a linear transformation L with only one XOR gate was used, then the matrix $[1, L, 1, L^2]_{gfs}$ constructed by us would cost only one XOR gate more than that of Wu *et al.*'s, whereas the matrix $[1, L, 1, L^2, 1, L^{-1}]_{gfs}$ constructed by us would cost two XOR gates less than that of Wu *et al.*'s. For example, when n is not a multiple of 8, there exists lots of irreducible trinomials of degree n. If the defining polynomial $f(x)$ was chosen as a trinomial satisfying the conditions of Theorem 1, Theorem 2 and Table 2, then the linear transformation $L : x \to \alpha \cdot x$ would cost only one XOR gate. On the other hand, when $n = 8, 16, 32, 64$, there does not exist irreducible trinomials of degree n, the linear transformation $L : x \to \alpha \cdot x$ would cost at least three XOR gates. However, in this case, we can find some linear transformations L with only two gates as shown in Table 1 and Table 3. Then the matrix $[1, L, 1, L^2]_{gfs}$ constructed by us would cost only two XOR gates more than that of Wu *et al.*'s, whereas the matrix $[1, L, 1, L^2, 1, L^{-1}]_{gfs}$ constructed by us would cost four XOR gates less than that of Wu *et al.*'s.

4 Conclusions

Maximum distance separable (MDS) matrices are widely used in the diffusion layers of block ciphers and hash functions. Inspired by Wu *et al.*'s recursive construction of MDS matrices from LFSRs, we further present some compact MDS matrices which have simple inverses. Compared with known constructions, the MDS matrices constructed by us have simple inverses which can be implemented with the same computational complexity, and the inverses are usually also MDS matrices. This property can provide much flexibility in the design of perfect diffusion layers.

References

1. Shannon, C.E.: Communication Theory of Secrecy Systems. Bell Syst. Technical J. 28, 656–715 (1949)
2. Sajadieh, M., Dakhilalian, M., Mala, H., Sepehrdad, P.: Recursive Diffusion Layers for Block Ciphers and Hash Functions. In: Canteaut, A. (ed.) FSE 2012. LNCS, vol. 7549, pp. 385–401. Springer, Heidelberg (2012)
3. Biham, E., Shamir, A.: Differential Cryptanalysis of DES-like Cryptosystems. Journal of Cryptology 4(1), 3–72 (1991)
4. Matsui, M.: Linear Cryptanalysis Method for DES Cipher. In: Helleseth, T. (ed.) EUROCRYPT 1993. LNCS, vol. 765, pp. 386–397. Springer, Heidelberg (1994)
5. Schnorr, C.-P., Vaudenay, S.: Black Box Cryptanalysis of Hash Networks Based on Multipermutations. In: De Santis, A. (ed.) EUROCRYPT 1994. LNCS, vol. 950, pp. 47–57. Springer, Heidelberg (1995)
6. Vaudenay, S.: On the Need for Multipermutations: Cryptanalysis of MD4 and SAFER. In: Preneel, B. (ed.) FSE 1994. LNCS, vol. 1008, pp. 286–297. Springer, Heidelberg (1995)
7. Daemen, J.: Cipher and Hash Function Design Strategies Based on Linear and Differential Cryptanalysis. PhD thesis, Elektrotechniek Katholieke Universiteit Leuven, Belgium (1995)
8. Daemen, J., Rijmen, V.: The Design of Rijndael: AES - The Advanced Encryption Standard. Springer (2002)
9. Guo, J., Peyrin, T., Poschmann, A.: The PHOTON Family of Lightweight Hash Functions. In: Rogaway, P. (ed.) CRYPTO 2011. LNCS, vol. 6841, pp. 222–239. Springer, Heidelberg (2011)
10. Guo, J., Peyrin, T., Poschmann, A., Robshaw, M.: The LED Block Cipher. In: Preneel, B., Takagi, T. (eds.) CHES 2011. LNCS, vol. 6917, pp. 326–341. Springer, Heidelberg (2011)
11. Wu, S., Wang, M., Wu, W.: Recursive diffusion layers for (Lightweight) block ciphers and hash functions. In: Knudsen, L.R., Wu, H. (eds.) SAC 2012. LNCS, vol. 7707, pp. 355–371. Springer, Heidelberg (2013)
12. MacWilliams, F.J., Sloane, N.J.A.: The Theory of Error-Correcting Codes. North-Holland Publishing Company (1978)
13. Chand Gupta, K., Ghosh Ray, I.: On Constructions of Involutory MDS Matrices. In: Youssef, A., Nitaj, A., Hassanien, A.E. (eds.) AFRICACRYPT 2013. LNCS, vol. 7918, pp. 43–60. Springer, Heidelberg (2013)
14. Roth, R.M., Lempel, A.: On MDS codes via Cauchy matrices. IEEE Trans. Inform. Theory 35(6), 1314–1319 (1989)
15. Lacan, J., Fimes, J.: Systematic MDS erasure codes based on vandermonde matrices. IEEE Trans. Commun. Lett. 8(9), 570–572 (2004)
16. Gupta, K.C., Ray, I.G.: On Constructions of MDS Matrices from Companion Matrices for Lightweight Cryptography. In: Cuzzocrea, A., Kittl, C., Simos, D.E., Weippl, E., Xu, L. (eds.) CD-ARES Workshops 2013. LNCS, vol. 8128, pp. 29–43. Springer, Heidelberg (2013)

Appendix

Proof (Proof of Theorem 2). We first show the result holds for $A = [1, \alpha, 1, \alpha + 1]_{gfs}$. In this case, we have

$$
A^4 = \begin{pmatrix}
1 & 1 & \alpha(\alpha+1) & \alpha(\alpha+1)^2 \\
\alpha(\alpha+1)^2 & (\alpha^2+\alpha+1)^2 & 1 & (\alpha+1)^2 \\
\alpha(\alpha+1) & \alpha^2(\alpha+1) & 1 & 1 \\
1 & \alpha^2 & \alpha^2(\alpha+1) & (\alpha^2+\alpha+1)^2
\end{pmatrix},
$$

and

$$
A^{-4} = \begin{pmatrix}
(\alpha+1)^4 & 1 & \alpha^2+\alpha+1 & \alpha^3 \\
\alpha^3 & 1 & 1 & \alpha^2 \\
\alpha^2+\alpha+1 & (\alpha+1)^3 & \alpha^4 & 1 \\
1 & (\alpha+1)^2 & (\alpha+1)^3 & 1
\end{pmatrix},
$$

where exactly all irreducible polynomials of degree less than 3 appear in entries of A^4 and A^{-4}. On the other hand, by calculation we find that exactly the following seven new irreducible polynomials $\alpha^3 + \alpha + 1$, $\alpha^3 + \alpha^2 + 1$, $\alpha^4 + \alpha + 1$, $\alpha^4 + \alpha^3 + 1$, $\alpha^4 + \alpha^3 + \alpha^2 + \alpha + 1$, $\alpha^5 + \alpha^3 + 1$, $\alpha^5 + \alpha^4 + \alpha^3 + \alpha^2 + 1$ appear in the determinants of 2×2 submatrices of A^4 and A^{-4} simultaneously. Thus from Proposition 2 we can deduce that A^4 and A^{-4} will be MDS matrices or non MDS matrices simultaneously, and they will be MDS matrices if and only if all the following ten irreducible polynomials respect to α are nonzero, that is,

$$
\begin{aligned}
\alpha &\neq 0, \\
\alpha + 1 &\neq 0, \\
\alpha^2 + \alpha + 1 &\neq 0, \\
\alpha^3 + \alpha + 1 &\neq 0, \\
\alpha^3 + \alpha^2 + 1 &\neq 0, \\
\alpha^4 + \alpha + 1 &\neq 0, \\
\alpha^4 + \alpha^3 + 1 &\neq 0, \\
\alpha^4 + \alpha^3 + \alpha^2 + \alpha + 1 &\neq 0, \\
\alpha^5 + \alpha^3 + 1 &\neq 0. \\
\alpha^5 + \alpha^4 + \alpha^3 + \alpha^2 + 1 &\neq 0,
\end{aligned}
\tag{2}
$$

Hence we can deduce that A^4 and A^{-4} will be MDS matrices if and only if $\deg f(x) \geq 5$ and $f(x) \neq x^5 + x^3 + 1$, $x^5 + x^4 + x^3 + x^2 + 1$. So the result holds for $A = [1, \alpha, 1, \alpha + 1]_{gfs}$.

Similarly we can show the result also holds for $A = [1, \alpha + 1, 1, \alpha]_{gfs}$.

On Constructions of Circulant MDS Matrices for Lightweight Cryptography

Kishan Chand Gupta and Indranil Ghosh Ray

Applied Statistics Unit, Indian Statistical Institute
203, B.T. Road, Kolkata 700108, India
{kishan,indranil_r}@isical.ac.in

Abstract. Maximum distance separable (MDS) matrices have applications not only in coding theory but are also of great importance in the design of block ciphers and hash functions. It is highly nontrivial to find MDS matrices which could be used in lightweight cryptography. In this paper we study and construct efficient $d \times d$ circulant MDS matrices for d up to 8 and consider their inverses, which are essential for SPN networks. We explore some interesting and useful properties of circulant matrices which are prevalent in many parts of mathematics and computer science. We prove that circulant MDS matrix can not be involutory. We also prove that $2^d \times 2^d$ circulant matrix can not be both orthogonal and MDS.

Keywords: Diffusion, InvMixColumn operation, Involutory matrix, MDS matrix, MixColumn operation, Orthogonal matrix.

1 Introduction

Claude Shannon, in his paper "Communication Theory of Secrecy Systems" [27], defined *confusion* and *diffusion* as two properties, required in the design of block ciphers. Nearly all the ciphers [1, 6, 7, 13, 21, 24, 25, 29, 31] use predefined MDS matrices for incorporating the diffusion property. Hash functions like Maelstrom [8], Grøstl [9] and PHOTON family of light weight hash functions [10] use MDS matrices as main part of their diffusion layers. In this context we would like to mention that in papers [10–12, 14, 17, 22, 23, 32, 34], different constructions of MDS matrices are provided. In Whirlpool hash function [3], the diffusion layer of underlying block cipher uses 8×8 circulant matrix.

In [33], authors proposed a special class of *substitution permutation networks (SPNs)* that uses same network for both the encryption and decryption operations. The idea was to use *involutory* MDS matrix for incorporating diffusion. It may be noted that for ciphers like FOX [15] and WIDEA-n [16] that follow the Lai-Massey scheme, there is no need of involutory matrices. In SPN networks, two modules are used for encryption and decryption. In SAC 2004 [14] paper, authors constructed efficient MDS matrices for encryption but the inverse of such matrices were not guaranteed to be efficient, which they left for the future work.

X. Huang and J. Zhou (Eds.): ISPEC 2014, LNCS 8434, pp. 564–576, 2014.

Our Contribution: In the AES MixColumn operation, the MDS matrix is a *circulant matrix* having elements of low hamming weights, but no general construction and study of $d \times d$ *circulant MDS matrices* for arbitrary d is available in the literature. We prove that *circulant MDS matrices* can not be involutory. We also prove that $2^d \times 2^d$ *circulant MDS matrices* are not orthogonal. We study some interesting properties of circulant matrices which are useful for efficient implementations of their inverses whenever the dimension is even. We also construct efficient $d \times d$ *circulant MDS matrices* over $\mathbb{F}_{2^n}$ for d up to 8 which are suitable for SPN networks and hash functions.

In Section 2 we provide definitions and preliminaries. In Section 3, we study some interesting and relevant properties of circulant matrices. In Section 4 we propose new efficient $d \times d$ *circulant MDS matrices* for $d = 3, 4, 5, 6, 7$ and 8.

2   Definition and Preliminaries

Let $\mathbb{F}_2 = \{0, 1\}$ be the finite field of two elements and $\mathbb{F}_{2^n}$ be the finite field of 2^n elements. Elements of $\mathbb{F}_{2^n}$ can be represented as polynomials of degree less than n over $\mathbb{F}_2$. For example, let $\beta \in \mathbb{F}_{2^n}$, then β can be represented as $\sum_{i=0}^{n-1} b_i \alpha^i$, where $b_i \in \mathbb{F}_2$ and α is the root of generating polynomial of $\mathbb{F}_{2^n}$. Another compact representation uses hexadecimal digits. Here the hexadecimal digits are used to express the coefficients of corresponding polynomial representation. For example $\alpha^7 + \alpha^4 + \alpha^2 + 1 = 1.\alpha^7 + 0.\alpha^6 + 0.\alpha^5 + 1.\alpha^4 + 0.\alpha^3 + 1.\alpha^2 + 0.\alpha + 1 = (10010101)_2 = 95_x \in \mathbb{F}_{2^8}$.

An MDS matrix provides diffusion properties that have useful applications in cryptography. The idea comes from coding theory, in particular from maximum distance separable code (MDS). In this context we state one important theorem from coding theory.

Theorem 1. *[19, page 33] If C is an $[n, k, d]$ code, then $n - k \geq d - 1$.*

Codes with $n - k = d - 1$ are called maximum distance separable code, or MDS code for short.

The following fact is another way to characterize an MDS matrix.

Fact 1. *A square matrix A is an MDS matrix if and only if every square submatrices of A are nonsingular.*

Fact 2. *If A is an MDS matrix over $\mathbb{F}_{2^n}$, then A', obtained by multiplying a row (or column) of A by any $c \in \mathbb{F}_{2^n}^*$ or by permutations of rows (or columns) is MDS. Also if A is MDS, so is A^T. Also if A is an MDS matrix over $\mathbb{F}_{2^n}$, then $c.A$ is MDS for any $c \in \mathbb{F}_{2^n}^*$.*

Recall that many modern block ciphers use MDS matrices as a vital constituent to incorporate diffusion property. In general two different modules are needed for encryption and decryption operations. In [33], authors proposed a special class of SPNs that uses same network for both the encryption and decryption operation. The idea was to use involutory MDS matrices for incorporating diffusion. In this paper we will prove that a circulant matrix can not be both involutory and MDS.

Definition 1. *[20, page 290] The $d \times d$ matrix of the form*

$$\begin{pmatrix} a_0 & a_1 & a_2 & \cdots & a_{d-1} \\ a_{d-1} & a_0 & a_1 & \cdots & a_{d-2} \\ \vdots & \vdots & \vdots & \vdots & \vdots \\ \vdots & \vdots & \vdots & \vdots & \vdots \\ a_1 & a_2 & a_3 & \cdots & a_0 \end{pmatrix}$$

is called a circulant matrix and will be denoted by $Circ(a_0, \ldots, a_{d-1})$.

Circulant matrix can also be written as a polynomial in some suitable permutation matrix. So we have the following fact.

Fact 3. *[20, page 290] A $d \times d$ circulant matrix $A = Circ(a_0, \ldots, a_{d-1})$ can be written in the form $A = a_0 I + a_1 P + a_2 P^2 + \ldots + a_{d-1} P^{d-1}$, where $P = Circ(0, 1, 0, \ldots, 0)$.*

Definition 2. *A square matrix A is called involutory matrix if it satisfies the condition $A^2 = I$, i.e. $A = A^{-1}$.*

For lightweight cryptographic application, it is desirable to have matrices whose elements are of low hamming weight with as many zeros as possible in the higher order bits. If such a matrix is orthogonal, then encryption and decryption can be implemented with almost same circuitry with same computational cost. We will prove that a $2^d \times 2^d$ circulant matrix can not be both orthogonal and MDS.

Definition 3. *A square matrix A is called orthogonal matrix if $AA^T = I$.*

For efficient implementation of perfect diffusion layer, it is desirable to have maximum number of 1's and minimum number of different entries in the MDS matrix. In [14], authors studied these two properties and proposed some bounds. Here we restate their definitions and few results, which we will use in our constructions.

Definition 4. *[14] Let $M = ((m_{i,j}))$ be a $q \times p$ MDS matrix over $\mathbb{F}_{2^n}$.*

- *Let $v_1(M)$ denotes the number of (i, j) pairs such that $m_{i,j}$ is equal to one. We call it the number of occurrences of one. Also let $v_1^{p,q}$ be the maximal value of $v_1(M)$.*
- *Let $c(M)$ be the cardinality of $\{m_{i,j} | i = 1, \ldots, q; j = 1, \ldots, p\}$. This is called the number of entries. Also let $c^{p,q}$ be the minimal value of $c(M)$.*
- *If $v_1(M) > 0$, then $c_1(M) = c(M) - 1$. Otherwise $c_1(M) = c(M)$. This is called the number of nontrivial entries.*

Fact 4. *[14] $v_1^{4,4} = 9$, $v_1^{5,5} = 12$, $v_1^{6,6} = 16$, $v_1^{7,7} = 21$, $v_1^{8,8} = 24$.*

Remark 1. High value of v_1 and low value of c and c_1 with low hamming weight elements are desirable for constructing efficient MDS matrices.

3   Some Useful Results on Circulant Matrices

In this section we study some important properties of circulant matrices. Recall that to design diffusion layers for lightweight application, efficient *involutory MDS matrices* are desirable as the same circuitry can be used for both encryption and decryption. Efficient orthogonal MDS matrices are also of similar interest as almost same circuitry can be used for both encryption and decryption. But we will see in this section that *circulant MDS matrices* can not be involutory or orthogonal. Also inverse of an efficient *circulant MDS matrix* may not be efficient. In [14], authors designed efficient MDS matrices but the inverse was not guaranteed to be efficient. In this context we study some interesting properties of circulant matrices which are useful for efficient implementation of inverse of efficient *circulant MDS matrices*.

MDS matrices of dimension $2^d \times 2^d$ are of special cryptographic interest. Note that in AES [7], a 4×4 MDS matrix is used. In MDS-AES [13], the proposed matrix is of dimension 16×16. In Lemma 1 and Corollary 1 we study two important properties of $2^d \times 2^d$ circulant matrices and using these results we show in Lemma 2 that $2^d \times 2^d$ circulant orthogonal matrices can not be MDS.

Lemma 1. $Circ(a_0, a_1, \ldots, a_{2^d-1})^{2^d} = (\sum_{i=0}^{2^d-1} a_i^{2^d})I$, where $a_0, \ldots, a_{2^d-1} \in \mathbb{F}_{2^n}$.

Proof. From Fact 3, $Circ(a_0, a_1, \ldots, a_{2^d-1}) = a_0 I + a_1 P + \ldots + a_{2^d-1} P^{2^d-1}$, where $2^d \times 2^d$ matrix $P = Circ(0, 1, 0, \ldots, 0)$. So, $Circ(a_0, a_1, \ldots, a_{2^d-1})^{2^d}$ $= (a_0 I + a_1 P + a_2 P^2 + \ldots + a_{2^d-1} P^{2^d-1})^{2^d} = a_0^{2^d} I^{2^d} + a_1^{2^d} P^{2^d} + a_2^{2^d} (P^{2^d})^2 + \ldots + a_{2^d-1}^{2^d} (P^{2^d})^{2^d-1} = (a_0^{2^d} + a_1^{2^d} + a_2^{2^d} + \ldots + a_{2^d-1}^{2^d})I.$ ☐

Remark 2. If $\sum_{i=0}^{2^d-1} a_i = 1$, then $Circ(a_0, a_1, \ldots, a_{2^d-1})^{2^d} = I.$

Corollary 1. $det(Circ(a_0, a_1, \ldots, a_{2^d-1})) = \sum_{i=0}^{2^d-1} a_i^{2^d}$, where $a_0, \ldots, a_{2^d-1} \in \mathbb{F}_{2^n}$.

Proof. Let $A = Circ(a_0, \ldots, a_{2^d-1})$ and $det(A) = \triangle$. So, $\triangle^{2^d} = (det(A))^{2^d}$ $= det(A^{2^d})$. From Lemma 1, $A^{2^d} = (\sum_{i=0}^{2^d-1} a_i^{2^d})I$. So, $\triangle^{2^d} = det((\sum_{i=0}^{2^d-1} a_i^{2^d})I) = (\sum_{i=0}^{2^d-1} a_i^{2^d})^{2^d}$. Therefore, $\triangle = \sum_{i=0}^{2^d-1} a_i^{2^d}$. ☐

Lemma 2. *Any $2^d \times 2^d$ circulant orthogonal matrix over $\mathbb{F}_{2^n}$ is non MDS.*

Proof. Let $A = Circ(a_0, a_1, \ldots, a_{2^d-1})$ be an orthogonal matrix, where $a_0, \ldots, a_{2^d-1} \in \mathbb{F}_{2^n}$. Let the row vectors of A are $R_0, R_1, \ldots, R_{2^d-1}$, where $R_0 = (a_0, a_1, \ldots, a_{2^d-1})$ and R_i can be obtained by rotating R_{i-1} one element to the right. Since A is orthogonal, $R_i.R_j = 0$ whenever $i \neq j$. Let us consider the cases $R_0.R_j = 0$ for $j = \{2k+1 : k = 0, \ldots, 2^{d-2}-1\}$, which give following 2^{d-2} equations:

$$\sum_{i=0}^{2^d-1} a_i a_{i+1} = 0, \sum_{i=0}^{2^d-1} a_i a_{i+3} = 0, \sum_{i=0}^{2^d-1} a_i a_{i+5} = 0, \ldots, \sum_{i=0}^{2^d-1} a_i a_{i+2^{d-1}-1} = 0,$$

where suffixes are computed modulo 2^d. Adding these equations, we get $\sum_{i,j} a_{2i} a_{2j+1} = (a_0 + a_2 + a_4 + \ldots + a_{2^d-2})(a_1 + a_3 + a_5 + \ldots + a_{2^d-1}) = 0$.

Note that A has a $(2^{d-1} \times 2^{d-1})$ submatrix $Circ(a_0, a_2, a_4, \ldots, a_{2^d-2})$ which is formed by 0th, 2nd, 4th, $\ldots$, $(2^d - 2)$th rows and 0th, 2nd, 4th, $\ldots$, $(2^d - 2)$th columns. From Corollary 1, $det(Circ(a_0, a_2, a_4, \ldots, a_{2^d-2}))$
$= a_0^{2^{d-1}} + a_2^{2^{d-1}} + a_4^{2^{d-1}} + \ldots + a_{2^d-2}^{2^{d-1}} = (a_0 + a_2 + a_4 + \ldots + a_{2^d-2})^{2^{d-1}}$.

Similarly it can be observed that A has $(2^{d-1} \times 2^{d-1})$ submatrix $Circ(a_1, a_3, a_5, \ldots, a_{2^d-1})$ which is formed by 0th, 2nd, 4th, $\ldots$, $(2^d - 2)$th rows and 1st, 3rd, 5th, $\ldots$, $(2^d - 1)$th columns and $det(Circ(a_1, a_3, a_5, \ldots,$
$a_{2^d-1})) = a_1^{2^{d-1}} + a_3^{2^{d-1}} + a_5^{2^{d-1}} + \ldots + a_{2^d-1}^{2^{d-1}} = (a_1 + a_3 + a_5 + \ldots + a_{2^d-1})^{2^{d-1}}$.

Now, $\sum_{i,j} a_{2i} a_{2j+1} = (a_0 + a_2 + a_4 + \ldots + a_{2^d-2})(a_1 + a_3 + a_5 + \ldots + a_{2^d-1}) = 0$, which implies that at least one of these submatrices is singular. So A is non MDS. □

Remark 3. Although $2^d \times 2^d$ *circulant MDS matrices are not orthogonal, but circulant MDS matrices* of other dimensions may be orthogonal. For example, let the irreducible polynomial $x^8 + x^4 + x^3 + x + 1$ be the constructing polynomial of $\mathbb{F}_{2^8}$, then the 3×3 matrix $Circ(\alpha, 1 + \alpha^2 + \alpha^3 + \alpha^4 + \alpha^6, \alpha + \alpha^2 + \alpha^3 + \alpha^4 + \alpha^6)$ and the 6×6 matrix $Circ(1, 1, \alpha, 1 + \alpha^2 + \alpha^3 + \alpha^5 + \alpha^6 + \alpha^7, \alpha + \alpha^5, \alpha^2 + \alpha^3 + \alpha^6 + \alpha^7)$ are orthogonal.

We next examine the possibility of constructing involutory MDS matrix from circulant matrices. Towards this we show that such *involutory circulant matrices* are non MDS in Lemma 5, but before that we study two useful properties in Lemma 3 and Lemma 4. When diffusion layer in SPN network is implemented using a $2d \times 2d$ *circulant MDS matrix*, Lemma 3 may be used for efficient implementation of its inverse (see Remark 4 and Remark 9).

Lemma 3. *Let* $(2d) \times (2d)$ *circulant matrix* $A = Circ(a_0, a_1, \ldots, a_{2d-1})$, *where* $a_0, \ldots, a_{2d-1} \in \mathbb{F}_{2^n}$. *Then* $A^2 = Circ(a_0^2 + a_d^2, 0, a_1^2 + a_{d+1}^2, 0, \ldots,$
$a_{d-1}^2 + a_{2d-1}^2, 0)$.

Proof. From Fact 3, $A = a_0 I + a_1 P + a_2 P^2 + \ldots + a_{2d-1} P^{2d-1}$, where $(2d) \times (2d)$ matrix $P = Circ(0, 1, 0, \ldots, 0)$. So $A^2 = a_0^2 I + a_1^2 P^2 + a_2^2 P^4 + \ldots + a_{2d-1}^2 P^{2(2d-1)} = (a_0^2 I + a_d^2 P^{2d}) + (a_1^2 P^2 + a_{d+1}^2 P^{2d+2}) + \ldots + (a_{d-1}^2 P^{2(d-1)} + a_{2d-1}^2 P^{2(2d-1)}) = (a_0^2 + a_d^2)I + (a_1^2 + a_{d+1}^2)P^2 + \ldots + (a_{d-1}^2 + a_{2d-1}^2)P^{(2d-2)} = Circ(a_0^2 + a_d^2, 0, a_1^2 + a_{d+1}^2, 0, \ldots, a_{d-1}^2 + a_{2d-1}^2, 0)$. □

Remark 4. For any $A = Circ(a_0, \ldots, a_{2^d-1})$ with $\sum_{i=0}^{2^d-1} a_i = 1$, from Remark 2, $A^{2^d} = I$. So $A^{-1} = A^{2^d-1} = \prod_{k=0}^{d-1} A^{2^k}$. Also note that matrices of the form A^{2^k} for $k > 0$ are efficient as most of the elements are zero. So the InvMixColumn operation can be implemented as a simple preprocessing step of multiplication by $A^2 \times A^4 \times \ldots \times A^{2^{d-1}}$ followed by the MixColumn step. For example, when $d = 2$, $A^{-1} = A \times A^2$.

Remark 5. In AES [7], the MDS matrix used in MixColumn operation is $M = Circ(\alpha, 1 + \alpha, 1, 1)$, where α is the root of $x^8 + x^4 + x^3 + x + 1$. P. Barreto observed that in the *InvMixColumn* operation [7] of decryption, instead of M^{-1}, $M \times M^{-2} = Circ(\alpha, 1 + \alpha, 1, 1) \times Circ(1 + \alpha^2, 0, \alpha^2, 0)$ can be used for more efficient implementation. This is a consequence of Lemma 1, Remark 2 and Remark 4.

Remark 6. In lightweight applications, major constraints are on processors and memory. If constraints on processor is more than that on memory, some prepro-cessing step as mentioned in Remark 4 may not be affordable. For such situations, at the cost of some additional memory, table lookup may be incorporated. The total number of operations and temporary variables may be reduced at the cost of such supplementary multiplication tables. But in a memory constraint system where scarcity of memory prevails over processor, if a little drop of performance due to this preprocessing step as mentioned in Remark 4 is acceptable, then no additional memory for multiplication table will be needed.

Lemma 4. *Let* $(2d+1) \times (2d+1)$ *circulant matrix* $A = Circ(a_0, \ldots, a_{2d})$, *where* $a_0, \ldots, a_{2d} \in \mathbb{F}_{2^n}$. *Then* $A^2 = Circ(a_0^2, a_{d+1}^2, a_1^2, a_{d+2}^2, \ldots, a_{d-1}^2, a_{2d}^2, a_d^2)$.

Proof. From Fact 3, $A = a_0 I + a_1 P + a_2 P^2 + \ldots + a_{2d} P^{2d}$, where $(2d+1) \times (2d+1)$ matrix $P = Circ(0, 1, 0, \ldots, 0)$. So $A^2 = a_0^2 I + a_1^2 P^2 + a_2^2 P^4 + \ldots + a_{2d}^2 P^{2(2d)} = a_0^2 I + a_{d+1}^2 P^{(2d+1+1)} + a_1^2 P^2 + a_{d+2}^2 P^{(2d+1+3)} + a_2^2 P^4 + \ldots + a_{d-1}^2 P^{2d-2} + a_{2d}^2 P^{(2d+1+2d-1)} + a_d^2 P^{2d} = a_0^2 I + a_{d+1}^2 P + a_1^2 P^2 + a_{d+2}^2 P^3 + \ldots + a_{d-1}^2 P^{(2d-2)} + a_{2d}^2 P^{(2d-1)} + a_d^2 P^{2d} = Circ(a_0^2, a_{d+1}^2, a_1^2, a_{d+2}^2, \ldots, a_{d-1}^2, a_{2d}^2, a_d^2)$. ∎

Lemma 5. *Circulant involutory matrices are non MDS.*

Proof. Let $A = Circ(a_0, a_1, \ldots, a_{2d-1})$ be a $(2d) \times (2d)$ involutory circu-lant matrix. Then $A^2 = I$. But from Lemma 3, $A^2 = Circ(a_0^2 + a_d^2, 0, a_1^2 + a_{d+1}^2, 0, \ldots, a_{d-1}^2 + a_{2d-1}^2, 0)$. So clearly $a_1^2 + a_{d+1}^2 = 0$. But A has a 2×2 subma-trix $Circ(a_1, a_{d+1})$ which can be obtained from 0th and dth rows and 1st and $(d+1)$th columns of A, and $det(Circ(a_1, a_{d+1})) = a_1^2 + a_{d+1}^2 = 0$. So A is not MDS.

Again for $(2d+1) \times (2d+1)$ involutory circulant matrix $A = Circ(a_0, \ldots, a_{2d})$, from Lemma 4, $A^2 = Circ(a_0^2, a_{d+1}^2, a_1^2, a_{d+2}^2, \ldots, a_{2d}^2, a_d^2)$. But since A is involutory, $A^2 = I$. So clearly $a_i = 0$ for all $i \in \{1, \ldots, 2d\}$. So A is not MDS. ∎

4   Efficient Circulant MDS Matrices

In this section we construct efficient *circulant MDS matrices* over finite field. By efficient MDS matrix we mean an MDS matrix with maximum number of 1's and minimum number of distinct elements with low hamming weights (see

Remark 1). MDS matrices with elements having low hamming weights are desirable for efficient implementations. It may be observed that in most of the cases, the inverse of an efficient *circulant MDS matrix* is not efficient. For lightweight application, $d \times d$ *circulant MDS matrices*, for d even, may be designed in such a way so that the inverse may also be implemented efficiently by using Lemma 3.

4.1 Efficient 4×4 Circulant MDS Matrices

In this subsection, we construct efficient 4×4 *circulant MDS matrices* $Circ(a_0, a_1, a_2, a_3)$ where $a_i \in \mathbb{F}_{2^n}$ for $i = \{0, 1, 2, 3\}$. Our target is to construct MDS matrices with high v_1 and low c_1 (see Remark 1). For efficient implementation, we aim to restrict a_i's to the form
$c_0 + c_1\alpha + c_2\alpha^{-1} + c_3\alpha^2 + c_4\alpha^{-2}$ where $c_i \in \{0, 1\}$.

Proposition 1. $A = Circ(\alpha, 1 + \alpha, 1, 1)$ *is MDS matrix for any* $\alpha \in \mathbb{F}_{2^n}$ *such that minimal polynomial of* α *is of degree* ≥ 4.

Proof. From Corollary 1, $det(A) = \alpha^4 + (\alpha+1)^4 + 1 + 1 = 1$. It can be checked that determinants of all 3×3 submatrices are $1 + \alpha^2 + \alpha^3, 1 + \alpha^3, \alpha + \alpha^2 + \alpha^3$ and $1 + \alpha + \alpha^3$. Also determinants of all 2×2 submatrices are $1, \alpha, 1 + \alpha, \alpha^2, 1 + \alpha^2, \alpha + \alpha^2$ and $1 + \alpha + \alpha^2$. Since the minimal polynomial of α is of degree ≥ 4, none of these determinants are zero. So A is MDS matrix.   □

Remark 7. Note that $v_1(Circ(\alpha, 1 + \alpha, 1, 1)) = 8 < v_1^{4,4}$ (See Fact 4). It is easy to check that in a 4×4 circulant matrix $Circ(a_0, a_1, a_2, a_3)$, if 1 is substituted in any three positions, then the matrix will be non MDS. So for 4×4 *circulant MDS matrices*, highest value of v_1 is 8.

Remark 8. When the underlying field is $\mathbb{F}_{2^8}$ with generating polynomial $x^8 + x^4 + x^3 + x + 1$ and α is the root of the generating polynomial, then the Proposition 1 gives the MDS matrix used in AES.

When minimal polynomial of α is the generating polynomial of underlying field, multiplication by A can be implemented using 15 XORs, 4 *xtime* (or 4 table lookups) and 3 temporary variables [7]. The multiplication by A^{-1} can be done by a small preprocessing followed by the multiplication by A (see Remark 4). If small drop of performance due to this preprocessing step is acceptable then no additional memory for multiplication table will be needed (see Remark 6). The preprocessing step can be implemented as follows using 6 XORs, 4 *xtimes* (or table lookups) and 2 temporary variables [7].

In Table 1, we provide an exhaustive list of efficient 4×4 *circulant MDS matrices* of the form $Circ(a_0, a_1, a_2, a_3)$ over $\mathbb{F}_{2^8}$ with generating polynomial $x^8 + x^4 + x^3 + x + 1$, up to the ordering of the elements of (a_0, a_1, a_2, a_3), where a_i's are restricted in $\{01_x, 02_x, \ldots, 07_x\}$ and $a_0 + a_1 + a_2 + a_3 = 1$ (so that the inverses can be implemented efficiently, see Remark 4).

Table 1. 4×4 *circulant MDS matrices over* $\mathbb{F}_{2^8}$ *with generating polynomial* $x^8 + x^4 + x^3 + x + 1$ *where elements of these matrices are polynomials in* α *of degree at most 2 and* α *is the root of the generating polynomial*

MDS Matrix A	Inverse Matrix $A^{-1} = A \times A^2$
$Circ(02_x, 03_x, 01_x, 01_x)$	$Circ(0E_x, 0B_x, 0D_x, 09_x) = Circ(02_x, 03_x, 01_x, 01_x) \times Circ(05_x, 00_x, 04_x, 00_x)$
$Circ(01_x, 04_x, 02_x, 06_x)$	$Circ(0D_x, 0C_x, 0E_x, 0E_x) = Circ(01_x, 04_x, 02_x, 06_x) \times Circ(05_x, 00_x, 04_x, 00_x)$
$Circ(01_x, 04_x, 03_x, 07_x)$	$Circ(0B_x, 0B_x, 09_x, 08_x) = Circ(01_x, 04_x, 03_x, 07_x) \times Circ(04_x, 00_x, 05_x, 00_x)$
$Circ(01_x, 05_x, 03_x, 06_x)$	$Circ(0B_x, 0A_x, 09_x, 09_x) = Circ(01_x, 05_x, 03_x, 06_x) \times Circ(04_x, 00_x, 05_x, 00_x)$

All matrices in Table 1 except $Circ(02_x, 03_x, 01_x, 01_x)$ have four 1's (i.e $v_1(A) = 4$) which could be maximized to eight (see Remark 7) with the proper choices of other elements. In Table 2, we provide some 4×4 *circulant MDS matrices* $A = Circ(a_0, a_1, a_2, a_3)$ with $v_1(A) = 8$ and generating polynomial $x^8 + x^4 + x^3 + x + 1$ (up to the ordering of the elements (a_0, a_1, a_2, a_3)), where $a_0 + a_1 + a_2 + a_3 = 1$. We restrict a_i's to the form $c_0 + c_1\alpha + c_2\alpha^{-1} + c_3\alpha^2 + c_4\alpha^{-2}$ where $c_i \in \{0, 1\}$.

Table 2. 4×4 *circulant MDS matrices over* $\mathbb{F}_{2^8}$ *with generating polynomial* $x^8 + x^4 + x^3 + x + 1$ *where elements of these matrices are of the form* $c_0 + c_1\alpha + c_2\alpha^{-1} + c_3\alpha^2 + c_4\alpha^{-2}$, $c_i \in \{0, 1\}$

MDS Matrix A	Inverse Matrix $A^{-1} = A \times A^2$
$Circ\left(\alpha + \alpha^{-1}, 1 + \alpha + \alpha^{-1}, 1, 1\right)$	$Circ\left(\alpha + \alpha^2 + \alpha^3 + \alpha^5 + \alpha^7, \alpha^2 + \alpha^5 + \alpha^6, \alpha + \alpha^5,\right.$ $\left. 1 + \alpha^3 + \alpha^5 + \alpha^6 + \alpha^7\right) = Circ\left(\alpha + \alpha^{-1}, 1 + \alpha + \alpha^{-1}, 1, 1\right)$ $\times Circ\left(1 + \alpha^2 + \alpha^{-2}, 0, \alpha^2 + \alpha^{-2}, 0\right)$
$Circ\left(1, 1, \alpha^2 + \alpha^{-2}, 1 + \alpha^2 + \alpha^{-2}\right)$	$Circ\left(\alpha^3 + \alpha^5 + \alpha^6, \alpha^3 + \alpha^4 + \alpha^5,\right.$ $\left. \alpha + \alpha^5 + \alpha^7, 1 + \alpha + \alpha^2 + \alpha^4 + \alpha^6 + \alpha^7\right) = Circ\left(1, 1, \alpha^2 + \alpha^{-2},\right.$ $\left. 1 + \alpha^2 + \alpha^{-2}\right) \times Circ\left(1 + \alpha^4 + \alpha^{-4}, 0, \alpha^4 + \alpha^{-4}\right)$
$Circ\left(1, 1, \alpha + \alpha^{-1} + \alpha^2 + \alpha^{-2},\right.$ $\left. 1 + \alpha + \alpha^{-1} + \alpha^2 + \alpha^{-2}\right)$	$Circ\left(1 + \alpha^2, \alpha + \alpha^3 + \alpha^4 + \alpha^5 + \alpha^7,\right.$ $\left. \alpha + \alpha^6, \alpha^2 + \alpha^3 + \alpha^4 + \alpha^5 + \alpha^6 + \alpha^7\right)$ $= Circ\left(1, 1, \alpha + \alpha^{-1} + \alpha^2 + \alpha^{-2}, 1 + \alpha + \alpha^{-1} + \alpha^2 + \alpha^{-2}\right) \times$ $Circ\left(1 + \alpha^2 + \alpha^{-2} + \alpha^4 + \alpha^{-4}, 0, \alpha^2 + \alpha^{-2} + \alpha^4 + \alpha^{-4}, 0\right)$

4.2 Efficient 8×8 Circulant MDS Matrices

Similar to the Subsection 4.1, we propose some efficient 8×8 *circulant MDS matrices* $Circ(a_0, a_1, a_2, a_3, a_4, a_5, a_6, a_7)$ where $a_i = c_0 + c_1\alpha + c_2\alpha^{-1} + c_3\alpha^2 + c_4\alpha^{-2}$, $c_i \in \{0, 1\}$ and $\sum_{i=0}^{7} a_i = 1$. It may be checked that if 1 is substituted in any of the four places, then $Circ(a_0, a_1, a_2, a_3, a_4, a_5, a_6, a_7)$ is not MDS. We record this in the following lemma without proof.

Lemma 6. $Circ(a_0, a_1, a_2, a_3, a_4, a_5, a_6, a_7)$ *is never an MDS matrix when any four or more elements from the set* $\{a_0, a_1, a_2, a_3, a_4, a_5, a_6, a_7\}$ *are 1.*

We next try to construct 8×8 *circulant MDS matrices* $A = Circ(a_0, a_1, a_2, a_3, a_4, a_5, a_6, a_7)$ where any three elements of $\{a_0, \ldots, a_7\}$ are 1. For that we fix $a_0 = a_1 = a_3 = 1$ and thus the matrix will be of the form $A' = Circ(1, 1, a_2, 1, a_4, a_5, a_6, a_7)$. So $v_1(A') = 24 = v_1^{8,8}$. For efficiency, the elements a_2, a_4, a_5, a_6 and a_7 are restricted to the form $c_0 + c_1\alpha + c_2\alpha^{-1} + c_3\alpha^2 + c_4\alpha^{-2}$ where $c_i \in \{0, 1\}$. There are 8×8 circulant MDS matrices with three elements as 1 in some other positions, but they will be equivalent to some matrices of the form A' up to the rotation and reverse ordering of the elements $(1, 1, a_2, 1, a_4, a_5, a_6, a_7)$ (see also the second paragraph of Section 4).

Proposition 2. $A = Circ(1, 1, \alpha^{-1}, 1, \alpha^{-2}, \alpha^{-1} + \alpha^{-2}, 1 + \alpha^{-1}, 1 + \alpha^{-1})$ is MDS matrix for any $\alpha \in \mathbb{F}_{2^n}$ such that minimal polynomial of α is $x^8 + x^4 + x^3 + x^2 + 1$.

Remark 9. The sum of the elements of the matrix A of Proposition 2 is 1 and $A^8 = I$ (see Remark 2), so $A^{-1} = A \times A^2 \times A^4$. From Lemma 3, $A^2 = Circ(1 + \alpha^{-4}, 0, 1 + \alpha^{-2} + \alpha^{-4}, 0, 1, 0, \alpha^{-2}, 0)$ and $A^4 = Circ(\alpha^{-8}, 0, 0, 0, 1 + \alpha^{-8}, 0, 0, 0)$. So for efficient implementation, the multiplication by A^{-1} can be replaced by $A \times A^2 \times A^4$ (see Remark 4).

Remark 10. Whirlpool [3] is a hash function which is based on an underlying dedicated block cipher with the block length of 512 bits. The diffusion layer of this block cipher uses 8×8 circulant matrix $C = Circ(1_x, 1_x, 3_x, 1_x, 5_x, 8_x, 9_x, 5_x)$ over $\mathbb{F}_{2^8}$ with the generating polynomial $x^8 + x^4 + x^3 + x^2 + 1$. In [28] authors proved that this matrix C is not MDS and proposed a new MDS matrix $M = Circ(1_x, 1_x, 2_x, 1_x, 5_x, 8_x, 9_x, 4_x)$ with $v_1(M) = 24 = v_1^{8,8}$ and $c_1(M) = 5$. Note that some elements of M are more expensive compared to the elements of the set $\{01_x, \ldots, 07_x\}$, but elements of matrix A of Proposition 2 are as efficient as the elements $\{1_x, \ldots, 7_x\}$ (see the first paragraph of Section 4). Also $c_1(A) = 4 < 5 = c_1(M)$ which is a better criteria for designing efficient matrix (see Remark 1).

The implementation of multiplication by the matrix A of Proposition 2 over $\mathbb{F}_{2^8}$ with generating polynomial $x^8 + x^4 + x^3 + x^2 + 1$ is given in the Appendix A. This implementation requires 71 XORs, 10 temporary variables and 24 $xtime\_inv$ operations (or 24 table lookup), which is the multiplication by α^{-1}. Also the implementation of multiplication by the matrix M of [28] is given in the Appendix B. This implementation requires 71 XORs, 12 temporary variables and 48 $xtime$ (or 48 table lookup) operations. Both the implementations require same number of XORs, but implementation of matrix A needs 24 $xtime$ operations which is half the number of $xtime$ operations needed for the implementation of matrix M. Also the matrix A needs lesser number of temporary variables than M. So the matrix A of Proposition 2, defined over $\mathbb{F}_{2^8}$ with generating polynomial $x^8 + x^4 + x^3 + x^2 + 1$, is more efficient compared the matrix M. Note that unlike our proposed matrix A in Proposition 2, $M^8 = (1 + \alpha^8)I$ and thus M^{-1} can not be implemented in the same way (see Remark 4). Also note that $M^{-1} = Circ(b5_x, 98_x, 23_x, fa_x, 23_x, a5_x, b6_x, 30_x)$ where all elements are of high hamming weights and not efficient, thus multiplication by M^{-1} is also costly.

We search for efficient 8×8 *circulant MDS matrices* $A = Circ(1, 1, a_2,$ $1, a_4, a_5, a_6, a_7)$ having $v_1(A) = 24 = v_1^{8,8}$ over $\mathbb{F}_{2^8}$ with generating polynomial $x^8 + x^4 + x^3 + x^2 + 1$, up to the ordering of the elements $(a_0, a_1, a_2, a_3, a_4,$ $a_5, a_6, a_7)$ with $a_2 + a_4 + a_5 + a_6 + a_7 = 0$, so that inverse matrices can also be implemented efficiently (see Remark 4). Here we restrict a_i's in the set of all polynomials in α^{-1} of degree at most 2. We get four such matrices which are given in Table 3.

Table 3. 8×8 *circulant MDS matrices* over $\mathbb{F}_{2^8}$ with generating polynomial $x^8 + x^4 + x^3 + x^2 + 1$ where elements of these matrices are polynomials in α^{-1} of degree at most 2 and α is the root of the generating polynomial

MDS Matrix A	Inverse Matrix $A \times A^2 \times A^4$
$Circ\left(1, 1, \alpha^{-1}, 1,\right.$ $\left.\alpha^{-2}, \alpha^{-1} + \alpha^{-2}, 1 + \alpha^{-1}, 1 + \alpha^{-1}\right)$	$Circ\left(1, 1, \alpha^{-1}, 1, \alpha^{-2}, \alpha^{-1} + \alpha^{-2}, 1 + \alpha^{-1}, 1 + \alpha^{-1}\right)$ $\times Circ\left(1 + \alpha^{-4}, 0, 1 + \alpha^{-2} + \alpha^{-4}, 0, 1, 0, \alpha^{-2}, 0\right)$ $\times Circ\left(\alpha^{-8}, 0, 0, 0, 1 + \alpha^{-8}, 0, 0, 0\right)$
$Circ\left(1, 1, \alpha^{-1}, 1,\right.$ $\left.1 + \alpha^{-2}, \alpha^{-1}, 1 + \alpha^{-1}, \alpha^{-1} + \alpha^{-2}\right)$	$Circ\left(1, 1, \alpha^{-1}, 1, 1 + \alpha^{-2}, \alpha^{-1}, 1 + \alpha^{-1}, \alpha^{-1} + \alpha^{-2}\right)$ $\times Circ\left(\alpha^{-4}, 0, 1 + \alpha^{-2}, 0, 1, 0, 1 + \alpha^{-2} + \alpha^{-4}, 0\right)$ $\times Circ\left(1 + \alpha^{-8}, 0, 0, 0, \alpha^{-8}, 0, 0, 0\right)$
$Circ\left(1, 1, 1 + \alpha^{-2}, 1,\right.$ $\left.\alpha^{-2}, 1 + \alpha^{-1}, \alpha^{-1} + \alpha^{-2}, \alpha^{-2}\right)$	$Circ\left(1, 1, 1 + \alpha^{-2}, 1, \alpha^{-2}, 1 + \alpha^{-1}, \alpha^{-1} + \alpha^{-2}, \alpha^{-2}\right)$ $\times Circ\left(1 + \alpha^{-4}, 0, \alpha^{-2}, 0, 1 + \alpha^{-2}, 0, 1 + \alpha^{-4}, 0\right)$ $\times Circ\left(\alpha^{-4} + \alpha^{-8}, 0, 0, 0, 1 + \alpha^{-4} + \alpha^{-8}, 0, 0, 0\right)$
$Circ\left(1, 1, \alpha^{-1} + \alpha^{-2}, 1,\right.$ $\left.1 + \alpha^{-2}, 1 + \alpha^{-1}, \alpha^{-1} + \alpha^{-2}, \alpha^{-1} + \alpha^{-2}\right)$	$Circ\left(1, 1, \alpha^{-1} + \alpha^{-2}, 1, 1 + \alpha^{-2}, 1 + \alpha^{-1}, \alpha^{-1} + \alpha^{-2},\right.$ $\left.\alpha^{-1} + \alpha^{-2}\right) \times Circ\left(\alpha^{-4}, 0, \alpha^{-2}, 0, 0, 0,\right.$ $\left.1 + \alpha^{-2} + \alpha^{-4}, 0\right) \times Circ\left(\alpha^{-8}, 0, 0, 0, 1 + \alpha^{-8}, 0, 0, 0\right)$

Remark 11. All MDS matrices in Table 3 are efficient and also their inverses can be implemented efficiently. So these matrices are suitable for SPN networks and can also be used in hash functions.

4.3 Efficient $d \times d$ MDS Matrices for $d = 3, 5, 6$ and 7

In Table 4 we present some $d \times d$ *circulant MDS matrices* over $\mathbb{F}_{2^8}$ for $d = 3, 5, 6$ and 7 with generating polynomial $x^8 + x^4 + x^3 + x^2 + 1$ where elements are restricted in $\{01_x, 02_x, \ldots, 07_x\}$. From Fact 4, $v_1^{5,5} = 12$. In case of 5×5 *circulant MDS matrices*, out of five positions, 1 can be substituted in maximum two positions, so highest value of v_1 in this case is 10. Similarly, $v_1^{6,6} = 16$ but maximum value of v_1 for 6×6 *circulant MDS matrices* is 12. In case of 7×7 *circulant MDS matrices*, v_1 can attain the highest value $v_1^{7,7}$ i.e 21. In Table 4, the 5×5, 6×6 and 7×7 *circulant MDS matrices* are having highest value of their respective v_1's.

Table 4. $d \times d$ *circulant MDS matrices* over $\mathbb{F}_{2^8}$ with generating polynomial $x^8 + x^4 + x^3 + x^2 + 1$ for $d = 3, 5, 6$ and 7

Dimension d	MDS Matrix A
3	$Circ(02_x, 01_x, 01_x)$
5	$Circ(01_x, 01_x, 02_x, 03_x, 02_x)$
5	$Circ(01_x, 01_x, 02_x, 03_x, 05_x)$
6	$Circ(01_x, 01_x, 02_x, 03_x, 05_x, 07_x)$
6	$Circ(01_x, 01_x, 02_x, 03_x, 07_x, 03_x)$
7	$Circ(01_x, 01_x, 02_x, 01_x, 05_x, 04_x, 06_x)$
7	$Circ(01_x, 01_x, 02_x, 01_x, 06_x, 07_x, 04_x)$

5 Conclusion

In this paper we studied the properties and constructions of $d \times d$ circulant MDS matrices for d up to 8, which are suitable for lightweight applications. We proved that circulant MDS matrices can not be involutory. We also proved that $2^d \times 2^d$ circulant MDS matrices are not orthogonal. We constructed efficient circulant MDS matrices with maximum number of 1's for which the inverse matrices can also be implemented efficiently.

Acknowledgements. We are thankful to the anonymous reviewers for their valuable comments. We also wish to thank Subhabrata Samajder for providing several useful and valuable suggestions.

References

1. Barreto, P., Rijmen, V.: The Khazad Legacy-Level Block Cipher, Submission to the NESSIE Project (2000), http://cryptonessie.org
2. Barreto, P.S., Rijmen, V.: The Anubis block cipher, NESSIE Algorithm Submission (2000), http://cryptonessie.org
3. Barreto, P.S.L.M., Rijmen, V.: Whirlpool, Encyclopedia of Cryptography and Security, 2nd edn., pp. 1384–1385 (2011)
4. Bosma, W., Cannon, J., Playoust, C.: The Magma Algebra System I: The User Language. J. Symbolic Comput. 24(3-4), 235–265 (1997); Computational algebra and number theory, London (1993)
5. Choy, J., Yap, H., Khoo, K., Guo, J., Peyrin, T., Poschmann, A., Tan, C.H.: SPN-Hash: Improving the Provable Resistance against Differential Collision Attacks. In: Mitrokotsa, A., Vaudenay, S. (eds.) AFRICACRYPT 2012. LNCS, vol. 7374, pp. 270–286. Springer, Heidelberg (2012)
6. Daemen, J., Knudsen, L.R., Rijmen, V.: The block cipher SQUARE. In: Biham, E. (ed.) FSE 1997. LNCS, vol. 1267, pp. 149–165. Springer, Heidelberg (1997)
7. Daemen, J., Rijmen, V.: The Design of Rijndael: AES - The Advanced Encryption Standard. Springer (2002)
8. Filho, G.D., Barreto, P., Rijmen, V.: The Maelstrom-0 Hash Function. In: Proceedings of the 6th Brazilian Symposium on Information and Computer Systems Security (2006)
9. Gauravaram, P., Knudsen, L.R., Matusiewicz, K., Mendel, F., Rechberger, C., Schlaffer, M., Thomsen, S.: Grøstl a SHA-3 Candidate, Submission to NIST (2008), http://www.groestl.info
10. Guo, J., Peyrin, T., Poschmann, A.: The PHOTON Family of Lightweight Hash Functions. In: Rogaway, P. (ed.) CRYPTO 2011. LNCS, vol. 6841, pp. 222–239. Springer, Heidelberg (2011)
11. Chand Gupta, K., Ghosh Ray, I.: On Constructions of Involutory MDS Matrices. In: Youssef, A., Nitaj, A., Hassanien, A.E. (eds.) AFRICACRYPT 2013. LNCS, vol. 7918, pp. 43–60. Springer, Heidelberg (2013)
12. Gupta, K.C., Ray, I.G.: On Constructions of MDS Matrices from Companion Matrices for Lightweight Cryptography. In: Cuzzocrea, A., Kittl, C., Simos, D.E., Weippl, E., Xu, L. (eds.) CD-ARES Workshops 2013. LNCS, vol. 8128, pp. 29–43. Springer, Heidelberg (2013)
13. Nakahara Jr. J., Abrahao, E.: A New Involutory MDS Matrix for the AES. International Journal of Network Security 9(2), 109–116 (2009)

14. Junod, P., Vaudenay, S.: Perfect Diffusion Primitives for Block Ciphers Building Efficient MDS Matrices. In: Handschuh, H., Hasan, M.A. (eds.) SAC 2004. LNCS, vol. 3357, pp. 84–99. Springer, Heidelberg (2004)
15. Junod, P., Vaudenay, S.: FOX: A new family of block ciphers. In: Handschuh, H., Hasan, M.A. (eds.) SAC 2004. LNCS, vol. 3357, pp. 114–129. Springer, Heidelberg (2004)
16. Junod, P., Macchetti, M.: Revisiting the IDEA philosophy. In: Dunkelman, O. (ed.) FSE 2009. LNCS, vol. 5665, pp. 277–295. Springer, Heidelberg (2009)
17. Lacan, J., Fimes, J.: Systematic MDS erasure codes based on vandermonde matrices. IEEE Trans. Commun. Lett. 8(9), 570–572 (2004) (CrossRef)
18. Lo, J.W., Hwang, M.S., Liu, C.H.: An efficient key assignment scheme for access control in a large leaf class hierarchy. Journal of Information Sciences: An International Journal Archive 181(4), 917–925 (2011)
19. MacWilliams, F.J., Sloane, N.J.A.: The Theory of Error Correcting Codes. North Holland (1986)
20. Rao, A.R., Bhimasankaram, P.: Linear Algebra, 2nd edn. Hindustan Book Agency
21. Rijmen, V., Daemen, J., Preneel, B., Bosselaers, A., Win, E.D.: The cipher SHARK. In: Gollmann, D. (ed.) FSE 1996. LNCS, vol. 1039, pp. 99–112. Springer, Heidelberg (1996)
22. Sajadieh, M., Dakhilalian, M., Mala, H., Omoomi, B.: On construction of involutory MDS matrices from Vandermonde Matrices in $GF(2^q)$. In: Design, Codes Cryptography 2012, pp. 1–22 (2012)
23. Sajadieh, M., Dakhilalian, M., Mala, H., Sepehrdad, P.: Recursive Diffusion Layers for Block Ciphers and Hash Functions. In: Canteaut, A. (ed.) FSE 2012. LNCS, vol. 7549, pp. 385–401. Springer, Heidelberg (2012)
24. Schneier, B., Kelsey, J., Whiting, D., Wagner, D., Hall, C., Ferguson, N.: Twofish: A 128-bit block cipher. In: The First AES Candidate Conference. National Institute for Standards and Technology (1998)
25. Schneier, B., Kelsey, J., Whiting, D., Wagner, D., Hall, C., Ferguson, N.: The Twofish encryption algorithm. Wiley (1999)
26. Schnorr, C.-P., Vaudenay, S.: Black Box Cryptanalysis of Hash Networks Based on Multipermutations. In: De Santis, A. (ed.) EUROCRYPT 1994. LNCS, vol. 950, pp. 47–57. Springer, Heidelberg (1995)
27. Shannon, C.E.: Communication Theory of Secrecy Systems. Bell Syst. Technical J. 28, 656–715 (1949)
28. Shiraj, T., Shibutani, K.: On the Diffusion Matrix Employed in the Whirlpool Hashing Function. NESSIE public report (2003)
29. Shirai, T., Shibutani, K., Akishita, T., Moriai, S., Iwata, T.: The 128-bit Block cipher CLEFIA. In: Biryukov, A. (ed.) FSE 2007. LNCS, vol. 4593, pp. 181–195. Springer, Heidelberg (2007)
30. Vaudenay, S.: On the Need for Multipermutations: Cryptanalysis of MD4 and SAFER. In: Preneel, B. (ed.) FSE 1994. LNCS, vol. 1008, pp. 286–297. Springer, Heidelberg (1995)
31. Watanabe, D., Furuya, S., Yoshida, H., Takaragi, K., Preneel, B.: A new keystream generator MUGI. In: Daemen, J., Rijmen, V. (eds.) FSE 2002. LNCS, vol. 2365, pp. 179–194. Springer, Heidelberg (2002)
32. Wu, S., Wang, M., Wu, W.: Recursive Diffusion Layers for (Lightweight) Block Ciphers and Hash Functions. In: Knudsen, L.R., Wu, H. (eds.) SAC 2012. LNCS, vol. 7707, pp. 355–371. Springer, Heidelberg (2013)

33. Youssef, A.M., Tavares, S.E., Heys, H.M.: A New Class of Substitution Permutation Networks. In: Workshop on Selected Areas in Cryptography, SAC 1996, Workshop Record, pp. 132–147 (1996)
34. Youssef, A.M., Mister, S., Tavares, S.E.: On the Design of Linear Transformations for Substitution Permutation Encryption Networks. In: Workshop On Selected Areas in Cryptography, SAC 1997, pp. 40–48 (1997)

Appendix A

The matrix $A = Circ(1, 1, \alpha^{-1}, 1, \alpha^{-2}, \alpha^{-1}+\alpha^{-2}, 1+\alpha^{-1}, 1+\alpha^{-1})$ of Proposition 2 over $\mathbb{F}_{2^8}$ with generating polynomial $x^8 + x^4 + x^3 + x^2 + 1$ can be implemented in the following way.

$t = a[0] \oplus a[1] \oplus a[2] \oplus a[3] \oplus a[4] \oplus a[5] \oplus a[6] \oplus a[7]$; $u0 = a[0]$; $u1 - a[1]$; $u2 = a[2]$; $u3 - a[3]$; $u4 = a[4]$; $u5 = a[5]$; /* a is the input vector */$z = a[4] \oplus a[5]$; $v = a[2] \oplus z$; $w = a[2] \oplus a[5] \oplus a[6] \oplus a[7]$; $w = xtime\_inv[w]$; $z = xtime\_inv[xtime\_inv[[z]]$; $a[0] = v \oplus w \oplus z \oplus t$; $z = a[5] \oplus a[6]$; $v = a[3] \oplus z$; $w = a[3] \oplus a[6] \oplus a[7] \oplus u0$; $w = xtime\_inv[w]$; $z = xtime\_inv[xtime\_inv[[z]]$; $a[1] = v \oplus w \oplus z \oplus t$; $z = a[6] \oplus a[7]$; $v = a[4] \oplus z$; $w = a[4] \oplus a[7] \oplus u0 \oplus u1$; $w = xtime\_inv[w]$; $z = xtime\_inv[xtime\_inv[[z]]$; $a[2] = v \oplus w \oplus z \oplus t$; $z = a[7] \oplus u0$; $v = a[5] \oplus z$; $w = a[5] \oplus u0 \oplus u1 \oplus u2$; $w = xtime\_inv[w]$; $z = xtime\_inv[xtime\_inv[[z]]$; $a[3] = v \oplus w \oplus z \oplus t$; $z = u0 \oplus u1$; $v = a[6] \oplus z$; $w = a[6] \oplus u1 \oplus u2 \oplus u3$; $w = xtime\_inv[w]$; $z = xtime\_inv[xtime\_inv[[z]]$; $a[4] = v \oplus w \oplus z \oplus t$; $z = u1 \oplus u2$; $v = a[7] \oplus z$; $w = a[7] \oplus u2 \oplus u3 \oplus u4$; $w = xtime\_inv[w]$; $z = xtime\_inv[xtime\_inv[[z]]$; $a[5] = v \oplus w \oplus z \oplus t$; $z = u2 \oplus u3$; $v = u0 \oplus z$; $w = u0 \oplus u3 \oplus u4 \oplus u5$; $w = xtime\_inv[w]$; $z = xtime\_inv[xtime\_inv[[z]]$; $a[6] = v \oplus w \oplus z \oplus t$; $z = u3 \oplus u4$; $v = u1 \oplus z$; $w = u1 \oplus u4 \oplus u5 \oplus u6$; $w = xtime\_inv[w]$; $z = xtime\_inv[xtime\_inv[[z]]$; $a[7] = v \oplus w \oplus z \oplus t$;

Appendix B

The matrix $M = Circ(1_x, 1_x, 2_x, 1_x, 5_x, 8_x, 9_x, 4_x)$ proposed in [28] can be implemented in the following way.

$t = a[0] \oplus a[1] \oplus a[2] \oplus a[3] \oplus a[4] \oplus a[5] \oplus a[6] \oplus a[7]$; $u0 = a[0]$; $u1 = a[1]$; $u2 = a[2]$; $u3 = a[3]$; $u4 = a[4]$; $u5 = a[5]$; $u6 = a[6]$; /* a is the input vector */$v = a[4] \oplus a[7]$; $w = a[5] \oplus a[6]$; $y = xtime[a[2]]$; $z = a[2] \oplus a[5] \oplus a[7]$; $v = xtime[xtime[v]]$; $w = xtime[xtime[xtime[z]]]$; $a[0] = t \oplus v \oplus w \oplus y \oplus z$; $v = a[5] \oplus u0$; $w = a[6] \oplus a[7]$; $y = xtime[a[3]]$; $z = a[3] \oplus a[6] \oplus u0$; $v = xtime[xtime[v]]$; $w = xtime[xtime[xtime[z]]]$; $a[1] = t \oplus v \oplus w \oplus y \oplus z$; $v = a[6] \oplus u1$; $w = a[7] \oplus u0$; $y = xtime[a[4]]$; $z = a[4] \oplus a[7] \oplus u1$; $v = xtime[xtime[v]]$; $w = xtime[xtime[xtime[z]]]$; $a[2] = t \oplus v \oplus w \oplus y \oplus z$; $v = a[7] \oplus u2$; $w = u0 \oplus u1$; $y = xtime[a[5]]$; $z = a[5] \oplus u0 \oplus u2$; $v = xtime[xtime[v]]$; $w = xtime[xtime[xtime[z]]]$; $a[3] = t \oplus v \oplus w \oplus y \oplus z$; $v = u0 \oplus u3$; $w = u1 \oplus u2$; $y = xtime[a[6]]$; $z = a[6] \oplus u1 \oplus u3$; $v = xtime[xtime[v]]$; $w = xtime[xtime[xtime[z]]]$; $a[4] = t \oplus v \oplus w \oplus y \oplus z$; $v = u1 \oplus u4$; $w = u2 \oplus u3$; $y = xtime[a[7]]$; $z = a[7] \oplus u2 \oplus u4$; $v = xtime[xtime[v]]$; $w = xtime[xtime[xtime[z]]]$; $a[5] = t \oplus v \oplus w \oplus y \oplus z$; $v = u2 \oplus u5$; $w = u3 \oplus u4$; $y = xtime[u0]$; $z = u0 \oplus u3 \oplus u5$; $v = xtime[xtime[v]]$; $w = xtime[xtime[xtime[z]]]$; $a[6] = t \oplus v \oplus w \oplus y \oplus z$; $v = u3 \oplus u6$; $w = u4 \oplus u5$; $y = xtime[u1]$; $z = u1 \oplus u4 \oplus u6$; $v = xtime[xtime[v]]$; $w = xtime[xtime[xtime[z]]]$; $a[7] = t \oplus v \oplus w \oplus y \oplus z$;

Author Index